Preface

WHY STUDY BUSINESS LAW?

The shift from a local to a world marketplace has created great incentive for uniformity in commercial transactions. As a result, laws governing business transactions everywhere are changing. *Law for Business*, Twelfth Edition, focuses on the developing laws regulating commercial activity to prepare students to conduct business in our dynamic world marketplace.

PURPOSE OF THE TEXT

Law for Business, Twelfth Edition, is a practical approach to law that emphasizes current and relevant issues students need to understand for business transactions, such as contracts. The basic concepts of business law are covered but without the excessive theory that often makes law seem incomprehensible. Practical coverage of law pertaining to business is the hallmark of this text.

Whereas the substantial breadth of this book's overview, laden with examples and cases, is an effective introduction to a variety of legal topics, it does not include the extensively detailed treatment of a law school text.

NEW AND SUCCESSFUL FEATURES

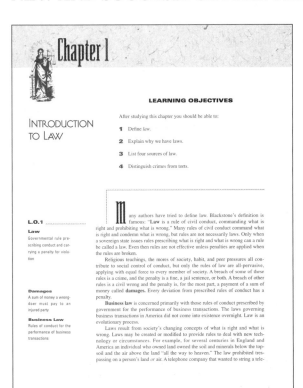

Feature: *Integrated Learning Objectives*

Benefit: Each chapter begins with learning objectives that outline for students what they will accomplish after reading the chapter. Marginal icons indicate where learning objectives are first discussed in the text. These learning objective icons create a natural outline to help students easily comprehend the information.

---

38   Part One · The Legal System and the Legal Environment of Business

1 Clean Air Act
2 Water Pollution and Control Act
3 Resource Conservation and Recovery Act
4 Comprehensive Environmental Response, Compensation, and Liability Act

CLEAN AIR ACT

The Clean Air Act was the first national environmental law. Under this law, the EPA sets minimum national standards for air quality and regulates hazardous air pollutants. These standards protect public health and welfare. The states apply and enforce these standards under state implementation plans setting limits on pollutants and approved by the EPA. The law provides civil and criminal penalties for its violation.

Under authority of the Clean Air Act, the EPA set an air-quality standard for ozone. The state of Michigan issued a state implementation plan, and the EPA approved the plan. Later, the United States sued in federal court to enforce the plan. A month later, Ford Motor Company sued the Michigan state pollution control agencies in a state court to keep them from enforcing the plan. The EPA was not a party to that suit. Ford and the state agencies negotiated a judgment in the state court changing the limits and thereby vacating the plan. Ford alleged the plan could not be enforced in the federal suit because the state court judgment invalidated it. The court said since state plans and any revisions to plans must be approved by the EPA, the state court action could not revise the plan.

WATER POLLUTION AND CONTROL ACT

Congress enacted the Water Pollution and Control Act (also referred to simply as the Clean Water Act) to restore and maintain the proper chemistry of United States waters. U.S. waters include adjacent wetlands. The law seeks to prevent the discharge of pollutants into navigable waters. The EPA has the primary administration and enforcement responsibility under the law. It sets limits on discharges, including pollutants into sewer systems, has the responsibility for wetlands protection, and can block or overrule the issuance of permits under the law. The EPA or private citizens may sue on the basis of the act, which even includes criminal liability for violation.

To expand a sanitary landfill, Orange County placed fill in the site, which included some wetlands. Orange Environment, Inc. (OEI) sued the county alleging violation of the Clean Water Act's prohibition against the discharge of fill materials into U.S. waters. In discussing the law, the court said the EPA has the ultimate authority for wetlands protection. The county had to obtain a permit to continue the landfill expansion.

Feature: *Environmental Protection Coverage*

Benefit: The tie between business and the environment has never been stronger. This edition has greatly expanded its coverage of environmental law and how it affects business. Environmental coverage has been moved forward to Chapter 4.

Chapter 3 · Business Crimes and Torts   31

L.O.1, 2   2 Anaheim Police detective Stockwell asked Diane Terry to help in a "sting" investigation of wrongful computer access. Terry worked for Trans Union, a credit reporting agency. She created a phony file in her company's credit data bank using the name Diane T. Wolfe, but without supplying any data. She phoned National Credit Service, which advertised as a service to help people with bad credit. Lelas Gentry told her he could create a new credit file for her with false information. She and Stockwell met with Gentry who gave Stockwell a full credit report on Diane T. Wolfe from Trans Union. Gentry did not have authorization for access to Trans Union's files, and only Gentry, Stockwell, and Terry knew of the fictitious Diane T. Wolfe. Gentry was charged with gaining access to a computer system and obtaining services with fraudulent intent. Was he guilty?

L.O.4   3 Pacific Gas and Electric Co. (PG&E) contracted with Placer County Water Agency to purchase hydroelectric power. Energy prices rose dramatically. Bear Stearns & Company tried to convince the Agency to make an effort to terminate the contract. The Agency contracted with Bear Stearns to pay it a percentage of any increase in revenue in return for Bear Stearns' paying for studies on the feasibility of terminating the power contract. Bear Stearns hired attorneys to draw up a plan for and litigate whether the Agency could terminate the contract. It also solicited buyers for the Agency's power and demanded PG&E arbitrate whether the contract could be terminated. PG&E sued alleging Bear Stearns had caused the Agency to breach promises to continue the contract for 50 years. Did Bear Stearns induce a breach of contract?

L.O.3, 4   4 Teilhaber Manufacturing Co. produced an industrial storage rack called the "Cue-Rack." It competed with one sold by Unarco Materials Storage, Inc. Unarco conducted tests on a hybrid rack composed of uprights manufactured by Teilhaber for the Cue-Rack and beams manufactured by another company. Unarco distributed a report on these tests written by Unarco's chief engineer. It stated the tests were performed on a Cue-Rack "furnished by Teilhaber." Teilhaber sued Unarco for product disparagement. Was the report false?

L.O.2   5 William Croft, an assistant professor at the University of Wisconsin–Madison, received a $130,000 grant from the Environmental Protection Agency to study cancer in cattle. He wanted to investigate the cancer-causing effects of asbestos. While working on the project, the town of Weston hired Croft to test the asbestos content of Weston's water supply. Croft hired Laurel Johnson to test Weston water samples during the summer. Johnson received $2,000 from EPA funds for her work on the Weston project. Croft's report to Weston included calculations prepared by Johnson. Croft was charged with larceny—misappropriating Johnson's services, paid for by the government, for his own, personal research project. Was he guilty?

L.O.4   6 Duo-Tint Bulb & Battery Co. supplied retailers with a bulb dispenser box containing an assortment of bulbs. With each box was an information chart listing the contents by manufacturer and bulb number and a reorder card. When a bulb ran out, the retailer mailed the card to Duo-Tint, which would ship a full bulb dispenser box. The retailer would return the old box for credit. After Lange was fired as a sales representative of Duo-Tint, he

Feature: *Real-World Cases*

Benefit: This book contains no make-believe cases. Every case example, problem, and summary is an actual U.S. court case, transferring theory into practice. These actual cases are exciting; they give students a way to relate to the subject. Citations give students further opportunities for research.

LAW FOR BUSINESS

12TH EDITION

JOHN D. ASHCROFT, J.D.
United States Senator
Member of the Missouri Bar

JANET E. ASHCROFT, J.D.
Member of the Missouri Bar

SOUTH-WESTERN College Publishing

An International Thomson Publishing Company

Acquisitions Editor: Gary Bauer
Developmental Editor: Tom Bormann
Production Editor: Shelley Brewer
Production House: Bookmark Media
Cover and Internal Designer: Michael H. Stratton
Photo Researcher: Debbie Leffert
Photo Editor: Jennifer Mayhall
Marketing Manager: Dreis Van Landuyt
Cover Photos: Tony Stone Images and Scott Barrow, Inc.

LA92LA

Photo Acknowledgments
Daryl Benson/Masterfile, xiii; Comstock, 42; Mike Dobel/Masterfile, 130; © Peter Poulides/Tony Stone Images, 160; Rosemary Weller, 212; Donovan Reese, 282; Greg Pease, 330; Comstock, 396; Chad Slattery, 444

Library of Congress Cataloging-in-Publication Data
Ashcroft, John D.,
  Law for business / John D. Ashcroft, Janet E. Ashcroft.—12th ed.
   p. cm.
  Includes index.
  ISBN 0-538-84545-7
   1. Commercial law—United States. I. Ashcroft, Janet E.
II. Title
KF889.3.A84 1995
346.73′07—dc20
[347.3067]   95-13763
                  CIP

 2 3 4 5 6 7 8 9 Ki 4 3 2 1 0 9 8 7 6
Printed in the United States of America

International Thomson Publishing
South-Western College Publishing is an ITP Company. The ITP trademark is used under license.

Feature: *Key Terms in Margin*

Benefit: Key terms are printed in the margin for easy identification and mastery. These terms are critical for students' mastery of business law. The terms are also compiled in a glossary at the end of the text.

---

6   Part One · The Legal System and the Legal Environment of Business

terms of the contract and sell the real estate. They also would provide for preventive action to protect individuals from a likely harm. In this type of case a court with equity powers might initially issue a **restraining order,** a temporary order forbidding a certain action. Upon a complete hearing, the court might issue an **injunction,** a permanent order forbidding activities that would be detrimental to others. Today only a few states maintain separate equity courts, or, as they are also called, Chancery Courts. In most states, courts apply legal and equitable principles to each case as the facts justify, without making any formal distinction between law and equity.

Restraining Order
Court's temporary order forbidding an action

Injunction
Court's permanent order forbidding an action

SOURCES OF LAW

L.O.3

Our laws come from several sources, which include the decisions of judges in cases they hear, federal and state constitutions, statutes, and administrative agency orders.

Judicial Decisions

Judicial interpretation is still an important element of the legal process. Because courts can interpret laws differently, the same law might have somewhat different consequences in different states. This happens because interpretations by the highest courts have the effect of precedents and under the doctrine of **stare decisis** (stand by the decision) bind the lower courts. These interpretations may concern a situation not previously brought before the court, or the court may decide to reverse a previous decision. Any state supreme court or the Supreme Court of the United States can reverse a decision of a lower court. For legal stability so that we can know our rights before we undertake a transaction, courts must generally adhere to the judicial precedents set by earlier decisions. However, changing situations or practices sometimes make it necessary for the previous case law to be overturned and a new rule or practice to be established.

Stare Decisis
Principle that a court decision controls the decision of a similar future case

Greg Batt was fired by Globe Engineering Co., Inc. He filed a suit against his former supervisor, Jack Johnson. In the appellate court, Batt asserted that Johnson had made false statements about Batt which led to the firing. Any statements by Johnson that could have helped Batt in the lawsuit could be admitted only if the court failed to follow a previous case decided by the state supreme court. The appellate court stated that it was duty bound to follow the law as established by supreme court decisions. The supreme court precedent was followed and judgment was for Johnson.

Constitutions

A **constitution** is the document that defines the relationships of the parts of the government to each other and the relationship of the government to its citizens or subjects. The U.S. Constitution is the supreme law of the land. State constitutions, as well as all other laws, must agree with the U.S. Constitution. The Supreme Court of the United States is the final arbiter in disputes about whether a state or federal law violates the U.S. Constitution. A state supreme court is the final judge as to whether a state law violates the constitution of that state.

Constitution
Document that contains fundamental principles of a government

---

Feature: *Four-color*

Benefit: As a pedagogical tool, color is a proven asset. Color has been used to clearly illustrate issues, cases, and key points of business law. It also enhances visual appeal and helps hold students' interest—the more students are interested, the more they learn.

Writ of Certiorari
Order to produce record of a case

The normal way a case gets to the Supreme Court is by application for a **writ of certiorari.** The party asking for the Supreme Court review of a case asks the court to issue a writ of certiorari. This writ requires the lower court that has decided the case to produce the record of the case for the Supreme Court's review. The court issues a writ for only a small number of the requests. The U.S. Supreme Court is the highest tribunal in the land, and its decisions are binding on all other courts. Its decisions are final until the Court reverses its own decision or until the effect of a given decision is changed by a constitutional amendment or an enactment by the Congress.

The Constitution created the Supreme Court and gave Congress the power to establish inferior courts.

State Courts

State courts (see Illustration 2-2) can best be classified into the following groups:

1 Inferior courts
2 Courts of original general jurisdiction
3 Appellate courts
4 Special courts

Illustration 2-2   Typical State Court System

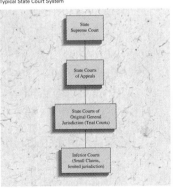

OTHER IMPORTANT NEW FEATURES:

Feature	Benefit
Ample Questions and Cases	The end-of-chapter materials include questions and case problems. This gives the teacher and the student the opportunity to check how well the student understands the material.
Earlier coverage of business crimes and torts	Criminal law generates a great deal of interest today. Because of this and the numerous lawsuits in today's society, this subject has been expanded and moved to Chapter 3. This chapter not only gives the student more information but deals with this high-interest topic early, thus helping engage the student in the text right from the start.
Improved Readability	Legal texts can often be dense and difficult to read. In *Law for Business*, special attention has been given to improving the readability of the text using such techniques as shortened sentences, active voice, and more information presented in list format rather than in paragraph form.
Short chapters	Extremely long chapters tend to dilute the critical points and confuse the reader. *Law for Business* is set up in short, easy-to-understand chapters so that critical points stand out.
Chapter Opening Vignette and Full-Page Color Picture	The beginning of every chapter has a high-interest case to involve students in the issues that will be discussed in the chapter.
Contracts, Commercial Paper/Negotiable Instruments, and Sales	In *Law for Business*, the coverage of the three most important topics of business law is second to none. In the Twelfth Edition it has been expanded and updated significantly.
New and Enhanced Content:	In the Twelfth Edition, we've reorganized the material to allow a more logical flow of business law topics. Our changes are as follows:
Special Bailments	Formerly, two chapters (19 and 20) covered this subject. They have been compacted into Chapter 15, combining the less important subjects and emphasizing the critical areas more.
Types of Insurance	Chapters 21, 40, and 42 have been combined into Chapter 39 to help students understand that insurance concepts cut across all types of insurance.

Bankruptcy	Moved from Chapter 49 to Chapter 41, discussion of bankruptcy now follows the security-devices chapter—a more logical progression of topics.
Part Nine: Real Property	This part has been reworded and retitled "Real Property." We've transferred the coverage of personal property to Chapter 14 and bankruptcy to Chapter 41; Part Nine is now more of a unit, as all of its chapters have a direct relationship with the topic of real property.
Nature of Personal Property	Transferred from Part Nine, this new Chapter 14 presents the various types of personal property and explains the special legal relationships involving personal property, including bailments.
Multiple Owners of Property	New Chapter 42 discusses joint tenancy, tenancy in common, tenancy by the entirety, and community property—topics that are critical in determining owners' property rights.
Ethics Coverage	First discussed in an appendix to Chapter 1, ethics has been expanded and moved forward in the book. It can also be found in other areas of the text relevant to ethics and business law.
International Coverage	Coverage of International law has been expanded. It is discussed throughout the text, especially in Chapters of 16, 17, and 18. Students will get the necessary exposure to this growing area of business law.
Technology and Business Law	This text features such technological topics as entering into a binding contract via a facsimile machine (Chapter 6), computer law (Chapter 3), and electronic fund transfers (Chapter 21).
Limited Liability Company	*Law for Business* discusses this new form of business organization (Chapter 32), which is now legal in some states.

FOR THE INSTRUCTOR

Law for Business comes with the most complete and integrated teaching package in the market. The following supplements are available to aid the teacher with this course:

• Instructor's Manual	This manual acts as a guide to the text and course, providing teaching suggestions, lesson outlines, explanations and citations for the example cases, and answers to the problems contained in the text. It also contains answers to the Student Workbook problems as well as the Achievement Tests and Exams. ISBN: 0-538-84548-2

• Achievement Tests	These tests provide an assessment opportunity for the instructor, showing the instructor what students have learned from using the text. ISBN: 0-538-84549-X
• Test Bank	Written by Janet Ashcroft, this supplement provides over 900 objective and case questions by chapter, giving the instructor additional assignments and questions to give the student. ISBN: 0-538-84550-3
• MicroExam 4.0	A computerized version of the test bank allows the instructor to quickly and efficiently produce professional-quality tests ISBN: 0-538-84551-1
• Study Guide Key	Provides answers to problems in the study guide. ISBN: 0-538-84552-X

FOR THE STUDENT

Also available are supplementary materials for the student that provide further opportunities to learn and review business law. The supplements include:

• Study Guide	Written by Ronald L. Taylor, from Metropolitan State College in Denver; this guide supplies chapter outlines and includes general rules, limitations on the rules, examples, and study hints. In addition, objective questions and case problems assist students in reviewing terms and applying concepts learned in each chapter. The Study Guide is available with and without the key. ISBN: 0-538-84576-7 (without key) ISBN: 0-538-85694-7 (with key)
• Student Workbook	Written by Janet Ashcroft, the Student Workbook reinforces students' understanding by reviewing the concepts and applying them to factual situations. It includes a variety of learning exercises including true/false questions, fill-in-the-blank statements, yes/no questions, questions referring to fact situations, and definitional exercises. Also included are legal forms, which give invaluable experience to students by familiarizing them with commonly used forms. ISBN: 0-538-84577-5 ISBN: 0-538-85695-5 (with Study Guide)

ABOUT THE AUTHORS

The authors both received their *Juris Doctor* degrees from the University of Chicago School of Law. Members of the Missouri Bar for more than twenty years, they practiced law in Spring-field, Missouri, and taught business law at Southwest Missouri State University in Springfield, Missouri. Both have been admitted to practice law in the Federal Court for the Western District of Missouri. Mrs. Ashcroft has taught additional law courses at other colleges and served as general counsel for the Missouri Department of Revenue. Senator Ashcroft was an assistant attorney general, later attorney general of Missouri for eight years, and governor of Missouri. He has presented cases at every level of the state and federal appellate courts in Missouri and in the U.S. Supreme Court, and has authored numerous articles for legal publications.

ACKNOWLEDGEMENTS

Marilyn S. Chernoff
Sawyer School

Robert D. Colestock
Indiana Vocational Technical College

Jay S. Hollowell
Commonwealth College, Virginia Beach

Susan Johnson
Central Wesleyan College

Esther M. Tremblay
Duff's Business Institute

Betty Young
Washington State Community College

Gamewell Gantt
Idaho State University

Linda B. Davis
Vance-Granville Community College

Clovie C. Quick
Columbus Technical Institute

Hugh L. Wink
Kilgore College

Lee Miller
Indiana Business College

Elizabeth Cummings
Mississippi Delta Community College

J. Franklin Lee
Pitt Community College

We would also like to thank all the people who have reviewed this text in past editions. It is your suggestions and comments that have helped make this text what it is today.

U.S. Senator John D. Ashcroft
Janet E. Ashcroft

Contents

Part 1

THE LEGAL SYSTEM AND THE LEGAL ENVIRONMENT OF BUSINESS

Chapter 1

INTRODUCTION TO LAW

LEARNING OBJECTIVES

After studying this chapter you should be able to:

1 Define *law*.

2 Explain why we have laws.

3 List four sources of law.

4 Distinguish crimes from torts.

L.O.1

Law
Governmental rule prescribing conduct and carrying a penalty for violation

Damages
A sum of money a wrongdoer must pay to an injured party

Business Law
Rules of conduct for the performance of business transactions

any authors have tried to define law. Blackstone's definition is famous: "**Law** is a rule of civil conduct, commanding what is right and prohibiting what is wrong." Many rules of civil conduct command what is right and condemn what is wrong, but rules are not necessarily laws. Only when a sovereign state issues rules prescribing what is right and what is wrong can a rule be called a law. Even then rules are not effective unless penalties are applied when the rules are broken.

Religious teachings, the mores of society, habit, and peer pressures all contribute to social control of conduct, but only the rules of law are all-pervasive, applying with equal force to every member of society. A breach of some of these rules is a crime, and the penalty is a fine, a jail sentence, or both. A breach of other rules is a civil wrong and the penalty is, for the most part, a payment of a sum of money called **damages.** Every deviation from prescribed rules of conduct has a penalty.

Business law is concerned primarily with those rules of conduct prescribed by government for the performance of business transactions. The laws governing business transactions in America did not come into existence overnight. Law is an evolutionary process.

Laws result from society's changing concepts of what is right and what is wrong. Laws may be created or modified to provide rules to deal with new technology or circumstances. For example, for several centuries in England and America an individual who owned land owned the soil and minerals below the topsoil and the air above the land "all the way to heaven." The law prohibited trespassing on a person's land *or* air. A telephone company that wanted to string a telephone wire through the air had to buy a right of way. When airplanes were invented, this law became a millstone around society's neck. Under this law, a transcontinental airline would have to buy a right of way through the air of every property owner in its path from New York to San Francisco. The modification of this rule by judicial decree shows the law changing when circumstances change.

OBJECTIVES OF LAW

L.O.2 .... We live in a very complex society. We constantly deal with other people—when doing our jobs, making a purchase, starting a business, traveling, renting an apartment, or trying to insure against loss. Every time we have business dealings with others, we have a potential for a dispute. The law seeks to establish rules so that we will be able to resolve any disputes that arise. The law also sets the rules of conduct for many transactions so we can know what we must do to avoid disputes. The law thus tries to establish a stable framework to keep society operating as smoothly as possible.

THE COMMON LAW

Common Law
English custom recognized by courts as binding

Common law is custom that has come to be recognized by the courts as binding on the community and therefore law. In eleventh-century England, there were no laws prescribing the proper rule of conduct in hundreds of situations. When a dispute came before the judge, the court prescribed a rule of its own based on the customs of the time. Over a period of several centuries, these court decisions developed into a body of law. The colonists brought this body of law from England to America. After the Untied States became a sovereign nation, most of these common laws were either enacted as statutory laws or continued as judge-made laws. Much of our law today follows from this common law.

EQUITY

Uniformity in the common law spread throughout England because judges tended to decide cases the same way other judges had decided them. But some wrongs occurred for which law provided no remedy. In the law courts practically the only remedy available was a judgment for money damages. In some cases, this was not an appropriate remedy. To obtain a suitable remedy, the parties began to petition the king for justice. The king delegated these matters to the chancellor, who did not decide the cases on the basis of the recognized legal principles, but on the basis of "equity"—what in good conscience ought to be done. Eventually an additional system of justice evolved that granted judicial relief when no adequate remedy at law existed, called **equity.**

Equity
Justice system based on fairness; provides relief other than merely money damages

Courts of equity, although they sometimes recognized legal rights, also provided new types of relief. For example, instead of merely ordering a person who had breached a contract agreeing to sell real estate to pay money damages, they would order "specific performance"—that is, require the seller to comply with the

Restraining Order

Court's temporary order forbidding an action

Injunction

Court's permanent order forbidding an action

terms of the contract and sell the real estate. They also would provide for preventive action to protect individuals from a likely harm. In this type of case a court with equity powers might initially issue a **restraining order,** a temporary order forbidding a certain action. Upon a complete hearing, the court might issue an **injunction,** a permanent order forbidding activities that would be detrimental to others. Today only a few states maintain separate equity courts, or, as they are also called, Chancery Courts. In most states, courts apply legal and equitable principles to each case as the facts justify, without making any formal distinction between law and equity.

SOURCES OF LAW

L.O.3 .... Our laws come from several sources, which include the decisions of judges in cases they hear, federal and state constitutions, statutes, and administrative agency orders.

Judicial Decisions

Stare Decisis

Principle that a court decision controls the decision of a similar future case

Judicial interpretation is still an important element of the legal process. Because courts can interpret laws differently, the same law might have somewhat different consequences in different states. This happens because interpretations by the highest courts have the effect of precedents and under the doctrine of **stare decisis** (stand by the decision) bind the lower courts. These interpretations may concern a situation not previously brought before the court, or the court may decide to reverse a previous decision. Any state supreme court or the Supreme Court of the United States can reverse a decision of a lower court. For legal stability so that we can know our rights before we undertake a transaction, courts must generally adhere to the judicial precedents set by earlier decisions. However, changing situations or practices sometimes make it necessary for the previous case law to be overturned and a new rule or practice to be established.

Greg Batt was fired by Globe Engineering Co., Inc. He filed a suit against his former supervisor, Jack Johnson. In the appellate court, Batt asserted that Johnson had made false statements about Batt which led to the firing. Any statements by Johnson that could have helped Batt in the lawsuit could be admitted only if the court failed to follow a previous case decided by the state supreme court. The appellate court stated that it was duty bound to follow the law as established by supreme court decisions. The supreme court precedent was followed and judgment was for Johnson.

Constitutions

Constitution

Document that contains fundamental principles of a government

A **constitution** is the document that defines the relationships of the parts of the government to each other and the relationship of the government to its citizens or subjects. The U.S. Constitution is the supreme law of the land. State constitutions, as well as all other laws, must agree with the U.S. Constitution. The Supreme Court of the United States is the final arbiter in disputes about whether a state or federal law violates the U.S. Constitution. A state supreme court is the final judge as to whether a state law violates the constitution of that state.

In 1791, after the U.S. Constitution had been adopted, it was amended by the addition of the Bill of Rights. The Constitution contained no specific guarantees of individual liberty. The **Bill of Rights** consists of ten amendments specifically designed to protect the civil rights and liberties of the citizens and the states. It is a part of the U.S. Constitution.

Bill of Rights
First ten amendments to
U.S. Constitution

Statutes

Statutes are laws enacted by legislative bodies. The federal Congress, the state legislatures, and city councils comprise the three chief classes of legislative bodies in the United States. City councils make laws called **ordinances,** a specific type of statutory law.

Statutes
Laws enacted by legislative bodies

Ordinances
Laws enacted by cities

In some cases statutes enacted by one legislative body conflict with statutes enacted by another legislative body. A constitutional federal statute prevails over a conflicting state statute.

Unlike constitutions, which are difficult to amend and are designed to be general rather than specific, statutes may be enacted, repealed, or amended at any regular or special session of the lawmaking body. Thus, statutes respond more to the changing demands of the people.

In the field of business law the most important statute is the Uniform Commercial Code (UCC).[1] The UCC regulates the fields of sales and leases of goods; commercial paper, such as checks; secured transactions; and particular aspects of banking and fund transfers, letters of credit, warehouse receipts, bills of lading, and investment securities. While all 50 states have enacted at least some portions of the UCC, individual states have made some changes. Therefore, variations exist from state to state, which in some cases are significant in the UCC as well as other laws.

Administrative Agency Orders

Administrative agencies set up by our legislative bodies carry on many of our governmental functions today. **Administrative agencies** are commissions or boards that have the power to regulate particular matters or implement laws. At the federal level alone there are almost 60 agencies involved in regulatory activity. The legislative branch of government enacts laws that prescribe the powers that may be exercised by administrative agencies, the principles that guide the agencies in exercising those powers, and the legal remedies available to those who want to question the legality of some administrative action.

Administrative Agencies
Governmental boards or commissions with authority to regulate matters or implement laws

Administrative agencies may be given practically the same power to make law as the legislature and almost the same power to decide cases as the courts. However, agencies are created by laws and have the power to enact law only if that power has been delegated to them by the legislature.

The heads of federal administrative agencies are appointed by the president of the United States with the consent of the Senate. Administrative agencies are given wide latitude in setting up rules of procedure. They issue orders and decrees that have the force of law unless set aside by the courts after being challenged.

[1]The UCC has been adopted at least in part in every state. The UCC also has been adopted in the Virgin Islands and for the District of Columbia.

The state department of revenue issued an order revoking Patrick Able's driver's license for five years. However, one of the convictions that was used to justify entry of the order should not have been so used. Three years later Able was arrested and charged with operating a motor vehicle while under revocation. Able said he was not guilty because the department of revenue order was not enforceable. The court said that the fact that the agency's order was erroneously made did not justify failure to obey it. Able should have challenged it in court.

CIVIL VERSUS CRIMINAL LAW

L.O.4

Civil Law
Law dealing with enforcement or protection of private rights

Criminal Law
Laws dealing with offenses against society

Crime
Punishable offense against society

Felony
A more serious crime

Misdemeanor
A less serious crime

Law may be classified as either **civil** or **criminal law**. A person may file a lawsuit in order to enforce or protect a private right by requesting compensation for damage suffered or other action for restoration of his or her property. This action in *civil law* is concerned with private or purely personal rights.

Criminal law is that branch of the law that has to do with crimes and the punishment of wrongdoers. A crime is an offense that tends to injure society as a whole.

Crimes are usually classified, according to the nature of the punishment, as felonies and misdemeanors. Generally speaking, **felonies** are the more serious crimes and are usually punishable by death or by imprisonment in a penitentiary for more than one year. **Misdemeanors** are offenses of a less serious character and are punishable by a fine or imprisonment in a county or local jail. Committing a forgery is a felony, but driving an automobile in excess of the speed limit is a misdemeanor. The criminal statutes define the acts that are felonies and those that are misdemeanors. Criminal statutes may vary from state to state.

TORT LAW

Tort
Private wrong for which damages may be recovered

Negligence
Failure to exercise reasonable care

Prosecutor or District Attorney
Government employee who brings criminal actions

A **tort** is a private or civil wrong or injury for which there may be an action for damages. A tort may be intentional or it may be caused by negligence. **Negligence** is the failure to exercise reasonable care toward someone. It is tort law that allows an innocent motorist who is the victim of a careless or negligent driver to sue the negligent driver for damages. Other torts include fraud, trespass, assault, slander, and interference with contracts.

A tort action must be brought by the injured person against the person alleged to be negligent. This contrasts with criminal actions in which an employee of the government—usually called the **prosecutor** or **district attorney**—brings the action.

QUESTIONS

1   What is *law*? What is *business law*?
2   How does law differ from religious teachings, the mores of society, habit, and peer pressure in controlling social conduct?
3   Why do we have laws?
4   What is common law, and why is it important?
5   Why did the equity courts develop?

6 Why are we justified in classifying law by judicial decision as a source of law? What are three other sources of law?

7 Describe the relationship between the U.S. Constitution, state constitutions, and state statutes.

8 What is the Bill of Rights?

9 Classify the following crimes into felonies and misdemeanors: murder, theft of one dollar, drunkenness, robbery, overtime parking, and forgery.

10 Distinguish crimes from torts.

Appendix 1A

ETHICS

Ethics
Study of morality of conduct, its motives, and duties

Chapter 1 has discussed the basis for laws. One of the most important ideas mentioned is that "laws are the result of society's changing concepts of what is right and what is wrong." That means laws are based on our judgment regarding what human conduct is right, and therefore should be encouraged, and what conduct is wrong, and therefore should be discouraged. We thus base our laws on our morals. The study of the morality of conduct, its motives, and duties is called **ethics.**

Bases for Ethical Judgment

Everyone has opinions on what behavior and thinking is right and what is wrong. Each person bases these ethical judgments on his or her own personal values. We develop our values from our religious beliefs, our experience, our cultural background, and our scientific knowledge.

Ethical Principles

In considering the way in which ethics relates to the law, several principles regarding the application of ethics emerge. These principles include:

1 Seriousness of consequences
2 Consensus of the majority
3 Change in ethical standards

Seriousness of Consequences. While law is based on what we believe is right and wrong, our laws do not reflect everything we believe is right or wrong. When unethical behavior can harm others—when the matter is of serious consequence to people—laws are usually enacted to regulate that behavior. Less serious matters can be right or wrong, but they are not addressed by laws. For example, rules of etiquette frequently reflect our ethical judgments about behavior, but they do not have serious enough consequences that laws should be passed to enforce them.

Consensus of the Majority. Our laws cannot express every individual's ethical principles since everyone does not agree on what is moral. When a conflict occurs, there may be no law reflecting a judgment on the matter, or the laws might reflect the judgment of some. For example, vegetarians and nondrinkers may not believe laws permitting the eating of meat or the consumption of alcoholic beverages are ethical. Their morality may not be reflected in law. In a democratic society such as ours, the laws are designed to reflect the ethical view of the majority.

Change in Ethical Standards. Ethical standards change over time. Behavior believed ethical in the past becomes unethical, and behavior previously viewed as immoral becomes acceptable. Consider the matter of cigarette smoking on airplanes. Many years ago airline passengers could smoke no matter where seated. Then the law mandated smoking, and nonsmoking sections on planes. Now all commercial planes in the United States prohibit smoking and the federal government uses the force of law to enforce this rule. This change in government rules reflects the change in the view of most people about the harmful effects of cigarette smoking. Our ethical standards have changed.

Business Ethics

Our ethical standards apply to every aspect of life. For businesspeople, this means that ethical standards help determine their business practices. In our competitive economic system, the standard people in business have been expected to follow in determining behavior is "the bottom line." Is the behavior something that will help the business financially? When studying ethics as applied to business, we ask, does a business have obligations other than simply to make a profit or maximize "the bottom line"?

Many types of businesses or professional organizations have adopted codes of ethics to guide the behavior of their members. Variety occurs not only in the types of business that have adopted such codes, but also in the impact of codes on business. Some are legally enforceable while others are strictly voluntary.

Legally Enforceable. A number of professions have codes of ethics, usually called codes of professional responsibility, which when violated provide the basis for penalties against members of the profession. For example, the American Bar Association has produced a model code and model rules for ethical behavior by lawyers. Although these particular models have not been adopted by every state, each state has adopted an ethical code for lawyers. A violation of legal ethics subjects a lawyer to discipline including suspension from practicing law or even disbarment.

Voluntary. Some businesses have adopted codes of ethics for themselves as guides for individuals employed in these businesses. Since government has not imposed them, they do not carry legal penalties for violation. They recognize that ethical business conduct is a higher standard than that required by law and encourage behavior that is fair, honest, and, if disclosed, would not be embarrassing to the individual or the business.

Chapter 2

COURTS AND COURT PROCEDURE

After studying this chapter you should be able to:

1 Explain the function of the courts.

2 Explain the relationships of the various courts in our society.

3 Describe the procedure for filing a lawsuit.

4 Describe the basic procedure for a jury trial.

While it may seem confusing at first, each state has two distinct court systems—federal courts and state courts. Federal courts are a part of the federal government headquartered in Washington, D.C. There are 50 different state court systems, each a part of a state government headquartered in its state capital. While the federal and state court systems are largely independent of each other, they have a similar function.

FUNCTION OF THE COURTS

L.O.1

A court declares and applies judicial precedents, or case law, and applies laws passed by the legislative arm of the government. This is not the whole story, however. Constitutions by their very nature must be couched in generalities. Statutes are less general than constitutions; however, they could not possibly be worded to apply to every situation that may arise. Thus, the chief function of the courts is to interpret and apply the law from whatever source to a given situation. For example, the U.S. Constitution gives Congress power to regulate commerce among the several states. Under this power Congress passes a law requiring safety devices on trains. If the law is challenged, the court must decide whether this is a regulation of interstate commerce.

Similarly, an Act of Congress regulates minimum wages for the vast majority of workers. A case may arise as to whether this applies to the wages paid in a sawmill located in a rural section of the country. The court must decide whether or not the sawmill owner engages in interstate commerce. The court's decision may become a judicial precedent that will be followed in the future unless the court changes its decision in a subsequent case.

JURISDICTION OF COURTS

Jurisdiction

Authority of a court to hear a case

The power or authority that each court has to hear cases is called its **jurisdiction.** Courts must have jurisdiction over the subject matter of the case and jurisdiction over the persons involved. If a claim is made for damages due to an automobile accident, a probate court does not have jurisdiction over the subject matter since a probate court deals with wills and the distribution of property of deceased persons. The damage action would have to be brought in a court of general jurisdiction. A court may have jurisdiction over the subject matter but not over the person. If a resident of Ohio is charged with trespassing on a neighbor's property in the same state, a court in Indiana does not have jurisdiction over the person of the accused. Nor does a court in Ohio have jurisdiction over the person of the accused if the accused has not been properly served with notice of the trial. Before any court can try a case, it must be established that the court has jurisdiction over both the subject matter and the person in the case at issue.

CLASSIFICATION OF COURTS

L.O.2 ....

Courts are classified for the purpose of determining their jurisdiction. This classification can be made in a variety of ways. One classification can be made according to the governmental unit setting up the court. Under this classification system, courts are divided into (1) federal courts, (2) state courts, and (3) municipal courts.

The same courts may be classified according to the method of hearing cases. Under this system they are classified as trial courts and appellate courts. **Trial courts** conduct the original trial of cases. **Appellate courts** review cases appealed from the decisions of lower courts. A losing party appeals to the higher court to review the lower court's decision by claiming the lower court made a mistake that caused the party to lose. Appellate courts include courts of appeals and supreme courts. Appellate courts exercise considerable authority over the courts under them. Lower courts are bound by the decisions of their appellate courts.

Trial Court

Court that conducts original trial of a case

Appellate Court

Court that reviews decision of another court

Federal Courts

The federal courts have exclusive jurisdiction of bankruptcy matters, claims against the United States, and patent and copyright cases. Federal courts (see Illustration 2-1) include:

1   Special federal courts
2   Federal district courts
3   Federal courts of appeals
4   United States Supreme Court

Special Federal Courts

Federal trial courts with limited jurisdiction

Special Federal Courts. The **special federal courts** are limited in their jurisdiction by the laws of Congress creating them. For example, the Court of International Trade hears cases involving the rates of duty on various classes of imported goods, the collection of the revenues, and similar controversies. The U.S. Claims Court hears cases involving claims against the U.S. government. The Tax Court hears

The Federal Court System

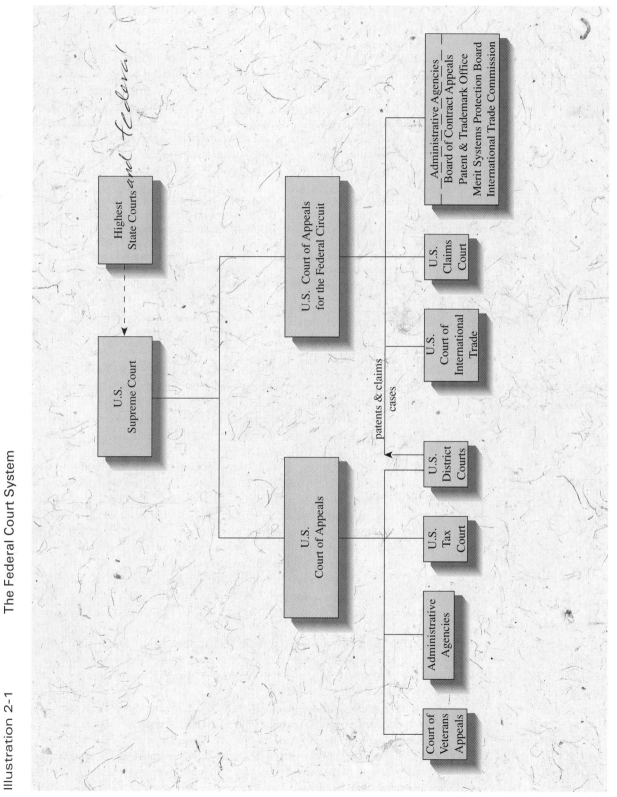

Illustration 2-1

cases involving tax controversies. Bankruptcy courts decide bankruptcy case. Most bankruptcy appeals are to the district courts.

Federal District Court

Trial court of federal court system

Federal District Courts. By far the largest class of federal courts consists of the **district courts.** These courts are strictly trial courts in which all criminal cases involving a violation of the federal law are tried. The district courts also have jurisdiction of civil suits that (1) are brought by the United States; (2) arise under the U.S. Constitution, federal laws, or treaties; or (3) are brought by citizens of different states or between citizens of one state and a foreign nation or one of its citizens where the amount in controversy is $50,000 or more.

Shortly after staying at Caesars Palace Resort Hotel in Las Vegas, Caesar Crimi formed a corporation that operated a beauty shop named "Caesars Palace" in New Jersey. A distinctive lettering style had been invented for the hotel's signs and they also contained a grammatical error—the apostrophe was missing from the possessive of the word *Caesar*. The main sign over the door at Crimi's shop had identical lettering and read "Caesars Palace"—also omitting the apostrophe. The hotel, which included a beauty salon, advertised nationally. The hotel sued for service mark infringement to prevent Crimi from using the words *Caesar's* with or without the apostrophe and the word *palace*. The hotel was a Florida corporation and the beauty shop was a New Jersey corporation. Because the corporations were of different states, the suit was brought by a citizen of one state against a citizen of another state and could be brought in a federal district court.

Federal Court of Appeals

Court that hears appeals in federal court system

Federal Courts of Appeals. The United States is divided into twelve federal judicial circuits. For each circuit there is a **court of appeals,** which hears appeals from cases arising in its circuit. The federal courts of appeals hear appeals from federal district courts and from federal administrative agencies and departments. A decision of a federal court of appeals is binding upon all lower courts within the jurisdiction of that circuit.

It is possible that one court of appeals could decide an issue one way and another court of appeals could decide it in another way. Because the lower courts within each court of appeals' jurisdiction must follow the decision of its court of appeals, courts in different circuits might decide similar cases differently. When this occurs, there is a conflict between the circuits. The conflict lasts until one circuit changes its decision or the U.S. Supreme Court rules on the issue.

There is also another court of appeals called the Court of Appeals for the Federal Circuit. It reviews decisions of special federal courts (such as the Court of International Trade and the U.S. Claims Court), decisions of four administrative agencies, and appeals from district courts in patent and claims cases.

U.S. Supreme Court

The highest court in the United States

United States Supreme Court. The **U.S. Supreme Court** has original jurisdiction in cases affecting ambassadors, public ministers, and consuls and in cases in which a state is a party. It has appellate jurisdiction in cases based on the U.S. Constitution, a federal law, or a treaty.

The majority of cases heard by the U.S. Supreme Court are cases appealed from the federal courts of appeals. Under certain circumstances a decision of a federal district court may be appealed directly to the Supreme Court. A state supreme court decision may also be reviewed by the U.S. Supreme Court if the case involves a federal constitutional question or if a federal law or treaty has been held invalid by the state court. Unlike the courts of appeals, the Supreme Court does not have to take all cases appealed. It chooses which appealed cases it will hear.

**Writ of
Certiorari**

Order to produce record
of a case

The normal way a case gets to the Supreme Court is by application for a **writ of certiorari**. The party asking for the Supreme Court review of a case asks the court to issue a writ of certiorari. This writ requires the lower court that has decided the case to produce the record of the case for the Supreme Court's review. The court issues a writ for only a small number of the requests. The U.S. Supreme Court is the highest tribunal in the land, and its decisions are binding on all other courts. Its decisions are final until the Court reverses its own decision or until the effect of a given decision is changed by a constitutional amendment or an enactment by the Congress.

The Constitution created the Supreme Court and gave Congress the power to establish inferior courts.

State Courts

State courts (see Illustration 2-2) can best be classified into the following groups:

1   Inferior courts
2   Courts of original general jurisdiction
3   Appellate courts
4   Special courts

Illustration 2-2   **Typical State Court System**

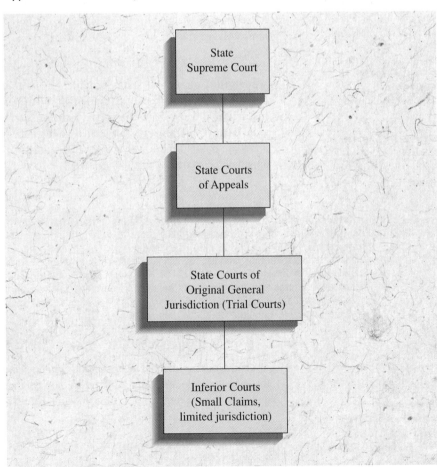

Inferior Courts
Trial courts that hear only cases involving minor offenses and disputes

Inferior Courts. Most states have **inferior courts** that hear cases involving minor criminal offenses and minor disputes between citizens. The names of inferior courts vary greatly from state to state. These courts are most frequently called district, magistrate, county, municipal, small claims, justice courts, or even taxi court. Some states have more than one of these named courts. Civil jurisdiction is limited to controversies involving a maximum amount of money, which generally varies from $1,000 to $25,000 or to a particular type of controversy. In addition, these courts may try all criminal cases involving misdemeanors. The loser in any of these courts may normally appeal to a court of original general jurisdiction.

Courts of Original General Jurisdiction
Court of record in which case is first tried

Courts of Original General Jurisdiction. Courts of original general jurisdiction are for the average citizen the most important courts of the state. These courts have broad jurisdiction over disputes between two or more parties as well as criminal offenses against the state. They are called **courts of original general jurisdiction** because the case is first instituted in them. On occasion they hear appeals from inferior courts, but this does not make them true appellate bodies because the entire case is retried at this level. Thus, such an appeal is actually treated as a case of original jurisdiction. These courts are also called trial courts, because they hear witnesses, receive evidence, and try the case.

An official, permanent record is kept of the trial showing the testimony, evidence, statements of counsel and the judge, the judgment, and the findings of the court. For this reason these courts are referred to as **courts of record.** The official name of such a court of original general jurisdiction varies from state to state, but in almost every state is one of the following: *circuit court, district court,* or *Superior Court.*[1]

Court of Record
Court in which an official record of the proceedings is kept

State Courts of Appeals
Intermediate appellate courts

State Supreme Court
Highest court in most states

Appellate Courts. All states provide for an appeal to an appellate court by the party dissatisfied with the final judgment of the trial court or any of its rulings and instructions. Most states have a system of intermediate appellate courts usually called **courts of appeals,** as well as one final appellate court. Decisions of the appellate courts bind lower courts. The **state supreme court** is usually the highest appellate court of a state.

> Jefferson Johnson, an attorney, represented Lillie McCoy in a claim against State Farm Insurance Co. State Farm offered to settle for $20,000. Someone in Johnson's office told State Farm McCoy would accept. State Farm gave Johnson a check for $20,000. McCoy's signature was forged on the check and deposited in Johnson's personal account. The prosecutor charged Johnson with stealing under state law. Johnson was tried in a state trial court in which witnesses were heard and documentary evidence was presented. He was found guilty. Johnson appealed to the state court of appeals. The state court of appeals found for Johnson. The state supreme court granted review of the appellate court decision and reversed that court finding Johnson guilty.

Probate Court
Court that handles estates

Domestic Relations Court
Court that handles divorce and related cases

Special Courts. Many states have additional special courts, such as **probate courts** that handle wills and estates; **juvenile courts** that are concerned with delinquent, dependent, and neglected children; and **domestic relations courts** that handle

[1]In New York this court is known as a Supreme Court, and in Ohio it is known as a Court of Common Pleas.

divorce and child custody cases. These are not courts of general jurisdiction, but of special jurisdiction. In some states these courts are of the same level as the trial courts. When this is the case, they, too, are properly called trial courts and are courts of record. In other states they are on the same level as the inferior courts and are not courts of record.

COURT OFFICERS

Constable or Bailiff
Executive officer of inferior state court

Sheriff
Executive officer of court of record

Clerk of Court
Recorder of court of record

Marshal
Executive officer of federal court

The chief officer of an inferior court is the **judge, justice of the peace, magistrate, trial justice,** or similar officer. The executive officer is the **constable** or **bailiff.** In a state court of record the chief officer is the **judge,** the executive officer is the **sheriff,** and the recorder is the **clerk of the court.** These titles are the same in the federal courts except that the executive officer is called a **marshal.**

Persons educated in the profession of the law and licensed to practice law, which means they may represent others in legal matters, are known as **lawyers** or **attorneys.** They are officers of the court and are subject to punishment for a breach of duty. Lawyers ordinarily represent the parties in a civil or a criminal action, although many states permit the parties to represent themselves. The practice of presenting one's own case, however, is usually not advisable.

PROCEDURE IN COURTS OF RECORD

Procedural law
Law specifying how actions are filed and what trial procedure to follow

Procedural law are laws that specify how parties are to proceed in filing civil actions and how these actions are to be tried. They must be followed if the parties wish to have the case settled by a court.

Filing Suit in a Civil Action

L.O.3

Complaint or Petition
Written request to court to settle dispute

Plaintiff
Person who begins a civil lawsuit

Defendant
Person against whom a case is filed

Summons or Process
Notice to appear in court

Answer
Response of defendant to a complaint

Courts with but few exceptions are powerless to settle disputes between individuals unless one of the parties so requests the court. The written request, called a **complaint** or **petition,** begins a civil suit. The individual who institutes a civil action is called the **plaintiff,** and the individual against whom action is brought is called the **defendant.** The order of events in bringing an action is generally as follows:

1. *Filing Suit.* The complaint or petition is filed with the clerk of the court. This petition sets forth the jurisdiction of the court, the nature of the claim, and the remedy sought.
2. *Notice of suit.* As soon as the petition is filed, the clerk issues a **summons** or, as it is sometimes called, a **process.** This gives the defendant notice of the complaint and informs the defendant of the time in which to respond.
3. *Response.* The defendant has a specified number of days available in which to file an **answer** or a *motion.* The answer admits or denies the facts alleged in the complaint. A motion is an application to the judge for an order requiring an act be done in favor of the moving party. The complaint and answer constitute the first pleadings.

Discovery

Means of obtaining information from other party before a trial

4   *Discovery.* To obtain information relevant to the subject matter of the action, the parties may request unprivileged information from another party in a number of ways, called **discovery**, including:

a.   Interrogatories: Written questions to be answered in writing.

b.   Deposition: Examination of a party or potential witness outside court and under oath.

c.   Admissions: Requests to agree that a certain fact is true or a matter of law is decided.

d.   Medical examination by a physician.

e.   Access to real and personal property.

If a court issues an order compelling discovery, failure to comply can result in punishment. The party who does not comply may be found in contempt of court or the judge may dismiss the case.

The parties may take other actions after a case has been instituted and before it goes to trial. A party may file a wide variety of motions, including a motion to dismiss the case, a motion for a judgment based solely on the pleadings, and a motion to obtain a ruling on the admissibility of certain evidence or to suppress evidence prior to trial.

5   *Fact Finding.* If disagreements occur about facts of the case, a jury may be impaneled to decide these facts. If neither party requests a jury, the case may be tried before a judge alone, who would act as both judge and jury.

Trial Procedure

L.O.4 ....

A typical jury trial proceeds in the following order:

1   The jury is selected and sworn in.

2   The attorney for the plaintiff makes an opening statement to the jury indicating the nature of the action and what the plaintiff expects to prove. This is usually followed by the defendant's attorney's opening statement.

3   The plaintiff presents evidence in the form of testimony of witnesses and exhibits designed to prove the allegations made in the plaintiff's petition. The plaintiff has the burden of proving facts adequate to support the petition's allegations. If this burden is not met, the case can be dismissed and the lawsuit ends. The plaintiff's evidence is followed by the defendant's evidence. The defendant tries to disprove the plaintiff's allegations. The defendant may also present evidence excusing the behavior complained of by the plaintiff.

4   The attorneys for each side summarize the evidence and argue their points in an attempt to win the jury to their version of the case.

5   The judge instructs the jury as to the points of law which govern the case. The judge has the sole power to determine the points of law, and the jury decides what weight is to be given to each point of evidence.

6   The jury adjourns to the jury room and in secret arrives at its decision, called the **verdict.** This verdict may be set aside by the court if it is contrary to the law and the evidence. Unless this is done, the judge enters a judgment in accordance with the verdict.

Verdict

Decision of a jury

Appeals

If either the plaintiff or the defendant is dissatisfied with the judgment and can cite an error of law by the court, an appeal may generally be taken to a higher court.

When an appeal is taken, a complete transcript or written record of the trial is given to the appellate court. Rather than hear testimony from witnesses, the appellate court reviews the entire proceedings from the transcript. The attorney for each side files a brief, setting forth the reasons that warrant the appellate court to either affirm or reverse the judgment of the lower court. The decision of the appellate court becomes judicial precedent and is binding upon lower courts. The appellate court may, however, reverse itself in a future case, although this seldom occurs.

PROCEDURE IN SMALL CLAIMS COURTS

Filing and trying a suit in an inferior court like a small claims court is a much simpler matter than filing and trying a suit in a court of record. A form for the complaint may be obtained from the court and filled out by the plaintiff without help from a lawyer. Frequently court employees will assist in filling out the forms. The defendant is then served with the complaint.

When the case is tried, the procedure is much more informal than in a court of record. The case is tried by a judge, so there is no jury. Since neither party has to be represented by an attorney, and in some courts may not be so represented, the judge asks the parties to state their positions. While witnesses and evidence may be presented, the questioning is more informal. The judge is likely to ask questions in order to assist in ascertaining the facts. The judge then renders the verdict and judgment of the court. Normally, either party may appeal the judgment to a court of record, in which case the matter is retried there.

QUESTIONS

1 Why does each state have two court systems?
2 What is the function of a court?
3 What is meant by a court's jurisdiction?
4 Is it ever possible for cases involving the same issue to be decided differently in different courts of a court system? Explain.
5 What are trial courts?
6 Name the court in which the following disputes would be settled:
   a. A dispute over the interpretation of a will
   b. A claim for an unpaid bill of $100
   c. The claim of a woman that her ex-husband refuses to support their child
   d. A damage suit for $2,500
   e. An appeal from a judgment
   f. A claim against the federal government under the Federal Tort Claims Act
7 Who are the officers of
   a. An inferior court?
   b. A state court of record?
   c. A federal court?
8 a. What is the first step in bringing a civil suit?
   b. What is the procedure in a civil suit tried by a jury?
9 How much of the proceedings of the trial court is reviewed by an appellate court?
10 How does trying a case in a small claims court differ from trying a case in a court of record?

Chapter 3

BUSINESS CRIMES AND TORTS

LEARNING OBJECTIVES

After studying this chapter you should be able to:

1 Explain what business crimes are.

2 Name and describe the crimes important to business.

3 Discuss the basis for intentional and negligent tort liability.

4 List and explain the generally recognized business torts.

The growth of businesses has caused concern about the way they relate to society and to other businesses. Is the activity of a business unfairly damaging another or even violating a criminal law? With some variations from state to state, courts have found some activities by businesses and some activities against businesses actionable.

CRIMES

The news media report on crimes every day so everyone hears about murders, robberies, assaults, and break-ins. While some of these crimes involve businesses or businesspeople, they pervade the entirety of society.

Business Crimes

L.O.1

Business Crimes

Crimes against a business or committed by using a business

Certain criminal offenses, such as arson, forgery, fraudulent conveyances, shoplifting, and embezzlement, closely relate to business activities. **Business crimes** consist of any crimes committed against a business or in which the perpetrator uses a business to commit the crime.

Gailon A. Joy owned Credit Management Services Corp. (CMS), a debt-collection agency. When CMS made a collection, it would deposit the money in a bank in Barre. CMS also had its own separate account. However, CMS began transferring funds from the Barre account to its own account to cover its expenses. CMS received a collection for Stacey Fuel and Lumber Co., but never even told Stacey the money had been collected. A year later, CMS filed for bankruptcy. The State charged Joy with the crime of embezzling the collection made for Stacey. Joy claimed he intended to repay the money. The court upheld Joy's conviction saying an intent to repay was irrelevant.

Types of Crimes

L.O.2 ....

The types of crimes committed by and against businesses appear to be limited only by the ingenuity of the human mind. Many include stealing or theft from the business. In this age of computers, wire transfers, and organized crime, the range of crime has been growing. Today, crimes affecting business include:

1 Theft
2 Computer crimes
3 RICO cases

Theft

Taking another's property without consent

Theft. Theft is the crime of stealing. It involves taking or appropriating another's property without the owner's consent and with the intention of depriving the owner of it. This definition includes taking and depriving another of property even when the thief initially obtains the property lawfully.

Some states use different terms to identify the various possible types of theft. As it relates to business, theft encompasses such crimes as shoplifting, embezzlement, and larceny. The elements of each of these offenses differs somewhat from state to state, but the crimes generally consist of the following:

Shoplifting

Taking unpurchased goods from a store

1 **Shoplifting**: Taking possession of goods in a store with the intent to use as the taker's own without paying the purchase price. In some states, merely concealing unpurchased goods while in a store constitutes shoplifting. The intent required for shoplifting is the intent to use the property as the taker's. This crime must be committed in a store by taking store merchandise, so it is always a business crime.

> At a supermarket, a police officer observed Victor Balboni remove two cartons of cigarettes from their rack and place them in an opened bag in his shopping cart. Balboni then put more cartons of cigarettes in the opened bag. The officer walked down the aisle where Balboni had the shopping cart and looked into the bag. He saw several cartons of cigarettes in it. The officer arrested Balboni since state law specified concealing merchandise with the intention of depriving the merchant of its use without payment constituted shoplifting. Balboni was searched and found to have no money. The court held he was guilty of shoplifting because he concealed the cartons and had no money to pay for them.

Embezzlement

Fraudulent conversion of property lawfully possessed

2 **Embezzlement**: Fraudulent conversion of another's property by someone in lawful possession of the property. Embezzlement requires the intent to defraud the owner of the property. Conversion here means the defendant handles the property inconsistently with the arrangement by which he or she has possession of it. Since many businesses rely on employees to receive payments and make disbursements, embezzlement is often a crime against a business.

Larceny

Taking and carrying away of property without consent

3 **Larceny**: Taking and carrying away the property of another without the consent of the person in possession and with the intention of depriving the possessor of the property. The intent to deprive the person in possession of the property must exist at the time the property is taken. For larceny to exist, the taker need not take the property from the owner—merely from the person in possession of it. Larceny can relate to business whenever someone takes any business property whether inventory, tools, or even office supplies.

Stephen Murray made false entries in his corporate employer's books and forged 180 of his employer's checks making them payable to himself. The amounts of the checks ranged from $2,000 to $60,000, and over five years Murray stole more than $4,000,000. The court found him guilty of 180 larcenies because 180 times he had taken his employer's property without consent and with the intention to deprive the employer of the money.

Computer Crimes

Computer Crimes

Crimes that are committed with aid of computers or that exist because of computers

Computer crimes are crimes committed with the aid of a computer or that exist because of computers. As more and more businesses rely on computers and as computer systems have become more interconnected, more opportunities exist for criminal behavior. Some computer offenses have been successfully prosecuted by using existing criminal laws prohibiting theft, mail fraud, wire fraud, and the transportation of stolen property.

McGraw operated a computer for the Indianapolis Department of Planning and Zoning. He used the city's computer for his private business of selling a dietary product. City employees did not have authorization to use the computer for private business. McGraw put his customer lists, inventory control, and other business records on the computer. After being fired, he asked another employee to get him a printout of his business records and then erase them. The other employee reported this and McGraw was charged under a traditional theft law with theft of computer services. The court said that computer time was services, which are a valuable asset. Therefore it was property and within the definition of property subject to theft.

Some courts have refused to apply traditional criminal laws to computer offenses. Both the federal government and the states have responded to the need for laws which clearly apply to computer crimes by enacting specific computer crime legislation.

One federal law is called the Computer Fraud and Abuse Act. This act makes it an offense to access a computer used by or for the U.S. government and to (1) fraudulently obtain anything of value; (2) intentionally alter, damage, or destroy information; (3) prevent authorized use of the computer or information; or (4) deal in computer passwords and thereby affect interstate commerce.

The laws enacted by the states vary considerably. However, they generally prohibit the intentional, unauthorized access to a computer regardless of the reason for the access.

Criminal activity relating to computers can be classified as of two types: trespass and fraud.

Computer Trespass

Unauthorized use of or access to computer

Trespass. As applied to business crime, **computer trespass** means unauthorized use of or access to a computer. A trespass can range from being harmless to being a threat to national security. Such activities as merely using a computer to play games or prepare personal documents constitute computer trespass. More serious trespasses include learning trade secrets, customer lists, and classified defense information. Computer trespass has been the focus of state computer crime laws.

A computer trespass may be committed in a number of ways, depending on who gains unauthorized access and the use made of the computer. The access might be by:

1 An employee not authorized to use a computer in the business
2 An employee authorized to use a computer who uses it for nonbusiness purposes
3 An outsider who gains access to the business's computer system

Since all computer trespass involves the use of computer time without permission, all trespass technically might be classified as theft of computer time. However computer trespass causes more serious problems. It ties up computers and prevents employees from doing their jobs, reveals trade secrets, customers' personal financial records, or confidential medical information. Because computers house so much information, it is helpful that the computer crime laws of the majority of jurisdictions protect the confidentiality of all information stored in computers.

Rogue Program

Set of software instructions that produces abnormal computer behavior

One of the most highly publicized methods of trespass involves damaging computer record systems by using rogue programs. A **rogue program** is a set of software instructions that produces abnormal or unexpected behavior in a computer. Various kinds of rogue programs have such colorful names as viruses, bacteria, worms, Trojan horses, and time bombs. They may cause computer users difficulty, inhibit normal use, or impose injury. The programs can be introduced to a computer by being attached to a useful program and spread to other computers through modems, disks, or network connections. Once introduced, a rogue program can alter the operations of a program, destroy data or screen displays, create false information, display a message, or even damage the computer.

Robert Morris, a graduate student at Cornell University, had authorization to use computers at Cornell. He wanted to demonstrate that security measures on computer networks were inadequate. Morris released a worm into the Internet from a computer at MIT. The worm was supposed to take up little computer time, but be difficult to detect. The worm duplicated and infected computers much faster than Morris expected. Many computers at universities, military sites, and medical research facilities all over the country crashed or would not work. The court found Morris guilty of violation of the Computer Fraud and Abuse Act.

Rogue programs may not show up for some time, so they can spread without alerting operators to their presence and damage all files in a computer system. One large computer software company inadvertently sent out copies of a software program containing a virus. The product had been accidentally infected after being loaded onto a computer that had received the virus from another program. In this case the virus merely caused a message to flash on computer users' screens. However, the software company had the expense of recalling thousands of copies of its software program.

Fraud. As applied to computer crime, fraud encompasses larceny and embezzlement. It includes causing bank deposits to be credited to just one individual's account. Such an action might be prosecuted under traditional crime statutes or new computer crime statutes.

Jones and an accomplice altered accounts payable documents fed into a computer. As a result, the computer issued checks to Jones totaling $130,000. They originated in Canada, and Jones cashed them in Maryland. Charged under a statute that made transporting securities known to be stolen, converted, or taken by fraud in interstate or foreign commerce a crime, Jones argued the securities were forgeries and as such the statute did not apply to them. The court said the checks were genuine but contained a false statement as to the true creditor. Jones was found guilty.

RICO Cases

The Racketeer Influenced and Corrupt Organizations Act, called RICO for short, is a federal law designed to prevent the criminal act of infiltration of legitimate businesses by organized crime. It prohibits investing income from racketeering to obtain a business, using racketeering to obtain a business (through conspiracy, extortion, and so on), using a business to conduct racketeering, and conspiring to do any of these. The law includes stiff criminal penalties for violation.

However, RICO includes civil sanctions as well as criminal ones. It has been applied to many business cases not involving organized crime. Although brought under RICO and based on the perpetration of criminal activity, these cases are technically civil cases. The injured party brings the action and requests damages. In criminal cases a government brings the action. To find a business violation of RICO, a plaintiff must show all of the following:

1 Conduct
2 Of an enterprise (at least two people)
3 Through a pattern (at least two acts within ten years)
4 Of racketeering activity

Racketeering activity means activity labeled criminal under state or federal laws. Examples of such activity include murder, kidnapping, arson, robbery, bribery, extortion, distribution of illegal narcotics, prostitution, and white-collar crime such as mail fraud, money laundering, and securities fraud. The defendant does not have to have been convicted. It is activity for which a conviction could be obtained. This makes it easier to win a civil RICO case than a criminal case.

Sedima and Imrex Company, Inc. formed a joint venture to sell electronic components. Once the buyer ordered parts, Imrex was to procure and ship them to Europe. Sedima and Imrex were to split the net proceeds. Orders were filled, but Sedima believed that Imrex was inflating expense bills and therefore cheating Sedima out of some of the proceeds. Sedima filed suit asserting claims under RICO. The trial court held that RICO did not apply because Imrex had not been convicted on criminal charges for a racketeering injury. The appellate court said only criminal activity, not a conviction, need be shown.

Civil suits under RICO have been very popular because of the liberal damages available. Rather than allowing merely compensatory damages, RICO provides recovery of three times the damages suffered. It also allows the recovery of attorneys' fees, which can be a substantial sum.

In addition to the federal RICO, many states have passed so-called *Baby RICO* laws. While similar to the federal law, these laws apply to activities in intrastate commerce. The federal law has jurisdiction over interstate commerce.

TORTS

Tortfeasor

Person whose action causes injury

Chapter 1 defined a tort as a private wrong or injury. The law permits people to sue for injuries caused by the intentional or negligent acts of others. The person who causes the injury is called a **tortfeasor.**

Intentional Torts

To recover for an intentional tort, the injured person must show three things:

1 An act by the defendant,
2 An intention to cause the consequences of the act, and
3 Causation—the injury was caused by the defendant's act or something set in motion by the act.

Intentional torts include such actions as assault, battery, trespass, and false imprisonment. While a business could be involved in these torts, parties involved in these types of cases come from every sector of the community.

Sears, Roebuck employed Lynn Malanga in the candy department. Sears knew that it had lost merchandise in the department. During her regular business hours in familiar surroundings, the store manager questioned Malanga about her involvement in a theft ring.

Malanga sued Sears for false imprisonment. The manager's act of questioning Malanga was clearly intentional, so Malanga claimed there had been an intentional tort.

Negligence Torts

To recover for a tort based on negligence, the injured party must show:

1 A duty of the tortfeasor,
2 Breach of that duty,
3 The breach was the actual and proximate cause of the injury, and
4 Injury or damage.

A person may recover in tort for negligence whenever these four elements occur. Courts frequently hear such cases involving automobile accidents, medical malpractice, injuries from products, and injuries resulting from the condition of a landowner's property.

Business Torts

Business Tort

Tort caused by or involving a business

Torts caused by a business or involving a business are **business torts.** Businesses become involved in a tort action in several common ways.

Product Liability. Manufacturers of products incur potential liability in tort for injuries caused by the products. A person injured through the use or condition of a product could sue on the basis of the manufacturer's negligence in the preparation or manufacture of the article. The plaintiff figuratively must go into the defendant's plant or factory, learn how the article was made, and prove negligence. Unless the plaintiff can show negligence in the design of the manufacturer's product or the general method of manufacture, it is unlikely the plaintiff will be able to prove negligence.

An overhead guard on a forklift fell and hit John Harper on the head. Harper sued Clark Equipment Co., the manufacturer of the forklift, for negligence in its design. Experts testified that the guard met all the industry standards. It had been tested at the equivalent of 10,000 hours of use for endurance and passed. The court said Harper had not shown negligence in the design so he could not recover.

Whenever a manufacturer as a reasonable person should foresee that a particular class of persons will be injured by the product, the manufacturer is liable to an injured member of that class without regard to whether such member purchased from the manufacturer or from anyone else.

Strict Tort Liability

Manufacturer of product liable without proof of negligence for dangerous product

The difficulty of proving negligence has helped lead the courts to expand a doctrine called **strict tort liability.** This doctrine makes a manufacturer liable without proof of negligence. It applies to anyone injured because of a defect in the manufacture of a product when such defect makes the use of the product dangerous to the user or persons in the vicinity of the product. The person injured or killed must be a user or person in the vicinity.

Business Activity. Several other business activities have been widely recognized as tortious. They may be based on state law, federal law, or the common law and are often intentional torts. While some variation exists among the states, an injured party may recover damages on the basis of four generally recognized business torts:

1   Inducing breach of contract
2   Interference with prospective advantage
3   Injurious falsehood
4   Confusion of source

Inducing Breach of Contract

Inducing Breach of Contract

Third party's causing a party to breach contract

Inducing breach of contract occurs when a third party in some way causes a party to a contract to breach that contract. If injured, the other party to the contract may have a cause of action against the party causing the breach.

While a breach is normally necessary for a cause of action, some states do not require that the contract actually be breached. They find a cause of action when the third party causes a party to a contract to exercise a right to terminate it. Competitors are usually privileged to do this, but noncompetitors are not. Normally inducing breach of contract requires that the injured party prove:

1   A valid contract existed
2   The defendant knew of the contract or the contract was readily apparent
3   Intentional interference designed to cause breach of the contract
4   Actual breach or disruption of the contract

A Valid Contract. Without a contract, there can be no breach, thus no tort.

Contract Known or Readily Apparent. A court imposes liability only if the defendant knew or a reasonable person would know there was a contract.

Intentional Interference Causing a Breach. Traditionally, proof of this tort only required a showing that the defendant knowingly interfered with a contract.

However, more and more states require that the intentional interference be improper. Improper interference can occur because of an improper motive, an improper means, or by acting other than in the legitimate exercise of the defendant's own rights. A defendant who protects its economic or safety interests or asserts an honest claim is not acting improperly.

Alyeska Pipeline Service Co. and Aurora Air Service had had a dispute. Later, RCA contracted with Alyeska to maintain a communications system along the Trans-Alaska Pipeline. RCA was to furnish all the transportation necessary; however, Alyeska was allowed to take over the transportation requirements. Aurora contracted with RCA to furnish a plane and pilot. About a year later, Alyeska took over the transportation requirements of its contract with RCA, so RCA termi-nated its contract with Aurora. Aurora sued Alyeska for intentionally interfering in its contractual relation-ship with RCA. It alleged Alyeska was motivated by spite from the earlier dispute. The court said that while Alyeska had the unilateral right to modify its contract with RCA, that right had to be exercised in good faith. Alyeska could not intentionally procure a breach of the contract between RCA and Aurora without justifica-tion. Judgment for Aurora.

In a free-market economy, competitors inevitably injure one another. Courts do not hold such injury tortious, even when intentional, if the action was taken to advance a person's economic interest and results from the competitive economic system.

Actual Breach or Disruption. Normally there can be no tort of inducing breach of contract unless a contract is actually breached. However, some courts do allow substantial interference with the contract's performance or reduction in the value of the contract to be actionable.

Interference with Prospective Advantage

Interference with prospective advantage is the unjustified interference with a person's reasonable expectation of future economic advantage. This tort involves an interest in prospective relationships not yet reduced to a formal contract. Examples of interference that can be actionable include interference with leasing opportunities, the opportunity of buying and selling goods or services, or the hiring of employees. Almost all jurisdictions define this tort to require:

1   Existence of a valid business relationship or expectancy
2   The defendant's knowledge of the relationship, or that it was readily apparent
3   A reasonable certainty that relationship would have continued or occurred
4   Intentional interference

Valid Business Relationship or Expectancy. The injured party must show either that a business relationship existed or that one would likely materialize. Negotiating with another regarding a business enterprise shows a business expectancy. A third party cannot interfere with a business relationship that has ended with no expectation it will resume.

Relationship Known or Readily Apparent. The person alleged to have interfered must have known of the business relationship or have been reasonably expected to know of it. The wrongdoer need not know with whom the injured party is dealing, only that the injured party does have a business relationship.

Care Enterprises operated a nursing home by lease with J & S Medical Group, Inc. The lease expired on June 30. Care wanted an extension. On April 28, J & S notified Care that the lease would not be renewed and that J & S was negotiating a new lease with an unnamed third party who would take possession of the home on July 1. Ramona, a partnership, was created and executed a lease of the facility with J & S on June 12. Care remained in possession of the home after June 30. Ramona sued Care for intentional interference with economic advantage. Care said that was impossible since it did not know of Ramona's name or existence on July 1. Care was liable. It knew that J & S had entered into a relationship with another party for the operation of the facility and knew the prospective operator's contractual rights would be frustrated by Care's actions.

Reasonable Certainty the Relationship Would Have Continued or Occurred. The defendant's action must have caused the plaintiff harm. A defendant incurs no liability if the business relationship would have terminated anyway.

Intentional Interference. A defendant must make a purposeful act designed to disrupt the business relationship. The interference must be for an improper purpose or committed by improper means. An improper means is contrary to law or designed to injure the other contracting party. This includes violence, threats, misrepresentation, bribery, unfounded litigation, or defamation. But a party may act reasonably to protect its own legitimate economic interest.

W. S. Leigh contracted to sell a furniture business to Richard Isom. The contract included a ten-year lease of a floor of the building housing the business. Leigh later wanted to sell the building, but could not because of the lease. Every week Leigh, his wife, and bookkeeper harassed Isom at the store, sometimes in front of customers. This interrupted sales activities, caused customers to comment and complain, and even to leave the store. Leigh filed two groundless lawsuits against Isom, refused to pay his share of bills, and threatened to cancel the sale contract. Leigh sued to repossess the building and terminate the lease. Isom alleged intentional interference with prospective economic relations. The court said by forcing Isom to defend groundless lawsuits, Leigh had employed an improper means to interference with Isom's business. Isom recovered damages.

Injurious Falsehood

Injurious falsehood occurs when a person makes false statements of fact that degrade the quality of another's goods or services. The false statement must be made to a third person. This is called **communication.** The hearer must understand the statement to refer to the plaintiff's goods or services and degrade their quality. The injured party must also show the statement was a substantial element in causing damage. In some states the plaintiff must identify specific customers lost as a result of the statement.

In a book, Time-Life Books Inc. reproduced Charles Atlas, Ltd.'s classic ad about a "97-pound weakling" who becomes a "real man" after using the Atlas exercise system. The caption above the reproduced ad described the Atlas system as isometric. The text of the book warned readers of the extreme dangers of isometric exercises. Atlas sued Time-Life alleging product disparagement. The court found that reading the caption in conjunction with the text, a reasonable reader could conclude that Atlas marketed an isometric exercise program, isometric exercises are dangerous, and therefore, Atlas' exercise program is dangerous. Time-Life falsely described the Atlas system as isometric, so Atlas stated a claim for injurious falsehood.

Finally, the statement must have been made maliciously. Malice can always be shown by proving that the statement was made as a result of ill will, spite, or hostility with the intention of causing harm to the plaintiff. In some jurisdictions, the plaintiff need only show that the false statement was made knowing it was false or with reckless disregard as to the truth or falsity of it.

Confusion of Source
Representing goods or services as those of another

Confusion of source occurs when a person attempts to represent goods or services as being the goods or services of someone else. The law assumes customers would be confused as to the source of the goods or services. Actual confusion need not be shown. This tort occurs from trademark or trade-name infringement or unfair competition.

Trademark
Word, symbol, device, or combination of them used to identify and distinguish goods

Trademarks. Federal law defines a **trademark** as a word, name, symbol, device, or any combination adopted and used by a person to identify and distinguish goods, including a unique product, from another's goods and to indicate the source of the goods. A trademark indicates that goods carrying that mark all come from one source.

Not all words or symbols qualify for protection as trademarks. Only those marks used by a business in a way that identifies its goods or services and differentiates them from others are entitled to protection. The mark normally must be inherently distinctive, which means the mark is unique, arbitrary, and nondescriptive.

Secondary Meaning
Special meaning of a mark that distinguishes goods

A mark not so distinctive, may be a trademark if it has acquired a **secondary meaning.** A secondary meaning is a special or trade meaning developed by usage that distinguishes the goods or services in such a way as to warrant trademark protection. A generic term can be protected if it has acquired a secondary meaning. If the right to trademark protection is based on the doctrine of secondary meaning, the geographical area of protection will be limited to the area in which the mark has such a secondary meaning.

Marks that are fanciful, arbitrary, or subtly suggest something about the product can be protected. Protected marks include words such as *Ivory* for soap, the letters *S* and *ECI*, abbreviations and nicknames such as *Coke*, made up words such as *Exxon* and *Rolex*, and the shapes of packages and products. Generic terms such as *super glue* and *softsoap* cannot be trademarks.

A trademark may be registered or unregistered. A trademark registered under the federal trademark law provides the holder with all the rights and remedies of that law. The holder of an unregistered trademark has some rights under the federal law and rights provided by the common law. Many states also have trademark laws; however, they vary greatly. In some states the holder of a mark may not get greater protection by registering than the common law affords an unregistered mark.

Courts examine a number of factors when deciding whether a likelihood of confusion between two marks exists. While the various courts do not always use the same factors, those factors most commonly considered include:

1 The similarity of the two marks
2 The similarity of the products represented by the marks
3 The similarity of marketing and customers
4 The similarity and amount of advertising used
5 The area of overlapping use
6 The intent of the parties in adopting the marks
7 The strength of the marks
8 Actual confusion by the public

The denomination's board of directors disaffiliated the First Church of Christ, Scientist, Plainfield, New Jersey. The church added the word *Independent* before its former name. The board sued for an injunction to keep the church from using *Christian Science* or *Church of Christ, Scientist* in relation to its church or reading room. The court said that the guidelines to determine the likelihood of confusion in reference to the sale of goods were equally applicable to religious associations. It then said that the addition of the qualifying adjective, *independent* to the name of a well-known prior organization was insufficient to avoid confusion. The injunction was granted.

Trademark or Trade-Name Infringement

Unauthorized use or imitation of another's mark or name

A trademark or trade name gives the owner the exclusive right to use a word or device to distinguish a product or a service. **Trademark or trade name infringement** is the unauthorized use or confusingly similar imitation of another person's mark or name. Because infringement is a tort, rather than a crime, the holder of the trademark or name has the duty of bringing any legal action to stop the alleged infringement and recover damages.

Trademarks identify and distinguish tangible goods; service marks identify and distinguish services. However, the same legal principles govern trademark infringement and service mark infringement.

Unfair Competition

Total impression of product results in confusion as to its origin

Unfair Competition. Unfair competition exists when the total impression a product gives to the consumer results in confusion as to the origin of the product. The impression of a product includes its packaging, size, color, shape, design, wording, any decorative indicia, and name. When unfair competition is claimed, the total physical image conveyed by the product and its name are considered together.

QUESTIONS

1   What is a business crime?
2   What crime is always a business crime and why?
3   What are some types of computer trespass that are serious for businesses?
4   Must there always be laws written specifically to punish computer crimes in order to convict a person of such a crime?
5   Why are injured parties eager to sue on the basis of RICO?
6   Explain the four generally recognized business torts.
7   Is it a business tort for competitors to injure one another?
8   What is a trademark?

CASE PROBLEMS

L.O.3, 4 ....

1   For 30 years, Draper Communications, Inc. operated a television station under the call letters *WBOC-TV*. It advertised by those call letters spending $150,000 annually. A new station managed by Delaware Valley Broadcasters chose the call letters *WBOT-TV*. WBOC and WBOT had some overlapping service area. Draper sued to prevent Broadcasters from using the call letters *WBOT-TV*. A witness testified that the call letters were overwhelmingly similar on phonetic grounds. WBOC had an extremely strong mark. WBOT posed a significant competitive threat, and television viewers were not likely to exercise great care in choosing a station. Could Draper keep Broadcasters from using the call letters *WBOT-TV*?

L.O.1, 2 ....

2   Anaheim Police detective Stockwell asked Diane Terry to help in a "sting" investigation of wrongful computer access. Terry worked for Trans Union, a credit reporting agency. She created a phony file in her company's credit data bank using the name Diane T. Wolfe, but without supplying any data. She phoned National Credit Service, which advertised as a service to help people with bad credit. Lelas Gentry told her he could create a new credit file for her with false information. She and Stockwell met with Gentry who gave Stockwell a full credit report on Diane T. Wolfe from Trans Union. Gentry did not have authorization for access to Trans Union's files, and only Gentry, Stockwell, and Terry knew of the fictitious Diane T. Wolfe. Gentry was charged with gaining access to a computer system and obtaining services with fraudulent intent. Was he guilty?

L.O.4 ....

3   Pacific Gas and Electric Co. (PG&E) contracted with Placer County Water Agency to purchase hydroelectric power. Energy prices rose dramatically. Bear Stearns & Company tried to convince the Agency to make an effort to terminate the contract. The Agency contracted with Bear Stearns to pay it a percentage of any increase in revenue in return for Bear Stearns' paying for studies on the feasibility of terminating the power contract. Bear Stearns hired attorneys to draw up a plan for and litigate whether the Agency could terminate the contract. It also solicited buyers for the Agency's power and demanded PG&E arbitrate whether the contract could be terminated. PG&E sued alleging Bear Stearns had caused the Agency to breach promises to continue the contract for 50 years. Did Bear Stearns induce a breach of contract?

L.O.3, 4 ....

4   Teilhaber Manufacturing Co. produced an industrial storage rack called the "Cue-Rack." It competed with one sold by Unarco Materials Storage, Inc. Unarco conducted tests on a hybrid rack composed of uprights manufactured by Teilhaber for the Cue-Rack and beams manufactured by another company. Unarco distributed a report on these tests written by Unarco's chief engineer. It stated the tests were performed on a Cue-Rack "furnished by Teilhaber." Teilhaber sued Unarco for product disparagement. Was the report false?

L.O.2 ....

5   William Croft, an assistant professor at the University of Wisconsin–Madison, received a $130,000 grant from the Environmental Protection Agency to study cancer in cattle. He wanted to investigate the cancer-causing effects of asbestos. While working on the project, the town of Weston hired Croft to test the asbestos content of Weston's water supply. Croft hired Laurel Johnson to test Weston water samples during the summer. Johnson received $2,000 from EPA funds for her work on the Weston project. Croft's report to Weston included calculations prepared by Johnson. Croft was charged with larceny—misappropriating Johnson's services, paid for by the government, for his own, personal research project. Was he guilty?

L.O.4 ....

6   Duo-Tint Bulb & Battery Co. supplied retailers with a bulb dispenser box containing an assortment of bulbs. With each box was an information chart listing the contents by manufacturer and bulb number and a reorder card. When a bulb ran out, the retailer mailed the card to Duo-Tint, which would ship a full bulb dispenser box. The retailer would return the old box for credit. After Lange was fired as a sales representative of Duo-Tint, he

contacted Moline Supply Co. about forming a business to distribute light bulbs. Moline adopted Duo-Tint's marketing system, and many retailers switched to it. Moline copied Duo-Tint's reorder card and bulb information chart. The bulb boxes were the same size and shape, but the color differed—Moline's was red, while Duo-Tit's was blue. Moline's items were labeled with its name. Duo-Tint sued Moline. Did Duo-Tint have a legally protectable interest in the chart, reorder card, box, or all three in a marketing system?

L.O.1, 2 ....

7   Mary Hyatt, president of R.A.G.S. Couture, Inc., ended association with the company on March 13. She and Oren Welborne told the stockholders that sewing machines used by R.A.G.S. were leased from Welborne. R.A.G.S. sued Hyatt and Welborne under RICO. It alleged both knew that on March 30 Welborne or Hyatt mailed fraudulent copies of invoices for rental fees on the sewing machines. It alleged the invoices were dated months earlier, but prepared after March 13. In August, Welborne's lawyer mailed copies of the invoices with a demand for payment to R.A.G.S.'s attorney. Did the plaintiff allege a pattern of racketeering activity?

L.O.4 ....

8   The program "60 Minutes" had a segment titled "Killer Wheels" about the use and safety of multi-piece tire rims. It stated that people had been injured and killed when pieces of metal from such rims separated. Redco Corp., a manufacturer of multi-piece tire rims, sued CBS for trade libel even though the program did not mention Redco. Redco admitted that some people had been killed in accidents involving multi-piece rims, although no one had died in an accident involving its rims. Redco claimed that the rims would not explode if properly serviced. Did Redco state a claim for product disparagement?

L.O.4 ....

9   Metalcraft, Inc. made a fire extinguisher sold to the military but not approved for other uses by Factory Mutual, an independent testing laboratory. It made Pratt an exclusive distributor of its products. Pratt could hardly sell the extinguisher because it lacked the approval. In early April, Joseph Ruiz, Metalcraft's president terminated the agreement with Pratt. On April 26, Ruiz called Robert Barr, a former employee of Pratt, and told him the relationship between Pratt and Metalcraft was over. Barr and Duane Henneman then organized a corporation called AMRIC. On May 1, in response to Barr's question, Ruiz told Barr that Pratt was not Metalcraft's distributor. Ruiz said AMRIC could have distributorship rights in Metalcraft. The extinguisher later received Factory Mutual approval. Pratt sued AMRIC and Metalcraft for interference with a business relationship. Should it recover?

L.O.4 ....

10   Since the mid-1960s, Ziebart International Corp. had sold a rustproofing compound to dealers who offered rustproofing services. When a Ziebart compound was applied to a car, a yellow and blue sticker would be placed on a car window. The sticker showed a knight helmet above a shield with the word *Ziebart* in a diagonal across the shield. The Protector Corp. began to market rustproofing compounds to new car dealers. They offered rustproofing when new cars were sold. Protector supplied window stickers that were red, black,

gray, and white for the dealers. They showed a helmet on top of a horizontal oval, which contained the words *The Protector.*

Ziebart sued Protector. Was there a likelihood of confusion by the consuming public of the two window decals?

Chapter 4

GOVERNMENT REGULATION OF BUSINESS

LEARNING OBJECTIVES

After studying this chapter you should be able to:

1 Explain why government regulates business.

2 List the major antitrust laws.

3 Discuss the types and powers of administrative agencies.

Government rules and regulations affect the operation of every business, no matter what type. The areas of business operation affected by government regulation, both state and federal, range from prices and the safety of any products produced to the relationship of the business to its employees. This chapter discusses some ways in which government regulates the operation of businesses. Some other aspects of governmental regulation of business are discussed in Chapter 20 (consumer protection) and in Chapters 30 and 31 (employers and employees).

PURPOSE OF REGULATION

L.O.1 ....

Government has undertaken the regulation of business in order to eliminate abuses and to regulate conduct considered to be unreasonable. The goal is to enhance the quality of life for society as a whole by setting the rules under which all businesses compete.

ADMINISTRATIVE AGENCIES

Chapter 1 defined administrative agencies as governmental boards or commissions with the authority to regulate or implement laws. Most governmental regulation of business takes place by means of administrative agencies.

Most administrative agency regulation occurs because of the complex nature of the area of regulation. Each administrative agency can become a specialist in its particular area of regulation. It can, if necessary, hire scientists and researchers to study industries or problems and set standards that businesses must follow. Administrative agencies conduct research on proposed drugs (the Food and Drug Administration), examine the safety of nuclear-power facilities (the Nuclear Regulatory Commission), certify the wholesomeness of meat and poultry (the Food Safety and Inspection Service), and set standards for aircraft maintenance (the Federal Aviation Administration). In all these areas, research has been necessary to determine a safe level for the public.

Some agencies investigate industries and propose rules designed to promote fairness to the businesses involved and the public. This occurs in the area of trading in stocks (the Securities and Exchange Commission), the granting of radio and television licenses (the Federal Communications Commission), and the regulation of banks (the Federal Deposit Insurance Corporation). The legislature thus can set up the guidelines and specify the research to be done by specialists in the field.

Structure of Administrative Agencies

Agencies may be run by a single administrator who serves at the pleasure of the executive—either the president of the United States in the case of federal agencies or the governor in the case of state agencies. Alternatively, agencies may be run by a commission, the members of which are appointed for staggered terms, frequently of five years.

Types of Agencies

L.O.2 ....

The two types of administrative agencies are usually referred to as regulatory and nonregulatory. Regulatory agencies govern to some degree the economic activity of businesses. They prescribe rules stating what should or should not be done in particular situations. They decide whether a law has been violated in individual cases and then proceed against those violating the law by imposing fines and, in some cases, ordering that the activity be stopped. Regulatory-type agencies include agencies such as the Environmental Protection Agency, the Securities and Exchange Commission, and the Federal Trade Commission.

Nonregulatory agencies dispense benefits for social and economic welfare. Also called social regulatory agencies, they also issue regulations governing the distribution of benefits. Such agencies would include the Railroad Retirement Board, the Farm Credit Administration, and the Department of Health and Human Services.

Powers of Agencies

Different regulatory agencies have different powers. However, the three major areas of regulations include:

1 Licensing power: Allowing a business to enter the field being regulated.

2 Rate-making power: Fixing the prices that a business may charge.

3 Power over business practices: Determining whether the activity of the entity regulated is acceptable or not.

Agencies such as the Federal Communications Commission, the Nuclear Regulatory Commission, and the Securities and Exchange Commission have licensing power. The Civil Aeronautics Board, the Federal Power Commission, and the Interstate Commerce Commission all have rate-making power. The primary powers of the Federal Trade Commission and the National Labor Relations Board are to control business practices.

Rule Making

Administrative agencies primarily set policy through the issuance of rules and regulations. When an agency's rule is challenged, the courts primarily focus on the procedures followed by the agency in exercising its rule-making power. The rule-making procedure followed by state agencies resembles that which must be used by federal agencies.

After investigating a problem, an agency will develop a proposed rule. A federal agency must publish in the *Federal Register* a notice of the proposed rule. This allows interested parties the opportunity to comment on the proposed rule. The agency might hold formal hearings on a proposed rule, but the informal **notice and comment rule making** has been more and more common. After time for comments, the proposed rule could be published as proposed, changed, or entirely abandoned by the agency. Once a rule or regulation is adopted, it has the force of a statute.

Notice and Comment Rule Making

Enacting administrative rules by publishing the proposed rule and then the final rule without holding formal hearings

State Agencies

While federal administrative agencies affect businesses throughout the country, states also have administrative agencies that affect businesses operated in their states. The most common state agencies include public service commissions, state labor relations boards or commissions, and workers' compensation boards.

ANTITRUST

Antitrust Laws

Statutes that seek to promote competition among businesses

L.O.3 ....

Government also regulates business by means of **antitrust laws,** which seek to promote competition among businesses.

The most important antitrust law, the federal Sherman Antitrust Act, declares that, "Every contract, combination in the form of trust or otherwise, or conspiracy, in restraint of trade or commerce among the several states, or with foreign nations is . . . illegal."[1] It further provides that anyone who monopolizes or tries to obtain a monopoly in interstate commerce is guilty of a felony.

[1] 15 U.S.C.§1

The Sherman Act applies to commerce or trade between two or more states and applies to both buyers and sellers. Most states also have antitrust laws, very similar to the Sherman Act, which prohibit restraints of trade within their states.

In interpreting the Sherman Act, the federal courts have said it prohibits only those activities that *unreasonably* restrain trade. The *rule of reason* approach means that the courts examine and rule on the anticompetitive effect of a particular activity on a case-by-case basis. The effect of the activity, not the activity itself, is the most important element in deciding whether the Sherman Act has been violated.

However, some activities are illegal under the Sherman Act without regard to their effect, called *per se* **violations.** They include price fixing, group boycotts, and horizontal territorial restraints.

Per Se
Violations
Activities illegal regardless of their effect

Many activities may lessen competition. Obviously, every business firm seeks to have cooperation within its firm. This is the basis of economic productivity, and this is lawful under the antitrust laws. Only when separate businesses make a commitment to a common plan or some type of joint action to restrain trade does an antitrust violation occur.

In addition to the Sherman Act, the federal government has enacted three other important antitrust laws. These include the Clayton Act, the Robinson-Patman Act, and the Federal Trade Commission Act.

The Clayton Act amends the Sherman Act by prohibiting certain practices if their effect may be to substantially lessen competition or tend to create a monopoly. The Clayton Act prohibits price discrimination to different purchasers where price difference does not result from differences in selling or transportation cost. The Clayton Act also prohibits agreements to sell on the condition that the purchaser shall not use goods of the seller's competitors, ownership of stock or assets in a competing business where the effect may be to substantially lessen competition, and interlocking directorates between boards of directors of competing firms.

The Robinson-Patman Act, an amendment to the Clayton Act, prohibits price discrimination generally and geographically for the purpose of eliminating competition. It also prohibits sales at unreasonably low prices in order to eliminate competition.

The Federal Trade Commission Act prohibits "unfair methods of competition in commerce and unfair or deceptive acts or practices in commerce."[2] In addition, this law prohibits false advertising. To prevent these unfair and deceptive practices, a federal administrative agency, the Federal Trade Commission, was established.

ENVIRONMENTAL PROTECTION

In recognition of the fact that the environment is the property of everyone, the federal government and many states have enacted a number of laws to protect our environment. A federal agency, the Environmental Protection Agency (EPA), administers many of these federal laws. The laws the EPA administers include the following:

[2]15 U.S.C.§45(a)(1)

1   Clean Air Act
2   Water Pollution and Control Act
3   Resource Conservation and Recovery Act
4   Comprehensive Environmental Response, Compensation, and Liability Act

CLEAN AIR ACT

The Clean Air Act was the first national environmental law. Under this law, the EPA sets minimum national standards for air quality and regulates hazardous air pollutants. These standards protect public health and welfare. The states apply and enforce these standards under state implementation plans setting limits on pollutants and approved by the EPA. The law provides civil and criminal penalties for its violation.

Under authority of the Clean Air Act, the EPA set an air-quality standard for ozone. The state of Michigan issued a state implementation plan, and the EPA approved the plan. Later, the United States sued in federal court to enforce the plan. A month later, Ford Motor Company sued the Michigan state pollution control agencies in a state court to keep them from enforcing the plan. The EPA was not a party to that suit. Ford and the state agencies negotiated a judgment in the state court changing the limits and thereby vacating the plan. Ford alleged the plan could not be enforced in the federal suit because the state court judgment invalidated it. The court said since plans and any revisions to plans must be approved by the EPA, the state court action could not revise the plan.

WATER POLLUTION AND CONTROL ACT

Congress enacted the Water Pollution and Control Act (also referred to simply as the Clean Water Act) to restore and maintain the proper chemistry of United States waters. U.S. waters include adjacent wetlands. The law seeks to prevent the discharge of pollutants into navigable waters. The EPA has the primary administration and enforcement responsibility under the law. It sets limits on discharges, including pollutants into sewer systems, has the responsibility for wetlands protection, and can block or overrule the issuance of permits under the law. The EPA or private citizens may sue on the basis of the act, which even includes criminal liability for violation.

To expand a sanitary landfill, Orange County placed fill in the site, which included some wetlands. Orange Environment, Inc. (OEI) sued the county alleging violation of the Clean Water Act's prohibition against the discharge of fill materials into U.S. waters. In discussing the law, the court said the EPA has the ultimate authority for wetlands protection. The county had to obtain a permit to continue the landfill expansion.

RESOURCE CONSERVATION AND RECOVERY ACT

The Resource Conservation and Recovery Act has the purpose of regulating the generation, storage, transportation, treatment, and disposal of hazardous waste. The law lists certain wastes defined as hazardous, but the term includes ignitable, corrosive, reactive, or toxic waste.

The law gives the EPA the duty of setting standards for individuals who own or operate hazardous waste disposal facilities. Anyone who generates or transports hazardous waste, and owners and operators of facilities for the treatment, storage, or disposal of such waste, must obtain a permit. Such persons must comply with the requirements of the permits when issued. The law requires individuals handling hazardous waste to keep extensive records in order to track it from generation to disposal. The law provides large civil and criminal penalties for its violation. This law also permits suits by private citizens.

COMPREHENSIVE ENVIRONMENTAL RESPONSE, COMPENSATION, AND LIABILITY ACT

Perhaps the most discussed federal environmental legislation, the Comprehensive Environmental Response, Compensation, and Liability Act (CERCLA) also called the "superfund" law, seeks the cleanup of waste from previous activities and requires notification of the release of hazardous substances. CERCLA, imposes liability for cleanup on past and current owners or operators of facilities where hazardous substances have been released, on anyone who arranged for disposal of substances where released, and on anyone who transported them. CERCLA imposes liability retroactively—acts that occurred before enactment of this law and were not negligent or illegal then can be the basis of liability.

Liability of Multiple Parties

Because CERCLA imposes liability on four groups of people—owners, operators, disposers, and transporters—several parties could be liable for one site. A liable party may take legal action to require other responsible or potentially responsible parties to pay a share of cleanup costs. Courts have stated that when several defendants are responsible under CERCLA, liability should be apportioned according to their contribution to the problem. However, if liability cannot be apportioned or only one liable party has any funds, one party could be liable for the entire cleanup cost. These costs can run into millions of dollars.

Business Costs

These provisions of CERCLA have resulted in concern by businesses and potential business owners because of the possibility of courts imposing huge cleanup costs on them as new owners of facilities who never released hazardous wastes there. If a hazardous substance was released 20 years ago by the then owner of a facility who sold the facility and then there was a series of sales, the current owner, who does not know about the release, might still have to pay for or help pay for the cleanup. Actually, some courts have found everyone in the chain of ownership of contaminated property, from disposal of the substance to the current owner, liable for cleanup. Thus, anyone buying contaminated land is potentially liable for cleanup costs. This can have serious repercussions for all landowners but particularly for businesses since business or manufacturing sites would be the most likely to have been the site of a release of hazardous substances.

Business costs could include not only possibly large cleanup costs but also legal fees. Litigation under the superfund law can be extremely expensive. A party responsible for cleanup costs can sue to require other "potentially" liable parties to share in the costs. Even if not ultimately found liable, the cost of defending against such a lawsuit can be very expensive. Legal fees have been reported to be 30% to 60% of superfund costs.

In addition to owners of facilities, courts have imposed CERCLA liability on business employees who had control over disposal decisions. Even lenders have been found liable for cleanup costs if the court found them adequately involved in running the business.

State Laws

A number of states have enacted state superfund laws. They also impose liability for cleanup costs and may require notification of release of hazardous substances to state environmental agencies.

Protection from Liability

A person can take some steps to help reduce the potential of liability under CERCLA and state superfund statutes. Banks and other lending institutions should require environmental assessments of properties before making a loan and before foreclosing on property. Before anyone buys or invests in property, an investigation should be made to identify any environmental risks and determine expected costs. When cleanup costs can be in the millions of dollars, they can be much greater than the value of the property involved.

QUESTIONS

1   Why does government regulate business?
2   What benefit can administrative agencies that regulate bring to their area of regulation?
3   Give an example of two agencies that regulate the economic activity of businesses.
4   What is the purpose of nonregulatory agencies?
5   What are the three types of powers possessed by regulatory agencies?
6   What must a federal agency do with a proposed rule before the rule can become effective?

7   What are antitrust laws?

8   Name the major antitrust laws.

9   What is the purpose of the Water Pollution and Control Act?

10   What four classes of people are potentially liable under the superfund law?

Part 2

CONTRACTS

Chapter 5

CONTRACTS: NATURE AND CLASSES

LEARNING OBJECTIVES

After studying this chapter you should be able to:

1 Describe what a contract is and how it differs from an agreement

2 List the different types of contracts.

3 State the five requirements for a valid contract.

Preview Case

Richard Iacomini contracted with Theodore Zadlo to tow, store, and repair a Mercedes. Zadlo said he owned the car and gave Iacomini a state registration certificate bearing his name. The police later notified Iacomini that the Mercedes was stolen. When the owner wanted to pick it up, Iacomini refused until he had been paid repair and storage fees. Must the owner pay the fees?

Contract

Legally enforceable agreement

L.O.1

A contract can be defined as a legally enforceable agreement between two or more competent persons. At first glance this seems like a very simple definition. Notice that this definition does not even require a written document. Chapters 5 through 13 are devoted exclusively to explaining and clarifying this definition. Making contracts is such an everyday occurrence that we often overlook their importance, except when the contracts are of a substantial nature. When one buys a cup of coffee during a coffee break, a contract has been made. When the purchaser agrees to pay 50¢ for the coffee, the seller agrees not only to supply one cup of coffee but also agrees by implication of law that it is safe to drink. If the coffee contains a harmful substance that makes the purchaser ill, a breach of contract has occurred that may call for the payment of damages.

Business transactions result from agreements. Every time a person makes a purchase, buys a theater ticket, or boards a bus, an agreement is made. Each party to the agreement obtains certain rights and assumes certain duties and obligations. When such an agreement meets all the legal requirements of a contract, the law recognizes it as binding upon all parties. If one of the parties to the contract breaches it by failing or refusing to perform, the law allows the other party an appropriate action for obtaining damages or enforcing performance by the party breaching the contract.

Contracts form the very foundation upon which all modern business rests. Business consists almost entirely of the making and performing of contracts. If the contract is a sale of goods, it is governed by the Uniform Commercial Code (see Chapter 16).

CONTRACTS CONTRASTED WITH AGREEMENTS

A contract must be an agreement, but an agreement need not be a contract. Whenever two or more persons' minds meet upon any subject, no matter how trivial, an agreement results. Only when the parties intend to be legally obligated by the terms of the agreement will a contract come into existence. Ordinarily, the subject matter of the contract must involve a business transaction as distinguished from a purely social transaction.

If Mary and John promise to meet at a certain place at 6 P.M. and have dinner together, this is an agreement not a contract, since neither intends to be legally bound to carry out the terms of the agreement.

If Alice says to David, "I will pay you $25 to be my escort for the Spring Ball," and David replies, "I accept your offer," the agreement results in a contract. David is legally obligated to provide escort service, and Alice is legally bound to pay the $25.

CLASSIFICATION OF CONTRACTS

L.O.2 ....

Contracts are classified by many names or terms. Unless you understand these terms, you cannot understand the law of contracts. For example, the law may state that executory contracts made on Sunday are void. You cannot understand this law unless you understand the words "executory" and "void." Every contract may be placed in the following classifications:

1 Valid contracts, void agreements, and voidable contracts
2 Express and implied contracts
3 Formal and simple contracts
4 Executory and executed contracts
5 Unilateral and bilateral contracts

Valid Contracts, Void Agreements, and Voidable Contracts

Valid Contract

Contract enforceable by law

Agreements classified according to their enforceability include valid contracts, void agreements, and voidable contracts.

A **valid contract** will be enforced by the courts against all parties. Such a contract must fulfill the following definite requirements:

1   It must be based on a mutual agreement by the parties to do or not to do a specific thing.
2   It must be made by parties who are competent to enter into a contract that will be enforceable against both parties.
3   The promise or obligation of each party must be supported by consideration (such as the payment of money, the delivery of goods, or the promise to do or refrain from doing some lawful future act) given by each party to the contract.
4   It must be for a lawful purpose; that is, the purpose of the contract must not be illegal, such as the unauthorized buying and selling of narcotics.
5   In some cases, the contract must meet certain formal requirements, such as being in writing or under seal.

You may test the validity of any contract using these five requirements. If the agreement fails to meet one or more of these requirements, the agreement may be void or the contract may be voidable.

Void

Of no legal effect

Unenforceable Contract

Agreement that is not currently binding

An agreement with no legal effect is **void.** An agreement not enforceable in a court of law does not come within the definition of a contract. A void agreement (sometimes referred to as a void contract) must be distinguished from an **unenforceable contract.** If the law requires a certain contract to be in a particular form, such as a deed to be in writing, and it is not in that form, it is merely unenforceable, not void. It can be made enforceable by changing the form to meet the requirements of the law. An agreement between two parties to perform an illegal act is void. Nothing the parties can do will make this agreement an enforceable contract.

Voidable Contract

Enforceable agreement that may be set aside by one party

Basically, a **voidable contract** would be an enforceable agreement; but, because of circumstances or the capacity of one party, it may be set aside by one or both of the parties. The distinguishing factor of a voidable contract is the existence of a choice by one party to abide by or to reject the contract. A contract made by an adult with a person not of lawful age (legally known as a minor or infant) is often voidable by the minor. Such a contract is enforceable against the adult but not against the minor. If both parties to an agreement are minors, either one may avoid the agreement. Until the party having the choice to avoid the contract exercises the right to set the contract aside, the contract remains in full force and effect.

Express and Implied Contracts

Express Contract

Contract with the terms of the agreement specified in words

Contracts classified according to the manner of their formation fall into two groups: express and implied contracts. In an **express contract,** the parties express their intentions by words, whether in writing or orally, at the time they make the agreement. Both their intention to contract and the terms of the agreement are expressly stated or written. Customary business terms, however, do not need to be stated in an express contract in order to be binding.

The Computer Shoppe, Inc. bid on a computer system for Tennessee sheriffs. After extended testing, state government representatives told the company it would get the contract for the computer system if it would modify its software. The company modified it as requested, and the state gave preliminary approval. The general assembly asked the attorney general to review the procurement process, and ultimately all the bids were rejected. Computer Shoppe filed a claim for its costs for software modification. State law allowed such claims based on an express contract. The state said no written contract existed, therefore no express contract existed. The company said an express oral contract existed to award it the contract if it modified the software. The court held an express contract could be oral.

Implied Contract

Contract with major terms implied by the parties' conduct

An **implied contract** (also called a *contract implied in fact*) is one in which the duties and the obligations that the parties assume are not expressed but are implied by their acts or conduct. The adage "actions speak louder than words" very appropriately describes this class of contracts. The facts of a situation imply that a contract exists. The parties indicate so clearly by their conduct what they intend to do that there is no need to express the agreement in words to make it binding.

Richardson hired the J. C. Flood Co. to correct a blocked sewer line. When the line was excavated, many leaks were found in a rusty, defective water pipe that ran parallel to the sewer line. Water district regulations required the pipe to be replaced. If the pipe were not replaced while it was exposed for the sewer-line repair, the yard would later have to be redug to replace the pipe. Flood told Richardson this and replaced the line. Richardson objected to paying for it. The court found that since Richardson inspected the work daily, knew the magnitude of the work being done, and made no objection until the work was done, there was an implied contract to replace the water line.

Formal and Simple Contracts

Formal Contract

Contract with special form or manner of creation

A **formal contract** must be in a special form or be created in a certain way. Formal contracts include contracts under seal, recognizances, and negotiable instruments.

When very few people could write, contracts were signed by means of an impression in wax attached to the paper. As time passed, a small wafer pasted on the contract replaced the use of wax. The wafer seal was in addition to the written signature. This practice is still used occasionally, but the more common practice is to sign formal contracts in one of these ways:

Jane Doe (Seal); Jane Doe [L.S.]

Today, it is immaterial whether these substitutes for a seal are printed on the document, typewritten before signing, or the persons signing write them after their respective names. In jurisdictions where the use of the seal has not been abolished, the seal implies consideration.

Marine Contractors Co., Inc. had a trust for its employees, but an employee who quit could not receive trust benefits for five years. When Thomas Hurley notified Marine he was quitting, they agreed upon immediate payment of his $12,000 in benefits for his promise not to compete in the Boston area for five years. The agreement stated the parties had "set their hands and seals" to it. Within a few months Hurley was competing. When sued by Marine, Hurley claimed there was no consideration since he was owed the $12,000 anyway. Marine alleged the agreement was a sealed instrument, which in that state implied consideration. The court held it was a sealed instrument.

In some states, the presence of a seal on a contract allows a party a longer time in which to bring suit if the contract is broken. Other states make no distinction between contracts under seal and other written contracts. The Uniform Commercial Code abolishes the distinction with respect to contracts for the sale of goods.

Recognizances, a second type of formal contract, are obligations entered into before a court whereby persons acknowledge they will do a specified act that is required by law. The persons acknowledge that they will be indebted for a specific amount if they do not perform as they agreed, such as the obligation undertaken by a criminal defendant to appear in court on a particular day.

Negotiable instruments, discussed in later chapters, are a third type of formal contract. They include checks, notes, drafts, and certificates of deposit.

All contracts other than formal contracts are informal and are called **simple contracts.** A few of these, such as an agreement to sell land or to be responsible for the debt of another, must be in writing in order to be enforceable; otherwise they need not be prepared in any particular form. Generally speaking, informal or simple contracts may be in writing, may be oral, or may be implied from the conduct of the parties.

A **written contract** is one in which the terms are set forth in writing rather than expressed orally. An **oral contract** is one in which the terms are stated in spoken, not written, words. Such a contract is usually enforceable; however, when a contract is oral, disputes may arise between the parties as to the terms of the agreement. No such disputes need arise about the terms of a written contract if the wording is clear, explicit, and complete. For this reason most businesspeople avoid making oral contracts involving matters of very great importance. Some types of contracts are required to be in writing and are discussed in Chapter 11.

Executory and Executed Contracts

Contracts are classified by the stage of performance as executory contracts and executed contracts. An **executory contract** is one in which the terms have not been fully carried out by all parties. If a person agrees to work for another for one year in return for a salary of $950 a month, the contract is executory from the time it is made until the 12 months expire. Even if the employer should prepay the salary, it would still be an executory contract because the other party has not yet worked the entire year, that is, executed that part of the contract.

An **executed contract** is one that has been fully performed by all parties to the contract. The Collegiate Shop sells and delivers a dress to Benson for $85, and Benson pays the purchase price at the time of the sale. This is an executed contract because nothing remains to be done on either side; that is, each party has completed performance of each part of the contract.

Recognizance

Obligation entered into before a court to do an act required by law

Negotiable Instrument

Document of payment, such as a check

Simple Contract

Contract that is not formal

Written Contract

Contract with terms in writing

Oral Contract

Contract with terms spoken

Executory Contract

Contract not fully carried out

Executed Contract

Fully performed contract

Lockheed sent M. B. Electronics a written purchase order to repair a shaker-amplifier system. The order stated if M.B. sent employees to Lockheed to perform the order, M.B. would indemnify Lockheed from injury arising out of the performance. While testing the amplifier system, Wichman, an employee of M. B., was electrocuted. Lockheed paid Wichman's heirs $115,000 and sued M. B. for reimbursement under the purchase order. Under the particular law, M. B. was not liable unless the purchase agreement was fully executed prior to the injury. Since Wichman was killed during the process of repairing the system, the repairs had not been completed nor had they been paid for; therefore, the purchase agreement was not fully executed.

Unilateral and Bilateral Contracts

Unilateral Contract

Contract calling for an act in consideration for a promise

When an act is done in consideration for a promise, the contract is a **unilateral contract.** If Smith offers to pay $100 to anyone who returns her missing dog, and Fink returns the dog, this would be a unilateral contract. It is unilateral (one-sided) in that only one promise is made. A promise is given in exchange for an act. Smith made the only promise, which was to pay anyone for the act of returning the dog. Fink was not obligated to find and return the dog, so only one duty existed.

Bilateral Contract

Contract consisting of mutual exchange of promises

A **bilateral contract** consists of a mutual exchange of promises to perform some future acts. One promise is the consideration for the other promise. If Brown promises to sell a truck to Adams for $5,000, and Adams agrees to pay $5,000, then the parties have exchanged a promise for a promise—a bilateral contract. Most contracts are bilateral because the law states a bilateral contract can be formed when performance is started. This is true unless it is clear from the first promise or the situation that performance must be completed. The test is whether there is only one right and duty or two.

Quasi Contract

Quasi Contract

Imposition of rights and obligations by law without a contract

Unjust Enrichment

One benefiting unfairly at another's expense

One may have rights and obligations imposed by law when no real contract exists. This imposition of rights and obligations is called a **quasi contract** or implied in law contract. It is not a true contract because the parties have not made an agreement. Rights and obligations will be imposed only when a failure to do so would result in one person unfairly keeping money or otherwise benefiting at the expense of another. This is known as **unjust enrichment**. For example, suppose a tenant is obligated to pay rent of $300 a month but by mistake hands the landlord $400. The law requires the landlord to return the overpayment of $100. The law creates an agreement for repayment even though no actual agreement exists between the parties. For the landlord to keep the money would mean an unjust enrichment at the expense of the tenant. An unjust enrichment offends our ethical principles, so the law imposes a contractual obligation to right the situation.

Richard Iacomini contracted with Theodore Zadlo to tow, store, and repair a Mercedes. Zadlo said he owned the car and gave Iacomini a state registration certificate bearing his name. The police later notified Iacomini that the Mercedes was stolen. When the owner wanted to pick it up, Iacomini refused until he had been paid repair and storage fees. The court said that although Iacomini and the car's owner did not have a contractual agreement, a court could and would impose one so there would not be an unjust enrichment.

QUESTIONS

1 What is a contract? How does it differ from an agreement?

2 Would it be possible to conduct a business without entering into contracts?

3 Relative to the enforceability of agreements, name the three groups into which they are classified. Define and give an example of each group.

4 Name the five requirements of a valid contract.

5 a. What is an implied contract?
   b. What is another name for such a contract?

6 a. Illustrate two ways by which one may indicate that a contract is under seal.
   b. Does a seal add anything of importance to a contract?

7 Do the terms *oral, simple,* and *informal* contracts refer to the same types of agreements?

8 a. Define an executory contract.
   b. Define an executed contract.

9 What is the difference between a unilateral and a bilateral contract?

10 What is unjust enrichment?

CASE PROBLEMS

When the concluding question in a case problem can be answered simply yes or no, state the legal principle or rule of law that supports your answer.

L.O.1, 2 ....

1 An irrigation district had a salary schedule with five steps—each step providing a higher wage. The announced practice of the district was to annually review each employee's work. Those who merited would be advanced to the next step. This practice was adopted by the district after negotiations with the employees' union. Youngman was employed by the district and after a year was advanced one step, as were almost all the employees. The next year, the district refused to advance any employees and discontinued its previously published, announced, and effected annual review. Youngman sued the district, claiming there was an implied contract for review and advancement. Was there?

L.O.2 ....

2 There was an agreement between the state welfare board and the state hospital association to provide hospital care for welfare patients according to a rate schedule. In April, the association told the board the schedule would have to be adjusted for all hospitals effective July 1. The welfare department prepared an adjustment. The association did not agree to it. Another adjustment was finally made and agreed to in September, but it did not cover July and August. The Bismarck Hospital Association, which had furnished hospital services to welfare patients, sued for the reasonable value of its services. The claim was for more than the amount provided in the original schedule. Was the new schedule an implied contract for the months of July and August?

L.O.2, 3 ....

3 Roy Miles was a retired judge and a member of the state retirement system. A law was enacted that changed the benefit base for judges' pensions. If there

was an executed contract between Miles and the state, the changes in the retirement base violated the constitution. The judge alleged that the state had made a promise of retirement benefits in accordance with the law then in effect, in return for his service as a judge. When he retired, he completed the contract with the state so that the contract was executed. Was this an executed contract?

L.O.2 .... **4** While employed by the Water Club, Patrick Kelly embezzled more than $450,000. Kelly used the money to buy land and build a house on it that he owned with his wife, Debra. The owners of the Water Club sued the Kellys for the money, claiming Debra was unjustly enriched by the embezzlement. Should a quasi contract be found?

L.O.1, 3 .... **5** Aberdeen White was employed full time by Hugh Chatham Memorial Hospital when she was fired because of a disabling illness. Three years before she left, the hospital distributed a personnel handbook that stated: "A full-time employee who becomes disabled during his employment will be able to maintain his group insurance." This statement was not withdrawn before White left. White knew about the statement, but was not allowed to continue the insurance. She sued saying she had a contract with the hospital requiring it to allow her to continue the insurance. The hospital said White had not promised to continue her employment after the handbook was issued. Was there a contract between White and the hospital?

L.O.2 .... **6** Gill entered into a verbal agreement to install sound equipment at a club. A written agreement was prepared for the club to sign, but it was never executed. After the equipment was installed, the club told Gill to bill the manufacturer of the equipment, who would pay Gill. Gill billed only the manufacturer. With Gill's knowledge, in March and May the club made payments to the manufacturer. When Gill was not paid he sued the manufacturer, who then went bankrupt and never paid him anything. He sued the club. Was there an enforceable contract between Gill and the club?

Chapter 6

OFFER AND ACCEPTANCE

LEARNING OBJECTIVES

After studying this chapter you should be able to:

1 List the requirements for a valid offer and acceptance.

2 Explain the difference between an offer and an invitation to make an offer.

3 Define a counteroffer.

4 State the way to accept an offer made by mail.

Preview Case

Stauffer Chemical Co. had a severance-pay policy that was explained to its management. The policy was not published or disseminated to other employees. The granting of severance pay was a voluntary, gratuitous benefit determined solely by Stauffer. Severance pay was not discussed with prospective employees. When Stauffer sold its plant as a going concern, 33 former employees sued Stauffer for severance pay. Was the granting of severance pay an offer that could have been accepted by the former employees?

A valid contract is created by the agreement of the parties. This agreement exists when one party makes an offer and the other party accepts the offer. The parties may expressly state, either orally or in writing, what they agree to do, or they may indicate their intentions by their actions. If A's conduct reasonably leads B to believe that A intends to enter into a binding contract, then A is bound as effectively as if the contract had been expressed. However, in business, a person seldom indicates every intention solely by acts. In most cases only a part of the contract is expressed, and the other part is implied.

Two essential elements of a contract are: (1) an offer, either expressed or implied; and (2) an acceptance, either expressed or implied.

REQUIREMENTS OF A VALID OFFER

L.O.1 ....

Offer

A proposal to make a contract

Offeror

Person who makes an offer

Offeree

Person to whom offer is made

The proposal to make a contract is the **offer.** The **offeror** is the person who makes the offer; the **offeree** is the person to whom the offer is made. An offer expresses the willingness of the offeror to enter into a contractual agreement. A valid offer includes three requirements:

1 The offer must be definite.
2 It must be seriously intended.
3 It must be communicated to the offeree.

The Offer Must Be Definite

A contract will not be enforced unless the court can ascertain what the parties agreed to. The offeror's intentions are ascertained from the offer, and these intentions cannot be ascertained unless the offer is definite. Terms usually required to be stated would include who the offeree is, the subject matter of the offer, price, quantity, and time of performance.

> Diversified Contractors agreed to build a warehouse for Fritz. The Bank of Marion agreed to loan Diversified money for the construction and told Diversified that Fritz's payments had to be payable to Diversified *and* the bank. Diversified prepared an instrument titled "Certification of Contract," which stated it was to confirm the contract between Fritz and Diversified in the amount of $115,409 which "... amount ... will be made jointly to the Bank of Marion and Diversified Contractors, Inc." Fritz did not know of the bank loan and issued checks payable only to Diversified, which did not pay off its loan. The bank claimed Fritz had contracted to make the payments jointly to it and Diversified. The court held the instrument, which was undated, recited no consideration, and contained no reference to anything to be done by the bank was not a definite offer, so the instrument could not be the basis of a contract between the bank and Fritz.

The Uniform Commercial Code modifies this strict rule somewhat as to contracts for the sale of goods. It is not always practical for a businessperson to make an offer for the sale of merchandise that is definite as to price. The offeror may state that the price will be determined by the market price at a future date or by a third party. If the contract does not specify the price, the buyer must ordinarily pay the reasonable value of the goods.

The Offer Must Be Seriously Intended

One may make an offer in jest, banter, fear, or extreme anger; and if this fact is known or should be known by the offeree because of the surrounding circumstances, no contract is formed. A business transaction is ordinarily not entered into in jest or because of extreme fear or anger, and the offeree has no right to think that the offer is seriously intended when it is made under these circumstances.

There are times when the offer is not seriously intended, but the offeree has no way of knowing this. In that event, if the offer is accepted, a binding contract results.

Lucy said to Zehmer, "I bet you wouldn't take $50,000 for . . ." the Ferguson farm. Zehmer replied, "Yes, I would, too; you wouldn't give $50." Lucy said he would and told Zehmer to write up an agreement to that effect. Zehmer took a restaurant check and wrote on the back that he agreed to sell it. Lucy told him he needed to change the "I" to "We" because Mrs. Zehmer would have to sign, too, and add a provision for having the title examined. Zehmer wrote on another check, "We hereby agree to sell to W. O. Lucy the Ferguson Farm complete for $50,000, title satisfactory to buyer." He and his wife both signed it, and Lucy took it with him. Zehmer later said he and Lucy had been drinking and the discussion about selling the farm was only a joke. The court held Zehmer's actions appeared to be a good faith acceptance of Lucy's offer, so there was a contract.

The Offer Must Be Communicated to the Offeree

Until the offeror makes the offer known to the offeree, it is not certain that it is intended that the offeree may accept and thereby impose a binding contract. Accordingly, an offer cannot be accepted by the offeree until the offeror has communicated the offer to the offeree. If one writes out an offer and the offer falls into the hands of the offeree without the knowledge or consent of the offeror, it cannot be accepted. Furthermore, an offer directed to a specific individual or firm cannot be accepted by anyone else. This is true because people have a right to choose the parties with whom they deal.

Stauffer Chemical Co. had a severance-pay policy that was explained in written instructions furnished to its management. The policy was not published or disseminated to other employees. The granting of severance pay was a voluntary, gratuitous benefit to be determined solely by Stauffer. Severance pay was not discussed with prospective employees. When Stauffer sold its plant as a going concern, 33 former employees sued Stauffer for severance pay. The court found that an offer of severance pay had not been made to the employees; thus, there was no contract to pay it.

INVITATIONS TO MAKE OFFERS

L.O.2 ....

In business, many apparent offers are not true offers. Instead, they are treated as invitations to the public to make offers at certain terms and prices. If the invitation is accepted by a member of the public, and an offer is submitted embodying all the terms set out in the invitation, the inviter may refuse to accept the offer. Ordinarily, however, as a practical matter and in the interest of maintaining goodwill, such an offer will be accepted. The most common types of general invitations are advertisements, window displays, catalogs, price lists, and circulars. If a merchant displays in a store window a coat for $95, there is no binding requirement to sell at this price. Most businesspeople would consider refusing to sell a very poor business policy, but nevertheless merchants may legally do so. Considering advertisements and window displays invitations to make offers rather than offers provides a protection to businesspeople. Otherwise they might find that they were subjected to many suits for breach of contract if they oversold their stock of goods.

Abraham and Strauss advertised a set of Sango china dishes for sale in *Newsday*. The ad listed a sale price for a service for twelve as $39.95 and the regular price as $280. Judith Geismar tried to buy the set for $39.95, but the store would not sell it at that price. She sued the store. The court stated that the ad was not an offer but an invitation to negotiate.

The general rule is that circulars are not offers but invitations to the recipients to make an offer. When in the form of a letter, however, it is often difficult to distinguish between a general sales letter and a personal sales letter. The fact that the letter is addressed to a particular individual does not necessarily make it a personal sales letter containing an offer. If the wording indicates that the writer is merely trying to evoke an offer on certain terms, it is an invitation to the other party to make an offer.

An advertisement, however, may be an offer when it clearly shows it is intended as an offer. This is primarily true with advertisements that offer rewards.

Weldon Hall sponsored a boat race for which the advertised first prize was a 14-foot boat, trailer, and 20-horsepower motor. After Gerald Bean called Hall's marina and verified the first prize, he won, but Hall offered a 6-horsepower motor as first prize. Bean sued to recover the advertised first prize. The court found that Hall had made an offer to the public, which Bean accepted by winning the race.

DURATION OF THE OFFER

Several rules affect the duration of an offer.

1 The offeror may revoke an offer any time prior to its acceptance. If it has been revoked, the offeree can no longer accept it and create a contract. Normally the offer can be revoked even if the offeror has promised to keep it open.

Richards, a real estate broker, found a prospective buyer, Baker, for Simpson's mining claims. Simpson had escrow instructions prepared that provided that they were to be signed by the buyer. They were not signed by Baker because of disagreement with Simpson over an access road. On April 2 Simpson canceled the escrow instructions and the listing of the property with Richards. On April 14 Baker signed the escrow instructions, but Simpson refused to sell. The court held Baker's acceptance of Simpson's offer was too late because the offer had been withdrawn.

2 The offer may state that it will be held open for a particular time. Ordinarily the offer may be revoked in spite of such a provision. However, if the offeror

Option

Binding promise to hold
an offer open

Firm Offer

A merchant's signed, written offer to sell or pur-
chase goods saying it will
be held open

receives something of value in return for the promise to hold the offer open, it is said to be an **option** and the offer cannot be revoked.

If the offer relates to the sale or purchase of goods by a merchant, a signed written offer to purchase or sell that states that it will be held open cannot be revoked during the time stated or if no time is stated, for a reasonable time, not to exceed three months. This type of offer is called a **firm offer.** It is valid even though no payment is made to the offeror.

In April, Mid-South Packers sent a letter to Shoney's listing prices at which Mid-South would supply bacon. The letter, titled "Proposal," stated Shoney's would have 45-day notice of price changes. In July, Shoney's began purchasing meat from Mid-South. In August, Mid-South told Shoney's that the price of bacon would be 7¢ per pound higher. Shoney's next order requested shipment at the old, lower price, but orders were filled and billed at the higher price. Shoney's reduced its payment by what it claimed it was overcharged by the price increase. Mid-South sued for payment. Shoney's argued that the proposal was an offer, which it accepted by placing orders. As a binding contract, it required 45-day notice of price increases. The court said, as a firm offer, the proposal was irrevocable for no more than 3 months, which expired in July, prior to Shoney's acceptance. Mid-South had the right to raise its price in August and collect full payment.

In states in which the seal has its common-law effect, an offer cannot be revoked when it is contained in a sealed writing that states that it will not be revoked.

3   A revocation of an offer must be communicated to the offeree prior to the acceptance. Mere intention to revoke is not sufficient. This is true even though the intent is clearly shown to persons other than the offeree, as when the offeror dictates a letter of revocation.

Notice to the offeree that the offeror has behaved in a way that indicates the offer is revoked, such as selling the subject matter of the offer to another party, revokes the offer.

Melvin Ingebretson, the major stockholder of the First State Bank of Thornton, sought to employ Glenn Emmons as manager. Ingebretson agreed to give Emmons an option to purchase his and some other stock if Emmons would work for the bank. Ingebretson signed an option agreement and sent it to Emmons. Before Emmons signed it, Ingebretson called and told him to "hold up on the contract" because he could not get all the stock to sell. Four days later Emmons signed the contract and returned it to Ingebretson with a check for the first payment. The court held that the obvious implication of Ingebretson's statement was that he would not be able to continue the offer to sell the stock and he therefore revoked the offer.

---

4   An offer is terminated by the lapse of the time specified in the offer. If no time is specified in the offer, it is terminated by a lapse of a reasonable time after being communicated to the offeree. A reasonable length of time varies with each case depending on the circumstances. It may be ten minutes in one case and 60 days in another. Important circumstances are whether the price of the goods or services involved are fluctuating rapidly, whether perishable goods are involved, and whether there is keen competition with respect to the subject matter of the contract.

5   Death or insanity of the offeror automatically terminates the offer. This applies even though the offeree is not aware of the death or the insanity of the offeror

and communicates an acceptance of the offer. Both parties must be alive and competent to contract at the moment the acceptance is properly communicated to the offeror.

6   Rejection of the offer by the offeree and communication of the rejection to the offeror terminates the offer.

7   If, after an offer has been made, the performance of the contract becomes illegal, the offer is terminated.

THE ACCEPTANCE

When an offer has been properly communicated to the party for whom it is intended and that party or an authorized agent accepts, a binding contract is formed. The acceptance must be communicated to the offeror, but no particular procedure is required. The acceptance may be made by words, oral or written, or by some act that clearly shows an intention to accept. Silence does not, except in rare cases, constitute an acceptance; nor is a mental intention to accept sufficient. If the offer stipulates a particular mode of acceptance, the offeree must meet those standards in order for a contract to be formed.

Albert Lewis ordered a yacht from Curtis Rudolph's marina. The agreement was signed by Lewis and Daniel Blake an employee of the marina. It stated, "this order is not valid unless signed by dealer." There was a signature line marked "dealer" and another marked "salesman." The dealer line was blank. Rudolph later refused to agree to the contract, and Lewis sued. The court stated that the mode of acceptance in the contract requiring the dealer's signature governed.

COUNTEROFFERS

L.O.3

Counteroffer

Offeree's response that rejects offer by varying its terms

An offer must be accepted without any deviation in its terms. If the intended acceptance varies or qualifies the offer, this **counteroffer** rejects the original offer. This rejection terminates the offer. This rule is changed to some extent where the offer relates to the sale or purchase of goods. In any case, a counteroffer may be accepted or rejected by the original offeror.

The Schoonovers offered to sell some real estate to Nance for $17,000 in cash. Nance told the Schoonovers he intended to give them a personal check in the amount of $17,000 to pay for the property. Since the offer specified payment in cash, not by personal check, Nance's statement was a counteroffer. The Schoonovers could either accept or reject this counteroffer.

INQUIRIES NOT CONSTITUTING REJECTION

The offeree may make an inquiry without rejecting the offer. For example, if the offer is for 1,000 shares of stock for $20,000 cash, the offeree may ask: "Would you be willing to wait 30 days for $10,000 and hold the stock as collateral security?" This mere inquiry does not reject the offer. If the offeror says no, the original offer may still be accepted, if it has not been revoked in the meantime.

MANNER OF ACCEPTANCE

L.O.4 ....

An offer that does not specify a particular manner of acceptance may be accepted in any manner reasonable under the circumstances. However, the offeror may stipulate that the acceptance must be written and received by the offeror in order to be effective. If there is no requirement of delivery, a properly mailed acceptance is effective when it is posted. This rule is called the "mailbox rule," and it applies even though the offeror never receives the acceptance.

National Old Line Insurance Company issued a $150,000 life insurance policy on John Bruegger. Premiums were not paid, and the policy lapsed. National sent an offer to reinstate the policy. On June 12, the documents required for reinstatement were properly mailed. The next day, Bruegger was shot. He died on June 24. The beneficiary requested the $150,000. National had to pay. Bruegger's acceptance of National's offer of reinstatement was effective upon mailing.

Similarly, the delivery of an acceptance to the telegraph company is effective unless the offeror specifies otherwise or unless custom or prior dealings indicate that acceptance by telegraph is improper. In former years the courts held that an offer could be accepted only by the same means by which the offer was communicated, called the "mirror-image rule." But this view is being abandoned in favor of the provision of the Uniform Commercial Code, Sec. 2–206(1)(a), relating to sales of goods: "Unless otherwise unambiguously indicated by the language or circumstances, an offer to make a [sales] contract shall be construed as inviting acceptance in any manner and by any medium reasonable in the circumstances." Under this principle, an acceptance can be made by telephone or even by fax. The contract is made on the date and at the place the fax acceptance is sent.

Nolt & Nolt in Pennsylvania faxed a contract to Rio Grande, Inc. at its New Jersey office. Rio Grande faxed a signed copy back to Nolt. The parties got into a disagreement over performance of the contract, and Nolt sued Rio Grande in a court in Pennsylvania. Rio Grande claimed it would have to be sued in New Jersey because the contract was accepted and signed in New Jersey. The court agreed. The contract was made when the fax acceptance was sent.

Careful and prudent persons can avoid many difficulties by stipulating in the offer how it must be accepted and when the acceptance is to become effective. For example, the offer may state, "The acceptance must be sent by letter and be received by me in Chicago by 12 noon on June 15 before the contract is complete." The acceptance is not effective unless it is sent by letter and is actually received by the offeror in Chicago by the time specified.

QUESTIONS

1   What are the three requirements of a valid offer?
2   What are the terms usually included in an offer?
3   What is the difference between an offer and an invitation to make an offer?
4   May an offeree accept a revoked offer?
5   What is an option?
6   How is a "reasonable time" after which an offer would "lapse" determined?
7   a.   When may an offer be revoked?
    b.   What is the effect of death or insanity of the offeror?
8   What are the requirements for an acceptance to the offeror?
9   What is a counteroffer?
10 How may an offer received by (a) letter, (b) telegraph, or (c) fax be accepted?

CASE PROBLEMS

L.O.1 ....

1   Carr agreed to sell specific property to the Savins for $18,500 plus a down payment, which was to be the Savins' efforts in restoring the property. The sale was to be made when the Savins had paid one-third of the purchase price. They did substantial work on restoration and made monthly payments for which Carr gave receipts reciting the payments were to apply towards purchase of the property. Carr later claimed the agreement was too indefinite as to time of performance and price to be binding. Was it?

L.O.1, 4 ....

2   Better Construction, Inc. was constructing a building. Meekis-Bamman Prestress bid $56,000 for the concrete roof structure for the building. It sent a printed form to Better stating, "The above quotation is subject to . . . approval by an officer of Meekins-Bamman Prestress, Inc. . . ." In another place it stated, "Note that this proposal . . . does not become a Contract until . . . approved as a Contract by Meekins-Bamman Prestress, Inc." The signature portion showed:

RICHARD CHATELLIER [typed]
MEEKINS-BAMMAN PRESTRESS, INC.

By: /s/   Richard Chatellier

Approved: Meekins-Bamman Prestress, Inc.

By   _____

                    _____ , 19 ____

Title   _____

The form was signed by Richard Chatellier, a Meekins sales representative. Better "accepted" the bid and returned copies of it to Meekins who never completed the blanks shown above because a miscalculation had caused an underestimate of the cost. Better sued claiming a contract existed. Did one exist?

L.O.3 ....

3 Roy Gilbert was an expert witness in a toxic tort lawsuit. When Gilbert sent his final bill to Akins & Pettiette lawyers they did not pay, so Gilbert's lawyer sent a letter demanding $5,448.25. Akins & Pettiette sent a check for $5,448.25 that stated: "Endorsement of this check constitutes . . . indemnity . . . of any and all claims and/or causes of action that arise or may arise out of" the toxic tort case and the present case. Gilbert rejected the check. The lawyers claimed he breached a contract to settle for $5,448.25. Did he?

L.O.4 ....

4 Medicine Shops Inc. (MSI) offered to allow Jayco to use MSI's trademark, trade name, logo, and services. On January 18, Jayco wrote a letter to MSI accepting its offer. Although properly addressed, stamped, and mailed on January 20, the letter was never delivered. On January 19, MSI wrote and mailed a letter to Jayco revoking the offer. This letter was received by Jayco on January 21. Was there a contract?

L.O.4 ....

5 A candidate in the Democratic primary election for the municipal council in Ridgefield, New Jersey, withdrew. A petition nominating Michael Madden was prepared, but because Madden was a student at Purdue University in Indiana he was not in New Jersey to sign the nomination acceptance. He signed the acceptance in Indiana and faxed it to New Jersey where it was properly and timely filed with the borough clerk. The clerk said the acceptance was defective because of the "facsimile" signature and refused to certify Madden as a candidate. Using principles of contract law, what is your opinion about the faxed document?

L.O.1, 2 ....

6 At the request of Nations Enterprises, Process Equipment made a proposal to supply some pumps for a project. Later Process got the specifications for the project and found out the pumps needed to withstand huge shock specifications. Nations sent a purchase order for some of the pumps in Process' proposal. The order said, "Execute acceptance [copy] . . . and return . . ." and, "This order is not valid until acceptance copy showing shipping date is received." Process never executed or returned the acceptance copy because it was not sure the pumps could meet the shock requirements. After some negotiation, the shock requirements were reduced and Process shipped nine pumps. It did not supply any more. Did Process breach a contract to supply the remaining pumps?

L.O.1 ....

7 Lynch received a contract to teach for the following school year. She signed the contract and delivered it in a sealed envelope to Chinn, the vice-president of the school board. Chinn took it to the school board meeting that evening and gave it to the secretary. Miner, the school superintendent, announced Lynch had returned the contract unsigned and recommended she be notified her services would be terminated at the end of the current school year. The board approved that recommendation. After the meeting, the secretary opened the envelope. When sued by Lynch, the board alleged there was no contract because its offer had been withdrawn before it was accepted. Was there a contract?

Chapter 7

DEFECTIVE AGREEMENTS

LEARNING OBJECTIVES

After studying this chapter you should be able to:

1 Describe the mistakes that do not invalidate a contract.

2 State what types of mistakes normally invalidate contracts.

3 Identify the situations in which fraud, duress, or undue influence are present.

4 Explain the remedies available to the victim of acts rendering contracts voidable.

Preview Case

Greenspan and Jacobsen built a duplex on a foundation that was constructed in violation of the building code. The foundation could not sustain the weight of the building. Massive cracks and severe settlement ensued. Greenspan and Jacobsen had plasterboard erected in the basement to cover the cracks. They then sold the duplex to Haberman and Ericksen. When the buyers discovered the cracks and settlement, they sought to invalidate the contract. May they?

Even when an offer and an acceptance have been made, situations exist in which the resulting contract is defective. Some mistakes make contracts defective. In addition, fraud, duress, or undue influence make contracts voidable because they are defective. A victim of an act rendering a contract defective has a choice of remedies.

MISTAKES

Unilateral Mistake
Mistake by one party to a contract

Mutual Mistake
Mistake by both parties to a contract

L.O.1 ....

Whether a mistake affects the validity of a contract normally depends on whether just one of the parties or both parties have made a mistake. A **unilateral mistake** occurs when only one party makes a mistake without the knowledge of the other. When both parties to a contract make the same mistake, a **mutual mistake** occurs.

Unilateral Mistakes

As a general rule, a unilateral mistake made at the time of contracting has no effect on the validity of a contract. This is true, for example, if a unilateral mistake occurs as to price or quantity. Even if the unilateral mistake as to price results from an error in typing or in misunderstanding an oral quotation of the price, the contract is valid.

Merritt had a survey made and used the description from the survey to convey some land to McIntyre. The surveyors had made a mistake and the description included more of his property than Merritt had intended. McIntyre had used the survey to have the land appraised so he would know what to pay for it. Merritt claimed the error in the description was a mutual mistake that should invalidate the contract. Only Merritt was mistaken; therefore, the contract was binding.

Mutual Mistakes

L.O.2 ....

When the mutual mistake concerns a material fact, some courts say such a contract is void because no genuine assent by the parties exists. Other courts say the contract is voidable. Some courts are not precise about whether the contract is void or voidable. However they classify a mutual-mistake contract, courts do not find them enforceable.

When contracting to buy the Last Chance Allotment—a ranching operation—from Robert Langston, neither L. Gurr McQuarrie, the buyer, nor Langston knew exactly how many cattle were involved in the sale. The contract provided for a cattle count to determine the exact number; however both parties thought the total number was 285, and at the agreed price per head, the total price would be $240,000. The cattle count showed only 246 head, so the total price was much less than $240,000. The court found a mutual mistake as to the number of cattle and the price. In this jurisdiction the contract was voidable, and Langston had it avoided.

The area of mistake is one in which significant variations exist among the states and also where exceptions to the general rules have been established in order to avoid harsh results. In some states it is much easier than in other states to get the courts to agree with a party that a contract should not be enforced when there has been a mistake.

Contract Terms Govern

It is important to remember that no matter what the law provides when a mistake occurs, the parties may specify a different outcome in their contract. And when the contract specifies what is to happen in the case of a mistake, the contract provision will apply even if the law would be otherwise. The contract could also indicate which party assumes the risk that the facts are not as believed. The law as to mistake applies only in the absence of a governing provision in the contract, so long as that governing provision is not unconscionable.

A. Cushman and Beresha Atkins purchased a residential lot from E. F. and Janice Kirkpatrick. Their contract stated that "this property is purchased 'as is.'" The Atkins tried to have a house built on the lot, but when the contractor dug footings, ground water seeped into the holes making it impossible to use them. The Atkins sued the Kirkpatricks claiming mutual mistake as to the suitability of the lot for use as a residential building lot. The court found mutual mistake of fact, but said the contract clearly allocated the burden of loss on the purchasers and the contract terms governed.

A contract could specify that it will be void if a specified fact is not as believed. *A*, owning a stone, could believe it to be worth very little money. However, if *A* wants to sell the stone to *B* for $100, the contract could recite that it is void if the stone is actually a valuable diamond. This applies in spite of the general rule announced above that a unilateral mistake does not invalidate a contract.

The contract could also make the realization of certain expectations a condition of the contract. If those expectations were not realized, even if only one party was mistaken about them, the contract would not be binding.

Frequently contracts are entered into orally and then reduced to writing. If, through an error in typing, the written form does not conform to the oral form, then the parties are not bound by the written form. The contract is what the parties agreed to orally.

Exceptions to General Rule

It is said that every rule has an exception, and the rule regarding unilateral mistake and mutual mistake of fact also has exceptions. Most states recognize the exceptions to the rule on mutual mistake; however, significant variation occurs among the states regarding whether exceptions to the unilateral-mistake rule are recognized.

Unilateral Mistakes. When there has been a unilateral mistake of a fact, the mistaken party sometimes receives relief. Courts will generally allow a unilateral mistake of fact to impair the enforceability of a contract if the nonmistaken party has caused the mistake or knew or should have known of the other party's mistake. Courts show extreme unwillingness to allow one party to hold the other to a contract if the first party knows that the other one has made a mistake.

Svalina, foreign-born and poorly educated, paid $5,160.40 to Big Horn National Life Insurance Co. Agents of the company had told him he could make an investment. He asked what would be paid in interest and they told him 10 percent. He entered into a contract with Big Horn thinking that the contract was primarily for the purchase of stock. It was solely for the purchase of insurance. When Svalina found out he had purchased insurance and no stock, he sued for the return of his money. The court found Svalina made a unilateral mistake caused and known by the agents. This entitled Svalina to relief.

A small number of states allow a party who has made a unilateral mistake of fact to raise the mistake as a defense when sued on the contract. This is allowed when the party has not been inexcusably negligent in making the mistake, and the other, nonmistaken, party has not taken actions in reliance on the contract so that failure to enforce it would be unconscionable.

To entitle a party to relief, the mistake must be one of fact, not mere opinion. If *A* buys a painting from *B* for $10 and it is actually worth $5,000, even if *A* knows *B* is mistaken as to its value, there is a valid contract. *B*'s opinion as to its value is erroneous, but there is no mistake as to a fact.

Since there are few exceptions to the rule that unilateral mistake does not affect a contract, it is clear that the law does not save us from the consequences of all mistakes. The exceptions cover a very small percentage of mistakes made in business transactions. Knowledge and diligence, not law, protect businesses against losses due to mistakes.

Mutual Mistakes

A mutual mistake will normally make a contract defective except in the case of mistake as to:

1 Value, quality, or price
2 The terms of the contract
3 The Law
4 Expectations

Mistakes as to Value, Quality, or Price. A contract is not affected by the fact that the parties made mistaken assumptions as to the value, quality, or price of the subject matter of the contract. Normally the parties assume the risk that their assumptions regarding these matters can be incorrect. If buyers do not trust their judgment, they have the right to demand a warranty from the seller as to the quality or value of the articles they are buying. Their ability to contract wisely is their chief protection against a bad bargain. If Snead sells Robinson a television set for $350, Robinson cannot rescind the contract merely because the set proved to be worth only $150. This is a mistake as to value and quality. Robinson should obtain as a part of the contract an express warranty as to the set's quality. Conversely, if the seller parts with a jewel for $50, thinking it is a cheap stone, a complaint cannot later be made if the jewel proves to be worth $2,500.

Mistakes as to the Terms of the Contract. A mistake as to the terms of the contract usually results from failure to read a written contract or a failure to understand a contract's meaning or significance. Such mistakes in both written and oral contracts do not affect their validity; otherwise anyone could avoid a contract merely by claiming a mistake as to its terms.

Lula and Martin signed a property settlement agreement giving Lula all the couple's property in California and Martin all the couple's property in Missouri. The agreement had been drawn up by Martin's lawyer. Martin later wanted the agreement voided because he had intended a note and a bank account in California to be his. Lula said she thought that property was to be hers. The court found Martin's mistake regarding the terms of the contract did not invalidate it.

Mistakes of Law. Ordinarily, when the parties make a mutual mistake of law, the contract is fully binding. The parties are expected to have knowledge of the law when making a contract.

Pupillo Brokerage Co. sold $146,000 of produce to Lombardo Fruit and Produce Co. Their agreement said payment was to be made within 30 days from the invoice date. Under the Perishable Agricultural Commodities Act (PACA), proceeds from the sale of perishable agricultural commodities are held for the benefit of unpaid suppliers. However, to receive PACA benefits, the payment time for transactions can be no more than 30 days after delivery. In the ensuing bank-ruptcy proceedings another creditor alleged Pupillo did not comply with PACA because most of the produce shipments were received before the invoices, giving Lombardo more than 30 days from delivery to pay. Pupillo said the parties mistakenly believed payment terms of 30 days from invoice date complied with PACA. The court said that this mistake of law did not affect the agreement.

Mistakes as to Expectations. When the parties to a contract are mutually mistaken as to their expectations, the contract is binding.

FRAUD

L.O.4

Fraud
Inducing another to contract as a result of an intentionally or recklessly false statement of a material fact

Fraud in the Inducement
Defrauded party intended to make a contract

Fraud in the Execution
Defrauded party did not intend to enter into a contract

Active Fraud
Party engages in action that causes the fraud

Passive Fraud
Failure to disclose information when there is duty to do so

One who intends to and does induce another to enter into a contract as a result of an intentionally or recklessly false statement of a material fact commits **fraud.** The courts recognize two kinds of fraud relating to contracts. These are fraud in the inducement and fraud in the execution.

Fraud in the Inducement

When the party defrauded intended to make the contract, **fraud in the inducement** occurs. Fraud in the inducement relates to the terms or obligations of the transaction between the parties and not to the nature of the document signed. The false statement might relate to the terms of the agreement, the quality of the goods sold, or the seller's intention to deliver goods. A contract so induced is voidable.

Fraud in the Execution

The defrauded party might also be tricked into signing a contract under circumstances in which the nature of the writing could not be understood. The law calls this **fraud in the execution** or fraud in the factum. In this case the victim unknowingly signs a contract. A person who cannot read or who cannot read the language in which the contract is written could be a victim of this type of fraud. When fraud in the execution occurs, the contract is void.

Fraud also may be classified according to whether a party engages in some activity that causes the fraud or does nothing. A party who actually does something or take steps to cause a fraud commits **active fraud.** Sometimes a party may be guilty of fraud without engaging in any activity at all. **Passive fraud** results from the failure to disclose information when there is a duty to do so.

Active Fraud

Active fraud may occur either by express misrepresentation or by concealment of material facts.

Express Misrepresentation. Fraud, as a result of express misrepresentation, consists of four elements, each of which must be present to constitute fraud:

Misrepresentation

False statement of a material fact

1   **Misrepresentation**: a false statement of a material fact.
2   Must be made by one who knew it to be false or made it in reckless disregard of its truth or falsity
3   Must be made with an intent to induce the innocent party to act.
4   The innocent party relies on the false statement and makes a contract.

If these four elements are present, a party who has been harmed is entitled to relief in court.

Brown was the administrator of a health-care clinic and a member of the board of directors of the corporation that owned the clinic. Knowing that the statement was false, Brown told several stockholders that pursuant to a corporate resolution they were required to sell their stock for $500. This amount was less than fair market value. After the stock was purchased by the corporation, Brown and the other remaining stockholders enjoyed a favorable income tax advantage and the retained earnings of the corporation were distributed to them. Brown was guilty of fraud.

Concealment of Material Facts. If one actively conceals material facts for the purpose of preventing the other contracting party from discovering them, such concealment results in fraud even without false statements.

Merely refraining from disclosing pertinent facts unknown to the other party is not fraud as a rule. There must be an active concealment.

Greenspan and Jacobsen built a duplex on a foundation constructed in violation of the building code and inadequate to sustain the weight of the building. Massive cracks and severe settlement ensued. Greenspan and Jacobsen had plasterboard erected in the basement to cover the cracks. They then sold the duplex to Haberman and Ericksen. When the buyers discovered the inadequate foundation, the contract was invalidated. The sellers' active concealment of the cracks constituted fraud.

Passive Fraud

If one's relationship with another relies on trust and confidence, then silence may constitute fraud. Such a relationship exists between partners in a business firm, an agent and principal, a lawyer and client, a guardian and ward, a physician and patient, and in many other trust relationships. In the case of an attorney-client relationship, for example, the attorney has a duty to reveal anything material to the client's interests, and silence has the same effect as making a false statement that there was no material fact to be told to the client. The client could, in such a case, avoid the contract.

Silence, when one has no duty to speak, is not fraud. If Lawrence offers to sell Marconi, a diamond merchant, a gem for $500 that is actually worth $15,000, Marconi's superior knowledge of value does not, in itself, impose a duty to speak.

Innocent Misrepresentation

Innocent Misrepresentation
False statement made in belief it is true

When a contract is being negotiated, one party could easily make a statement believing it to be true when it is in fact false. Such a statement, made in the belief that it is true, is called an **innocent misrepresentation.** Courts generally hold that if it was reasonable for the misled party to have relied on the innocent misrepresentation, the contract is voidable.

Statements of Opinion

Statements of opinion, as contrasted with statements of fact, do not, as a rule, constitute fraud. The person hearing the statement realizes or ought to realize that the other party is merely stating a view and not a fact. But if the speaker is an expert or has special knowledge not available to the other party and should realize that the other party relies on this expert opinion, then a misstatement of opinion or value, intentionally made, would amount to fraud.

Such expressions as "This is the best buy in town," "The price of this stock will double in the next 12 months," "This business will net you $25,000 a year" are all statements of opinion, not statements of fact. If one says, "This business has netted the owner $25,000," this is not an opinion or a prophecy, but a historical fact.

DURESS

Duress
Obtaining consent by means of a threat

For a contract to be valid, all parties must enter into it of their own free wills. **Duress** is a means of destroying another's free will by one party obtaining consent to a contract as a result of a wrongful threat to do the other person or family members some harm. Duress causes a person to agree to a contract he or she would not otherwise agree to. Normally, to constitute duress, the threat must be made by the other party and must be illegal or wrongful. A contract made because of duress is voidable.

One Saturday Carrie Ekl called James Knecht's plumbing company to fix a slow tub drain. Knecht and his helper, Reginald Wagner, cut open a pipe in the basement and removed the obstruction. They replaced the sawed off pipe and installed a PVC trap and tail assembly in case of future blockage. They spent 60 to 90 minutes. Knecht's bill was $480. Ekl said it was ridiculous and the amount outrageous. Knecht said if Ekl did not pay, he would undo the work and turn off the water in her home. Because she was afraid of Knecht, Ekl wrote a check to him for $480. Carrie and her husband sued Knecht claiming it was a contract entered into under duress. The court said it would have been illegal for Knecht to turn off the water therefore there was duress.

Duress is classified according to the nature of the threat as physical, emotional, or economic.

Physical Duress

When one party makes a threat of violence to another person who then agrees to a contract to avoid injury, physical duress occurs. Holding a gun to anther's head or threatening to beat a person up clearly risks injury to a human being and is unlawful.

Emotional Duress

Emotional duress occurs when one party's threats result in such psychological pressure that the victim does not act under free will. Courts will consider the age and health of the victim in determining whether emotional duress occurred.

Barrett financed the purchase of cars, which Sovine then sold. They divided the profit. After Sovine gave Barrett two worthless checks, Barrett had two warrants issued against Sovine. Barrett repeatedly visited Sovine's 70-year-old mother, waving the two checks at her and saying Sovine would go to jail. On February 20, Mrs. Sovine signed a note and mortgage on her home to Barrett. On March 5, the warrants were dismissed. When Barrett sought to foreclose on the home, Mrs. Sovine successfully alleged duress by Barrett.

Financial Duress

When one party wrongly threatens to injure another person financially in order to get agreement to a contract, economic duress occurs. However, duress does not exist when a person agrees to a contract merely because of difficult financial circumstances that are not the fault of the other party. Also, duress does not exist when a person drives a hard bargain and takes advantage of the other's urgent need to make the contract.

UNDUE INFLUENCE

Undue Influence

Person in special relationship causing another's action contrary to free will

One person may exercise such influence over the mind of another that the latter does not exercise free will. Although there is no force or threat of harm (which would be duress), a contract between two such people is nevertheless regarded as voidable. If a party in a confidential or fiduciary relationship to another induces the execution of a contract against the other person's free will, the agreement is voidable because of **undue influence.** If, under any relationship, one is in a position to take undue advantage of another, undue influence may render the contract voidable. Relationships that may result in undue influence are family relationships, a guardian and ward, an attorney and client, a physician and patient, and any other relationship where confidence reposed on one side results in domination by the other. Undue influence may result also from sickness, infirmity, or serious distress.

In undue influence there are no threats to harm the person or property of another as in duress. The relationship of the two parties must be such that one relies on the other so much that he or she yields because it is not possible to hold out against the superior position, intelligence, or personality of the other party. Whether undue influence exists is a question for the court (usually the jury) to determine. Not every influence is regarded as undue; for example, a nagging spouse is ordinarily not regarded as exercising undue influence. In addition, persuasion and argument are not per se undue influence. The key element is that the dominated party is helpless in the hands of the other.

Caleb Patterson, age 85 and in poor mental and physical health, wanted to give his home to the university. After numerous visits from employees of the university, he was told his house was wanted, but not for the use he proposed. The visits were not always cordial. At times there would be arguing and the voices would get loud. After the visitors left, Patterson would be nervous, shaky, upset, and confused. He told his housekeeper the university was going to take all his money and he did not want that. Patterson did deed his home and almost all his property to the university. The court held the gift to be the result of undue influence by university employees.

REMEDIES FOR BREACH OF CONTRACT BECAUSE OF FRAUD, DURESS, OR UNDUE INFLUENCE

L.O.4 ....

Since some mistakes, such as fraud in the inducement, duress, and undue influence, render contracts voidable, not void, you must know what to do if you are a victim of one of these acts. If you do nothing, your right to avoid the contract's provisions may be lost. Furthermore, you may ratify the contract by some act or word indicating an intention to be bound. After you affirm or ratify the contract, you are as fully bound by it as if there had been no mistake, fraud, duress, or undue influence. But still you may sue for whatever damages you have sustained.

Rescind

To set a contract aside

If the contract is voidable, you might elect to **rescind** it or set it aside. Recission seeks to put the parties in the position they were in before the contract was made. In order to rescind, you must first return or offer to return what you received under the contract. After this is done, you are in a position to take one of four actions depending upon the circumstances:

1 You may bring a suit to recover any money, goods, or other things of value, plus damages.
2 If the contract is executory on your part, you may refuse to perform. If the other party sues, you can plead mistake, fraud, duress, or undue influence as a complete defense.
3 You may bring a suit to have the contract judicially declared void.
4 If a written contract does not accurately express the parties' agreement, you may sue for **reformation**, or correction, of the contract.

Reformation

Judicial correction of a contract

In no case can the wrongdoer set the contract aside and thus profit from the wrong. If the agreement is void, neither party may enforce it; no special act is required for setting the agreement aside.

QUESTIONS

1 What mistakes do not invalidate a contract?
2 When a contract provision specifies what will happen in the case of mistake and the law provides otherwise, does the contract or the law govern?
3 What types of mistakes invalidate contracts?
4 If an oral contract is made and then incorrectly reduced to writing, which contract is binding—the oral or the written one?
5 Explain the effect on a contract of:
   a. Fraud in the inducement.
   b. Fraud in the execution.
6 If one does not rely on a misrepresentation, may fraud exist?
7 May an innocent misrepresentation make a contract defective?
8 What is the difference between duress and undue influence?
9 What remedies are available to victims of acts that render contracts voidable?
10 What is the effect of ratifying a contract made as a result of mistake, fraud, duress, or undue influence?

CASE PROBLEMS

L.O.3, 4 ....

1 Larry and Shirley McDaniel paid American Independent Management Systems, Inc., (AIMS) $1,500 to open an AIMS agency. AIMS had told the McDaniels that it had agencies nationwide; it would provide extensive training for them; it offered a variety of financial management services; and it would provide a monthly management bulletin and advertising material. In fact, AIMS had only 14 agents in seven states; it provided a two-day training session; it supplied no advertising material and only one monthly bulletin; and it did not provide the financial management services. The McDaniels sued for $1,500 and their expenses in setting up the office, alleging fraud. Was AIMS guilty of fraud?

L.O.1 ....

2 Donna and Clifford Murray, divorced, agreed to a judgment that awarded Clifford their home and custody of the younger of their two sons. The older son attended college in another state. The older son returned home and the two boys fought, so the younger went to live with Donna. She asked the court to set aside the judgment because she had given up her right to the home thinking Clifford would totally support the younger son. Donna claimed the judgment was based on mutual mistake of fact that the younger son would live with Clifford. By law, the judgment was a contract which could only be rescinded on the same grounds as any other contract. Should the judgment be set aside?

L.O.3 ....

3 After being fired from her job with Hilton Hotels Corp., Marcia Evans filed charges with government agencies and a grievance with Hilton through her union. Evans claimed she was fired because she refused her supervisor's sexual advances. A hearing was held on the grievance. Evans was represented by a lawyer and an agreement was signed. Evans was to get $2,750 and be allowed to quit. She was to withdraw all her filings. Evans then filed suit

against Hilton under the Civil Rights Act. Evans could not sue if the agreement she signed was binding. She alleged undue influence by her attorney caused her to sign the agreement. Was the agreement binding?

L.O.2 .... 4 After Olga Mestrovic died, the 1st Source Bank was appointed to handle her property. The bank contracted to sell Mestrovic's house to Terrence and Antoinette Wilkin. After closing, the Wilkins complained that the house was cluttered with "junk," "stuff," or "trash." The bank said it would hire a rubbish removal service to clean the house or the Wilkins could clean it out and keep any items they wanted. The Wilkins chose to clean the property and found eight drawings and a sculpture created by Mestrovic's husband, a well-known artist. The Wilkins said they cleaned the house, so they had ownership of the art works. The bank said the parties shared the assumption that the items were "junk" and therefore were both mistaken about a vital fact on which the agreement was made. Who owned the art works?

L.O.1 .... 5 Betty Tarrant left a diamond engagement ring with Monson Jewelry for repairs. When Tarrant called for it, Monson told her it was lost and offered to replace it with another wedding set. Tarrant chose a replacement set, which Monson said was worth $450 more than Tarrant's ring. Six months later Monson found the ring in his safe. He offered to exchange the rings. Tarrant and Monson did not agree on an exchange, so Monson sued to rescind the replacement agreement claiming mutual mistake of fact. Was it?

L.O.3 .... 6 When Nancy and William Blodgett divorced, the court ordered Nancy to be paid $2,765,000 as her share of the marital assets if she agreed to a judgment in that amount promptly. Nancy appealed claiming she should get more money. While the appeal was pending, Nancy asked the appellate court to order that either $2,765,000 be released to both her and William or some other amount that would put them on an equal financial footing during the appeal. The court refused. While the appeal was pending, Nancy signed the judgment, so $2,765,000 was released to her and William deeded her the family home. William asked the court to dismiss Nancy's appeal since such a payment takes away the right to appeal. Nancy argued that she signed the judgment involuntarily as the victim of economic duress. Who wins, William or Nancy?

L.O.2 .... 7 D.R. was a multiply handicapped student needing special education. D.R.'s parents and the school board signed an agreement that required the board to pay the placement costs for D.R. at a residential school, the Benedictine School, at the current annual rate of $30,000. The agreement required the board to pay for the next year, 90% of any increase over the previous rate. The board was to pay no other costs for D.R.'s placement. Several months later the board received an estimate of $62,487 for the next year's cost at Benedictine for D.R. The $62,487 included the services of a one-to-one aide for D.R. during his waking hours. The board refused to pay for the aide. In the proceedings that followed, D.R.'s parents asserted that because the need for the aide was not anticipated when the agreement was signed, there was a mutual mistake of fact and the agreement was defective. Was it?

L.O.1 ....

8 A partnership defaulted on a note given to South Washington Associates for the purchase of a building, so Washington foreclosed. The foreclosure recovered $1.2 million less than was owed, so Washington sued the partners. Before trial the parties agreed to arbitration. The agreement provided that for the purpose of any appeal, the arbitrators' award should be reviewed like a trial court's decision. Washington did not like the arbitrators' award and appealed to the state court of appeals. The court stated that the law did not give it jurisdiction to review such an award. Washington argued that the agreement to arbitrate was then based on mutual mistake and was invalid. Was the agreement to arbitrate valid?

L.O.2 ....

9 The Sweetwater County School District had a rule incorporated in its contracts that read, "New teachers being hired by the district will be expected to reside in the community at least five days a week. . . ." Joseph Roush was hired to teach and did live in the community. In a subsequent year he moved to another town and commuted. Two other teachers also commuted. The district tried to terminate Roush, saying that the rule dealing with "new teachers" was meant to apply to teachers hired after the adoption of the rule. Roush had assumed that the rule applied only to first-year teachers. The superintendent testified that the rule had not been enforced. Was Roush's mistake justified?

L.O.3, 4 ....

10 Dimou advertised for sale a used car "in very good condition." McGregor took the car for a short test-drive and discovered it could start only in reverse. Dimou said it was an electrical problem and denied that the car had ever been in an accident. McGregor bought the car and took it to an auto dealer for a complete inspection and evaluation. He was told it was seriously defective, hazardous, and not repairable. The car had been "totaled" in an accident. Dimou had purchased it from a salvage operator and had done extensive work on it. Can McGregor rescind the contract of sale?

Chapter 8

CAPACITY TO CONTRACT

LEARNING OBJECTIVES

After studying this chapter you should be able to:

1 Identify classifications of individuals who may not have the capacity to contract.

2 Define disaffirmance.

3 Explain how a minor's contract can be ratified.

Preview Case

When Jacqueline Flowers was four years old she was severely injured in an automobile accident. She received medical treatment for her injuries from East Tennessee Baptist Hospital, and the unpaid bill for this treatment was $5,271.29. A settlement in the amount of $7,125 was made for Jacqueline with the person alleged to have caused the accident. The hospital tried to subject the settlement to the payment of the hospital bill. Can the hospital recover?

L.O.1

In order that an agreement may be enforceable at law, all parties must have the legal and mental capacity to contract. This means that the parties must have the ability to understand that a contract is being made, have the ability to understand its general nature, and have the legal competence to contract. The general rule presumes that all parties have this capacity. However, in the eyes of the law some parties lack such capacity because of age, physical condition, or public policy. Among those whom the law considers to be incompetent, at least to some degree, include minors, mentally incompetent persons, intoxicated persons, and convicts.

MINORS

Minor

Person under the legal
age to contract

The common-law rule that persons under 21 years of age are **minors** has been abolished by most of the states. Most states have enacted statutes making persons competent to contract at 18 years of age, and a few set the age at 19. In some states, all married minors are fully competent to contract. In still other states minors in business for themselves are bound on all their business contracts.

Contracts of Minors

Almost all of a minor's contracts are voidable at the minor's option. That is, if a minor so desires, the minor can avoid the contract. If a minor wishes to treat a contract made with an adult as valid, the adult is bound by it. An adult cannot avoid a contract on the ground that the minor might avoid it. If a contract is between two minors, each has the right to avoid it. Should the minor die, the personal representative of the estate may avoid the contract that the minor could have avoided.

Firms that carry on business transactions in all the states must know the law dealing with minors in each of the 50 states. Mail-order houses and correspondence schools are particularly susceptible to losses when dealing with minors. The significance of the law is that, with but few exceptions, people deal with minors at their own risk. The purpose of the law is to protect minors from unscrupulous adults, but in general the law affords the other party no more rights in scrupulous contracts than in unscrupulous ones. The minor is the sole judge as to whether a voidable contract will be binding.

Contracts That Cannot Be Avoided

While most contracts made by minors are voidable, a few are not. These include contracts for necessaries, business contracts, and other specially enforced contracts such as student loan agreements.

Necessaries

Items required for living at
a reasonable standard

Contracts of Minors for Necessaries. If a minor contracts for **necessaries**, the minor is liable for the reasonable value. Necessaries include items required for a person to have a reasonable standard of living. The dividing line between necessaries and luxuries is often a fine one. Historically necessaries included food, clothes, and shelter. With the raising of standards of living, courts now hold that necessaries also include medical services such as surgery, dental work, and medicine; education through high school or trade school, and in some cases through college; working tools for a trade; and other goods that are luxuries to some people but necessaries to others because of peculiar circumstances.

The minor's liability is quasi-contractual in nature. The reasonable value of what is actually received must be paid in order to prevent the minor from being unjustly enriched. The minor is not, however, required to pay the contract price.

When Jacqueline Flowers was four years old she was severely injured in an automobile accident. She received medical treatment from East Tennessee Baptist Hospital, and the unpaid bill for this treatment was $5,271.29. A settlement of $7,125 was made for Jacqueline with the person alleged to have caused the accident. The hospital tried to subject the settlement to the payment of the hospital bill. The court found that the treatment was necessary. Because of the inability of Jacqueline's parents to pay for the needed medical treatment, Jacqueline was required to pay the reasonable value of the services from the settlement.

L.O.2

Disaffirmance

Repudiation of a voidable contract

Disaffirmance. The term **disaffirmance** means the repudiation of a contract, that is, the election to avoid it or set it aside. A minor has the legal right to disaffirm a voidable contract at any time during minority or within a reasonable time after becoming of age.

If the contract is wholly executory, a disaffirmance completely nullifies the contract.

Minors, upon electing to disaffirm contracts, must return whatever they may have received under the contracts, provided they still have possession of it. The fact that the minor does not have possession of the property, however, regardless of the reason, does not prevent the exercise of the right to disaffirm the contract. In most jurisdictions, an adult may not recover compensation from a minor who returns the property in damaged condition.

Halbman, a minor, agreed to purchase a car from Lemke. He made a down payment and took possession of the car. An engine rod broke, and Halbman had the car repaired at a garage. Lemke endorsed the car's title to Halbman, but shortly thereafter Halbman returned the title to Lemke, disaffirmed the contract, offered to return the car, and demanded the return of all his money. The repair bill had never been paid, so the garage removed the engine and transmission. The car was vandalized, making it unsalvageable. Halbman sued Lemke for the money he had paid him. Lemke argued that he should be entitled to recover for the damage to the vehicle up to the time of disaffirmance. Halbman was entitled to recover his payments without liability for the use, depreciation, or damage to the car.

If an adult purchases personal property from a minor, the adult has only a voidable title to the property. If the property is sold to an innocent third party before the minor disaffirms the contract, the innocent third party obtains good title to the property. However, the minor may recover from the adult the money or the value of property received from the third party. Statutes in some states make minors' contracts void, not merely voidable. In these states, disaffirmance is not necessary.

L.O.3

Ratification

Adult indicating contract made while a minor is binding

Ratification. A minor may ratify a voidable contract only after attaining majority. **Ratification** means indicating one's willingness to be bound by promises made during minority. It is in substance a new promise and may be oral, written, or merely implied by conduct.

After majority is reached, silence ratifies an executed contract.

William Jones, a minor, signed a contract with Free Flight Sport Aviation allowing Jones to use an airplane ferrying skydivers. The contract included an agreement not to sue and an exemption of liability for Free Flight. A month later Jones attained majority. Ten months after that he was seriously injured when a Free Flight skydiving plane crashed. He sued Free Flight for his injuries. The court held that Jones had ratified the contract by accepting the benefits of it when he used Free Flight's facilities the day of the crash.

A minor cannot ratify part of a contract and disaffirm another part; all or none of it must be ratified. Ratification must be made within a reasonable time after reaching majority. A reasonable time is a question of fact to be determined in light of all surrounding circumstances.

Minors' Business Contracts. Many states, either by special statutory provision or by court decisions, have made a minor's business contracts fully binding. If a minor engages in a business or employment in the same manner as a person having legal capacity, contracts that arise from such business or employment cannot be set aside.

Young Gibson was a minor and in the business of selling and delivering gasoline and motor oil for Rubin Kyle. Under their agreement, Gibson was not authorized to extend credit to anyone unless approved by Kyle. Gibson did extend credit without approval to customers. After the business arrangement ended, Gibson admitted he owed Kyle the amount of unapproved credit extended and Gibson's father executed a note in that amount. The note was enforceable only if Kyle could enforce payment from young Gibson. State law made a minor's business contracts binding, so the court found Kyle could enforce payment from the minor.

Other Enforceable Contracts. A number of states prevent a minor from avoiding certain, specified contracts. These contracts include educational loan agreements, contracts for medical care, contracts made with court approval or in performance of a legal duty, and contracts involving bank accounts.

Contracting Safely with Minors

Since in general one deals with minors at risk, every businessperson must know how to be protected when contracting with minors. The safest way is to have an adult (usually parent or guardian) join in the contract as a cosigner with the minor. This gives the other party to the contract the right to sue the adult who cosigned. A merchant must run some risks when dealing with minors. If a sale is made to a minor, the minor may avoid the contract and demand a refund of the purchase price years later. Since few minors exercise this right, businesspersons often run the risk of contracting with minors than to seek absolute protection against loss.

Minors' Torts

As a general rule, a minor is liable for torts as fully as an adult. If minors misrepresent their age, and the adults with whom they contract rely upon the misrepresentation to their detriment, they commit a tort. The law is not uniform throughout the United States as to whether or not minors are bound on contracts induced by misrepresenting their age. In some states, when sued, they cannot avoid their contracts if they fraudulently misrepresented their age. In some states they may be held liable for any damage to or deterioration of the property they received under the contract. If minors sue on the contracts to recover what they paid, they may be denied recovery if they misrepresented their age.

MENTALLY INCOMPETENT PERSONS

A number of reasons beyond a person's control result in mental incompetence. These include insanity or incompetence as a result of stroke, senile dementia, and retardation. In determining a mentally incompetent person's capacity to contract, the intensity and duration of the incompetency must be determined. In most states, if a person has been formally adjudicated incompetent, contracts made by the person are void without regard to whether they are reasonable or for necessaries. Such a person is considered incapable of making a valid acceptance of an offer no matter how fair the offer is. When a person has been judicially declared insane and sanity is later regained and a court officially declares the person to be competent, the capacity to contract is the same as that of any other normal person. If a person is incompetent but has not been so declared by the court, then the person's contracts are voidable, not void. Like a minor, the person must pay the reasonable value of necessaries that have been supplied. Upon disaffirmance, anything of value received under the contracts and which the person still has must be returned.

After being asked by Mary Bradshaw to oppose her guardian's annual accounting of her estate, Wendell Snell sought compensation for his legal services. Bradshaw had been declared incompetent. In the judicial proceedings that followed, the court determined that an incompetent did not have capacity to contract for such services. Recovery for the services was not allowed.

A person who has not been declared by a court to be insane and has only intervals of insanity or delusions can make a contract fully as binding as that of a normal person if it is made during a sane or lucid interval. The person must be able to understand that a contract is being made.

In September, Ruby Bonham and her daughter, Pauline Olson, signed an agreement to sell land. They had rejected the buyer's first offer of $50,000 and countered with $52,500, which the buyer accepted. Two months before, Bonham had shown Jay Uribe, the buyer, around and correctly answered all his questions. In December, Olson was declared conservator of Bonham's property and claimed Bonham had not been competent in September. Uribe sued. Testimony at the trial was that Bonham's mental acuity had gradually deteriorated prior to the agreement and that she had had periods of disorientation, paranoia, eccentric habits, and delusions about friendships with Barry Goldwater and Frank Sinatra. Her sister said that before signing the agreement Bonham had told the realtor, "I don't care what you do with this property. You can give it back to the Indians if you want to." But Bonham had also had the agreement explained to her, read it, and appeared to understand. The court found Bonham competent because she had negotiated the sale, listened to the explanation, and read the agreement.

INTOXICATED PERSONS

People may also put themselves in a condition that destroys contractual capacity. Contracts made by people who have become so intoxicated that they cannot understand the meaning of their acts are voidable. Upon becoming sober, they may affirm or disaffirm contracts they made while drunk. If one delays unreasonably in disaffirming a contract made while intoxicated, however, the right to have the contract set aside may be lost.

Marvin and Mercedes Olsen were the beneficiaries of Hobart Turner's life insurance policy. Turner changed the beneficiary to Charles Hawkins. Turner had been committed because of alcoholism to the state hospital for six months two years prior to the beneficiary change. After Turner died, the Olsens sued for the insurance proceeds alleging Turner signed the change of beneficiary while an alcoholic and not in control of his faculties. Witnesses said about that time Turner was properly dressed and behaved; he conversed normally; they did not know he was an alcoholic, and he told them he had changed the beneficiary and why. A witness to Turner's signing said he seemed perfectly normal at the time. The court found he was sober and could understand what he was doing at the time of the beneficiary change.

That a contract is foolish and would not have been entered into if the party had been sober does not make the contract voidable.

A person who has been legally declared to be a habitual drunkard cannot make a valid contract but is liable for the reasonable value of necessaries furnished. If a person is purposely caused to become drunk in order to be induced to contract, the agreement will be held invalid.

The rule regarding the capacity of an intoxicated person also applies to people using drugs.

J. Gerald and Martha R. Hudson executed a mortgage on real estate to Ralph B. and Virginia I. Poole. There was a default, and the Pooles sued to foreclose. Martha Hudson defended on the basis that she was "under the influence of opiates and did not know the nature and character of the papers she signed." The court stated that mental incapacity resulting from the use of drugs may be a ground for avoiding a contract. However, merely being under the influence of drugs is not enough. Reasoning powers must be so impaired as to render the person incapable of comprehending and acting rationally in the transaction. The foreclosure was permitted.

CONVICTS

Convict

Person found guilty by court of major criminal offense

While many states have repealed their former laws restricting the capacity of a **convict** (one convicted of a major criminal offense, namely, a felony or treason) to contract, some jurisdictions still have limitations. These range from depriving convicts of rights as needed to provide for the security of the penal institutions in which they are confined and for reasonable protection of the public, to classifying convicts as under a disability, as are minors and insane persons. In these instances, the disability lasts only as long as the person is imprisoned or supervised by parole authorities.

QUESTIONS

1   What classes of persons are considered by the law to lack full capacity to make contracts?

2   Who is a minor?

3   Are contracts made by minors binding?

4   If a minor wishes to treat as binding a contract with an adult, can the adult avoid it because the other party is a minor?

5   If a minor contracts to purchase necessaries, must the contract price be paid?

6   What is disaffirmance?

7   If Sally purchases a car from Henry, a minor, and then sells it to Watson, can Henry demand that Watson return the car to him?

8   When can a minor ratify a voidable contract?

9   In what situations is a minor bound on contracts?

10 If Gordon, a minor, lies about his age to induce an adult to enter a contract, is he guilty of a tort?

11 If a person judicially declared insane becomes sane, is the capacity to contract restored?

12 Is a contract made by an intoxicated person valid?

CASE PROBLEMS

L.O.3 ....

1   Seventeen-year-old Charles Edward Smith bought a car from Bobby Floars Toyota. Smith made 11 monthly payments on the car, of which 10 were made after he turned 18. He then took the car back to Floars. The car was sold, but for less than Smith owed on it and Floars sued him for the difference. Smith claimed returning the car 10 months after reaching majority constituted a timely disaffirmance of the contract. What do you think the court should find?

L.O.2 ....

2   The parents of Marilyn Calhoun, age 13, were divorced. Marilyn's mother and two other people came to an apartment where Marilyn was babysitting. Marilyn was told that her father was dead and that she needed to sign certain documents for the body to be picked up. She signed the documents while one person covered the written portion. She was not told they were documents that indicated her agreement to turn over the proceeds of an insurance policy for $1,944.72 and her promise to pay for her father's funeral and allow a judgment to be entered against her if the money was not paid. Eight months later an action was filed and a judgment for the funeral costs was entered. A year after Marilyn attained majority, a prospective employer informed her that her credit record was impaired. Upon further inquiry, she first learned of the judgment. Two months later she sought to challenge it. Was this a disaffirmance of the documents she had signed, and, if so, must she return anything to the holder of the note?

L.O.1 ....

3   Edward Daubert, a minor, married, and a father, had a car to get to work. He was injured in an automobile accident and signed a release contract for the injuries. He then sued James Mosley, the motorist who caused the accident. Mosley argued the release prevented the suit and Daubert pled disaffirmance and revocation of the release. The court had to decide whether a car was a necessary for a married minor. Is it?

L.O.1, 2 ....

4   When 17 years old, Cindy Farrar signed a form at Swedish Health Spa for a two-year membership for $324.31. As payment she used her father's

MasterCard credit card. The father paid his MasterCard bill but then told the spa that Cindy was a minor and asked that the money be refunded. Cindy never used the facilities or services of the spa after signing the form. Did the payment of the MasterCard bill by the father constitute ratification?

L.O.1 ....

5 On April 1, Bobby Joe Clardy, a manic-depressive, negotiated the purchase of a truck from Shoals Ford. Visiting his daughter, Leslie, Bobby Joe went out of control, throwing his medicine into a fire. On April 3 Shoals told him his bad credit rating required a down payment of $10,500 instead of $5,000. At 5 A.M. on April 5 he banged on the doors and windows of Leslie's house, threatened everyone there, and forced Leslie to write him a check for $500. As soon as possible, she arranged to have Bobby Joe involuntarily committed. She called Shoals Ford to explain that a "buying spree" was a symptom of his illness and he was being committed. She said he could not make the truck payments and was not insurable. Bobby Joe returned to Shoals with the down payment, and Shoals gave him the truck. Bobby Joe's wife, Maxine, was appointed to handle Bobby Joe's funds and sued to have the sale set aside. A psychiatrist testified that Bobby Joe was incompetent on April 6 and he could not imagine him otherwise on April 5. Was Bobby Joe competent to buy the truck?

L.O.3 ....

6 While a minor, Jerry Ray borrowed money from Acme Finance Corp. to buy a car and signed a loan agreement. Six payments were made, some after Ray achieved majority. Ray wrecked the car and refused to make any further payments. State law provided that ratification after majority of a debt contracted during minority had to be in writing. Acme sued on the unpaid loan. Analyze and decide the case.

L.O.1 ....

7 While married to Olivia, George Lloyd bought an annuity and made his daughters from a previous marriage, Betty Lou Jordan and Marion Pitts, the beneficiaries. George and Olivia divorced. George showed evidence of mental instability and dementia in April and was declared incompetent in September. Meanwhile, in August he remarried Olivia who got a form to change the beneficiary of the annuity to her. After George died, Jordan and Pitts asked the court to declare them the beneficiaries. Olivia testified she "couldn't say" George "knew what he was doing" when he signed the form. Who should get the benefits from the annuity?

L.O.2 ....

8 Melvin Parrent was 15 when he was injured while working for Midway Toyota. Midway accepted liability and paid temporary total disability payments for more than a year. Several months later Parrent and Midway signed a final settlement for disability benefits totaling $6,136.40. Parrent and his mother negotiated the settlement, and she was present at the time he signed. She did not object, but no one of legal age signed in Parrent's behalf. Parrent later filed a petition to reopen his claim. Midway claimed that because of the close relation and continuous awareness of the mother the settlement is enforceable. Is it?

Chapter 9

CONSIDERATION

After studying this chapter you should be able to:

1 Define consideration.

2 Explain when part payment constitutes consideration.

3 Give three examples of insufficient or invalid consideration.

4 Recognize when consideration is not required.

Preview Case

Richard Runyan, age 53, was told his employment would be terminated. He told his employer that it was age discrimination. His employer said it was due to inadequate job performance. After discussing the termination, Runyan and the employer agreed Runyan would have a one-year consulting arrangement that provided a minimum monthly compensation. Later Runyan asked that the written consulting agreement be extended and the compensation be increased. The company agreed to increase the monthly compensation by $1,667 in consideration for Runyan's releasing the company from all other debts and claims relating to his termination. Both parties signed this agreement. After the consulting agreement expired, Runyan sued the company for $450,000 claiming he was terminated because of age discrimination. Did the release agreement bar the suit?

L.O.1

Consideration
What promisor requires
as the price for a promise

Courts will compel compliance with an agreement only when it is supported by consideration. Consideration distinguishes mere agreements from legally enforceable obligations. **Consideration** is whatever the promisor demands and receives as the price for a promise. This could be money, personal property, a service, or a promise of any of these items.

NATURE OF CONSIDERATION

In most contracts, the parties require and are content with a promise by the other party as the price for their own promises. For example, a homeowner may promise to pay a painter $1,000 in return for the promise of the painter to paint the house. Correspondingly, the painter makes the promise to paint in return for the promise of the homeowner to make such payment. By its nature, this exchange of a promise for a promise occurs at the one time.

For a promise to constitute consideration, the promise must impose an obligation upon the person making it. If a merchant promises to sell a businessperson all of the computer paper ordered at a specific price in return for the businessperson's promise to pay that price for any computer paper ordered, there is no contract. There is no certainty that any computer paper will be needed.

A promise may be made that is conditional. Such a promise is consideration even if the condition is unlikely to occur. If *A* promises to sell *B* paint if the paint shipment arrives, the promise is consideration.

Consideration may also be the doing of an act or the making of a promise to refrain from doing an act that can be lawfully done. Thus, a promise to give up smoking or drinking can be consideration for a promise to make a certain payment in return therefor. In contrast, a promise to stop driving an automobile in excess of the speed limit is not consideration because a person does not have a right to drive illegally. The promise to drive lawfully does not add anything to that already required.

ADEQUACY OF CONSIDERATION

As a general rule, the adequacy of the consideration is irrelevant. The law does not prohibit bargains. Except in cases where the contract calls for a performance or the sale of goods that have a standard or recognized market value, it is impossible to fix the money value of each promise. If the consideration given by one party is grossly inadequate, this is a relevant fact in proving fraud, undue influence, duress, or mistake.

Emanuel Watson, when he was 100 years old and unable to handle his business affairs because of a stroke, sold some land worth $6,750 to Stewart and Gloria Landes for $200. Emanuel's widow, Reather, asked a court to set the transaction aside saying Emanuel was not competent at the time of the sale. Reather alleged the inadequate consideration was evidence of Emanuel's incompetence. The court held that such a gross inadequacy of consideration proved Emanuel's incapacity. The sale was set aside.

Part Payment

L.O.2 .... A partial payment of a past-due debt is not consideration to support the creditor's promise to cancel the balance of the debt. The creditor is already entitled to the part payment. Promising to give something to which the other party is already entitled is not consideration.

Several exceptions apply to this rule:

1   If the amount of the debt is in dispute, the debt is canceled if a lesser sum than that claimed is accepted in full settlement.

> Richard Runyan, age 53, was told his employment would be terminated. He told his employer that was age discrimination. His employer said it was due to inadequate job performance. After discussing the termination, Runyan and the employer agreed that Runyan would have a one-year consulting arrangement that provided a minimum monthly compensation. Later Runyan asked that the agreement be extended and the compensation increased. The company agreed to increase the monthly compensation by $1,667 in consideration for Runyan's releasing the company from all other debts and claims relating to his termination. Both parties signed this agreement. After the consulting agreement expired, Runyan sued the company for $450,000, claiming he was terminated because of age discrimination. The court found a bona fide dispute existed concerning the reason for the termination. Therefore, any greater amount potentially owed by the company because of age discrimination was waived when the increased compensation was given in full settlement of any claims by Runyan regarding his termination.

Composition of Creditors

When all of multiple creditors settle in full for a fraction of the amount owed

2   If there is more than one creditor, and each one agrees, in consideration of the others' agreement, to accept in full settlement a percentage of the amount due, this agreement will cancel the unpaid balance due these creditors. This arrangement is known as a **composition of creditors.**

> The Henry B. Gilpin Company agreed to pay David Moxley $56,390 and signed a note to Moxley in that amount. When interest came due, Gilpin could not make the payment. It proposed a composition of creditors by which it would pay 60% of all debts owed in full settlement. Moxley and a majority of the creditors agreed. Two months later, Gilpin offered a new plan to ensure it continued in business. This offer stated it superseded the previous offer, which it withdrew. This offer also precluded Gilpin from paying any creditor under the previous offer. All creditors except Moxley accepted the second offer. Moxley demanded payment of the whole amount due including interest. Gilpin paid only interest, and Moxley sued claiming Gilpin had breached its agreement. The court found that the first composition was a binding contract, and Moxley was entitled to sue on it.

3   If the debt is evidenced by a note or other written evidence, cancellation and return of the written evidence cancels the debt.

4   If the payment of the lesser sum is accompanied by a receipt in full and some indication that a gift is made of the balance, the debt may be canceled.

5   If a secured note is given and accepted in discharge of an unsecured note for a greater amount, the difference between the two notes is discharged. The security is the consideration to support the contract to settle for a lesser sum.

Insufficient or Invalid Consideration

L.O.3 ....

Many apparent considerations lack the full force and effect necessary to make enforceable agreements. Consideration of the following classes is either insufficient or invalid:

1 Performing or promising to perform what one is already obligated to do.

2 Refraining from doing or promising to refrain from doing what one has no right to do.

3 Past performance.

Performing or Promising to Perform What One Is Already Obligated to Do. If the supposed consideration consists merely of a promise to do what one is already legally obligated to do, consideration is invalid. If the consideration is invalid, the contract is invalid. In such case, the promise gives nothing new to the other contracting party.

Wendell Anderson purchased a herbicide and applied it to farmland. He later became aware of a weed-control problem on the farm. The company that produced the herbicide offered to settle Anderson's claim by providing an alternative herbicide equal to the value of the original herbicide plus a cash allowance for application. Anderson accepted the offer. He later sued for $10,228 for the failure of the original herbicide to control the growth of weeds. Anderson alleged that the producer's settlement offer was a promise to perform a pre-existing duty (weed control), so the compromise agreement was invalid for lack of consideration. The court held that the producer's act of providing an alternative herbicide plus cash and Anderson's promise not to sue provided consideration, and the compromise agreement was valid.

Parties to a contract may at any time mutually agree to cancel an old contract and replace it with a new one. For this new contract to be enforceable, there must be some added features that benefit both parties though not necessarily to an equal extent. If a contractor agrees to build a house of certain specifications for $80,000, a contract of the homeowner to pay an additional $1,000 is not binding unless the contractor concurrently agrees to do something the original contract did not require as a consideration for the $1,000. The value of the additional act by the contractor need not be $1,000. It merely must have a monetary value.

If unforeseen difficulties arise that make it impossible for the contractor to complete the house for $80,000, these unforeseen difficulties may, in rare cases, be consideration. Unforeseen difficulties include underground rock formations or a change in the law relative to the building codes and zoning laws. The homeowner is not bound to agree to pay more because of unforeseen difficulties; but if such an agreement is made, these difficulties will constitute a consideration even though the contractor does not agree to do anything additional. Strikes, bad weather, and a change in prices are examples of foreseeable difficulties, which would not be consideration.

Refraining or Promising to Refrain from Doing What One Has No Right to Do. When one refrains or promises to refrain from doing something, this conduct is called **forbearance.** If the promisor had a right to do the act, forbearance is a valid consideration. Consideration is invalid when it consists of a promise to forbear doing something that one has no right to do, such as to commit an unlawful act.

Forbearance

Refraining from doing something

Often the forbearance consists of promising to refrain from suing the other party. Promising to refrain from suing another constitutes consideration if one has a reasonable right to demand damages and intends to file a suit. Such a promise is even valid when a suit lacks merit if the promisor mistakenly, but honestly and reasonably, believes a suit would be valid.

Desmarais purchased a farm from Huberdeau for $40,000 down and $5,000 of principal and accrued interest yearly. Desmarais failed to make several principal payments. Huberdeau agreed to accept only the interest if Desmarais would continue farming. Then they agreed if the farm were forfeited because Desmarais breached the contract of sale, Desmarais would transfer the allotment base under which he received federal payments to Huberdeau. In return, Huberdeau agreed to forbear suing for the timely payment of the principal installments. The second agreement was not binding. Huberdeau did not have a valid ground of forbearance.

Past Performance. An act performed prior to the promise does not constitute valid consideration. If a carpenter gratuitously helps a neighbor build a house with no promise of pay, a promise to pay made after the house is completed cannot be enforced. The promise to pay must induce the carpenter to do the work, and this cannot be done if the promise is made after the work is completed.

For 30 years Virginia Sigler resided with Helen Mariotte and shared expenses. After Mariotte was hospitalized, Sigler was eager for her to return home and told Mariotte's son she would care for her at no charge. Sigler assisted in caring for Mariotte and paid $200 per month for food and rent. Three years later Mariotte signed a document in which she instructed that from the time of her return from the hospital, Sigler was to be paid $85 per week plus room and board. After a conservator was appointed for Mariotte, Sigler filed a claim for $85 per week and reimbursement for rent and food after Mariotte's return from the hospital. The claim was disallowed. Sigler agreed to care for Mariotte free of charge. Past benefits did not constitute consideration for the subsequent promise by Mariotte.

A debt that is discharged by bankruptcy may be revived under certain circumstances, usually by the debtor's agreeing, with approval from the bankruptcy court, to pay it. Such promises are enforceable even though the creditor, the promisee, gives no new consideration to support the promise. The debtor is said to have waived the defense of discharge in bankruptcy; and the original debt, therefore, is deemed to remain in force.

EXCEPTIONS TO REQUIREMENT OF CONSIDERATION

L.O.4 .... As a general rule, a promise must be supported by consideration. Certain exceptions to the rule involve voluntary subscriptions, debts of record, promissory estoppel, and modification of sales contracts.

Voluntary Subscriptions

When charitable enterprises are financed by voluntary subscriptions of many persons, the promise of each person is generally held to be enforceable. When a number of people make pledges to or subscribe to a charitable association or to a church, for example, the pledges or subscriptions are binding. One theory for enforcing the promise is that each subscriber's promise is supported by the promises of other subscribers. Another theory is that a subscription is an offer of a unilateral contract that is accepted by creating liabilities or making expenditures. Despite the fact that such promises lack the technical requirements of ordinary contracts, the courts in most states will enforce the promises as a matter of public policy.

> To encourage doctors to settle in Parkersburg and to provide a medical building, P.H.C.C.C. was formed to solicit contributions. At a meeting P.H.C.C.C. held, B. J. Johnston spoke favorably about the project and said he would give $50,000. He read and signed a subscription card that said "I _____ do hereby subscribe and promise to pay P.H.C.C.C. . . . the total sum of $50,000."
>
> Johnston gave only $12,750. The building was completed using borrowed money. Johnston's subscription was used as collateral for the loan. P.H.C.C.C. sued for the remainder of the pledge. Johnston claimed the subscription agreement was unenforceable. The court said it was enforceable.

Debts of Record

Consideration is not necessary to support an obligation of record, such as a judgment, on the basis that such an obligation is enforceable as a matter of public policy.

Promissory Estoppel

Promissory Estoppel

Substitute for consideration when another acts in reliance on promisor's promise

Although not supported by considerations, courts enforce some promises on the basis of **promissory estoppel.** According to this doctrine, if one person makes a promise to another and that other person acts in reliance upon the promise, the promisor will not be permitted to claim lack of consideration. Enforcement is held to be proper when the promisor should reasonably expect to cause and does cause action by the promisee and the promisee would be harmed substantially if the promise is not enforced. The theory has gained support as a means of realizing justice. The elements of promissory estoppel include:

1   A promise is made.
2   The promisor reasonably expects the promise to induce action by the promisee.
3   The promisee does act.
4   Justice requires enforcement of the promise.

Courts will find that justice requires enforcement of the promise when the promisee would be substantially harmed if it were not enforced.

> McNeill and Associates was a general agent for ITT Life Insurance. Insurance Marketing, Inc. (IMI) owed ITT a large amount of money and was failing. ITT asked McNeill to purchase IMI's business. McNeill refused. IMI had ten times as many accounts as McNeill. Later ITT again asked McNeill to purchase IMI's business. A written agreement of sale was signed by IMI, McNeill, and ITT. ITT separately promised McNeill it would not
>
> terminate the general agency if McNeill purchased IMI. McNeill purchased IMI's business for $510,000. ITT later terminated the agency. McNeill sued and alleged that promissory estoppel required enforcement of the promise not to terminate the agency. The court said justice required enforcing the promise because of liabilities McNeill incurred by purchasing a much larger business in reliance on ITT's promise.

Modification of Sales Contracts

Sales of goods are regulated by the Uniform Commercial Code (see Chapter 16). The Code provides that when a contract for the sale of goods is modified by agreement of the parties, no consideration is necessary to make it enforceable.

QUESTIONS

1   What is the importance of *consideration*?
2   What is necessary for a promise to constitute consideration?
3   If a boy promises his father that he will not own and operate an automobile until he is 18 in exchange for his father's promise to pay him $2,000, is this a valid contract?
4   Does the adequacy of consideration determine if a contract is valid?
5   When does part payment constitute consideration?
6   If Davis owes Dennis $10,000, and Dennis offers to settle for $7,000, what must be done to make the contract binding?
7   What are three situations in which consideration is insufficient or invalid?
8   May refraining from suing someone be valid consideration?
9   What are the four situations in which a promise not supported by consideration will be enforced?
10   What is *promissory estoppel*?

CASE PROBLEMS

L.O.1, 4   1   Gordon Hayes offered Kathleen Hunter a job, to begin on a specified date, as a flag girl on a construction job. He also told her to quit her job at the telephone company. Hunter did quit her job, but Hayes did not employ her, and she was out of work for two months. She sued Hayes for her lost wages. Hayes said there was no consideration for his promise, therefore it was unenforceable. How should the court decide?

L.O.3   2   Walter and Martha Crown agreed, in writing, to buy William and Ann Cole's house and put down $1,500, of which $500 was a note. The Crowns asked the broker to condition their purchase on them selling their own house; however they knew the agreement did not say that. When they had difficulty selling their house, they sued for return of their $1,500 alleging they had an oral agreement that their purchase was conditioned on their house selling. They claimed the consideration for the oral agreement was that they gave up the legal right to contest the validity of the note and not pay it. Was this a forbearance and valid consideration?

L.O.2   3   William Coester had a beer distributorship agreement with H.H.B. Company. The parties entered into a Termination of Business Agreement, which included a full release of H.H.B. from Coester. H.H.B. agreed to purchase all Coester's inventory at retail price and pay off a $44,164.10 mortgage on a warehouse rented by Coester from his mother for use in his business. H.H.B. performed all its obligations under the Agreement. Coester sued H.H.B., arguing that the release was invalid because it was not supported by adequate consideration because the retail price of the beer was not much and he did not receive the benefit of the $44,164.10 paid on the mortgage. Was the release valid?

L.O.3 ....

4   Two corporations of which Samuel Bogley was an officer passed resolutions or motions stating ". . . in consideration of past services and services to be rendered by Samuel E. Bogley . . . the Corporation is authorized upon . . . death . . . to pay (his) estate or named beneficiary the total compensation received by the officer for the past two years prior to his death." After Bogley's death the corporations paid his estate $126,300. The IRS claimed it should be included in computing federal estate tax because the corporations made offers that were accepted by Bogley's continuing to serve as an officer of the corporations until his death. Thus, the IRS argued, the money was paid under binding contracts and it should be included in his estate for tax purposes. Were there binding contracts?

L.O.2 ....

5   Carl Evans Boyd and Luther Claud Boyd died leaving two sets of wills. The beneficiaries of the earlier wills contested the later wills, claiming the Boyds did not have the testamentary capacity to make them. While the will contest was pending, all the parties entered into written agreements resolving all the questions regarding the distribution of the estates of the Boyds. They then asked the judge to enter an order confirming the agreements and disposing of the will contest in accordance with the agreements. The judge claimed he could not enter a judgment declaring the later wills void without finding that the Boyds lacked capacity to make them. Was there sufficient consideration for the agreements?

L.O.3 ....

6   After having surgery, Roman Hladun needed personal care upon leaving the hospital. Hladun entered a written agreement with Tender Loving Care Agency to provide the care. A week later, Hladun's daughter, Vira Goldman, returned from Hong Kong. When Tender Loving Care Agency was not fully paid, it sued Goldman claiming she had orally promised to pay for the care. Was Goldman liable?

L.O.1, 4 ....

7   At a meeting of the board of trustees of the Oral Roberts Evangelistic Association, Nicholas Timko proposed that a building in Detroit be purchased. He stated that a down payment of $25,000 could buy it, and if the association made payments for five years, he would then pay any unpaid balance. The association bought the building with Timko making the arrangements and reiterating his promise to pay the balance remaining after five years. Less than five years after the purchase Timko died having made no payment. The association filed a claim for the unpaid balance against Timko's estate alleging his voluntary subscription was enforceable on the basis of promissory estoppel. Is the promise enforceable?

Chapter 10

ILLEGAL AGREEMENT/

LEARNING OBJECTIVES

After studying this chapter, you should be able to:

1 Explain the consequences of a contract for an unlawful purpose or a purpose achieved illegally.

2 Explain what types of contracts are void for illegality.

3 Identify the types of contracts which are contrary to public policy.

Preview Case

Before their marriage, Richard J. Reynolds executed a prenuptial agreement with Marianne O'Brien. In it he conveyed all the common stock of Sapelo Plantation, Inc., by bill of sale and agreed to transfer the stock upon the books of the corporation in consideration of $10 and O'Brien's agreement to marry him. At the time he was married to Elizabeth Dillard Reynolds. The stock was not transferred on the books of the corporation. After Richard's death, Marianne Reynolds claimed title to the stock. Was the agreement to marry another when already married valid?

L.O.1

A contract must be for a lawful purpose, and this purpose must be achieved in a lawful manner. Otherwise the contract is void. If this were not true, the court might force one party to a contract to commit a crime. If the act itself is legal, but the manner of committing the act that is called for in the contract is illegal, the contract is void.

A contract that is void because of illegality does not necessarily involve the commission of a crime. It may consist merely of a private wrong—the commission of a tort—such as an agreement by two persons to slander a third. A contract contrary to public policy is also illegal.

If the parties are not equally guilty, courts may assist the less guilty party.

If the contract is indivisible, that is, it cannot be performed except as an entity, then illegality in one part renders the whole contract invalid. If the contract is divisible, so that the legal parts can be performed separately, the legal parts of the contract are enforceable. For example, when one purchases several articles, each priced separately, and the sale of one article is illegal because the price was illegally set by price-fixing, the whole contract will not fall because of the one article.

Savin Corporation entered into a contract with Copy Distributing Company to sell Copy copiers, parts, and supplies. In paragraph 3(a), Copy agreed to sell Savin products "only to bona fide retail end users." Wayne Marcy agreed to pay under the contract if Copy did not. All payments were not made, and Savin sued. The provision to sell only at retail was illegal under state antitrust law, so Copy was not required to pay. Savin argued Marcy was still liable. The court disagreed. An agreement to pay on an illegal contract was not enforceable.

CONTRACTS PROHIBITED BY STATUTE

L.O.2 .... There are many types of contracts declared illegal by statute. Some common ones include:

1 Gambling contracts
2 Sunday contracts
3 Usurious contracts
4 Contracts of an unlicensed operator
5 Contracts for the sale of prohibited articles
6 Contracts in unreasonable restraint of trade

Gambling Contracts

Gambling Contract

Agreement in which parties win or lose by chance

A **gambling contract** is a transaction wherein the parties stand to win or to lose based on pure chance. What one gains, the other must lose. Under the early common law, private wagering contracts were enforceable, but they are now generally prohibited in all states by statute. In recent years certain classes of gambling contracts regulated by the state, such as state lotteries and pari-mutuel systems of betting on horse races and dog races, have been legalized in many states.

In general the courts will leave the parties to a private gambling contract where it finds them and will not allow one party to sue the other for the breach of a gambling debt. If two parties to a gambling contract give money to a stakeholder with instructions to pay the money to the winner, the parties can demand a return of their money. If the stakeholder pays the money to the winner, then the loser may sue either the winner or the stakeholder for reimbursement. No state will permit the stakeholder, who is considered merely a trustee of the funds, to keep the money. The court in this event requires the stakeholder to return each wagerer's deposit.

During a campaign to fluoridate the water in Codahy, James Quirk was opposed and the Jaycees in favor. Quirk challenged the Jaycees by offering to give them $1,000 if four daily glasses of fluoridated water could not "cause 'dermatologic, gastrointestinal, and neuro-logical disorders.'" He added that he would also pay $1,000 if the Jaycees found he had misrepresented matters. The Jaycees checked up somewhat and were satisfied fluoridation was not so harmful and demanded the $1,000. The court said the challenge was a bet or wager—essentially Quirk was gambling his $1,000 against the Jaycees proving him wrong. Since the court will not settle a dispute for the partici-pants in a wager, the Jaycees lost.

Closely akin to gambling debts are loans made to enable one to gamble. If *A* loans *B* $100 and then wins it back in a poker game, is this a gambling debt? Most courts hold that it is not. If *A* and *B* bet $100 on a football game and *B* wins, and if *A* pays *B* by giving a promissory note for the $100, such a note may be declared void.

Trading on the stock exchange or the grain market represent legitimate busi-ness transactions. But the distinction between such trading and gambling contracts is sometimes very fine.

Alewine and Goodnoe could form a contract whereby Alewine agrees to sell Goodnoe 10,000 shares of stock one month from date at $42 a share. If they do not actually intend to buy and sell the stock, but agree to settle for the difference between $42 a share and the closing price on the date fixed in the contract, this is a gambling contract.

However, Ripetto could agree to sell Bolde 10,000 bushels of wheat to be delivered six months later at $1.70 a bushel. Ripetto does not own any wheat, but expects to buy it for delivery. If at the end of the six-month period the seller does not actually deliver the wheat, and if the price of wheat has gone up, the seller may pay the buyer the difference between the current price and the contract price. If the seller does not deliver the wheat and the price of wheat has gone down, the buyer may pay the seller the difference. Such a contract is legal because the intention was to deliver. The primary difference between the Alewine case and Ripetto case is the intention to deliver. In the case of trading, the seller (Ripetto) intended at the time of the contract to deliver the wheat and the buyer to accept it. In the gambling case, the seller (Alewine) did not intend to deliver.

Sunday Contracts

The laws pertaining to Sunday contracts resulted from statutes and judicial interpre-tation. They vary considerably from state to state. Most states have repealed their statutes that had made Sunday contracts illegal.

The violators of Sunday acts are seldom prosecuted. For this reason the types of transactions one observes being carried on Sunday do not necessarily indicate restrictions imposed by these laws.

Usury
Charging higher rate of interest than law allows

Maximum Contract Rate
Highest legal rate of inter-est

Usurious Contracts

State laws that limit the rate of interest that may be charged for the use of money are called **usury** laws. Frequently there are two rates, the maximum contract rate and the legal rate. The **maximum contract rate** is the highest rate that may be

Legal Rate

Interest rate applied when no rate specified

charged; any rate above that is usurious. In some states this rate fluctuates depending on the prime rate. The **legal rate,** which is a rate somewhat lower than the contract rate, applies to all situations in which interest may be charged but in which the parties were silent as to the rate. If merchandise is sold on 30 days' credit, the seller may collect interest from the time the 30 days expire until the debt is paid. If no rate is agreed upon in a situation of this kind, the legal rate may be charged.

The courts will treat transactions as usurious when there is in fact a lending of money at a usurious rate even though disguised. Such activities as requiring the borrower to execute a note for an amount in excess of the actual loan and requiring the borrower to antedate the note so as to charge interest for a longer period than that agreed on could make a loan usurious.

The penalty for usury varies from state to state. In most states the only penalty might prohibit the lender from collecting the excess interest. In other states the entire contract is void, and in still others the borrower need not pay any interest but must repay the principal. If the borrower has already paid the usurious interest, the court will require the lender to refund to the borrower any money collected in excess of the contract rate.

In all states special statutes govern consumer loans by pawnbrokers, small loan companies, and finance companies. In some states these firms may charge much higher rates of interest.

The Walkers executed an agreement with Nationwide Financial Corporation for a loan of $15,537.64 secured by a first deed of trust against real property. The interest rate was 18 percent. In the state where they borrowed the money, the maximum permissible interest rate for loans that did not come within the Uniform Consumer Credit Code was 10 percent. The Code recited that a loan secured by an interest in land was a consumer loan and also that a loan primarily secured by an interest in land was a consumer loan if the interest rate exceeded 10 percent. Thus, the loan was a consumer loan, and its rate of 18 percent was not usurious.

Contracts of an Unlicensed Operator

Statutes make it illegal to operate certain types of businesses or professions without a license. Most of these statutes are made to protect the public from incompetent operators. The most common types of professional persons who must be licensed to operate include doctors, lawyers, certified and licensed public accountants, dentists, and insurance and real estate salespeople. A person who performs these services without license not only cannot sue to collect for the services but also may be guilty of a crime.

Cebe Loomis and her sons, Andrew, Christian, and Just, signed an agreement for Lange Financial Corporation (LFC) to find a buyer for real estate the Loomises owned. The agreement required the Loomises to pay LFC a 10 percent commission on the sale. William Lange signed for LFC with John Valentine to market the land, although neither had a state real estate broker's license. Valentine found a buyer who then rescinded its offer. The Loomises finally sold part of the land to Allright Sierra Parking. LFC claimed a commission on the sale. The Loomises asserted LFC could not collect because of violation of the real estate licensing law. The court agreed because the law was enacted to protect people when dealing with individuals in the real estate profession.

A licensing law may be designed solely as a revenue measure by requiring payment of a fee for a license. Contracts made by an unlicensed person operating in one of the fields or businesses covered by such a law are normally held valid. However, the unlicensed operator may still be subject to fine or imprisonment for violating the law.

Contracts for Sale of Prohibited Articles

If a druggist sells morphine or a similar drug to one who does not have a prescription, a suit to collect the price would not be successful. One who sells cigarettes or alcoholic beverages to a minor when such a sale is prohibited cannot recover on the contract. In such cases, the court will not interfere to protect either party.

Contracts in Unreasonable Restraint of Trade

Government policy encourages competition. Any contract, therefore, intended to unreasonably restrain trade is null and void. The dividing line between reasonable and unreasonable restraint of trade is often dim, but certain acts have by judicial decision become well established as being an unreasonable restraint of trade. The most common acts in this class include:

1 Contracts not to compete
2 Contracts to restrain trade
3 Contracts to fix the resale price
4 Unfair competitive practices

Contracts Not to Compete. Normally a contract not to compete is illegal; however, it can be valid when buying a business or making an employment contract.

When one buys a going business, not only are the physical assets acquired, but also the goodwill, which is often the most valuable asset of the firm. In the absence of a contract prohibiting the seller from attempting to retake the asset "goodwill," the seller may engage in the same business again and seek to retain former customers. It is customary and highly desirable when purchasing a business to include in the contract a provision prohibiting the seller from entering the same business again in the trade territory for a specified length of time. Such a contract not to compete is legal if the restriction is reasonable as to both time and place.

The restriction as to territory should not go beyond the trade area of the business. Since the restriction is sustained to protect the buyer of the business from competition of the seller, it follows that the restriction should not reach out into areas where the buyer's reputation has not reached, nor should the seller be subjected to the restriction longer than is reasonably necessary for the buyer to become established in the new business. When the restriction goes further or longer than necessary to protect the buyer of the business, it is unlawful not only because it burdens the seller but also because it deprives the business community and society in general of the benefit of the activities of the seller.

Closely allied to this type of contract is one whereby an employee, as a part of the employment contract, agrees not to work for a competing firm for a certain period of time after terminating employment. These contracts must be reasonable as to time and place.

James Dagata was employed by Timenterial, Inc., under a contract that provided that he would not "engage . . . in any business venture having to do with the sale or rental of mobile homes . . . in a 50-mile radius from any existing Timenterial, Inc., sales lot" for one year after leaving Timenterial. He terminated his employment with Timenterial and continued to engage in the mobile home business. Timenterial sued Dagata. The court found that the one-year restriction was reasonable, but the area covered by the 50-mile radius from any Timenterial lots would include parts of six states and was unreasonable.

Contracts to Restrain Trade. Contracts to fix prices, divide up the trade territory, limit production so as to reduce the supply, or otherwise limit competition are void. Such contracts, which affect interstate commerce and which are therefore subject to regulation by the federal government, are specifically declared illegal by the Sherman Antitrust Act and the Clayton Act. Most of the states have similar laws applicable to intrastate commerce.

Contracts to Fix the Resale Price. An agreement between a seller and a buyer that the buyer shall not resell below a stated price is generally illegal as a price-fixing agreement. The original seller (manufacturer) can, of course, control the price by selling directly to the public through outlet stores.

Unfair Competitive Practices. The Robinson-Patman Act attempted to eliminate certain unfair competitive practices in interstate commerce. Under this act it is unlawful to discriminate in price between competing buyers if the goods are of like grade, quantity, and quality. Most states have passed similar laws for intrastate commerce. Some state statutes go further and prohibit the resale of goods at a loss or below cost for the purpose of harming competition.

Administrative Agency Orders

As was mentioned in Chapter 4, many government administrative agencies have the authority to issue rules and regulations that have the force of law. A contract that violates such a rule is illegal.

CONTRACTS CONTRARY TO PUBLIC POLICY

L.O.3 ....

Contracts contrary to public policy are unenforceable. The courts must determine from the nature of the contract whether or not it is contrary to public policy.

One court, in attempting to classify contracts contrary to public policy, defined them thus: "Whatever tends to injustice, restraint of liberty, restraint of a legal right, whatever tends to the obstruction of justice, a violation of a statute, or the obstruction or perversion of the administration of the law as to executive, legislative, or other official action, whenever embodied in and made the subject of a contract, the contract is against public policy and therefore void and not susceptible to enforcement." (*Brooks* v. *Cooper*, 50 N. J. Eq. 761, 26 A. 978.)

The most common types of contracts contrary to public policy include:

1   Contracts limiting the freedom of marriage
2   Contracts obstructing the administration of justice
3   Contracts injuring the public service

Contracts Limiting the Freedom of Marriage

It is contrary to public policy to enter into any contract the effect of which is to limit freedom of marriage. Such contracts are void. The following provisions in contracts have been held to render the contract a nullity: (1) an agreement whereby one party promises never to marry; (2) an agreement to refrain from marrying for a definite period of time (an agreement not to marry during minority, however, is valid); (3) an agreement not to marry certain named individuals.

Before their marriage, Richard J. Reynolds executed a prenuptial agreement with Marianne O'Brien. In it he conveyed all the common stock of Sapelo Plantation, Inc., by bill of sale and agreed to transfer the stock upon the books of the corporation in consideration of $10 and O'Brien's agreement to marry him. At the time he was married to Elizabeth Dillard Reynolds. The stock was not transferred on the books of the corporation. After Richard's death, Marianne Reynolds claimed title to the stock. The agreement to marry another when already married is contrary to public policy, which encourages the preservation of marriage. The agreement was void.

Also, in order to preserve and protect marriages it is held that an agreement to seek a divorce for a consideration is void as against public policy. However, property settlement agreements made in contemplation of divorces are valid.

Contracts Obstructing the Administration of Justice

Any contract that may obstruct our legal processes is null and void. It is not necessary that justice actually be obstructed. If the contract has the tendency to do so, the courts will not enforce it.

The following provisions have been held to render contracts void: (1) an agreement to pay a witness a larger fee than that allowed by law, provided the promisor wins the case; (2) an agreement by a candidate for sheriff that a certain individual will be appointed deputy sheriff in return for aid in bringing about the promisor's election; (3) an agreement to pay a prospective witness a sum of money to leave the state until the trial is over; (4) an agreement not to prosecute a thief if the stolen goods will be returned.

Contracts Injuring the Public Service

Any contract that may, from its very nature, injure public service is void. A person may contract as an attorney to appear before any public authority to obtain or oppose the passage of any bill. But a contract to use improper influence such as bribery to obtain the desired results is void.

Contracts to use one's influence in obtaining a public contract that by statute must be let to the lowest responsible bidder, to obtain pardons and paroles, or to pay a public official more or less than the statutory salary are also void.

QUESTIONS

1   Does a contract that is void for illegality necessarily involve the commission of a crime?
2   What is the effect of an illegal part of a contract?
3   What are some of the types of contracts that have been declared illegal by statute?
4   What is a gambling contract?
5   May one party to a private gambling contract sue the other for breach of contract?
6   What is the difference between the maximum contract rate of interest and the legal rate of interest?
7   Give two illustrations of attempts to disguise transactions to avoid the usury laws.
8   If a real estate agent who is not licensed secures a buyer for a house, is the owner bound to pay the commission?
9   What is the effect of a contract that unreasonably restrains trade?
10   What is the effect of a contract that violates an administrative agency regulation?
11   What types of contracts are contrary to public policy?
12   Donald promises to pay Henry $1,000 if he will leave the state so that he cannot be called as a witness against Donald. Is this a valid contract?

CASE PROBLEMS

L.O.1 ....

1   To pay a judgment and other debts, Vernon Ai and Sandra Fukuhara signed a note. The amount of the judgment included an award of attorney's fees. The note stated that if it were not paid, it would be given to an attorney to collect and Ai and Fukuhara would "pay attorney's fees at the rate of 33-1/3 percent of the amount due thereon, whether suit be instituted or not." Ai and Fukuhara asked a court to declare the note void as a violation of the law limiting attorney's fees in these cases to 25 percent after a suit is filed against the debtor. Does the provision regarding attorney's fees make the note void?

L.O.3 ....

2   Barbara Weiss Lurie and Bertram S. Lurie, while married but living apart, entered into a property settlement agreement. Bertram was to give Barbara real and personal property and $23,000 cash, $750 for all attorneys' fees, support prior to any divorce, and child support and alimony thereafter. She was to release certain property rights in jointly or separately owned property and resign as requested by Bertram from any position as "Trustee, Officer and/or Director of any trust, corporation, or other entity" in which he was involved. All of this was "[u]pon and in the event of the entry of issuance of a final decree in divorce . . ." within four months. The divorce was not final within

four months but Barbara asked the court to require Bertram to comply with the agreement. Was the agreement against public policy and therefore illegal?

L.O.2 .... 3 David Ford paid an entry fee of $1,500 to Celia and Ernesto Henry to join an illegal pyramid scheme. The pyramid device was supposed to result in payments to Ford every time he got another entrant. Ford wanted his money back, so he sued the Henrys. As the judge, how do you decide?

L.O.2 .... 4 George and Linda Vordenbaum contracted to sell a residence to Barry and Patricia Rubin. The contract obligated the Rubins to sign a note that would have been usurious. When the Vordenbaums refused to convey the property, the Rubins asked the court to order them to do so. May the Vordenbaums avoid the contract because of usury?

L.O.3 .... 5 Arthur Wells agreed to sell the stock he owned in Ramson, Inc., back to the corporation for $52,500. He also agreed not to compete with Ramson in the New Bedford and Fall River areas, which are in southeastern Massachusetts— between and not distant from the areas of Ramson's existing business activity. Arthur then formed a corporation that provided the same kind of services as Ramson. Both corporations contracted with regional, nonprofit corporations to provide social services to people. At the time of Arthur's agreement with Ramson no such nonprofit corporations had been organized in the Fall River or New Bedford areas, but they later were. Ramson contracted to provide services with a newly formed New Bedford corporation. Arthur's corporation advertised for a director of a New Bedford office. Ramson sought to have the agreement not to compete enforced. Is the agreement enforceable in Fall River and New Bedford?

L.O.2 .... 6 Polk County Memorial Hospital entered into a recruitment agreement with Dr. Kenneth Peters. Under the agreement the hospital made an interest-free loan of $30,684 to Peters, provided him free office space, gave him rent and utility subsidies, and reimbursed some malpractice insurance. This assistance was given for Peters using the hospital for his patients who required hospitalization. Federal law prohibited kickbacks from hospitals to doctors. When sued by the hospital for the amount of the loan, Peters raised the defense of illegality. Can the agreement to repay the loan be enforced?

Chapter 11

THE WRITTEN CONTRACT

LEARNING OBJECTIVES

After studying this chapter, you should be able to:

1 Identify which contracts the Statute of Frauds requires to be in writing.

2 Distinguish adequate from inadequate writings when a written contract is required.

3 Explain the parol evidence rule.

Preview Case

General Federal Construction, Inc., was awarded a contract for the construction of a hospital. The project was so large General expected to use subcontractors for some work. James A. Federline, Inc., had submitted a bid to General for the mechanical work. General used Federline's bid in figuring out its bid for the project, but Federline was not awarded the subcontract. Federline sued General, alleging breach of an oral agreement for it to do the mechanical work. By the terms of the contract the mechanical subcontractor was to provide all preventive maintenance for the equipment for one year after substantial completion of the contract and a complete water treatment service for one year after acceptance of the condensor water system. Was this contract enforceable?

Contracts may be in written or oral form. All contracts of importance ought to be in writing, but only a few must be written in order to be enforceable. An oral contract is just as effective and enforceable as a written contract unless it is one of the few types specifically required by statute to be in writing.

REASONS FOR WRITTEN CONTRACTS

A written contract has advantages over an oral contract, provided it includes all the terms and provisions of the agreement. In the first place, the existence of a contract cannot be denied if it is in writing. If there were no witnesses when an oral contract was formed, one of the parties might successfully deny that any contract was formed. In the second place, one of the parties may die or become insane. The administrator or executor of an estate in case of death, or the committee or guardian in case of insanity, is tremendously handicapped in enforcing an oral agreement made previously by the deceased or insane person. Even when there are witnesses present at the time an oral contract is formed, the testimony may vary considerably as to the actual terms of the contract. Written evidence, composed in clear and unambiguous language, is always better than oral evidence.

For these reasons most business people prefer to have contracts pertaining to matters of importance reduced to writing as a matter of caution even when not required by law.

STATUTE OF FRAUDS

L.O.1 ....

Statute of Frauds

Law requiring certain contracts to be in writing

In the year 1677 the English Parliament enacted a statute known as the **Statute of Frauds.** The statute listed certain classes of contracts that could not be enforced unless their terms were evidenced by a writing. Most of our states have adopted this list with but slight variations.

The Statute of Frauds applies only to executory contracts. If two parties enter into an oral contract that comes within the Statute of Frauds and both parties have fully performed according to its terms, neither party can seek to set aside the transaction on the ground that there was no writing.

The Statute of Frauds provides that the following types of agreements must be in writing:

1. An agreement to sell land or any interest in or concerning land.
2. An agreement the terms of which cannot be performed within one year from the time it is made.
3. An agreement to become responsible for the debts or default of another.
4. An agreement of an executor or administrator to pay debts of the estate from the executor's or the administrator's personal funds.
5. An agreement in which the promise of one person is made in consideration of marriage.
6. An agreement to sell goods for $500 or more. (This is discussed in detail in Chapter 17.)

An Agreement to Sell Land or Any Interest in or Concerning Land

An agreement to sell any interest in land comes within the Statute of Frauds. The required writing differs from the deed, which will be executed later and by which the seller makes the actual transfer of title to the buyer.

One may wish to sell not the land itself, but only an interest in the land. Evidence of this contract also must be in writing. These sales usually involve rights of way, joint use of driveways, mineral rights, or timber. A lease for more than one year must be evidenced by a writing to be binding.

The Hulbers orally agreed to sell the standing timber on their land to W. S. Hundley for $64,000. They subsequently executed a written agreement to convey the timber to J. T. Butler for $68,500. Hundley sued the Hulbers to require them to comply with the oral contract, alleging that the sale of the timber was the sale of personal, not real, property. The court held that the sale of the timber was the sale of real property. Since the contract was not in writing, it was voidable by the sellers.

Frequently, oral contracts relative to land are performed before any question of their validity is raised. For example, one leases a building by oral contract for two years. The building is occupied for that period, and then the rent is not paid on the ground that the oral contract is invalid. The law will compel payment of the rent orally agreed to for the time that the premises were occupied. If one has paid money or performed a service under an oral contract, the money or the value of the service may be recovered even though the executory part of the contract cannot be enforced. This recovery is not based on the terms of the contract but on the theory of preventing the unjust enrichment of one party.

An Agreement the Terms of Which Cannot Be Performed Within One Year from the Time It Is Made

The terms of a contract that cannot be performed in one year might easily be forgotten before the contract is completed. To minimize the need to resort to the courts, the law requires all contracts that cannot be performed within one year to be in writing.

This provision of the Statute of Frauds means that if the terms of the contract are such that, by their nature, they cannot be performed within one year from the date of the contract, then the contract must be in writing. The contract can be so worded that it may not be completed for 50 years, yet if it is physically possible to complete it within one year, it need not be in writing. If John agrees in consideration of $50,000 to care for Chen for "as long as he (Chen) lives," this contract need not be in writing because there is no certainty Chen will live one year. But an agreement to manage a motel for five years will, by its terms, require more than one year for performance; therefore, it comes within the Statute of Frauds.

General Federal Construction, Inc., was awarded a contract for the construction of a hospital. The project was so large General expected to use subcontractors for some work. James A. Federline, Inc., had submitted a bid to General for the mechanical work. General used Federline's bid in figuring out its bid for the project, but Federline was not awarded the subcontract. Federline sued General, alleging breach of an oral agreement for it to do the mechanical work. By the terms of the contract the mechanical subcontractor was to provide all preventive maintenance for the equipment for one year after substantial completion of the contract and a complete water treatment service for one year after acceptance of the condensor water system by the owner. By the terms of this contract, it could not be performed within one year; therefore, the oral agreement was not enforceable.

An Agreement to Become Responsible for the Debts or Default of Another

Debt

Obligation to pay money

Default

Breach of contractual obligation other than money

The term **debt** refers to an obligation to pay money; **default** refers to a breach of contractual obligations other than money, such as a contract to build a house. Under such an agreement, the promisor undertakes to make good the loss that the promisee would sustain if another person does not pay the promisee the debt owed or fails to perform a duty imposed by contract or by law. If *A* promises *C* to pay *B*'s debt to *C* if *B* fails to pay, *A*'s promise must be in writing; *A*'s promise is to be responsible for the debt of another.

The Statute of Frauds does not apply to the promise if in fact it is an original promise by the promisor rather than a promise to pay the debt of another. For example, if *A* buys on credit from *B* and tells *B* to deliver goods to *C*, *A* is not promising to pay the debt of another; the promise is to pay *A*'s own debt. *A*'s promise does not have to be in writing.

The Statute of Frauds does not apply if the main purpose of the promise is to gain some advantage for the promisor. This provision of the Statute of Frauds was designed especially for those situations where one promises to answer for the debt of another person purely as an accommodation to that person. Situations exist where one person promises to answer for the debt or default of another because it is in the promisor's personal financial interest to do so.

Modern Electric Co. contracted with Warren Reese to install heating and air conditioning equipment in Reese's building. The equipment installed was not at all satisfactory and did not meet the specifications in the contract. Air Engineers, Inc., told Reese that if he would delay suing the installer, it would correct the problem. The heating and air conditioning never became adequate.

Nearly two years after the requested delay, Reese filed suit. The court found that the forbearance of suit was beneficial to Air Engineers and so was not within the Statute of Frauds.

The Statute of Frauds does not apply where the promisor promises the debtor that the promisor will pay the debt owed to the third person.

To pay for his political campaign, George Meeker, the Democratic nominee for Congress, arranged for the Farmers State Bank of Ingalls to loan up to $25,000 on a note signed by supporters. Meeker told the people getting the signatures to tell the supporters they would have no liability to pay because Meeker would pay any balance remaining after the election. Meeker lost; the note was not paid, and the bank sued. Meeker said he was not liable because under the Statute of Frauds, his oral promise to pay the debt of another was not enforceable. The court held the promise was made to the debtor to pay a debt to a third person, thus not within the Statute of Frauds and binding.

An Agreement of an Executor or Administrator to Personally Pay the Debts of the Estate

When a person dies, an executor or administrator takes over all the deceased's assets. From these assets the executor or administrator pays all the debts of the deceased before distributing the remainder according to the terms of the decedent's will or, in the absence of a will, to the heirs. The executor or the administrator is not obligated to pay the debts of the deceased out of the executor's personal funds. For this reason, a promise to pay the debts of the estate from personal funds is in reality a contract to become responsible for the debts of another and must be in writing to be enforceable.

An Agreement in Which the Promise of One Person Is Made in Consideration of Marriage

An agreement by which one person promises to pay a sum of money or to give property to another in consideration of marriage or a promise to marry must be in writing. This requirement of the Statute of Frauds does not apply to mutual promises to marry.

Henry and Wilma Tatum married after Henry orally promised Wilma to leave her whatever he owned when he died if Wilma married him. The Tatums signed a joint will leaving all the property of either one to the survivor. A month before he died, Henry revoked his will and made a new one leaving everything to Rupert Tatum and Margie Rodriguez. Wilma sued and Rupert claimed the oral promise was made in consideration of marriage and therefore unenforceable. The court agreed.

NOTE OR MEMORANDUM

L.O.2
....

The Statute of Frauds requires either that the agreement be in writing and signed by both parties or that there be a note or memorandum in writing signed by the party against whom the claim for breach of promise is made. With the exception of the case of the sale of goods (Chapter 17), the contract and the note or memorandum required by the Statute of Frauds must set forth all the material terms of the transaction. For example, in the case of the sale of an interest in real estate the memorandum must contain the names of the parties, the subject matter of the contract, the basic terms of the contract, including the price and the manner of delivery, and it must be signed by the one to be charged.

The law states that the memorandum must contain all the essential terms of the contract; yet the memorandum differs materially from a written contract. Probably the chief difference is that one may introduce oral testimony to explain or complete the memorandum. The court held the following receipt was an adequate memorandum: "Received of Sholowitz $25 to bind the bargain for the sale of Moorigan's brick store and land at 46 Blackstone Street to Sholowitz. Balance due $1,975."

The memorandum need not be made at the time of the contract. It needs to be in existence at the time suit is brought. The one who signs the memorandum need not sign with the intention of being bound. If Jones writes Smith, "Since my agreement to pay you the $500 Jacobson owes you was oral, I am not bound by it," this is a sufficient memorandum and removes the objection based on the Statute of Frauds.

OTHER WRITTEN CONTRACTS

The five classes of contracts listed by the Statute of Frauds are not the only contracts required by law to be in writing in order to be enforceable. Every state has a few additional requirements. The more common ones are contracts for the sale of securities, agreements to pay a commission to real estate brokers, and a new promise to extend the statute of limitations.

PAROL EVIDENCE RULE

L.O.3 ....

Parol Evidence
Oral testimony

Parol Evidence Rule
Complete, written contract may not be modified by oral testimony unless evidence of fraud, accident, or mistake

Spoken words, or **parol evidence,** will not be permitted to add to, modify, or contradict the terms of a written contract that appears to be complete unless evidence of fraud, accident, or mistake exists so that the writing is in fact not a contract or is incomplete. This is known as the **parol evidence rule.**

If a written contract appears to be complete, the parol evidence rule will not permit modification by oral testimony or other writing made before or at the time of executing the agreement. However, an exception is made when the contract refers to other writings and indicates they are considered as incorporated into the contract.

The parol evidence rule assumes that a written contract represents the complete agreement. If, however, the contract is not complete, the courts will admit parol evidence to clear up ambiguity or to show the existence of trade customs that are to be regarded as forming part of the contract.

Thomas leased a farm from Clark. The lease contained this uncompleted provision: "Lessor does hereby rent and lease to the Lessee the following described property . . . for a term commencing on the ___ day of _____, 19 ___, and ending on the ___ day of _____, 19 ___." Clark later sued to regain possession. Thomas wanted to prove an oral agreement that the lease was to run as long as a note, but the maturity date of the note had not been known when the lease was signed. The court found that the written contract (the lease) was clearly incomplete, so parol evidence was permitted to establish the term of the lease.

A contract that appears to be complete may, in fact, have omitted a provision that ought to have been included. If the omission is due to fraud, alteration, typographical errors, duress, or other similar conduct, oral testimony may be produced to show such conduct.

QUESTIONS

1   As a general rule, an oral contract is just as enforceable as a written contract. Why, then, should all important contracts be in writing?

2   What does it mean to say that the Statute of Frauds applies to executory contracts?

3   Name the types of contracts that must be in writing to be enforceable.

4   If one assumes an original obligation, even though the benefits go to another party, must the contract be in writing to be enforceable?

5   Must an agreement for the estate to pay burial costs be in writing to be enforceable?

6   Does the Statute of Frauds apply to mutual promises to marry?

7   Who must sign a note or memorandum required by the Statute of Frauds?

8   What must be included in a note or memorandum required by the Statute of Frauds?

9   What is the parol evidence rule?

10   May oral evidence ever be admitted to contradict a complete written contract?

CASE PROBLEMS

L.O.1 ....

1   Howard E. Johnson and Loren Ward orally contracted to form a partnership to operate a dental supply business. Johnson later sued for a dissolution of the partnership. The parties had originally agreed that termination of the partnership would occur on default, withdrawal, or death of Ward or the closing of other branches operated by Johnson. Ward asked the court to dismiss the suit because the contract was not in writing and not performed within one year. Was the contract in violation of the Statute of Frauds?

L.O.1 ....

2   Kenneth Gross, the primary unsecured creditor of Wind Surfing, Inc., asked White Stag Manufacturing Co. to extend credit to Wind Surfing. White Stag said not until a past-due balance was paid. After negotiations, Gross personally sent $14,000 to White Stag to apply to the past-due account. When calling to check on whether further merchandise would be sent, Gross promised White Stag he had signed a guaranty form, which was in the mail. White Stag shipped goods worth a total of $49,637.87 to Wind Surfing. Gross's guaranty never arrived and Wind Surfing never paid its accounts. In a suit by White Stag, Gross argued that he was not liable because his agreement to pay the debt of Wind Surfing was not in writing. Was he liable?

L.O.3 ....

3   Limited partners had sued their former law firm. The parties agreed to a written partial settlement that dismissed some of the parties' claims, and stated the parties would "enter into good faith settlement negotiations" on the remaining claims. It also stated, "This agreement . . . constitute[s] the entire agreement of the parties. There are no additional promises . . . except those expressly set forth in this agreement." The law firm finally offered to fully settle for $80,000 when the partners had expected $275,000 to $550,000. Since the agreement gave no anticipated settlement, the higher amount was a result of an oral promise made by the law firm prior to the signing of the agreement. Should the promise modify the settlement agreement?

L.O.3 .... **4** The Jabberwock Band contracted in writing with Jeanette Johnson to perform for two months at The Riverbend Lounge. Before the contract was signed, the leader of the band orally promised Johnson she could terminate upon giving two weeks' notice if the band did not draw well. This promise was not in the written contract. The band failed to draw patrons. Johnson gave two weeks' termination notice and then fired the band. The band sued her for the amount due for the remaining time under the written contract. Was evidence of the two-week termination agreement admissible?

L.O.1 .... **5** Anna Blumer orally rented a building to Martin Dorfman for ten years. Dorfman occupied the building for almost three years, but did not pay rent for the last year. Dorfman vacated the premises and Blumer sued for unpaid rent. Dorfman claimed the Statute of Frauds made the oral lease unenforceable. How should the case be decided?

L.O.1 .... **6** When Simon Smith died, Hunt's Golden State Funeral Parlor was notified, and it handled the funeral. Insurance did not cover all the costs, so Hunt's sued Smith's daughter, Irma Howard, alleging she had orally promised to pay any amount not covered by insurance. Must Howard pay?

L.O.1 .... **7** Robert Sickinger owned the motion picture rights to a novel and was required to direct the first motion picture based on it. Sickinger and David Sawyer orally agreed that if the author would allow Sawyer to direct the first movie, Sickinger would give Sawyer an option to acquire a screenplay and all of Sickinger's rights under his agreements with the author. The option required Sawyer to pay Sickinger 1.5 percent of the producer's share of the net profits from the movie forever. Sawyer obtained the required permission from the author, but Sickinger refused to perform the agreement. Sawyer sued Sickinger, who alleged the agreement could not be performed within one year. Could it?

L.O.2 .... **8** After negotiating about the sale of her cottage to Betty Jean Sprague, Laura Johnson signed a piece of note paper on which was written:

Check 7414 is for down payment on cottage

42,000.00
−1,000.00
41,000.00

I will relinquish if I don't buy or finish in one month—Aug. 13

Johnson received a check for $1,000 from Sprague on which was written "down payment on cottage." Johnson later tried to return the check claiming that under the Statute of Frauds they did not make an enforceable contract to sell the cottage. Sprague sued to enforce the sale. Should she win?

Chapter 12

THIRD PARTIE/ AND CONTRACT/

LEARNING OBJECTIVES

After studying this chapter you should be able to:

1 Explain the difference between assignment of a contract and delegation of duties under it.

2 State the effects of an assignment and the difference between an assignment and a novation.

3 Describe the different types of contracts involving more than two people.

Preview Case

Equilease Corporation leased seven trucks to Henry Oil Company, Inc. To secure the lease payments, Henry Oil assigned six savings certificates issued by State Federal Savings and Loan Association to Equilease. State Federal was not notified of the assignment. Henry Oil told State Federal that the savings certificates had been lost and was allowed by State Federal to withdraw the deposits represented by the certificates. Henry Oil defaulted on its lease with Equilease, which then discovered that the funds had been withdrawn. Equilease sued State Federal for the amount of the savings certificates. Can it recover?

A contract creates both rights and obligations. Ordinarily, one who is not a party to the contract has no right to the benefits to be derived from the contract nor responsibility for any of the duties or obligations. However, parties may intend to benefit a third person when they make a contract. Also, third parties may acquire rights or assume duties.

WAYS TO INVOLVE A THIRD PARTY

L.O.1 ....

A third party can become involved in a contract in several common ways. These include: as a third-party beneficiary, by novation, by assignment, and by delegation.

Third-Party Beneficiary

Third-Party Beneficiary

Person not party to contract but whom parties intended to benefit

Creditor Beneficiary

Person to whom promisee owes obligation, which is discharged if promisor performs

Donee Beneficiary

Third-party beneficiary for whom performance is a gift

Incidental Beneficiary

Person who unintentionally benefits from performance of contract

At common law only the parties to a contract could sue upon or seek to enforce the contract. Courts held that strangers to a contract had no rights under a contract. But courts began to make exceptions to the rule when it seemed evident that the contracting parties intended to benefit a third person, called a **third-party beneficiary.**

The rule today specifies that a third person expressly benefited by the performance of the contract may enforce it against the promisor if benefit to the third party was intended by the contracting parties. The third person may be either a creditor beneficiary or a donee beneficiary. A **creditor beneficiary** is a person to whom the promisee owes an obligation or duty that will be discharged to the extent that the promisor performs the promise. If *A* makes a contract to pay *B*'s debt to *C*, *C* is the creditor beneficiary of the contract between *A* and *B*. A **donee beneficiary** is one to whom the promisee owes no legal duty but to whom performance is a gift, such as the beneficiary named in a life insurance contract. When an event must occur before the donee beneficiary is benefited, the contracting parties may change the beneficiary.

Not everyone who benefits by the performance of a contract between others is properly considered a third-party beneficiary with rights under the contract. If a person merely incidentally benefits by the performance of a contract, suit for breach or for performance will not be successful. For example, a town contracts with a contractor for the paving of a certain street and the contractor fails to perform. The property owners whose property would have been improved by the paving are not entitled to sue for damages for nonperformance because they were to be only incidentally benefited. The contract for the paving of the street was designed essentially to further the public interest, not to benefit individual property owners. They are merely **incidental beneficiaries.**

Novation

L.O.2 ....

Novation

Termination of a contract and substitution of new one with same terms but new party

The party entitled to receive performance under a contract may agree to release the party who is bound to perform and to permit another party to render performance. When this occurs, it is not just a matter of delegating the duties under the contract; rather, it is a matter of abandoning the old contract and substituting a new one in its place. The change of contract and parties is called **novation.** To be more precise, novation substitutes a new party for one of the original parties at the mutual agreement of the original parties, such that the prior contract terminates and a new one substitutes for it. The terms of the contract remain the same but with different parties. For example, if Koslov and Burnham have a contract, they, together with Caldwell, may agree that Caldwell shall take Koslov's place, and a novation occurs. Koslov is discharged from the contract, and Burnham and Caldwell are bound. It must be shown that a novation was intended. When a novation occurs, the original obligor drops out of the picture, and the new party takes the original obligor's place and is alone liable for the performance.

Hemisphere National Bank loaned Fancy Foods $72,000, and Wisconsin Surety Corporation guaranteed the loan. Fancy Foods defaulted and Wisconsin Surety could not pay. Monte and Marietta Bourjaily, the only shareholders of Fancy Foods, then executed a mortgage on real estate to the bank. The mortgage was ultimately foreclosed and the bank received only $30,000. During the foreclose proceedings, the bank executed a sworn statement that the mortgage was "to replace the guarantee provided by Wisconsin Surety." On the basis of the affidavit and the $30,000 from the foreclosure sale, there was a novation and the bank had no further claim against anyone.

Assignment

Assignment
Conveyance of rights in a contract to person not a party

Assignor
Person making an assignment

Assignee
Person to whom contract right is assigned

A party to a contract may wish to assign the rights or to delegate the duties under the contract or to do both. If one party transfers the contract in its entirety, it is "an assignment of rights and a delegation of duties." An **assignment** means that one party conveys rights in a contract to another who is not a party to the original undertaking.

As a general rule, a party's rights under a contract may be assigned. One's rights under a contract may be transferred almost as freely as property. The party making the assignment is known as the **assignor;** the one to whom the right is transferred is the **assignee.**

Statutes may impose some restrictions on the assignment of rights. Statutes in a number of states prohibit employees from assigning their wages. Statutes also prohibit the assignment of future pay by soldiers, sailors, and marines. Many states and cities also prohibit the assignment of the pay of public officials. Employees on public works are in many states prohibited by law from assigning a certain minimum percentage of their wages. This protects wage earners and their families from hardpressing creditors.

Often one's right under a contract is to receive the services of the other party, such as a bookkeeper, salesperson, or other employee. A right to personal services cannot be assigned because an employee cannot be required to work for a new employer without the employee's consent.

The parties may include in the original contract a prohibition of the assignment of rights thereunder. Such a prohibition, however, is not effective in some states when only the right to money has been assigned.

Thus, whether rights may be assigned depends upon their nature and the terms of the contract.

Delegation

Delegation
Transfer of duties

The term **delegation** describes a transfer of the duties alone without a transfer of rights. The duties under a contract cannot be delegated by a party a readily as the rights can be assigned because more frequently a "personal" element exists in the performance aspect of a contract. It would change the obligation thereof if it were performed by another. If Allen retains Bentley, an attorney, to obtain a divorce for a fee of $350, Bentley can assign the right to receive the $350 to anyone and Allen must pay. The duty to represent Allen in the divorce proceeding, however, may not be delegated. In those contracts that involve trust and confidence, one may not delegate the duties. If one employs the Local Wonder Band to play for a dance, the contract cannot be assigned, even to a nationally known band. Taste, confidence, and trust cannot be scientifically measured. It is not material that a reasonable person would be satisfied or content with the substitution.

But if one hires Horne to paint a house for $900, whether or not the house has been painted properly can readily be determined by recognized standards in the trade. Therefore, this task could be delegated.

> The Atlanta Tile & Marble Company contracted with H. S. Huggins to lay a tile floor in a building being constructed. The contract stated that Atlanta's work was subject to approval or disapproval of A. Thomas Bradbury, the architect. After the floor was down, Ralph Slay, an architect associated with Bradbury, disapproved the job. Huggins tore the tile up and sued Atlanta for that cost. The court held that an architect is chosen because of personal skill and judgment and that cannot be delegated. Atlanta did not have to pay.

Only when the performance is standardized may one delegate its performance to another. In the construction industry, for example, many instances of delegation of duties occur because the correct performance can be easily ascertained. Contracts calling for unskilled work or labor may in most instances be delegated.

In all cases of delegation, the delegating party remains fully liable under the contract. Suit may be brought for any breach of contract even though another party actually performed. In such an event, the delegating party may in turn sue the party who performed inadequately.

The parties to the original contract may expressly prohibit the delegation of duties thereunder.

Rights transferred by assignment and duties transferred by delegation cannot be modified by the assignment or transfer. They remain the same as though only the original parties to the contract were involved.

TECHNICALITIES OF AN ASSIGNMENT

Even if a contract may be assigned, there may be some technical requirements that must be met to make sure the assignment is effective. It is also important to understand what the legal position of the three parties is as a result of the assignment.

Notice of an Assignment

Notice need not be given to the other party in order to make the assignment effective as between the assignor and the assignee. Business prudence demands that the original promisor be notified, however. The assignee may not receive payment if notification of the assignment is not given to the original promisor. The promisor has a right to assume that the claim has not been assigned unless otherwise notified. For example, F. Gonzales promised to pay Hodges $500 in 30 days. When the account came due, Gonzales, since no notice of assignment had been given, was safe in paying Hodges. But if Hodges had assigned the account to Wilson and

Wilson had not given Gonzales notice, then Wilson would not have been able to collect from Gonzales.

Equilease Corporation leased seven trucks to Henry Oil Company, Inc. To secure the lease payments, Henry Oil assigned six savings certificates issued by State Federal Savings and Loan Association to Equilease. State Federal was not notified of the assignment. Henry Oil told State Federal that the savings certificates had been lost and was allowed by State Federal to withdraw the deposits represented by the certificates. Henry Oil defaulted on its lease with Equilease, which then discovered that the funds had been withdrawn. Equilease sued State Federal for the amount of the savings certificates. Since State Federal had not been notified of the assignment, it was not liable for allowing Henry Oil to withdraw the funds.

In most jurisdictions, if a party to a contract makes more than one assignment and the assignees all give notice, the law gives priority in the order in which the assignments were made.

In the event the assignor assigns a larger sum than the debtor owes, the debtor has no obligation to pay the entire assignment. When the creditor assigns only part of a claim, the debtor has no obligation to make payment thereof to the assignee, although such payment may be made and it reduces the debtor's liability to the creditor to the extent of such payment.

Form of the Assignment

An assignment may be made either by operation of law or by the act of the parties. In the event of death, the law assigns the rights and duties (except for personal services) of the deceased to the executor or administrator of the estate. In the event of bankruptcy, the law assigns the rights and duties of the debtor to the trustee in bankruptcy. These two types of assignments are effective without any act of the parties.

When the assignment is made by act of the parties, it may be either written or oral; however, it must be clear that a present assignment of an interest held by the assignor is intended. If the original contract must be in writing, the assignment must be in writing; otherwise, it may be made orally. It is always preferable to make an assignment in writing. This may be done in the case of written contracts by writing the terms of the assignment on the back of the written contract. Any contract may be assigned by executing an informal written assignment. The following written assignment is adequate in most cases:

> In consideration of the Local Finance Company's canceling my debt of $500 to it, I hereby assign to the Local Finance Company $500 owed to me by the Dale Sand and Gravel Company.
>
> Signed at noon, Friday, December 16, 1995, at Benson, Iowa.
>
> (Signed) Harold Locke

While an assignment may be made for consideration, consideration is not necessary.

Effect of an Assignment

An assignment transfers to the assignee all the rights, title, or interest held by the assignor in whatever is being assigned. The assignee does not receive any greater right or interest than the assignor held.

> On November 10, John and Catherine Licciardi contracted to buy 144 pounds of meat from V & B Discount Meats. V & B would store the meat, and the Licciardis could draw out meat as they needed. The agreement obligated the Licciardis to make monthly payments. The contract was assigned to Rainbow Commercial Alliance, Inc. The Licciardis withdrew meat in November, but when they went to get some meat in December, V & B was out of business. The Licciardis had made one payment. Rainbow sued for the remainder. The court said Rainbow was subject to all the defenses the Licciardis had against V & B and the Licciardis would not have to pay V & B for meat they did not get.

The nonassigning party retains all rights and defenses as though there had never been an assignment. For example, if the nonassigning party lacked competence to contract or entered into the contract under duress, undue influence, fraud, or misrepresentation, these defenses may be raised by the nonassigning party against the assignee as effectively as they could have been raised against the assignor.

Warranties of the Assignor

When one assigns rights under a contract to an assignee for value, the assignor makes three implied warranties:

1. That the assignor is the true owner of the right.
2. That the right is valid and subsisting at the time the assignment is made.
3. That there are no defenses available to the debtor that have not been disclosed to the assignee.

If the assignor commits a breach of warranty, the assignee may seek to recover any loss from the assignor.

Most assignments involve claims for money. The Fair Deal Grocery Company assigned $10,000 worth of its accounts receivable to the First National Bank. The assignor warranted that the accounts were genuine. If a customer, therefore, refused to pay the bank and proved that no money was owed, the grocery company would be liable. If payment was not made merely because of insolvency, most courts would hold that the assignor was not liable.

In the absence of an express guarantee, an assignor does not warrant that the other party will perform the duties under the contract, that the other party will make payment, or that the other party is solvent.

If the Harbottle Distributing Company owes the Norfolk Brewery $10,000, it could assign $10,000 of its accounts receivable to the Norfolk Brewery in full satisfaction of the debt. If the assignee is able to collect only $7,000 of these accounts because the debtors were insolvent, the brewery would have no recourse against Harbottle. If the $3,000 is uncollectible because the debtors had valid defenses to the claims, the Harbottle Distributing Company would have to make good the loss.

The Norfolk Brewery Company should not take these accounts receivable by assignment. An assignment allows Harbottle Distributing Company to pay its debt, not with cash, but by a transfer of title of its accounts receivable. From the brewery company's standpoint, the same result can be obtained not by taking title to these accounts but by taking them merely as collateral security for the debt with a provision that the brewery is to collect the accounts and apply the proceeds on the $10,000. Under this arrangement, the brewery can look to the distributing company for the balance of $3,000.

JOINT, SEVERAL, AND JOINT AND SEVERAL CONTRACTS

L.O.3 ....

When two or more persons enter into a contract with one or more other persons, the contract may be joint, several, or joint and several. The intention of the parties determines the type of contract.

Joint Contracts

Joint Contract

Contract obligating or entitling two or more people together to performance

A **joint contract** is a contract in which two or more persons jointly promise to carry out an obligation. A joint contract is also a contract in which two or more persons are jointly entitled to the performance of another party or parties. If Sands and Cole sign a contract stating "we jointly promise . . . ," the obligation is the joint obligation of Sands and Cole. Unless otherwise expressed, a promise by two or more persons is generally presumed to be joint and not several.

Several Contracts

Several Contract

Two or more people individually agree to perform obligation

A **several contract** arises when two or more persons individually agree to perform the same obligation even though the individual agreements are contained in the same document. If Sands and Cole sign a contract stating "we severally promise" or "each of us promises" to do a particular thing, the two signers are individually bound to perform.

Joint and Several Contracts

Joint and Several Contract

Two or more people bound jointly and individually

A **joint and several contract** is one in which two or more persons are bound both jointly and severally. If Sands and Cole sign a contract stating "we, and each of us, promise" or "I promise" to perform a particular act, they are jointly and severally obligated.

The other party to the contract may treat the obligation as either a joint obligation or as a group of individual obligations and may bring suit against all or any one or more of them at one time. Statute in some states interprets a joint contract to be a joint and several contract.

QUESTIONS

1 May the contracting parties change who a donee beneficiary is?
2 What is the difference between an assignment of a contract and the delegation of duties under it?
3 Name and identify the parties to an assignment.
4 Why may rights to personal services not be assigned?
5 If one delegates duties under a contract, what is the delegating party's liability under the contract?
6 Must notice of an assignment be given to the other party to the original contract?
7 If a party becomes dissatisfied with a contract, does assigning it to someone else rid the party of all obligations?
8 What is the effect of an assignment upon each party involved?
9 What is the difference between an assignment and a novation?
10 Explain the meaning of *joint, several,* and *joint and several contracts* to pay $1,000.

CASE PROBLEMS

L.O.1, 2 ....

1 Verlin and Loretta Wippert agreed to sell Stone Ranch to the Robertsons. By a written supplemental agreement, the Robertsons agreed to carry out the terms of a summer pasturage lease to Larry Whitford, and the Robertsons were to ". . . be entitled to payment from Larry Whitford of the remaining $12,000 . . ." rent. The ranch was conveyed to the Robertsons. The $12,000 was not paid, and the Robertsons sought to recover the $12,000 from the Wipperts. Was the agreement an assignment? Could the Robertsons recover from the Wipperts?

L.O.3 ....

2 Raymond F. Robson Sr., and Raymond F. Robson Jr., entered into a contract that required a monthly payment be made to Ray Sr.'s wife for her lifetime upon Ray Sr.'s death. It required the same payment for five years, or until she remarried, to Ray Jr.'s wife, Birthe Lise Robson, in the event of his death. Ray Jr. and Birthe later separated, and Ray Jr. filed for divorce. He and Ray Sr. then deleted the portion of the contract providing for payments to Birthe. Ray Jr. died and Birthe sued claiming she was a donee beneficiary of the contract. Is she entitled to collect?

L.O.2 ....

3 A partnership, Boger-Hare Manufacturing, and its partners, Mike Boger and J. O. Hare, got a loan from American Bank of Commerce and signed a note. Hare signed a guaranty contract agreeing to pay the partnership debts. A second loan was made and note executed by Hare. Seven months later a third note in the amount due on the partnership notes was prepared to be executed by Boger-Hare, Inc., although the business had not, in fact, been incorporated. Both Hare and Boger signed it, without indicating any corporate titles. The first two notes were not canceled. The bank sued the partnership and the partners for payment of the first two notes. They argued the third note was a novation. Was it?

L.O.2 ....

4   Klimate-Pruf Paint Company, Inc. sold its assets including its accounts receivable to a new company that then became Klimate-Pruf. The selling company took the name the Klein Corporation. In the sale contract, the seller promised that "the said assets . . . are free and clear of all liens and encumbrances and claims of every nature." Two of the accounts were uncollectible since the debtors went bankrupt. The new Klimate-Pruf sued Klein alleging the promise in the contract was a warranty of the collectibility of the accounts. Decide the case.

L.O.2 ....

5   At a contempt-of-court hearing, Thomas C. Vaughn said he planned to pay his child support arrearages out of his inheritance from the estate of Marvin Everett Vaughn. Nine days later, Vaughn executed a written assignment of his interest in the estate to Homemaker's Finance and Real Estate Loans. The personal representative of the estate asked the court which of the assignments he should honor. Was Vaughn's action at the contempt hearing a present assignment of his interest in the estate or merely an agreement to transfer the funds sometime in the future?

L.O.2 ....

6   Johnny Turcich owed Louisiana Materials Company $3,838. When payment was not made Louisiana sued. Turcich and Louisiana executed a document that assigned to Louisiana a claim for $3,810 owed to Turcich by Mike Bradford and Co. Bradford was declared bankrupt so Louisiana again demanded payment from Turcich. He claimed he had paid Louisiana an additional $150, and, since $28 constituted payment in full, his obligation was discharged. The court had to decide whether the document Turcich and Louisiana executed was an assignment or a novation. What was it?

Chapter 13

TERMINATION OF CONTRACTS

LEARNING OBJECTIVES

After studying this chapter you should be able to:

1 List the methods of terminating contracts.

2 Explain the potential remedies for breach of contract.

3 Define malpractice.

Preview Case

Jerry and Ann Beachum conveyed land to Rancho Camille. Rancho Camille agreed to pay a note secured by a deed of trust on the property, to pay the taxes, and to keep the property insured. The Beachums sued to rescind (set aside) the conveyance and to recover court costs, alleging that a payment on the note was past due and unpaid, the taxes were delinquent, and the insurance policy had not been renewed. After part of the trial, Rancho Camille offered to pay the taxes. It alleged that the note and insurance had been paid. At the end of the trial it offered to pay the taxes and the still unpaid note payment and insurance. Was there a valid tender?

While it is important to know how a contract is formed and who is bound on it, it is also important to know when it is ended, or terminated, and when the parties are no longer bound.

METHODS BY WHICH CONTRACTS ARE TERMINATED

L.O.1

Five common methods by which contracts may be terminated include: (1) by performance of the contract, (2) by operation of law, (3) by voluntary agreement of the parties, (4) by impossibility of performance, and (5) by acceptance of a breach of contract.

Performance

When all the terms of a contract have been fulfilled, the contract is discharged by performance. Not all the parties, however, need to perform simultaneously. Parties are discharged from further liability as soon as they have done all that they have agreed to do. The other party or parties are not discharged, nor is the contract, if any material thing remains to be done by them.

Several factors determine whether there has been performance:

1 Time of performance
2 Tender of performance
3 Tender of payment
4 Satisfactory performance
5 Substantial performance

Time of Performance. If the contract states when performance is to be rendered, the contract provisions must be followed unless under all the circumstances performance on the exact date specified is not vital. When performance on the exact date is deemed vital, it is said that "time is of the essence." If the contract states no time for performance, then performance must ordinarily be rendered within a reasonable time.

Tender of Performance | Offer to perform in satisfaction of terms of contract

Tender of Performance. An offer to perform an obligation in satisfaction of the terms of a contract is called a **tender of performance.** If a contract calls for the performance of an act at a specified time, a tender of performance will discharge the obligation of the one making the tender so long as the tender conforms to the agreement.

Tender of Payment | Offer and ability to pay money owed

Tender of Payment. An offer to pay money in satisfaction of a debt or claim when one has the ability to pay is a **tender of payment.** The debtor must offer the exact amount due, including interest, costs, and attorneys' fees, if any are required. If the debtor says, "I am now ready to pay you," a sufficient tender has not been made. The debtor must pay or offer the creditor the amount due.

Jerry and Ann Beachum conveyed land to Rancho Camille, which agreed to pay a note secured by a deed of trust on the property, to pay the taxes, and to keep the property insured. The Beachums sued to rescind the conveyance and to recover court costs, alleging that a payment on the note was past due and unpaid, the taxes were delinquent, and the insurance policy had not been renewed. After part of the trial, Rancho Camille offered to pay the taxes. It alleged that the note and insurance had been paid. At the end of the trial it offered to pay the taxes and the still unpaid note payment and insurance. The court found there was not a valid tender since, even after offering to pay the note payment and insurance, Rancho Camille had never offered to pay the accrued court costs.

Legal Tender | Any form of lawful money

A tender in the form of a check is not a proper tender. The payment must be made in **legal tender.** With but few minor exceptions, this is any form of United States money. If a check is accepted, the contract is performed as soon as the check is honored by the bank on which it is drawn.

If the tender is refused, the debt is not discharged. However, proper tender does stop the running of interest. In addition, if the creditor should bring suit, the person who has tendered the correct amount is not liable for court costs after the date of the tender. The debtor must, however, be in readiness to pay at any time. If a tender is made after a suit, the debtor frequently pays the money over to the court.

Satisfactory Performance. It frequently happens that contracts specifically state that the performance must be "satisfactory to" or "to the satisfaction of" a certain person. What constitutes satisfactory performance is frequently a disputed question. The courts generally have adopted the rule—especially when a definite, objective measure of satisfaction exists—that if the contract is performed in a manner that would satisfy an ordinary, reasonable person, the terms of the contract have been met sufficiently to discharge it. If the performance is clearly intended to be subject to the personal taste or judgment of one of the parties, however, it may be rejected on the ground that it is not satisfactory to that party.

Medivox Productions contracted with Hoffmann-LaRoche to produce a radio series about events in medical history. The contract stated, "Roche reserves the right to review and approve all programs." Roche terminated the contract and Medivox sued. The evidence at trial was that in the advertising field it was understood that the client's right to reject any advertising copy was absolute. In this case, Roche was the client. The court found that in view of the understanding in advertising and the fact that the contract did not limit Roche's right to approval by any definite or objective measure, it was a satisfaction contract. Since Roche was not satisfied, it could terminate.

Substantial Performance. Under the early common law, each party to a contract had to perform to the last letter of the contract before a demand for the party's rights under the contract could be made. Such a rule was often extremely inequitable. If a contractor builds a $50 million office building, it might be grossly unfair to say that none of the $50 million could be collected because of a relatively minor breach.

The law today can be stated as follows: If a construction contract is substantially performed, the party performing may demand the full price under the contract less the damages suffered by the other party. In the case of the office building, if the contract price is $50 million and the damages are $5,000, the contractor will be allowed to collect $49,995,000. Suppose, however, that the contractor completed the excavation and then quit. The contractor would be entitled to collect nothing. Just how far the contractor must proceed toward full performance before there has been substantial performance is often difficult to determine. The performance must be so nearly complete that it would be a great injustice to deny the contractor any compensation for the work. There must have been an honest attempt to perform. A court will weigh all the circumstances surrounding the deviation, including the significance of and reasons for it.

Dorothy E. Converse sold her equipment-rental business to John and Beverly Zinke for cash and a note secured by a lien on the business property. The Zinkes failed to make the required note payments, so Converse sued. The Zinkes alleged failure of consideration because 71 of the 273 items of inventory purchased were in need of repair or inoperable. This was not a total failure of consideration. The contract was substantially performed by Converse.

Discharge by Operation of Law

Under certain circumstances the law will effect a discharge of the contract, or at least the law will bar all right of action. The most common conditions under which the law operates to discharge contracts include:

1   Discharge in bankruptcy
2   Running of the statute of limitations
3   Alteration of written contract

Bankruptcy. Individuals and business firms overwhelmed with financial obligations may petition the court for a decree of voluntary bankruptcy. Creditors may, under certain circumstances, force one into involuntary bankruptcy. In either event, after a discharge in bankruptcy, creditors' rights of action to enforce the contracts of the debtor are barred.

Statute of Limitations. A person's right to sue must be exercised within the time fixed by a statute called the **statute of limitations.** This time varies from state to state, for different types of suits, and for different types of debts. For open accounts, accounts receivable, and ordinary loans, the time varies from 2 to 8 years, while for notes it varies from 4 to 20 years.

Statute of Limitations

Time within which right to sue must be exercised or lost

After a person has brought suit and obtained judgment, the judgment must be enforced by having the property of the debtor levied upon and sold. If this is not done, a statute of limitations operates even against judgments in some states. In those states where a statute applies to judgments, the time varies from 5 to 21 years from date of judgment. If a payment is made on a judgment, the payment constitutes an acknowledgment of the debt and the statute starts to run again from the date of payment.

The time is calculated from the date the obligation is due. In the case of running accounts, as purchases from department stores, the time starts from the date of the last purchase. If a part payment is made, the statute begins to run again from the date of such payment. If the promisor leaves the state, the statute ceases to run while the promisor is beyond the jurisdiction of the court.

Jack Slayton purchased items from Oras Taylor on an open account. Five years after the last purchase, Slayton made two $5 payments on the account. Two years after the payments, Taylor sued to collect the amount owed. Slayton defended the suit on the basis of a three-year statute of limitations. The court ruled that on an open account, part payment made after the statute of limitations has barred suit starts the statute running again.

A debt that has been outlawed by a statute of limitations may be revived. Some states do this by a written acknowledgment of or a promise to pay the debt, in others by part payment after the debt has been outlawed, and on still others by the mere payment of the interest. After the debt is revived, the period of the statute of limitations begins to run again from the time of the revival.

Alteration of Written Contract. If one of the parties alters the written contract, it is discharged if the alteration was done intentionally and without the consent of the other party. In most states the alteration must also be material or important. If a contractor who has undertaken to build a house by January 15, realizing that because of winter conditions it cannot be finished by that date, erases and changes the date to March 15, there is a material alteration that will discharge the contract.

Voluntary Agreement of the Parties

A contract is a mutual agreement. The parties are as free to change their minds by mutual agreement as they are to agree in the first place. Consequently, whenever the parties to a contract agree not to carry out its terms, the contract is discharged. The contract itself may recite events or circumstances that will automatically terminate the agreement. The release of one party to the contract constitutes the consideration for the release of the other.

Impossibility of Performance

If the act called for in a contract is impossible to perform at the time the contract is made, no contract ever comes into existence. Frequently, impossibility of performance arises after a valid contract is formed. This type of impossibility discharges the contract under certain circumstances. However, the fact that performance has merely become more difficult does not discharge the contract. The most common causes of discharge by impossibility of performance occurring after the contract is made include:

1   Destruction of the subject matter
2   New laws making the contract illegal
3   Death or physical incapacity of person to render personal services
4   Act of other party

Destruction of the Subject Matter. If the contract involves specific subject matter, the destruction of this specific subject matter without the fault of the parties discharges the contract because of impossibility of performance. This rule applies only when the performance of the contract depends on the continued existence of a specified person, animal, or thing.

The contract is not discharged if an event occurs that it is reasonable to anticipate. Any payment made in advance must be returned when performance of the contract is excused.

An agreement provided that Ishikawajima-Harima Heavy Industries Co., Ltd., would manufacture and deliver small boats of particular types and sizes ordered by Charles Goddard. Goddard transmitted a written order for a number of boats. Ishikawajima-Harima's factory where the boats were to be manufactured was completely destroyed by fire, and it was impossible to manufacture the boats in time. The court held destruction of the factory excused performance for the order.

New Laws Making the Contract Illegal. If an act is legal at the time of the contract but is subsequently made illegal, the contract is discharged.

Death or Physical Incapacity. If the contract calls for personal services, death or physical incapacity of the person to perform such services discharges the contract.

The personal services must be such that they cannot readily be performed by another or by the personal representative of the promisor.

Such acts as the painting of a portrait, representing a client in a legal proceeding, and other services of a highly personal nature are discharged by death or incapacity. In general, if the performance is too personal to be delegated, the death or disability of the party bound to perform will discharge the contract.

Winfred Mullen agreed to purchase Rufus Wafer's "accounting business and equipment, including all accounts in connection therewith." Wafer agreed "to remain active in the accounting business with Buyer for a period of two years" and "cooperate fully with the Buyer in effecting a satisfactory transfer of accounts . . . and giving all encouragement possible to the continuation of business relations." Wafer moved from his offices and occupied offices with Mullen. They executed a promissory note and security agreement. Less than a month later, Wafer died. Mullen asked the court to rescind the contract of sale and cancel the note, claiming the contract was contingent on Wafer's providing personal services. The executrix of Wafer's estate argued the contract was for the sale of the accounting business, and the transfer was made before Wafer's death. The court found the contract embodied and provided for the personal services of Wafer, so his death cancelled the sale of the accounting business.

Act of Other Party. When performance of a contract by a party is made impossible by the wrongful act of the other party, the performance is excused. The party who cannot perform has not breached the contract by the failure to perform.

Anne E. McCabe decided to build a shopping center. On her behalf, Rubin Co. executed a written lease of space in the center to Bernard Levicoff. The lease provided that Levicoff's store was to be built in accordance with plans prepared by McCabe, but she was required to incorporate Levicoff's "requirements" as submitted by him. Immediately after the lease was signed, Rubin told Levicoff to submit a plan for his intended store so it could be incorporated into the plan for the shopping center. Levicoff agreed to do so, but five months later had not, even though Rubin had repeatedly asked for the plan. Finally, Rubin wrote Levicoff that the lease was cancelled. Eight months later Levicoff sued to require McCabe to lease the store. The court refused saying Levicoff had made it impossible for her to perform her part of the contract, which was to build a store suitable for Levicoff's purposes.

Breach
Failure or refusal to perform contractual obligations

Anticipatory Breach
One party announces intention not to perform prior to time to perform

Acceptance of Breach of the Contract by One of the Parties

When one of the parties fails or refuses to perform the obligations assumed under the contract, there is a **breach** of the contract.

If one party, prior to the time the other party is entitled to performance, announces an intention not to perform, **anticipatory breach** of the contract occurs. If the innocent party accepts the breach of the contract, the contract is thereby discharged.

REMEDIES FOR BREACH OF CONTRACT

L.O.2 ....

If a breach of contract occurs, the innocent party has three courses of action that may be followed:

1   Sue for damages
2   Rescind the contract
3   Sue for specific performance

Sue for Damages

Damages

Sum of money awarded to injured party

Nominal Damages

Small amount awarded when there is technical breach but no injury

The usual remedy for breach of contract is to sue for **damages** or a sum of money to compensate for the breach. A suit for damages really consists of two suits in one. The first requires proving breach of contract. The second requires proving damages. Four kinds of damages include: (1) nominal, (2) compensatory, (3) punitive, and (4) liquidated.

Nominal Damages. If the plaintiff in a breach of contract suit can prove that the defendant broke the contract but cannot prove any loss was sustained because of the breach, then the court will award **nominal damages,** generally one dollar, to symbolize vindication of the wrong done to the plaintiff.

William DeVries stocked a truck with auto parts and supplies and developed customers for them along a specified route. He sold his truck with the name "William DeVries Co." painted on it, its merchandise, and the business and good will of the route to Albert and Norma Shields. He agreed not to sell merchandise to anyone trying to sell on the route who drove a William DeVries truck. DeVries developed and sold other routes. Three years later, after Shields had removed the name "DeVries" from his truck, trucks painted "William DeVries Co." started to appear on the route. Three years after that, the Shields sued DeVries for breach of contract. The court said while the contract was breached, if DeVries had not sold to the others they would have purchased the supplies elsewhere. It found that only nominal damages would be awarded for breach of a promise which, if kept, would not have helped the Shields. The trial court was instructed to fix damages of $1 to $25.

Compensatory Damages

Amount equal to the loss sustained

Compensatory Damages. The theory of the law of damages is that an injured party should be compensated for any loss that may have been sustained but should not be permitted to profit from the other party's wrongdoing. The law, when a breach of contract occurs, entitles the injured party to compensation for the exact amount of loss, but no more. Such damages are called **compensatory damages.** Sometimes the actual loss is easily determined, but at other times it is very difficult to determine. As a general rule, the amount of damages is a question to be decided by the jury.

Punitive Damages

Amount paid to one party to punish the other

Punitive, or Exemplary, Damages. In most breach-of-contract cases, the awarding of compensatory damages fully meets the ends of justice. Cases occur, however, where compensatory damages are not adequate. In these instances the law may permit the plaintiff to receive punitive damages. **Punitive damages** are damages paid to the plaintiff in order to punish the defendant, not to compensate the plaintiff. Punitive damages are more common in tort than contract actions. For example, if a tenant maliciously damages rented property, the landlord may frequently recover as damages the actual cost of repairs plus additional damages as punitive damages.

Liquidated Damages. When two parties enter into a contract, they may, in order to avoid the problems involved in proving actual damages, include a provision fixing

Liquidated Damages

Sum fixed by contract for breach where actual damages difficult to measure

the amount of damages to be paid in the event one party breaches the contract. Such a provision is called **liquidated damages.** Such a clause in the contract specifies recoverable damages in the event that the plaintiff establishes a breach by the defendant. Liquidated damages must be reasonable and should be provided only in those cases where actual damages are difficult or impossible to prove. If the amount of damages fixed by the contract is unreasonable and in effect the damages are punitive, the court will not enforce this provision of the contract.

John Deere Leasing Company leased a combine to Reuben Blubaugh under an agreement that gave Blubaugh the option to purchase the combine for $27,191.25 at the end of the lease. Blubaugh defaulted, the combine was sold, and Deere sued under the liquidated damages clause of the lease. These damages were found by adding the option purchase price to the rental deficiency and subtracting the sale proceeds. The court found this amount excessive in view of the fact that there was no requirement that Blubaugh purchase the combine for $27,191.25 at the end of the lease. The provision was unenforceable.

Rescind the Contract

Rescind

Set aside or cancel

The aggrieved party, when a contract is breached, may elect to **rescind** the contract which releases this party from all obligations not yet performed. If this party has executed the contract, the remedy is to sue for recovery of what was parted with. If the aggrieved party rescinds a contract for the sale of goods, damages for the breach may also be requested.

Sue for Specific Performance

Specific Performance

Carrying out the terms of contract

Sometimes neither a suit for damages nor rescission will constitute an adequate remedy. The injured party's remedy under these circumstances is a suit in equity to compel **specific performance,** that is, the carrying out of the specific terms of the contract.

This remedy is available in most contracts for the sale of real estate or any interest in real estate and for the sale of rare articles of personal property, such as a painting or an heirloom, the value of which cannot readily be determined. There is no way to measure sentimental value attached to a relic. Under such circumstances mere money damages may be inadequate to compensate the injured party. The court may compel specific performance under such circumstances.

Albert and Mae Madariaga leased their business, which manufactured "Albert's Famous Mexican Hot Sauce," to James Morris. The lease required rental payments totaling $54,000 and then Morris would have an option to purchase the business and hot sauce formula for $1,000. Morris finally paid the $54,000 and then $1,000 to buy the business. The Madariagas refused to convey it, so Morris sued for specific performance. The court said that the business, which included the hot sauce formula, had a peculiar and unique character and Morris could not get it anywhere else.

As a general rule, contracts for the performance of personal services will not be specifically ordered. This is both because of the difficulty of supervision by the courts and because of the Constitution's prohibition of involuntary servitude except as a criminal punishment.

MALPRACTICE

L.O.3

Malpractice
Failure to perform with ability and care normally exercised by people in the profession

A professional person, such as a lawyer, accountant, or doctor who makes a contract to perform professional services has a duty to perform with the ability and care normally exercised by others in the profession. A contract not so performed is breached because of **malpractice.**

An accountant is liable to a client who suffers a loss because the accountant has not complied with accepted accounting practices.

For five years Boris Elieff had done all the accounting and tax work for Jerry Clark Equipment. Elieff sold the business to Roger Hibbits, a CPA and tax attorney, and Clark agreed to have him continue to do the accounting work. Three years later Clark ended Hibbits' services because Hibbits had failed to prepare Clark's last three corporate income tax returns. Interest and penalties for that failure were $8,033, so Clark sued Hibbits. The court held that Hibbits was negligent and awarded damages.

In some cases, a person other than a party to the contract may sue a professional person for malpractice. In the case of a contract for accounting services, a third party may, under certain circumstances, recover when the negligence or fraud by the accountant causes a loss to that party.

QUESTIONS

1 What are five common methods of terminating a contract?
2 Must all parties perform a contract simultaneously? Explain.
3 If a contract contains no provision for time of performance, when must performance be rendered?
4 If a contract calls for an act, what is the effect of a tender of performance?
5 What is the effect of a tender of payment?
6 What is the rule regarding satisfactory performance?
7 What is the effect on a contract of an alteration?
8 If one cannot perform a contract on time because of a strike in the trucking industry, is this a legal impossibility?
9 If a singer contracts to sing at a party, is the contract released if the singer develops laryngitis just before the party starts?
10 When will a court order specific performance of a contract?
11 Why are punitive damages awarded? Are punitive damages common in contract actions?
12 What is malpractice?

CASE PROBLEMS

L.O.2

1 Melvin and Sybil Evenson contracted to buy a mobile home from Pierce-Odom. They were to trade in a lot they owned as part of the new mobile home's price and they made a down payment. They cashed a certificate of deposit, had a deed to the lot prepared, sold their old mobile home, and had it removed. The day before the new home was to be delivered, Jerry Odom,

who owned Pierce-Odom, called for directions to the lot they were trading in. Later a salesman for Pierce-Odom said the lot would not be taken in on trade. The Evensons sued for specific performance. Should it be ordered?

L.O.1 ....

2 Lukens Tool & Die Company agreed to construct a machine to manufacture hay-rake teeth for Alliance Tractor & Implement Company. The machine was to "have capabilities to manufacture the rake teeth . . . at the average rate of 100 per hour during a period of 100 hours" and the teeth were to have "no less degree of usability and performance than rake teeth . . . produced by International Harvester Company." The machine never operated 5 hours. International Harvester teeth had a sharp 90-degree bend, and teeth manufactured by the Lukens machine had a round bend that would not fit as tightly into the clamp that fastened them to the rake frame. When sued by Alliance, Lukens alleged substantial performance. Was there substantial performance?

L.O.1 ....

3 Florida Federal held a mortgage on property owned by Summa Investing Crop. Florida Federal told Summa if it did not pay the $2,505 it owed by April 2 by certified or cashier's check, the entire debt plus collection costs and additional interest would be due. No funds were received by April 2, so Florida Federal began foreclosure proceedings. Summa then tendered an ordinary check for $3,032. Florida Federal returned the check saying the amount was now $4,373 and the funds must be certified. Summa sent another ordinary check, which was returned. Did Florida Federal reject a valid tender?

L.O.1 ....

4 Kaldenbach & Wysong, Inc., contracted to do all the plumbing work on a new building according to certain specifications. These required that all pipes laid in filled ground had to be supported by brick piers or some other approved supports. After the building was completed, the service pipe running from the public water main broke. As required by law, this pipe had been laid by the District of Columbia. It was in filled ground without the required support. Kaldenbach refused to pay for the damage and was sued. It defended citing impossibility of performance because the law required the pipe to be laid by the District. You decide if Kaldenbach is excused on the basis of impossibility.

L.O.1 ....

5 George Booth contracted to renovate a kitchen for Ray Parker. Parker sued Booth for failure to complete the job in a workmanlike manner, alleging recovery should be the amount paid to have the kitchen work redone by others. Booth alleged damages for defective performance should be the difference between the value of the performance contracted for and the value of the performance actually rendered. What is the correct measure of damages?

L.O.1 ....

6 When Willie and Londia Weatherspoon were divorced, Willie was granted custody of their seven children, and Londia was ordered to pay $520-a-month child support. Years later Willie sued for past-due child support. More than three years before, Londia had failed to pay child support for two months. No other payments had been missed that year. She argued that the three-year statute of limitation barred recovery for the two missed payments. Did it?

L.O.1 ....

7 Freeport Minerals Co. was the tenant of a lease under which it had the right to mine kaolin and bauxite in exchange for a royalty of "12½ cents per ton . . . of refined kaolin and bauxite (railroad weight) removed . . . by tenant." Freeport told Minnie Belle Dennard, the holder of the lease, that it intended to pay her 12½ cents per ton on each ton of crude ore rather than on refined kaolin or bauxite. Did payment on the basis of crude ore rather than refined kaolin constitute substantial compliance?

L.O.2 ....

8 For many years, Neil DeWerff was employed as a teacher and basketball coach by Unified School District No. 315. On June 28, he resigned and was told by the district he must pay $400 as required by the contract. DeWerff refused and the district sued. The contract provided liquidated damages of $400 if a teacher broke a contract before August 1. If it was later, the amount was $75 for each month left on the contract. DeWerff said the amount was punitive. The district said it was very difficult and time-consuming to locate qualified replacements that late—in fact no exact replacement was found. Were the damages enforceable?

L.O.1 ....

9 Marshall County Redi-Mix, Inc., and Wright-Denaut Construction Co. contracted to pour and finish a concrete floor for a building being constructed by La Verne and Martha Matthew. The floor was poured but not yet sealed. The concrete froze, leaving the top 1/16-inch of the 4-inch base in a crumbling and powdery condition. When the Matthews refused to pay for the floor, Redi-Mix and Wright-Denaut sued. The Matthews argued that because of the destruction of the subject matter of the contract (the floor) they should not have to pay as required by the contract. Do they?

L.O.2 ....

10 Howard Beckman contracted with Vassall-Dillworth Lincoln-Mercury for the purchase of a new Lincoln Continental. Four weeks later, Beckman asked about the car and Vassall-Dillworth said the order could not be found; therefore, the car had not been ordered. The dealer offered to order another car, but at a higher price than that in the contract. Beckman sued Vassall-Dillworth for specific performance of the contract. Is this an appropriate remedy?

Summary Cases

CONTRACTS

1 McLeish Ranch signed an agreement to list land for sale with Reinhold Schauer. The agreement stated the terms would be "cash upon delivery of deed. Sale includes ½ of the mineral rights, oil, gas." Erwin Grossman signed a "contract for sale" to purchase the land for the full price in the listing agreement, subject to financing, and stating coal and gravel were included minerals. The ranch would not sell the land. Grossman sued for specific performance alleging the listing agreement constituted an offer to sell that was accepted by Grossman's signing of the "contract for sale." Was there a contract? [*Grossman* v. *McLeish Ranch,* 291 N.W.2d 427 (N.D.)]

2 In January, Edward Hayes, an employee of Plantations Steel Company, announced his intention to retire in July because he had worked continuously for 51 years. One week before his retirement, an officer of Plantations told him the company "would take care" of him. The following January and for the following three years Plantations paid Hayes $5,000. After the company refused to make any further payments, Hayes filed suit alleging an implied contract to pay him a yearly pension of $5,000. Was there an implied contract? [*Hayes* v. *Plantations Steel Company,* 438 A.2d 1091 (R.I.)]

3 When speaking before the Washington State Gambling Commission, Warren Treece, the vice president of a punchboard company, stated he would pay $100,000 to anyone who could find a crooked punchboard. Vernon Barnes heard Treece's statement. He called Treece and told him he had two fraudulent punchboards and asked if the statement about the crooked punchboards was serious. Treece said it was, that $100,000 was being held in escrow, and directed Barnes to bring a punchboard to his office for inspection. Barnes brought in one punchboard, was given a receipt for it and told it would be taken to Chicago for inspection. When Treece refused to pay, Barnes sued for breach of contract. Treece said his statement was a joke so it was not an offer Barnes could accept. Should Treece have to pay? [*Barnes* v. *Treece,* 549 P.2d 1152 (Wash. Ct. App.)]

4 A schizophrenic and manic-depressive, G.A.S. was recommitted to the state hospital by his wife, S.I.S., on December 23. S.I.S. filed for divorce, and G.A.S. was served with divorce papers on January 10. He did not have his own attorney and had limited success trying to work days. He was unable to sit or concentrate for any significant time as a result of taking drugs that negatively affected his reasoning powers. While committed, he was dependent on his wife for transportation, cigarettes, money, and permission to leave the hospital. He did not want his wife to get a divorce and therefore was extremely cooperative. On February 20, while still committed, he signed, without reading, a separation agreement prepared by her attorney, at his office. It required G.A.S. to pay $750 a month child support and a $155 mortgage payment from take-home pay of $1,300 and to give S.I.S. their beach property and the use of their home. He complied for several years and then sued to rescind the agreement. Is there any basis on which this contract could be rescinded? [*G.A.S.* v. *S.I.S.*, 407 A.2d 253 (Del. Fam. Ct.)]

5   The Midtown Motors employed Wise as an expert automobile mechanic for three years at a stated salary that increased each year. After eight months Wise was discharged without justifiable cause. He sued for damages and obtained a judgment. He went to work in the meantime for another auto firm. To collect his judgment Wise garnisheed the Midtown Motors' bank account. The owner of the Midtown Motors went to Wise's new place of employment and engaged in considerable verbal abuse of Wise. He threatened him with legal action for garnisheeing the bank account. Wise's present employer joined in the verbal abuse and told him he was "fired" unless he accepted the proffered $200 in full settlement and signed a release for the balance. While in a state of extreme mental confusion as to what to do, he signed the release. The next day he changed his mind and repudiated the release and demanded the full amount due him. May he repudiate the signed release? [*Wise* v. *Midtown Motors*, 42 N. W. 2d 404 (Minn.)]

6   American Family Life Assurance Company filed an action to prevent six former employees from violating the nondisclosure covenants in written agreements. Paragraph seven of the agreements, titled "Covenant Not to Compete," contained six subparagraphs, two of which were nondisclosure covenants and two of which were noncompetitive covenants. The two noncompetitive covenants were overly broad and unenforceable. Could the nondisclosure covenants be enforced? [*American Family Life Assurance Company* v. *Tazelaar*, 468 N.E.2d 497 (Ill. App. Ct.)]

7   Parker sold his bakery business to Thomas. As a part of the sales agreement, this clause appeared: "together with goodwill and bakery machinery in said bakery." Another clause stipulated, "Parker agrees that he will not engage in the bakery business directly or indirectly for a period of seven years within a radius of seven miles of Boston." About one year later Parker began working as a baker for the Boston Syrian Baking Company. Thomas brought suit asking that Parker be enjoined from working for the Syrian Baking Company. Is he entitled to the injunction? [*Thomas* v. *Parker*, 98 N. E. 2d 640 (Mass.)]

8   Andrew Truebenbach owned two adjoining tracts of land. He sold one to Edward Pick, and the deed stated, "Grantors also guarantee grantees . . . a right-of-way across the 25-acre tract sold to Walter Bartel." The other tract, consisting of 25 acres, was sold to Bartel five days later. Since an easement is an interest in land and therefore subject to the Statute of Frauds, was the language in Pick's deed sufficient to establish an easement? [*Pick* v. *Bartel*, 659 S.W.2d 636 (Tex.)]

9   Babylon Associates contracted to build a water-pollution-control plant for Suffolk County. It hired Lizza Industries, Inc., as subcontractor to install reinforced "102-inch" pipe. Lizza subcontracted with Clearview Concrete Products Corp. to manufacture the "102-inch" pipe. Clearview was convicted of making defective pipe used in the water-pollution-control plant. The EPA's reduction in its grant for the project and test to determine the soundness of the pipes delayed construction. The contract with Suffolk County provided that the contractor agreed "to be fully and directly responsible . . . for all acts

and omissions of his Subcontractors and of any other person employed directly or indirectly by the . . . Subcontractors." In claiming breach of contract the county alleged it was entitled to recission of the whole contract and all the money it had paid Babylon. Is it? [*Babylon Associates* v. *County of Suffolk,* 475 N.Y.S.2d 869 (N.Y. App. Div.)]

10 After a divorce decree was entered, Richard Pressley was ordered to pay $20-per-week child support. He made payments directly to his ex-wife. A year later she applied for public assistance and was required to assign her right to support to the Commonwealth of Pennsylvania, Department of Public Welfare. Pressley was never notified of the assignment and continued to make payments to his ex-wife. Four years later the Department of Public Welfare sought to collect the support payments from Pressley. Was Pressley bound on the assignment? [*Commonwealth* v. *Pressley,* 479 A.2d 1069 (Pa. Super. Ct.)]

11 Hobbs Trailers and Arnett Grain executed a written contract involving three trailers. They later disagreed over the nature of their transaction. Hobbs said it was a lease and Arnett said it was a lease-purchase with an oral agreement for Arnett to purchase the trailers for one dollar each at the end of 60 payments. A lawsuit resulted. The contract stated: "This transaction is a leasing and not a sale" and "Lessee does not acquire . . . any right, title, or interest in . . . said equipment . . . except the right to possess and use said equipment so long . . . as Lessee shall not be in default hereunder." Another provision stated: "This instrument contains the entire agreement between the parties." What was their agreement? [*Hobbs Trailers* v. *J. T. Arnett Grain Co., Inc.,* 560 S.W.2d 85 (Tex.)]

12 Kelley entered into a contract with Hance whereby Kelley was to construct a sidewalk and curb in front of Hance's property. The price for the work was to be $3 a running foot, or $420 for the 140 feet. Kelley was to start work within one week and complete it before cold weather. Although the contract was entered into in September, Kelley did not begin work until December 4. He continued to work until he had removed dirt to a width of 12 feet. He then discontinued the work and never returned. In March the following year, Hance notified Kelley that the contract was canceled. Kelley then brought suit to recover for the value of the work he already had done at the time the contract was terminated by Hance. Is Kelley entitled to any compensation? [*Kelley* v. *Hance,* 142 A. 683 (Conn.)]

13 While employed at the Stardust Hotel, Gilbert Smith thought that a recreational vehicle park, built and operated as a part of the hotel, would be a profitable idea. He devised a brochure indicating his plan and met with the manager of the Stardust, Allan Sachs. After explaining his idea, Smith stated he wanted to be paid either in money or by being an executive in the operation. The only interest Sachs expressed was to suggest Smith contact him later. Smith could not arrange another meeting and finally received a note from Sachs' secretary saying he was not interested. The Stardust opened a recreational vehicle park two years later. Smith's demands for compensation were refused, so he sued, alleging an implied contract. Was there such a contract? [*Smith* v. *Recrion Corporation,* 541 P.2d 663 (Nev.)]

14 Silverstein and Silverstein held a three-year written lease on space in Dohoney's property to be used for cigarette vending machines. The lease provided for the payment of rent by means of a commission on all cigarettes sold, but the amount of the commission was not stated. Prior to this lease the plaintiff had a machine in Dohoney's property and had paid him commissions on all sales of cigarettes. In a suit involving this contract, the key question was whether or not oral testimony could be introduced to prove the amount of commissions that were to be paid. Should the oral testimony be admitted? [*Silverstein* v. *Dohoney*, 108 A. 2d 451 (N.J. Super. Ct. App. Div.)]

Part 3

Personal Property

Chapter 14

NATURE OF PERSONAL PROPERTY

LEARNING OBJECTIVES

After studying this chapter you should be able to:

1 Define and name the two classes of personal property.

2 Explain the difference between lost and abandoned property.

3 Define and give examples of a bailment.

4 Distinguish the three types of bailments.

Preview Case

Police in Miami responded to reports of a shooting at the apartment of Carlos Fuentes, who had been shot in the neck and shoulder and was removed to a hospital. During an ensuing search of Fuentes' apartment, police found assorted drug paraphernalia, a gun, and $58,591 in cash. Fuentes left the hospital and never came forward to claim the property. The police could not find him. Four years later, James Green and Walter Vogel, the owners of the apartment building, sued the city of Miami for the cash. Green and Vogel claimed they were entitled to the money because it was abandoned on their premises. Was the cash abandoned at the apartment?

Property

Anything that may be owned

nything that may be owned is **property**. A person may enter into a contract with another to use property without becoming the owner of the property. The law protects not only the right to own property but also the right to use it. Property includes not only physical things but such things as bank deposits, notes, and bonds that give the right to acquire physical property or to use such property.

PERSONAL PROPERTY

L.O.1 ....

Personal Property
Movable property; interests less than complete ownership in land or rights to money

Property is frequently classified according to its movability. If it is movable property, it is **personal property.** Thus clothing, food, TV's, theater tickets, and even house trailers are personal property.

While land is not personal property, an interest in land less than complete ownership, such as a leasehold, is normally classified as personal property. In addition to movable physical property, personal property includes rights to money such as notes, bonds, and all written evidences of debt. Personal property is divided into two classes:

1 Tangible
2 Intangible

Tangible Personal Property

Tangible Personal Property
Personal property that can be seen, touched, and possessed

Tangible personal property is personal property that can be seen, touched, and possessed. Tangible personal property includes animals, merchandise, furniture, annual growing crops, clothing, jewelry, and similar items.

Intangible Personal Property

Intangible Personal Property
Evidences of ownership of rights or value

Intangible personal property consists of evidences of ownership of rights or value. Some common forms of intangible personal property include checks, stocks, contracts, copyrights, and savings account certificates.

When Elizabeth H. Plummer died, her will left her tangible personal property to her brother, Paul Higgins, and sister-in-law, Adelaide Higgins. All property not left to specific persons was left to eight charities. In her safe deposit box were found 240 gold coins— 57 Kruggerands and 183 Canadian maple leaf coins. The executors believed the coins were intangible personal property because they were purchased for investment. The court said the coins could be felt and touched, thus were tangible property. They went to the Higginses not the charities.

METHODS OF ACQUIRING PERSONAL PROPERTY

The title to personal property may be acquired by purchase, will, gift, descent, accession, confusion, and creation.

Purchase

Purchase
Ownership by payment

Ownership most commonly occurs through **purchase.** The buyer pays the seller, and the seller conveys the property to the buyer.

Will

The owner of property may convey title to another by will. Title does not transfer by will until the person who made the will dies and appropriate judicial proceedings have taken place.

Descent

When a person dies without leaving a will, that person dies intestate. The person's heirs acquire title to the personal property according to the laws existing in the decedent's state of residence.

Gift

Gift
Transfer without consideration

A **gift** is a transfer made without consideration in return.

Accession

Accession
Adding property of another

Accession is the acquiring of property by means of the addition of personal property of another. If materials owned by two people are combined to form one product, the person who owned the major part of the materials owns the product.

Confusion

Confusion
Inseparable mixing of goods of different owners

Confusion is the mixing of the personal property of different owners so that the parts belonging to each owner cannot be identified and separated. Grain, lumber, oil, and coal are examples of the kinds of property susceptible to confusion. The property, belonging to different owners, may be mixed by common consent, by accident, or by the willful act of some wrongdoer.

When confusion of the property occurs by common consent or by accident, each party will be deemed the owner of a proportionate part of the mass. If the confusion is willful, the title to the total mass passes to the innocent party, unless it can be clearly proven how much of the property of the one causing the confusion was mingled with that of the other person.

Wesley West was entitled to a royalty from Humble Oil & Refining Co. on gas produced from certain land. After years of gas production, Humble concluded that the gas reservoir on the land was approaching depletion. It concluded that the injection of extraneous gas was necessary to preserve the reservoir from destruction by water encroachment. A lawsuit between West and Humble resulted. West alleged that injecting extraneous gas into the reservoir resulted in the willful confusion of the two gasses. He claimed that Humble must pay a royalty on all gas produced whether native or injected. The court found that the burden was on Humble—the party mingling the goods—to properly identify the share of each owner in the gas. Unless Humble could do so, West was entitled to royalty on all gas produced from the land.

Creation

Creation

Bringing property into being

One may acquire personal property by **creation.** This applies to inventions, paintings, musical compositions, and other intellectual productions. Title to these may be obtained for a period of years through patents and copyrights.

The one who first applies for and obtains a patent gets title to the production. Creation alone does not give absolute title; it gives only the right to obtain absolute title by means of a patent, which protects the creator for seven years. Songs, books, and other compositions fixed in any tangible medium of expression are protected by copyright from their creation. A copyright gives the owner the exclusive right to reproduce, copy, perform, or display the work or authorize another to do so. While the copyright provides protection from the time of creation of the work, the copyright must be registered in order to sue for infringement. Copyrights protect authors for their lifetime plus 50 years.

Lost and Abandoned Property

L.O.2 ....

Abandon

Discard with no intention to reclaim

The difference between abandoned and lost property lies in the intention of the owner to part with title to it. **Abandoned** property arises when the owner actually discards it with no intention of reclaiming it.

A person who discovers and takes possession of property that has been abandoned and that has never been reclaimed by the owner acquires a right thereto. The finder of abandoned goods has title to them and thus has an absolute right to possession. The prior owner, however, must have completely relinquished ownership.

Police in Miami responded to reports of a shooting at the apartment of Carlos Fuentes, who had been shot in the neck and shoulder and was removed to a hospital. During an ensuing search of Fuentes' apartment, police found assorted drug paraphernalia, a gun, and $58,591 in cash. Fuentes left the hospital, never came forward to claim the property, and the police could not find him. Four years later, James Green and Walter Vogel, the owners of the apartment building, sued the city of Miami for the money. Green and Vogel claimed they were entitled to the money because it was abandoned on their premises. The court held they had not proven Fuentes voluntarily gave up his right to the money with the intention of terminating his ownership of it at the time he was removed from the apartment. The money was not abandoned at the apartment.

A number of states have enacted the Uniform Disposition of Unclaimed Property Act. This law provides that holders of property that the law presumes is abandoned turn over the property to the state.

Lost Property

Property unintentionally left with no intention to discard

Property is considered to be **lost** when the owner, through negligence or accident, unintentionally leaves it somewhere.

The finder of lost property has a right of possession against all but the true owner as long as the finder has not committed a wrong of some kind. No right of possession exists against the true owner except in instances when the owner cannot be found through reasonable diligence on the part of the finder and certain statutory requirements are fulfilled.

Leonard and Bernard Kapiloff collected stamps. They purchased two sets of stamps and for years thought the stamps remained in their possession. Then they saw an ad in a nationally circulated catalogue offering them for sale for $150,400. They demanded the stamps back from Robert L. Ganter, the alleged owner. When Ganter refused, the Kapiloffs sued for the stamps. Ganter said that he found them in a dresser he had bought at a used furniture store. The court held that the finder of lost personal property holds it against all except the rightful owner. Once the true owners were determined, Ganter's possessory interest ceased, and the Kapiloffs were entitled to the stamps.

In a few cases the courts have held that if any employee finds property in the course of the employment, the property belongs to the employer. Also, if property is mislaid, not lost, then the owner of the premises has first claim against all but the true owner. This especially applies to property left on trains, airplanes, in restaurants, and in hotels.

BAILMENTS

L.O.3 ....

Bailment

Transfer of possession of personal property on condition property will be returned

Bailor

Person who gives up possession of bailed property

Bailee

Person in possession of bailed property

The transfer of possession, but not the title, of personal property by one party, usually the owner, to another party is called a **bailment**. The transfer is on condition that the same property will be returned or appropriately accounted for either to the owner or designated person at a future date. The person who gives up possession, the **bailor,** is usually the owner of the property. The **bailee** accepts possession of the property but not the title.

Some typical transactions resulting in a bailment include:

1   A motorist leaves a car with the garage for repairs.
2   A family stores its furniture in a warehouse.
3   A student borrows a tuxedo to wear to a formal dance.
4   A hunter leaves a pet with a friend for safekeeping while going on an extended hunting trip.

THE BAILMENT AGREEMENT

A true bailment is based upon and governed by a contract, express or implied, between the bailor and the bailee. When a person checks a coat upon entering a restaurant, nothing may be said, but the bailment is implied by the acts of the two parties. A bailment can be created by the conduct of the parties, whether spoken or written.

Melvin Delzer leased a paylogger from Rapid City Implement. The lease stated: "Lessee further agrees to protect the Lessor on this contract with full insurance coverage" and "Lessee agrees to pay the Lessor for all loss and damages to the equipment arising from any cause . . . during the life of this leave." During the lease, the paylogger was damaged by fire. It was returned and Rapid City's insurer paid Rapid City for the damage. The insurer then sued Delzer. The court found Delzer liable since he had failed to obtained the insurance required by the agreement.

DELIVERY AND ACCEPTANCE

A bailment can be established only if delivery occurs accompanied by acceptance of personal property. The delivery and acceptance may be actual or constructive. Actual delivery and acceptance results when the goods themselves are delivered and accepted. Constructive delivery and acceptance results when no physical delivery of the goods occurs but when control over the goods is delivered and accepted.

Ovie O. Farmer was employed by Machine Craft as a machinist. As a condition of employment, employees had to furnish their own sets of tools. Farmer's toolbox weighed more than 100 pounds. For the employees' convenience, they were allowed by Machine Craft to keep the toolboxes at the shop overnight. Although other employees took their tools home, Farmer left his at the shop. Farmer's tools were stolen. Farmer sued Machine Craft for the value of the tools alleging Machine Craft was the bailee of the tools and had not taken adequate care of them. The judge ruled that to have a bailment, the alleged bailee must have intended to exercise control of the property. Machine Craft never exercised any control so there was no bailment and no liability.

Constructive Bailment

Bailment imposed when a person controls lost property

A **constructive bailment** arises when someone finds and takes possession of lost property. The owner does not actually deliver the property to the finder, but the law holds this to be a bailment. A constructive bailment can also occur when property of one person is washed ashore. The finder becomes a bailee if some overt act of control over the property occurs.

RETURN OF THE BAILED PROPERTY

In some cases a bailment may exist when the recipient does not return the actual goods.

In the case of fungible goods, such as wheat, a bailment exists if the owner expects to receive a like quantity and quality of goods. If the goods are to be processed in some way, a bailment arises if the product made from the original goods is to be returned.

When a consignment exists, the property may be sold by the consignee and not returned to the consignor. Finally, when property is left for repair, the property returned should be repaired and therefore not be identical to the property left. In each case, a bailment arises although the identical property is not returned.

Fred Peterson asked Nathan Shay, who was in business as a jeweler, to sell some jewelry. Shay picked up the jewelry at Peterson's house and gave him a receipt listing the items and an estimated value for each. At the bottom of the receipt was written, "To be sold at the agreed prices above." Two days later Peterson told Shay to return the jewelry, but one item had been stolen. Peterson sued his insurance company for the loss. The company denied liability claiming the jewelry had been sold to Shay and was not owned by Peterson when it was stolen. The court held that the transaction was a bailment because any unsold jewelry was to be returned to Peterson.

TYPES OF BAILMENTS

L.O.4 .... The three types of bailments include:

1 Bailments for the sole benefit of the bailor.
2 Bailments for the sole benefit of the bailee.
3 Mutual-benefit bailments.

Bailments for the Sole Benefit of the Bailor

If one holds another's personal property only for the benefit of the owner, a bailment for the sole benefit of the bailor exists. The bailee receives no benefits or compensation.

Such a bailment arises when a person asks a friend to keep a piano until the owner finds a larger apartment. The friend may not play the piano or otherwise receive any benefits of ownership during the bailment. The bailee may only use the property if the use will benefit or preserve it.

A constructive bailment exists for the sole benefit of the bailor. The bailor lost the property, and the bailee found the property. In a bailment for the sole benefit of the bailor, most states hold that the bailee need exercise slight care and is liable only for gross negligence with respect to the property.

William and Betty Martin asked Barbara Bell and Ellen Christian to "house sit" while the Martins were on vacation. The Martins left a few dollars for groceries but otherwise did not pay Bell and Christian. Personal property of the Martins was damaged when Christian left a pan of grease unattended on a range burner. The Martins sued Bell and Christian for the damages. The court found that the arrangement was a bailment for the sole benefit of the bailor. It also found that Bell and Christian had not been grossly negligent and were therefore not liable for the damage to the personal property.

Bailments for the Sole Benefit of the Bailee

If the bailee holds and uses another's personal property, and the owner of the property receives no benefit or compensation, a bailment for the sole benefit of the bailee exists. This type of bailment arises when someone's property is borrowed.

While alive, Leo B. Dorfman had received some bonds from Austin S. Brunjes on the promise to return them. The bonds were transferred to Colonial Trust Co. by Dorfman to secure a loan. After Dorfman's death Colonial still had the bonds even though the loan was paid. Brunjes claimed the bonds as did Dorfman's personal representative and creditors. The transaction between Dorfman and Brunjes was a bailment for the sole benefit of the bailee. Dorfman was obligated to return the bonds to the owner. The personal representative and creditors were in no better position than Dorfman so the bonds were ordered to Brunjes.

The bailee must exercise great care over the property. However, any loss or damage due to no fault of the bailee falls upon the owner. If Petras borrows Walker's diamond ring to wear to a dance and is robbed on the way to the dance, the loss falls upon Walker, the owner, as long as Petras was not negligent.

The bailee must be informed of any known defects in the bailed property. If the bailee is injured by reason of such a defect, the bailor who failed to inform the bailee is liable for damages.

John Maurer Painting and Decorating Company contracted to paint a highway overpass bridge that was under construction. To do this, a wooden scaffold was constructed of planks from a pile of lumber at the worksite. The lumber had presumably been used by Calhoun County Contracting Corporation when it poured the concrete deck of the bridge. When the scaffold was being dismantled, the plank on which Frank Rynders, an employee of Maurer, was standing broke, and Rynders fell to the ground. The board had an obvious knothole on one side. Rynders sued Calhoun for damages for his injuries. Even if Calhoun did loan the lumber to Maurer, the bailment was for the sole benefit of the bailee. Calhoun's only duty was to warn of known defects, so it was not liable.

Mutual-Benefit Bailments

Most bailments exist for the mutual benefit of both the bailor and the bailee. Some common bailments of this type include: a TV left to be repaired; laundry and dry cleaning contracts; and the rental of personal property, such as an automobile or furniture. The bailor of rented property must furnish safe property, not just inform the bailee of known defects.

In mutual-benefit bailments, the bailee renders a service and charges for the service. This applies to all repair jobs, laundry, dry cleaning, and storage bailments. The bailee has a lien against the bailed property for the charges. If these charges are not paid after a reasonable time, the bailee may advertise and sell the property for the charges. Any money remaining after paying expenses and the charges must be turned over to the bailor.

A bailee rendering services may receive a benefit other than a fee or monetary payment. For example, a skating rink may offer to check shoes for its customers without charging for the service. A mutual-benefit bailment exists. The customer (bailor) receives storage service and the skating rink (bailee) gains the benefit of a neater, safer customer area.

In mutual-benefit bailments, the standard of care required of the bailee for the property is reasonable care under the circumstances. Such care means the degree of care that a reasonable person would exercise in order to protect the property from harm. The bailee is liable for negligence.

When John Chambers left his car at Apco Transmission for repair of the transmission the body of the car was undamaged. When the car was returned, the body was damaged. Chambers sued for the damage. The court found that the transaction was a mutual-benefit bailment. Where goods are in good condition when delivered to a bailee and damaged when returned, negligence is shown. The claim for damages was granted.

SPECIAL MUTUAL-BENEFIT BAILMENTS

A mutual-benefit bailment includes the deposit of personal property as security for some debt or obligation. Tangible property left as security, such as livestock, a

Pawn

Tangible personal property
left as security for a debt

radio, or an automobile, is a **pawn.** Intangible property left as a security, such as notes, bonds, or stock certificates, is a **pledge.**

CONVERSION OF BAILED PROPERTY BY THE BAILEE

Pledge

Intangible property serv-
ing as security for a debt

Conversion

Unauthorized exercise of
ownership rights

Not being the owner of the property, a bailee normally has no right to convert the property. **Conversion** is the unauthorized exercise of ownership rights over another's property. Thus, the bailee may not sell, lease, or even use the bailed property as security for a loan, and one who purchases such property from a bailee ordinarily does not get good title to it.

> Johnson hired O. J. Drake to haul wheat from his farm in Colorado to a wheat elevator in Cherokee, Oklahoma, for storage. Instead, Drake took the wheat to the Woodward Co-Operative Elevator Association's elevator in Woodward, Oklahoma. There, he said he owned the wheat; sold it to the Association; took the money, and absconded. Johnson sued for the value of the wheat alleging it was converted by the Association. The court found no evidence of authority in Drake to sell the wheat. Since the Association acquired the wheat by the wrongful act of the bailee, Johnson was allowed to recover its value from the Association.

However, when the purpose of the bailment is to have the property sold and the proceeds remitted to the bailor, the bailee has the power to sell all goods regardless of any restriction upon the right to sell, unless the buyer knows of the restriction.

A bailor may mislead an innocent third person into believing that the bailee owns the bailed property. In this situation, the bailee may convey good title.

QUESTIONS

1　What is personal property?
2　Name three types of intangible personal property.
3　Who owns the product of an accession?
4　What difference does it make whether confusion of personal property is willful or by accident?
5　What is the difference between lost and abandoned property?
6　What is a *bailment*?
7　May a bailment exist without any verbal or written communication between the bailor and the bailee?
8　If the owner of a car has it in *B*'s garage and gives the keys to *C* with the instruction to get the car, is this a bailment?
9　What are the three types of bailments based on benefits? What are the characteristics of each type?
10　a.　Define a *pawn*.
　　b.　Define a *pledge*.

CASE PROBLEMS

L.O.1 ....

1　In 1767 and 1768, while he was the attorney for the king, William Hooper, who later signed the Declaration of Independence, signed and filed two indictments. They were purchased at an auction by B. C. West over 200 years later. The state sued to recover possession of them, alleging it was the lawful custodian of and had the right to possess all court records and documents of the state. By an act of the Colonial Assembly the chief justice was authorized to appoint clerks responsible for the safekeeping of records. West alleged the indictments were abandoned, and since he now had possession, he had title to them. Were the indictments abandoned?

L.O.4 .... **2** Marzano Construction Company leased a backhoe from Ausdale Equipment Rental Corporation. At the time, there was a worn sheave on the backhoe, which had the effect of cutting and weakening the fiber of the cables. On September 6, the steel cable that supported the backhoe's boom and bucket snapped. The cable was replaced, and ten days later the backhoe was being used to lower concrete pipe into a trench. The cable snapped again. The bucket fell, glanced off a section of pipe and struck Augustine Brimbau, who was working in the trench. Brimbau was severely injured and sued Ausdale. Backhoe cables generally have a useful life of three to four months. Was Ausdale liable?

L.O.2 .... **3** Dottie Kitchen had moved her personal belongings out of her mobile home. She told the manager of the trailer park that because she was pregnant, she would be back with help "the next day or over the weekend" to get an air conditioner, a lawn mower, a ladder, and a grill located outside the trailer. While repossessing Kitchen's trailer for the Wachovia Bank and Trust Company, the items were taken. Kitchen returned and discovered the loss, so she sued for conversion. The bank alleged she had abandoned them. Had she?

L.O.4 .... **4** James Smith delivered his motorcycle to the main building of McRary Harley-Davidson for a warranty check and servicing. Smith knew the building had a burglar alarm system. On previous visits he had seen other motorcycles being repaired and stored in that building. McRary gave no indication the motorcycle would be stored in a separate, smaller building. The smaller building was broken into and Smith's motorcycle stolen. Smith sued McRary for failure to return the motorcycle. Smith asked the judge to instruct the jury that if there was agreement that the motorcycle was to be stored at the main building and McRary stored it at another building without the consent of Smith, McRary would be liable. Should the instruction be given?

L.O.2 .... **5** In 1776, some American colonists toppled a statue of King George III in New York. The statue was hacked apart and the pieces taken to Wilton, Connecticut, where the colonists stopped to imbibe. A group of loyalists stole a load of the pieces, which were scattered about in the area of a swamp. Fragments had occasionally turned up since then. Two hundred years later, Louis Miller entered property owned by Fred Favorite without permission and with a metal detector discovered a 15-inch square statuary fragment 10 inches below the soil. Miller dug it up and removed it. Favorite did not know about the piece found on his property until he read about it in the newspaper much later. He sued for return of the fragment. Miller, who wanted to sell the fragment to a museum, argued that his rights as a finder were superior to those of anyone except the true owner—the British government. Who was entitled to the fragment?

L.O.3, 4   **6**   Edwards took her car to Crestmont Cadillac Corporation to have a tire changed and the wheels aligned. She told the service order man that she and her family were packed and ready to leave on a vacation. She was told to wait in the outer lobby. Several hours later she was told the car had been stolen. Edwards had had personal property valued at more than $2,500 in the car's trunk. She sued Crestmont for the value of the personal property, alleging there had been a bailment of the property. Was Crestmont liable for the personal property in the trunk?

L.O.4   **7**   In danger of sinking, the MV *Harry Adams* was towed to Norfolk Shipbuilding and Drydock's wharf. Emergency repairs were made. Norfolk asked John Mosele, the owner, to pay for the repairs and remove the ship. Mosele replied he would. Norfolk had to install two pumps because the ship still leaked. In March, Norfolk asked Mosele to move the vessel and stated there would be a $25-per-day storage charge. Mosele said he hoped to move the ship soon and asked if it could be left a short time longer without storage charges. In August, the pumps failed and the *Harry Adams* was partially submerged. Norfolk refloated the ship and made emergency repairs. Norfolk then sued for these repairs and dockage from the date of the repairs. Could it recover even though the pumps it installed had failed?

L.O.2   **8**   Owen Flora got a judgment against Arthur Myles for $1,500. The court ordered Valley Federal Savings and Loan to pay $942.46, which Myles had on deposit, toward the judgment minus $100. State law exempted $100 if the deposit was intangible property. Myles alleged the deposit was cash and therefore tangible personal property, which was subject to a $4,000 exemption. Was the deposit intangible or tangible personal property, and how much of it was exempt?

L.O.3, 4   **9**   J. D. Butler borrowed a tractor from Don Shirah to help in driving cattle. Several people rode on the tractor as passengers. After going a short distance, the left rear wheel of the tractor fell off, causing injuries to Butler. Butler died from these injuries, and Butler's mother sued for wrongful death. Was Shirah, who knew of no defects on the tractor, liable?

L.O.3   **10**   By written agreement, Clifton Taylor took possession of a Buick from Mark Singleton Buick, Inc., a Buick dealer, for 48 months. The agreement obligated Taylor to make monthly payments, pay the taxes and insurance, make all necessary repairs, and return the car at the expiration of the agreement. The agreement preserved the warranties made by the manufacturer "or its dealers." Singleton repaired and serviced the car numerous times, but after 15 months refused to make any further repairs. The court had to decide if the transaction was a sale or a lease and whether Singleton had any obligation to repair the car. You decide.

L.O.3, 4 .... **11**   When Gayle Benz left her husband Jeffrey, she left personal property valued at $10,000 at their residence. After Gayle and Jeffrey got a divorce, she sued for the value of the property. The court found that Gayle had abandoned the property. Gayle appealed. As the appellate judge faced with these facts, how do you decide?

Chapter 15

SPECIAL BAILMENTS

LEARNING OBJECTIVES

After studying this chapter you should be able to:

1 Explain what a carrier does and name the two categories of carriers.

2 Identify the exceptions to the normal rule of a common carrier being an insurer of the safety of goods.

3 Explain what a hotelkeeper does.

4 Distinguish a boardinghouse keeper from a hotelkeeper.

5 Name the duties and liabilities of a hotelkeeper

Preview Case

Jean King and Miriam Kelley were robbed in Room 821 of the Ilikai Tower Building. The Tower Building of the Ilikai Hotel was operated by Ilikai Properties, Inc., as a hotel, but it also contained condominium units. Room 821 was a condominium owned by Melvin Shigeta, who had rented it to King. Kelley was visiting King. King and Kelley sued Ilikai Properties, alleging their losses were caused by Ilikai's failure to make the premises safe. Did Ilikai have a duty to protect them from robbers?

There are several types of mutual-benefit bailments in which the bailor, under the common law, was held to a higher than normal standard of care for the bailed property. These bailments, sometimes called extraordinary bailments, include common carriers and hotelkeepers.

CARRIERS

L.O.1

Carrier
Transporter of goods, people, or both

A **carrier** engages in the business of transporting either goods or persons, or both. A carrier of goods is a bailee. Since a carrier charges a fee for such service, the bailment exists for the mutual benefit of both parties.

Classification of Carriers

Carriers are usually classified into two groups:

1   Private carriers
2   Common carriers

Private Carriers

Private Carrier
Carrier that transports under special arrangements for a fee

A **private carrier,** for a fee, undertakes to transport goods or persons. It transports only under special instances and special arrangements and may refuse service that is unprofitable. The most usual types of private carriers are trucks, moving vans, ships, and delivery services. A carrier owned by the shipper, such as a truck from a fleet owned and operated by an industrial firm for transporting its own products, is a private carrier.

Private carriers' contracts for transporting goods are mutual-benefit bailments, and the general law of bailments governs them. They are liable only for loss from the failure to exercise ordinary care. By contract a private carrier may further limit liability for loss to the goods.

Common Carriers

Common Carrier
One that undertakes to transport without discrimination for all who apply for service

Consignor
One who ships by common carrier

Consignee
One to whom goods are shipped

Bill of Lading
Receipt and contract between consignor and carrier

A **common carrier** undertakes to transport goods or persons, without discrimination, for all who apply for that service. The goods to be transported must be proper, and facilities must be available for transport. One who ships goods by a common carrier is called the **consignor**; the one to whom the goods are shipped is called the **consignee**; and the receipt and contract between the carrier and the consignor is called a **bill of lading.**

A common carrier must serve without discrimination all who apply. If it fails to do so, it is liable for any damages resulting from such a refusal. A common carrier may, however, refuse service because the service is not properly equipped. For example, an express company does not have to accept lumber for transportation. Also, a common carrier may refuse service if its equipment is inadequate to accommodate customers in excess of the normal demands. A common carrier of persons is not required to transport (1) any person who requires unusual attention, such as an invalid, unless that person is accompanied by an attendant; (2) any person who intends or is likely to cause harm to the carrier or the passengers; or (3) any person who is likely to be offensive to passengers, such as an intoxicated person.

The usual types of common carriers of persons are trains, buses, airplanes, ships, and subways. Common carriers are public monopolies and are subject to regulations as to prices, services, equipment, and other operational policies. This public regulation is in lieu of competition as a determinant of their prices and services.

LIABILITY OF COMMON CARRIERS OF GOODS

L.O.2 .... While common carriers of goods and common carriers of persons are alike in that they must serve all who apply, they differ sharply in their liability for loss. Common carriers of goods are insurers of the safety of the transported goods and are liable for loss or damage regardless of fault, unless the loss arises from:

1   Acts of God
2   Acts of a public authority
3   Inherent nature of the goods
4   Acts of the shipper
5   Acts of a public enemy

These exceptions do not excuse the carrier if the carrier failed to safeguard the goods from harm.

Acts of God

The carrier is not liable for unusual natural occurrences such as floods, snowstorms, tornadoes, lightning, or fire caused by lightning, since these are considered acts of God. Normal weather such as a rainstorm is not.

Ozark White Lime Co. shipped a carload of lime from Johnson, Arkansas, to Okmulgee, Oklahoma, by the St. Louis–San Francisco Railway Company. The railway car got as far as McBride, Oklahoma. The train could not proceed beyond McBride because a landslide covered the tracks. While there, excessive rains caused the Grand River to flood the track and the lime was destroyed. When Ozark sued the railroad for the value of the lime, the court held that the unprecedented flood was an act of God.

Acts of a Public Authority

An act of a public authority occurs if illicit goods are seized by public officials, or if goods that are a menace to health are seized by health officials. The carrier is not liable for such loss.

Inherent Nature of the Goods

The carrier is not liable for damage due to the inherent nature of the goods, such as decay of vegetables, fermentation or evaporation of liquids, and the death of livestock as a result of natural causes or the fault of other animals.

Acts of the Shipper

Acts of the shipper that can cause loss include misdirection of the merchandise, failure to indicate fragile contents, and improper packing. If improper packing is noticeable, the carrier can refuse to accept the goods.

Semi Metals, Inc., delivered two cartons of germanium to Pinter Brothers for shipment under a straight bill of lading. The germanium was worth $85 a pound, but to avoid higher freight charges Semi Metals described it as electronic material and no value was stated in the bill of lading. The tariff for electronic materials had a maximum value of $5 a pound. The two cartons were lost. Semi Metals sued Pinter for $19,280, the full value of the germanium. The court held that the intentional misdescription of the shipper to avoid higher shipping charges limited Semi Metals' recovery to $5 a pound.

Acts of a Public Enemy

Organized warfare or border excursions of foreign bandits constitute acts of a public enemy. Mobs, strikers, and rioters are not classified as public enemies in interpreting this exclusion.

Contractual Limitations on Liability

A common carrier may attempt to limit or escape the extraordinary liability imposed upon it by law, often by a contract between the shipper and the carrier. As the written evidence of the contract, the bill of lading sets out the limitations on the carriers' liability. Since the shipper does not have any direct voice in the preparation of the bill of lading, the law requires every carrier to have its printed bill-of-lading form approved by a government agency before adoption.

In addition to uniform limitations set out in the printed form of a bill of lading, additional limitations may be added that the shipper and the carrier may agree upon. The Federal Bills of Lading Act governs this matter as to interstate shipments, while the Uniform Commercial Code controls with respect to intrastate shipments. In general, the limitations upon the carrier's liability permitted by these acts fall into the following classes:

1   A carrier may limit by agreement its loss to a specified sum or to a specified percent of the value of the goods. However, a carrier must give the shipper the choice of shipping at lower rates subject to the limited liability or at a higher rate without limitation of liability.

Richard Alteri Jr., shipped two packages containing computer equipment from New York to Illinois by Greyhound Lines with a declared value of $1,100. Both packages were lost so Alteri sued Greyhound for their alleged true value of $8,000. Greyhound asserted its liability was limited as stated on the bus bills to $100 for a two-package shipment unless the shipper declares and pays for a greater value, not to exceed $1,000, at the time of shipment. The court agreed with Greyhound that its liability was limited to $1,000.

2 Most states permit carriers to exempt themselves from liability due to certain named hazards. The most common named hazards include fire, leakage, breakage, spoilage, and losses due to riots, strikes, mobs, and robbers. Some states specifically prohibit an exemption for loss by fire. These exemptions must be specifically enumerated in the bill of lading or shipper's receipt. The exemptions are not effective if the loss is due to the negligence of the carrier.

3 Delay in transportation of livestock may result in serious losses or extra expense for feed. Most states allow some form of limitation upon the carrier's liability if the loss is due to a delay over which the carrier has no control.

In those cases where the carrier is held liable only for loss due to negligence, the Uniform Commercial Code provides for liability only for ordinary negligence.

Duration of the Special Liability

The carrier's high degree of liability lasts only during transportation. If the goods are delivered to the carrier ready for shipment and are received from the carrier promptly upon arrival, the goods are regarded as being transported during the entire transaction.

Carrier as Bailee Before Transportation

Frequently, goods are delivered to the carrier before they are ready for transportation. The carrier is liable only as a mutual-benefit bailee until the goods are ready for transportation.

Carrier as Bailee After Transportation

When the goods arrive at their destination, the consignee has a reasonable time to accept delivery of the goods. Railroads need only place the goods in the freight depot, or, in case of car lots, set the car on a siding where the consignee can unload the goods. If the consignee does not call for the goods within a reasonable time after being notified by the carrier that the goods have arrived, the carrier is liable only as a mutual-benefit bailee.

Connecting Carriers

The initial carrier and the final, or terminal, carrier are each liable for a common-carrier loss occurring on the line of a connecting carrier. Whichever of these carriers has been held liable may then compel the connecting carrier to reimburse it.

Bills of Lading

The bill of lading not only sets forth the contract between the shipper and the carrier, it is a document of title. Title to the goods described in the bill of lading may be passed by transferring it to the purchaser. There are two types of bills of lading:

1 Straight, or nonnegotiable, bills of lading
2 Order, or negotiable, bills of lading

Straight Bills of Lading

Straight Bill of Lading
Contract requiring delivery of shipped goods to consignee only

Under a **straight bill of lading** (see Illustration 15.1), the consignee alone is designated as the one to whom the goods are to be delivered. The consignee's rights may be transferred to another, but the third party normally obtains no greater rights than the shipper or the consignee had. However, if the bill of lading contains a recital as to the contents, quantity, or weight of the goods, the carrier is bound to a bona fide transferee as to the accuracy of these descriptions unless the bill of lading itself indicates that the contents of packages are unknown to the carrier.

The assignee should notify the carrier of the assignment when the original consignee sells the goods before receipt. The carrier is justified in delivering goods to the consignee if it has not received notice of assignment.

Illustration 15-1

Bill of Lading

21040

ALWAYS LIST HAZARDOUS MATERIALS FIRST IN DESCRIPTION OF ARTICLES COLUMN.

STRAIGHT BILL OF LADING - SHORT FORM - Original-Not Negotiable
RECEIVED, subject to the classification and tariffs in effect on the date of issue of this Original Bill of Lading

NOT to be used for ORDER NOTIFY SHIPMENTS. DATE

BIG BEAR Transfer Company

BIG BEAR TRANSFER COMPANY
NOTE: DRIVER AFIX PRO NUMBER LABEL HERE

(NAME OF CARRIER) (SCAC)

CUSTOMER P.O. NO. ROUTE SHIPPER'S NUMBER

TO: CONSIGNEE
on COD Shipments the letters "COD" must appear before consignee's name.
FROM: SHIPPER

STREET STREET

(DESTINATION) CITY, STATE, ZIP
(ORIGIN) CITY, STATE, ZIP

C.O.D. AMT $ ____ FEE PPD ☐ COL ☐ IS CUSTOMER'S CHECK ACCEPTABLE FOR C.O.D.? YES ☐ NO ☐

NO. SHIPPING UNITS	(X) HM	RATE AND CLASS	kIND OF PACKAGING, DESCRIPTION OF ARTICLES, SPECIAL MARKS AND EXCEPTIONS (LIST HAZARDOUS MATERIALS FIRST)	WEIGHT LBS (Subject to Correcitons)
	◄ TOTAL		TOTAL ►	

NOTE: Where the rate is dependent on value, shippers are required to state specifically in writing the agreed or declared value of the property.
The agreed or declared value of the property is hereby specifically stated by the shipper to be not exceeding
$ ____
per ____

Subject to Section 7 of the conditions, if this shipment is to be delivered to the consignee without recourse on the consignor, the consignor shall sign the following statement:
The carrier shall not make delivery of this shipment without payment of freight and all other lawful charges.
____
(Signature of Consignor

FREIGHT CHARGES
WRITE IN PREPAID OR COLLECT

RECEIVED, subject to the classifications and tariffs in effect on the date of the issue of this Bill of Lading, the property described above in apparent good order, except as noted (contents and condition of contents of packages unknown), marked, consigned and destined as indicated above which said carrier (the word carrier being understood throughout this contract as meaning any person or corporation in possession of the property under the contract) agrees to carry to its usual place of delivery at said destination, if on its route, otherwise to deliver to another carrier on the route to said destination. It is mutally agreed as to each carrier of all or any of, said property over all or any to all the bill of lading terms and conditions in the governing classification on the date of shipment.

Shipper hereby certifies that he is familiar with all the bill of lading terms and conditions in the governing classification and the said terms and conditions are hereby agreed to by the shipper and accepted for himself and his assigns.

This is to certify that the above-named materials are properly classified, described, packaged, marked and labeled, and are in proper condition for transportation according to the applicable regulations of the Department of Transportation	SHIPPER:	BIG BEAR TRANSFER COMPANY	
	PER:	DRIVER	TRAILER
		PIECES	DATE

MARK "X" IN "HM" COLUMN FOR HAZARDOUS MATERIALS.

Richard Hightower, an army officer, shipped goods on a U.S. government bill of lading by Bekins Van Lines Co. After shipment, some articles were missing and others were damaged. Hightower sued Bekins for the full loss of $14,868.83. The bill of lading limited the value of the goods to 60 cents per pound "unless otherwise specifically annotated" and there was no annotation. An "Order for Services" contained a written and signed agreement by Hightower limiting losses to 60 cents per pound and a condition that in the space provided the shipper had to insert the declared value or the words "60 cents per pound" in his own handwriting or "the shipment will be deemed released to a maximum value equal to $1.25 times the weight of the shipment in pounds." An insertion of "60 cents per pound" was made but not in Hightower's handwriting. Since Bekins treated Hightower as the shipper in the Order for Service and Hightower had not written "60 cents per pound" on the Order, Hightower was allowed to recover $1.25 times the weight, or $6,650.

Order Bills of Lading

Order Bill of Lading

Contract allowing delivery of shipped goods to bearer

The bill of lading may set forth that the goods are shipped to a designated consignee or order, or merely "to the bearer" of the bill of lading. In such case, the bill of lading is an **order,** or negotiable, **bill of lading** and must be presented to the carrier before the carrier can safely deliver the goods. If the goods are delivered to the named consignee and later a bona fide innocent purchaser of the order bill of lading demands the goods, the carrier is liable to the holder of the bill of lading.

Nissho, a Japanese corporation, ordered hog grease from Amkor Corporation in the United States. Nissho reserved space on Iino Kaiun Kaisha Ltd.'s ship bound for Kobe, Japan, and Amkor purchased the grease from Swift and Company. Amkor asked Chase Manhattan Bank to finance the sale. Chase agreed if it got a signed mate's receipt issued in its name. Grease was pumped aboard Iino's ship, and on May 8 an order bill of lading was issued showing Nissho as owner. While the ship was enroute to Japan, Chase was working on the details of financing including receiving a receipt from Swift. It was not until May 26 that Chase wrote Iino claiming to own the goods. Iino replied that upon delivery of the order bill of lading, Iino had released the grease to Nissho. Chase sued. The court said the carrier, Iino, properly delivered the merchandise to the holder when the order bill of lading was presented.

Common Carriers of Persons

Common carriers of persons have the right to prescribe the place and time of the payment of fares, usually before boarding the plane, train, bus, or other vehicle. They also have the right to prescribe reasonable rules of conduct for transporting passengers. They may stop the vehicle and remove any passenger who refuses to pay the fare or whose conduct offends the other passengers. They also have the right to reserve certain coaches, seats, or space for special classes of passengers, as in the case of first-class seats in the forward cabin of aircraft.

J. W. Adams boarded a train for a trip from Greenville to Gastonia. When the conductor asked for his ticket, Adams could not locate it. He was put off the train. He sued the railroad for damages after he later located his ticket. He did not succeed in his claim for damages since he could not produce a ticket when required. The carrier was not required to take his word that he had a valid ticket.

Liability of Common Carriers of Persons

The liability of a carrier for the passengers' safety begins as soon as passengers enter the terminal or waiting platform and does not end until they have left the terminal at the end of the journey. A carrier must provide only ordinary care while passengers are in the terminal. After passengers board the bus, train, plane, or other vehicle, the highest degree of care consistent with practical operation is required.

Duties of Common Carriers of Persons

A carrier's duties to its passengers consist of:

1 Duty to provide reasonable accommodations and services.
2 Duty to provide reasonable protection to its passengers.

Duty to Provide Reasonable Accommodations and Services

A carrier is required to furnish adequate and reasonable service. A passenger is not necessarily entitled to a seat; however, the carrier must make a reasonable effort to provide sufficient facilities so that the public can be accommodated, which may be merely standing room. A passenger may make an express reservation that requires the carrier to provide a seat. The carrier must notify the passenger of the arrival of the train, bus, or airplane at the destination and stop long enough to permit the passenger to disembark.

For two weeks during the summer, Burton Fendelman was a passenger on Conrail trains that were late; overcrowded; lacking in air conditioning, water facilities, and electricity; and which had dirty toilets and noxious odors. He sued Conrail and testified that these "atrocious conditions" had existed for years. The court found that as a common carrier, Conrail was required to furnish such service and facilities as shall be safe and adequate and in all respects just and reasonable. This it did not do, and it was required to pay Fendelman damages.

Duty to Provide Reasonable Protection to Its Passengers

Common carriers of passengers need not insure the absolute safety of passengers but must exercise extraordinary care to protect them. Any injury to the passenger by an employee or fellow passengers subjects the carrier to liability for damages, provided the injured passenger is without blame. The vehicle must stop at a safe place for alighting, and passengers must be assisted when necessary for alighting.

Baggage
Articles necessary for personal convenience while traveling

Baggage

Baggage consists of those articles of personal convenience or necessity usually carried by passengers for their personal use at some time during the trip. Articles carried by travelers on similar missions and destinations constitute the test. For example, fishing paraphernalia is baggage for a person who expects to go fishing while away, but not for the ordinary traveler. Any article carried for one who is not a passenger is not baggage.

A reasonable amount of baggage may be carried as a part of the cost of the passenger's fare. The carrier may charge extra for baggage in excess of a reasonable amount.

The liability of a common carrier for checked baggage historically was the same as that of a common carrier of goods—an insurer of the baggage with the five exceptions previously mentioned. The liability for baggage retained in the possession of the traveler was only for lack of reasonable care or for willful misconduct of its agents or employees. However, today carriers are allowed to limit their liability for loss of baggage to a fixed maximum amount. This amount will be stated on the ticket. Such limitations are binding on passengers.

On the way to her Delta Airlines flight, Felice Lippert took a handbag containing $431,000 worth of jewelry through a Palm Beach International Airport security checkpoint. She placed the bag on the conveyer belt and walked through the archway magnetometer. The alarm sounded and she was briefly inspected by security personnel. Lippert then discovered her handbag was missing. She sued Delta and Wackenhut who operated the security checkpoint for Delta. They asserted the $1,250 limitation of liability, printed on the back of Lippert's ticket, should apply. It covered "baggage or other property (including carry-on baggage . . . delivered into the custody of [Delta])." The court held that the $1,250 limitation applied because the handbag clearly was delivered into the custody of Delta at the security checkpoint.

HOTELKEEPERS

L.O.3 ....

L.O.4 ....

Hotelkeeper
One engaged in business of offering lodging to transients

Boardinghouse Keeper
Person in business to supply accommodations to permanent lodgers

Guest
Transient received by hotel for accommodations

A **hotelkeeper** regularly engages in the business of offering lodging to all transient persons. The hotelkeeper may also supply food or entertainment, but providing lodging to transients is the primary business.

A person who provides rooms or room and board to permanent lodgers but does not behave as able and willing to accommodate transients is not a hotelkeeper. Such persons are **boardinghouse keepers** and the laws of hotelkeepers do not apply to them. The owner of a tourist home is not a hotelkeeper if the establishment does not advertise as willing to accommodate all transients who apply. Most people who run hotels and motels are hotelkeepers. A hotel that caters to both permanent residents and transients is a hotelkeeper only with respect to the transients.

Who Are Guests?

To be a **guest** one must be a transient obtaining lodging, not a permanent resident or visitor. One who enters the hotel to attend a ball or other social function, to visit a guest, or to eat dinner is not a guest. A guest need not be a traveler nor come from a distance. A guest might be a person living within a short distance of the hotel who rents a room and remains there overnight.

The relationship of guest and hotelkeeper does not begin until the hotelkeeper receives the person seeking lodging as a guest. The relationship terminates when the guest leaves or makes arrangements for permanent residence at the hotel.

Jean King and Miriam Kelley were robbed in Room 821 of the Ilikai Tower Building. The Tower Building of the Ilikai Hotel was operated by Ilikai Properties, Inc., as a hotel, but it also contained condominium units. Room 821 was a condominium owned by Melvin Shigeta, who had rented it to King. Kelley was visiting King. King and Kelley sued Ilikai Properties, alleging their losses were caused by Ilikai's failure to make the premises safe for them as guests. The court found that King and Kelley were not guests of the hotel.

Duties of a Hotelkeeper

L.O.5 ....

The duties of a hotelkeeper include:

1   To serve all who apply
2   To protect a guest's person
3   To care for the guest's property

Duty to Serve All Who Apply

The basic test of hotelkeepers is that they hold themselves out as willing to serve without discrimination all who request lodging. However, this does not require hotelkeepers to serve drunken persons, someone criminally violent, someone not dressed in a manner required by reasonable hotel regulations applied to all or when no rooms are available. If a hotel refuses lodging for an improper reason, it is liable for damages, including exemplary damages, to the person rejected.

In addition, a hotel may be liable for discrimination under a civil rights or similar statutory provision and may also be guilty of a crime if a court has issued an injunction prohibiting such discrimination. By virtue of the Federal Civil Rights Act of 1964, neither a hotel nor its concessionaire can discriminate against patrons nor segregate them on the basis of race, color, religion, or national origin. When there has been improper discrimination or segregation or it is reasonably believed that such action may occur, the federal act authorizes the institution of proceedings in the federal courts for an order to stop such practices.

Duty to Protect a Guest's Person

A hotelkeeper must use reasonable care for the guests' personal safety. The same standard applies to the personal safety of a visitor or a patron of a newsstand or lunchroom.

Reasonable care requires that a hotelkeeper provide fire escapes and also have conspicuous notices indicating directions to the fire escapes. If a fire starts due to no negligence of the hotelkeeper or employees, there is no liability to the guests for their personal injuries unless they can show that the fire was not contained because of a failure to install required fire safety features. In one case the court held the hotelkeeper was not liable for the loss of life on the floor where the fire started, but was liable for all personal injuries on the four floors to which the fire spread because of the negligence of the hotel.

If a hotelkeeper knows of prior criminal acts on or near the hotel premises, additional security measures may be required. However, the hotelkeeper is not liable if the guest's behavior increases the risk of criminal attack.

Dula McCarty, a guest at a hotel, left her room to go to dinner. A sliding glass door equipped with a lock and a safety chain was closed and chained, but not locked. An intruder pried open the door from the outside, broke the security chain, and, when McCarty returned to the room, attacked and beat her. McCarty sued the hotel alleging it had breached its duty of care. The court found that the hotel was not liable because McCarty had failed to take the elementary precaution of locking the sliding glass door before leaving the room.

Duty to Care for the Guest's Property

Traditionally, the hotelkeeper had a very high duty and was an insurer of the guest's property except for losses occurring from:

1 An act of God
2 The act of a public enemy
3 An act of a public authority
4 An act of the guest
5 The inherent nature of the property

In every state this liability has been modified to some extent. The statutes vary greatly but most limit a hotel's liability to a designated sum or simply declare that the law of mutual-benefit bailments applies.

Some states permit the hotelkeeper to limit liability by posting a notice in the guest's room. Some of the statutes require that the hotelkeeper, in order to escape full liability, provide a vault or other safe place of deposit for valuables such as furs and jewelry. If a guest fails to deposit valuable articles when notice of the availability of a safe has been posted, the hotelkeeper is released from liability as an insurer.

Hotelkeeper's Lien

A hotelkeeper has a lien on the baggage of guests for the value of the services rendered. This lien extends to all wearing apparel not actually being worn, such as an overcoat or an extra suit.

If hotel charges are not paid within a reasonable time, the hotelkeeper may sell the baggage to pay the charges. Any residue must be returned to the guest. The lien terminates if the property is returned to the guest even though the charges are unpaid.

The lien usually attaches only to baggage. It does not apply to an automobile, for example, in most states. If a hotelkeeper charges separately for car storage, this charge (but not the room charge) must be paid before the car can be removed.

QUESTIONS

1 a. What is a *carrier*?
   b. Name the two categories of carriers.
2 a. What is a *bill of lading*?
   b. What is the difference between a *straight bill of lading* and an *order bill of lading*?

3   Is a common carrier liable for all loss or damage to goods being transported regardless of negligence?

4   When does the common carrier's liability begin?

5   When goods must be transported by two or more carriers before reaching their destination, which carrier is liable if the goods are damaged?

6   Are common carriers insurers of the safety of passengers?

7   What is baggage and the liability of a common carrier for baggage carried by a passenger?

8   a. What is a *hotelkeeper*?
    b. Who is a *guest*?

9   What are the duties and liabilities of a hotelkeeper to guests?

10 Is the hotelkeeper liable for the injury to a guest by fire if the hotel was in no way negligent?

11 How may a hotelkeeper frequently limit liability for loss of a guest's property?

12 a. What is a hotelkeeper's lien?
    b. How can the lien be enforced?

CASE PROBLEMS

L.O.1, 2 ....

1   Containers of plywood shipped by Masonite Corporation on Norfolk & Western Railway Company tilted so much during transit they almost fell from the flatcar and required extraordinary handling to unload. The railroad told Masonite that improper internal bracing allowed the plywood to move and that subsequent containers were to be sent to a facility for inspection prior to shipment. Later, Masonite sent two containers that were poorly packed and were not sent to the inspection facility. The containers received only a routine inspection at the yard. They fell from the flatcar and derailed another car in the train. Masonite sued Norfolk & Western alleging that it was strictly liable for the damages because it knew of the defective bracing. Norfolk & Western alleged it had no duty to discover defects in Masonite's packing. Did it?

L.O.1, 2 ....

2   Gensplit Finance Corporation bought the right to collect on three shipments from D.E.C. Western Distributors, Inc., to Corporacion Intercontinental, C.A. in Venezuela. Three Pan American straight air waybills [bills of lading issued by an airline] had been issued and D.E.C.'s rights under them had been transferred to Gensplit. Gensplit relied on these air waybills to advance $117,568 to D.E.C. The shipments never arrived, so Gensplit sued Pan Am. Pan Am had filed tariffs with the government. If they were effective against Gensplit, Pan Am would win the suit. Pan Am alleged since the tariffs were binding on D.E.C., they would be binding on Gensplit. How should the case be decided?

L.O.1, 2 ....

3   Iowa Beef Processors, Inc., shipped meat to Standard Meat Company by American Trucking Company, a common carrier. The meat was loaded into a trailer that Iowa sealed. It was Standard's responsibility to break the seal upon arrival. When the shipment arrived, the meat was tendered to Standard but not unloaded for two days because of a lack of freezer space. It was dis-

covered during unloading that much of the meat was spoiled. The shipment was rejected. Iowa sued American for damages, alleging American was liable as an insurer because the meat was in good condition when it was shipped. Is American liable?

L.O.1, 2 ....

4 K. C. Mah bought a full-fare ticket from New York to Radford on Greyhound Lines, Inc. She checked three pieces of baggage and was given three claim checks. Each claim check stated: "BAGGAGE LIABILITY LIMITED TO $50.00 (SEE OVER)." Language on the back stated Greyhound's liability was limited to $50 for all baggage checked on one full-fare ticket unless a greater value was declared in writing and additional charges were collected at the time of checking. It added, "This check is accepted subject to all conditions of published tariffs." The tariff had the same limitation of liability. Mah boarded a bus and upon arrival in Radford her baggage could not be found. Three days later one piece was delivered. She sued for $1,000, the value of the lost bags and their contents. For what, if anything, was Greyhound liable?

L.O.1, 2 ....

5 During the daytime Phyllis Parlato alighted from a Connecticut Transit bus and started to cross the bus-stop area. She stepped into a hole that was covered by leaves and broke her leg. The bus driver had stopped at the area five or six times previously that day and did not know about the hole. Parlato sued for breach of Connecticut's duty of utmost care for its passengers. Did Connecticut Transit breach its duty?

L.O.3 ....

6 An individual rented and paid for an efficiency apartment on a weekly basis for four weeks. Apartments were not rented on a daily basis as regular motel rooms were. After leaving some of his belongings in the unit and failing to return the key for two extra days, he was convicted of the crime of theft of services. The law defines theft of services as failure to pay for services rendered as a "transient guest at a hotel, motel, . . . or comparable establishment." The defendant appealed claiming he was not a "transient guest." The unit had cooking facilities and no maid service as regular motel rooms had. Was the defendant a transient guest?

L.O.1, 2 ....

7 David Lloyd, an independent trucker, contracted with East Texas Motor Freight to haul a load of insulation from California to Ohio. During his trip, Lloyd ran into a severe rainstorm that damaged the load. East Texas sued Lloyd who argued that an "act of God" was responsible for the damage. He testified that the storm was a little worse than storms he had previously been in. Should Lloyd be excused from liability because of an act of God?

L.O.4, 5 ....

8 Mary Weaver had been staying at the Sea Esta Motel for about four months and paid a monthly rate. She was injured when a chair in her motel room collapsed. She sued the motel. Was she a guest?

L.O.3 ....

9 Mr. and Mrs. Andrew Laubie were guests at the Royal Sonesta Hotel. They locked the doors and windows and secured the chain lock to their room, but during the night burglars opened the door and severed the chain lock. Valuable jewelry was stolen. The hotel provided a safety deposit vault for its guests. State law provided that an innkeeper was not liable to guests for loss of property in any sum exceeding $100 if a copy of the law was conspicuously posted in the guest's room or unless greater liability was contracted for in writing. In a suit brought by the Laubies against the hotel, the question was whether the statute limited the hotel's liability for negligence as well as its liability as a depositary. Did it?

Summary Cases

PERSONAL PROPERTY

1. Cerreta parked his automobile in the Kinney Corporation parking lot. On the back seat of the car were some valuable drawings and sporting equipment. The articles on the back seat were not visible from the outside of the car. When Cerreta returned to pick up the car, the articles were missing. He sued the Kinney Corporation as a bailee. Decide. [*Cerreta* v. *Kinney Corp.*, 142 A. 2d 917 (N.J. Super. Ct. App. Div.)]

2. Georgia Best Sales Company delivered cases of Cornish hens to H & M Motor Lines, Inc., for transport from Chattanooga to South Carolina. When the truck arrived, ninety-four cases of hens were missing. The bill of lading signed by H & M stated, "WSHE L. CARRIER COUNT," which wording required the carrier to count the actual load rather than goods placed on the dock for later loading. Georgia Best sued H & M for the missing hens. Was H & M liable for the loss? [*H & M Motor Lines, Inc.* v. *Georgia Best Sales Company*, 253 S.E.2d 841 (Ga. Ct. App.)]

3. State law provided that all intangible property remaining unclaimed by the owner for more than seven years after it was payable was presumed abandoned. Such intangible property could be claimed by the state. Blue Cross and Blue Shield (BC/BS) held $125,000 in uncashed checks issued by it to pay benefits and premium refunds. The state demanded the funds. Were they intangible property? [*Revenue Cabinet* v. *Blue Cross and Blue Shield*, 702 S.W.2d 433 (Ky.)]

4. American Cyanamid Co. shipped 12 large boxes of heavy machinery and oil by Seatrain Lines of Puerto Rico, Inc., and then by land with Francisco Vega Otero, a common carrier. The boxes were loaded onto three platforms owned by Seatrain, and the platforms were loaded aboard Seatrain's ship. Upon arrival in Puerto Rico the platforms were unloaded and each mounted on a chassis with wheels. Later they were attached to three Vega Otero trucks. The cargo on the platforms was so high the truck drivers could not pass under a bridge on the normal route. They blocked off a one-way exit ramp and went up the ramp the wrong way intending to make a U-turn at the top. When the first driver carefully and cautiously tried to turn, the platform tipped onto its side causing the chassis and truck to overturn, damaging the cargo. It was the custom of the parties for the land carrier to accept goods in the trailers chosen by the sea carrier. Cyanamid's insurance company sued Seatrain and Vega Otero. What is the liability of either or both carriers? [*American Foreign Insurance Association* v. *Seatrain Lines of Puerto Rico, Inc.*, 689 F.2d 295 (1st Cir.)]

5. The painter Alphonse Mucha had more than 20 of his paintings, including a large one called "Quo Vadis," delivered to the Newcomb-Macklin gallery for the gallery to try to sell for him. Mucha had occasional contact by letter with

the gallery, but died 19 years after the delivery. His son, Jiri, thought he had recovered all the remaining paintings after Alphonse's death. Fifty-nine years after receiving the paintings, the gallery was liquidating and Rupprecht asked the owner for the rolled-up paintings in the basement. One of the paintings was "Quo Vadis," which Rupprecht sold to an art dealer who sold it to Charles King. A year later a friend of King's wrote Jiri, asking about the symbolism in the painting. Jiri found out King had it and sued for its return claiming a conversion by the gallery. Was there a 59-year bailment and a conversion of "Quo Vadis"? [*Mucha* v. *King,* 792 F.2d 602 (7th Cir.)]

6 While she was a passenger in a motor home leased from BCJ Corporation, Jayne Miles was severely burned when the motor home caught fire. It had collided with a guard rail causing the gas tanks to rupture, and the leaking gas caught fire. Miles sued BCJ, alleging it knew the motor home was defectively designed because the only exit door was directly over the gas tanks, and the tires were overloaded and likely to rupture. The trial court dismissed the suit before any evidence was heard. Did Miles allege a cause of action against BCJ? [*Miles* v. *General Tire & Rubber Co.,* 460 N.E.2d 1377 (Ohio Ct. App.)]

7 After checking into his motel room late at night, Thomas Urbano went to his car in the motel parking lot to get his luggage. He was assaulted and seriously injured by unidentified people. There had been 42 episodes of criminal activity at the motel in the prior three years, and 12 of the episodes had occurred in the previous three and one-half months. The parking lot was not enclosed, and the area of Urbano's room was dimly lighted. Urbano sued the motel, alleging it was negligent in not providing adequate lighting, not fencing the parking lot, not notifying him of criminal activity, and not monitoring and protecting the premises. The motel argued the case should be dismissed. Should it? [*Urbano* v. *Days Inn of America, Inc.,* 295 S.E.2d 240 (N.C. Ct. App.)]

8 At the Yuma County Airport there was a "tie down" area operated by Aero International, Inc., for planes using the airport. They were fastened with cables or chains at the underside of each wing and the tail section to two parallel, long, metal cables attached to the parking surface. Dale F. Webb paid Aero for use of the area and left one of several keys to his plane with Aero employees so they could move the plane when he requested maintenance on it. Franklin Fry rented Webb's plane and returned it to the tie down area, securing it with Aero's chains and a rope. Shortly thereafter, record winds hit the area. The plane was tossed upside down seriously damaging it. Webb sued Aero as bailee of the plane. Was it? [*Webb* v. *Aero International, Inc.,* 633 P.2d 1044 (Ariz. Ct. App.)]

Part 4

SALES

Chapter 16

/ALE/ OF PER/ONAL PROPERTY

After studying this chapter you should be able to:

1 Define *goods*.

2 Define a *sale* of goods and distinguish it from a contract to sell.

3 Distinguish between existing and future goods.

Preview Case

John Van Sistine contracted with Jan Tollard to install some windows; reposition an air conditioner, a range, and a cabinet; install siding; and perform certain finishing. Van Sistine was referred to in the contract as a contractor, and most of the price was for labor. The parties agreed to additional work but then disagreed on the value of the work. Van Sistine sued Tollard for more money. Tollard defended on the basis of the law of sales. Since Van Sistine furnished both goods and services, the test was whether the predominant factor of the contract was the rendition of a service or a sale. Which was it?

L.O.1

Goods
Movable personal property

In terms of the number of contracts as well as in the dollar volume, contracts for the sale of **goods**—movable personal property—constitute the largest class of contracts in our economic system. Every time one purchases a package of gum, one makes a sales contract. If the gum contained some harmful substance, the sale could be the basis of a suit for thousands of dollars in damages. Article 2 of the Uniform Commercial Code (UCC), effective in all states except Louisiana, governs sales of movable personal property.

PROPERTY SUBJECT TO SALE

**Movable
Personal
Property**
All physical items except
real estate

Real Property
Land and things perma-
nently attached to land

**Intangible
Personal
Property**
Evidences of ownership
of personal property

As used in the UCC and in these chapters, *sale* applies only to the sale of movable personal property. Thus, it does not apply to (1) real property or (2) intangible personal property. **Movable personal property** consists of all physical items that are not real estate. Examples include food, vehicles, clothing, and furniture. **Real property** is land, interests in land, and things permanently attached to land. **Intangible personal property** consists of evidences of ownership of personal property, such as contracts, copyrights, certificates of stock, accounts receivable, notes receivable, and similar assets.

Sales contracts must have all the essentials of any other contract, but they also have some additional features. Many rules pertaining to sales of personal property have no significance to any other type of contract, such as a contract of employment.

SALES AND CONTRACTS TO SELL

L.O.2 ....

Sale
Transfer of title to goods
for a price

Contract to Sell
Agreement to transfer
title to goods for a price

Title
Ownership

A sale differs from a contract to sell.

A **sale** of goods involves the transfer of title to goods from the seller to the buyer for a consideration called the price. The ownership changes hands at the moment the bargain is made regardless of who has possession of the goods.

A **contract to sell** goods is a contract whereby the seller agrees to transfer the title to goods to the buyer for a consideration called the price. In this type of contract individuals promise to buy and to sell in the future.

An important distinction exists between a sale and a contract to sell. In a sale the **title,** or the ownership of the subject matter, is transferred at once; in a contract to sell it will be transferred at a later time. A contract to sell is not in the true sense of the word a sale; it is merely an agreement to sell.

David M. Lide Sr. and Pel-Star Oil Corporation leased farmland to E. E. Day. The lease provided that the lessors (Lide and Pel-Star) were to receive as rent one-fourth of the cotton produced from the land. Day had the right to sell that one-fourth interest and give the proceeds to the lessors, unless notified in writing not to. For eight years the cotton was sold and the proceeds given to the lessors. The following June 6th, Day signed a "Sale and Purchase Agreement" with Massony Cotton Co. The agreement stated Day ". . . agrees to sell and the buyer agrees to buy . . ." the cotton produced on the land. In July, the lessors gave written notice that the cotton was to be delivered to them, not sold. Day filed a suit to determine who was entitled to the cotton. The court held that by the terms of the agreement, the parties had not made a sale, but a contract to sell. The cotton belonged to the lessors.

In order to determine who has title to goods, a sale must be distinguished from a contract to sell. Title always rests with either the seller or the buyer. Since the owner normally bears the risk of loss, the question of whether the seller or buyer has title must be answered. Also, any increase in the property belongs to the one who has the title. It is essential, therefore, to have definite rules to aid the courts in determining when title and risk of loss pass if the parties to the contract are silent as to these matters. If the parties specify when title or risk of loss passes, the courts will enforce this agreement.

SALES OF GOODS AND CONTRACTS FOR SERVICES

An agreement to perform some type of service must be distinguished from a sale of goods since Article 2 of the UCC governs sales of good but not agreements to perform services. When a contract includes the supplying of both services and articles of movable personal property, the contract is not necessarily considered a contract of sale of goods. The test is which factor is predominant. If the predominant factor is supplying a service, with the goods being incidental, the contract is considered a service contract, not covered by Article 2. For example, the repair of a television set is not a sale even though new parts are supplied.

John Van Sistine contracted with Jan Tollard to install some windows; reposition an air conditioner, a range, and a cabinet; install siding; and perform certain finishing. Van Sistine was referred to in the contract as a contractor, and most of the price was for labor. The parties agreed to additional work but then disagreed on the value of the work. Van Sistine sued Tollard for more money. Tollard defended on the basis of the law of sales. Since Van Sistine furnished both goods and services, the test was whether the predominant factor of the contract was the rendition of a service or a sale. Since Van Sistine was referred to in the contract as a contractor, most of the money claimed was for labor, and the work was to "install," "reposition," and "finish," the transaction was not a sale of goods.

PRICE

Price

Consideration in a sales contract

The consideration in a sales contract is generally expressed in terms of money or money's worth and is known as the **price.** The price may be payable in money, goods, or services.

The sales contract is ordinarily an express contract, but some of its terms may be implied. If the sales contract does not state the price, it will be held to be the reasonable price. For goods sold on a regulated market, such as a commodity exchange, the price on such market will be deemed the reasonable price. If the parties indicate that the price must be fixed by them or by a third person at a later date, no binding contract arises if the price is not thus fixed. If the price can be computed from the terms of the contract, the contract is valid.

A. P. Leonards employed an architect to renovate a building. While Leonards was out of the country, his wife selected bay windows for the building, and the architect ordered them from Benglis Sash & Door Co. The price of the windows was not discussed. When they arrived Leonards refused to accept them. Benglis sued for the price of the windows. Leonards argued there was no contract because the parties had never agreed on the price. Since the parties had a history of dealings in which Leonards ordered things and paid the invoice price, and since he did not object to the price charged, consent to buy at a reasonable price may be implied and the contract was enforceable.

EXISTING GOODS

L.O.3 ....

Existing Goods

Goods that are in being and owned by the seller

In order to be the subject of a sale, the goods must be existing. **Existing goods** are those both in existence, as contrasted with goods not yet manufactured, and then owned by the seller. If these conditions are not met, the only transaction that can be made between the seller and the buyer will be a contract to sell goods.

Identified Goods

Goods picked to be delivered to the buyer

Identified goods are those that the seller and buyer have agreed are to be received by the buyer or have been picked out by the seller.

> Matthew Serra agreed to buy a Lincoln Continental *Mark V* from Suburban Ford Lincoln Mercury. Serra paid a portion of the price, got a title certificate, registered the car, and paid the necessary sales tax. Serra wanted to store the Lincoln for several years because it was in a collectors' series. Since he had no room in his garage, Suburban agreed to keep it on its lot. Suburban stored the car for more than a year when the car Serra drove was damaged in an accident and he went to Suburban to get the Lincoln. The car was not there because Suburban was in financial trouble and its main creditor had repossessed all the cars. Serra's suit for possession of the Lincoln was successful because the court said the Lincoln was identified goods.

Future Goods

Goods not both existing and identified

Future goods are goods that are not both existing and identified. The buyer expects to acquire the goods in the future by purchase or by manufacture. Any contract purporting to sell future goods is a contract to sell and not a contract of sale. Title to the goods does not pass to the buyer when the goods come into existence. Some further action, such as shipment or delivery, must be taken by the seller.

BILL OF SALE

Bill of Sale

Written evidence of title to tangible personal property

A **bill of sale** provides written evidence of one's title to tangible personal property (see Illustration 16-1). No particular form is required for a bill of sale. It can simply state that title to described property has been transferred to the buyer.

Generally, a buyer does not need a bill of sale as evidence of title; but if a person's title is questioned, such evidence is highly desirable. If an individual buys a stock of merchandise in bulk, livestock, jewelry, furs, or any other relatively expensive items, demand should be made to the seller for a bill of sale. The bill of sale serves two purposes:

1 If the buyer wishes to resell the goods and the prospective buyer demands proof of title, the bill of sale can be produced.

2 If any question arises as to whether or not the buyer came into possession of the goods legally, the bill of sale is proof.

> Alda Lee Souza signed a bill of sale transferring the contents of her home to Zeuxis Ferreira Neves for several thousand dollars. Neves and Souza agreed that Souza would keep possession and use of the items, but that Neves could take any of the items whenever he wished. After Souza's death, the person handling her estate refused to let Neves have the property. Neves sued alleging the bill of sale transferred title to the property to him. The court agreed.

ILLEGAL SALES

Many difficulties arise over illegal sales, that is, the sale of goods prohibited by law, such as alcoholic beverages in a "dry" locality. If the sale is fully executed, the court will not intervene to aid either party. If an innocent party through fraud is induced to enter into an illegal sale, the court will compel a restoration of the goods or money the innocent party has transferred.

Illustration 16-1   Bill of Sale

BILL OF SALE OF CATTLE

Purchaser Mickey Bedrosian

Address Bedrosian Farms

Rt. 3 Box 1246-A

Miller, KS

Date March 26 19 --

Animals	Tattoo #	Sex	Price
Simmental cow with heifer by side	6783	F	$950
Simmental heavy heifer	17302	F	$725

By receipt of above, which is hereby acknowledged, the undersigned grants, bargains, sells and assigns all its rights, title and interest in and to the cattle described above; if check or draft is given in full or part payment of said described animal(s), title and ownership shall remain with Seller until check is cleared by the bank on which drawn.

Seller ___ Cadaret & Co. ___

Address Rt. 1 Box 1793-C

Wichita, KS

Signed _Curt McCaskill_

If the illegal sale is wholly executory, the transaction is a contract to sell and will not be enforced. If it is only partially executory, the court will still leave the parties where it finds them unless the one who has performed is an innocent victim of a fraud.

A Better Place, Inc. (ABP) manufactured and distributed gifts and souvenirs including pipes and accessories, snuff products, T-shirts, and posters. The state passed a law that made the sale of drug paraphernalia a crime. Giani Investment Co., a retailer, bought items from ABP. Giani's main store was raided by the police. Under the authority of a search warrant for drug paraphernalia, the police seized merchandise. Giani refused to pay ABP for the seized goods. The court said since the goods were drug paraphernalia it would not enforce Giani's obligation to pay for them.

If the sale is divisible with a legal part and an illegal part, the court will enforce the legal part. If the individual items are separately priced, the sale is divisible. If the sale involves several separate and independent items but is a lump-sum sale, then the sale is indivisible. An indivisible sale with an illegal part makes the entire sale illegal.

INTERNATIONAL SALES CONTRACTS

Questions may arise about what law governs an international contract for the sale of goods. These questions could present major problems to the parties if any litigation arises on the contract. Of course, the parties may specify in the contract what law governs. However, many international sales contracts are made without such a specification. To help in this type of situation, the United States has ratified the United Nations Convention on Contracts for the International Sale of Goods. This convention, or agreement, applies to contracts for the sale of goods if the buyer and seller have places of business in different countries agreeing to the convention. Several dozen countries have ratified or acceded to the convention.

Businesses may choose to indicate in their international contracts that they will not be governed by the convention. However, unless the parties state that the contract will not be governed by the convention, it will be. The convention does not cover contracts between two parties unless their places of business are in countries that have adopted the convention. It also does not cover consumer transactions.

QUESTIONS

1   What are *goods*?
2   Explain the types of property Article 2 of the UCC applies to and does not apply to.
3   a.   What is the difference between a sale and a contract to sell?
    b.   Why is it important to make a distinction between a sale and a contract to sell?
4   What is the difference between an agreement to perform services and a sale of goods?
5   Is an offer to sell a specified amount of wheat at the Chicago market closing price on June 7 an acceptable offer?
6   If goods are not existing, may a buyer and seller make a sale?
7   a.   What are *future goods*?
    b.   How do future goods differ from existing goods?
8   a.   What is a *bill of sale*?
    b.   Is a bill of sale necessary to pass title?

CASE PROBLEMS

L.O.2 ....

1   Harvey, Inc., agreed to sell restaurant equipment to Ruby Brown. After Brown accepted the equipment, a dispute arose about the price. Brown had agreed to pay the amount owed a bank on the equipment. Harvey asserted that Brown had agreed to pay both the principal and the interest owed and sued him for this amount. Brown said the price was not fixed. The president

of the bank testified that Brown agreed to pay the outstanding principal but that there was a dispute about who was to pay the outstanding interest. Was there a fixed price and, if so, what was it?

L.O.3 ....

2 Champion Manufacturing Industries ordered from Electrodyne four 104-foot, 210,000-pound masts used in the oil and gas industry. Three masts were completed and accepted by Champion and the fourth was 60 percent complete when Champion canceled the order. The fourth mast was never completed, accepted, or even shipped. Electrodyne sued for the order price, of it. Under state law, Electrodyne could not recover on its suit unless the mast had been sold to Champion. Analyze the situation and explain whether Electrodyne could recover.

L.O.2 ....

3 Lois and Arthur McNeil owned a registered quarter horse named Freckles Beachboy. Arthur executed a note to Doug Brink in the amount of $10,000. Arthur failed to pay it, and Brink sued him to collect. Lois and Arthur began a dissolution of marriage suit, and Lois paid Arthur $5,000 for his interest in the horse. Arthur made out and gave Lois, who had possession, a bill of sale to Freckles Beachboy. Then Brink got a judgment against Arthur, a dissolution of marriage decree was entered, and the sheriff seized the horse. Who owned Freckles Beachboy?

4 Kune Junde Haby signed a contract not to make a will. The contract provided that if she were permitted to use her children's land, her property would pass on her death according to the plan in the contract. The plan violated the law, and no element of it could be removed without destroying the whole plan. After she died her children disputed the validity of the contract, with one arguing that the illegal provisions were separable from the valid provisions. Were they?

L.O.2 ....

5 Stewart & Stevenson Services contracted to buy from Enserve, Incorporated 50 well-servicing pumps, used in the oil industry. The price for the first 10 pumps was to be the price S & S paid to another manufacturer for such pumps. The parties were to set the price of the remaining pumps from a cost analysis of the first ones. After S & S had approved the first pumps the oil industry suffered a business reversal. S & S refused to buy more than 11 pumps. Enserve sued for breach of contract. S & S said there was no contract because the price was left open. Was there a contract?

Chapter 17

FORMALITIES OF A SALE

LEARNING OBJECTIVES

After studying this chapter you should be able to:

1 List the requirements of the Statute of Frauds for sales, and explain the exceptions to it.

2 Define an auction sale, and describe its peculiarities to the law of sales.

3 Describe the nature of the writing required by the Statute of Frauds.

Preview Case

Each fall, Oakland Gin Co. asked Tennessee Valley Cotton Oil Mill what it would pay for seed. Tennessee always said it would pay whatever prices and rebates were paid by its competitors. During two years Oakland was not paid the rebates the other cotton-seed oil mills had paid. Oakland requested Tennessee pay the rebates, but Tennessee refused. A lawsuit was brought over the unpaid rebates. Would Tennessee be required to pay them?

L.O.1

All contracts for the sale of goods must be evidenced by a writing when the sales price is $500 or more. This Statute of Frauds' requirement has been included in the UCC. If the sales price is less than $500, the contract may be oral, written, implied from conduct, or a combination of any of these.

A sales contract that does not meet the requirements of the UCC is unenforceable. If both parties elect to abide by its terms even though not legally bound to do so, neither one can later avoid the contract.

Tube City Iron and Metal Co. contracted with A1 Ferro Commodities Corp. to buy 8,500 tons of scrap steel for $977,500. Tube City was required to nominate a ship to A1 on which the scrap was to be loaded prior to the date of delivery. After many delays, Tube City had not nominated a ship, and the delivery date had passed. On December 22, Tube City's president and CEO had a telephone conference with A1's lawyer, Michael Mesnik, in which they stated Tube City wanted to nominate a ship. Mesnik called A1 who would accept a nomination if it were done no later than December 23. Mesnik orally relayed this to Tube City. No communication followed, so A1 sold the scrap to someone else and sued for breach of contract. Tube City alleged that although the original contract was breached, the December 22 telephone calls created a new contract. The court said no enforceable new contract was made.

MULTIPLE PURCHASES AND THE STATUTE OF FRAUDS

Frequently one makes several purchases the same day from the same seller. The question may then be raised as to whether there is one sale or several sales. If one contracts to purchase five items from the same seller in one day, each one having a sale price of less than $500, but in the aggregate they exceed $500, must this contract meet the requirement of the Statute of Frauds? If the several items are part of the same sales transaction, it is one sale and must meet the requirement of the statute. If all the contracts to purchase are made during the same shopping tour and with the same salesperson who merely adds up the different items and charges the customer with a grand total, the several items are considered to be part of the same transaction. If a separate sales slip is written for each purchase as an individual goes through a department store and buys in different departments, each transaction is a separate sale.

WHEN PROOF OF ORAL CONTRACT PERMITTED

In some instances the absence of a writing does not bar the proof of a sales contract for $500 or more.

Receipt and Acceptance of Goods

Receipt
Taking possession of goods

Acceptance
Assent of buyer to become owner of goods

An oral sales contract may be enforced if it can be shown that the goods were delivered by the seller and were received and accepted by the buyer. Both a receipt and an acceptance by the buyer must be shown. **Receipt** is taking possession of the goods. **Acceptance** is the assent of the buyer to become the owner of specific goods. The contract may be enforced only insofar as it relates to the goods received and accepted.

Each fall, Oakland Gin Co. asked Tennessee Valley Cotton Oil Mill what it would pay for seed. Tennessee always said it would pay whatever prices and rebates were paid by its competitors. During two years Oakland was not paid the rebates the other cottonseed oil mills had paid. Oakland requested that Tennessee pay the rebates, but Tennessee refused. A lawsuit was brought over the unpaid rebates. The court held that although the contract agreeing to pay the rebates was oral, it was enforceable because Tennessee had received and accepted the seed.

Payment

An oral contract may be enforced if the buyer has made full payment on the contract. In the case of part payment, a contract may be enforced only with respect to goods for which payment has been made and accepted.

Some uncertainty occurs under this rule as to the effectiveness of payment by check or a promissory note executed by the buyer. Under the law of commercial paper, a check, draft, or note is conditional payment when delivered. It does not become absolute until the instrument is paid. However, since business people ordinarily regard the delivery of a check or note as payment, the delivery of such an instrument is normally sufficient to make the oral contract enforceable. A check or promissory note tendered as payment but refused by the seller does not constitute a payment under the Statute of Frauds.

Harry Kaufman and George Solomon discussed the sale of Solomon's loader. Kaufman believed a price of $60,000 was agreed upon, and the same day he delivered a check to Solomon in that amount. When Kaufman later asked for delivery of the loader, Solomon refused. He kept Kaufman's check for 30 days and then returned it unaltered in any way. Kaufman sued. The court held that the check constituted payment because payment by check was consistent with the reality of common business usage.

When the buyer has negotiated or assigned to the seller a negotiable instrument executed by a third person, and the seller has accepted the instrument, a payment has been made within the meaning of the Statute of Frauds.

Judicial Admission

Judicial Admission
Fact acknowledged in course of legal proceedings

When a person voluntarily acknowledges a fact during the course of some legal proceedings, this is a **judicial admission**. No writing is required when the person against whom enforcement of the contract is sought voluntarily admits in the course of legal proceedings to having made the contract.

Nonresellable Goods

No writing is required when the goods are specifically made for the buyer and are of such an unusual nature that they are not suitable for sale in the ordinary course of the seller's business. For this exception to apply, however, the seller must have made a substantial beginning in manufacturing the goods or, if a middleman, in procuring them, before receiving notice of a repudiation by the buyer.

P. N. Hirsch & Co. Stores, Inc., bought its paper bags from Smith-Scharff Paper Co. for 36 years. The bags were imprinted with the P. N. Hirsch logo. Smith-Scharff kept a supply of the bags in stock so it could promptly fill Hirsch's purchase orders. Hirsch was aware of this practice and even provided a generalized profile of its business forecasts to Smith-Scharff to help it judge how many bags to have on hand. Hirsch was sold and refused to purchase $20,000 worth of bags left in Smith-Scharff's inventory. Smith-Scharff sued Hirsch for breach of contract. Hirsch argued that it was not liable because there was no written contract. The court held the bags were nonresellable goods, so the contract did not have to be in writing.

Auction Sales

L.O.2

Auction
Sale of property to the
highest bidder

Bidder
Person who makes offer
at auction

Without Reserve
Auction goods may not be
withdrawn after bidding
starts

With Reserve
Auction goods may be
withdrawn after bidding
starts

An **auction** is a sale in which a seller or an agent of the seller orally asks for bids on goods and orally accepts the highest bid. A sale by auction for any amount is valid even though it is, by necessity, oral. In most states the auctioneer is the special agent for both the owner and the bidder. When the auctioneer or the clerk of the auction makes a memorandum of the sale and signs it, this binds both parties. The **bidder** is the one who makes the offer. There is no contract until the auctioneer accepts the offer, which may be done in several ways. The most common way is the fall of the hammer, with the auctioneer saying, "Sold" or "Sold to (a certain person)." In most auctions the final bid is preceded by several lower bids. When a person makes a bid to start the sale, the auctioneer may refuse to accept this as a starting bid. If the bid is accepted and a higher bid is requested, the auctioneer can later refuse to accept this starting bid as the selling price.

If a bid is made while the hammer is falling in acceptance of a prior bid, the auctioneer has the choice of reopening the bid or declaring the goods sold. The auctioneer's decision is binding.

Goods may be offered for sale with reserve or without reserve. If they are **without reserve,** then the goods cannot be withdrawn after the bidding starts unless no bid is received within a reasonable time after the auctioneer calls for bids. Goods are presumed to be offered **with reserve,** or they may be withdrawn, unless the goods are explicitly put up without reserve.

NATURE OF THE WRITING REQUIRED

L.O.3 The UCC does not have stringent requirements for the sufficiency of a writing to satisfy the Statute of Frauds for sales contracts.

Terms

The writing need only give assurance that a transaction existed. Specifically, it need only indicate that a sale or contract to sell has been made and state the quantity of goods involved. Any other missing terms may be shown by parol evidence in the event of a dispute.

Signature

When a suit is brought against an individual on the basis of a transaction, the terms of which must be in writing, the writing must be signed by the person being sued or an authorized agent of that person. The signature must be placed on the writing with the intention of authenticating the writing. It may consist of initials; it may be printed, stamped, or typewritten. The important thing is that it was made with the necessary intent.

The UCC makes an exception to the requirement of signing regarding a transaction between merchants. It provides that the failure of a merchant to repudiate within ten days a confirming letter sent by another merchant is binding just as though the letter or other writing had been signed. This ends the possibility of a situation under which the sender of the letter was bound but the receiver could safely ignore the transaction or could hold the sender as desired depending upon which alternative gave the better financial advantage.

Time of Execution

To satisfy the Statute of Frauds, a writing may be made at or any time after the making of the sale. It may even be made after the contract has been broken or a suit brought on it. The essential element is the existence—at the time the trial is held— of written proof of the transaction.

Particular Writings

The writing that satisfies the Statute of Frauds may be a single writing or it may be several writings considered as a group. Formal contracts, bills of sale, letters, and telegrams are common forms of writings that satisfy the Statute of Frauds. Purchase orders, cash register receipts, sales tickets, invoices, and similar papers generally do not satisfy the requirements as to a signature, and sometimes they do not specify any quantity or commodity.

QUESTIONS

1   If a contract for the sale of goods is for less than $500, in what form must it be to be enforceable?
2   What facts would be relevant to determining whether the purchase of a number of items is one sale or many sales?
3   a.   What is *receipt*?
    b.   What is *acceptance*?
4   Does part payment make an oral contract enforceable?
5   What is a judicial admission?
6   How does a contract for goods that are specifically manufactured for the buyer and not suitable for sale to others in the seller's ordinary course of business differ from an ordinary contract of sale?
7   What is an auction sale, and why is it peculiar to the law of sales?
8   In order to satisfy the Statute of Frauds for sales, what must a writing include?

CASE PROBLEMS

L.O.3 ....

1   Donald Fisher orally agreed to buy a sloop from Albert Cohn for $4,650. He gave Cohn a check for $2,325 on which was written, "deposit on aux. sloop, D'Arc Wind, full amount $4,650." They agreed to meet later for Fisher to pay the remainder of the purchase price and Cohn to transfer title. They had a disagreement and Fisher stopped payment on the check. Cohn readvertised the boat, sold it for the highest offer, $3,000, and sued Fisher for breach of contract. Did the check satisfy the memorandum requirements of the Statute of Frauds?

L.O.3 ....

2   After negotiations, Quality Oil Co. sent a letter to Pee Dee Oil Co. saying, "We propose to purchase your Shell contract for $75,000.00 and the Fastway station . . . for $140,000.00 . . . [W]e would pay you a reasonable market value for the equipment located at the Rockingham Self Service and Holiday Shell. We would . . . assume the leases on these locations . . . Please contact us as soon as you have made your decision on our proposal." Quality prepared a written contract, which Pee Dee signed and returned to Quality. Four months later, Quality had not signed the contract and Pee Dee had to sell some of the assets at a loss. When Pee Dee sued for breach of contract, Quality said the contract was not binding because quality had not signed it. Was there an enforceable contract?

L.O.1 ....

3   Wendell Ray, president of Raelyn International, placed an oral order for furniture from LEA Industries at a trade show. Raelyn sent a check in partial payment to LEA, which LEA accepted and deposited to its bank account. The check bounced. LEA sued for payment of this and other orders. Raelyn defended on the basis that the contract was unenforceable because it was oral. As the judge in the case, how would you decide?

L.O.1 ....

4   At a stockholders' meeting, Leonard Pirilla offered to buy all the outstanding shares of stock held by the shareholders in two corporations for $525,000 plus a $15,000 commission. The minutes of the meeting indicated that all the shareholders of the corporations were present in person or by proxy, all voted to accept the offer, and the officers of the corporations were authorized to implement the sale. They signed a Letter of Intent containing the terms of the sale. Pirilla tendered a Stock Purchase Agreement to the shareholders, but some refused to sign it. Pirilla sued for specific performance of the sale. The defense was the Statute of Frauds. Is there an enforceable contract?

L.O.1 ....

5   Mitchell Swerdloff was the manager of a Station Managers, Inc. (SMI), service station under a written agreement that could be terminated at will by either party. He alleged that Mobile Oil Corporation, which owned SMI, orally promised him that he would be granted a dealership of the station if and when it was converted from an SMI station to a straight dealership. Was the oral promise enforceable?

L.O.1 ....

6   Colorado Carpet Installation was in the business of buying carpet from manufacturers or wholesalers and reselling it to retail buyers. It submitted a proposal to Fred and Zuma Palermo to supply and install carpet in their home for $4,778. Believing Mrs. Palermo orally accepted its proposal, Colorado ordered that carpet, which, although a stock item, was to come from out-of-state suppliers. It was delivered to a warehouse. When the Palermos would not take the carpet, Colorado returned or sold the carpeting to others and sued the Palermos for breach of contract. Colorado alleged that the oral contract was enforceable because the carpeting was nonresellable goods. Was it?

L.O.1 ....

7   Larry Teel wanted to buy a 28-foot cruiser from Peoria Harbor Marina, but had a bad credit rating. However, his mother, Wilma McGlasson, agreed to buy the boat and he would pay her. The parties agreed on a price of $19,900,

a warranty, the slip rental, $200 deposit, and the balance due. These terms were written on a blank bill of sale form which also described the boat and which McGlasson and Peoria signed. Teel used the boat every week until it was stored for the winter. McGlasson could not find a bank that would finance the sale, so Teel attempted to pay rental and storage fees as if there had been a rental instead of a purchase. Peoria refused the payment, sold the boat, and sued for the amount it lost on the sale. McGlasson claimed no written contract existed, therefore the sale was not enforceable. Was there a written contract?

Chapter 18

TRANSFER OF TITLE AND RISK IN SALES CONTRACTS

LEARNING OBJECTIVES

After studying this chapter you should be able to:

1 Explain the importance of determining when title and risk of loss pass.

2 Distinguish between a sale on approval, a sale or return, and a consignment.

3 Explain the application of the law of sales to fungible goods.

4 Discuss the rule regarding attempted sales by people who do not have title to the goods, and list exceptions to the rule.

Preview Case

Roger and Sharon Russell agreed to sell Robert Clouser a boat for $8,500. Clouser made an initial payment of $1,700, with the balance to be paid upon possession. The Russells were to retain the boat to replace an engine and drive train, after which Clouser was to take delivery at their marina. No documents of title were required to sell a boat. Prior to delivery to Clouser, while being tested by the Russells' employees, the boat hit a seawall and was destroyed. The Russells' insurance policy with Transamerica Insurance Company did not cover damage resulting from watercraft hazard unless the watercraft was not owned by the Russells. Transamerica refused to pay, claiming the boat was owned by the Russells at the time of the accident. Who owned the boat?

L.O.1

Title
Evidence of ownership of property

hen a person owns a television set, that owner holds all the power to control the set. If desired, the set may be kept or sold. To signify ownership we say that the owner has **title** to the set. When sold, title to—and, normally, physical possession of—the set passes to the buyer who then has control over it. Normally, if the TV set is damaged or lost, the owner bears any loss. In business transactions, because of the large volume of goods dealt in and the need to arrange the sale of goods before they may even be in existence, all of which may make physical possession of the goods difficult or impossible, some problems may arise regarding title to goods and risk of loss.

POTENTIAL PROBLEMS

In the vast majority of sales transactions, the buyer receives the proper goods and makes payment, which completes the transaction. However, several types of problems may arise. For the most part, problems can be avoided if the parties expressly state their intentions in their sales contract. When the parties have not specified the results they desire, however, the rules in this chapter apply.

Creditors' Claims

Creditors of the seller may seize the goods as belonging to the seller, or the buyer's creditors may seize them on the theory that they belong to the buyer. In such a case it must be determined who owns the goods. The question of ownership is also important in connection with resale of the buyer, liability for or computation of certain kinds of taxes, and liability under certain registration and criminal statutes.

Insurance

Until the buyer has received the goods and the seller has been paid, both the seller and buyer have an economic interest in the sales transaction. The question arises as to whether either or both have enough interest to entitle them to insure the property involved; that is, whether they have an insurable interest.

Damage to Goods

If the goods are damaged or totally destroyed without any fault of either the buyer or the seller, must the seller bear the loss and supply new goods to the buyer? Or must the buyer pay the seller the purchase price even though the buyer now has no goods or has only damaged goods?

CLASSIFICATION OF SALES TRANSACTIONS

The nature of the transaction between the seller and the buyer determines the answer to be given to each question in the preceding section. Sales transactions may be classified according to (1) the nature of the goods and (2) the terms of the transaction.

Nature of Goods

As explained in Chapter 16, goods may be existing goods, identified goods, or future goods. Goods are existing goods even if the seller must do some act or complete the manufacture of the goods before they satisfy the terms of the contract.

Terms of the Transaction

**Warehouse
Receipt**

Document of title issued
by storage company for
goods stored

Bill of Lading

Carrier's receipt showing
terms of contract of transportation

The terms of the contract may require that the goods be sent or shipped to the buyer, that is, that the seller make shipment. In that case, the seller's part is performed when the goods are handed over to a carrier for shipment.

Instead of calling for actual delivery of goods, the transaction may involve a transfer of the document of title representing the goods. For example, the goods may be stored in a warehouse, the seller and the buyer having no intention of moving the goods, but intending that there should be a sale and a delivery of the **warehouse receipt** that stands for the goods. In this case the seller must produce the proper paper as distinguished from the goods themselves. The same is true when the goods are represented by a **bill of lading** issued by a carrier or by any other document of title.

TRANSFER OF TITLE, SPECIAL PROPERTY INTERESTS, AND RISK IN PARTICULAR TRANSACTIONS

The kinds of goods and transaction terms may be combined in a number of ways. Only the more common types of transactions will be considered here. The following rules of law apply only in the absence of a contrary agreement by the parties concerning these matters.

Existing Goods Identified at Time of Contracting

The title to existing goods identified at the time of contracting and not to be transported passes to the buyer at the time and place of contracting.

Roger and Sharon Russell agreed to sell Robert Clouser a boat for $8,500. Clouser made an initial payment of $1,700, with the balance to be paid upon possession. The Russells were to retain the boat to replace an engine and drive train, after which Clouser was to take delivery at their marina. Prior to delivery to Clouser, while being tested by the Russells' employees, the boat hit a seawall and was destroyed. The Russells' insurance policy with Transamerica Insurance Company did not cover damage resulting from watercraft hazard unless the watercraft was not owned by the Russells. Transamerica refused to pay, claiming the boat was owned by the Russells at the time of the accident. The court said that since the boat had been identified at the time of contracting, no documents were to be delivered, and delivery was to be made without the boat being moved, titled passed at the time of contracting.

If existing goods require transporting, title to the goods passes when the seller has completed delivery.

The buyer, who becomes the owner of the goods, has an insurable interest in them when title passes. Conversely, the seller no longer has an insurable interest unless by agreement a security interest has been reserved to protect the right to payment.

If the seller is a merchant, the risk of loss passes to the buyer when the goods are received from the merchant. If the seller is a nonmerchant seller, the risk passes when the seller tenders or makes available the goods to the buyer. Thus, the risk of loss remains longer on the merchant seller on the ground that the merchant seller, being in the business, can more readily arrange to be protected against such continued risk.

The fact that "title" to a motor vehicle has not been transferred because of a statute making the issuance of a title certificate essential for that purpose does not affect the transfer of the risk of loss as between the seller and buyer.

Negotiable Documents Representing Existing Goods Identified at Time of Contracting

When documents that can transfer title represent existing, identified goods, the buyer has a property interest, but not title, and an insurable interest in such goods at the time and place of contracting. The buyer does not ordinarily acquire the title nor become subject to the risk of loss until delivery of the documents is made. Conversely, the seller has an insurable interest and title up to that time.

Seller's Marking Future Goods for Buyer

A buyer may send an order for goods to be manufactured by the seller or to be filled from inventory or by purchases from third persons. If so, one step in the process of filling the order is the seller's act of marking, tagging, labeling, or in some way doing an act for the benefit of the shipping department or for the seller to indicate that certain goods are the ones to be sent or delivered to the buyer under contract. This act gives the buyer a property interest in the goods and the right to insure them. However, neither title nor risk of loss passes to the buyer until some event, such as a shipment or delivery, occurs. The seller, as continuing owner, also has an insurable interest in the goods until shipment or delivery.

Contract for Shipment of Future Goods

In this situation the buyer has placed an order for goods that will be shipped later. The contract is performed by the seller when the goods are delivered to a carrier for shipment to the buyer. Under such a contract the title and risk of loss pass to the buyer when the goods are delivered to the carrier, that is, at the time and place of shipment.

Home Liquors ordered whiskey valued at $21,302 from Black Prince Distillery. When the order was ready, Black Prince informed Royal Trucking that the goods were available to be picked up. Home confirmed the order in a writing that asked that the order be released to Royal. There was no direction regarding where the order was to be delivered. While Royal was on the way to a destination directed by Home, the shipment was hijacked. Black Prince sued Home for the contract price. The court said the transaction was clearly a shipping contract so title and risk of loss passed when the whiskey was released to the carrier, Royal.

DAMAGE TO OR DESTRUCTION OF GOODS

Damage to or the destruction of the goods affects the transaction as follows:

Damage to Identified Goods Before Risk of Loss Passes

When goods identified at the time of contracting suffer some damage or are destroyed without the fault of either party before the risk of loss has passed, the contract is avoided if the loss is total. If the loss is partial or if the goods have so deteriorated that they do not conform to the contract, the buyer has the option, after inspecting the goods, (1) to treat the contract as avoided, or (2) to accept the goods subject to an allowance or deduction from the contract price. In either case, the buyer cannot assert any claims against the seller for breach of contract.

Damage to Identified Goods After Risk of Loss Passes

If partial damage or total destruction occurs after the risk of loss has passed, it is the buyer's loss. The buyer may, however, be able to recover the amount of the damages from the person in possession of the goods or from a third person causing the loss. For example, in many instances the risk of loss passes at the time of the transaction even though the seller will deliver the goods later. During the period from the transfer of the risk of loss to the transfer of possession to the buyer, the seller has possession of the goods and is liable to the buyer for failure to exercise reasonable care.

Damage to Unidentified Goods

So long as the goods are unidentified, no risk of loss has passed to the buyer. If any goods are damaged or destroyed during this period, the seller bears the loss. The buyer may still enforce the contract and require the seller to deliver the goods according to the contract. A seller who fails to deliver the goods is liable to the purchaser for the breach of the contract. The only exception arises when the parties have provided in the contract that destruction of the seller's supply shall release the seller from liability or when the parties clearly contracted for the purchase and sale of part of the seller's supply to the exclusion of any other possible source of such goods.

Reservation of Title or Possession

When the seller reserves title or possession solely as security to make certain that payment will be made, the buyer bears the risk of loss if the circumstances are such that the buyer would bear the loss in the absence of such reservation.

SALES ON APPROVAL AND WITH RIGHT TO RETURN

Sale on Approval
Sale that is not completed until buyer approves goods

A sales transaction may give the buyer the privilege of returning the goods. In a **sale on approval,** the sale is not complete until the buyer approves the goods. A

L.O.2 ....

Sale or Return

Completed sale with right
to return goods

sale or return is a completed sale with the right of the buyer to return the goods and thereby set aside the sale. The agreement of the parties determines whether the sale is a sale on approval or a sale or return. If the parties fail to indicate their intention, a returnable-goods transaction is deemed a sale on approval if the goods are purchased for use, that is, by a consumer. It is deemed a sale or return if the goods are purchased for resale, that is, by a merchant.

Consequence of Sale on Approval

Unless agreed otherwise, title and risk of loss remain with the seller under a sale on approval. Use of the goods by the buyer consistent with the purpose of trial does not constitute approval. An approval occurs, however, if the buyer acts in a manner inconsistent with a reasonable trial, or if the buyer fails to express a choice within the time specified or within a reasonable time if no time is specified. If the buyer returns the goods, the seller bears the risk and the expense involved. Since the buyer is not the "owner" of the goods while they are on approval, the goods may not be claimed by the buyer's creditors.

Consequence of Sale or Return

Commercial Unit

Quantity regarded as separate unit

In a sale or return, title and risk of loss pass to the buyer as in the case of an ordinary sale. In the absence of a contrary agreement, the buyer under a sale or return may return all of the goods or any commercial unit thereof. A **commercial unit** includes any article, group of articles, or quantity commercially regarded as a separate unit or item, such as a particular machine, a suite of furniture, or a carload lot. The goods must still be in substantially their original condition, and the option to return must be exercised within the time specified by the contract or within a reasonable time if not specified. The return under such a contract is at the buyer's risk and expense. As long as the goods are in the buyer's possession, the buyer's creditors may treat the goods as belonging to the buyer.

Other Transactions

Consignment

Agency in which goods are in the possession of a nonowner in order to be sold

A **consignment** is not a sale on approval or a sale with right to return. In the absence of any contrary provision, it is merely an agency and denotes that property is in the possession of the consignee for sale. In the absence of some restriction, the consignor may revoke the agency at will and retake possession of the property. Whether goods are sent to a person as buyer or on consignment to sell for the owner is a question of the intention of the parties.

SALES OF FUNGIBLE GOODS

L.O.3 ....

Fungible Goods

Goods of a homogeneous nature sold by weight or measure

Fungible goods are goods of a homogeneous or like nature that may be sold by weight or measure. They include goods of which any unit is from its nature or by commercial usage treated as the equivalent of any other unit. Fungible goods include wheat, oil, coal, and similar bulk commodities, since any one bushel or other unit of the mass will be the same as any other bushel or similar unit within the same grade.

The UCC provides that title to an undivided share or quantity of an identified mass of fungible goods may pass to the buyer at the time of the transaction. This makes the buyer an owner in common with the seller. For example, when one person sells to another 600 bushels of wheat from a bin that contains 1,000 bushels, title to 600 bushels passes to the buyer at the time of the transaction. This gives the buyer a 6/10ths undivided interest in the mass as an owner in common with the seller. The courts in some states, however, have held that the title does not pass until a separation has been made.

SALE OF UNDIVIDED SHARES

The problem of the passage of title to a part of a larger mass of fungible goods differs from the problem of the passage of title when the sale is made of a fractional interest without any intention to make a later separation. In the former case the buyer will become the exclusive owner of a separated portion. In the latter case the buyer will become a co-owner of the entire mass. Thus, there may be a sale of a part interest in a radio, an automobile, or a flock of sheep. The right to make a sale of a fractional interest is recognized by statute.

AUCTION SALES

When goods are sold at an auction in separate lots, each lot is a separate transaction, and title to each passes independently of the other lots. Title to each lot passes when the auctioneer announces by the fall of the hammer or in any other customary manner that the auction is completed as to that lot.

FREE ON BOARD

F.O.B. (Free on Board)
Designated point to which seller bears risk and expense

A contract may call for goods to be sold **f.o.b., (free on board)** a designated point. Goods may be sold f.o.b. the seller's plant, the buyer's plant, an intermediate point, or a specified carrier. The seller bears the risk and expense until the goods are delivered at the f.o.b. point designated.

Saul Boyman contracted to buy a boat. The contract required the boat to be delivered "F.O.B. Stuart, Florida." The boat was manufactured in North Carolina and shipped by ocean freight to Stuart, Florida. A dispute about the sale resulted in a lawsuit in which the seller of the boat alleged that Boyman was required to pay the freight charge. The court held the term "F.O.B. Stuart" required the seller to pay freight charges until the boat reached its destination, Stuart, Florida.

C.O.D. SHIPMENT

In the absence of an extension of credit, a seller has the right to keep the goods until paid. The seller loses this right if possession of the goods is delivered to anyone for the buyer. However, where the goods are delivered to a carrier, the seller may keep the right to possession by making the shipment C.O.D., or by the addition of any other terms indicating that the carrier is not to surrender the goods to the buyer until the buyer has paid. The C.O.D. provision does not affect when title or risk of loss passes.

TRANSFER OF TITLE

L.O.4 ....

Bailment

Temporary transfer of possession of personal property

As a general rule, people can sell only such interest or title in goods as they possess. If property is subject to a **bailment** (personal property temporarily in the custody of another person), a sale by the owner is subject to the bailment. Thus, if the owner of a rented car sells the car to another person, the person who has rented the car, the bailee, may still use the car according to the terms of the bailment. Similarly, bailees can only transfer their individual rights under the bailments, assuming that the bailment agreements permit the rights to be assigned or transferred.

A thief or finder generally cannot transfer the title to property. Only that which a person has—possession in the case of a thief or finder—can be passed. In fact, the purchaser from the thief not only fails to obtain title but also becomes liable to the owner as a converter of the property. Liability occurs even though the property may have been purchased in good faith.

W. A. Andres rented his motor home to Phillip Robertson, who was really Lewis Murphy. Murphy obtained an Alabama registration for the motor home under the name L. E. Boggs. Nebraska provided Boggs a certificate of title, which was transferred to Murphy. Murphy traded the home to McDonald's Chevrolet, Inc., after applying for an Indiana certificate of title. Otis Johnson purchased the motor home from McDonald's. It was seized by the Indiana State Police and given to Andres' insurer, Foremost Insurance Company. Johnson sued Foremost to recover the home. Since Murphy did not have title, he could not convey title to McDonald's, and McDonald's could not convey title to Johnson. Even though Johnson did not know the motor home was stolen and even though he had paid for it, Johnson was not entitled to it.

Certain instances occur, however, when because of the conduct of the owner or the desire of society to protect the bona fide purchaser for value, the law permits a greater title to be transferred than the seller possesses.

Sale by Entrustee

If the owner entrusts goods to a merchant who deals in goods of that kind, the merchant has the power to transfer the entruster's title to anyone who buys in the ordinary course of business. This is true as long as the merchant is not doing business in the entrusting owner's name. Similarly, the goods are subject to the claims of the merchant's creditors.

It is immaterial why the goods were entrusted to the merchant. Hence the leaving of a watch for repairs with a jeweler who sells new and secondhand watches would give the jeweler the power to pass the title to a buyer in the ordinary course of business. The entrustee is, of course, liable to the owner for damages caused by the sale of the goods and may be guilty of a statutory offense such as embezzlement.

If the entrustee is not a merchant, but merely a prospective customer, no transfer of title occurs when the entrustee sells to a third person.

Consignment Sales

Consignment

Transfer of possession of goods for purpose of sale

A manufacturer or distributor may send goods to a dealer for sale to the public with the understanding that the manufacturer or distributor is to remain the owner and the dealer is, in effect, to act as an agent. This is a **consignment.** Title does not normally pass to the consignee. However, when the dealer maintains a place of business at which dealings are made in goods of the kind in question under a name other than that of the consigning manufacturer or distributor, the creditors of the dealer may reach the goods as though the dealer owned the goods.

Estoppel

The owner of property may be estopped (barred) from asserting ownership and denying the right of another person to sell the property to a good-faith purchaser. A person may purchase a product and have the bill of sale made out in the name of a friend who receives possession of the product and the bill of sale. This might be done in order to deceive creditors or to keep other persons from knowing that the purchase had been made. If the friend should sell the product to a bona fide purchaser who relies on the bill of sale, the true owner is estopped or barred from denying the friend's apparent ownership.

United Road Machinery Co. leased a truck scale to Consolidated Coal Co. United paid for the scale and told the supplier of the scale that Consolidated would take possession, which it did. United sent a contract for the lease to Consolidated, which never returned the contract. Consolidated took the scale to its place of business in Laurel County, added decking, and then sold it to Kentucky Mobile Homes of Pulaski County. Kentucky had had the records of Laurel and Pulaski Counties checked and found there was no encumbrance shown against the scale. Kentucky then sold the scale to Clyde Jasper, who had also searched the records for an encumbrance on the scale. Neither Kentucky nor Jasper knew of any dispute between United and Consolidated. When it failed to receive any payment from Consolidated, United sued Jasper for the scale. The court found that there was nothing to suggest that Consolidated was not the owner of the scale as against Jasper, a good-faith purchaser. United was estopped from asserting its title against Jasper.

Documents of Title

Document of Title

Document that shows ownership

Documents that show ownership are called **documents of title.** They include bills of lading and warehouse receipts. By statute, certain documents of title, when executed in the proper form, may transfer title. The holder of such a document may convey the title of the person who left the property with the issuer of the document if all of the following conditions are met:

1   The document indicates it may be transferred.
2   The transferee does not know of any wrongdoing.
3   The transferee has purchased the document by giving up something of value.

In such cases, it is immaterial that the transferor had not acquired the documents in a lawful manner.

Recording and Filing Statutes

In order to protect subsequent purchasers and creditors, statutes may require that certain transactions be recorded or filed. The statutes may provide that a transaction not recorded or filed has no effect against a purchaser who thereafter buys the goods in good faith from the person who appears to be the owner or against creditors who have lawfully seized the goods of such an apparent owner. Suppose a seller makes a credit sale and wants to be able to seize and sell the goods if the buyer does not make payment. The UCC requires the seller to file certain papers. If they are not filed, the buyer will appear to own the goods free from any interest of the seller. Subsequent bona fide purchasers or creditors of the buyer can acquire title, and the seller will lose the right to repossess the goods.

Voidable Title

If the buyer has a voidable title, as when the goods were obtained by fraud, the seller can rescind the sale while the buyer is still the owner. If, however, the buyer resells the property to a bona fide purchaser before the seller has rescinded the transaction, the subsequent purchaser acquires valid title. It is immaterial whether the buyer having the voidable title had obtained title by fraud as to identity, or by larceny by trick, or that payment for the goods had been made with a bad check, or that the transaction was a cash sale and the purchase price has not been paid.

QUESTIONS

1 What is title and why is it normally important?
2 If the terms of a sales transaction require that the goods be shipped by the seller to the buyer, when is the seller considered to have completed performance?
3 Must the goods themselves always be transferred from seller to buyer in order for there to be a sale?
4 When does title to existing and identified goods that are not to be transported pass?
5 If the seller of identified goods is a merchant, when does risk of loss pass?
6 If damage occurs to identified goods before risk of loss passes, what options does the buyer have?
7 Distinguish among a *sale on approval,* a *sale or return,* and a *consignment.*
8 a. What are *fungible goods*?
   b. When does title to fungible goods pass?
9 a. What is the rule regarding attempted sales by people who do not have title to the goods?
   b. List six exceptions.
10 If Holmes leaves a portable television set for repair with Ace TV (repair shop and dealer in new and used sets), and Ace sells the set to Lodder, would the buyer get good title?

CASE PROBLEMS

L.O.1 ....

1 Andrew Pruitt, a supervisor of the commissary meat department at Fort Lewis, diverted meat ordered for Fort Lewis to his two restaurants. Pruitt instructed Randy's Meats to set aside an order of meat for Fort Lewis in a "will-call" trailer to be picked up later. Randy's marked the top boxes "Fort Lewis" and entered the number on each box on the invoices for Fort Lewis. A person who told Randy's he was acting for Pruitt picked up the meat and delivered it to the restaurants. When charged with conspiracy and theft, the restaurants alleged the meat was not government property. Was it?

L.O.1 ....

2 Tri-State Contracting & Trading Corporation contracted with Saudi Arabian importers for the sale of Pepsi-Cola. The containers of soda were sealed at the warehouse and delivered to ocean terminals to be put on ocean carriers. The ocean carriers issued negotiable bills of lading for the soda to Tri-State, which was fully paid for the sale. When the shipment arrived in Saudi Arabia the cans of soda had sustained significant leakage and were not merchantable. Would the carriers be liable to Tri-State?

L.O.1 ....

3 Russ Bullock met with Parkes Shewmake, an official of Joe Bailey Auction Company, to arrange for Shewmake to act as a bidder for Bullock at an auction. Verification of financing was received, and Shewmake successfully bid on the equipment for Bullock. The equipment was not in operable condition. It was left at the auction site until after Bullock performed extensive repairs and removed it to Utah. Bullock's financing was delayed, and he gave Shewmake a check which stated, "Not to be presented to the bank for collection until adequate financing is completed." When the check could not be negotiated, Bailey indicated he intended to reclaim the equipment, alleging no sale occurred because payment had not been made. Was there a sale?

L.O.2 ....

4 Danny Fuller opened a store called Danny's Drapery Outlet. Sixteen days later a fire destroyed its contents. Some of Fuller's inventory had been received from Amcrest Textiles. When sued for the price of the Amcrest goods, Fuller claimed his arrangement with Amcrest was a consignment— that he was to get a percentage of anything he sold. Amcrest had sent Fuller invoices which said "PAY BY THIS INVOICE" and "no returns will be accepted unless authorized in writing" by Amcrest. If the transaction was a sale, Fuller had title and had to pay for the goods. If it was a consignment, title had not passed to Fuller and Amcrest would bear the risk of loss. What was the transaction?

L.O.2 ....

5 Anthony Coppola ordered some coins from First Coinvestors, Inc., under an agreement that the coins would be paid for or returned within ten days. Coppola was not in the business of selling coins but was a collector. The package of coins was delivered to a person on Coppola's property who signed for them, but no one knew who he was or what happened to the coins. Coinvestors sued Coppola for the value of the coins. Is he liable?

L.O.4 .... **6** A farmer, Carl Davidson, leased 100 head of cattle from Matthew Bauer. Davidson "sold" some of them to R. D. Curran. When sued by Bauer, Curran alleged that Davidson was a merchant who dealt in cattle; therefore, he had the power to transfer title to the cattle. Evidence at the trial was that Davidson had previously sold part of the cattle he leased, but at Bauer's direction and in his name. Davidson had only bought or sold his own cattle occasionally. Who owns the cattle?

L.O.1 .... **7** A & M Engineering Plastics in Pinellas County contracted to supply plastic parts and moldings to Energy Saving Technology in Broward County. The contract called for prices to be f.o.b. Clearwater in Pinellas County. Several shipments were made, but then a machinery breakdown resulted in a shutdown. Technology sued A & M in Broward County. A & M alleged the suit had to be filed in Pinellas County. The suit had to be filed in the county in which the covenant alleged to have been breached was supposed to be performed. If the breached covenant was failure to supply the parts, where was the contract breached?

L.O.2 .... **8** Kenneth Stevenson, a car dealer, doing business as T & S Enterprises, asked Peter Pan Motors if it could find a certain kind of white BMW. Peter Pan said it could and located and bought one. T & S picked up the car. The parties had made previous deals in which Peter Pan would sell T & S cars and T & S would resell them. T & S deposited payment for the BMW in Peter Pan's bank account, but stopped payment on the check and told Peter Pan it did not want the car. While T & S had the BMW, a creditor, Wayne Minor claimed it. He said the transaction was a sale or return, so the BMW's title passed to T & S and Minor had a valid claim against it. Was there a sale or return?

Chapter 19

WARRANTIES AND PRODUCT LIABILITY

LEARNING OBJECTIVES

After studying this chapter you should be able to:

1 Define a warranty, and distinguish between express and implied warranties.

2 Specify the warranties that apply to all sellers and those that apply only to merchants.

3 Explain how warranties may be excluded or surrendered.

4 List the different theories by which a person may be entitled to recover damages for personal injury or property damage.

Preview Case

Gerard Construction, Inc., executed a bill of sale for a towboat to Phillip Mossesso and Donald Fix. Paragraph 2 of the bill of sale stated, "Seller warrants title to be good and marketable and free of all debts, liens, and encumbrances." Paragraph 5 stated, "Seller states that it is its belief that the vessel is now operative and in a safe condition and is not in violation of any federal regulation." Mossesso and Fix used the boat and then tried to rescind the transaction, claiming Paragraph 5 constituted a warranty. Did the language of Paragraph 5 create a warranty?

L.O.1

Warranty
Assurance article conforms to a standard

In making a sale, a seller often makes a **warranty**: an assurance that the article will conform to a certain standard or will operate in a certain manner. By the warranty the seller agrees in effect to make good any loss or damages that the purchaser may suffer if the goods are not as represented.

A warranty made at the time of the sale is considered to be a part of the contract and is therefore binding. A warranty made after a sale has been completed is binding even though not supported by any consideration; it is regarded as a modification of the sales contract.

EXPRESS WARRANTIES

Express Warranty

Statement of guarantee by seller

The statement of the seller in which the article is warranted or guaranteed is known as an **express warranty.** The UCC specifically provides that any affirmation of fact or promise made by the seller to the buyer that relates to the goods and becomes part of the basis of the bargain creates an express warranty. The seller actually and definitely states an express warranty either orally or in writing.

The seller needs no particular words to constitute an express warranty. The words "warranty" or "guarantee" need not be used. If a reasonable interpretation of the language of a statement or a promise leads the buyer to believe a warranty exists, the courts will construe it as such. A seller is bound by the ordinary meaning of the words used not by any unexpressed intentions.

The seller can use the word "warrant" or "guarantee" and still not be bound by it if an ordinary, prudent person would not interpret it to constitute a warranty. If the seller of a car says, "I'll guarantee that you will not be sorry if you buy the car at this price," no warranty exists. This is mere sales talk, even though the seller used the word "guarantee."

Seller's Opinion

The law holds that sellers may praise their wares, even extravagantly, without being obligated on their statements or representations. A person should not be misled by "puffing." Such borderline expressions as "best on the market for the money," "these goods are worth $10 if they are worth a dime," "experts have estimated that one ought to be able to sell a thousand a month of these," and many others, which sound very convincing but which have been held to be mere expressions of opinion, are not warranties.

Gerard Construction, Inc., executed a bill of sale for a towboat to Phillip Mossesso and Donald Fix. Paragraph 2 of the bill of sale stated, "Seller warrants title to be good and marketable and free of all debts, liens, and encumbrances." Paragraph 5 stated, "Seller states that it is its belief that the vessel is now operative and in a safe condition and is not in violation of any federal regulation." Mossesso and Fix used the boat and then tried to rescind the transaction, claiming Paragraph 5 constituted a warranty. The court found the language of Paragraph 5 was clearly drafted in pursuance of the UCC provision regarding a seller's opinion not creating a warranty. Also, Paragraph 2 clearly indicated that the parties knew how to embody a warranty when they wanted to.

The rule that a statement of opinion or belief does not constitute a warranty must be qualified. Although an expression by the seller of what is clearly an opinion does not normally constitute either a warranty or a basis for fraud liability, the seller may be liable for fraud if, in fact, the seller does not believe the opinion. Also, a representation by the seller is a warranty if the seller asserts a fact of which the buyer is ignorant. If the seller merely states an opinion on a matter of which the seller has no special knowledge and on which the buyer may be expected also to have an opinion and exercise judgment, it is not a warranty.

Defects

If defects are actually known to the buyer, or defects are so apparent that no special skill or ability is required to detect them, an express warranty may not cover them. The determining factor is whether the statement becomes a part of the basis of the bargain. If it does, an express warranty results. This would not be true if the seller used any scheme or artifice to conceal the defect such as covering the defect with an item of decoration. The seller must not do anything for the purpose of diverting the attention of the buyer from the defects.

IMPLIED WARRANTIES

Implied Warranty
Warranty imposed by law

An **implied warranty** is one that was not made by the seller but which is imposed by the law. The implied warranty arises automatically from the fact that a sale has been made. Express warranties arise because they form part of the basis on which the sale has been made.

Express warranties do not exclude implied warranties. When both express and implied warranties exist, they should be construed as consistent with each other. When not construed as consistent, an express warranty prevails over an implied warranty as to the same subject matter, except in the case of an implied warranty of fitness for a particular purpose.

FULL OR LIMITED WARRANTIES

Full Warranty
Warranty with unlimited duration of implied warranties; any limits on consequential damages conspicuous; and if product defective, free repair

Limited Warranty
Written warranty not a full warranty

A written warranty made for a consumer product may be either a full warranty or a limited warranty. The seller of a product with a **full warranty** must remedy any defects in the product in a reasonable time without charge, place no limit on the duration of implied warranties, not limit consequential damages for breach of warranty unless done conspicuously on the warranty's face, and permit the purchaser to choose a refund or replacement without charge if the product contains a defect after a reasonable number of attempts by the warrantor to remedy the defects. All other written warranties for consumer products are **limited warranties** (see Illustration 19-1).

WARRANTIES OF ALL SELLERS

L.O.2 ....

The following warranties apply to all sellers:

Warranty of Title

All sellers, by the mere act of selling, make a warranty that they have good titles and make rightful transfers. A warranty of title may be excluded or modified by the specific language or the circumstances of the transaction. The latter situation occurs

Illustration 19-1   Limited Warranty

ONE YEAR LIMITED WARRANTY

ABC Company warrants this product, to original owner, for one year from purchase date to be free of defects in material and workmanship.

Defective product may be brought or sent (freight prepaid) to an authorized service center listed in the phone book, or to Service Department, ABC Company, Main and First Streets, Riverdale, MO 65000, for free repair or replacement at our option.

Warranty does not include: cost of inconvenience, damage due to product failure, transportation damages, misuse, abuse, accident or the like, or commercial use. IN NO EVENT SHALL THE ABC COMPANY BE LIABLE FOR INCIDENTAL OR CONSEQUENTIAL DAMAGES. Some states do not allow exclusion or limitation of incidental or consequential damages, so above exclusion may not apply.

This warranty is the only written or express warranty given by The ABC Company. This warranty gives specific legal rights. You may have other rights which vary from state to state.

For information, write Consumer Claims Manager, at the Riverdale address. Send name, address, zip, model, serial number, and purchase date.

Keep this booklet. Record the following for reference:

Data purchased _____

Model Number _____

Serial Number _____

---

when the buyer has reason to know that the seller does not claim title or that the seller is purporting to sell only such right or title as the seller or a third person may have. For example, no warranty of title arises when the seller makes the sale in a representative capacity, such as a sheriff, an auctioneer, or an administrator. Likewise no warranty arises when the seller makes the sale by virtue of a power of sale possessed as a pledgee or mortgagee.

Warranty Against Encumbrances

In addition to a warranty of title, every seller makes a warranty that the goods shall be delivered free from any security interest or any other lien or encumbrance of which the buyer at the time of making the sales contract had no knowledge. Thus, a breach of warranty exists when the automobile sold to the buyer is already subject to an outstanding claim that had been placed against it by the original owner and which was unknown to the buyer at the time of the sale.

The warranty against encumbrances applies to the goods only at the time they are delivered to the buyer. It is not concerned with an encumbrance that existed before or at the time the sale was made. For example, a seller may not have paid in full for the goods being resold, and the original supplier may have a lien on the goods. The seller may resell the goods while that lien is still on them. The seller's only duty is to pay off the lien before the goods are delivered to the buyer.

A warranty against encumbrances does not arise if the buyer knows of the existence of the encumbrance in question. Knowledge must be actual knowledge as contrasted with constructive notice. **Constructive notice** is information that the law

Constructive Notice

Information or knowledge imputed by law

presumes everyone knows by virtue of the fact that it is filed or recorded on the public record.

Warranty of Conformity to Description, Sample, or Model

Sample

Portion of whole mass of transaction

Model

Replica of an article

Any description of the goods, sample, or model made part of the basis of the sales contract creates an express warranty that the goods shall conform in kind and quality to the description, sample, or model. Ordinarily, a **sample** is a portion of a whole mass that is the subject of the transaction. A **model** is a replica of the article in question. The mere fact that a sample is exhibited in the course of negotiations does not make the sale a sale by sample. There must be an intent shown that the sample is part of the basis of contracting.

Warranty of Fitness for a Particular Purpose

When the seller has reason to know at the time of contracting that the buyer intends to use the goods for a particular or unusual purpose, the seller may make an implied warranty that the goods will be fit for that purpose. Such an implied warranty arises when the buyer relies on the seller's skill or judgment to select or furnish suitable goods and when the seller has reason to know of the buyer's reliance. For example, where a government representative inquired of the seller whether the seller had a tape suitable for use on a particular government computer system, there arose an implied warranty, unless otherwise excluded, that the tape furnished by the seller was fit for that purpose. This warranty of fitness for a particular purpose does not arise when the goods are to be used for the purpose for which they are customarily sold or when the buyer orders goods on particular specifications and does not disclose the purpose.

The fact that a seller does not intend to make a warranty of fitness for a particular purpose is immaterial. Parol evidence is admissible to show that the seller had knowledge of the buyer's intended use.

ADDITIONAL WARRANTIES OF MERCHANT

Merchant

Person who deals in goods of the kind or by occupation is considered to have particular knowledge or skill regarding goods involved

A seller who deals in goods of the kind or who is considered, because of occupation, to have particular knowledge or skill regarding the goods involved is a **merchant.** Such a seller makes additional implied warranties.

Warranty Against Infringement

Unless otherwise agreed, a merchant warrants that goods shall be delivered free of the rightful claim of any third person by way of patent or trademark infringement. A buyer sued for infringement must notify the seller. A buyer who supplies the seller with specifications must protect the seller against claims growing out of compliance with the specifications. If the buyer has provided specifications, the seller must notify the buyer of an infringement suit.

Warranty of Merchantability or Fitness for Normal Use

Unless excluded or modified, merchant sellers make an implied warranty of merchantability, which results in a group of warranties. The most important is that the goods are fit for the ordinary purposes for which they are sold. Consequently, when the seller of ice-making and beverage-vending machines is a merchant of such machines, an implied warranty of fitness for use arises. Also included are implied warranties as to the general or average quality of the goods and their packaging and labeling.

The implied warranty of merchantability relates to the condition of the goods at the time the seller is to perform under the contract. Once the risk of loss has passed to the buyer, no warranty exists as to the continuing merchantability of the goods unless such subsequent deterioration or condition is proof that the goods were in fact not merchantable when the seller made delivery.

Warranty of merchantability relates only to the fitness of the product made or sold. It does not impose upon the manufacturer or seller the duty to employ any particular design or to sell one product rather than another because another might be safer.

Gina and Douglas Felde bought a new car from Schaumburg Dodge and signed a contract to make 48 monthly payments to Chrysler Credit Corp. Three weeks later, Gina noticed the car occasionally surged forward and accelerated by itself. She took it to the dealer who replaced the throttle sensor. The problem continued and Gina took the car back two or three times more, but the acceleration continued. Gina took the car to another dealer five times for the problem. The throttle sensor was replaced three times, but the sudden acceleration was not corrected. A year after buying the car, it lurched forward from a stop when Gina took her foot off the brake and it hit a truck. Gina had the car towed to Schaumburg Dodge. The manager called her the next day and told her she would be charged for storage. Gina told him to keep the car. The Feldes sued for breach of the implied warranty of merchantability. At trial a certified mechanic testified that the car was not safe to drive. The court said the warranty was breached.

WARRANTIES IN PARTICULAR SALES

As discussed in the following sections, particular types of sales may involve special considerations.

Sale of Food or Drink

The sale of food or drink, whether to be consumed on or off the seller's premises, is a sale. When made by a merchant, the sale carries the implied warranty that the food is fit for its ordinary purpose or human consumption. Under the prior law some authorities held that no breach of warranty occurred when a harmful object found in the food was natural to the particular kind of food, such as an oyster shell in oysters, a chicken bone in chicken, and so on.

Other cases regarded the warranty as breached when the presence of the harm-causing substance in the food could not be reasonably expected, without regard to whether the substance was natural or foreign, as in the case of a nail or piece of glass. In these cases a determination of fact must be made, ordinarily by the jury, to determine whether the buyer could reasonably expect the object in the food. The UCC does not end the conflict between the courts applying the "foreign/natural" test and those applying the "reasonable expectation" test.

It is, of course, necessary to distinguish the foregoing situations from those in which the preparation of the foods contemplates the continued presence of some element such as prune stones in cooked prunes.

Ginger Lee Jeffries ordered a "crab melt" sandwich from Clark's Restaurant Enterprises, Inc. It contained a piece of crab shell one inch in diameter, which Jeffries did not see. The crab shell lodged in her esophagus and had to be removed surgically. Jeffries filed suit for damages. The court held that it was a question for the jury whether Jeffries should have reasonably expected to find such a piece of shell in the sandwich.

Sale of Article with Patent or Trade Name

The sale of a patent- or trade-name article is treated with respect to warranties in the same way as any other sale. The fact that the sale is made on the basis of the patent or trade name does not bar the existence of a warranty of fitness for a particular purpose or of merchantability when the circumstances giving rise to such a warranty otherwise exist.

It is a question of fact, however, whether the buyer relied on the seller's skill and judgment when making the purchase. If the buyer asked for a patent- or trade-name article and insisted on it, the buyer clearly did not rely on the seller's skill and judgment. Therefore the sale lacks the factual basis for an implied warranty of fitness for the particular purpose. If the necessary reliance upon the seller's skill and judgment is shown, however, the warranty arises in that situation.

Sperry Rand Corp. agreed to convert the record-keeping system of Industrial Supply Corp. so that it could be maintained by a computer. Sperry Rand also agreed to sell a computer and nine other items necessary for such a record-keeping system. The computer and the equipment were ordered by identified trade name and number. When the system did not work, Industrial Supply sued Sperry Rand for breach of implied warranty of fitness. Sperry Rand raised the defense that no such warranty existed because the equipment had been ordered by trade name and number. The court held that the fact that the equipment was ordered by trade name and number did not automatically extinguish the warranty of fitness. The circumstances showed the sale was made in reliance on the seller's skill, and with appreciation of the buyer's problems, and the sale of the particular equipment to the buyer was made as constituting the equipment needed by it. Under such circumstances, a warranty of the fitness of the equipment for such purpose was implied.

The seller of automobile parts is not liable for breach of the implied warranty of their fitness when the parts were ordered by catalog number for use in a specified vehicle and the seller did not know that the lubrication system of the automobile had been changed so as to make the parts ordered unfit for use.

Sale on Buyer's Specifications

When the buyer furnishes the seller with exact specifications for the preparation or manufacture of goods, the same warranties arise as in the case of any other sale of such goods by the particular seller. No warranty of fitness for a particular purpose can arise, however, since the buyer is clearly purchasing on the basis of a decision made without relying on the seller's skill and judgment.

In sales made upon the buyer's specifications, the merchant seller makes no implied warranty against infringement. Conversely, the buyer in substance makes a warranty to protect the seller from liability should the seller be held liable for patent violation by following the specifications of the buyer.

Sale of Secondhand or Used Goods

No warranty arises as to fitness of used property for ordinary use from a sale made by a casual seller. If made by a merchant seller, such a warranty may exist. A number of states follow the rule that implied warranties may apply in connection with the sale of used or secondhand goods, particularly automobiles and equipment.

EXCLUSION AND SURRENDER OF WARRANTIES

L.O.3 .... Warranties can be excluded or modified by the agreement of the parties, subject to the limitation that such a provision must not be unconscionable.

The jury may consider the purchase price in determining the scope of the warranty of fitness, as where coal was bought for one half or less the price of standard coal.

If a warranty of fitness is to be excluded, the exclusion must be in writing and so conspicuous as to assure that the buyer will be aware of its presence. If the implied warranty of merchantability is excluded or modified, the exclusion clause must expressly mention the word "merchantability" and if in writing must be conspicuous.

Particular Provisions

Such a statement as "there are no warranties that extend beyond the description on the face hereof" excludes all implied warranties of fitness. Normally, implied warranties are excluded by the statement "as is," "with all faults," or other language that in normal common speech calls attention to the warranty exclusion and makes it clear that no implied warranty exists. An implied warranty that a steam heater would work properly in the buyer's dry cleaning plant was effectively excluded by provisions that "the warranties and guarantees herein set forth are made by us and accepted by you in lieu of all statutory or implied warranties or guarantees, other than title. . . . This contract contains all agreements between the parties, and there is no agreement, verbal or otherwise, that is not set down herein," and the contract had only a "one-year warranty on labor and material supplied by seller."

In order for a disclaimer of warranties to be a binding part of an oral sales contract, the disclaimer must be called to the attention of the buyer. When the contract as made does not disclaim warranties, a disclaimer of warranties accompanying goods delivered later is not effective because it is a unilateral attempt to modify the contract.

Examination

No implied warranty exists with respect to defects in goods that an examination should have revealed when, before making the final contract, the buyer has examined as fully as desired the goods, or a model or sample, or has refused to make such examination.

Dealings and Customs

An implied warranty can be excluded or modified by course of dealings, course of performance, or usage of trade.

> Standard Structural Steel Co. contracted to remove the truss spans of a bridge. It decided to use a derrick system utilizing a cable to remove the sections of the span. A number of derricks and barges were involved in the system. Standard consulted with Bethlehem Steel Corp. and then telephoned an order for bridge strand cable to Bethlehem. Bethlehem had been a major supplier of Standard's for 62 years. Standard knew it was Bethlehem's policy to sell products only with disclaimers of the warranties of merchantability and fitness for a particular purpose. When Standard was removing the first section of bridge span, some strands of the cable broke and an accident occurred that seriously damaged Standard's equipment. Standard sued Bethlehem for breach of the warranties of merchantability and fitness for a particular purpose. The court held that the oral agreement by telephone included Standard's understanding from the 62-year course of dealing that Bethlehem would not sell products without excluding the implied warranties.

CAVEAT EMPTOR

Caveat Emptor

Let the buyer beware

In the absence of fraud on the part of the seller or circumstances in which the law imposes a warranty, the relationship of the seller and the buyer is described by the maxim **caveat emptor** (let the buyer beware). Courts at common law rigidly applied this rule, requiring purchasers in ordinary sales to act in reliance upon their own judgment except when sellers gave express warranties. The trend of the earlier statutes, the UCC, and decisions of modern courts have been to soften the harshness of this rule, primarily by establishing implied warranties for the protection of the buyer. Consumer protection statutes have also greatly soften this rule. The rule of caveat emptor still applies, however, when the buyer has full opportunity to make such examination of the goods as would disclose the existence of any defect and the seller has not committed fraud.

PRODUCT LIABILITY

L.O.4 ....

When harm to person or property results from the use or condition of an article of personal property, the person injured may be entitled to recover damages. This right may be based on the theory of breach of warranty.

Breach of Warranty

Privity of Contract

Relationship between contracting parties

At common law there could be no suit for breach of warranty unless **privity of contract** (a contract relationship) existed between the plaintiff and the defendant. A growing trend exists to allow recovery by the "stranger" on the theory of breach of warranty. For example, it has been held that a mechanic injured because of a defect in the automobile being fixed may sue the manufacturer for breach of implied warranty of fitness.

In most states an exception to the privity rule allows members of the buyer's family and various other persons not in privity of contract with the seller or manufacturer to sue for breach of warranty when injured by the harmful condition of food, beverages, or drugs.

The UCC expressly abolished the requirement of privity against the seller by members of the buyer's family, household, and guests in actions for personal injury. Apart from the express provision made by the UCC, a conflict of authority exists as to whether other cases require privity of contract. The trend leans toward the abolition of the privity requirement. Many states flatly reject the doctrine when a buyer sues the manufacturer or a prior seller. In many instances, recovery by the buyer against the remote manufacturer or seller is based on the fact that the defendant had advertised directly to the public and therefore made a warranty to the purchasing consumer of the truth of the advertising. Although advertising by the manufacturer to the consumer is a reason for not requiring privity when the consumer sues the manufacturer, the absence of advertising by the manufacturer frequently does not bar such action by the buyer. While most jurisdictions have modified the privity requirement beyond the exceptions specified in the UCC, each state has retained limited applications of the doctrine.

> While William Bernick was playing hockey for Georgia Tech he was struck in the face by a hockey stick. His mouthguard was shattered, his upper jaw fractured, three teeth knocked out, and a part of a fourth tooth broken off. The manufacturer of the mouthguard, Cooper of Canada, Ltd., had promoted it through hockey catalog advertisements and parent guides as giving "maximum protection to the lips and teeth." The language was such as to induce the purchase of the mouthguard by Bernick's mother for his use while playing. Bernick did rely on an express warranty.

Recovery may also be allowed when the consumer mails to the manufacturer a warranty registration card that the manufacturer had packed with the purchased article.

Effect of Reprocessing by Distributor

Liability of the manufacturer or supplier to the ultimate consumer for breach of warranty or negligence does not arise when the manufacturer or supplier believes or has reason to believe that the immediate distributor or processor will complete processing or will take further steps to remove an otherwise foreseeable danger.

Emil Suhrmann operated a delicatessen at which he sold mettwurst, a pork sausage. Suhrmann's supplier had been heating the sausage to 137º to destroy any trichinae. The supplier informed Suhrmann that it could no longer supply him with mettwurst because it could no longer heat it. Suhrmann replied, "I will finish" the mettwurst. "What you cannot do I will complete." The supplier then processed the mettwurst without heating it and delivered the unfinished product to Suhrmann. Kurt Schneider purchased mettwurst from Suhrmann and after eating it contracted trichinosis. He sued Suhrmann and the supplier. While Suhrmann was liable, the supplier was not because it did not know or have any reason to suspect that Suhrmann would fail to process the sausage.

IDENTITY OF PARTIES

The existence of product liability may be affected by the identity of the claimant or of the defendant.

Third Persons

While the UCC permits recovery for breach of warranty by the guests of the buyer, it makes no provision for recovery by employees or strangers.

A conflict of authority exists as to whether an employee of the buyer may sue the seller or manufacturer for breach of warranty. Some jurisdictions deny recovery on the ground that the employee is outside of the distributive chain, not being a buyer. Others allow recovery in such a case. By the latter view, an employee of a construction contractor may recover for breach of the implied warranty of fitness made by the manufacturer of the structural steel that proved defective and fell, injuring the employee.

Manufacturer of Component Part

Many items of goods in today's marketplace were not made entirely by one manufacturer. Thus, the harm caused may result from a defect in a component part of the finished product. Since the manufacturer of the total article was the buyer from the component-part manufacturer, the privity rule barred suit against the component-part manufacturer for breach of warranty by anyone injured. In jurisdictions in which privity of contract is not recognized as a bar to recovery, it is not material that the defendant manufactured merely a component part. In these cases, the manufacturer of a component part cannot defend from suit by the ultimate purchaser on the ground of absence of privity. Thus, the purchasers of a tractor trailer may recover from the manufacturer of the brake system of the trailer for damages sustained when the brake system failed to work. Likewise, a person injured while on a golf course when an automobile parked on the club parking lot became "unparked" and ran down hill can sue the manufacturer of the defective parking unit.

NATURE AND CAUSE OF HARM

The law is more concerned in cases where the plaintiff has been personally injured as contrasted with economically harmed. Thus, the law places protection of the person of the individual above protection of property rights. The harm sustained must have been "caused" by the defendant.

To prove a case for breach of warranty, only facts of which the plaintiff has direct knowledge or about which information can readily be learned need be proven. Thus, the plaintiff need show only that a sale and a warranty existed, that the goods did not conform to the warranty, and that injury resulted from the goods.

A manufacturer or seller may assume by the terms of a contract a liability broader than would arise from a mere warranty.

Spiegel purchased a jar of skin cream from Saks 34th Street. It had been manufactured by National. The carton and the jar stated that the cream was chemically pure and absolutely safe. When Spiegel used the cream, it caused a severe skin rash. She sued Saks and National. Judgment was for Spiegel. The statements on the carton and the jar constituted an express warranty binding both the seller and the manufacturer. The statement that it was safe was an absolute undertaking that it was safe for everyone; as distinguished from merely an implied warranty of reasonable fitness, which would be subject to an exception of a particular allergy of a plaintiff.

LEASED GOODS

Rather than purchase expensive goods, many people and businesses lease such goods. The users of the goods could suffer personal injury or property damage from the use or condition of leased property. Most states have adopted Article 2A of the UCC, which applies to personal property leasing. Article 2A treats lease transactions similarly to the way Article 2 treats sales, which includes express and implied warranty provisions. However, a warranty of possession without interference replaces the warranty of title.

QUESTIONS

1. a. What is a warranty?
   b. How do express and implied warranties differ?
2. Is the statement, "This fish bait is so good you will have to hide behind a tree to put it on a hook," a warranty?
3. What is a full warranty?
4. List the warranties that apply to all sellers and those that apply only to merchants.
5. When does a warranty against encumbrances apply?
6. Distinguish by examples the difference between an implied warranty of fitness for a particular purpose and an implied warranty of merchantability.
7. Explain the difference in the "foreign/natural" test and the "reasonable expectation" test as applied to the sale of food or drink.

8 When a sale of goods is made on the buyer's specifications are there any warranties?

9 How may warranties be excluded or surrendered?

10 Under what different theories may a person be entitled to recover for personal injury or property damage?

CASE PROBLEMS

L.O.1 ....

1 Fuqua Chrysler-Plymouth bought a used Chevrolet from Alfred Dirico, and Fuqua then sold the car at retail. The car odometer showed 50,864 miles, but it had more than 128,000. After being sued by the buyer, Fuqua sued Dirico for breach of express warranty contending that the odometer mileage statement received when it purchased the car from Dirico formed an express warranty. Since the mileage was incorrect, Fuqua claimed it was a breach of the warranty. After giving the mileage, a box was checked on the mileage statement form by the statement, "I hereby certify to the best of my knowledge the odometer reading . . . reflects the actual mileage." Did the mileage statement create an express warranty?

L.O.2 ....

2 David Duff bought tongue-and-groove lumber from Bonner Building Supply, Inc., a dealer in lumber products. Bonner represented that the lumber was kiln-dried, which meant its moisture content would not exceed 19 percent and shrinkage would be minimal. Duff installed the lumber as wall paneling and significant shrinkage occurred. Some boards shrank one-half inch, which was enough to pull the wood tongues from their grooves leaving gaps between the boards. Duff sued Bonner for the cost of repair and replacement, alleging breach of implied warranty of merchantability. Was it?

L.O.2 ....

3 Daniel Shaffer ordered a glass of wine at the Victoria Station restaurant. The wine glass broke in his hand, resulting in injury. Shaffer sued the restaurant for breach of warranty. Victoria Station argued the UCC did not apply because it was not a merchant with respect to wine glasses, and the glass itself was not sold. Does the UCC apply?

L.O.1 ....

4 Kevin Woods purchased a car from Robert Secord. Their oral agreement stated that Woods purchased it in "as is" condition without guarantee. Woods was only willing to purchase the car "as is" based upon Secord's representation that the car was in good condition and ran properly. Immediately after the sale Woods had severe problems with the car. Secord refused to cure the problems, so Woods sold the car for salvage. Woods sued, alleging the car was not fit for its intended use at the time of sale. Can he recover?

L.O.3 ....

5 St. Croix Printing Equipment, in Minnesota, contracted with Tobi's Graphics, in California, to find a used printer for Tobi to buy "as is." By phone, Deborah Sexton of St. Croix agreed to buy a used Adast press from Rockwell Graphics in Illinois. Sexton wanted the press shipped directly to Tobi's without inspecting it. The press was supposed to be capable of four-color printing, and Sexton was told it was in working condition. The contract between

Rockwell and St. Croix conspicuously said the press was sold "as is" and disclaimed any warranties express or implied. After it was shipped to Tobi's, it was found it did not work properly and could not do four-color printing. St. Croix sued Rockwell for breach of warranty. Decide the case.

L.O.1 ....

6 Jose Martinez looked at a used Volkswagen at Valley Datsun. When asked about strange "engine noises," Valley's salesman told Martinez that the car was in "excellent condition" and the noise was normal. Relying on the superior knowledge of the salesman, Martinez bought the car. Two days after the purchase, the clutch burned out and the engine threw a rod. Martinez sued Valley for breach of express warranty. Was there a breach?

L.O.1 ....

7 Lorraine Hinchliffe bought a new Jeep Wagoneer from Lipman Motors, Inc. Hinchliffe had told the seller she wanted a vehicle capable of hauling her camper trailer. The jeep was advertised as having "full-time four-wheel drive" when it had just a system for transmitting power to the wheels using a limited slip differential mechanism. Hinchliffe had many problems with the Jeep and sued, alleging breach of warranty. Could she establish a case?

L.O.2 ....

8 Ronald and Wyman Robinson did business as Friendly Discount Auto Sales. They bought a classic Chevrolet Camaro and then sold it to Mike Durham. Shortly thereafter, the F.B.I. seized the car. It had been stolen, and the FBI returned it to its original owner. Durham sued for breach of warranty. Did he have a valid claim? Why or why not?

L.O.2 ....

9 Kwikee Enterprises manufactured and sold automatic extendable/retractable steps for motor homes and recreational vehicles. It had problems with the control unit and described the problems to Controltek. It supplied Controltek with a unit and a brochure describing the step. Kwikee told Controltek it wanted an electronic control device that would make the step "work every time," but gave no written specifications for the control. Controltek designed and built an electronic control unit. Kwikee bought 1,000 units and sold the steps with these controls. Almost all the steps sold were returned because they did not work when installed on vehicles. Kwikee found another control unit that worked and returned units to Controltek for credit. Controltek sued Kwikee for payment for all the controls. Kwikee said breach of a warranty of fitness for a particular purpose existed. Did a warranty of fitness for a particular purpose arise in this sale?

L.O.1 ....

10 Michael Booher purchased 128 copying machines from Royal Business Machines, Inc. Royal had told Booher that the machines were of high quality, experience and testing had shown the frequency of repairs was very low, and replacement parts were readily available; experience had shown that the purchase of the machines and leasing of them to customers would give substantial profits to Booher and that the machines were safe and could not cause fires. In a suit for breach of warranty, Booher alleged all the statements were express warranties. Were any of them warranties?

Chapter 20

CONSUMER PROTECTION

After studying this chapter you should be able to:

1 Explain the purpose of consumer protection laws.

2 List the traditional consumer protective measures.

3 State the objectives of laws requiring disclosure and uniformity.

Preview Case

Porter & Dietsch, Inc., marketed "X-11" tablets, which were nonprescription, weight-reduction tablets. Advertisements for the tablets stated, in capital letters, "EAT WELL . . . AND LOSE THAT FAT" and "EAT WHAT YOU WANT—AND SLIM DOWN." They continued to state that "no starvation dieting" was necessary and loss of weight could be accomplished without "suffering through starvation dieting hunger" or "boring reducing diets." In fact, use of the tablets would not cause weight loss unless a severely restricted caloric diet was followed. Is the advertising deceptive?

L.O.1

Consumer protection laws are designed to protect the parties to a contract from abuse, sharp dealing, and fraud. They are based on the awareness that the bargaining power of the parties many times is unequal. Frequently the consumer-buyer is a total novice in the area of business dealings, whereas the seller is a virtual professional in regard to the particular transaction.

Consumer protection does more than protect "consumer" interests. It strengthens legitimate business interests. Laws requiring fairness and full disclosure of business dealings make it more difficult for unscrupulous business people to operate and thereby infringe upon the trade of those with sound business practices. This area of the law continues to grow and to protect the consumer from unfair practices.

TRADITIONAL PROTECTION

L.O.2 .... Of the protective measures, some have been in existence for many years. Such traditional protections include usury laws, antitrust laws, and regulatory agencies.

Usury Laws

Among the oldest measures designed to protect parties to business transactions are the laws that fix the maximum rate of interest that may be charged on loans. Such laws, called usury laws, recognize that the borrower is frequently in a weak position and therefore unable to bargain effectively for the best possible rates of interest.

Most states provide for several rates of interest. The legal rate, which varies from state to state from 5 percent to 15 percent, applies when interest must be paid but no rate has been specified. The maximum contract rate is the highest rate that can be demanded of a debtor. This rate varies from 8 percent to as much as 45 percent. Some states allow the parties to set any rate of interest. Statutes usually permit a higher rate to be charged on small loans on the theory that the risks and costs per dollar loaned are greater in making small loans.

The laws vary regarding the damages awarded to a person charged a usurious rate of interest. Some laws allow recovery of the total interest charged and others allow recovery of several times the amount charged.

In many states, corporations are prohibited from raising the defense of usury. In an effort to reflect fluctuating market rates of interest, a number of jurisdictions have recently adopted a fluctuating maximum rate of interest based on such rates as the Federal Reserve discount rate, the prime rate, or the rate on U.S. Treasury Bills.

Antitrust Laws

Antitrust laws are designed to prevent any individual, corporation, or group from controlling too large a share of the market for a product. These laws are based on the theory that monopolists would charge higher prices than exist in a competitive market and might not seek to improve the product so as to provide the consumer with the best possible goods. Antitrust laws prohibit corporations from actions that lessen competition or result in a restraint of trade.

The Brown Shoe Co. and the G. R. Kinney Co., which together would have controlled 5 percent of the United States shoe market, attempted to merge. The federal government sought to stop the merger on the grounds that it violated the Clayton Act, which prohibits corporations from acquiring other corporations where the effect of the acquisition might substantially lessen competition or tend to create a monopoly. The U.S. Supreme Court prohibited the merger holding that the proposed merger would tend to lessen competition.

Regulatory Agencies

Most jurisdictions regulate a wide variety of professions that serve the public. Those supervised and regulated by governmental agencies in an effort to protect the interests of consumers include barbers, doctors, insurance agents, morticians, cosmetologists, fitters of hearing aids, and restaurateurs. In order to be licensed to practice a regulated profession, an individual must meet the requirements set by the appropriate regulatory agency.

Public utility companies, which are granted monopoly status, are regulated to assure that they charge fair rates and render adequate service. Such businesses include natural gas, electric, and water companies. A Public Service Commission or Public Utilities Commission regulates these companies in most states.

EXPANSION OF CONSUMER PROTECTION

The most recent consumer emphasis includes product safety, disclosure and uniformity, statutes prohibiting unconscionable contracts, warranty protection, fair credit reporting, and state consumer protection agencies.

Product Safety

Laws requiring that goods meet safety standards have become increasingly widespread in recent years. Probably the most well known of these product design requirements applies in the case of automobiles. Standards for bumpers, tires, and glass have been set by the federal government. The range of products affected by safety standards is substantial. It includes toys, television sets, insecticides, and drugs. Substandard products are often subject to recall at the instigation of federal agencies. In some instances fines and imprisonment may be imposed on corporate executives whose businesses have distributed clearly hazardous, substandard goods.

In 1972 the federal government implemented the Consumer Product Safety Act which established the Consumer Product Safety Commission. The Commission has broad power to promulgate safety standards for many products. Federal courts have the power to review these standards to make sure they are necessary to abolish or decrease the risk of injury and that they do so at a reasonable cost. The commission may order a halt to the manufacture of unsafe products. Certain products, inherently dangerous or hazardous, may be banned by the Commission if there appears to be no way to make the product safe. The law requires manufacturers, distributors, and retailers of consumer products to immediately notify the Commission if a product fails to comply with an applicable safety standard or contains a defect that creates a substantial risk of injury to the public.

A sizable number of people were injured every year from accidental ignition of matchbooks. The Consumer Product Safety Commission issued matchbook safety regulations. They stated that "the friction shall be located on the outside back cover near the bottom of the matchbook." A manufacturer of paper matchbooks, D. D. Bean & Sons, asked for federal court review of the regulations. While the matchbook industry would have to modify its equipment to put the friction for lighting matches on the back of the covers, it was a one time cost. The court said that the rule was reasonable in view of the injury likely to be reduced and the relatively small cost to the industry.

The 1972 act does not cover motor vehicles, pesticides, airplanes, boats, food and drugs, and similar items usually regulated by other federal agencies.

Disclosure and Uniformity

L.O.3 ....

The objectives of disclosure and uniformity include trust in advertising, truth in lending, and product uniformity.

Truth in Advertising. Under authorization initially granted in the Federal Fair Trade Acts shortly after the turn of the century, the Federal Trade Commission (FTC) has been active in demanding that advertisements be limited to those statements that can be substantiated about products. The FTC may seek voluntary agreement from a business to stop false or deceptive advertising and in some instances to agree to corrective advertising. Such agreement is obtained by a business's signing a consent order. The FTC also has the power to order businesses to "cease and desist" from unfair trade practices. The business has the right to contest an FTC order in court.

The FTC has the authority to require the name of a product be changed if it misleads or tends to mislead the public regarding the nature or quality of the product. If an advertisement actually misstates the quality of a product or makes the product appear to be what it is not, the FTC can prohibit the advertising.

Porter & Dietsch, Inc., marketed "X-11" tablets, which were nonprescription, weight-reduction tablets. Advertisements for the tablets stated, in capital letters, "EAT WELL . . . AND LOSE THAT FAT" AND "EAT WHAT YOU WANT—AND SLIM DOWN." They continued to state that "no starvation dieting" was necessary and loss of weight could be accomplished without "suffering through starvation dieting hunger" or "boring reducing diets." In fact, use of the tablets would not cause weight loss unless a severely restricted caloric diet was followed. The FTC found the advertising deceptive and required the phrase "Dieting is required" to be included in future advertising.

Truth in Lending. The federal Truth in Lending Act requires lenders to make certain written disclosures to borrowers before extending credit. These disclosures include:

1   The finance charge.

2   The annual percentage rate.

3   The number, amount, and due dates of all payments, including any **balloon payments**—payments that are more than twice the normal installment payments.

Balloon Payment
Payment more than twice the normal one

Finance Charge
Total amount paid for credit

Annual Percentage Rate (APR)
Amount charged for loan as percentage of loan

The **finance charge** is the total dollar amount the borrower will pay for the loan. The finance charge includes all interest and any other fees or charges required to be paid in order to get the loan.

The **annual percentage rate (APR)** is the dollar amount charged for the loan expressed as a percentage of the amount borrowed. The APR must be on a yearly rate. This helps a borrower "comparison shop" among different lenders when seeking credit.

Advertisements indicating any credit terms must also meet substantially the same requirements regarding disclosure. The law provides that when the purchase of consumer products is financed by executing a mortgage on the debtor's principal dwelling, the debtor has three days in which to rescind the mortgage agreement. Both criminal penalties and civil recovery are available against those who fail to comply with the Truth in Lending Act.

Product Uniformity. A number of required practices give consumers the ability to make intelligent choices when comparing competing products. For years, some states have required certain products to be packaged in specifically comparable quantities.

Unit Pricing

Price stated per unit of measurement

Some local governments require **unit pricing.** In unit pricing the price for goods sold by weight is stated as the price per ounce or other unit of measurement of the product as well as a total price for the total weight. Thus, all products sold by the ounce would be marked with not only a total price but also with a price per ounce that could be compared to competing products even if the competing products were not packaged in an equal number of ounces.

In order to allow consumers to compare various makes of automobiles more easily, the federal government requires sellers of automobiles to publish mileage test data in marketing new cars.

Statutes Prohibiting Unconscionable Contracts

Section 2-302 of the UCC provides courts with authority to refuse to enforce a sales contract or a part of it because it is "unconscionable." Some courts have described this section as an enactment into law of the community's moral awareness. If the terms of the contract are so harsh or the price so unreasonably high as to shock the conscience of the community, the courts may rule the contract to be unconscionable.

The Reynosos purchased a refrigerator-freezer from the Frostifresh Corporation for a cash price of $900 plus a credit charge of $245.88 for a total price of $1,145.88. The contract was negotiated orally in Spanish, and during the conversation Mr. Reynoso stated he had only one week left on his job and could not afford the appliance. The signed retail installment contract covering the sale was entirely in English. Frostifresh had paid $348 for the appliance. When sued for the contract price the Reynosos argued that the contract was unconscionable. The New York courts set aside the contract price and required the Reynosos to pay only the net cost of the refrigerator-freezer to Frostifresh along with a reasonable profit and trucking and service charges.

Warranty Protection

In 1975 the Congress passed the Magnuson-Moss Warranty and Federal Trade Commission Improvement Act. The Act does not require sellers to give written warranties for consumer goods, but if the seller chooses to give a warranty, it must meet certain requirements. The FTC requires clear disclosure of all warranty provisions and statement of the legal remedies of the consumer under the warranty to be a part of the warranty. According to the Act, the consumer must be informed of the warranty prior to the sale. In order to satisfy the law, the language of warranties of goods costing more than $15 must not be misleading to a "reasonable, average consumer."

The Act allows the FTC to provide for an extension of the warranty time in the event repairs require that the product be out of service for an unreasonable length of time.

Roxanne Sadat bought a new car covered by a full written warranty. Unfortunately, the brakes faded or were hard to engage, the steering column vibrated excessively, the transmission slipped from park to reverse, the car leaked oil and dieseled after the engine was turned off, and the passenger compartment smelled of exhaust. Sadat took the car in to the dealer seven times for repair of these problems, but they were never cured. Sadat asked to have her car replaced at no cost. American Motors refused, so Sadat sued for relief under the Magnuson-Moss Act. The court said the law gave Sadat a right to sue for breach of warranty.

Further, when repairs take an unreasonable amount of time, the consumer may recover incidental expenses. If after a reasonable number of opportunities the manufacturer is unable to remedy the defect in a product, the consumer must be permitted to elect to receive a refund or a replacement when the product has been sold with a full warranty.

A significant aspect of the Act requires that no written warranty may waive the implied warranties of merchantability and fitness for a particular purpose during the term of the written warranty or unreasonably soon thereafter. Thus, the previously common practice of replacing the implied warranties of fitness and merchantability with substandard written warranties has been significantly limited. The Act also curtails the limitation of implied warranties on items for which a service or maintenance contract is offered within 90 days after the initial sale. The Act also extends the coverage of a warranty to those who purchase consumer goods secondhand during the term of the warranty.

Enforcement of the Act occurs through civil suits authorized in the Act. Attorney fees as well as damages may be awarded to plaintiffs who successfully sue to enforce the provisions of the statute.

FAIR CREDIT REPORTING

Another of the recent federal enactments protecting the rights of consumers includes the Fair Credit Reporting Act. It requires creditors to notify a potential recipient of credit whenever any adverse action or denial of credit was based on a credit report. It permits the consumer about whom a credit report is written to obtain from a credit agency the substance of the credit report. An incorrect credit report must be corrected by the credit agency. In some cases, if the consumer disagrees with a creditor about the report the consumer may be permitted to add an explanation of the dispute to the report. Certain types of adverse information may not be maintained in the reports for more than seven years. The reports may be used for legitimate business purposes only.

Individuals whose rights under the Act have been violated may sue and recover ordinary damages if the harm resulted from negligent noncompliance. If the injury resulted from willful noncompliance with the Fair Credit Reporting Act, the aggrieved party may seek punitive damages.

Terry Fischl applied for credit. General Motors Acceptance Corp. (GMAC) obtained a consumer report on him. It erroneously referred to one of Fischl's jobs as past employment and an account in good standing with Sears, Roebuck & Co. as a credit inquiry. GMAC sent Fischl a form letter rejecting his application and indicating the reason was "credit references are insufficient." The section of the form designed to report the use of information from outside sources was marked "disclosure inapplicable." When sued for violation of the Fair Credit Reporting Act, GMAC argued credit was not refused because of what was in the report, but because of what was not in the report. The court held that disclosure under the Act was not conditioned on derogatory or negative information in a report, but disclosure was required when a decision is based wholly or in part on information in the report.

State Consumer Protection Agencies

Injunctive Powers

Power to issue cease-and-desist orders

A number of states have enacted laws giving either the state attorney general or a special consumer affairs office the authority to compel fairness in advertising, sales presentations, and other consumer transactions. State officials will investigate complaints received from consumers. If the complaint appears valid, efforts will be made to secure voluntary corrective action by the seller. Frequently these agencies have **injunctive powers**, which means that they may issue cease-and-desist orders similar to those of the FTC. In a limited number of jurisdictions the agencies may prosecute the offending business, and significant criminal penalties may be imposed that substantially augment the operation of these efforts.

QUESTIONS

1   What is the relative bargaining power of the consumer-buyer and the seller in many business transactions?
2   What recovery does the law allow to a victim of usury?
3   Explain how antitrust laws benefit consumers.
4   Give examples of some professions that are regulated by government to protect the public.
5   What are the objectives of laws requiring disclosure and uniformity?
6   What methods may the FTC use to curtail unfair trade practices?
7   Explain how the disclosure provisions of the Truth in Lending Act benefit consumers.
8   a.   What is *unit buying*?
     b.   Why is it considered beneficial to consumers?
9   How does the Magnuson-Moss Warranty Act assist a consumer?
10   What state governmental agencies are usually empowered to assist with consumer complaints?

CASE PROBLEMS

L.O.1 ....

1   As a result of Hurricane Gloria, widespread power outages occurred on much of Long Island. Electric generators were in demand. A state price-gouging statute prohibited charging unconscionably excessive prices for products during any abnormal disruption of the market. Numerous consumers who had bought generators to get a source of electric power for their homes claimed

they had to pay exorbitant prices. During the power outages, the prices charged by Honda-Yamaha of Mineola were uniformly higher than before. Some prices of generators had increased as much as 67 percent. Who might help the consumers?

L.O.3 .... **2** Advance Machine Company owned Commercial Mechanisms, Inc., which manufactured automatic baseball-pitching machines. The Consumer Product Safety Commission notified Advance it had decided to issue an administrative complaint seeking a penalty for failure to immediately report a defect in the pitching machine. Regulations defined "immediately" as 24 hours. Advance argued that the duty to report ended after 24 hours. Did it?

L.O.2 .... **3** Triton Oil & Gas contracted with Marine Contractors & Supply to drill, complete, equip, and maintain an oil and gas well. Marine agreed to pay one-third of the cost and Triton agreed to pay two-thirds. The contract did not make any provision for charging interest. Marine refused to pay its share of the costs when it became dissatisfied with Triton's performance. Triton billed Marine and charged 10 percent interest on the unpaid balance. Triton sued to collect the unpaid costs and Marine alleged usury. It stated that since no interest was provided in the contract, 6 percent was the highest interest allowed by law. The legal rate in the state was 6 percent. Was the interest usurious?

L.O.3 .... **4** The Flemings applied to the Federal Land Bank of Columbia for a loan on real estate which they said was not their residence. When they defaulted on the loan, the Land Bank foreclosed on the real estate and then brought an action against the Flemings for a deficiency judgment. The Flemings argued that under the Truth in Lending Act the Land Bank wrongfully denied them the right to rescind the loan transaction. Should they have had the right to rescind within three days following the loan transaction?

L.O.3 .... **5** Kenneth McDonald saw an ad for a Hunter 45 sailboat in *Yachting,* a national magazine. The ad had two lists separated by empty space. The first list was headed "Specifications." The second was titled "Cruise Pac." Below both lists appeared the statement, "Specifications subject to change without notice." By written contract, McDonald bought a Hunter 45 for $109,500. The contract listed equipment that came with the boat and stated, "plus . . . all equipment . . . nationally advertising in *Yachting*." Two items listed as included in the Cruise Pac were not included. McDonald sued for false advertising. Was there false advertising?

Summary Cases

SALES

1 Songbird Jet Ltd., Inc., and Jet Leasing Corporation, acting together, negotiated with Amax Inc. for the purchase of a jet airplane. Songbird and Jet Leasing claimed that an oral agreement was reached by which they would purchase the jet for $8,850,000. Jet Leasing sent Amax a check for $250,000, which it claimed was a deposit on the sale. Amax later notified Jet Leasing the jet was not for sale and that no contract had been made. Songbird and Jet Leasing sued Amax claiming the $250,000 check was partial performance of the alleged contract. Amax alleged that claim was barred by the Statute of Frauds. Was it? [*Songbird Jet Ltd., Inc.* v. *Amax Inc.*, 581 F. Supp. 912 (S.D.N.Y.)]

2 Halstead Hospital, Inc., ordered bond forms from Northern Bank Note Company. Northern was advised that the bond closing was scheduled for December 18. Northern accepted the order stating it would complete its work for shipment December 16. It arranged for the delivery of the bond forms to a specific location in New York City, the Signature Company, so that they could be inspected and signed prior to the closing. Northern printed the bonds, boxed them into four cartons, and arranged for a common carrier to deliver them to New York. One of the boxes did not arrive until after December 18, so the closing was canceled for that day. Halstead sued for breach of contract, alleging that the contract required shipment and timely delivery by Northern. Did it? [*Halstead Hospital, Inc.*, v. *Northern Bank Note Co.*, 680 F.2d 1307 (10th Cir.)]

3 Plummer sold a car for $800 cash to Davis. Davis paid for the car by check. Plummer delivered the car to Davis together with a certificate of title but with the understanding that there was to be no sale until the check was cleared through the bank. The check turned out to be a bad check. Davis in the meantime had sold the car to Kingsley, who knew nothing about the arrangement between Plummer and Davis. Plummer brought suit against Kingsley to recover the car, claiming that since Davis did not have good title to the car, he could not transfer good title to Kingsley. Did Kingsley obtain good title? [*Plummer* v. *Kingsley*, 226 P. 2d 297 (Or.)]

4 Conida Warehouses sold light red kidney bean seed to Larry Mallory. After Mallory planted the seeds, the beans developed halo blight, a disease. Mallory sued Conida for breach of warranty. Conida claimed it had effectively disclaimed the warranty of merchantability by attaching a tag to the bag of seed. That tag showed the word "warranty" in capital letters at the top and the rest of the letters were in standard size type. The disclaimer tag contained no contrasting color or other emphasis. That tag was attached with two other tags at the bottom of the bag and under the other two bags. Was this an effective disclaimer? [*Mallory* v. *Conida Warehouses, Inc.*, 350 N.W.2d 825 (Mich. Ct. App.)]

5 Hodge Chile Co. negotiated for the purchase of food cartons from Interstate Folding Box Co. Interstate sent samples of its boxes to Hodge without making any statement as to their qualifications. Hodge subjected the samples to various tests and then placed an order for the boxes with Interstate. Hodge did not pay for the boxes. When sued for their purchase price, Hodge claimed there was a breach of an implied warranty of fitness of the boxes for a particular purpose. It was shown that the defects of which Hodge complained had not been revealed in the tests because the cartons had been filled by hand instead of by machine and the chile put in the boxes was poured at a lower temperature than when poured by machine. Did Hodge have a valid defense? [*Interstate Folding Box Co.* v. *Hodge Chile Co.*, 334 S.W.2d 408 (Mo. Ct. App.)]

6 At an auction, Gaylen Bennett bought 55 head of cattle from Tony Jansma. The next day some of the cattle were sick. Eventually 19 of the 55 cattle died. Jansma regularly dealt in the buying and selling of cattle and held himself out as having knowledge peculiar to cattle transactions. Bennett sued for breach of the warranty of merchantability. Was Jansma a merchant? [*Bennett* v. *Jansma*, 329 N.W.2d 134 (S.D.)]

7 Central Credit Bureau issued a credit report on Barbara Johnson that contained an item relating to Johnson's outstanding obligation to Beneficial Finance Corp. The obligation had been discharged by Johnson's bankruptcy. At Johnson's request, Central had reinvestigated and made a note that the debt had been discharged. It then corrected the report. Johnson sued for damages, alleging a violation of the Fair Credit Reporting Act. Was there such a violation? [*Johnson* v. *Beneficial Finance Corp.*, 466 N.Y.S.2d 553 (N.Y.)]

Part 5

COMMERCIAL PAPER/ NEGOTIABLE INSTRUMENTS

Chapter 21

NATURE OF COMMERCIAL PAPER/ NEGOTIABLE INSTRUMENTS

LEARNING OBJECTIVES

After studying this chapter you should be able to:

1 Explain what a negotiable instrument is.

2 Discuss how negotiable instruments are transferred.

3 Differentiate between bearer paper and order paper.

4 Name the types of negotiable instruments and the parties to them.

Preview Case

Enterprises, Inc., and George Becker entered into a contract. Enterprises agreed to do certain work on a residence for Becker, and Becker agreed to pay for the work done. Enterprises later sued for breach of contract, alleging it was not allowed to perform the contract. Becker moved to dismiss the suit, arguing that the contract violated state law. The law required that a promissory "note . . . given in respect of a home solicitation sale" had to include certain statements. These statements were not included in the contract. Was the contract a promissory note?

L.O.1

Commercial Paper or Negotiable Instrument

Writing drawn in special form that can be transferred as substitute for money or as instrument of credit

ommercial paper or **negotiable instruments** are writings drawn in a special form that can be transferred from person to person as a substitute for money or as an instrument of credit. Such an instrument must meet certain definite requirements in regard to form and the manner in which it is transferred. Two types of negotiable instruments include checks and notes. Since a negotiable instrument is not money, the law does not require a person to accept one in payment of a debt.

HISTORY AND DEVELOPMENT

The need for instruments of credit that would permit the settlement of claims between distant cities without the transfer of money has existed as long as trade has existed. References to bills of exchange or instruments of credit appeared as early as 50 B.C. Their widespread usage, however, began about A.D. 1200 as international trade began to flourish in the wake of the Crusades. At first these credit instruments were used only in international trade, but they gradually became common in domestic trade.

Law Merchant

Rules applied by courts set up by merchants in early England

In England prior to about A.D. 1400, all disputes between merchants were settled on the spot by special courts set up by the merchants. The rules applied by these courts became known as the **law merchant.** Later the common-law courts took over the adjudication of all disputes, including those between merchants, but these courts retained most of the customs developed by the merchants and incorporated the law merchant into the common law. Most, but by no means all, of the law merchant dealt with bills of exchange or credit instruments.

In the United States each state modified in its own way the common law dealing with credit instruments so that eventually the various states had different laws regarding credit instruments. The American Bar Association and the American Banks Association appointed a commission to draw up a Uniform Negotiable Instruments Law. In 1896 the commission proposed a uniform act. This act was adopted in all the states, but it was then displaced by Article 3 of the UCC.

Revised Article 3

In 1990, a commission that writes uniform laws issued a revised Article 3. Because a significant number of states have adopted the revision, this text explains major changes made by the revision in separate paragraphs. The revision uses the term *negotiable instruments* and not *commercial paper*.

NEGOTIATION

L.O.2 ....

Negotiation

Act of transferring ownership of negotiable instrument

Indorsement

Signature of owner on back of negotiable instrument

Holder in Due Course

Person who acquires rights superior to those of original owner of negotiable instrument

Negotiation is the act of transferring ownership of a negotiable instrument to another party. A negotiable instrument owned by and payable to a person may be negotiated by the owner. The owner negotiates it by signing the back of it and delivering it to another party. The signature of the owner made on the back of a negotiable instrument before delivery is called an **indorsement.**[1]

When a negotiable instrument is transferred to one or more parties, these parties may acquire rights superior to those of the original owner. Parties who acquire rights superior to those of the original owner are known as **holders in due course.** It is mainly this feature of the transfer of superior rights that gives negotiable instruments a special classification all their own.

[1]Indorsement is the spelling used in the UCC, although endorsement is commonly used in business.

ORDER PAPER AND BEARER PAPER

L.O.3 ....

Order Paper

Commercial paper payable to order

Bearer Paper

Commercial paper payable to bearer

Commercial paper is made payable either to the order of a named person, in which case it is called **order paper,** or to bearer, in which case it is called **bearer paper.** Order paper must use the word *order*, as in the phrase "pay to the order of John Doe," or some other word to indicate it may be paid to a transferee. Order paper is negotiated only by indorsement of the person to whom it is then payable and by delivery of the paper to another person. In the case of bearer paper, the transfer may be made merely by handing the paper to another person.

Payment is made on a different basis with order paper than with bearer paper. Order paper may be paid only to the person to whom it is made payable on its face or the person to whom it has been properly indorsed. However, bearer paper may be paid to any person in possession of the paper.

Rob-Glen Enterprises executed promissory notes for a $46,000 loan and delivered them to the Dolly Cam Corp. Before the notes were due, Dolly Cam indorsed them payable to bearer and delivered them to First National Bank of Long Island. When the notes were due, Rob-Glen refused to pay claiming it had paid them by paying a third party. The court held that since the notes were payable to bearer and First National had possession of them, it was entitled to be paid.

CLASSIFICATION OF COMMERCIAL PAPER

L.O.4 ....

The basic negotiable instruments are:

1. Drafts
2. Promissory notes

Drafts

Draft or Bill of Exchange

Written order by one person directing another to pay sum of money to third person

Promissory Note

Unconditional written promise to pay sum of money to another

A **draft** is also called a **bill of exchange.** It is a written order signed by one person and requiring the person to whom it is addressed to pay on demand or at a particular time a sum certain in money to order or to bearer. Checks and trade acceptances are special types of drafts.

Promissory Notes

A **promissory note** is an unconditional promise in writing made by one person to another, signed by the promisor, engaging to pay on demand, or at a definite time, a sum certain in money to order or to bearer (see Illustration 21-1).

Enterprises, Inc., and George Becker entered into a contract. Enterprises agreed to do certain work on a residence for Becker, and Becker agreed to pay for the work done. Enterprises later sued for breach of contract, alleging it was not allowed to perform the contract. Becker moved to dismiss the suit, arguing that

Illustration 21-1

Promissory Note
Parties: maker, Jan L. Hendricks: payee, Ana Nieves

NOTE

$ _7,000.00_   Greenfield, Missouri _____April 1,_____ 19 _--_

_____One (1) year_____ after date, for value received, _____I_____ promise

to pay to the order of _Ana Nieves_____

the sum of _Seven Thousand Dollars ($7,000.00)_____

with interest thereon from data at the rate of _fifteen percent (15%)_____

per annum, interest payable _____semiannually_____ and if interest

is not paid _____semiannually_____ to become as principal and bear

the same rate of interest.

Payable at _Northside Bank_____

_____ _Jan L. Hendricks_____

the contract violated state law. The law required that a promissory "note . . . given in respect of a home solicitation sale" had to include certain statements. These statements were not included in the contract. The court held that the law did not apply to the contract because it was not a promissory note. The contract did not make an unconditional promise to pay, but merely a promise to pay when the other party performed.

PARTIES TO NEGOTIABLE INSTRUMENTS

Each party to a negotiable instrument is designated by a certain term, depending upon the type of instrument. Some of these terms apply to all types of negotiable instruments, whereas others are restricted to one type only. The same individual may be designated by one term at one stage and by another at a later stage through which the instrument passes before it is collected. These terms include payee, drawer, drawee, acceptor, maker, bearer, holder, indorser, and indorsee.

Payee

Payee
Party to whom instrument is payable

The party to whom any negotiable instrument is made payable is called the **payee**.

Drawer

Drawer
Person who executes a draftt

The person who executes or signs any draft is called the **drawer** (see Illustration 21-2).

Drawee

Drawee
Person ordered to pay draft

The person who is ordered to pay a draft is called the **drawee**.

Illustration 21-2

Draft
Parties: drawer, Lee W. Richardson; drawee, Walter Evans; payee, Community Bank

$ __450.00__	__December 22,__ 19 __--__
__Six months after date__	PAY TO THE
ORDER OF __Community Bank__	
__Four hundred fifty dollars and no/100__	
VALUE RECEIVED AND CHARGE TO ACCOUNT OF	FOR CLASSROOM USE ONLY DOLLARS
TO __Walter Evans__	
No. __27 Walden, Virginia__	__Lee W. Richardson__

Acceptor

Acceptor
Person who agrees to pay a draft

A drawee who accepts a draft, thus indicating a willingness to assume responsibility for its payment, is called the **acceptor**. Drafts not immediately payable are accepted by writing upon the face of the instrument these or similar words: "Accepted, Jane Daws." This indicates that Jane Daws will perform the contract according to its terms.

Maker

Maker
Person who executes a note

The person who executes a promissory note is called the **maker.** The maker contracts to pay the amount due on the note. This obligation resembles that of the acceptor of a draft.

Bearer

Bearer
Payee of instrument made payable to whoever is in possession

Any negotiable instrument may be made payable to whoever possesses it. The payee of such an instrument is the **bearer**. If the instrument is made payable to the order of "Myself," "Cash," or another similar name, it is payable to bearer.

Holder

Holder
Person in possession of instrument payable to bearer or that person

Any person who possesses an instrument is the **holder** if it has been delivered to the person and it is either bearer paper or it is payable to that person as the payee or by indorsement. The payee is the original holder of an instrument.

Holder in Due Course

Holder in Due Course
Holder who takes instrument in good faith and for value

A holder who takes a negotiable instrument in good faith and for value is a **holder in due course**.

Indorser

Indorser

Payee or holder who
signs back of instrument

When the payee of a draft or a note wishes to transfer the instrument to another party, it must be indorsed. The payee is then called the **indorser**. The payee makes the indorsement by signing on the back of the instrument.

Indorsee

Indorsee

Named holder of indorsed
negotiable instrument

A person who becomes the holder of a negotiable instrument by an indorsement that names him or her as the person to whom the instrument is negotiated is called the **indorsee**.

Several hundred people invested in a Cayman Islands entity called Tradecom, Ltd. They used cashier's checks payable to the order of Tradecom. Tradecom's purported agent, Arvey Drown, indorsed the checks and deposited them in an account at Central Bank and Trust Company. Tradecom deposited one $57,000 check without indorsement into that same account, owned by Equity Trading Corporation. An officer of Central indorsed the check:

"For deposit only
072 575
Tradecom by
Mark E. Thomson
Commercial Loan Officer"

Tradecom had no account at Central. The investors lost most of their money. They sued Central, alleging it had permitted Drown to divert checks payable to Tradecom to Equity's account. By state law, a bank could supply an indorsement for a customer. Since the check was order paper it could be negotiated only by indorsement of the holder, Tradecom.

NEGOTIATION AND ASSIGNMENT

The right to receive payment of instruments may be transferred by negotiation or by assignment. Nonnegotiable paper cannot be transferred by negotiation. The rights to them are transferred by assignment. Negotiable instruments may be transferred by negotiation or assignment. The rights given the original parties are alike in the cases of negotiation and assignment. In the case of a promissory note, for example, the original parties are the maker (the one who promises to pay) and the payee (the one to whom the money is to be paid). Between the original parties, both a nonnegotiable and a negotiable instrument are equally enforceable. Also, the same defenses against fulfilling the terms of the instrument may be set up. For example, if one party to the instrument is a minor, the incapacity to contract may be set up as a defense against carrying out the agreement.

However, the rights given to subsequent parties differ depending on whether an instrument is transferred by negotiation or assignment. When an instrument is transferred by assignment, the assignee receives only the rights of the assignor and no more. (See Chapter 12.) If one of the original parties to the instrument has a defense that is valid against the assignor, it is also valid against the assignee.

When an instrument is transferred by negotiation, however, the party who receives the instrument in good faith and for value may have rights that are superior to the rights of the original holder. Defenses that may be valid against the original holder may not be valid against a holder who has received an instrument by negotiation.

CREDIT AND COLLECTION

Negotiable instruments are called instruments of credit and instruments of collection. If A sells B merchandise on 60 days' credit, the buyer may at the time of the sale execute a negotiable note or draft due in 60 days in payment of the merchandise. This note or draft then is an instrument of credit.

If the seller in the transaction above will not extend the original credit to 60 days, a draft may be drawn on the buyer, who would be the drawee. In this case, the drawer may make a bank the payee, the bank being a mere agent of the drawer, or one of the seller's creditors may be made the payee so that an account receivable will be collected and an account payable will be paid all in one transaction. When the account receivable comes due, the buyer will mail a check to the seller. In this example, the draft is an instrument of collection.

ELECTRONIC FUND TRANSFERS

Electronic Fund Transfer

Fund transfer initiated electronically, telephonically, or by computer

More and more transfers of funds occur today in which a paper instrument is not actually transferred and the parties do not have face-to-face, personal contact. An **electronic fund transfer** (EFT) is any transfer of funds initiated by means of an electronic terminal, telephonic instrument, or computer or magnetic tape that instructs or authorizes a financial institution to debit or credit an account. An EFT does not include a transfer of funds begun by a check, draft, or similar paper instrument.

EFTs are popular because they are faster and less expensive than the transfer of paper instruments. EFTs also reduce the risk of problems resulting from lost instruments. If a check, for example, does not have to make the entire trip from the payee to the drawee bank to the drawer customer, costs and delays can be reduced.

A federal law, the Electronic Fund Transfer Act, defines and regulates EFTs. A transfer initiated by a telephone call between a bank employee and a customer is not an EFT unless it is in accordance with a prearranged plan.

The law requires disclosure of the terms and conditions of the EFTs involving a customer's account at the time the customer contracts for an EFT service. This notification must include:

1   What liability could be imposed for unauthorized EFTs.
2   The type of EFTs the customer may make.
3   The charges for EFTs.

Several widely used types of EFTs include check truncation, preauthorized debits and credits, automated teller machines, and point-of-sale systems.

Check Truncation

Check Truncation
Shortening check's trip from payee to drawer

A system of, in some way, shortening the trip a check makes from the payee to the drawee bank and then to the drawer is called **check truncation**. Many banks no longer return canceled checks to their customers with the monthly statement. Instead, the form of the statements to customers has been revised to list the check numbers. As before, the dollar amount on the checks is shown, but the transactions are now printed in numerical order. The customer can easily reconcile the account without having the canceled checks. This is a type of check truncation.

Preauthorized Debits and Credits

Preauthorized Debit
Automatic deduction of bill payment from checking account

Preauthorized Credit
Automatic deposit of funds to account

Checking account customers may authorize that recurring bills, such as home mortgage payments, insurance premiums, or utility bills, be automatically deducted from their checking accounts each month, called a **preauthorized debit**. It allows a person to avoid the inconvenience and cost of writing out and mailing checks for these bills.

A **preauthorized credit** allows the amount of regular payments to be automatically deposited in the payee's account. This type of EFT is frequently used for depositing salaries and government benefits, such as social security payments. It benefits the payor who does not have to issue and mail the checks. The payee does not have to bother depositing a check and normally has access to the funds sooner.

Automated Teller Machines

Automated Teller Machine
EFT terminal that performs routine banking services

An **automated teller machine** (ATM) is an EFT terminal capable of performing routine banking services. Many thousands of such machines exist at locations designed to be accessible to customers. The capabilities of the machines vary; however, some ATMs do such things as dispense cash and account information and allow customers to make deposits, transfer funds between accounts, and pay bills. ATMs are conveniently found at many locations, even in foreign countries, and are open when banks are not.

Point-of-Sale Systems

Point-of-Sale System
EFTs begun at retailers when customers pay for goods or services

Electronic fund transfers that begin at retailers when consumers want to pay for goods or services are called **point-of-sale systems** (POS). These transactions occur when the person operating the POS terminal enters information regarding the payment into a computer system. The entry reduces the consumer's bank account and credits the retailer's account by the amount of the transaction.

QUESTIONS

1 Is a person required to accept commercial paper in payment of a debt? Why or why not?
2 What is a negotiable instrument?

3   How are negotiable instruments transferred?

4   How does one indorse a negotiable instrument?

5   What is the difference in the wording of "bearer" paper and "order" paper?

6   What are the two types of negotiable instruments and the parties to them?

7   What does the maker of a promissory note contract to do?

8   Who is the indorser of a negotiable instrument? Who is the indorsee?

9   What is the difference in the rights of the subsequent parties in cases of negotiation and assignment?

10 Why are EFTs popular?

CASE PROBLEMS

L.O.2

1   The Second National Bank of North Miami took a note executed by G.M.T. Properties by assignment. The payee did not indorse the note to Second. When the note was not paid, Second tried to foreclose on the property that was the security for the note. In the ensuing lawsuit, G.M.T. tried to raise a defense that the note was procured by fraud. What difference does it make to Second whether the note was transferred by negotiation or by assignment?

L.O.2, 3

2   Flight Training Center operated a flight school and aircraft rental business. Russell Lund and William Rubin owned and rented planes to FTC. Lund and Rubin decided to sell two jet planes to FTC. A check drawn on Chemical Bank and payable to FTC for $716,946 was indorsed by FTC and made payable to the order of William Rubin and Russell Lund. FTC's lawyer had prepared a power of attorney purporting to authorize Rubin to indorse the check for Lund. It was a forgery. Rubin indorsed the check in his own name and as attorney-in-fact for Lund. The check was given to Laidlaw Adams & Peck, Inc., which deposited it in its account at Chemical. When he learned of this, Lund sued Chemical. Had there been a negotiation of the check?

3   June Wachter went to Denver National Bank and paid the bank cash to make a wire transfer to California. Denver's personnel transferred the funds, which were received in California the same day. Wachter later asked for confirmation. Denver gave Wachter a copy of the actual wire transfer and orally advised her the transfer had been made. Denver even provided her with a copy of a letter from the California bank indicating that the intended recipient had received the funds. Wachter was still not convinced and went to California to make sure. She then sued Denver under the Electronic Fund Transfer Act. Did the Act apply?

L.O.1

4   Jacobson, Inc., sued Walter Burris personally on a charge account. The application for the charge account indicated Oak Tree Homes as the applicant, but at the end it was signed by Walter Burris with no indication it was signed other than by him individually. At trial the judge entered judgment against Burris, relying on a law that referred to negotiable instruments. Was this the proper law to rely upon?

L.O.3

5   C. C. Lamb executed five promissory notes to Opelika Production Credit Association (OPCA), which was directly supervised by the Federal

Intermediate Credit Bank of New Orleans (FICB). The notes became in default, so OPCA made demand for payment and then filed suit. Lamb alleged that OPCA could not sue on the notes because it was not the holder of them. Although the notes remained in OPCA's vaults, they had a prestamped indorsement to the FICB. Was OPCA the holder of the notes?

Chapter 22

E//ENTIAL/ OF NEGOTIABILITY

LEARNING OBJECTIVES

After studying this chapter you should be able to:

1 List the seven requirements of negotiability.

2 Explain the requirements for delivery of a negotiable instrument.

3 State whether a negotiable instrument must be dated and whether the location of making payment must be indicated.

Preview Case

George Werner, Stan Fejta, and August Werner, as well as two witnesses, signed the following document:

> Promissory Note
> Werner Enterprises, Inc., by resolution and signature acknowledges that a debt of $8000.00 is owed to Mr. Stan Fejta (Fejta Construction Company) regarding the construction of "Pontchartrain Plaza," 1930 West End Park.
> This note is payable at maturity on or before May 19, 19--, plus 10% (percent) interest.
>
> Date: April 4, 19--

After unsuccessful attempts to collect this indebtedness, Fejta filed suit. Werner alleged that the writing was nothing more than an acknowledgment of a preexisting debt since it did not contain an unconditional promise to pay. Was this a note?

Negotiability

Transferability

An important characteristic of negotiable instruments is their transferability or **negotiability.** However, instruments must meet certain requirements in order to be negotiable.

REQUIREMENTS

L.O.1 ....

An instrument must comply with seven requirements in order to be negotiable. If it lacks any one of these requirements, the document is not negotiable even though it may be valid and enforceable as between the original parties to it. These seven requirements include the following :

1   The instrument must be in writing and signed by the party executing it.
2   The instrument must contain either an order to pay or a promise to pay.
3   The order or the promise must be unconditional.
4   The instrument must provide for the payment of a sum certain in money.
5   The instrument must be payable either on demand or at a fixed or definite time.
6   The instrument must be payable to the order of a payee or to bearer.
7   The payee (unless the instrument is payable to bearer) and the drawee must be designated with reasonable certainty.

A Signed Writing

A negotiable instrument must be written. The law does not, however, require that the writing be in any particular form. The instrument may be written with pen and ink or with pencil; it may be typed or printed; or it may be partly printed and partly typed. An instrument executed with a lead pencil meets the legal requirements of negotiability. However, a person executing an instrument with pencil takes a risk because of the ease with which the instrument could be altered without detection.

A signature must be placed on a negotiable instrument in order to indicate the intent of the promisor to be bound. The normal place for a signature is in the lower right-hand corner, but the location of the signature and its form are wholly immaterial if it is clear that a signature was intended. The signature may be written, typed, printed, or stamped. It may be a name, a symbol, a mark, or a trade name. The signature, however, must be on the instrument. It cannot be on a separate paper attached to the instrument.

Some odd but valid signatures follow:

1   Richard **X** Cooper — His / Mark. This type of signature might be made by a person who does not know how to write. The signer makes the X in the center. A witness writes the signer's name, Richard Cooper, and the words, *His Mark* to indicate who signed the instrument and that it was intended as a signature.
2   "I, Tammy Morley," written by Morley in the body of the note but with her name typed in the usual place for the signature.
3   "Snowwhite Cleaner," the trade name under which Glendon Sutton operates his business.

The instrument may be signed by an agent—another person who has been given authority to perform this act.

An Order or a Promise to Pay

A draft, such as a trade acceptance or a check, must contain an order to pay. If the request is imperative and unequivocal, it is an order even though the word *order* is not used.

A promissory note must contain a promise to pay. The word *promise* need not be used—any equivalent words will answer the purpose—but the language used must show that a promise is intended. Thus, the words *I will pay*, *I guarantee to pay*, and *This is to certify that we are bound to pay* were held to be sufficient to constitute a promise. A mere acknowledgment of a debt does not suffice.

George Werner, Stan Fejta, and August Werner, as well as two witnesses, signed the following document:

> **Promissory Note**
> Werner Enterprises, Inc., by resolution and signature acknowledges that a debt of $8000.00 is owed to Mr. Stan Fejta (Fejta Construction Company) regarding the construction of "Pontchartrain Plaza," 1930 West End Park.
> This note is payable at maturity on or before May 19, 19--, plus 10% (percent) interest.
>
> Date: April 4, 19--

After unsuccessful attempts to collect this indebtedness, Fejta filed suit. Werner alleged that the writing was nothing more than an acknowledgment of a preexisting debt since it did not contain an unconditional promise to pay. The court held that examination of the entire writing showed a promise to pay. It was titled "Promissory Note" and stated it was "payable at maturity"; therefore, it was intended to be a promise to pay money.

Unconditional

The order or the promise must be absolute and unconditional. Neither must be contingent upon any other act or event. If Baron promises to pay Noffke $500 "in 60 days, or sooner if I sell my farm," the instrument is negotiable because the promise itself is unconditional. In any event, a promise to pay the $500 in 60 days exists. The contingency pertains only to the time of payment, and that time cannot exceed 60 days. If the words "or sooner" were omitted, the promise would be conditional, and the note would be nonnegotiable. As stated previously, however, an instrument may be binding on the parties even though nonnegotiable.

If the order to pay is out of a particular fund or account, the instrument is normally nonnegotiable. For example, "Pay to the order of Leonard Cohen $5,000 out of my share of my mother's estate" would be a conditional order to pay. The order or the promise must commit the entire credit of the one primarily liable for the payment of the instrument. There is an exception made in the case of instruments issued by a government or a governmental agency or unit.

Revised Article 3 changes this rule. Under the revision, an order to pay is not conditional if payment is restricted to a specified fund or account.

A reference to the consideration in a note that does not condition the promise does not destroy negotiability. The clause "This note is given in consideration of a typewriter purchased today" does not condition the maker's promise to pay. If the clause read, "This note is given in consideration for a typewriter guaranteed for 90 days, breach of warranty to constitute cancellation of the note," the instrument would not be negotiable. This promise to pay is not absolute, but conditional. Also, if the recital of the consideration is in such form as to make the instrument subject to another contract, the negotiability of the instrument is destroyed.

Thus, a mere reference to a separate agreement or a statement that the instrument arises out of a separate agreement, does not make the promise or order conditional. However, if the promise or order states it is subject to or governed by another agreement, it is conditional.

Koyt Everhart executed a note to Jane Everhart in which he promised to pay $150,000 "in lieu of a property settlement supplementing that certain Deed of Separation and Property Settlement . . . the terms of which are incorporated herein by reference." Jane signed a document prepared by her attorneys that purported to assign one-third of the note to them. After default, they sued for collection of the note. For them to recover, the note had to be negotiable. It was not. Incorporating the Deed of Separation and Property Settlement into the note made it subject to any conditions in those documents, and therefore the promise was conditional.

A Sum Certain in Money

The instrument must call for the payment of money. It need not be American money, but it must be some national medium of exchange that is legal tender at the place payment is to be made. Thus it could be payable in dollars, yen, marks, pounds, pesos, or rubles. It cannot be in scrip, gold bullion, bonds, or similar assets. The instrument may provide for the payment of either money or goods. If the choice lies with the holder, such a provision does not destroy its negotiability.

To buy a new Buick, Susan Kellar executed an installment note to Society National Bank. Kellar stopped making payments on it shortly after making the note. She asked for the payoff balance in order to pay off the loan. The balance was $19,297.87. By mail, Society received a "certified draft" for $19,300 drawn on International Credit Exchange in Acapulco, Mexico. The draft stated, "This draft is redeemable in current funds (credit) when presented . . ." After forwarding the instrument for payment, Society found out that the draft was returned unpaid and International Credit Exchange did not exist. Society sued Kellar who claimed the draft was a negotiable instrument. The court held that it was not negotiable because it was not payable in money but in credit.

The sum payable must be a certain amount not dependent upon other funds or upon future profits.

Not only must the contract be payable in money to be negotiable, but the amount must be certain from the wording of the instrument itself. If a note for $5,000 provides that all taxes that may be levied upon a certain piece of real estate will be paid, it is nonnegotiable. The amount to be paid cannot be determined from the note itself. A provision providing for the payment of interest or exchange charges, however, does not destroy negotiability. Other terms that have been held not to destroy negotiability are provisions for cost of collection, a 10 percent attorney's fee if placed in the hands of an attorney for collection, and installment payments.

All jurisdictions do not agree how a variable rate of interest affects negotiability. Most find instruments with such rates negotiable.

Revised Article 3 requires the instrument to call for payment of a "fixed amount" of money. Since the fixed amount refers to principal, the revision specifically permits the rate of interest to be a variable one without destroying negotiability.

Orel and Mildred Hershiser executed a $10.5 million promissory note to Westwood Mortgage Corporation. When sued on the note by the subsequent holder, the Federal Savings and Loan Insurance Corporation, the Hershisers and subsequent obligors argued the note was not negotiable. The note provided for a variable interest rate tied to a commercial index. Hershiser said that the promise to pay was therefore not a "sum certain." The court found that because the interest rate was readily ascertainable and the interest owed could be easily calculated, the promise was indeed a sum certain.

Sometimes, through error of the party writing the negotiable instrument, the words on the instrument may call for the payment of one amount of money, while the figures call for the payment of another. The amount expressed in words prevails because one is less likely to err in writing this amount. Also, if anyone should attempt to raise the amount, it would be much simpler to alter the figures than the words. By the same token, handwriting prevails over conflicting typewriting, and typewriting prevails over conflicting printed amounts.

Payable on Demand or at a Definite Time

An instrument meets the test of negotiability as to time if it is payable on demand (as in a demand note) or at sight (as in a sight draft). If no time is specified (as in a check), the commercial paper is considered payable on demand.

If the instrument provides for payment at some future time, the due date must be fixed.

Charles and Alice Faulkner signed a promissory note payable to the order of Elmer E. Miller and Ronald Rotert. It provided for 8 percent interest "from the date of death of Elmer E. Miller." Monthly payments of principal and interest were to be made starting one month after Miller's death. The Faulkners made no payments even after Miller's death, and Rotert sued them for payment. The decision in the case rested on whether the note was negotiable. The court held that since payments were to begin one month after Miller's death, the note was not payable at a definite time and therefore not negotiable.

Promissory notes often include either an acceleration clause or a prepayment clause. An acceleration clause protects the payee, and the prepayment clause benefits the party obligated to pay. A typical acceleration clause provides that in the event one installment is in default, the whole note shall become due and payable at once. This does not destroy its negotiability. Most prepayment clauses give the maker or the drawee the right to prepay the instrument in order to save interest. This also does not affect the negotiability of the instrument.

Payable to Order or Bearer

The two most common words of negotiability are *order* and *bearer*. The instrument is *payable to order* when some person is made the payee, and the maker or drawer wishes to indicate that the instrument will be paid to the person designated or to anyone else to whom the payee may transfer the instrument by indorsement.

It is not necessary to use the word *order*, but it is strongly recommended. The law looks to the intention of the maker or the drawer. If the words used clearly show an intention to pay either the named payee or anyone else whom the payee designates, the contract is negotiable. A note payable to "Smith and assigns" was held to be nonnegotiable. If it had been payable to "Smith or assigns," it would have been negotiable.

Revised Article 3 provides that a *check* reading "Pay to Smith" is negotiable. This applies only to checks and not to other drafts or notes.

The other words of negotiability, *payable to bearer,* indicate that the maker or the acceptor of a draft is willing to pay the person who possesses the instrument at maturity. The usual form in which these words appear is *Pay to bearer* or *Pay to Lydia Lester or bearer*. Other types of wording make an instrument a bearer instrument. For example, *pay to the order of cash*, and *pay to the order of bearer*, or any other designation that does not refer to a natural person or a corporation is regarded as payable to bearer.

Payee and Drawee Designated with Reasonable Certainty

When a negotiable instrument is payable "to order," the payee must be so named that the specific party can be identified with reasonable certainty. For example, a check that reads, *Pay to the order of the Treasurer of the Virginia Educational Association* is not payable to a specific named individual, but that person can be ascertained with reasonable certainty. Therefore the check is negotiable. If, on the other hand, the check is payable "to the order of the Treasury of the Y.M.C.A." and the city has three such organizations, it would not be possible to ascertain with reasonable certainty who the payee is. This check would not be negotiable.

The drawee of a draft must likewise be named or described with reasonable certainty so that the holder will know who will accept or pay it.

DELIVERY

L.O.2 ....

Issue

To release control over negotiable instrument to payee

A negotiable instrument written by the drawer or maker does not have any effect until it is "issued." **Issued** ordinarily means that the drawer or maker mails it or hands it over to the payee or does some other act that releases control over it and sends it on its way to the payee. To negotiate order paper, it must be both indorsed by the person to whom the paper is then payable and delivered to the new holder. Bearer payer requires no indorsement, and negotiation is effected by a physical transfer of the instrument alone.

Whenever delivery is made in connection with either the original issue or a subsequent negotiation, the delivery must be absolute, as contrasted with conditional. If it is conditional, the issuing of the instrument or the negotiation does not take effect until the condition is satisfied; although, as against a holder in due course, a defendant will be barred from showing that the condition was not satisfied.

DELIVERY OF AN INCOMPLETE INSTRUMENT

If a negotiable instrument is only partially filled in and signed before delivery, the maker or drawer is liable if the blanks are filled in according to instructions. If the holder fills in the blanks contrary to authority, the maker or drawer is liable to the original payee or an ordinary holder for only the amount actually authorized. A holder in due course, however, can enforce the paper according to the filled-in terms even though they were not authorized.

DATE AND PLACE

L.O.3 ....

Various matters not of commercial significance do not affect the negotiable character of a negotiable instrument.

1   *The instrument need not be dated.* The negotiability of the instrument is not affected by the fact it is undated, antedated, or postdated. The omission of a date may cause considerable inconvenience, but the date is not essential. The holder may fill in the correct date if the space for the date is left blank. If an instrument is due 30 days after date and the date is omitted, the instrument is payable 30 days after it was issued or delivered. In case of dispute, the date of issue may be proved.

2   *The name of the place where the instrument was drawn or where it is payable need not be specified.* For contracts in general, the law where the contract is made or where it is to be performed governs one's rights. This rule makes it advisable for a negotiable instrument to stipulate the place where it is drawn and where it is payable, but neither is essential for its negotiability.

QUESTIONS

1   If an instrument lacks a requirement of negotiability, is it totally unenforceable?
2   State the seven requirements of negotiability.
3   Must the signature of the maker on a negotiable contract be in the lower right-hand corner?
4   Must a draft contain the word *order* to be negotiable?
5   Will a reference to the consideration in a note destroy negotiability?
6   When must a negotiable instrument be payable?
7   When the amount in words in an instrument conflicts with the amount in figures, which prevails?
8   Explain the difference between negotiation of an instrument that is *payable to order* and one that is *payable to bearer.*
9   What are the requirements for delivery of a negotiable instrument?
10   Must a negotiable instrument be dated and the location of payment be indicated?

CASE PROBLEMS

L.O.2 ....

1   Kathryn McCain was employed near a safety deposit box to which she and other employees had access at the front desk of a motel. Money ($110) was stolen from the safety deposit box, and McCain was investigated as a suspect.

Following a polygraph test, McCain was fired. She went to the motel to pick up a payroll check due her and was told $110 was to be withheld from her wages, pending the results of the police investigation. While there, she saw her payroll check and refused a check for the amount of her wages less $110. After being refused a written demand for the payroll check, she filed suit, alleging wrongful conversion of her payroll check. Conversion requires the taking or a detention, interference, illegal assumption of ownership, or illegal use or misuse of property. Was there a wrongful conversion?

L.O.1 .... **2** Air Terminal Gifts, Inc., executed a $125,000 promissory note. The note stated it was secured by a separate agreement and, "Reference is made to the Purchase and Security Agreement for additional rights of the holder hereof." When sued for payment of the note, Air Terminal claimed the quoted language made it nonnegotiable. Decide this case.

L.O.1 .... **3** Charles Cox, Morris Grossman, Thomas King, and Melvin Gittleman formed a partnership named G.G.C. Co. to build and operate an apartment complex. Cox, Grossman, and King then formed a corporation, also named G.G.C. Co., which was designated by the partnership as attorney-in-fact to secure financing for the complex. The corporation, Cox, Grossman, and King signed a promissory note in favor of First National Bank of St. Paul to secure a $1,250,000 loan. The corporation defaulted on the note, and the Bank foreclosed on the complex. The Bank alleged that Gittleman should be liable on the note because he was a partner in the partnership that dominated the corporation that executed the note. Should he be liable?

L.O.2 .... **4** Catherine Wagner received a check for $17,400. She indorsed it in blank and left it and two letters on the kitchen table in the apartment she shared with Robert Scherer. In one of the letters, Wagner stated she "bequeathed" the check to Scherer. Wagner left the apartment and jumped from the roof of the building to her death. In the lawsuit that ensued, the court had to decide whether Wagner had delivered the check to Scherer. How do you decide?

L.O.1 .... **5** S. Gentilotti wrote a check for $20,000 payable to the order of his son. It was postdated 15 years and delivered to the boy's mother. Before his death, Gentilotti frequently asked the mother if she had the check. After his death demand for payment was made and refused. The mother and son sued the executrix of Gentilotti's estate for payment of the check. Was it negotiable?

L.O.1 .... **6** Charles and Joan Valentine executed a note to First National City Bank, payable to First National "or order." When sued for payment of the note, the Valentines argued that it was not negotiable. The UCC requires an instrument to be payable "to order or to bearer," and the note did not contain those exact words. Did the language impair the negotiability of the note?

Chapter 23

PROMISSORY NOTES AND DRAFTS

LEARNING OBJECTIVES

After studying this chapter you should be able to:

1 Distinguish among the different types of notes.

2 Identify the two different kinds of drafts.

3 Explain how drafts are accepted and what admissions are made by acceptance.

4 Describe the characteristics of a check.

Preview Case

At about three-thirty Friday afternoon, Marcia Garcia purchased jewelry from Shaw's of San Antonio, Inc., by a check for $1,328.20 drawn on Groos National Bank. Before delivering the jewelry, Shaw's telephoned the bank and was told the check was good. On Saturday Garcia returned to Shaw's and tried to buy more jewelry. Finding out that the address Garcia used on her check was nonexistent, Shaw's became suspicious and sent an employee to the bank at nine o'clock Monday when it opened for business. Garcia's account lacked enough money to pay the check. When Shaw's sued the bank for payment, the bank alleged it was not liable because it had not accepted the check. Had there been a proper acceptance?

Notes and drafts are negotiable instruments widely used in commercial and personal transactions. Each has unique features.

NOTES

Any written promise to pay money at a specified time is a promissory note, but it may not be a negotiable instrument. To be negotiable, a note must contain the essential elements discussed in Chapter 22.

The two original parties to a promissory note are the maker, the one who signs the note and promises to pay, and the payee, the one to whom the promise is made.

Liability of the Maker

The maker of a promissory note (1) expressly agrees to pay the note according to its terms, (2) admits the existence of the payee, and (3) warrants that the payee is competent to transfer the instrument by indorsement.

Thomas Sessions bought farm machinery from Charles McCarthy to use on the farms he owned and operated with his wife Dorothy. The Sessions signed a promissory note to McCarthy in the amount due on the machinery on February 8. Thomas Sessions died on March 31. McCarthy sued to collect on the note.	Dorothy said she was not liable because Thomas purchased the machinery, not her, and Thomas was liable on the underlying debt. The court stated she was a maker of the note. As a maker, Dorothy contracted to pay the note according to its terms at the time she signed it and was liable to McCarthy.

Types of Notes

L.O.1 ....

Many types of notes known by special names include:

1. Bonds
2. Collateral notes
3. Real estate mortgage notes
4. Debentures

Bond

Sealed, written contract obligation with essentials of note

Bonds. A **bond** is a written contract obligation, usually under seal, generally issued by a corporation, a municipality, or a government, that contains a promise to pay a sum certain in money at a fixed or determinable future time. In addition to the promise to pay, it will generally contain certain other conditions and stipulations. A bond issued by a corporation is generally secured by a deed of trust on the property of the corporation. A bond may be a coupon bond or a registered bond.

Coupon Bond

Bond with detachable individual coupons representing interest payments

A **coupon bond** is so called because the interest payments that will become due on the bond are represented by detachable individual coupons to be presented for payment when due. Coupon bonds and the individual coupons are usually payable to the bearer; as a result, they can be negotiated by delivery. There is no registration of the original purchaser or any subsequent holder of the bond.

Registered Bond

Bond payable to specific person, whose name is recorded by issuer

A **registered bond** is a bond payable to a named person. The bond is recorded under that name by the organization issuing it to guard against its loss or destruction. When a registered bond is sold, a record of the transfer to the new bondholder must be made under the name of the new holder of the bond.

Collateral Note

Note secured by personal property

Collateral Notes. A **collateral note** is a note secured by personal property. The collateral usually consists of stock, bonds, or other written evidences of debt, or a security interest in tangible personal property given by the debtor to the payee-creditor.

The transaction may vary in terms of whether the creditor keeps possession of the property as long as the debt is unpaid or whether the debtor may keep possession of the property until default. When the creditor receives possession of collateral, reasonable care must be taken of it, and the creditor is liable to the debtor for any loss resulting from lack of reasonable care. If the creditor receives any interest, dividend, or other income from the property while it is held as collateral, such amount must be credited against the debt or returned to the debtor.

Regardless of the form of the transaction, the property is freed from the claim of the creditor if the debt is paid. If not paid, the creditor may sell the property in the manner prescribed by law. The creditor must return to the debtor any excess of the sale proceeds above the debt, interest, and costs. If the sale of the collateral does not provide sufficient proceeds to pay the debt, the debtor is liable for any deficiency.

Real Estate Mortgage Note

Note secured by mortgage on real estate

Real Estate Mortgage Notes. A **real estate mortgage note** is given to evidence a debt that the maker-debtor secures by giving to the payee a mortgage on real estate. As in the case of a real estate mortgage, generally the mortgagor-debtor retains possession of the property. If the real estate is not freed by payment of the debt, the holder may proceed on the mortgage or the mortgage note to enforce the maker-mortgagor's liability. Chapter 44 more thoroughly describes real estate mortgages.

Debenture

Unsecured bond issued by a business

Debentures. An unsecured bond or note issued by a business firm is called a **debenture.** A debenture, like any other bond, is nothing more or less than a promissory note, usually under seal. It may be embellished with gold-colored edges, but this does not in any way indicate its value. A debenture is usually negotiable in form.

CERTIFICATES OF DEPOSIT

Certificate of Deposit

Acknowledgment by bank of receipt of money with engagement to repay it

While the UCC does not classify a certificate of deposit (CD) as a note, a CD has all the elements of a note except it does not contain the word *promise*. The UCC defines a **certificate of deposit** as "an acknowledgement by a bank of a receipt of money with an engagement to repay it." Normally the money is repaid with interest. A CD is not a draft because it does not contain an order to pay.

Revised Article 3 treats certificates of deposit as notes.

George Robinson bought a money market certificate from the West Greeley National Bank and named his stepdaughter, Loretta Wygant, as the pay-on-death (P.O.D.) beneficiary. George later married Hope Robinson and orally asked the bank to change the beneficiary to his wife. After George died, Hope and Loretta both claimed the proceeds of the certificate.

Loretta claimed the certificate was a negotiable instrument and her indorsement was required to change the beneficiary. In order to be negotiable, there must be an unconditional promise to pay. Here, the P.O.D. clause conditioned payment to Loretta on the death of George Robinson; thus, it was not negotiable.

DRAFTS

L.O.2 ....

The drawer draws or executes a draft in favor of the payee, who has the drawer's authority to collect the amount indicated on the instrument. It must be clear that the signature is intended to be that of a drawer; otherwise the signature will be construed to be that of an indorser. A draft is addressed to the drawee, who is the person ordered by the drawer to pay the amount of the instrument. The drawee pays the amount to the payee or some other party to whom the payee has transferred the instrument by indorsement. The drawee, after accepting the instrument, that is, after agreeing to pay it, becomes the acceptor.

An **inland,** or *domestic,* **draft** is one that shows on its face that it is both drawn and payable within the United States. A **foreign draft** shows on its face that it is drawn or payable outside the United States.

Forms of Drafts

Two kinds of drafts exist to meet the different needs of business:

1 Sight drafts
1 Time drafts

Sight Drafts. A **sight draft** is a draft payable at sight or upon presentation by the payee or holder. By it the drawer demands payment at once. Special types of sight drafts include money orders and checks.

Time Drafts. A **time draft** has the same form as a sight draft except regarding the date of payment. The drawer orders the drawee to pay the money a certain number of days or months after the date on the instrument or a certain number of days or months after presentation.

In the case of a time draft, the holder cannot require payment of the paper until it has matured. The holder normally presents the draft to the drawee for acceptance. However, whether or not the draft has been accepted does not affect the time when it matures if it is payable a certain length of time after its date.

A time draft payable a specified number of days after sight must be presented for acceptance. The due date is calculated from the date of the acceptance, not from the date of the draft.

Trade Acceptance

A **trade acceptance** is a type of draft used in the sale of goods. It is a draft drawn by the seller on the purchaser of goods sold and accepted by such purchaser. The drawer draws a trade acceptance at the time goods are sold. The seller is the drawer, and the purchaser is the drawee. A trade acceptance orders the purchaser to pay the face of the bill to the order of the named payee, who is frequently the seller.

Presentment for Acceptance

L.O.3 ....

All trade acceptances and all time drafts payable a specified time after sight must be presented for acceptance by the payee to the drawee. In case of other kinds of drafts, presentment for acceptance is optional and is made merely to determine the intention of the drawee and to give the paper the additional credit strength of the acceptance. A qualified acceptance destroys the negotiability of the instrument. An

---

Inland Draft

Draft drawn and payable in the U.S.

Foreign Draft

Draft drawn or payable outside the U.S.

Sight Draft

Draft payable upon presentation by holder

Time Draft

Draft payable certain number of days or months after date or presentation

Trade Acceptance

Draft drawn by seller on purchaser of goods

acceptance could be qualified by adding additional terms such as "if presented for payment within 24 hours" or "in ten days from date."

Place. The instrument should be presented at the drawee's place of business. If there is no place of business, it may be presented at the drawee's home or wherever the drawee may be found.

Party. A draft must be presented to the drawee or to someone authorized either by law or by contract to accept it. If there are two or more drawees, the draft must be presented to all of them unless one has authority to act for them all.

Form of Acceptance

The usual method of accepting a draft is to write on the face:

> Accepted
> John Doe.

The word *accepted* and the drawee's signature are all that is normally necessary to constitute a valid acceptance. If an acceptance on a sight draft does not include a date, the holder may supply the date. The drawee may use other words of acceptance, but the words used must indicate an intention to be bound by the terms of the instrument and must be written on the instrument.

At about three-thirty Friday afternoon, Marcia Garcia purchased jewelry from Shaw's of San Antonio, Inc., by a check for $1,328.20 drawn on Groos National Bank. Before delivering the jewelry, Shaw's telephoned the bank and was told the check was good. On Saturday Garcia returned to Shaw's and tried to buy more jewelry. Finding out that the address Garcia used on her check was nonexistent, Shaw's became suspicious and sent an employee to the bank at nine o'clock Monday when it opened for business. Garcia's account lacked enough money to pay the check. When Shaw's sued the bank for payment, the bank alleged it was not liable because it had not accepted the check. The court agreed, saying that an acceptance must be in writing and on the instrument.

If the drawee refuses to accept a draft or to accept it in a proper way, the holder of the draft has no claim against the drawee but can return the draft to the drawer. Any credit given the drawer by the delivery of the draft is thereby canceled. If the draft is a trade acceptance, the refusal of the drawee to accept means that the buyer refuses to go through with the financing terms of the transaction; unless some other means of financing or payment is agreed upon, the transaction falls through.

Admissions of the Acceptor

A draft presented to a drawee for acceptance must be either accepted or returned. If not returned, the drawee is treated as having stolen the paper form the holder. By accepting the instrument, the drawee assumes liability for the payment of the paper. This liability of the acceptor runs from the due date of the paper until the statute of limitations bars the claim.

When the drawee accepts a draft, two admissions concerning the drawer are made:

1   That the signature of the drawer is genuine
2   That the drawer has both the capacity and the authority to draw the draft.

> B. C. Dahl offered a check drawn on First State Bank of Rollingstone to Lou Hodnik, a supervisor of Greyhound Lines, in payment of a debt to Greyhound. Hodnik refused to take the check unless the bank confirmed the funds were in the account. Dahl returned with the check signed by Duane Klein, vice president of the bank. Hodnik talked with Klein by phone. Klein assured him the money was in the bank. Hodnik took the check, which bounced. Greyhound sued First State. The court held that First State had accepted the check and had to pay it.

The drawee, by accepting a draft, also admits the payee's capacity to indorse, but not the genuineness of the payee's indorsement.

Having made these admissions, the acceptor cannot later deny them against a holder of the instrument.

Acceptance by the Buyer's Financing Agency

Another financing technique employed in the sale of goods is "acceptance by the buyer's financing agency." As a variation of the pattern in which the buyer is the drawee of the trade acceptance, the buyer may arrange with a bank or finance company to accept the trade acceptance that the buyer will draw upon. When this occurs, the buyer will have worked out some loan or financing arrangements with the bank or finance company. The buyer will name the bank or finance company as drawee, and the bank or finance company will accept the draft.

Money Orders

Money Order

Instrument issued by business indicating payee may receive indicated amount

A **money order** is an instrument issued by a bank, post office, or express company indicating that the payee may request and receive the amount indicated on the instrument. When paid for, issued, and delivered to the payee, the issuer has made a contract to pay.

CHECKS

L.O.4

Check

Draft drawn on a bank and payable on demand

A **check** is a type of draft. To be a check, the draft must be drawn on a bank and payable on demand. It is a type of sight draft with the drawee a bank and the drawer a depositor—a person who has funds deposited with a bank. Just like other drafts, a check is an order by the *drawer,* upon the *drawee,* to pay a sum of money to the order of another person, the *payee.*

The numbers at the bottom of a check (see Illustration 23-1) are printed in magnetic ink. The numbers identify the specific account and the bank that holds the account. Since the numbers are printed in magnetic ink, the check may be sorted by electronic data processing equipment. The Federal Reserve System requires that all

Illustration 23-1   Check

CURTRON HEATING/AIR CONDITIONING
1401 Dixie Highway
Newport, Kentucky

No. **83**   46-0039
                0420

May 28, 19 --

PAY TO THE
ORDER OF ___Ashland Oil_____ $ 243 21

Two hundred forty-three 21/100 _____ DOLLARS
                        FOR CLASSROOM USE ONLY

PROVIDENCE NATIONAL BANK
Covington, Kentucky

Jane E. Congdon

⑆0420C0392⑆ 2461705⑈

checks passing through its clearinghouses be imprinted with such identifying magnetic ink. In most cases, however, the drawee bank will accept checks that do not carry the magnetic ink coding. In fact, the material upon which a check is written does not affect the validity of a check.

Special Kinds of Checks

Five special types of checks include:

1 Certified checks
2 Cashier's checks
3 Bank drafts
4 Voucher checks
5 Traveler's checks

Certified Check

Check accepted by bank's writing "certified" on it

Certified Checks. A **certified check** is an ordinary check accepted by an official of the drawee bank. The official accepts it by writing across the face of the check the word *certified*, or some similar word, and signing it. Either the drawer or the holder may have a check certified. The certification of the check by the bank has the same effect as an acceptance. It makes the bank liable for the payment of the check and binds it by the warranties made by an acceptor.

A certification obtained by a holder releases the drawer from liability. The rationale for releasing the drawer from liability is that the holder will accept the obligation of the bank to pay rather than require payment at the time. Had payment been made, all other parties would have been discharged from all possible future liability. Having failed to free the other parties by accepting the certification in place of payment, the holder loses the right to proceed against the other parties.

Revised Article 3 provides that the drawer of a draft accepted by a bank is relieved of liability on the instrument. It does not matter when or by whom acceptance was obtained.

The Bank of New York certified a $60,000 check payable to Charles and Jean Thornton drawn by White Plains Hospital Medical Center. BNY later stopped payment on the check at the request of White Plains. The Thorntons then opened an account at Casco Bank and Trust Company using the check. BNY refused to pay the check because of the stop payment order. The Thorntons withdrew all the funds from the account at Casco, so Casco sued BNY. The court found that Casco was entitled to the $60,000 check amount.

Cashier's Check

Check drawn by bank on its own funds

Cashier's Checks. A check that a bank draws on its own funds and that the cashier or some other responsible official of the bank signs is called a **cashier's check.** It is accepted for payment when issued and delivered. Such a check may be used by a bank in paying its own obligations, or it may be used by anyone else who wishes to remit money in some form other than cash or a personal check.

Bank Draft

Check drawn by one bank on another

Bank Drafts. A **bank draft** is a check drawn by one bank on another bank. Banks customarily keep a portion of their funds on deposit with other banks. A bank, then, may draw a check on these funds ars freely as any corporation may draw checks.

Voucher Check

Check with voucher attached

Voucher Checks. A **voucher check** is a check with a voucher attached. The voucher lists the items of an invoice for which the check is the means of payment. In business the drawer of the check customarily writes on the check such words as *In full of account, For invoice No. 1622,* or similar notations. These notations make the checks excellent receipts when returned to the drawer. A check on which additional space is provided for the drawer to make a notation for which the check is issued is sometimes referred to as a voucher check. A payee who indorses a check on which a notation has been made agrees to the terms of the check, which include the terms written in the notation by the drawer.

Traveler's Checks. A traveler's check is an instrument much like a cashier's check of the issuer except that it requires signature and counter-signature by its purchaser. Traveler's checks, sold by banks and express companies, are payable on demand. The purchaser of traveler's checks signs each check once at the time of purchase and then countersigns it and fills in the name of the payee when the check is to be used.

Charles Gray, who owned a wholesale grocery business, received an order from Ernie's Truck Stop for $4,900 worth of cigarettes. Gray delivered the cigarettes to Ernie's, which gave them to Joseph Faillance. Faillance paid Ernie's with $4,900 in American Express traveler's checks. Gray saw Faillance countersign the checks, but they were not dated or made payable to anyone. Ernie's gave the checks to Gray in payment for the cigarettes. The next day Gray turned them in to a bank and was refused payment because they were stolen. Gray sued American Express for payment. The court found that although an instrument need not be dated, the name of the payee is essential. Since the checks were incomplete, they were unenforceable.

Postdated Checks

Postdated Check

Check drawn prior to its date

A check drawn prior to the time it is dated is a **postdated check.** If it is drawn on June 21, but dated July 1, it is, in effect, a ten-day draft. There is nothing unlawful about a postdated check as long as it was not postdated for an illegal or fraudulent purpose. It is payable on demand on or any time after its date. As a practical matter the payee may refuse to accept it because payment is desired now rather than at a later date.

Revised Article 3 and its amendments to other parts of the UCC change the rule on postdated checks. A bank on which such a check is drawn may pay it *before* its date unless the customer/drawer has properly notified the bank of the postdated check.

Mr. and Mrs. Charles Wilson signed and gave to Steven Anny, a real estate salesman, printed forms of "offer to buy real estate," which Anny filled out. They also gave him a postdated check dated February 14 for $500 payable to the real estate company. On February 11, Anny visited Eileen Lewis, who owned the real estate the Wilsons wanted to buy, and after about two hours of discussion she accepted the offer. The offer stated the company had "Received from (the Wilsons) herein called Buyer, the sum of Five Hundred dollars ($500.00) evidenced by . . . personal check" to be held as a deposit. Lewis did not examine the check and was not told that it was postdated. The next day Lewis called Anny and said she wanted to rescind. The Wilsons, the company, and Anny sued for breach of contract. The court found a postdated check was merely a promise to pay in the future and not payment as had been recited in the offer. Lewis was entitled to rescind.

Bad Checks

Bad Check

Check the drawee bank refuses to pay

If a check is drawn with intent to defraud the payee, the drawer is civilly liable, as well as subject to criminal prosecution in most states under so-called *bad check* laws. A **bad check** is a check that the holder sends to the drawee bank and the bank refuses to pay, normally for insufficient funds. Usually these statutes state that if the check is not made good within a specific period, such as ten days, a presumption arises that the drawer originally issued the check with the intent to defraud.

Duties of the Bank

The bank owes several duties to its customer, the depositor-drawer. It must maintain secrecy regarding information acquired by it in connection with the depositor-bank relationship.

The bank also has the duty of comparing the signature on the depositor's checks with the signature of the depositor in the bank's files to make certain the signatures on the checks are valid. If the bank pays a check that does not have the drawer's signature, it is liable to the drawer for the loss.

Refusal of Bank to Pay. The bank is under a general contractual duty to its depositors to pay on demand all of their checks to the extent of the funds deposited to their credit. When the bank breaches this contract, it is liable to the drawer for damages. In the case of a draft other than a check, there is ordinarily no duty on the drawee to accept the draft or to make payment if it has not been accepted. Therefore, the drawee is not liable to the drawer when an unaccepted draft is not paid.

Even if the normal printed form supplied by the bank is not used, the bank must pay a proper order by a depositor. Any written document that contains the substance of a normal printed check must be honored by the bank.

A divorced man making his last alimony payment wrote a check out on a T-shirt to send a message to his ex-wife that she was taking "the shirt off his bank." She did not care for the technique, but the T-shirt check was valid.

The liability of the drawee bank for improperly refusing to pay a check only runs in favor of the drawer. Even if the holder of the check or the payee may be harmed when the bank refuses to pay the check, a holder or payee has no right to sue the bank. However, the holder has a right of action against the person from whom the check was received. This right of action is based on the original obligation, which was not discharged because the check was not paid.

Stale Check

Check presented more than six months after its date

A check that is presented more than six months after its date is commonly called a **stale check.** A bank that acts in good faith may pay it. However, unless the check is certified, the bank is not required to pay it.

Stopping Payment. Drawers have the power of stopping payment of checks. After a check is issued, a drawer can notify the drawee bank not to pay it when presented for payment. This is a useful procedure when a check is lost or mislaid. A duplicate check can be written, and to make sure that the payee does not receive payment twice or that an improper person does not receive payment on the first check, payment on the first check can be stopped. Likewise, if payment is made by check and the payee defaults on the contract, payment on the check can be stopped, assuming that the payee has not cashed it.

A stop-payment order may be written or oral. The bank is bound by an oral stop-payment order only for 14 calendar days unless confirmed in writing within that time. A written order is effective for no more than six months unless renewed in writing.

Unless a valid limitation exists on its liability, the bank is liable for the loss the depositor sustains when the bank makes payment on a check after receiving proper notice to stop payment. However, the depositor has the burden of proving the loss sustained.

The Georgia Motor Club maintained a checking account at First National Bank & Trust Company of Augusta. On April 10 the Club informed First National that checks numbered 293 through 307 had been stolen and ordered that payment be stopped on them. The Club sent a written stop payment order on these checks on April 13, which First National received. In September, First National disregarded the stop payment order and honored six of the checks. The Club sued to recover the amount of the six checks. First National had to pay.

A depositor who stops payment without a valid reason may be liable to the payee. Also, the depositor is liable for stopping payment with respect to any holder in due course or other party having the rights of a holder in due course unless payment is stopped for a reason that may be asserted against such a holder as a defense. The fact that the bank refuses to make payment because of the drawer's instruction does not make the case any different from any other instance in which the drawee refuses to pay, and the legal consequences of imposing liability upon the drawer are the same.

When the depositor makes use of a means of communication such as the telegraph to give a stop-payment notice, the bank is not liable if the notice is delayed in reaching the bank and the bank makes payment before receiving the notice. The depositor can, however, sue the telegraph company if negligence on its part can be shown.

A payee who wants to avoid the potential of payment being stopped may require a certified check of the buyer or a cashier's check from the buyer's bank because neither the buyer nor the buyer's bank can stop payment to the payee on such checks.

Payment After Depositor's Death. Usually a check is ineffective after the drawer dies. However, until the bank knows of the death and has had a reasonable opportunity to act, the bank's agency is not revoked. A bank may even continue to pay or certify a depositor's checks for ten days unless a person claiming an interest in the estate orders it to stop.

QUESTIONS

1   What is a promissory note?
2   What are the obligations of the maker of a promissory note?
3   What is the difference between a bond, a collateral note, a real estate mortgage note, and a debenture?
4   What is a certificate of deposit?
5   What is the difference between sight drafts and time drafts?
6   Must a time draft payable 30 days after sight be presented for acceptance?
7   Must all drafts be presented for acceptance?
8   How are drafts accepted?
9   When the drawee accepts a draft, what admissions are made concerning the drawer?
10   What is a check?
11   If the holder of a check has it certified, who is liable for its payment?
12   Is it illegal to postdate a check?
13   If the drawer's signature is forged on a check and the check is cashed, must the bank reimburse the depositor?
14   Does the payee of a check have a cause of action against a bank that, without giving any reason for its refusal, refuses to honor a check when presented for payment?

CASE PROBLEMS

L.O.1 1   Dolanson Company, a partnership, and the partners individually, executed a promissory note to C & S National Bank in order to finance some property. When the Bank sued them on the note, the partners alleged that C & S's president, Mills Lane, orally agreed to look solely to the property for payment of the note and not require the partners to pay until the property could be sold or refinanced. Would an oral agreement by Lane change the terms of the note?

L.O.1 2   Philip Fazio sued Dominic Loweth for payment of a purported promissory note. The document in question was dated and stated: "This is to certify that I borrowed $15,000 from Philip N. Fazio on this day to be returned within ten days." The signature of Dominic Loweth appeared below the statement. Does this document meet the requirements for a negotiable promissory note?

L.O.1 .... **3** Peoples Protective Life Insurance Company sued to recover $50,000 deposited with the Bank of Alamo and represented by a certificate of deposit. The certificate stated:

> Peoples Protective Life Insurance Company has deposited in this bank exactly $50,000 dollars payable to themselves in current funds on the return of this certificate properly endorsed six months after date with interest at the rate of 5 ½ percent per annum for the time specified only.
> s/Patricia Nolen
> Authorized Signature

When the bank was sued for payment of the certificate there was an issue as to whether it was a negotiable note. Was it?

L.O.2 .... **4** National Bank of Austin sent North Valley Bank a letter authorizing North Valley to execute a sight draft on it for $75,000 within seven months. Based on that, North Valley loaned Donald Chambers $75,000 for six months. Chambers defaulted, so North Valley drew a draft on National for $75,000. The line for the signature of the drawer on the draft was blank; however, on the back was a stamp that said, "Pay to the Order of Any Bank, Banker or Trust Co. All Prior Endorsements Guaranteed. North Valley State Bank . . ." Also on the back was the signature of the vice president of North Valley. National notified North Valley it would not honor the draft. North Valley sued. National alleged the instrument was not a draft because it did not contain a proper signature of the Drawer. Did it?

L.O.3 .... **5** Cotton States Mutual Insurance Company executed a draft payable to the order of B. C. Baum and drawn on First National Bank of Atlanta. When presented for payment the draft was not accepted. Baum then sued Cotton States for payment. Cotton States defended by saying the draft was conditional on acceptance, and since it was not accepted, Cotton States was not liable. Was this defense good?

L.O.3 .... **6** When Galaxy Boat Manufacturing Company sold boats to B. L. Romans, it required Romans to pay C.O.D. The parties developed a procedure that when Galaxy received an order for boats from Romans, it would call Romans' bank, East End State Bank. East End would call Romans to make sure he had ordered the boats. East End would call Galaxy back, tell it to send the boats and that a check would be honored upon delivery. On April 29, Romans paid Galaxy upon a delivery with a check drawn on East End for $24,121. Romans stopped payment on the check on May 6. East End refused to pay the check when it was presented on May 11. Galaxy sued East End alleging an oral promise to pay the check. Must East End pay?

L.O.2, 3 .... **7** The following draft was sent by Security State Bank to Midland National Bank for collection.

COLLECT DIRECTLY THROUGH <u>MIDLAND NATIONAL BANK</u>   559499
<u>Billings, Montana 59101</u>

September 30, 19--

<u>One Hundred Sixty</u> (160) Days After Sight and Subject to Approval of Title

Pay to the
Order of ___<u>Tim Clawson</u>_____ $ 5,400.00

_____<u>---Five Thousand Four Hundred and No/100---</u>_____ DOLLARS

Consideration for <u>Balance of bonus consideration - executing oil & gas lease</u>

To: Ronald D. Berklund
   605 Midland Bank Bldg.   /s/ **Ruth L. Berklund**
   Billings, Montana 59101   Ruth L. Berklund

Midland acknowledged receipt on October 4, but no date of present-ment was written on the draft. Ronald Berklund attempted to pay on March 15 of the following year. In the lawsuit that followed, Clawson claimed that since Berklund never indicated the date of presentment, Clawson may supply the presentment date of October 4. He further alleged that since presentment was October 4, the due date was March 13 of the following year, 160 days after the 4th; therefore the draft was dishonored since payment was not attempted until March 15. Was he correct?

L.O.4 ....

8 On September 14, David Siegel wrote out and delivered to Peter Peters a $20,000 check, postdated November 14. Peters deposited the check in his bank, which forwarded it to the drawee, New England Merchants National Bank. It failed to notice the date, paid the check, and debited Siegel's account on September 17. In late September, another of Siegel's checks bounced and he discovered New England's error. It refused to credit the $20,000 to Siegel's account. He sued New England. Under pre-1990 Article 3, did it have a right to pay the check on September 17 and debit Siegel's account $20,000?

L.O.4 ....

9 Erma Brown, who owed taxes to the state, purchased from the Bank of the Commonwealth on August 29 a cashier's check payable to the state. On May 17 of the following year, the state served a warrant-notice of levy on the bank advising it of Brown's debt. On May 22, at one of the bank's branches, Brown indorsed the check to herself and received full payment. The state sued the bank, alleging that once a cashier's check has been issued it cannot be countermanded. Could the cashier's check be canceled by Brown and the bank?

L.O.4 ....

10 Robert Kaiser rented space from Northwest Shopping Center, Inc., under a lease that gave Kaiser the exclusive right to operate a pharmacy in the shop-ping center. The term expired on December 31, but a letter gave Kaiser the right to extend at an increased rental of $750. Another letter, dated January 22 after the original termination date, told Kaiser that he was a month-to-month tenant at $600 per month because he had not extended. Starting in January after the original termination date, Kaiser sent checks in the amount of $750, but Northwest held Kaiser's rent checks while it negotiated with another tenant who wanted to put in a pharmacy. The negotiations collapsed, so in October Northwest presented the checks to Kaiser's bank. It refused to honor some because they were stale. Northwest sued. Kaiser alleged that since the checks were held more than a reasonable time, they and the underlying debt were discharged. Were they?

Chapter 24

LIABILITIE/ OF THE PARTIE/ TO COMMERCIAL PAPER

LEARNING OBJECTIVES

After studying this chapter you should be able to:

1 Specify who is primarily and who is secondarily liable on commercial paper.

2 Discuss the requirements for presentment and notice of dishonor.

3 Explain the procedures for an agent to use when executing a negotiable instrument.

Preview Case

Community Bank and Trust loaned Pitrolo Pontiac Company $400,000, and Paul and Janice Pitrolo executed a "Guarantee of Payment" of the promissory note. Pitrolo Pontiac defaulted and Community sued the Pitrolos as guarantors. They asserted they were not liable on the note because it was a corporate note, and they did not receive any direct consideration for signing. Did the lack of consideration relieve the Pitrolos from liability?

T he law of commercial paper imposes liability on parties to negotiable instruments depending on the nature of the paper; the role of the party as maker, acceptor, indorser, or transferor; and the satisfaction of certain requirements of conduct by the holder of the instrument. Two basic categories of liability incidental to commercial paper include: (1) the liability created by what is written on the face of the paper (contractual liability), and (2) the liability for certain warranties regarding the instrument.

LIABILITY FOR THE FACE OF THE PAPER

Parties whose signatures do not appear on commercial paper are not liable for its payment. A signature can be any name including a trade or assumed name and may be handwritten, typed, or printed. It can even be a word or logo in place of a signature. For those whose signatures do appear, two types of contractual liability exist regarding the order or promise written on the face of the instrument: primary liability and secondary liability.

Primary Liability

L.O.1 ....

Primary Liability
Liability without conditions for commercial paper that is due

A person with **primary liability** may be called upon to carry out the specific terms indicated on the paper. Of course, the paper must be due, but no other conditions need be met by the holder of commercial paper prior to the demand being made upon one primarily liable. The two parties who ordinarily have the potential of primary liability on commercial paper include makers of notes and acceptors of drafts.

The maker of a note is primarily liable and may be called upon for payment. The maker has intended this by the unconditional promise to pay. Such a promise to pay contrasts sharply with the terms used by drawers of drafts who order drawees to pay.

The drawer of a draft does not expect to be called upon for payment; the drawer expects that payment will be made by the drawee. However, it would be unreasonable to expect that the drawee could be made liable by a mere order of another party, the drawer. Understandably then, the drawee of a draft who has not signed the instrument has no liability on it. Only when a drawee accepts a draft by writing "accepted" and signing it does the drawee have liability on the instrument. By acceptance the drawee in effect says, "I promise to pay. . . ." This acceptance renders the drawee primarily liable just as the maker of a note is primarily liable.

Secondary Liability

Indorsers and drawers are the parties whose liability on commercial paper is ordinarily secondary.

Secondary Liability
Liability for commercial paper that has been presented, dishonored, and notice of dishonor given

When the conditions of **secondary liability** have been met, a holder may require payment by any of the indorsers who have not limited their liability by the type of indorsement used or by the drawer. Generally, three conditions must be met for a party to be held secondarily liable:

1   The paper must be properly presented for payment.
2   The paper must be dishonored.
3   Notice of the dishonor must be given to the party who is to be held secondarily liable.

L.O.2 ....

Presentment
Demand for acceptance or payment

Presentment. Presentment is the demand for acceptance or payment made upon the maker, acceptor, drawee, or other payor of commercial paper. In order for indorsers to remain secondarily liable, the instrument must be properly presented.

This means the instrument should be presented to the right person, in a proper and timely manner.

Presentment of instruments that state a specified date for payment should be made on that date. Other instruments must be presented for payment within a reasonable time after a party becomes liable on the instrument. The nature of the instrument, existing commercial usage, and the partial facts of the case determine what length of time is reasonable. The UCC specifies that for drawers on uncertified checks, a presentment within 30 days after the date of the check or the date it was issued, whichever is later, is presumed to be reasonable. As to indorsers, the UCC specifies presentment within 7 days of the indorsement is presumed to be reasonable.

On August 22, Karvin Kilmer applied for auto insurance with MFA Mutual Insurance Company and wrote out a check for the first premium. An MFA agent sent the application and check to MFA's home office. On September 5 that office presented the check for payment. The bank dishonored the check, but before MFA knew that, it approved the application for insurance. The next day, Kilmer had an accident. In the resulting lawsuit the court had to decide whether MFA acted reasonably in waiting 14 days to present the check for payment. The court said that since the UCC presumed 30 days to be reasonable, a 14-day delay was also reasonable.

If presentment is delayed, drawers and makers of the instruments payable at a bank may no longer have funds in the bank to cover the instruments if the bank fails. If the bank failure occurs after presentment should have been made, drawers and indorsers may be excused from secondary liability on the basis that no proper presentment was made. To be so excused, the drawers or makers must make a written assignment of their rights against the bank, to the extent of the funds lost, to the holders of the paper.

Proper presentment is not a condition to secondary liability on a note when the maker has died or has been declared insolvent. A draft does not require presentment if the drawee or acceptor has died or gone into insolvency proceedings. Commercial paper may contain terms specifying that the indorsers and the drawer agree to waive their rights to the condition of presentment. Further, the holder is excused from the requirement of presentment if, after diligent effort, the drawee of a draft or the maker of a note cannot be located.

Stancel Kirkland was the attorney for, and an officer in, Cecil Development Company. He also owned 30 percent of its stock. Cecil executed a note to American Bank and Trust Company in the amount of $127,700. Kirkland signed the note as an indorser. When the note was due, Cecil did not pay it, and American did not present it for payment. Kirkland knew of the default. When American sued for payment of the note, Kirkland said he was discharged because of the failure of presentment. The court said the UCC excuses presentment when the indorser has no reason to expect a note to be paid. Since Kirkland knew Cecil had not paid and knew it would not pay the note, presentment was unnecessary.

Finally, if the secondary party knows that the draft or note will not be paid or has no reason to believe that the paper will be honored, presentment is excused.

Dishonor

Presentment made, but acceptance or payment not made

Dishonor. The UCC states that **dishonor** occurs when a presentment is made and a due acceptance or payment is refused or cannot be obtained within the prescribed time.

This occurs when, for example, a bank returns a check to the holder stamped "insufficient funds" or "account closed." Return of a check lacking a proper indorsement does not constitute dishonor.

Notice of Dishonor. A holder desiring to press secondary liability upon an indorser or drawer must inform that party of the dishonor. Notice of dishonor must be conveyed promptly to parties who are secondarily liable. The UCC provides that such notice shall be given by midnight of the third business day following the dishonor or receipt of notice of dishonor. This time limit applies to all holders except banks. The UCC requires that a bank give notice of dishonor to those it wishes to hold liable by midnight of the next banking day following the day on which it receives notice of dishonor. In order to avoid unduly burdening holders, the UCC provides that notice may be given by mail and that proof of mailing conclusively satisfies the requirement that notice be given.

Generally, notice of dishonor does not need to be in any special form. However, if the dishonored instrument is drawn or payable outside the United States of America, notice of dishonor must be certified by a public official authorized to do so. This requirement is known as **protest.**

Protest

Certification of notice of dishonor by authorized official

Revised Article 3 requires notice of dishonor only to hold indorsers liable. The drawer of an unaccepted draft has primary liability, and the holder does not have to give notice of dishonor to such a drawer.

Delay or failure to give notice of dishonor is excused in most cases where timely presentment would not have been required. Basically, this occurs when notice has been waived; when notice was attempted with due diligence but was unsuccessful; or if the party to be notified had no reason to believe that the instrument would be honored, for example because of death or insolvency.

Liability of Agents

L.O.3 ....

A negotiable instrument may be signed by an agent, and the principal, not the agent, will be bound. If the agent, authorized by the principal, signs the instrument. "John Smith, Principal, by Jane Doe, Agent," or more simply, "John Smith by Jane Doe," the principal will be bound, but the agent will not be bound by the terms of the instrument.

The agent, in these cases, has signed the instruments, but has indicated a representative capacity and identified the person represented.

Three general types of signature situations occur that could present problems for the agent. The result might be that the agent would be bound while the principal might not be bound.

1   The agent could sign the instrument in such a way that the instrument did not name the principal, nor indicate that it was signed by an agent. For example, if the agent simply signed, "Jane Doe," the principal would not be bound, since the principal's signature does not appear on the instrument. The agent would be bound because nothing existed to indicate that she did not sign in her own capacity.

Benchmark Computer Systems contracted to purchase property known as the PCA building from Mid-America Real Estate and Investment Corp. In lieu of immediate cash as earnest money from Benchmark, Dwight Lund, Gerald Horning, and Michael Possehl, officers of Benchmark, signed a promissory note for $24,000 to Mid-America. Benchmark decided not to buy the building and Mid-America sued Lund, Horning, and Possehl. They said the note was executed for Benchmark. But Benchmark's name was not on the note, and no indication existed the signers signed in a representative capacity. The three officers were personally liable.

2 The agent could sign the instrument in such a way that the principal was named, but it was not shown that the agent was acting merely as an agent. If the agent signed, "John Smith" and immediately below that "Jane Doe," the agent and the principal would both be bound. The agent would be bound because she did not indicate that she was an agent, and the other party to the instrument might have relied on the signature of the agent as an individual.

3 The agent could sign the instrument in such a way that the principal was not named, but it would be clear that the agent signed as an agent. Such a case would occur if the agent signed, "Jane Doe, Agent." In this situation, only the agent would be bound by the instrument, since it would not be evident from the face of the instrument who the principal might be.

However, in these last two examples, there is ambiguity about the agent's status. When a party to the instrument sues for payment, parol evidence may be introduced to prove the agency. So if the parties to the instrument knew that John Smith was the principal and Jane Doe was merely an agent, then only the principal would be bound on the instrument.

Financial Directors Corporation delivered a promissory note for $125,000 to Wise. The note was signed "Financial Directors Corporation by John Rauckhorst and Douglas Duker." Under these signatures was typed the line "Financial Directors Corporation." The note consistently identified Financial as the sole maker. Rauckhorst and Duker were not named or referred to in the note. When sued by Wise for payment, Rauckhorst and Duker said they signed in a representative capacity. The court held that ambiguity existed about the signers status, and Wise was a party to the note. Thus parol evidence was admissible to show the agency.

Revised Article 3 changes this rule about agent liability somewhat. In all of these three examples, a holder in due course without knowledge the agent was not supposed to be liable can enforce liability against the agent. However, if a holder in due course is not involved, the revision states the undisclosed principal is liable. In addition, the agent will not be liable if she can prove that the original parties did not intend her to be liable.

Revised Article 3 also has a special rule for checks signed by agents. If an agent signs a check in a representative capacity without indicating that capacity, but the check is on the principal's account and the principal is identified, the agent is not liable. Almost all checks today are personalized to identify the individual on whose account the check is drawn. So the agent does not deceive anyone by signing such a check.

In the case of a corporation or other organization, the authorized agent should sign above or below the corporation or organization's name and indicate the position held after the signature. For example, Edward Rush, the president of Acme Industries should sign:

ACME INDUSTRIES
By Edward Rush, President

If the instrument were signed this way, Acme Industries, not Edward Rush, would be bound.

If an individual signs an instrument as an agent, "John Smith, Principal, by Jane Doe, Agent," but the agent is not authorized to sign for the principal, the principal would not be bound. It would be as if the agent, Jane Doe, had forged John Smith's signature. However, the agent who made the unauthorized signature would be bound. This protects innocent parties to the instrument who would not be able to enforce their rights against anyone if the unauthorized agent was not bound.

Guarantors

Indorsers can escalate their liability to primary status by indorsing an instrument "Payment guaranteed." These words indicate that the indorser agrees to pay the instrument if it is not paid when due. The holder does not need to seek payment from anyone else first.

If the transferor indorses the instrument with the words "Collection guaranteed," secondary liability is preserved. However, the contingencies that must be met by the holder in order to hold this type of guarantor liable change from presentment, dishonor, and notice of dishonor to obtaining against the maker or acceptor a judgment that cannot be satisfied.

People usually act as guarantors in order to increase the security of commercial paper. Frequently, if someone liable has a poor credit rating, the instrument could not be negotiated without having an additional party sign as a guarantor of the instrument.

Community Bank and Trust loaned Pitrolo Pontiac Company $400,000, and Paul and Janice Pitrolo executed a "Guarantee of Payment" of the promissory note. Pitrolo Pontiac defaulted and Community sued the Pitrolos as guarantors. They asserted they were not liable on the note because it was a corporate note, and they did not receive any direct consideration for signing. The court held that lack of consideration merely established them as accommodation guarantors. Accommodation guarantors agree to pay if the principal debtor defaults. They sign the instrument for the purpose of lending their names to the other party to it. The liability of an accommodation guarantor is supported by the consideration received by the principal debtor. The Pitrolos were, therefore, liable on the note.

LIABILITY FOR WARRANTIES

Contractual liability required a signature on the paper. However, warranty liability is created by transferring negotiable instruments. Every transferor of commercial paper warrants the existence of certain facts. Unless specifically excluded, these warranties are automatically charged to every transferor of commercial paper. Note that one's signature or even one's name does not have to appear on the instrument in order to be liable as a warrantor, as for example, when a person negotiates bearer paper by delivery alone.

The UCC specifies that each transferor who receives consideration and does not specifically limit liability warrants that:

1   The transferor has good title to the instrument, authorization to obtain acceptance or payment on behalf of the rightful owner, and that the transfer is otherwise rightful.
2   All signatures are genuine or authorized.
3   The instrument has not been materially altered.
4   No defense of any party is good. (Explained in Chapter 27.).
5   The transferor has no knowledge of any insolvency proceedings instituted with respect to the maker or acceptor or the drawee of an unaccepted instrument.

QUESTIONS

1   What is the difference between contractual liability and warranty liability?
2   Must a signature on a negotiable instrument be a handwritten name?
3   What parties to commercial paper might be
    a.   primarily liable?
    b.   secondarily liable?
4   What conditions must be met in order for a party to be held secondarily liable?
5   If there is no specified date for payment, when must an instrument be presented for payment?
6   When does a dishonor occur?
7   When is notice of dishonor excused?
8   How should an agent execute a negotiable instrument in order to bind the principal and not the agent?
9   If someone signs a commercial paper as guarantor, what is the effect of this act:
    a.   If the words *Payment guaranteed* are used?
    b.   If the words *Collection guaranteed* are used?
10 What warranties are made by a transferor of commercial paper?

CASE PROBLEMS

L.O.2 ....

1   Betty Jean Wright and her husband, Verlon, opened a joint checking account at the Commercial Savings Bank in the name of Level Building Supply. Either party could draw on the account with only one signature. After Betty and Verlon had marital problems, Verlon instructed the bank to remove Betty's name from the account, which it did. Betty went to the bank and asked for a counter check to withdraw $500 from the account. The teller refused because her name no longer appeared on the account. Betty sued the bank, alleging wrongful dishonor because it refused the counter check. Was there a wrongful dishonor?

L.O.3 ....

2 George Avery sent a letter to Jim Whitworth. Printed on the stationery was the name of Avery's employer, V & L Manufacturing Co., and the words *George Avery, President*. The letter stated, "This is your note for $45,000.00, secured individually and by our Company. . . ." Avery had signed the letter. V & L did not pay the entire $45,000, so Whitworth sued Avery. He said the stationery showed V & L was the debtor and he signed only in a representative capacity. Must Avery pay?

L.O.1 ....

3 Gus Stathis agreed to sell real estate to Edgar, Rintz, and Grandinetti. As consideration, he received a promissory note for $575,000 executed by the purchasers and their wives. This debt was secured by First Arlington National Bank's letter of credit, which guaranteed payment of $575,000 upon default of the note if Stathis indorsed the note to the bank. There was default in the payment of interest. When Stathis sought payment on the letter of credit and presented the indorsed note, the bank refused to pay. In a lawsuit over payment of the letter of credit, the bank contended that the warranties of transferors of negotiable instruments were applicable because Stathis was required to transfer the note to it. Were they?

L.O.1 ....

4 Tours by Irene, Inc., signed a promissory note to Chemical Bank. Bernadetta Ciszewska signed a guaranty of the note, which stated, "the undersigned hereby guarantees, absolutely and unconditionally, to the Bank the payment of all liabilities." Tours failed to pay the note, so Chemical sued Ciszewska. She claimed Chemical had to enforce the note against Tours first. Did Chemical have a valid suit against Ciszewska?

L.O.3 ....

5 Mestco Distributors sued Ralph Stamps for payment of four notes. The notes were signed as follows:

1. I.T.S. Inc.
   by Ralph W. Stamps
   Secty. Treas.
2. Ralph W. Stamps
   Secty-Treas. I.T.S. Inc.
3. Innovative Timber Specialties Inc.
   by Secty-Treas
   Ralph W. Stamps
4. Ralph W. Stamps
   Innovative Timber Specialties, Inc.
   by: Secretary

Stamps argued that he executed the notes in a representative capacity. Decide whether Stamps executed each note as an agent or personally.

L.O.2 ....

6 Bridgecrest, Inc., executed a promissory note to Custom Craft Tile, Inc. It was signed by Fred Chapman as president of Bridgecrest and indorsed personally by Chapman. When Custom sued him on the note, Chapman denied receiving timely notice of dishonor. The note was due on October 6 and Bridgecrest went into bankruptcy proceedings two years later. Custom said notice of dishonor was excused because of the bankruptcy. Was it?

L.O.2 .... **7** Eugene Weiss was an indorser on a promissory note for $20,000 made by a business associate. The terms of the note stated Weiss waived presentment, demand, notice, and all other demands related to performance, default, or enforcement of the note. After the note came due, the holder gave no notice to Weiss and spent several years trying to enforce payment against the maker. When that was unsuccessful, the holder finally sought payment from Weiss. Must Weiss pay?

Chapter 25

NEGOTIATION AND DISCHARGE

After studying this chapter you should be able to:

1 State what negotiation involves.

2 Discuss how indorsements are made, and identify the different types of indorsements.

3 Describe the liabilities of an indorser.

4 Explain how negotiable instruments may be discharged.

Preview Case

Mahmoud Halloway bought an insurance policy from Home Life Insurance Company through Home's field underwriter for $2,551. He executed and delivered a note for that amount payable to Madison Bank & Trust Company. Duane Wolfram, the manager of a branch office of Home, signed the note "without recourse" as an accommodation party. When Halloway defaulted on the note, Wolfram paid the $2,551. Halloway refused to reimburse Wolfram. Wolfram sued Halloway, who alleged that Wolfram had no obligation to pay the note because he had indorsed it "without recourse." Did the qualified indorsement absolve the indorser from liability on the instrument?

L.O.1

Indorsement
Signature of holder on back of instrument with any directions or limitations

egotiation involves the transfer of a negotiable instrument in such a way that the transferee becomes the holder of the instrument. Bearer instruments may be negotiated by delivery. Delivery effectively vests ownership in the transferee. Practice usually requires an indorsement. An **indorsement** is a signature on the back of an instrument (usually the holder's) along with any directions or limitations regarding use of or liability for the instrument. Although not required for negotiation, a transferee may require it for bearer paper because this adds the liability of the new indorser to the paper and thus makes it a better credit risk. It also preserves a written chronological record of all negotiations.

An instrument payable to "order" can be negotiated only by indorsement and delivery. Indorsing or transferring a negotiable instrument creates certain liabilities, depending upon the nature of the indorsement or transfer.

PLACE OF INDORSEMENT

L.O.2

Trailing Edge
Left side of front of check

Allonge
Paper so firmly attached to instrument as to be part of it

Banks require that an indorsement on a check be on the back and within 1½ inches of the **trailing edge.** The trailing edge is the left side of a check when looking at it from the front. (See Illustration 25-1). If the indorser's signature appears elsewhere and it cannot be determined in what capacity the signature was made, it will be considered an indorsement. In any event, the indorsement must be on the instrument or on a paper firmly attached to it. An **allonge** is a paper so firmly attached to an instrument as to become a part of it. If a party does not wish to be liable as an indorser, the instrument can be assigned by a written assignment on a separate piece of paper.

Occasionally, the name of the payee or indorsee of an instrument is misspelled. If a paycheck intended for, and delivered to, John F. Smith is made out to "John K. Smith" through clerical error, John F. Smith may ask his employer for a new check properly made out to him or he may keep the check and indorse in any of the following ways:

1   "John K. Smith"
2   "John F. Smith"
3   "John K. Smith, John F. Smith"

If he intends to receive value for the check, the person to whom it is negotiated may require him to sign both names.

Illustration 25-1   Indorsed Check Folded to Show the Position of the Indorsement

However, if John F. Smith obtains a check made payable to, and intended for, John K. Smith, it would be illegal for the latter to indorse it and receive payment for it. Only when the check is actually intended for John F. Smith may he make a corrective indorsement.

It is not always necessary to correct an irregularity in the name of a party to an instrument. An irregularity does not destroy negotiability. Only if shown that different people were actually identified by the different names, as opposed to the different names standing for one person, must the irregularity be considered. It has been held that a note was correctly negotiated when indorsed "Greenlaw & Sons by George M. Greenlaw," although payable to "Greenlaw & Sons Roofing & Siding Co." Nothing indicates that the two enterprises were not the same firm.

KINDS OF INDORSEMENTS

Four types of indorsements include:

1 Blank indorsements
2 Special indorsements
3 Qualified indorsements
4 Restrictive indorsements

Blank Indorsements

Blank Indorsement

Indorsement consisting of signature of indorser

As the name indicates, a **blank indorsement** is one having no words other than the name of the indorser. (See Illustration 25-2.) If the instrument is bearer paper, it remains bearer paper when a blank indorsement is made. Thus, the new holder may pass good title to another holder without indorsing the instrument. The one primarily liable on the instrument is bound to pay the person who presents it for payment on the date due, even if the person is a thief or other unauthorized party.

Illustration 25-2   Blank Indorsement and Special Indorsement

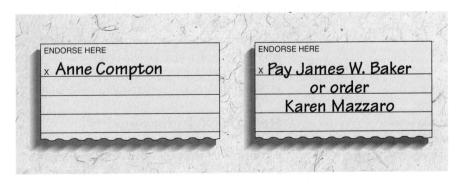

Katherine Warnock bought a cashier's check payable to her order in the amount of $53,542. On the back she indorsed it "Katherine Warnock." Her lawyer, Jerry Quick, wrote "deposit only" underneath her signature and deposited the check in an account he had at La Junta State Bank. Warnock did not have an account there. After Warnock's death several years later, the representatives of her estate discovered these facts. The account had been depleted so they sued La Junta alleging it had wrongfully deposited the cashier's check. The court concluded that when Warnock indorsed the check in blank and gave it to Quick, he became the holder of bearer paper. He could therefore negotiate it by delivery, and his subsequent writing did not change the fact that he was the holder of bearer paper.

If the instrument is order paper, a blank indorsement converts it to bearer paper; if thereafter indorsed to someone's order, it becomes order paper again. Risks involved in handling instruments originally payable to bearer or indorsed in blank can be minimized by converting the instruments to order paper.

Special Indorsements

Special Indorsement
Indorsement that designates particular person to whom payment to be made

A **special indorsement** designates the particular person to whom payment should be made. (See Illustration 25-2.) After making such an indorsement, the paper is order paper, whether or not it was originally so payable or was originally payable to bearer. The holder must indorse it before it can be further negotiated. Of course, the holder may indorse the instrument in blank, which makes it bearer paper. Each holder has the power to decide to make either a blank or a special indorsement.

An indorsee by a blank indorsement may convert it to a special indorsement by writing the words *pay to the order of [indorsee]* above the indorser's signature. Such an instrument cannot now be negotiated except by indorsement and delivery. This in no way alters the contract between the indorser and the indorsee.

Qualified Indorsements

Qualified Indorsement
Indorsement that limits liability of indorser

A **qualified indorsement** has the effect of qualifying, thus, limiting, the liability of the indorser. This type of indorsement is usually used when the payee of an instrument is merely collecting the funds for another. For example, if an agent receives checks in payment of the principal's claims but the checks are made payable to the agent personally, the agent can and should elect to use a qualified indorsement. The agent does this merely by adding to either a blank or special type of indorsement the words *without recourse* immediately before the signature. (See Illustration 25-3.) This releases the indorser from liability for payment if the instrument remains unpaid because of insolvency or mere refusal to pay.

A qualified indorser still warrants that the signatures on the instrument are genuine, that the indorser has good title to the instrument, that the instrument has not been altered, that no defenses are good against the indorser, and that the indorser has no knowledge of insolvency proceedings with respect to the maker, acceptor, or drawer (as was mentioned in Chapter 24). An indorser may avoid these warranties as well by indorsing the instrument "without recourse or warranties."

Restrictive Indorsements

Restrictive Indorsement
Indorsement that restricts use of instrument

A **restrictive indorsement** is an indorsement that attempts to prevent the use of the instrument for anything except the stated use. (See Illustration 25-3.) The indorse-

Illustration 25-3   Qualified Indorsement and Restrictive Indorsement

ment may state that the indorsee holds the paper for a special purpose or as an agent or trustee for another or it may impose a condition that must occur before payment. Such an indorsement does not prohibit further negotiation of the instrument.

Revised Article 3 makes conditional indorsements ineffective with respect to anyone other than the indorser and indorsee. Since conditional and transfer limiting indorsements are not effective as restrictive indorsements, revised Article 3 does not include "restrictive indorsements."

As against a holder in due course, it is immaterial whether the restrictions have in fact been recognized by the indorsee. A bank receiving a check for deposit with a restrictive indorsement, such as "for deposit" or "for collection" must honor the restriction.

One of Mary Ann Hunsberger's duties as bookkeeper for the Lehigh Presbytery required her to rubber-stamp an indorsement on checks received by the Presbytery. She also deposited them in the Presbytery's account with Merchants Bancorp. The indorsement read, "For Deposit Only To The Credit of Presbytery of Lehigh, Ernest Hutcheson, Treas." Over about five years, Hunsberger deposited 153 checks in her account in spite of the rubber-stamp restrictive indorsement. She filled out deposit slips in the Presbytery's name, but put her account number on the slips. The Presbytery sued Merchants contending the restrictive indorsements bound it to obey the indorsements on the 153 checks deposited in Hunsberger's account. The court said the UCC required that the amount of the checks be applied consistently with the indorsement. Lehigh could recover.

LIABILITY OF INDORSER

L.O.3 ....   By indorsing a negotiable instrument, a person can become secondarily liable for payment of the face amount and responsible for certain warranties.

Liabilities for Payment of Instrument

By making an indorsement, an indorser, with the exception of a qualified indorser, agrees to pay any subsequent holder the face amount of the instrument if the holder presents the instrument to the primary party when due and the primary party refuses to pay. The holder must then give the indorser in question notice of such default.

This notice may be given orally or it may be given by any other means, but it must be given before midnight of the third full business day after the day on which the default occurs.

Warranties of the Indorser

Chapter 24 listed warranties of the indorser. They differ from liability for the face of the paper in that they are not subject to the requirements of presentment and notice. The distinction is also important for purposes of limiting liability; for an indorsement "without recourse" destroys only the liability of the indorser for the face of the instrument. It does not affect all warranties. Such an indorsement does limit the warranty that there are no good defenses. This becomes a warranty that the indorser has no knowledge of any good defenses.

Revised Article 3 changes this rule. It provides that an indorsement "without recourse" does *not* limit the warranty that there are no good defenses.

A "without recourse" indorsement does not limit the other warranties. An indorsement "without warranties" or a combined "without recourse or warranties" is required to exclude warranty liability.

Mahmoud Halloway bought an insurance policy from Home Life Insurance Company through Home's field underwriter for $2,551. He executed and delivered a note for that amount payable to Madison Bank & Trust Company. Duane Wolfram, the manager of a branch office of Home, signed the note "without recourse" as an accommodation party. When Halloway defaulted on the note, Wolfram paid the $2,551. Halloway refused to reimburse Wolfram. Wolfram sued Halloway, who alleged that Wolfram had had no obligation to pay the note because he had indorsed it "without recourse." The court held that the qualified indorsement did not necessarily absolve the indorser from liability on the instrument because it does not protect from liability for breach of warranty.

OBLIGATION OF NEGOTIATOR OF BEARER PAPER

Bearer paper need not be indorsed when negotiated. Mere delivery passes title. One who negotiates a bearer instrument by delivery alone does not guarantee payment, but is liable to the immediate transferee as a warrantor of the genuineness of the instrument, of title to it, of the capacity of prior parties, and of its validity. These warranties are the same as those made by an unqualified indorser, except that the warranties of the unqualified indorser extend to all subsequent holders, not just to the immediate purchaser. But since negotiable instruments are not legal tender, no one is under any obligation to accept bearer paper without an indorsement. By requiring an indorsement even though not necessary to pass title, the holder is gaining protection by requiring the one who wishes to negotiate it to assume all the obligations of an indorser.

DISCHARGE OF THE OBLIGATION

L.O.4 .... Negotiable instruments may be discharged by payment, by cancellation, or by renunciation. Payment at or after the date of the maturity of the instrument by the

Cancellation
Act that indicates intention to destroy validity of an instrument

Renunciation
Unilateral act of holder giving up rights in the instrument or against a party to it

party primarily liable constitutes proper payment. **Cancellation** consists of any act that indicates the intention to destroy the validity of the instrument. A cancellation made unintentionally, without authorization, or by mistake is not effective. A holder of several negotiable instruments might intend to cancel one upon its payment and inadvertently cancel an unpaid one. This does not discharge the unpaid instrument. **Renunciation** is a unilateral act of a holder of an instrument, usually without consideration, whereby the holder gives up rights on the instrument or against one or more parties to the instrument.

The obligations of the parties may be discharged in other ways, just as in the case of a simple contract. For example, parties will no longer be held liable on instruments if their debts have been discharged in bankruptcy or if there has been the necessary lapse of time provided by a statute of limitations.

A negotiable instrument may be lost or accidentally destroyed. This does not discharge the obligation. A party obligated to pay an instrument has a right to demand its return if possible. If this cannot be done, then the payor has a right to demand security from the holder adequate to protect the payor from having to pay the instrument a second time. The holder usually posts an indemnity bond. This is an agreement by a bonding company to assume the risk of the payor's having to pay a second time.

QUESTIONS

1 What is an indorsement?
2 What is *negotiation*, and how are the two kinds of commercial paper negotiated?
3 If a check for Susan L. Grey is made out to Suzanne E. Grey, how might Grey indorse it?
4 Name four kinds of indorsements, and give an example of the proper use of each one.
5 Why is it usually undesirable to indorse a check in blank?
6 If an instrument that is payable to "bearer" is indorsed by special indorsement, what must the second holder do in order to negotiate it?
7 If a check is indorsed "without recourse," is the indorser absolved from all liability on the instrument?
8 Is a restrictive indorsement on a check binding on a bank in which it is deposited?
9 How may negotiable instruments be discharged?
10 If one loses a negotiable instrument, is there any way it can be collected?

CASE PROBLEMS

L.O.2

1 Olga Blaire bought a Hamburg Savings Bank teller's check [draft drawn by a bank on another bank] payable to her order for $3,000. She indorsed it "Pay to Simone Travel Bureau, Inc." and turned it over to S. Reiss. Reiss added his name above the special indorsement and signed it. He then gave the check to University Funding Corp., which deposited it in its account at Manufacturers Hanover Trust. The back of the check then read:

S. Reiss to
Pay to Simone Travel
Bureau, Inc.
   Olga Blair
July 28, 19__
   S. Reiss
University Funding Corporation
X 22-058828

University claimed to be a holder of the check. Was it?

L.O.2 ....

2 Over a period of years, Rosemary McCormick embezzled from her orthodontist employer, Dr. Gus Angelos. McCormick took patient checks that Angelos had indorsed in blank and deposited them in her account at First Interstate Bank of Utah. When Angelos discovered the thefts, he sued First Interstate for wrongfully accepting checks with forged indorsements. Did First Interstate wrongfully credit McCormick's account with the amount of these checks?

L.O.4 ....

3 Paul Reid contracted to sell land to Bruce Cramer. The contract stated earnest money in the form of a promissory note for $4,000 due at closing was received, and the earnest money would be forfeited if Cramer failed to buy the land. The note was payable to Home Realty, the seller's agent, and indorsed to Reid. When Cramer refused to buy the land, Reid sued to enforce the note. The note had been marked "void" without authorization by an employee of Home. Cramer alleged the marking made the note unenforceable. Did it?

L.O.2 ....

4 To obtain a loan for George Richardson from Liberty National Bank, where he had been employed, Michael Johnson executed a standard form blank guaranty agreement. The loan was not obtained from Liberty, and Johnson was so notified. Instead, a renewal note guaranteed by Johnson was issued to Richardson by Shepherd Mall State Bank, and about seven months later another renewal note was issued to him. When the second note went into default, the bank sent Johnson a demand letter regarding the guaranty agreement and then sued. The letter was the first notice Johnson had that the agreement had been used for a loan from this bank. Did the agreement impose the liability of an indorser on Johnson?

L.O.1, 2 ....

5 Dean and Vickie Ferguson executed a $230,000 note, secured by a mortgage on land, to John Muskopf. Later Muskopf executed an $80,000 note to Bremen Bank and Trust Co. secured by written assignment of the Ferguson note and mortgage. Muskopf gave the note to Bremen, but did not indorse it. Eventually the Fergusons defaulted and Muskopf foreclosed the mortgage. He bought the land at the foreclosure sale and conveyed it to Eugene and Joanne Hoffmann. They conveyed the property to Paul Faix. Muskopf failed to pay his note to Bremen, which then found out about the foreclosure. Bremen tried to set the sale aside arguing it was the holder of the note and mortgage. Decide the case.

L.O.1   6   Corporacion Venezolana de Fomento was the guarantor of promissory notes in the total amount of $5,813,950 executed by Venezolana de Cruceros del Caribe, C.A. (Cariven), to The Merban Corporation. Merban indorsed the notes in blank and delivered them to Security Pacific International Bank. Some of the notes were then transferred to Chemical Bank to be held for the benefit of any people to whom participating interests in the notes might be sold. Merban sold participations in the notes to four Canadian banks, and Chemical issued each one a certificate of ownership in the notes to the extent of the interest purchased. Cariven defaulted, and in the subsequent lawsuit, Corporacion alleged that the Canadian banks were not holders of the notes because Chemical and Security had physical possession of them. Were the Canadian banks holders?

Chapter 26

HOLDER/ IN DUE COUR/E

After studying this chapter you should be able to:

1 Explain the prime significance of negotiability.

2 Define holder in due course and holder through a holder in due course.

3 Discuss the special rules for holders of consumer paper.

Preview Case

Farmers Insurance Group delivered a draft payable "On Acceptance of Commerce Bank of Kansas City" to the order of Deborah Crippen. Crippen indorsed the draft for deposit in her checking account at Friendly National Bank of Southwest Oklahoma City. Friendly credited her account with the amount of the draft, and Crippen wrote checks against it. When Friendly had paid out $490.15 on Crippen's checks, the draft was returned to Friendly with the notation "Payment Declined by Farmers Insurance: Payment Stopped." Friendly sued Farmers, alleging it was a holder in due course because it had given value for the draft. Had Friendly given value?

L.O.1

Holder in Due Course

Holder for value and in good faith with no knowledge of dishonor, defenses, or claims or that paper is overdue.

Negotiable instruments would have no advantage over ordinary contracts if the remote parties could not be given immunity against many of the defenses that might be made against simple contracts. To enjoy this immunity, the holder of a negotiable instrument must be a **holder in due course.** The term *innocent purchaser* is also used to describe a person who is a holder in due course.

HOLDERS IN DUE COURSE

L.O.2

Neither the term *holder in due course* nor *innocent purchaser* describes anyone but the holder of a negotiable instrument who has obtained it under these conditions:

1   The holder must take the instrument in good faith and for value.

2   The holder must have no notice the instrument is overdue or has been dishonored.

3   At the time the instrument is negotiated, the holder must have had no notice of any defense against or adverse claim to the instrument.

For Value and in Good Faith

The law of commercial paper is concerned only with persons who give something for the paper. Thus, to attain the specially favored status of being a holder in due course, the holder must give value for the paper. Conversely, one who does not do so, as a niece receiving a Christmas check from an uncle, cannot be a holder in due course. A mere promise does not constitute value.

The requirement that value be given does not mean that one must pay full value for a negotiable instrument in order to be a holder in due course. Thus, one who purchases a negotiable contract at a discount can qualify as a holder in due course. The law states that it must be taken "for value and in good faith." If the instrument is offered at an exorbitant discount, that fact may be evidence that the purchaser did not buy it in good faith. It is the lack of good faith that destroys one's status as a holder in due course, not the amount of the discount.

If the payee of a negotiable instrument for $3,000 offered to transfer it for a consideration of $2,700, and the purchaser had no other reason to suspect any infirmity in the instrument, the purchaser can qualify as a holder in due course. The instrument was taken in good faith. If, on the other hand, the holder had offered to discount the note $1,000, the purchaser could not take it in good faith because it should be suspected that there is some serious problem with the contract because of the large discount.

As often occurs, the purchaser may pay for the instrument in cash and other property. The inflated value placed on the property taken in payment conceals the discount. The test always is: Were there any circumstances that should have warned a prudent person that the instrument was not genuine and in all respect what it purported to be? If there were, the purchaser did not take it in good faith.

If the holder is notified of a problem with the instrument or a defect in the title of the transferor before the full purchase price has been paid, the holder will be a holder in due course to the extent of the amount paid before notification.

Farmers Insurance Group delivered a draft payable "On Acceptance of Commerce Bank of Kansas City" to the order of Deborah Crippen. Crippen indorsed the draft for deposit in her checking account at Friendly National Bank of Southwest Oklahoma City. Friendly credited her account with the amount of the draft, and Crippen wrote checks against it. When Friendly had paid out $490.15 on Crippen's checks, the draft was returned to Friendly with the notation "Payment Declined by Farmers Insurance: Payment Stopped." Friendly sued Farmers, alleging it was a holder in due course because it had given value for the draft. The court held that crediting Crippen's account for the amount of the draft and allowing her to draw checks on it meant Friendly had given value.

No Knowledge Instrument Past Due or Dishonored

One who takes an instrument known to be past due cannot be an innocent purchaser. However, a purchaser of demand paper on which demand for payment has

Uncured Default
Not all payments on in-
strument fully made and
not all made by due date

been made and refused is still a holder in due course if the purchaser had no notice of the demand. A purchaser who has reason to know that any part of the principal is overdue, that an **uncured default** exists in payment of an instrument in the same series, or that acceleration of the instrument has been made has notice that the instrument is overdue. A note dated and payable in a fixed number of days or months itself indicates whether or not it is past due.

An instrument transferred on the date of maturity is not past due but would be overdue on the day following the due date. If payable on demand, it is due within a reasonable time after issuance. For checks drawn and payable in the United States, 30 days is presumed to be a reasonable time.

No Knowledge of Any Defense or Adverse Claim to the Instrument

Fiduciary
A person in relationship of
trust and confidence

When one takes a negotiable instrument by negotiation, to obtain the rights of an innocent purchaser there must be no knowledge of any defense against or claim adverse to the instrument. Notice of a claim may be inferred if the holder has knowledge that a **fiduciary** has negotiated an instrument in payment of a personal debt. As between the original parties to a negotiable instrument, any act, such as fraud, duress, mistake, illegality, that would make any contract either void or void-able will have the same effect on a negotiable instrument. Many of these defenses, as will be seen in the next chapter, are eliminated as defenses if the instrument is negotiated to an innocent purchaser. Knowing that an instrument has been ante-dated or postdated, was incomplete and has been completed, that default has been made in the payment of interest, or that it was issued or negotiated in return for an executory promise or accompanied by a separate agreement does not give a holder notice of a defense or claim.

Palmetto Leasing Company sued Winifred Crespo. Harry Chiles represented her and negotiated a settle-ment with Palmetto's attorney. The settlement required Crespo to pay Palmetto $9,000. Palmetto refused to accept an uncertified check or Crespo's check drawn on an out-of-state bank. The parties agreed that Chiles would write out a check from his trust account for $9,000, but that time would be needed to allow Crespo to get funds to Chiles to cover the check. Chiles wrote out the check and gave it to Palmetto who held the check for six days. Palmetto deposited the check, but the next day Chiles stopped payment on it because Crespo had not supplied the funds to cover it. Palmetto sued Chiles alleging it was a holder in due course. The court held Palmetto was not a holder in due course because it knew there was no consideration for the check when it took it.

HOLDER THROUGH A HOLDER IN DUE COURSE

**Holder Through
a Holder in Due
Course**
Holder subsequent to
holder in due course

The first holder in due course brings into operation for the first time all the protec-tions that the law has placed around negotiable instruments. When these protections once accrue, they are not easily lost. Consequently, a subsequent holder, known as a **holder through a holder in due course,** may benefit from them even though not a holder in due course. For example, Doerhoff, without consideration, gives Bryce a negotiable note due in 60 days. Before maturity, Bryce indorses it to Cordell under conditions that make Cordell a holder in due course. Thereafter, Cordell transfers the note to Otke. Otke is not a holder in due course, since she did not give any consideration for the note. If Otke is not a party to any wrongdoing or illegality affecting this instrument, she acquires all the rights of a holder in due course. This is true because Cordell had these rights, and when Cordell transferred the note to Otke, he transferred all of his rights, which include the right to collect the amount due and the right to be free from the defense of no consideration.

HOLDERS OF CONSUMER PAPER

Consumer Goods or Services
Goods or services primarily for personal, family, or household use

L.O.3 ....

Setoff
A claim by the party being sued against the party suing

The UCC rules regarding the status of a holder in due course have been modified for holders of negotiable instruments given for consumer goods or services. **Consumer goods or services** are defined as goods or services for use primarily for personal, family, or household purposes. The changes resulted from both amendment to the UCC by the states—which means that the rules vary somewhat from state to state—and the adoption of an FTC rule.

Generally, the rights of the holder of consumer paper are subject to all defenses and setoffs of the original purchaser or debtor arising from the consumer transaction. A **setoff** is a claim a party being sued makes against the party suing. In the case of consumer sales, the FTC rule requires that consumer credit contracts contain specified language in bold print indicating that holders of the contracts are subject to all claims and defenses the debtor could assert against the seller. The language is:

NOTICE

ANY HOLDER OF THIS CONSUMER CREDIT CONTRACT IS SUBJECT TO ALL CLAIMS AND DEFENSES WHICH THE DEBTOR COULD ASSERT AGAINST THE SELLER OF GOODS OR SERVICES OBTAINED PURSUANT HERETO OR WITH THE PROCEEDS HEREOF. RECOVERY HEREUNDER BY THE DEBTOR SHALL NOT EXCEED AMOUNTS PAID BY THE DEBTOR HEREUNDER.

The state laws generally make holder in due course rules inapplicable to consumer sales or limit the cutoff of consumer rights to a specified number of days after notification of assignment.

Normally these rights of the debtor are available only when the loan was arranged by the seller or lessor of the goods or was made directly by the seller or lessor. The state laws do not apply to credit card sales on a credit card issued by someone other than the seller. However, federal law allows a credit card holder to refuse to pay credit card issuers in some cases when an earnest effort at returning the goods is made or a chance to correct a problem is given the seller.

Modifying or abolishing the special status of a holder in due course for consumer goods prevents frauds frequently practiced upon consumers by unscrupulous business people. Such individuals would sell shoddy merchandise on credit and immediately negotiate the instrument of credit to a bank or finance company. When the consumer discovered the defects in the goods, payment could not be avoided, because the new holder of the commercial paper had purchased it without knowledge of the potential defenses and was therefore a holder in due course. Further, the seller who had frequently left the jurisdiction or gone bankrupt was unavailable to be sued. Thus, the consumer would be unable to assert a defense or rescind the transaction against either the seller or the holder. The modifications based on changes to the UCC and adoption of the FTC rule have remedied this problem. A consumer who purchases goods that are not delivered or worthless can avoid paying more and recover what has been paid.

Rose and William Morgan bought a new car from Neponset Lincoln Mercury. To finance the car with Ford Credit, they signed a retail installment contract that contained the bold print language required by the FTC. The Morgans used the car for 18 months. They had such problems as water leaking into the trunk, a defective head gasket, rust, misaligned hood, and when left unattended the transmission shifting into reverse from park so it would have to be shifted back to park to start it. They missed car payments, and let the insurance lapse. William hid the car until he was found in contempt of court, so he surrendered it. Ford got court approval to sell the car, but William delayed the sale for an inspection. By then the car was vandalized and worthless. Ford sued the Morgans for the amount due on the contract. They said the dealer had made false representations on which they had relied. The court agreed that the Morgans' defenses against the dealer could be raised against Ford.

Allowing the consumer to have such rights against a holder who would otherwise be a holder in due course protects consumers who usually do not have knowledge of negotiable instruments laws. Usually the bank or finance company, which may buy many instruments from the seller, can more easily ascertain whether the seller is reliable than individual consumers can.

QUESTIONS

1 What special immunity does a holder in due course have?
2 Who is a holder in due course?
3 May a holder in due course obtain possession by receiving the instrument at less than face value?
4 What does it mean to take a negotiable instrument in good faith?
5 What constitutes notice that an instrument is overdue?
6 What is presumed to be a reasonable time within which checks drawn and payable in the United States are not overdue?
7 Does knowledge that an instrument was postdated constitute knowledge of a defense or adverse claim?
8 Who is a holder through a holder in due course?
9 Under what circumstances is an innocent holder of consumer paper denied the status of a holder in due course?

CASE PROBLEMS

L.O.2 ....

1 Kenneth Hessler raised hogs for John Smith Grain Co. Smith or J & J Farms would deliver hogs and Hessler would sign a promissory note payable to Smith to cover the cost of the hogs and feed. J & J delivered hogs that had been mortgaged to Producer's Livestock Association. After Hessler signed a note, an officer of Smith told him to sign his wife's name, Carla Hessler, too. Hessler did so and put his initials, K. H., after her name. Smith assigned the note to Arcanum National Bank. Shortly thereafter, Producer's took the hogs from Hessler's farm because of Smith's financial problems. Smith could not pay the note, so Arcanum sued Hessler. Arcanum handled the Hesslers' personal finances. Hessler alleged that Arcanum was not a holder in due course. He said it took the note with notice of a defense, since he added Carla's signature and the note was irregular on its face. Was the note irregular on its face?

L.O.2 .... **2** The General Services Administration (GSA) contracted with Almark, Inc., to buy bulletin boards. Almark and A. C. Davenport & Son Co. agreed that Davenport would supply the bulletin boards. Davenport later had doubts about Almark's ability to pay. It insisted that Almark and the GSA modify their contract to change the payment address from "Almark, Inc., 542 South 23rd Street, Arlington, Virginia 22202" to "Almark, Inc. c/o Davson, 306 East Helen Road, Palatine, IL 60067" and provide that checks under the contract be deposited in a special account from which only Davenport could withdraw the funds. Despite the contract modification, the GSA sent checks to Almark's Virginia address. When Davenport wrote the GSA that it had not received checks for shipments, it was advised that the checks had been sent to Almark, but a stop-payment had been put on them. The GSA issued a duplicate check, which was deposited in the special account, and Davenport withdrew the money. The stop order was ineffective as to checks totaling $11,822.89. The GSA demanded the money. When Davenport did not pay, the GSA withheld payments due Davenport on unrelated contracts as setoffs against the amount it claimed was owed. Davenport sued to recover the money. For Davenport to be a holder in due course it must have taken the check without notice of any defense or claim. Did Davenport have such notice?

L.O.1, 2 .... **3** M-H Enterprises and Michael Holmes requested a loan from Brookwood National Bank to buy some real estate. To get the loan, Brookwood required M-H and Holmes to buy a title insurance policy on the property naming Brookwood as beneficiary. M-H and Holmes bought the property, signed a note to Brookwood, and gave it a mortgage. They also bought a title policy from American Title Insurance Co. with Brookwood as insured. A year later, a prior mortgage on the property, which American had failed to notice, was foreclosed. M-H and Holmes told Brookwood they would make no more payments on the note and asked it to file a claim with American. American learned this and paid the claim, so Brookwood assigned its note and mortgage to American. It sued M-H and Holmes for the balance on the note. To win, American had to be a holder in due course. Was it?

L.O.3 .... **4** Eugene Perez hired Perma-Stone to install siding, new windows, screen doors, and vents at his house. To finance the improvements, Perez signed a promissory note and retail improvement contract containing the FTC required language. Perma-Stone sold the note to Briercroft Service Corp. Several months later, the siding started to fall off the house, the new windows fell apart, the doors would not shut, and the sewer vents stopped in the attic instead of going through the roof. Perez stopped paying on the note. In the resulting lawsuit, Briercroft said Perez was entitled only to a refund of the money he had paid but not to cancellation of the note. How should the court rule?

L.O.2 .... **5** For one and a half years, Ranchers Exploration and Development Corp. made monthly payments to American Express Company (AmEx), which covered both its corporate credit card bills and unknowingly covered personal debts of Linda Rodriguez, an employee of Ranchers. After paying Ranchers for its loss, Travelers Indemnity Company sued AmEx for the payments made on Rodriguez's behalf. AmEx said the court should find for it without a trial because, on the basis of the facts, it was clearly a holder in due course of the payments, since there was no evidence it received Ranchers' payments with knowledge of the defense that the payments on Rodriguez's account were unauthorized. Was it clearly a holder in due course?

L.O.2 .... **6** After making a loan, the Valley National Bank held an interest in all accounts, including checks, payable to Van Dyck Heating and Air Conditioning, Inc., but indorsed to a third party. Van Dyck was owned and operated by Shirley and Kenneth Horn. A loan was in default, but Valley allowed Van Dyck to operate for five months. Kenneth Horn was contacted by Fred Couch, an IRS officer, because Van Dyck's federal tax payments were slow. Couch advised Horn to pay the taxes before other creditors to avoid civil and criminal penalties for delinquent tax payments. To avoid writing bad corporate checks to the IRS because of cash flow problems, Horn indorsed checks received from customers directly to the IRS. In accord with IRS policy, because Van Dyck's tax account was not classed as delinquent, no search for interests of others was made. Valley sued. Did the IRS take the checks in good faith?

Chapter 27

DEFENSES

After studying this chapter you should be able to:

1 State the chief advantage of being a holder in due course of commercial paper.

2 Identify the defenses that are universal, those that are limited, and those that may be either universal or limited.

3 Distinguish between limited and universal defenses to holders.

Preview Case

James and Marie Estepp wanted to get a loan from United Bank and Trust Company of Maryland. United required an additional signature by an owner of real estate. Estepp brought Marvin Schaeffer to the bank saying he needed Schaeffer to sign a character reference. Estepp supervised Schaeffer at work and had helped Schaeffer make funeral arrangements when his wife had died. Schaeffer had a learning disability and could not read or write. The bank officer handling the transaction did not explain to Schaeffer that he was assuming a financial responsibility. Schaeffer signed the note. The Estepps defaulted, so United sued Schaeffer. Did Schaeffer have an effective defense?

When the holder of commercial paper is refused payment, a lawsuit may be brought. Chapter 24 discussed the parties liable for the payment of the face of the paper. What defense can be raised by the defendant being sued? This question does not arise until it has first been determined that the plaintiff is the holder of the paper and that the defendant is a person who would ordinarily have liability for payment of the face of the paper. Assuming that those two questions have been decided in favor of the plaintiff, the remaining question concerns whether this defendant has a particular defense that may be raised.

Assume there are four successive indorsers and the holder who comes at the end of these four indorsers sues the first indorser. Can the first indorser raise against the holder a defense that the first indorser has against the second indorser? For example, can the defense be raised that the first indorser was induced by fraud to make the indorsement? More commonly the situation will arise in which the remote holder sues the drawer of a check. The drawer then defends on the ground that the check had been given in payment for goods or services that the drawer never got, did not work, or were not satisfactory. Can the drawer now raise against the remote holder the defense that the drawer has against the payee of the check, namely, the defense of failure of consideration? The answer to this depends on the nature of the defendant's defense against the person with whom the dealings were made and the character of the holder. If the defense is a **limited defense** and the remote holder is a holder in due course, the defendant cannot raise such a defense. If the defense is a **universal defense** or the holder is an ordinary holder, the defendant may raise that defense.

Limited Defense
Defense that cannot be used against holder in due course

Universal Defense
Defense against any holder

CLASSIFICATION OF DEFENSES

L.O.2 ....

Certain defenses are limited to being raised against ordinary holders and cannot be raised against holders in due course. Limited defenses include:

1 Ordinary contract defenses
2 Fraud that induced the execution of the instrument
3 Conditional delivery
4 Improper completion
5 Payment or part payment
6 Nondelivery
7 Theft

Limited Defenses

L.O.1 ....

A significant number of defenses cannot be raised against a holder in due course or a holder through a holder in due course. Limited defenses, also called personal defenses, must be distinguished from universal ones.

Ordinary Contract Defenses. In general, the defenses available in a dispute over a contract may be raised only against holders who do not qualify as holders in due course. Accordingly, if the instrument is held by a holder in due course, the defense of failure of consideration is not effective when raised by the maker who alleges that no consideration was received for the paper. In an action on an ordinary contract, the promisor may defend on the ground that no consideration existed for the promise; or that if consideration did exist in the form of a counterpromise, the promise was never performed; or that the consideration was illegal. Thus, if Smith agreed to paint Jones's house but did not do it properly, Jones would have a right of action against Smith for breach of contract, or Jones could refuse to pay Smith the price agreed upon. If Smith assigned the right to payment, Jones would be able to raise against the assignee the defenses available against Smith.

However, if Jones paid Smith by check before the work was completed, and the check was negotiated to a holder in due course, Jones could not defend on the ground of failure of consideration. The check would have to be paid. Jones' only right of action would be against Smith for the loss.

Fraud that Induced the Execution of the Instrument. When a person knows a commercial paper is being executed and knows its essential terms but is persuaded or induced to execute it because of false representations or statements, this is not a defense against a holder in due course. For example, if Randolph persuades Drucker to buy a car because of false statements made by Randolph about the car, and Drucker gives Randolph a note for it that is later negotiated to a holder in due course, Drucker cannot defend on the ground that Randolph lied about the car. Drucker will have to pay the note and seek any recovery from Randolph.

Donald Mertens sold the personal property of a laundromat to Cliff Coffman, who sold it to Elna Phillips. The sale to Phillips was subject to a financing and security agreement between Mertens and Coffman that Phillips assumed and agreed to pay. Part of the security agreement included a promissory note. After Phillips went broke, Mertens sued for the balance on Coffman's note. Coffman had told Phillips that the business was profitable and the equipment in good working order, and Phillips relied on these representations. They were false. Phillips raised the defense of fraud in the inducement. The defense was good because Mertens was not a holder in due course. He was a creditor beneficiary of the Coffman-Phillips agreement.

Conditional Delivery. As against a holder in due course, an individual who would be liable on the instrument cannot show that the instrument, absolute on its face, was delivered subject to an unperformed condition or that it was delivered for a specific purpose but was not used for it. If Sims makes out a check for Byers and delivers it to Richter with instructions not to deliver it until Byers delivers certain goods, but Richter delivers it to Byers, who then negotiates it to a holder in due course, Sims will have to pay on the check.

Improper Completion. If any term in a commercial paper is left blank, for example, the payee or the amount, and the drawer then delivers the instrument to another to complete it, the drawer cannot raise the defense of improper completion against a holder in due course. In this case, the holder in due course may require payment from the drawer.

Payment or Part Payment. Upon payment of commercial paper the party making the payment should demand the surrender of the instrument. If not surrendered, the instrument may be further negotiated, and a later holder in due course would be able to demand payment successfully. A receipt is not adequate as proof of payment, because the subsequent holder in due course would have no notice of the receipt; whereas, surrender of the instrument would clearly prevent further negotiation.

Florida City Express executed a promissory note due in three months for $3,292 to Latin American Tire Co. Two months later it executed another note to Latin American due in two months for $3,500. Latin American sold the notes to the Bank of Miami. When the notes came due, it turned out that unknown to the bank, Florida City had paid the full amount of the notes to Latin American. The bank sued Florida City, which raised the defense of payment. The court said the bank was a holder in due course because it paid for the notes and had no notice of Florida City's payments. Florida city had to pay again.

If only partial payment is made, a holder would not and should not be expected to surrender the instrument. In such a case the person making the payment should note the payment on the instrument, thereby giving notice of the partial payment to any subsequent transferee.

Nondelivery. Normally, a negotiable instrument fully or partially completed but not delivered to the payee is not collectible by the payee. However, if a holder in due course holds the instrument, payment of it may be required. For example, if one person makes out a note to another person and that other person takes the note from the maker's desk without the maker's permission and negotiates the note to an innocent purchaser, or holder in due course, the holder in due course would be entitled to recover the amount of the note against the maker. This applies in spite of the nondelivery of the note.

Theft. A thief may not normally pass good title; however, an exception occurs when the thief conveys an instrument to a holder in due course. Such a purchaser will be able to enforce the obligation in spite of the previous theft of the paper. The thief or any ordinary holder cannot require payment of stolen paper.

Universal Defenses

L.O.3 ....

Those defenses thought to be so important that they are preserved even against a holder in due course are called "universal" or "real." Universal defenses can be raised regardless of who is being sued or who is suing. Thus, they can be raised against the holder in due course as well as an ordinary holder. The more common universal defenses include:

1 Minority
2 Forgery
3 Fraud as to the nature of the instrument or its material terms
4 Discharge in bankruptcy proceedings

Minority. The fact that the defendant is a minor capable of avoiding agreements under contract laws is a defense that may be raised against any holder.

Forgery. Except in cases where the defendant's negligence made the forgery possible, forgery may be raised successfully against any holder. However, a forged signature operates as the signature of the forger in favor of a holder in due course.

Fraud as to the Nature of the Instrument and Its Essential Terms. The defense that one was induced to sign an instrument when one did not know that it was in fact commercial paper is available against any holder. For example, an illiterate person told that a note is a receipt and thereby induced to sign it may successfully raise this defense against any holder. The defense is not available, however, to competent individuals who negligently fail to read or give reasonable attention to the details of the documents they sign.

James and Marie Estepp wanted to get a loan from United Bank and Trust Company of Maryland. United required an additional signature by an owner of real estate. Estepp brought Marvin Schaeffer to the bank saying he needed Schaeffer, whose wife had died, to sign a character reference. Estepp supervised

Schaeffer at work and had helped Schaeffer make funeral arrangements. Schaeffer had a learning disability and could not read or write. The bank officer handling the transaction did not explain to Schaeffer that he was assuming a financial responsibility. Schaeffer signed the note. The Estepps defaulted, so United sued Schaeffer. The court found fraud existed as to the nature and essential terms of the note.

Discharge in Bankruptcy Proceedings. Even holders in due course are subject to the defense that a discharge in bankruptcy has been granted.

Hybrid Defenses

Several defenses may be either universal or limited. These include:

1 Duress
2 Incapacity other than minority
3 Illegality
4 Alteration

Duress. Whether or not duress is a valid defense against a holder in due course depends upon whether the effect of such duress under the state law makes a contract void or voidable. When the duress nullifies a contract, the defense is universal. When the duress merely makes the contract voidable at the option of the victim of the duress, the defense is limited.

Incapacity Other than Minority. In cases of incapacity other than minority, if the effect of the incapacity makes the instrument void, a nullity, the defense is universal. If the effect of the incapacity does not make the instrument a nullity, the defense is limited.

Illegality. The fact that the law makes certain transactions illegal gives rise to a defense against an ordinary holder. Such a defense would be unavailable against a holder in due course unless the law making the transaction illegal also specifies that instruments based upon such transactions are unenforceable.

Alteration. An altered instrument has no effect if the plaintiff is an ordinary holder. If the plaintiff is a holder in due course, the instrument can be sued upon according to its terms before it was altered. An **alteration** exists only if (1) a party to the instrument (2) fraudulently made (3) a material change. If any one of these elements is lacking, the modification of the instrument is not called an alteration and has no legal effect. As a practical matter, however, there may be some difficulty in proving just what the instrument said before it was modified.

Alteration

Material change fraudulently made by party to instrument

Milton Turner and his companies had executed promissory notes to United American Bank. Jacob Butcher, president of UAB told Turner UAB was being audited and Turner needed to sign a guaranty for one of his company's files. Turner signed a guaranty form that had blanks for the name of the debtor and the amount of the guaranty. As part of Butcher's fraud, the name Lovell Road Properties Limited Partnership was put in as the debtor and the amount as $2 million. UAB's name, which was printed on the form, was erased with correction fluid and replaced with City and County Bank (CCB). Turner had no connection with Lovell or CCB and no knowledge of the improper completion or alteration. A holder in due course acquired Lovell's notes and the altered guaranty and sued Turner. The court said Turner was not liable.

MISCELLANEOUS MATTERS

In addition to the defenses described above, remember that every lawsuit presents certain standard problems. Any defendant may, under appropriate circumstances, raise the defense that the suit is not brought in the proper court, that no service of process existed, or that the statute of limitations has run and bars suit. Any defendant in a suit on commercial paper can claim that the instrument is not negotiable; that the plaintiff is not the holder; and that the defendant is not a party liable for payment of the paper. If the holder claims that the defendant is secondarily liable for the payment of the face of the paper, the defendant may also show that the paper had not been properly presented to the primary party and that proper notice of default had not been given to the secondary party.

QUESTIONS

1   Is it any advantage to be the holder of a negotiable instrument even though one is not a holder in due course?

2   What is a limited defense?

3   What is a real or universal defense?

4   State in one sentence the chief advantage of being the holder in due course of commercial paper.

5   Name and explain three limited defenses.

6   Name and explain three universal defenses.

7   Which defenses may be either universal or limited?

8   If partial payment of a note is made, how can the payor be protected against being required to pay the full amount of the note?

9   What is the effect upon a holder in due course if the instrument was not completed or delivered by the maker thereof but was subsequently filled in naming an inappropriate party as payee and specifying an unduly large sum?

10   What effect does alteration of an instrument have against a holder in due course?

CASE PROBLEMS

L.O.2, 3 ....

1   Jacqueline Quazzo purchased some real estate and during the next half dozen years spent $100,000 to renovate it. Although the funds used did not belong to her sister-in-law, Ada Quazzo, after the remodeling, Jacqueline executed a note for that amount to Ada. When Jacqueline did not pay the note, Ada sued her. Jacqueline tried to defend on the basis of failure of consideration. Should she succeed?

L.O.1,2, 3 ....

2   Matthew Roarke executed three promissory notes payable to the order of State Bank of Albany. Roarke defaulted on the notes, and the bank sued for payment of them. Roarke raised the defense of fraud as to the nature or essential terms of the instruments. He alleged that Maurice O'Connell, then a vice president of the bank, and Frank Kindlon conspired in a fraudulent scheme, that Kindlon misrepresented the nature of the instruments and their purpose when Roarke executed them at Kindlon's request. Was this defense good?

L.O.2, 3 ....

3 Troy Garrison Sr. sued his son, Troy Jr. and daughter-in-law, Erika Garrison, on a note they had signed in the amount of $96,000. Erika alleged that she had never received any money from Troy Sr. She stated it had been given to Troy Jr. as a gift and they had only signed the note so Troy Sr. would have it for tax purposes. What defense did Erika allege? Discuss its effectiveness against various types of holders.

L.O.2, 3 ....

4 Raejean and Robert Stotler bought a lot from SilverCreek Development Company. They signed a promissory note in payment. SilverCreek assigned the note to Geibank Industrial Bank. SilverCreek went bankrupt, and the Stotlers defaulted on the note. In the ensuing lawsuit, the Stotlers alleged they were induced to buy the lot and sign the note on the basis of false representations that SilverCreek would develop the surrounding property with condominiums, a golf course, and western theme park. The court said Geibank was a holder in due course. Are the Stotlers allegations good against Geibank?

L.O.2, 3 ....

5 Colonial Bank was the holder of a note in the amount of $75,000. Colonial sued Philip Robin for enforcement of the note. A signature appeared on the note in the name "Philip Robin," but Robin proved to the satisfaction of the court that it was not his signature on the note. If Colonial is a holder in due course, may it enforce the note?

Summary Cases

COMMERCIAL PAPER

1 Public Relations Enterprises, Inc., paid Melco Products Corporation for goods by means of personal money orders purchased from Nassau Trust Company and Republic National Bank of New York. When Melco presented them for payment, the banks dishonored them on the ground that Public had stopped payment. Melco sued the banks for payment, alleging that the banks had no right to stop payment on the personal money orders. Did they? [*Melco Products Corp.* v. *Public Relations Enterprises, Inc.,* 460 N.Y.S.2d 466 (N.Y. Sup. Ct.)]

2 Dallas County State Bank sold a personal money order on a forged check. It then stopped payment on the money order and refused to accept and pay it when it was presented by Northpark National Bank of Dallas. The money order had a checkwriting imprint, "Dallas County State Bank," as well as the name of the Bank printed on it. Northpark sued for payment. Dallas alleged it was not liable on the money order since its signature did not appear on it. Was it liable? [*Interfirst Bank Carrollton* v. *Northpark National Bank of Dallas,* 671 S.W.2d 100 (Tex. Ct. App.)]

3 The Board of Commissioners for the Pontchartrain Levee District executed a warrant to the State Comptroller payable to Farmer Construction Co., Inc. Farmer negotiated it to St. James Bank and Trust Co. Before the State Comptroller received it, the Board stopped payment, and the warrant was returned to St. James unpaid. St. James sued the Board, alleging it was a holder in due course. The Board defended that the warrant was not negotiable because it was paying out of a particular fund. Was the warrant conditional? [*St. James Bank & Trust Co.* v. *Board of Commissioners, Pontchartrain Levee District,* 354 So.2d 233 (La. Ct. App.)]

4 A check was drawn by the Havana Canning Company for $125 payable to George Wells. The check was regular in every detail except that in the lower left-hand corner were the words: *For berries to be delivered to us June 8th.* This check was indorsed by George Wells to an innocent purchaser. The drawer wished to raise a defense to the payment of a breach of warranty that, being a failure of consideration, was a limited defense. In order to raise this defense, he had to establish that this check was nonnegotiable because of this notation. Did this notation make the order to pay conditional? [*First National Bank of Marianna* v. *Havana Canning Company,* 195 So. 188 (Fla.)]

5 Berry executed a promissory note payable to William C. Stepp. The note was in perfect order. Stepp indorsed the note before maturity as follows: "I hereby transfer my right to this note over to W. E. McCullough. (signed) William C. Stepp." The maker failed to pay the note, and McCullough brought suit against Stepp, the indorser. Stepp's defense was that the indorsement was a

qualified indorsement, and therefore, he was not liable, since the maker's only reason for not paying was insolvency. Was this a qualified indorsement? [*McCullough* v. *Stepp*, 85 S.E.2d 159 (Ga. Ct. App.)].

6 Omega Electronics, Inc., executed a promissory note to the order of State Bank of Fisk. It was signed on the front by two officers of the corporation and on the back by five individuals. The note stated: "We, the makers, . . . endorsers and guarantors of this note, hereby severally waive presentment for payment, notice of nonpayment, protest and notice of protest." When the note was not paid, the Bank sued the individuals. They alleged they were not liable because they had not been given notice of dishonor and protest. Were they liable? [*State Bank of Fisk* v. *Omega Electronics, Inc.*, 634 S.W.2d 234 (Mo. Ct. App.)]

7 A check was drawn by Fellsway Motors, Inc., on October 25, made payable to Therrien. Therrien then drew a line through the "5" in "25" to make it look like Oct. 28. The line was in a different color of ink from the rest of the check, and the change in the number was perfectly evident. On October 29 Therrien indorsed the check to Manuel Medeiros for value and in good faith. Before the check was paid, the drawer stopped payment. The key question to be decided in the case was whether or not Medeiros was a holder in due course. [*Medeiros* v. *Fellsway Motors Inc.*, 96 N.E.2d 170 (Mass.)]

8 In August, Hier executed a negotiable note for $1,075, payable to the Washington Fixtures and Equipment Company. The note was to be paid in installments, the first installment to be due December 1, with a provision that if any installment was not paid on time, the entire balance should become due and payable at once. The first installment was not paid. On December 23, the payee indorsed the note to the Federal Glass Company, Inc., for value. When Hier was sued by the holder, he wished to plead fraud and a breach of warranty. The holder claimed he was not required to defend against such a defense. What fundamental error did some employee for the Federal Glass Company commit in this case? [*Hier* v. *Federal Glass Co., Inc.*, 102 A.2d 840 (D.C.)]

9 Blas Garcia told Arthur and Lucy Casarez he was a representative of Albuquerque Fence Company, so they contracted with the Company to build a home for them. Blas introduced them to Cecil Garcia, who said he would make a loan for the home. The Garcias were in no way affiliated with Albuquerque. Cecil got a $25,000 loan from Rio Grande Valley Bank in the form of a cashier's check. The Casarezes signed a note, and Cecil indorsed the check: "Pay to the order of Lucy N. Casarez, Cecil Garcia." Lucy indorsed it: "Pay to the order of Albuquerque Fence Co., Lucy N. Casarez." She handed the check to Blas who indorsed the check: "Alb. Fence Co." Cecil signed his own name under that and presented the check to Rio Grande in return for $5,000 and four cashier's checks for $5,000. The Casarezes sued Rio Grande, alleging the words "Pay to the order of Albuquerque Fence Co." constituted a special indorsement and the check could be negotiated only by indorsement by an authorized official of the company. Was this a valid assertion? [*Casarez* v. *Garcia*, 660 P.2d 598 (N.M. Ct. App.)]

10 Mr. Schafer, the chief operating officer of The Heights Bank, called Clifford Lee, told him he needed a favor, and asked him to come to the bank. Schafer asked Lee to cosign a note with Gordon, Lee's brother-in-law. Lee refused.

Schafer told Lee the note was fully secured by a $10,000 bond and showed Lee a copy of the Security Agreement. Lee asked why he was needed if the loan was secured. Schafer said it would help him with the bank examiners. Schafer stated, "You've made a loan request and I am going to help you out, too." After deliberating, Lee agreed to cosign. Three months later Lee was told Gordon's note was in default. Lee told Schafer to sell the bond. Schafer told him there was none. The Bank told Lee if he did not pay the Gordon note, it would ruin Lee's excellent credit rating. Lee paid the note and sued the Bank for reimbursement. Was the bank guilty of fraud in the inducement? [*Lee* v. *Heights Bank,* 446 N.E.2d 248 (Ill. App. Ct.)]

11 George Weast borrowed $140,000 from State National Bank of Maryland (SNB), and his wife, Ruth, cosigned for him. This debt later was in default, so George indorsed and delivered some notes made by Francis and Josephine Arnold and Randall Co. to the order of SNB. Payments were made on these notes for several years before default. Ruth and George got divorced. When Ruth paid off the amount owed on their debt, SNB indorsed the notes of the Arnolds and Randall to Ruth. She sued them for payment on the notes. They alleged she was subject to a defense regarding the transaction that gave rise to the notes. Ruth claimed to be a holder through a holder in due course, so the defense would not be valid against her. Was Ruth a holder through a holder in due course when the notes had been indorsed to her after default? [*Weast* v. *Arnold,* 474 A.2d 904 (Md.)]

12 South Carolina Insurance Company issued a draft to Kevlin Owens drawn on the account of Seibels, Bruce Group at South Carolina National Bank. Owens negotiated the draft to First National Bank of Denham Springs, which paid him the entire amount and delivered it to South Carolina National Bank. The insurance company alleged fraud in Owens' claim and issued a stop-payment order. South Carolina National Bank did not honor the draft. The draft stated it was payable as follows: "Upon acceptance, pay to the order of Kevlin Owens." South Carolina Insurance Company was a wholly owned subsidiary of Seibels, Bruce Group. Therefore, South Carolina was both drawer and drawee. First National sued South Carolina for payment. South Carolina said the words *upon acceptance* made the draft conditional, therefore the draft was not negotiable, First National is not a holder in due course, and the defense of fraud may be raised. Was the draft conditional? [*First National Bank of Denham Springs* v. *South Carolina Insurance Company,* 432 So. 2d 417 (La. Ct. App.)]

Part 6

AGENCY
AND
EMPLOYMENT

Chapter 28

NATURE AND CREATION OF AN AGENCY

LEARNING OBJECTIVES

After studying this chapter you should be able to:

1 Explain the nature of an agency and identify the parties involved.

2 Describe the different classifications of agents and the corresponding authority of each.

3 Discuss how an agency is usually created.

4 Distinguish between an agency and independent contractor or employer-employee relationships.

Preview Case

Robert Weeks was employed as an electrician by Howard P. Foley Company during construction of a power plant by Alabama Electric Cooperative, Inc. (AEC). He was injured when a scaffold collapsed. He sued AEC as the owner of the premises, alleging there was an employer-employee relationship, and AEC had breached its duty of care. By contract AEC had retained the right to supervise or inspect the work of each independent contractor to determine whether the work was being done according to the plans and specifications. Were AEC and Weeks in an employer-employee relationship?

L.O.1

Principal
Person who appoints another to contract with third parties

Agent
Person appointed to contract on behalf of another

When one party, known as a **principal,** appoints another party, known as an **agent,** to enter into contracts with third parties in the name of the principal, a contract of **agency** is formed. By this definition every contract that an agent negotiates involves at least three parties, the principal, the agent, and the third party. It is this making of contracts with third persons on behalf of the principal that distinguishes an agency from other employment relationships. The principal, the agent, or the third party may be an individual, a partnership, or a corporation.

IMPORTANCE OF AGENCY

Agency
Contract under which one party is authorized to contract for another

Because of the magnitude and the complexity of our modern industry, many of the important details pertaining to business transactions must be delegated by the owners of businesses to agents. The general principles of law pertaining to contracts governs the relation creating this delegation of powers.

Even in the performance of routine matters by individuals, agents are necessary in order to bring one person into a business contractual relationship with other persons. Thus, a farmer who sends an employee to town to have a piece of machinery repaired gives the employee the authority to enter into a contract that binds the farmer to the agreement.

WHAT POWERS MAY BE DELEGATED TO AN AGENT?

As a general rule, a person may do through an agent all of those things that could otherwise be done by the person. However, the courts will not permit certain acts of such a personal nature to be delegated to others. Some of these acts that may not be performed by an agent include voting in a public election, executing a will, or serving on a jury.

What one may not lawfully do may not be done through another. Thus, no person can authorize an agent to commit a crime, to publish a libelous statement, to perpetrate a fraud, or to do any other act judged illegal, immoral, or opposed to the welfare of society.

Robert Miner, a prisoner serving a life sentence, applied to participate in a department of corrections family reunion program, claiming he was legally married. Under state law, a person serving a life sentence was considered civilly dead. Miner had executed a document appointing Michael Foster his agent for the purpose of entering into a proxy marriage, which Foster had done. The court held that Miner was not legally married. As a civilly dead person, he could not lawfully marry. Since he could not marry, Miner could not appoint an agent to enter into that relationship on his behalf.

WHO MAY APPOINT AN AGENT?

All people legally competent to act for themselves may act through an agent. This rule is based upon the principle that whatever a person may do may be done through another. Hence corporations and partnerships, as well as individuals, may appoint agents.

The contract by which a minor appoints an agent to act for the minor is normally voidable. Some states, however, find such contracts void, not voidable.

WHO MAY ACT AS AN AGENT?

Ordinarily, any person who has sufficient intelligence to carry out a principal's orders may be appointed to act as an agent. The law does not impose this requirement. It arises from the practical consideration of whether the principal wants to have the particular person act as agent. Corporations and partnerships may act as agents.

Some types of transactions cannot be performed by an agent without meeting certain requirements. For example, in many states a real estate agent must possess certain definite qualifications and must, in addition, secure a license to act in this capacity. Failure to do this disqualifies a person to act as an agent in performing the duties of a real estate agent.

CLASSIFICATION OF AGENTS

L.O.2 ....

Agents may be classified as:

1   General agents
2   Special agents

General Agents

General Agent

Agent authorized to carry out particular kind of business or all business at a place

A **general agent** is one authorized to carry out the principal's business of a particular kind or all the principal's business at a particular place even though not all of one kind. Examples of general agents who perform all of the principal's business of a particular kind include a purchasing agent and a bank cashier. A general agent who transacts all of the principal's business at a particular place include a manager in full charge of one branch of a chain of shoe stores. A general agent buys and sells merchandise, employs help, pays bills, collects accounts, and performs all other duties. Such an agent has a wide scope of authority and the power to act without express direction from the principal.

A general agent has considerable authority beyond that expressly stated in the contract of employment. In addition to express authority a general agent has that authority that one in such a position customarily has.

Special Agents

Special Agent

Agent authorized to transact specific act or acts

A **special agent** is one authorized by a principal to transact some specific act or acts. Such an agent has only limited powers that may be used only for a specific purpose. The authorization may cover just one act, such as buying a house; or it may cover a series of merely repetitious acts such as selling admission tickets to a movie.

Flushing Operating Corp. leased a building to Dutch Treat Bakers. The lease stated Flushing would spend $45,000 to renovate the building. Dutch Treat hired contractors, including Rowen & Blair Electric Co. Dutch Treat sent the bills to Flushing, which issued checks in payment to Dutch Treat and the appropriate contractor. Rowen received a check from Flushing for $7,040. Five months after executing the lease, Flushing sent its last check because the $45,000 figure had been reached. After that date, Rowen did more work and Dutch Treat paid it $10,000. When Rowen finished, it demanded $39,033 more. Dutch Treat had gone bankrupt, so Rowen sued Flushing. The court stated that Dutch Treat acted as a special agent for Flushing. In the lease, Flushing limited the agency to expending $45,000 for the renovations. Since Flushing had spent that much, it had no liability for any more.

ADDITIONAL TYPES OF AGENTS

There are several additional types of agents. Most of these are special agents, but because of the nature of their duties, their powers may exceed those of the ordinary special agent:

1 Factors
2 Factors del credere
3 Brokers
4 Attorneys in fact

Factors

Factor

Bailee seeking to sell property on commission

A **factor** is one who receives possession of another's property for the purpose of sale on commission. Factors, also called *commission merchants*, may sell in the name of the principal, but normally they sell in the merchant's own name. When factors collect the sale price, they deduct the commission, or factorage, and remit the balance to the principal. The third party, as a rule, is aware that the dealings are with an agent by the nature of the business or by the name of the business. The words *commission merchant* usually appear on all stationery. Commission merchants have the power to bind the principal for the customary terms of sale for the types of business they are doing. In this regard their powers are slightly greater than those of the ordinary special agent.

Factors del Credere

Factor del Credere

Factor who sells on credit and guarantees price will be paid

A **factor del credere** is a commission merchant who sells on credit and guarantees to the principal that the purchase price will be paid by the purchaser or by the factor. This is a form of contract of guaranty, but the contract need not be in writing as required by the Statute of Frauds, since the agreement is a primary obligation of the factor.

Brokers

Broker

Agent with job of bringing two contracting parties together

A **broker** is a special agent whose task is to bring the two contracting parties together. Unlike the factor, the broker does not have possession of the merchandise. In real estate and insurance a broker normally acts as the agent of the buyer rather than the seller. If the job merely consists of finding a buyer or, sometimes, a seller, the broker has no authority to bind the principal on any contract.

Attorneys in Fact

Attorney in Fact

General agent appointed by written authorization

An **attorney in fact** is a general agent who has been appointed by a written authorization. The writing, intended to be shown to third persons, manifests that the agent has authority.

EXTENT OF AUTHORITY

Express Authority

Authority of agent stated in agreement creating agency

Implied Authority

Agent's authority to do things in order to carry out express authority

Customary Authority

Authority agent possesses by custom

As a rule, a general agent has authority to transact several classes of acts: those clearly within the scope of the express authority, those customarily within such an agent's authority, and those outside of express authority but which appear to third parties to be within the scope of the agent's authority.

Express authority is the authority specifically delegated to the agent by the agreement creating the agency. It amounts to the power to do whatever the agent is appointed to do.

Frequently, in order to carry out the purposes of the agency, the agent must have the authority to do things not specifically enumerated in the agreement. This authority is called **implied authority.** An agent appointed to manage a retail shoe store has implied authority to purchase shoes from wholesalers in order to have a stock to sell.

Authority to act on behalf of another arises when by custom such agents ordinarily possess such powers. This is sometimes called **customary authority.**

Clyde Thomas managed the Russell Dry Goods Company store. Over a period of five months, he placed several orders of furniture items from Kyle Furniture Company and had them shipped and charged to Russell. Thomas made another order on April 28. When the truck arrived with the shipment, the store was on fire, so Thomas asked that the truck be taken to his garage and unloaded there. Later, the owner of the store refused to pay for the shipment, saying Thomas did not have the authority to purchase merchandise. Kyle sued Russell. Testimony at trial stated that store managers normally had authority to buy merchandise. The court held that Thomas had the authority customary for store managers to have, including the purchase of merchandise.

Apparent Authority

Authority agent believed to have because of principal's behavior

In addition, without regard to custom, the principal may have behaved in a way or made statements that caused the third person to believe that the agent has the authority. This is called **apparent authority.** For example, the Pardalos Insurance Company might advertise "For all your insurance problems see your local Pardalos Insurance agent." This would give the local Pardalos Insurance Company agent apparent authority to arrange any insurance matters even though the agents did not actually have such authority or had been told that certain kinds of cases had to be referred to the home office.

As to innocent third parties, the powers of a general agent may be far more extensive than those actually granted by the principal. Limitations upon an agent's authority do not bind a third party who has no knowledge of them; but they do bind a third party who knows of them.

In every case the person who would benefit by the existence of authority on the part of the alleged agent has the burden of proving the existence of authority. If a person appears to be the agent of another for the purpose of selling the car of that other person, the prospective purchaser must seek assurance from the principal as to the agent's authority.

Once the third party has learned the actual scope of an agent's express authority from the principal, the agent has no greater authority than the principal's actions and statements indicate, together with such customary authority as would attach.

CREATION OF AN AGENCY

L.O.3 ....

Usually the relationship of agency may be created by:

1 Appointment
2 Ratification
3 Estoppel
4 Necessity

Appointment

The usual way of creating an agency is by the statement of the principal to the agent. In most cases the contract may be either oral or written, formal or informal. In some instances, however, the appointment must be made in a particular form. The contract appointing an agent must be in writing if the agency is created to transfer title to real estate. Also, to extend an agent's authority beyond one year from the date of the contract, the Statute of Frauds requires the contract to be in writing. The appointment of an agent to execute a formal contract, such as a bond, requires a formal contract of appointment.

A written instrument indicating the appointment of an agent is known as a *warrant* or **power of attorney.** To record a power of attorney, it must also be acknowledged before a notary public or other officer authorized to take acknowledgments. Illustration 28-1 shows an ordinary form of power of attorney.

Power of Attorney

Writing appointing an agent

Ratification

Ratification is the approval by one person of the unauthorized act of another done in the former's name. The unauthorized act may have been done by an assumed agent who purported to act as an agent without actual or apparent authority, or it may have been done by a real agent who exceeded actual and apparent authority. Such an act does not bind the supposed principal in such a case unless and until it is ratified. Ratification relates back to the date of the act done by the assumed agent. Hence, ratifying the act puts the assumed agent in the same position as if there had been authority to do the act at the time the act was done.

A valid ratification requires:

Ratification

Approval of unauthorized act

1 The one who assumed the authority of an agent must have made it known to the third person that he or she was acting on behalf of the party who attempts to ratify the act.
2 The one attempting to ratify must have been capable of authorizing the act at the time the act was done. Some jurisdictions apply this rule to corporations so that an act of a promoter cannot be ratified by a corporation formed subsequent to the time of the act. Other states have ignored this requirement in regard to ratification of the acts of corporate promoters.
3 The one attempting to ratify must be capable of authorizing the act at the time approval of the act is given.
4 The one attempting to ratify must have knowledge of all material facts.

Illustration 28-1   Power of Attorney

Know All Men by These Presents:

That I, Amelia Clermont

of Portland

County of Multnomah   , *State of* Oregon

have made, constituted and appointed, and by these presents do make, constitute and appoint James Turner

of Vancouver

County of Clark   , *State of* Washington

my true and lawful attorney   *in fact, for me and in my name, place and stead,* to manage, operate, and let my rental properties in the City of Vancouver, County of Clark, State of Washington

giving and granting unto my said attorney full power and authority to do and perform all and every act and thing whatsoever requisite and necessary to be done in and about the premises, as fully to all intents and purposes as I might or could do, if personally present, with full power of substitution and revocation; hereby ratifying and confirming all that my said attorney——or his   *substitute——shall lawfully do, or cause to be done, by virtue hereof.*

In Witness Whereof, *I have hereunto set my hand this* tenth   *day of* July   *, 19* --

Signed and acknowledged in presence of:

Amelia Clermont

Samuel Adamick

Teresa Romano

---

5   The one attempting to ratify must approve the entire act.
6   The ratified act must be legal, although a forgery on commercial paper may be ratified by the person whose name was forged.
7   The ratification must be made before the third party has withdrawn from the transaction.

Estoppel

Agency by estoppel arises when a person by words or conduct leads another person to believe that a third party is an agent or has the authority to do particular acts. The principal who has made representations is bound to the extent of those representations for the purpose of preventing an injustice to parties who have been misled by the acts or the conduct of the principal.

Diamond Kamvakis & Co. had done business with Ace Fastener Company for many years. Paul Slepp, the salesman for Ace, offered to sell merchandise to Diamond at a substantial discount conditioned on immediate payment directly to Slepp. Diamond suspected a problem with this arrangement, so its president called Fred Riley, Ace's national sales manager. Riley had authority over making discounts and setting the terms of sale and method of payment. Riley okayed the arrangement, so Diamond bought the merchandise. It turned out that Slepp and Riley engaged in a criminal conspiracy to sell Ace merchandise and pocket the proceeds. When sued for payment for the merchandise, Diamond alleged Ace was estopped to deny Slepp's authority to make the deal because Riley, who had authority, said it was okay. The court agreed.

Necessity

The relationship of agency may be created by necessity. Parents must support their minor children. If they fail to provide their children with necessaries, the parents' credit may be pledged for the children, even against their will. Agency by necessity may also arise from some unforeseen emergency. Thus, the driver of a bus operating between distant cities may pledge the owner's credit in order to have needed repairs made and may have the cost charged to the owner.

OTHER EMPLOYMENT RELATIONSHIPS

Two types of employment relationships differ from agency relationships:

1   Independent contractor
2   Employer and employee, originally referred to in law as master and servant

Independent Contractor

L.O.4 ....

Independent Contractor
One who contracts to do jobs and is controlled only by contract as to how performed

An **independent contractor** is one who contracts to perform some tasks for a fixed fee. The other contracting party does not control an independent contractor as to the means by which the contractor performs except to the extent that the contract sets forth requirements to be followed. The independent contractor is merely held responsible for the proper performance of the contract. Because one who contracts with an independent contractor has much less control over the performance of the work, the contract does not create either a principal-agent relationship or an employer-employee relationship. The most usual type of independent contractor relationship is in the building trades.

Robert Weeks was employed as an electrician by Howard P. Foley Company during construction of a power plant by Alabama Electric Cooperative, Inc. (AEC). He was injured when a scaffold collapsed. He sued AEC as the owner of the premises, alleging there was an employer-employee relationship, and AEC had breached its duty of care. By contract AEC had retained the right to supervise or inspect the work of each independent contractor to determine whether the work was being done according to the plans and specifications. The court ruled this right did not include control over the employees of the contractors; thus, no employer-employee relationship existed.

Employer and Employee

An employee performs work for an employer. The employer controls the employee both as to the work to be done and as to the manner in which it is done. One contracting with an independent contractor does not have such control. The degree of control that the employer or principal exercises over the employee or agent and the authority the agent has to bind the principal to contracts constitute the main differences between an employee and an agent.

There are many reasons why a contract of employment must not be confused with a contract of an independent contractor. An employer may be held liable for any injuries employees negligently cause to third parties. This is not true for injuries caused by independent contractors. Second, employers must comply with laws relative to their employees. Employers must, for example, withhold social security taxes on employees' wages, pay a payroll tax for unemployment compensation, withhold federal income taxes, and, when properly demanded, bargain with their employees collectively. None of these laws apply when one contracts with independent contractors. Independent contractors are the employers of those employed by them to perform the contract.

QUESTIONS

1   What is an agency and who is involved in it?
2   Why are most business transactions carried on by agents?
3   What acts can be delegated to an agent?
4   Discuss the effectiveness of a contract by a minor to appoint an agent.
5   What are the two basic types of agents and their authority?
6   What is a factor?
7   What is the difference between express authority and implied authority?
8   What is apparent authority?
9   How is an agency usually created?
10   How does an agency by estoppel arise?

CASE PROBLEMS

L.O.1, 2 ....

1   Charles Beasley bought cotton seed and other items at the "Kerr-McGee Field Office," a separate part of a larger general store named "Houser's Supermarket." John Houser operated the businesses. Beasley charged all the items to his established account with Kerr-McGee. Houser gave Beasley a printed Kerr-McGee delivery ticket that had at the bottom Houser's signature above the printed name "Kerr-McGee Chemical Corp." Kerr-McGee billed Beasley and he paid Kerr-McGee. The seed did not germinate properly, so Beasley sued Kerr-McGee arguing that Houser acted as its agent in selling the seed. Kerr-McGee argued that it did not have an agency agreement with Houser. Did Houser have apparent authority from Kerr-McGee?

L.O.2 ....

2   Nelson, Hesse, Cyril, Weber & Sparrow hired Susan Blackmon as a secretary who later inquired of Ms. Steeves, the office manager, about coverage under

the firm's group health insurance plan. Blackmon stated she told Steeves she needed surgery but would wait until she had coverage. She further stated that Steeves told her upon completion of the application form that coverage began immediately, and Steeves made deductions from Blackmon's salary for premiums to start coverage that day. Eight days later, thinking she had coverage, Blackmon had the surgery. Steeves had just mailed the application, and the company did not approve it until five days after the surgery. Blackmon sued the firm, alleging Steeves was its agent and acted negligently in advising when the coverage took effect. Was Steeves the firm's agent?

L.O.4 ....

3 Lisa Millsap suffered injuries when a car driven by Christopher Pence hit her car. North County Express (NCE) paid Pence to deliver packages to its customers. In making deliveries, Pence used his own car, supplied his own gas and oil, liability insurance, and paid for his car repairs. NCE paid him a lump sum based on distance for the deliveries. NCE would call when needing packages delivered or Pence would stop in. He received no employee benefits and had no taxes withheld from his paychecks. He would give NCE invoices when he wanted. Pence received no instruction from NCE about how to make the deliveries. It did require him to get a signed confirmation of them. Millsap sued Pence and NCE for her injuries. NCE incurred no liability if Pence contracted with it as an independent contractor. Decide the independent contractor issue.

L.O.2 ....

4 William Savary who operated an insurance agency, helped Rodney Carney fill out an application for "assigned risk" auto insurance through the Automotive Plan in New York. Neither knew which company would be assigned. Concord General Mutual Insurance Company sent a policy directly to Rodney, and the Plan notified Savary it had assigned Rodney to Concord. While driving Rodney's car, his brother, Brian, had an accident with Gilbert Libby. Libby's attorney tried to contact the Carneys and their insurers, but could not. Suit was filed against Rodney. Savary was not Concord's authorized agent, but Carney made the insurance payments to Savary who received a commission on the insurance. At Rodney's request, Savary had sent statements and letters to Concord. Can Savary be held an express or implied agent of Concord?

L.O.3 ....

5 George and Emily Zeese assigned Max Siegel a written lease of property they owned. Siegel owned Trailer Mart, Inc., which did business on the property. After Trailer Mart took possession of the property, Siegel died. Eva Siegel, his widow and executrix, sent a letter to the Zeeses exercising an option to renew the lease for ten years. During the next four years, George Zeese visited the property on numerous occasions to observe the business, and during this time Trailer Mart sent monthly rental checks to the Zeeses and paid the property taxes. The Zeeses then served a notice-to-quit on Trailer Mart, alleging Eva Siegel was not the agent of Trailer Mart when she exercised the option to renew the lease. Trailer Mart alleged that even if she was not an agent, it had ratified her acts. Had Trailer Mart renewed the lease?

6   Mr. and Mrs. Howard Anderson wanted to obtain a consolidation loan to reduce their monthly payments on their loans. They consulted First National Bank of Pine City. Mrs. Anderson went to First National and brought home papers for Mr. Anderson to sign. He refused because there were unfilled blanks in the papers. Mrs. Anderson signed his name as well as her own to a note and mortgage deed on their home and delivered them to First National. When the Andersons fell behind on their payments on the note, First National began foreclosure proceedings. The Bank alleged Mr. Anderson ratified his wife's forgery by being silent and failing to notify it. Mr. Anderson stated he was silent because he feared his wife would be prosecuted for forgery. He had learned about her signing his name three months later and thought she had forged his name to a loan secured by personal property, not a mortgage. Had he ratified the forgery?

7   Joyce Koven incurred injuries while at the Legend City Amusement Park. She sued the owner of the park, Saberdyne Systems, Inc. (SSI). Her attorney examined the public state corporation records to find out who to serve with the legal papers. The most recent information was a two-year-old annual report filed by SSI that showed Morry Spitz as vice president. SSI had not appointed a statutory agent for service. Service of process was made on Spitz, but he had resigned and cut all connection with SSI two years previously. Koven claimed Spitz was the apparent agent for SSI. What should the court hold?

Chapter 29

OPERATION AND TERMINATION OF AN AGENCY

LEARNING OBJECTIVES

After studying this chapter you should be able to:

1 Specify the duties an agent owes the principal and the principal owes the agent.

2 Describe an agent's liabilities to third parties.

3 Explain when a principal is liable for contracts made by an agent.

4 State how an agency may be terminated, either by the parties or by operation of law.

Preview Case

John Kennon, doing business as Kennon Adjustment Company, was hired by Commercial Standard Insurance Company to investigate a workers' compensation claim. There was no agreement as to the amount to be paid Kennon. After an award was made to the claimant, Kennon submitted a bill for more than three times the amount of the award. Commercial refused to pay the bill, saying that it was too high. Kennon sued. In the absence of an agreement for compensation, how much, if anything, must be paid an agent?

In a contract of agency, the law imposes upon the agent certain duties not set out in the contract. Likewise, the relationship of agency creates duties and obligations that the principal owes to an agent even though not specifically enumerated in the contract. In turn, the agency relationship imposes upon both principal and agent certain duties and obligations to third parties. An examination of these duties and obligations will reveal the importance of the relationship of agent and principal as well as the necessity for each party in the relationship to be fully cognizant of both the rights and duties that exist.

AGENT'S DUTIES TO PRINCIPAL

L.O.1 .... An agent owes the following important duties to the principal:

1. Loyalty and good faith
2. Obedience
3. Reasonable skill and diligence
4. Accounting
5. Information

Loyalty and Good Faith

The relationship of principal and agent is fiduciary in nature; thus, the principal must be able to trust the agent to perform the duties according to contract. The relationship of agent and principal calls for a higher degree of faith and trust than do most contractual relationships. For this reason the law imposes upon agents the duty of loyalty and good faith and deprives them of their right to compensation, reimbursement, and indemnification when they prove disloyal to their principal or act in bad faith. The interests of the principal must be promoted by agents to the utmost of their ability.

Loyalty and good faith are abstract terms. Thus, the courts have wide latitude in interpreting what acts constitute bad faith or a breach of loyalty. Such acts as secretly owning an interest in a firm that competes with the principal, disclosing confidential information, selling to or buying from the agent without the knowledge of the principal, and acting simultaneously as the agent of a competitor constitute acts that the courts have held to be breaches of good faith. An agent who acts in bad faith not only may be discharged but the principal may also recover any damages that have been sustained. Also, the principal may recover any profits the agent has made while acting in bad faith even though the act did not damage the principal.

A business entity, Del Rayo, asked Byron Culver & Associates, realtors, to find property to buy. Culver's agent, Frank Whiteside, contacted Joseph Jaoudi about selling 33.5 acres. Jaoudi said the property was for sale, but Arthofer Industries had a contract on five of its lots. After negotiation, Jaoudi gave Whiteside a one-time listing on the property. Jaoudi eventually signed an offer from Del Rayo that included a commission to Culver, but mentioned that the Arthofer deal had to be canceled. Jaoudi also asked if Culver had any association with Del Rayo. Whiteside said no. When Jaoudi reached Arthofer, it refused to cancel its deal. Arthofer contacted Del Rayo and objected to its purchase. Whiteside told Jaoudi to sign a deed to Del Rayo before Arthofer did anything else, and Jaoudi did. Jaoudi had the sale closed but without Culver's commission. Culver sued for the commission. The court said Culver acted as the agent for Del Rayo to find property, held a listing on it from Jaoudi, and had advised him how to handle the sale. Since Culver acted as agent for both parties, it did not perform in good faith. The court held that Culver could not require a commission.

Obedience

An agent may have two types of instructions from the principal: one routine and the other discretionary. The agent must carry out all routine instructions to the letter as long as compliance would not defeat the purpose of the agency, be illegal, or perpetrate a fraud on others. An instruction not to accept any payments made by check illustrates a routine instruction. The agent incurs liability for any losses caused by disobeying these instructions. There is no justification for disobeying such instructions under any conditions.

Agents must use the best judgment of which they are capable regarding discretionary instructions. For example, an agent instructed to accept checks, incurs no liability for a bad check when in the agent's judgment the drawer of the check is solvent and reliable. If an agent accepts a check that the agent has reason to believe is bad, the agent incurs liability for any loss that the principal sustains by reason of this act.

Reasonable Skill and Diligence

One who acts as an agent must possess the skill required to perform the duties and must be diligent in performing the skill. An implied warranty exists that the agent has such skill and will exercise such diligence. Any breach of this warranty subjects the agent to a liability for damages for the loss by reason of the breach.

Because it is assumed that agents are appointed in reliance on their individual skills, talents, and judgment, agents may not generally appoint subagents. This, of course, is not true if the agency agreement provides for the appointment of subagents, if the work delegated is merely clerical, or if the type of agency is one in which it is customarily assumed that subagents would be appointed. Whenever appointing subagents, the agent must use skill and diligence in appointing competent subagents and remains liable to the principal for their breach of good faith or lack of skill.

Accounting

The duties of an agent include the keeping of a record of all money transactions pertaining to the agency. An accounting must be made to the principal for any of the principal's money and property that may come into the agent's possession. Money should be deposited in a bank in the name of the principal, preferably in a bank other than that in which the agent keeps personal funds. If the deposit is made in the name of the agent, any loss caused by the failure of the bank will fall on the agent. Personal property of the principal must be kept separate from property of the agent.

Information

Agents have a duty to keep principals informed of all facts pertinent to the agency that may enable the principals to protect their interests. In consequence, an agent cannot enforce a principal's promise to pay a bonus to the agent for information secured by the agent in the performance of agency duties on the ground that the principal was entitled to the information anyway. The promise was therefore not supported by consideration.

PRINCIPAL'S DUTIES TO AGENT

The principal has four important duties in respect to the agent:

1   Compensation
2   Reimbursement
3   Indemnification
4   Abidance by the terms of the contract

Compensation

The contract of agency determines the compensation due the agent. As in most other contracts, this provision may be either express or implied. If the amount is clearly and expressly stated, disputes seldom arise. When an agency agreement does not state the amount of compensation, the agent may obtain reasonable or customary compensation for the services provided. In the absence of customary rates of compensation, a reasonable rate will be fixed by the court according to the character of the services rendered. Frequently, the parties set the compensation on a contingent basis, such as a percentage of the selling price, provided a sale occurs. In such a case, the agent cannot collect compensation from the principal unless a sale actually occurs.

Commercial Standard Insurance Company hired John Kennon, doing business as Kennon Adjustment Company, to investigate a workers' compensation claim. They made no agreement as to the amount to be paid Kennon. After the claimant received an award, Kennon submitted a bill for more than three times the amount of the award. Commercial refused to pay the bill, saying that it was too high. Kennon sued. The court held that in the absence of an agreement for compensation, an implied promise arises for a principal to pay a reasonable amount for such services rendered in the location where they were furnished.

Reimbursement

The principal must reimburse an agent for any expenses incurred or disbursements made by the agent from personal funds as a necessary part of the agency. If, for example, the agent had to pay from personal funds a $100 truck repair bill before a trip on behalf of the principal could be continued, the agent would be entitled to reimbursement. If, on the other hand, a $50 fine for speeding had to be paid, the principal would not be required to reimburse this expense. Any expense incurred as a result of an agent's unlawful act must be borne by the agent.

Indemnification

A contractual payment made by the agent for the principal is an expense of the principal. If the agent makes the payment not by reason of a contract but as a result of a loss or damage due to an accident, the principal must indemnify the agent. The principal must reimburse expenses and indemnify for losses and damages. If the principal directs the agent to sell goods in the stock room that already belong to the principal's customer, that customer can sue both the principal and the agent. If the agent must pay the customer damages, the agent can in turn sue the principal for giving the instructions that caused the loss.

Abidance by the Terms of the Contract

The principal must abide by the terms of the contract in all respects including any implied compliance. Thus, the agent must be employed for the period stated in the contract unless justification exists for terminating the contract at an earlier date. If the cooperation or participation of the principal is required in order to enable the agent to perform duties, the principal must cooperate or participate to the extent required by the contract. For example, if an agent sells by sample and receives a commission on all sales, the agent must be furnished samples, and the opportunity to earn the fee or commission must be given.

AGENT'S LIABILITIES TO THIRD PARTIES

L.O.2 .... Ordinarily, whenever an agent performs duties, the principal is bound but not the agent. In relations with third parties, however, an agent may be personally liable on contracts and for wrongs in several ways:

1   Agents who contract in their own names and do not disclose the names of the principals become liable to the same extent as though they were the principals. For this reason, agents who sign contracts in their own names will be held liable. The proper way for an agent to sign so as to bind only the principal is to sign "principal, by agent." A signing of the principal's name alone will likewise protect the agent, although the third person may require the placing of the agent's name under the name of the principal so that at a later date it can be determined which agent had obtained the contract.
2   Agents may make themselves personally liable to third parties by an express agreement to be responsible.
3   People who assume to act for others but actually have no authority, or who exceed or materially depart from the authority they were given, incur personal liability to those with whom they do business. The latter situation may arise when overzealous agents affect what they may think is a desirable contract.
4   An agent incurs personal liability for fraud or any other wrongdoing, whether caused by disobedience, carelessness, or malice, or whether committed on the order of the principal.

PRINCIPAL'S DUTIES AND LIABILITIES TO THIRD PARTIES

L.O.3 .... The principal ordinarily has liability to third parties for contracts made within the actual or the apparent scope of the agent's authority. When the agent enters into an unauthorized contract not within the apparent scope of authority, the principal is not bound unless the contract is subsequently ratified.

The test of when an agent has apparent authority is whether, on the basis of the conduct of the principal, a reasonable person would believe that the agent had the authority to make the particular contract. If such a person would, the contract binds the principal. For example, if the manager of a furniture store sells a suite of furniture on credit contrary to the authority granted, the principal must fulfill the contract with the third party, provided the third party did not know of the limitation upon the agent's authority. The agent has liability to the principal for any loss sustained.

The principal, as well as the agent, has liability for an injury to the person or the property of a third party caused by the negligence or the wrongful act of the agent in the course of employment. When the agent steps aside from the business of the principal and commits a wrong or injury to another, the principal is not liable for an unratified act.

TERMINATION OF AN AGENCY BY ACTS OF THE PARTIES

L.O.4 ....

An agency may be terminated by acts of the parties by:

1. Original agreement
2. Subsequent agreement
3. Revocation
4. Renunciation by the agent

Original Agreement

The contract creating the agency may specify a date for the termination of the agency. In that event, the agency automatically terminates on that date. Most special agencies, such as a special agency to sell an automobile, terminate because their purpose has been accomplished.

Subsequent Agreement

An agreement between the principal and the agent may terminate an agency at any time.

Revocation

The principal may revoke the agent's authority at any time, thereby terminating the agency. One must distinguish between the right to terminate the agency and the power to do so. The principal has the right to terminate the agency any time the agent breaches any material part of the contract of employment. If the agent, for example, fails to account for all money collected for the principal, the agent may be discharged, and the principal incurs no liability for breach of contract. The principal, on the other hand, has the power, with one exception, to revoke the agent's authority at any time. Under these circumstances, however, the principal becomes liable to the agent for any damage sustained by reason of an unjustifiable discharge. This is the agent's sole remedy. The agent cannot insist upon the right to continue to act as an agent even though nothing has been done to justify a termination before the end of the contract period.

The only exception to this rule that the principal has the power to terminate the agency occurs in the case of an **agency coupled with an interest.** Interest may take one of two forms: (1) interest in the authority and (2) interest in the subject matter. An agent has interest in the authority when authorized to act as an agent in collecting funds for the principal with an agreement not to remit the collections to the principal but to apply them on a debt owed to the agent by the principal. In the second case, the agent has a lien on the property of the principal as security for a debt and is appointed as agent to sell the property and apply the proceeds on the debt.

Agency Coupled with an Interest

Agency in which agent has financial stake in performance of agency because of having given consideration to principal

---

Boring Montgomery and others contracted with J. Y. Foreman, a realtor, to develop property they owned as he saw fit. The owners had to pay the taxes, but Foreman had to pay all development costs. When a lot sold, Foreman had to pay the owners a set amount per front foot of the lot. He kept any excess to cover his costs and profit. The contract ran for 15 years, but 6 years into it, Foreman died. Montgomery asked a court to declare the contract void arguing that as an agency contract, it expired at the death of the agent. The court said that the parties intended that Foreman would recover his investment in improvements from his share of the selling price. Therefore his agency to sell was coupled with an interest in the property over which he had power, making the agency irrevocable. Since the principals could not revoke the agency, the death of the agent could not revoke it.

Renunciation

Like the principal, the agent has the power to renounce the agency at any time. An agent who abandons the agency without cause before fulfillment of the contract incurs liability to the principal for all losses due to the unjustified abandonment.

TERMINATION BY OPERATION OF LAW

An agency may also be terminated by operation of law. This may occur because of:

1   Subsequent illegality
2   Death or incapacity
3   Destruction
4   Bankruptcy
5   Dissolution
6   War

Subsequent Illegality

Subsequent illegality of the subject matter of the agency terminates the agency.

Death or Incapacity

Death or incapacity of either the principal or agent normally terminates the agency. For example, when the agent permanently loses the power of speech so that the principal's business cannot be performed, the agency automatically terminates.

An exception to the rule of termination by incapacity has been enacted by states that provide for **durable powers of attorney.** A durable power of attorney is a written appointment of agency designed to be effective even though the principal is incapacitated. Such a power of attorney may allow an agent to make health-care decisions for the principal such as admission to a hospital or nursing home, authorization of a medical procedure, or insertion of a feeding tube. It may also direct the attorney in fact to withhold certain, specified medical treatments or procedures.

Durable Power of Attorney

Appointment of agency that survives incapacity of principal

Destruction

Destruction of the subject matter, such as the destruction by fire of a house to be sold by the agent, terminates the agency.

Bankruptcy

Bankruptcy of the principal terminates the agency. In most cases bankruptcy of the agent does not terminate the agency.

Dissolution

Dissolution

Termination of corporation's operation except activities needed for liquidation

Dissolution of a corporation terminates an agency in which the corporation is a party. This is similar to death, since a **dissolution** of a corporation is a complete termination of operation except for the activities necessary for liquidation.

War

When the country of the principal and that of the agent are at war against each other, the agent's authority usually terminates or at least lapses until peace occurs. A war that makes performance impossible terminates the agency.

NOTICE OF TERMINATION

When principals terminate agencies, they must give notice to third parties with whom the agents have previously transacted business and who would be likely to deal with them as an agent. If such notice is not given, the principal might still be bound on any future contracts negotiated by the agent.

When operation of law terminates an agency, notice need not be given either to the agent or to third parties.

QUESTIONS

1 What does it mean to say that the relationship of principal and agent is fiduciary in nature?

2 What is the difference between a routine instruction and a discretionary instruction from a principal to an agent?

3 When may an agent appoint subagents?

4 If the agent and the principal do not set the amount of the agent's compensation in the agency contract, on which basis is the amount determined if the agent and the principal cannot agree?

5 If an agent must pay agency expenses out of personal funds in order to complete the mission, what is the liability of the principal?

6 How should an agent sign a contract so that it binds the principal and not the agent?

7 What is the test of when an agent has apparent authority?

8 When does a principal have the right to terminate the agency?

9 How does a durable power of attorney change the ordinary rules of agency?

10 When must notice of termination of an agency be given?

CASE PROBLEMS

L.O.2 ....

1 Robert Westlake and Glenn Shepherd, partners in real estate projects, had used the services of Dunn & Wendel Architects. Shepherd asked Wendel to visit apartment projects similar to one called "Village in the Woods" that Shepherd and Westlake wanted to develop. Wendel did so and at Shepherd's request sent a proposal to his home for architectural services for the project. Westlake rejected the proposal, but formed a corporation, Shelter Concepts, to develop the Village in the Woods. Dunn & Wendel never knew about Shelter. Westlake eventually accepted a proposal for architectural work and Dunn & Wendel prepared and revised drawings and finally sent a bill. Westlake said the bill would be paid. But the Village in the Woods project was given up. Dunn & Wendel received no payment and it sued Westlake. Westlake claimed he acted as agent for Shelter and thus had no personal liability. Should the court hold Westlake personally liable?

L.O.1 ....

2 Foster Winans and another wrote a daily column, "Heard on the Street," for *The Wall Street Journal*. Because investors respected the column, it could potentially affect the price of stocks discussed. Winans knew that the *Journal's* practice and policy required that the columns were its confidential information before publication. He engaged in a plot with two brokers to give them advance information about the column so they could trade stock based on the expected impact of the column and all split the profits. In four months they made $690,000. Charged with fraud, Winans claimed he had really only violated a workplace rule. The court discussed Winans' obligation to the *Journal* as an agent to his principal. Evaluate Winans' behavior under agency principles.

L.O.1 ....

3   As the agent of Judy Hiller, Helen L. Lips Realty, Inc., negotiated the sale of Hiller's home and accepted checks totaling $2,400 as a deposit. Lips never cashed the checks. The purchaser refused to close the sale and then stopped payment on the checks. Hiller sued Lips for $2,400. Lips alleged that Hiller had not stated a basis for a suit and moved to have it dismissed. Had Hiller presented grounds for a lawsuit?

L.O.1, 4 ....

4   Thomas and Cassandra Tackett were agents of Montgomery Ward. They would purchase merchandise from Wards, resell it to customers, and be paid commissions from Wards. The franchise agreement was terminated by Wards. In the resulting lawsuit, the Tacketts alleged wrongful termination. Many errors had been made by Wards in shipments, and while the policy of Wards was to act upon claims for credit within ten days, they were actually delaying some claims for months and refusing to pay some valid claims. The Tacketts withheld credits due Wards because of the trouble getting their claims approved. Several times they asked for an audit to settle the financial questions. When an auditor arrived without explanation, they assumed it was in response to their requests. Thomas told the auditor he was withholding credits because his claims were not properly approved. After the audit Thomas was asked to sign a statement agreeing to remit $1,586.49 to Wards. After signing, the agency was terminated. Was it wrongfully terminated?

L.O.1 ....

5   Stanley Sadler and James Cisar had an idea for a label that recorded the number of times a person needed to take medication and called their device "Medi-Dot." They asked Commercial Sales Network, Inc. (CSN), to help. CSN found a company to produce the labels. Rather than Sadler and Cisar paying CSN for the printing, their agreement provided that the printer paid CSN a commission on the labels printed. By contract, Sadler and Cisar named CSN the exclusive sales and production agent for Medi-Dot with commissions on sales. It turned out CSN had marked up the costs for printing the labels contrary to the agreement, and when CSN got a very large contract for labels it entered into the contract in its own name and received a check payable to CSN. CSN also developed a competing reminder device and marketed it to Medi-Dot customers. A lawsuit followed. Who should recover against whom and for what?

L.O.1 ....

6   Bak-a-Lum Corporation of America (BAL) had an agreement with Alcoa Building Products, Inc., by which BAL was the exclusive distributor in Northern New Jersey for ALCOA's aluminum siding. At a time when ALCOA had already secretly decided to terminate the exclusive nature of the distributorship, BAL, with ALCOA's knowledge, made a major expansion in its warehouse facilities at substantial expense. Just before the announcement of the termination, ALCOA's salespeople induced BAL to place an extremely heavy order. BAL sued ALCOA, alleging breach of good faith. Was there a breach of good faith?

L.O.4 ....

7   There were 55 transactions in which William Kirchberg contacted George Arakelian Farms, Inc., and ordered lettuce on behalf of his principal, Leonard O'Day. The custom in the business was for the orders to be oral. Arakelian

would ship the lettuce for delivery to O'Day's customers. A bill of lading, signed by the carrier, would be sent to Arakelian, which would prepare an invoice and send it and a copy of the bill of lading to O'Day. O'Day paid all but the last three invoices. They were paid by checks from O.K. Distributors Company, a firm owned by Kirchberg. Arakelian never dealt directly with O'Day. Unknown to Arakelian, O'Day and Kirchberg parted company. Twenty additional orders for lettuce were made by Kirchberg. Arakelian proceeded in its normal manner, and O'Day denied any connection with the 20 shipments. Arakelian sued O'Day for payment of them. Was he liable?

L.O.1 8   Gerard Zell, a real estate agent, filed suit against his broker to recover commissions on sales. Zell had breached his fiduciary duty to his broker. The broker alleged Zell should lose the commission "earned" on a fraudulent transaction as well as all commissions earned thereafter. Should Zell receive any commissions for transactions unrelated to the fraudulent one and subsequent to it?

Chapter 30

EMPLOYER AND EMPLOYEE

LEARNING OBJECTIVES

After studying this chapter you should be able to:

1 Recognize how the relationship of employer and employee arises.

2 Identify the statutory modifications of an employer's defenses under the common law.

3 Describe the liability an employer has to third parties for acts of employees.

4 Name the duties an employee owes the employer.

Preview Case

Under a written contract, Alex Mumford was employed by Hutton and Bourbonnais Company. Mumford's annual salary was to be increased in 60 and 90 days for satisfactory performance. In addition, Hutton was to advance money each month to Mumford's override account as follows: for the first year, 1 percent on all new accounts, and in the second and third years, 1/2 of 1 percent; at the end of the third year these would become house accounts. Mumford was discharged, and he sued, alleging the employment contract was to be for three years. Was it?

Over a period of many decades, the common law developed rules governing the relationship between an employer and employees. These rules governing their relationship have been greatly modified by statute. In every state remnants of the common law still apply to the employer-employee relationship. Many of the common-law features dealing with safe working conditions and other aspects of the employment contract have been retained in labor legislation. These laws do not cover all employees. In every state a small number of employees still have their rights and duties determined largely by common-law rules. This chapter deals with the common law and statutory modifications of it as they relate to employers and employees. However, the law regarding employers and employees varies significantly from state to state.

CREATION OF EMPLOYER AND EMPLOYEE RELATIONSHIP

L.O.1 ....

The relationship of employer and employee arises only from a contract of employment, either express or implied. The common law allowed employers the right to hire whom they pleased and employees the right to freely choose their employers. The relationship of employer and employee could not be imposed upon either the purported employer or employee without consent. One who voluntarily performs the duties of an employee, cannot by that act subject the employer to the liability of an employer. But the relationship may be implied by conduct that demonstrates the parties agree that one is the employer and the other the employee.

Length of Contract

An employee discharged without cause may recover wages due up to the end of the contract period from the employer. However, when creating an employer-employee relationship seldom does either party mention the length of the contract period. In some jurisdictions, the terms of compensation determine the contract period. In such jurisdictions, an employee paid by the hour may be discharged without liability at the end of any hour. An employee paid by the week or by the month, as are many office employees, has a term of employment of one week or one month as the case may be. With monthly paid employees, the term of employment may depend upon the way the employer specifies the compensation. A stated salary of $27,500 a year gives a one-year term of employment, even though the employer pays once a month. In other jurisdictions, employment at a set amount per week, month, or year does not constitute employment for any definite period but amounts to an indefinite hiring.

Under a written contract, Hutton & Bourbonnais Company employed Alex Mumford. The annual salary was to be increased in 60 and 90 days for satisfactory performance. In addition, Hutton was to advance money each month to Mumford's override account as follows: for the first year, 1 percent on all new accounts, and in the second and third years, 1/2 of 1 percent; at the end of the third year these were to become house accounts. Hutton fired Mumford, and he sued, alleging a three-year employment contract. The court held that the time specified in the contract was just a formula for crediting the override account and did not establish a definite term of employment. Since the term was not specified, the contract was for an indefinite period and could be ended at will.

Employment at Will

Employment terminable by employer or employee for any reason

Many employer-employee situations have an indefinite length for the contract, and either the employer or the employee may terminate the employment for any reason or for no reason. This situation is called an **employment at will.** However, as a result of labor legislation, union or other employment contracts, or other exceptions that have developed to employment at will, many employees have significant job security. They may not be discharged except for good cause. As in the case of an employee discharged without cause who is employed for a specified period, such an employee may sue the employer for money damages. In some cases the employee may also sue to be restored to the job.

Determination of Contract Terms

Employer-employee contracts frequently do not state terms other than the compensation. Terms are determined by law, custom, and possibly by union contracts. In some cases, courts have held that statements in employer's written policy manuals constitute terms of employer-employee contracts.

Union Contracts

Formerly the employer contracted individually with each employee. However, as the union movement developed and collective bargaining became commonplace, employers began agreeing with unions to provisions of employment that applied to large numbers of employees. The signed contract between them embodied this agreement between the employer and the union. An agent of the employees, the union, speaks and contracts for all the employees collectively. As a general rule, the employer still makes a contract individually with each employee, but the union contract binds the employer to recognize certain scales of union wages, hours of work, job classifications, and related matters.

DUTIES AND LIABILITIES OF THE EMPLOYER

The employer under the common law had five well-defined duties:

1   Duty to exercise care
2   Duty to provide a reasonably safe place to work
3   Duty to provide safe tools and appliances
4   Duty to provide competent and sufficient employees for the task
5   Duty to instruct employees with reference to the dangerous nature of employment

Duty to Exercise Care

This rule imposes liability on employers if their negligence causes harm to an employee. Employers have exercised proper care when they have done what a reasonable person would have done under the circumstances to avoid harm.

Duty to Provide a Reasonably Safe Place to Work

The employer must furnish every employee with a reasonably safe place to work. What constitutes a safe place depends upon the nature of the work. Most states have statutes modifying the common law for hazardous industries.

Duty to Provide Safe Tools and Appliances

The tools furnished employees by their employer must be safe. This rule applies also to the machinery and appliances.

Duty to Provide Competent and Sufficient Employees for the Task

Both the number of employees and their skill and experience affect the hazardous nature of many jobs. The employer has liability for all injuries to employees directly caused by either an insufficient number of workers or the lack of skill of some of the workers.

Duty to Instruct Employees

In all positions that use machinery, chemicals, electric appliances, and other production instruments, there are many hazards. The law requires the employer to give that degree of instruction to a new employee that a reasonable person would give under the circumstances to avoid reasonably foreseeable harm that could result from a failure to give such instructions.

COMMON-LAW DEFENSES OF THE EMPLOYER

Under the common law, when an injured employee sued the employer, the employer could raise the following defenses:

1   The employee's contributory negligence
2   The act of a fellow servant
3   A risk assumed by the employee

Contributory Negligence Rule

The contributory negligence rule states that an employer can escape liability for breach of duty if it can be established that the employee's own negligence contributed to the accident. An employee who could have avoided the injury by the exercise of due diligence has no right to collect damages from the employer.

The Fellow-Servant Rule

Fellow Servant
Employee with same status and working with another worker

The fellow-servant rule allows an employer to avoid liability by providing that the injury was caused by a fellow servant. A **fellow servant** is an employee who has the same status as another worker and works with that employee. This rule has been abrogated or so severely limited that it now very rarely has any significance.

Assumption-of-Risk Rule

Every type of employment in industry has some normal risks. The assumption-of-risk rule states that employees assume these normal risks by voluntarily accepting employment. Therefore, if the injury results from the hazardous nature of the job, the employer cannot be held liable.

STATUTORY MODIFICATION OF COMMON LAW

L.O.2 .... The rules of the common law have been greatly altered by the enactment of laws modifying an employer's defenses when sued by an employee, laws providing for workers' compensation, and the Occupational Safety and Health Act.

Modification of Common-Law Defenses

Statutes have modified the defenses an employer may use when sued for damages by an employee. For example, the Federal Employers' Liability Act and the Federal Safety Appliance Act apply to common carriers engaged in interstate commerce. A plaintiff suing under these laws must still bring an action in a court and prove negligence by the employer or other employees. However, winning the case is easier because of limits on the employer's defenses. An employer has liability even if the employee is contributorily negligent. However, such negligence may reduce the amount of damages. Many states have also modified the common-law defenses of employers of employees engaged in hazardous types of work.

Workers' Compensation

Every state has adopted workers' compensation statutes that apply to certain industries or businesses. These statutes allow an employee, or certain relatives of a deceased employee, to recover damages for injury to or death of the employee. They may recover whenever the injury arose within the course of the employee's work from a risk involved in that work. An injured party receives compensation without regard to whether the employer or the employee was negligent. Generally no compensation results for a willfully self-inflicted injury or a harm sustained while intoxicated. However, the employer has the burden of proving intentional self-inflicted injury. The law limits the amount of recovery and sets it in accordance with a prescribed schedule.

Workers' compensation laws generally allow recovery for accident-inflicted injuries and occupational diseases. Some states limit compensation for occupational diseases to those specified by name in the statute. These would include silicosis, lead poisoning, or injury to health from radioactivity. Other states compensate for any disease arising from the occupation.

Whether based on the common law or an employer's liability statute, courts of law try damages actions. Workers' compensation proceedings differ because a special administrative agency or workers' compensation board hears them. However, either party may appeal the agency or board decision to the appropriate court of law.

Workers' compensation statutes do not bar an employee from suing another employee for the injury.

Occupational Safety and Health Act

In 1970, the federal government enacted the Williams-Steiger Occupational Safety and Health Act to ensure safe and healthful working conditions. This federal law applies to every employer engaged in a business affecting interstate commerce except governments. The Occupational Safety and Health Administration (OSHA) administers the Act and issues standards that must be complied with by employers and employees. In order to ensure compliance with the standards, OSHA carries out jobsite inspections. Detailed records of work-related deaths, injuries, and illnesses must be maintained by employers. The Act provides fines for violations, including penalties of up to $1,000 per day for failure to correct violations within the allotted time.

LIABILITIES OF THE EMPLOYER TO THIRD PARTIES

L.O.3

An employer has liability under certain circumstances for injuries that are caused by employees to third parties. To be liable, the employee must have committed the injury in the course of employment. An employee, who, without any direction from the employer, injures a third party and causes injury not as a result of the employment, has personal liability, but the employer does not. The employer has liability, however, if it ordered the act that caused the injury or had knowledge of the act and assented to it. Finally, the employer has liability for the torts of employees due to the employer's negligence in not enforcing safe working procedures; providing safe equipment, such as trucks; or employing competent employees.

Nationwide Personal Security Corporation employed Arthur Hinton. While on the job at a supermarket, he got into an argument about the job with the supermarket manager. A cashier, Marta Rivas, screamed for help when Hinton started choking the manager. To silence Rivas, Hinton struck her. Rivas sued Nationwide for assault and battery arguing that Hinton committed the attack in the course of his employment. The court agreed and ordered judgment for Rivas.

EMPLOYEE'S DUTIES TO THE EMPLOYER

L.O.4 ....

The employee owes certain duties to the employer. The failure to comply with these duties may result in discharge. An employee's duties include:

1. Job performance
2. Business confidentiality
3. Granting of right to use inventions

Job Performance

The duties required by the job must be performed faithfully and honestly and to advance the employer's interests. In skilled positions, the worker must perform the task with ordinary skill.

Business Confidentiality

An employee has a duty of confidentiality regarding certain business matters. Trade secrets or other confidential business information must not be revealed.

Inventions

In the absence of an express or implied agreement to the contrary, inventions belong to the employee who devised them, even though the time and property of the employer were used in their discovery, provided that the employee was not employed for the express purpose of inventing the things or the processes that were discovered.

Shop Right

Employer's right to use employee's invention without payment of royalty

If the invention is discovered during working hours and with the employer's material and equipment, the employer has the right to use the invention without charge in the operation of the business. If the employee has obtained a patent for the invention, the employer must be granted a nonexclusive license to use the invention without the payment of royalty. This **shop right** of the employer does not give the right to make and sell machines that embody the employee's invention; it only entitles the employer to use the invention in the operation of the plant.

Stair Glide manufactured elevator chairs that, if a gear stripped, would accelerate and throw their occupants out. Richard Dewey, employed by Stair Glide to weld and not to do engineering or design-concept work, heard about the problem through "shop talk." While at work, he had an idea for a safety device. He gathered some scrap material during lunch hour and built a model. He used the company welder and cutting torch as well as some of his own tools. Employees were allowed to take scrap home. At home, he made a drawing of his safety device. The next day he showed his drawing to Stair Glide officials and fully explained his idea and its operation. Stair Glide never returned his drawing but manufactured and used the device despite being told Dewey wanted compensation for the use of his idea. Dewey sued Stair Glide. The court found he worked on his own time and at home where he fully developed his idea. He made only minimal use of Stair Glide's equipment, so Stair Glide did not have a shop right to the device.

When an employer employs a person to secure certain results from experiments to be conducted by that employee, the courts hold that the inventions equitably belong to the employer. Courts base this result on a trust relation or an implied agreement to make an assignment.

In any case, an employee may expressly agree that inventions made during employment will be the property of the employer. Such contracts must be clear and specific, or else courts normally rule against the employer. The employee may also agree to assign to the employer inventions made after the term of employment.

EMPLOYEES' RIGHTS

Many federal and state laws, municipal ordinances, and court decisions grant specific rights to employees. However, because of the variations in state laws, court decisions, and local ordinances, all employee rights vary. Some rights extend to all or almost all employees, and the law is extending other rights to cover ever larger numbers of employees. The more recently sought-for rights relate to polygraph testing, AIDS testing, smoking, and drug testing.

Polygraph Testing

Testing with lie detector devices

Polygraph Testing

In 1988, the federal government enacted the Employee Polygraph Protection Act. A **polygraph** is a lie detector. The law limits the use of lie detector devices in the workplace. Private employers may not use polygraphs unless: they have reason to believe an employee has committed a theft or industrial espionage, the employer provides security services, or the employer is a drug company. The law does not prohibit federal, state, and local governments from subjecting their employees to polygraphs.

AIDS Testing

With the spread of the AIDS virus, employees have been concerned about contamination from afflicted co-workers. At the same time, workers with the virus have been concerned that they could be stigmatized and even lose their jobs. There is no uniform national standard to assist employers and employees dealing with the impact of the AIDS virus at the job site. Some employees of federal contractors, public employees, and employees of some hospitals may be protected from discrimination for carrying the AIDS virus by federal law. Protection may also be afforded by state law or judicial decision.

Smoking

The disclosure of the damaging effects of breathing second-hand smoke has resulted in some protections of employees. Some employers have taken the initiative by prohibiting or restricting smoking at their workplaces. In addition, a number of states and municipalities have enacted restrictive smoking legislation. This legislation varies greatly. No state law totally bans smoking at the job site. Some laws merely require employers to formulate and publicize a written policy about smoking in the workplace. Others require employers to designate smoking and nonsmoking areas.

Drug Testing

There has been concern about the ability of employees in certain jobs to properly do their jobs while under the influence of drugs. This concern has resulted in several federal administrative agencies' requiring drug testing of employees or prospective employees. Customs Service employees seeking transfers or promotions to sensitive positions and railroad workers involved in major railroad accidents or who violate certain safety rules are tested for drug use. Courts have upheld random drug testing for employees in order to promote safety.

The Federal Aviation Administration (FAA) issued a rule requiring random testing of airline employees for marijuana, cocaine, opiate, phencyclidine (PCP), and amphetamine use. The employees covered included flight crew members, attendants, instructors, and flight testing and maintenance personnel. Employees who tested positive and could not offer a satisfactory alternative explanation had to be removed from their positions. Employees subject to the FAA drug testing rules, labor organizations, and an organization of aviation employees and employers sued the FAA arguing that the regulations were unreasonable searches in violation of the Constitution. The court held that the FAA's decision that safety concerns outweighed privacy concerns was reasonable and could not be overturned.

FEDERAL SOCIAL SECURITY ACT

The federal Social Security Act has four major provisions:

1   Old-age and survivors' insurance
2   Assistance to persons in financial need
3   Unemployment compensation
4   Disability and Medicare benefits

Old-Age and Survivors' Insurance

The Social Security Act provides payment of decreasing term life insurance to the dependents of covered workers who die before the age of retirement. This part constitutes the survivors' benefits. If workers live to a specified age and retire, then they and their spouses draw retirement annuities known as joint and survivor annuities. This part constitutes the old-age benefits. Both parts are called insurance because they constitute risks that could be insured against by life insurance companies. The survivors' insurance covers the risk of the breadwinner's dying and leaving dependents without a source of income. Old-age benefits cover the risk of outliving one's savings after retirement.

Who Is Covered? The life and annuity insurance provisions of the Social Security Act cover practically everyone except federal employees. Employees in state and local governments, including public school teachers, may be brought under the coverage of the Act by means of agreements between the state and the federal government.

This provision of the Act also covers farmers, professional people (such as lawyers), and self-employed business people. The Act does not cover certain types of work of close relatives, such as a parent for a child, work by a child under 21 for parents, and employment of a spouse by a spouse.

Eligibility for Retirement Benefits. To be eligible for retirement benefits, one must meet these requirements:

1   Be fully insured (40 quarters or the equivalent of 10 years) at the time of retirement
2   Be 62 years of age or older
3   Apply for retirement benefits after reaching the age of retirement. To be entitled to the maximum retirement benefits, one must wait until age 65 to apply for them.

Eligibility for Survivors' Benefits. The family of a worker who dies has a right to survivors' benefits while fully insured or currently insured at the time of death. Currently insured means the person had worked at least 6 quarters in the 13-quarter period ending with death.

Assistance to Persons in Financial Need

People over 65 who have financial need may be eligible for federal supplemental security income payments. These monthly payments go to blind or disabled people in financial need. No one contributes specifically to this system based only on need.

Unemployment Compensation

In handling unemployment compensation, the federal government cooperates with the states, which set up their own rules, approved by the federal government, for the payment of unemployment benefits. Payments of unemployment compensation are made by the states and not by the federal government.

The unemployment compensation laws of the various states differ, although they tend to follow a common pattern. They all provide for raising funds by levies upon employers. The federal government pays the cost of running the programs.

State unemployment compensation laws apply in general to workers in commerce and industry. Agricultural workers, domestic servants, government employees, and employees of nonprofit organizations formed and operated exclusively for religious, charitable, literary, educational, scientific, or humane purposes may not be included.

To be eligible for benefits, a worker generally must meet the following requirements:

1 Be available for work and registered at an unemployment office.
2 Have been employed for a certain length of time within a specified period in an employment covered by the law.
3 Be capable of working.
4 Not have refused reasonably suitable employment.
5 Not be self-employed.
6 Not be out of work because of a strike or a lockout still in progress or because of voluntarily leaving a job without cause.
7 Have served the required waiting period.

Disability and Medicare Benefits

The government makes monthly cash benefits, called disability insurance benefits, to disabled persons under the age of 65 and their families. A disabled person is someone unable to engage in any substantial gainful activity because of a medically determinable physical or mental impairment expected to end in death or has lasted or will last continually for 12 months.

Medicare is insurance designed to help pay a large portion of personal health-care costs. Virtually everyone aged 65 and over may be covered by this contributory hospital and medical insurance plan. The program covers only specified services.

Taxation to Finance the Plan

To pay the life insurance and the annuity insurance benefits of the Social Security Act, both the employer and the employee pay a payroll tax (FICA) of an equal percentage of all income earned in any one year up to a specified maximum. The maximum income and the rate may be changed at any session of Congress. A payroll tax finances the unemployment compensation part of the Act. In most states the employer bears this entire tax. The assistance to persons in need is paid for by general taxation. No specific tax is levied to meet these payments. Disability and Medicare benefits are funded from a combination of four sources. These sources are: FICA, a Medicare tax on people who are not covered by the life and annuity insurance, premiums paid by the people covered, and the general federal revenue.

QUESTIONS

1 Discuss the impact of the common law on the rules governing the employer-employee relationship.

2 How does the relationship of employer and employee arise?

3 If employers make contracts individually with employees, what is the significance of a union contract?

4 What are the basic provisions of workers' compensation statutes with regard to injury or death of an employee?

5 What methods does OSHA use to try to ensure safe and healthful working conditions?

6 When may an employer be liable for injuries to third parties caused by employees?

7 Does an employee who invents a device on the employer's time have an exclusive right to it?

8 Do all employees have the same rights? Explain.

9 What employers have the right to require employees to take polygraph tests?

10 What are the four major provisions of the Social Security Act?

11 What are the general requirements for a person to be eligible for unemployment benefits under typical state laws governing unemployment compensation?

12 For what Social Security programs are employees taxed?

CASE PROBLEMS

L.O.2 ....   **1** William Roundtree was a cab driver for Dotty Cab Co. Dotty's radio dispatcher told him to pick up a fare on Bell Street. Two hours later his body was found a block away from the cab by the police. He and another person had been shot. The homicide was not solved. His dependents sought workers' compensation benefits. Was Roundtree's death sufficiently related to his employment that workers' compensation should have been awarded?

L.O.1 ....   **2** Marine Midland Bank recruited Patricia Feeney to work as a vice resident. After a restructuring several years later, Marine fired her. She sued Marine arguing that she had a contract of employment. Marine had sent a letter confirming the offer of employment. The letter mentioned a bonus payable the following January. Marine's two employee handbooks provided to Feeney stated Marine had no contractual arrangement with its employees and that employees were employed at will. Did the letter's reference to a January bonus set a guaranteed term of employment?

L.O.4 ....   **3** Leslie Hubbell worked as a salesman for St. Cloud Aviation. A competitor told St. Cloud that Hubbell sent a customer to it and Hubbell had asked for a commission on the sale. St. Cloud fired Hubbell because it could have made the sale and therefore lost business. Did St. Cloud have a right to fire Hubbell?

L.O.2 .... **4** John Leffler was employed by Fluor Corporation in Iran. The employment agreement stated Fluor would provide housing and utilities. Leffler and his wife lived on the third floor of an apartment complex occupied by Fluor employees. There was a swimming pool beneath the balcony of their apartment. At a party, Leffler made a $20 bet with his new boss that he could dive off the balcony of the apartment into the pool. Leffler was a skilled high diver, but the balcony was 10 to 20 feet higher than any dive he had made. The next day Leffler dove from his balcony into the pool. He returned to the building, announcing he was the first person to dive from the third floor. At his apartment he complained of back and chest pain. He collapsed and was taken to the hospital, where he died. Death was due to a ruptured aorta as a result of the dive. Leffler's widow sought workers' compensation benefits. Should they be awarded?

L.O.3 .... **5** Welsh Manufacturing made gold sunglass frames and kept quantities of gold at its plant. Pinkerton's, Inc., provided a security guard. In a 45-day period, three thefts at the plant caused gold loss of $200,000. A Pinkerton's guard, Donald Lawson, 21, admitted the thieves the first two times and gave them vital information the third time. Lawson took the job to help a neighbor steal from Welsh. Welsh sued Pinkerton's. When applying for the job, Lawson had filled out a general application form asking for former employers and three people who had known him for more than five years. Pinkerton's did not contact the three references. It sent forms to Lawson's high school principal and the hospital at which he had worked for two months. This form did not inquire about the applicant's honesty. How do you think the jury decided this case?

L.O.4 .... **6** Vigitron, Inc., manufactured and sold electronic flame safety controls for industrial boiler systems. The business involved trade secrets and confidential proprietary information. Vigitron employed James Ferguson to supervise all research and development and James Weeden to develop new products and improve on flame safeguard controls. Vigitron started its "9003" project to develop an improved flame safeguard control box. The president of Vigitron told Ferguson about the project and asked him to keep it secret. Weeden worked on the project at home in response to instructions from Ferguson. Ferguson and Weeden formed a partnership to market electronic systems. Ferguson resigned from Vigitron, and the two attempted to sell to a distributor of Vigitron products a flame safeguard control device they had developed. The distributor told Vigitron, which then sued Ferguson and Weeden. To whom does the new control device belong?

L.O.1 .... **7** Anchor Media, Ltd., employed Charles Wing as vice president and general manager of a television station. Anchor had given Wing an employee handbook that stated all employees could be fired at any time. Wing had also signed a statement that unequivocally stated Anchor could end his employment anytime. Shortly thereafter, Anchor fired Wing who sued asserting Anchor breached a written employment contract. How should the court decide?

Chapter 31

Labor Legislation

After studying this chapter you should be able to:

1 Discuss the objectives and coverage of the Fair Labor Standards Act.

2 State the five major provisions of the Labor Management Relations Act.

3 Name the three major provisions of the Labor-Management Reporting and Disclosure Act.

4 List the bases stated in the Civil Rights Act of 1964 and the Age Discrimination in Employment Act upon which an employer may not discriminate against employees.

Preview Case

The law firm of Humphreys, Hutcheson & Moseley represented Southern Silk Mills, Inc., which was facing an election to determine whether its employees would be represented by the Amalgamated Clothing and Textile Workers Union. Before the election, two attorneys from the firm made speeches to groups of Southern's employees to persuade them to vote against the union in the election. They were introduced as attorneys in the law firm representing Southern. The law firm refused to comply with the disclosure requirements of the Labor-Management Reporting and Disclosure Act. It alleged that the requirements did not apply because the intent of the law was to discourage secret persuader activities and that its relationship to Southern was announced before the presentation. Did the disclosure requirements apply to the law firm?

ince 1930, the federal government has enacted more laws dealing with industrial relations than had been enacted during the prior history of the republic. Although the scope of a course in business law does not include all of these laws together with the court interpretations of them, some basic knowledge of them is valuable. This chapter covers the Fair Labor Standards Act, the Labor Management Relations Act, the Labor-Management Reporting and Disclosure Act, the Civil Rights Act of 1964, and the Age Discrimination in Employment Act.

THE FAIR LABOR STANDARDS ACT

L.O.1 ....

The federal Fair Labor Standards Act had two major objectives. The first objective placed a floor, regardless of economic conditions, under wages of employees engaged in interstate commerce (trade among or between states). The second objective discouraged a long work week and thus spread employment. Setting a minimum wage accomplished the first objective. This wage by successive amendments has increased to a rate of $4.25 per hour. Requiring employers to pay time and a half for all hours over 40 achieved the second objective. An employer may work employees, other than children, any number of hours a week if the employer pays the overtime wage.

Exclusions from the Act

The Fair Labor Standards Act does not cover the following:

1 Employees working for firms engaged in intrastate commerce (trade within a state). This results from the constitutional provision giving Congress power to regulate interstate, not intrastate, commerce.
2 Employees working for firms engaged in interstate commerce but in a business excluded from the Act, such as agriculture.
3 Employees in certain positions such as executives, administrators, and outside salespeople.
4 The workweek provisions do not apply to employees in that part of the transportation industry over which the Interstate Commerce Commission has control, to any employee engaged in the canning of fish, and to persons who are employed as outside buyers of poultry, eggs, cream, or milk in their natural state.

Child Labor Provisions

The Fair Labor Standards Act forbids "oppressive child labor." It prohibits or severely limits the employment of children under 16 years of age. This rule does not apply to certain agricultural employment, to parents or guardians employing their children or wards, to children employed as actors, or to certain types of employment specified by the Secretary of Labor as being excepted by the regulations. Youth between the ages of 16 and 18 are not permitted to work in industries declared by the Secretary of Labor to be particularly hazardous to health.

The Fair Labor Standards Act permits employers to ask the Secretary of Labor for a waiver of child labor laws so 10 and 11 year olds may harvest certain crops. The secretary must grant the waivers if: "the employment . . . would not be deleterious to their health or well-being" and "the level and type of pesticides and other chemicals used would not have an adverse effect on the health or well-being of" the children. After reviewing existing scientific literature, the Department of Labor issued regulations. They allowed the use of certain pesticides a set time before harvesting by 10 and 11 year olds. Two private, nonprofit organizations representing farm worker families asked the court to rule that the approval of pesticide use violated the statutory waiver provision. None of the scientific literature had addressed the risk to children. The court ruled that because there was no objective proof of the safety of the regulations, they were invalid.

Contingent Wages

Many types of employment call for the payment of wages on a commission basis or on a piece-rate basis. Many salespeople receive a commission on their sales rather than a salary. For employees covered by the Act, if commissions earned in any one week are less than the minimum wages for the hours worked, the employer must add to the commission enough to bring the total earnings to the minimum wage. The same applies to employees being paid on a piece-rate basis. The Act allows these types of incentive wages, but they cannot be used to evade the minimum-wage provisions of the Act.

THE NATIONAL LABOR RELATIONS ACT AND THE LABOR MANAGEMENT RELATIONS ACT

Collective Bargaining
Process by which employer and union agree on terms of employment

The National Labor Relations Act of 1935 (the Wagner Act), expanded by the federal Labor Management Relations Act of 1947, also known as the Taft-Hartley Act, sought to create bargaining equality between employers and employees. It requires that the employer recognize and bargain with (**collective bargaining**) the representative selected by the employees. The employees' representative is typically a union. The Act also sought to eliminate certain forms of conduct from the scene of labor negotiations and employment by condemning them as unfair practices.

With the following specific exceptions, the Act applies to all employers engaged in interstate commerce:

1 The railroad industry, which the Railway Labor Act of 1947 covers
2 Agricultural laborers
3 Domestic servants
4 Supervisory employees, who are considered a part of management
5 Government employees

L.O.2 ....

The Labor Management Relations Act has the following five major provisions:

1 Continuation of the National Labor Relations Board (NLRB) created by the National Labor Relations Act.
2 A declaration as to the rights of employees.
3 A declaration as to the rights of employers.
4 A prohibition of employers' unfair labor practices.
5 A prohibition of unfair union practices.

The National Labor Relations Board

The Labor Management Relations Act provides a continuation of the National Labor Relations Board (NLRB) of five members appointed by the president. This board hears and conducts investigations of complaints of employer and union unfair labor practices. If the board finds that an unfair practice exists, it has the power to seek an injunction to stop the practice. When a strike threatens national health or safety, the president may appoint a five-person board of inquiry and upon the basis of their findings may apply to the federal court for an injunction that will postpone the strike for 80 days. The NLRB supervises elections to determine the bargaining representative for the employees within each bargaining unit. In case of dispute, the NLRB determines the size and nature of the bargaining unit.

In addition to appointing the NLRB, the president appoints a general counsel. This general counsel has complete independence from the board in prosecuting complaint cases but in most other matters acts as the chief legal advisor to the board.

Declaration as to the Rights of Employees

The Labor Management Relations Act sets forth the following rights of employees:

Strike

Temporary, concerted action of workers to withhold their services from employer

1   To organize.
2   To bargain collectively through their own chosen agents.
3   To engage in concerted action; that is, **strike,** for their mutual aid and protection.
4   To join or not to join a union unless a majority of all workers vote for a **union shop** and the employer agrees thereto.

Union Shop

Work setting in which all employees must be union members

Declaration as to the Rights of Employers

The Labor Management Relations Act gives the employer many important rights:

1   To petition for an investigation when questioning the union's right to speak for the employees.
2   To refuse to bargain collectively with supervisory employees.
3   To institute charges of unfair labor practices by the unions before the board.
4   To sue unions for breaches of the union contract whether the breach is done in the name of the union or as an individual union member.
5   To plead with workers to refrain from joining the union, provided the employer uses no threats of reprisal or promises of benefits.

Prohibition of Employers' Unfair Labor Practices

The chief acts prohibited as unfair practices by employers comprise:

1   Interfering in the employee's exercise of the rights granted by the Act.
2   Refusing to bargain collectively with employees when they have legally selected a representative.
3   Dominating or interfering with the formation or administration of any labor organization or contributing financial support to it.
4   Discriminating against or favoring an employee in any way because of membership or lack of membership in the union. An employee may be fired for non-membership in a union when the union has a valid union shop contract.

5 Discriminating against an employee who has filed charges against the employer under the Act.

When the National Labor Relations Board finds the employer guilty of any of these acts, it usually issues a "cease and desist order." If the cease and desist order does not prove effective, an injunction may be obtained.

Prohibition of Unfair Union Practices

The Labor Management Relations Act lists seven specific acts that unions and their leaders may not engage in:

1 Coercion or restraint of workers in the exercise of their rights under the Act.

2 Picketing an employer to force bargaining with an uncertified union (one that has not been elected to represent the employees).

3 Refusal to bargain collectively with the employer.

4 Charging excessive initiation fees and discriminatory dues and fees of any kind.

5 Barring a worker from the union for any reason except the nonpayment of dues.

Secondary Boycott

Attempt by employees to stop third party dealing with employer

6 Secondary boycotts or strikes in violation of law or the contract, although certain exceptions are made in the construction and garment industries. A **secondary boycott** is an attempt by employees to cause a third party to stop dealing with the employer. The third party would normally be a customer or supplier of the employer. The most common ways the boycott is carried out are by a strike or by picketing.

7 Attempts to exact payment from employers for services not rendered.

THE LABOR-MANAGEMENT REPORTING AND DISCLOSURE ACT

L.O.3

In 1959, Congress passed the Labor-Management Reporting and Disclosure Act, also called the Landrum-Griffin Act. The purpose of this Act was to protect union members from improper conduct by union officials. The Act contains a bill of rights for union members, it classifies additional actions as unfair labor practices, and it requires unions operating in interstate commerce and their officers and employers to file detailed public reports.

Bill of Rights

The bill of rights provisions of the Labor-Management Reporting and Disclosure Act guarantee union members the right to meet with other union members, to express any views or opinions at the union meetings, and to express views on candidates for union office or business before the meeting.

Additional Unfair Labor Practices

In addition to the unfair labor practices outlawed by the Labor Management Relations Act, the Labor-Management Reporting and Disclosure Act declares the following acts unfair labor practices:

1   Picketing by employees in order to extort money and for recognition when another union is the legally recognized bargaining agent, and there is no question regarding union representation.

2   To close loopholes, an expanded range of activities defined as secondary boycotts, except in the garment industry.

3   "Hot cargo agreements," except in the construction and garment industries. A **hot cargo agreement** is an agreement between a union and an employer that the employer will not use nonunion materials.

Hot Cargo Agreement

Agreement employer will not use nonunion materials

Reporting Requirements

The very detailed reporting requirements of the Act require unions to file copies of their bylaws and constitutions in addition to reports listing the name and title of each officer; the fees and dues required of members; and the membership qualifications, restrictions, benefits, and the like. Financial information required to be reported includes a complete listing of assets and liabilities, receipts, and disbursements. The union reports must be signed by the officials of the union, and the information contained in them must be made available to the union members.

The officials of the union must each file a report indicating any financial interest in or benefit they have received from any employer whose employees the union represents. They must also report whether they have received any object of value from an employer.

In addition to the requirement of annual reports by the union and its officials, employers must file annual reports listing any expenditures made to influence anyone regarding union organizational or bargaining activities. Certain information must be disclosed by everyone involved in labor persuader activities. As public information, anyone who requests these reports may obtain them.

The law firm of Humphreys, Hutcheson & Moseley represented Southern Silk Mills, Inc., which was facing an election to be conducted by the NLRB to determine whether its employees would be represented by the Amalgamated Clothing and Textile Workers Union. Before the election, two attorneys from the firm made speeches to groups of Southern's employees to persuade them to vote against the union in the election. They were introduced as attorneys in the law firm representing Southern. The law firm refused to comply with the disclosure requirements of the Labor-Management Reporting and Disclosure Act. It alleged that the requirements did not apply because the intent of the law was to discourage secret persuader activities and that its relationship to Southern was announced before the presentation. The court held the goal of the law was disclosure, and since the activities of the law firm were persuader activities, it must comply with the disclosure requirements.

The Act also contains a number of additional provisions aimed at making unions more democratic and at protecting union funds from embezzlement and misappropriation.

CIVIL RIGHTS ACT OF 1964

L.O.4

The federal Civil Rights Act of 1964 is designed to prevent job discrimination on the basis of race, color, religion, sex, or national origin. The Act applies to every employer engaged in an industry affecting interstate commerce who has 15 or more employees and to labor unions with 15 or more members. It does not apply to the U.S. government or certain private membership clubs exempt from federal taxation.

This law makes it an unlawful employment practice for an employer to fail to hire, to discharge, or to in any way discriminate against anyone with respect to the terms, conditions, or privileges of employment because of the individual's race, color, religion, sex, or national origin. (Discrimination because of sex includes discrimination because of pregnancy, childbirth, or related medical conditions.) The employer also may not adversely affect an employee's status because of one of these factors. In addition, it is an unlawful employment practice for an employment agency or a labor organization to in any way discriminate, classify, limit, or segregate individuals on any one of these bases. Economic harm does not necessary have to be proved.

Mechelle Vinson was employed by Meritor Savings Bank. She took indefinite sick leave and later was fired for excessive use of that leave. She sued the bank claiming that while working at the bank she had constantly been subjected to sexual harassment by Sidney Taylor, her supervisor. She did not claim any economic damages, merely a hostile work environment. The bank claimed the Civil Rights Act was not concerned with the psychological aspects of the workplace environment. The court said the law was violated if sexual harassment altered the conditions of the victim's employment and created an abusive working environment. Vinson did not have to show economic loss.

The Act establishes the Equal Employment Opportunity Commission (EEOC), which hears complaints alleging violations of this Act. The complaints may be filed by individuals, or the EEOC itself may issue charges. If the EEOC verifies the charge, it must seek by conference, conciliation, and persuasion to stop the violation. If this fails, the EEOC may bring an action in federal court.

THE AGE DISCRIMINATION IN EMPLOYMENT ACT

In order to protect persons aged 40 or above, the federal government enacted the Age Discrimination in Employment Act (ADEA). This statute prohibits discrimination by employment agencies, employers, or labor unions against persons aged 40 or above. Employers are prohibited from firing or failing to hire persons in this age group, and they may not limit, segregate, or classify their employees so as to discriminate against persons in this age group solely because of their age.

However, this law excludes from the definition of employee persons elected to state or local office and persons appointed at the policymaking level.

OTHER FEDERAL LEGISLATION

Many other federal laws affect labor. These include the Immigration Reform and Control Act of 1986, which makes it illegal for an employer to knowingly hire undocumented aliens or to continue to employ an alien no longer authorized to work. The Equal Pay Act of 1963 requires an employer to pay men and women equal pay for equal work. The Americans with Disabilities Act of 1990 prohibits employment discrimination against people with disabilities. It applies to employers of 15 or more employees.

QUESTIONS

1 What two objectives does the Fair Labor Standards Act have?
2 Are all workers covered by the Fair Labor Standards Act?
3 May an employer use incentive wages and still comply with the Fair Labor Standards Act? Explain.
4 What was the chief purpose of the Labor Management Relations Act?
5 What does the National Labor Relations Board do?
6 a. If an employer refuses to bargain collectively with employees, is this an unfair labor practice?
   b. Name some unfair labor practices by employers.
7 What is a secondary boycott and how is one usually carried out?
8 What was the purpose of the Labor-Management Reporting and Disclosure Act?
9 To whom are the reports required by the Labor-Management Reporting and Disclosure Act available?
10 The Civil Rights Act of 1964 and the Age Discrimination in Employment Act prohibit job discrimination based on what?

CASE PROBLEMS

L.O.1

1 Williams Chemical Co. operated self-service gasoline stations and hired married couples to manage some stations where living quarters were located on the premises. Employees were instructed to keep the stations open 80 hours a week, but there was no written policy regarding the number of hours each employee was to work. Instructions about whether they were to work together or alone were vague. Generally, both spouses were at the station for the total number of hours the station was open. However, paychecks were evenly split between them, paying each spouse for 40 hours of work. Only one person was needed to manage the station during a shift. The Secretary of Labor filed suit, alleging the husband-wife teams were entitled to back wages for all the hours they were at the stations. Should they get this back pay?

L.O.4

2 The Missouri Constitution made retirement mandatory for judges at age 70. The governor appointed Judge Ellis Gregory and other judges to office. When they reached 70, they sued John Ashcroft, the governor, alleging mandatory retirement violated the Age Discrimination in Employment Act. Gregory argued that as judges they just resolved factual issues and decided legal questions, therefore the exception for persons appointed at the policymaking level did not apply to them. Ashcroft argued that in applying the common law to cases judges made policy. They also had supervisory authority over inferior courts and the state bar. Does the ADEA apply to these judges?

L.O.2 ....

3 Limbach Constructors, Inc. (LCI), had wholly owned subsidiaries Limbach Company, a union contractor, and Jovis Construction. Jovis bought Harper Plumbing and Heating, Inc., a nonunion contractor. Union employees warned LCI that labor troubles would ensue for Limbach if it did not make Harper sign a collective bargaining agreement with the union. After more of such threats, the union terminated its collective bargaining agreement with Limbach. All Limbach's employees left their job sites and quit. Limbach filed unfair labor practice charges alleging the union had engaged in secondary boycott activity because it and Harper constituted separate employers. As such, a labor dispute between Harper and the union did not involve Limbach. Did the union's activity amount to coercion to get a secondary objective?

L.O.1 ....

4 Scott Hageman worked for several years as a maintenance person for Park West Gardens apartments. He had no other employment. He performed various jobs including electrical, plumbing, heating, and air conditioning repairs. The apartment management gave Hageman a check for $100 or $150 each month for supplies. It paid him $7 an hour, $10 a week for gas, and reduced his rent $125 a month. Hageman had no set hours, but went to the office daily at 10 A.M. for work orders. He had a voice pager so Midwest could page him in emergencies. He sued Park West for overtime compensation alleging he was an employee subject to the Fair Labor Standards Act. The trial court found that as an independent contractor, the act did not cover Hageman. Should Hageman get overtime compensation?

L.O.4 ....

5 The Edward Malley Company fired Walter Parcinski, a buyer aged 63, after Malley was purchased by The Outlet Company. Malley was debt-ridden, and Outlet hoped to make it profitable by having buying handled through its central purchasing office. This arrangement meant eliminating Malley's buying staff, including Parcinski. The decision to eliminate the buyers was made prior to any consideration of their ages. Only four of 30 buyers were given new positions with Malley, and three of these four were within the protected age range of the Age Discrimination in Employment Act (ADEA). Parcinski sued under the ADEA. Was his discharge a violation of the Act?

L.O.1 ....

6 Silent Woman sold women's and children's outerwear sewed and embroidered by women part-time in their homes. Nine of these women, who had worked for Silent for several years, filed a suit for a declaration that the Fair Labor Standards Act did not cover them as employees. The women owned their own sewing machines and worked regularly except when ill or Silent did not have work. They had identical contracts with Silent, which supplied them with pre-cut cloth kits for each garment including specifications and appliqué designs. Silent had the right to reject garments that did not conform. It paid them on piece rates identical for all seamstresses. None of them worked for anyone else. Did this arrangement make them independent contractors or employees covered by the Fair Labor Standards Act?

Summary Cases

AGENCY AND EMPLOYMENT

1 In response to a newspaper ad, Helen Campbell looked at a car at Duncan's residence. She believed he was the only person who had owned the car and that the right door had been dented but was fixed and all right. She purchased the car, believing it was basically brand-new. After receiving her title and finding out the transferor was Hamilton Auto Company, she learned the car had not been a one-owner car owned by Duncan. The car had been totaled, sold as salvage, and transferred through a series of dealers. It was worth $3,000 less than she had paid, considering its actual condition. Had she known all this, she would not have bought it. Gordon Hamilton authorized Duncan to buy cars with drafts drawn on Hamilton Auto Company. The purchase was financed at a bank with Hamilton's credit. Hamilton held title to the cars and he limited Duncan to buying three cars at any time. Hamilton required him to dispose of them within 30 days. Campbell sued Hamilton, alleging that his agent, Duncan, committed fraud. Should she recover? [*Campbell* v. *Hamilton,* 632 S.W.2d 633 (Tex. Ct. App.)]

2 Joseph and Frida Friedman owned adjoining lots, No. 3 and No. 5, with Leonard and Bernice Feldman. They retained Lam and Buchsbaum as their agent to sell the lots. Charles Samter, a salesman for Lam and Buchsbaum, showed Lot No. 3 to Victor and Barbara Kasser. The Friedmans had left the sale of the lots to Leonard Feldman, so Samter told Feldman the Kassers liked Lot No. 3. He asked Feldman to meet them at the lot to show them its dimensions. The meeting could not be arranged, but Feldman met Samter, gave him a plot plan, and paced off the lot's boundaries, which they staked off. Feldman told Samter the staking was probably a bit off, and any purchaser should have the lot surveyed. Samter showed the lot to the Kassers, pointed out the stakes, and gave them a copy of the plot plan. They bought the lot and built a house. The Friedmans got full title to adjoining Lot No. 5 and moved into the house there. They had parking pads built within the area designated by the stakes. A survey showed the Kassers' carport was 5.8 feet on Lot No. 5, and their driveway was up to 45 feet on the lot. The Friedmans sued to have removed the Kassers' carport, driveway, and so much of their house as was within 15 feet of Lot No. 5 in violation of zoning ordinance. Are the Friedmans bound by the property line as demonstrated by Samter? [*Friedman* v. *Kasser,* 481 A.2d 886 (Pa. Super. Ct.)]

3 Alfred S. Dale was the owner of an apartment building in Bismarck. He ordered some beds from Sears, Roebuck and Company. When the beds arrived, he contracted with Nelson to install one of them in one of the apartments. Claude Newman rented the apartment. The bed collapsed and Newman was seriously injured. Nelson had not followed instructions in installing the bed. He used wood screws instead of the lag screws that the seller had recommended for the installation. This was the direct cause of the collapse. Was Nelson an employee of Dale or an independent contractor? [*Newman* v. *Sears Roebuck Co. and Dale*, 43 N.W.2d 411 (N.D.)]

4 Mr. and Mrs. Miles contracted to buy a house and met with Frederick Russell, president of Perpetual Savings & Loan Company, to arrange a mortgage loan. The Mileses asked about a termite inspection and were told it was Perpetual's policy to require one and that these matters were usually handled by Perpetual. A termite inspection company was hired by Perpetual to inspect the house. For the closing, Russell prepared a real estate Disclosure/Settlement Statement indicating a termite inspection had been made. A copy was given to the Mileses. Later that day Russell was told the inspection showed termite infestation, and treatment would cost $460. Russell did not tell the Mileses. After they took possession of the house, they discovered the termite damage, which was estimated to cost $5,962.50 to repair. They sued Perpetual. It alleged that the obligation of a savings and loan to appraise property prior to approving a loan did not impose a duty to disclose to the buyer information about the property obtained from the appraisal. Was it liable? [*Miles* v. *Perpetual Savings & Loan Co.*, 388 N.E.2d 1364 (Ohio)]

5 Edrel Clinkenbeard contracted to have Central Southwest Oil Corporation help him participate in a lottery conducted by the Department of the Interior to award leases of federal land. Central was to select valuable tracts coming up for leasing, do the paper work required to enter Clinkenbeard's name, and notify him if he won a lease. Tom Allen, the president of Central, called to say Clinkenbeard had won a lease. Allen stated that the lease was not particularly valuable and that there had been few filings on it but offered Clinkenbeard $5,020 for it. Clinkenbeard finally agreed to assign the lease for $7,020 and an overriding royalty. Later Clinkenbeard found out the lease was one of the most heavily filed on in the lottery and was worth several times what Central paid him. He sued for rescission of the assignment, alleging that Central, as his agent, violated its duty to disclose material facts to him. Should he be allowed to rescind? [*Clinkenbeard* v. *Central Southwest Oil Corporation*, 526 F.2d 649 (5th Cir.)]

6 Harry Hager was the former minister of a church and was sued by the church for possession of the parsonage he occupied. Hager alleged that his contract of employment with the church provided for him to be their minister for his life; therefore, he was entitled to occupy the parsonage. The written contract of employment was not available, but a form copy's only provision that applied to the term of employment stated: "We promise and oblige ourselves . . . to pay you the sum of $___ in ___ payments Yearly and every year so long as you continue the minister of the Church." Did the contract provide that employment was for the duration of Hager's life? [*Bethany Reformed Church of Lynwood* v. *Hager*, 406 N.E.2d 93 (Ill. App. Ct.)]

7 While employed as a professor of food science and microbiology at the University of North Carolina, Marvin Speck, with the assistance of Stanley Gilliland, professor of food science, developed a new procedure by which lactobacillus acidophilus could be added to milk without causing a sour taste. Both were employed to teach and do research on the use of high temperature for pasteurization and sterilization of foods. It was in the course of this research that the new procedure was developed. The process was discovered at the University, and resources provided for their research by the University made it possible for them to discover it. They sued the University to share in the royalties from the commercial use of the process. Are they entitled to payment? [*Speck* v. *North Carolina Dairy Foundation,* 319 S.E.2d 139 (N.C.)]

8   Billy Forrester sued Roth's IGA Foodliner to recover unpaid overtime compensation. Officials of Roth's did not know Forrester had worked uncompensated overtime hours. Forrester admitted he did not mention unpaid overtime to any store official. He knew that overtime was to be reported on time sheets and that the store paid for such reported overtime. He was paid for all overtime he reported. He stated that if he had reported the additional overtime he claimed in the suit he would have been paid. Was Roth's in violation of the Fair Labor Standards Act? [*Forrester* v. *Roth's I.G.A. Foodliner, Incorporated,* 646 F.2d 413 (9th Cir.)]

9   The Duke Power Co. required all new employees and employees requesting a transfer to have a high school diploma or to have passed an intelligence test. These requirements were not directed at or intended to measure ability to learn or perform a particular job or category of jobs. Because of these requirements, a disproportionate number of black applicants were denied employment. A group of black employees brought an action charging discrimination under the 1964 Civil Rights Act. Were the requirements discriminatory? [*Griggs* v. *Duke Power Co.,* 401 U.S. 424]

10   John P. Finnegan was the driver of a truck for the New York Tribune, Inc. On his way to deliver a truckload of paper, he collided with a bus driven by Sauter. When Sauter got out of the bus, an argument ensued between Sauter and Finnegan. Finnegan became very angry and kicked Sauter in the face, causing a very painful injury. Sauter then sued the employer of Finnegan, the New York Tribune, Inc., for damages for this unprovoked assault. Was the employer liable for this act of its employee? [*Sauter* v. *New York Tribune, Inc. et al.,* 113 N.E.2d 790 (N.Y.)]

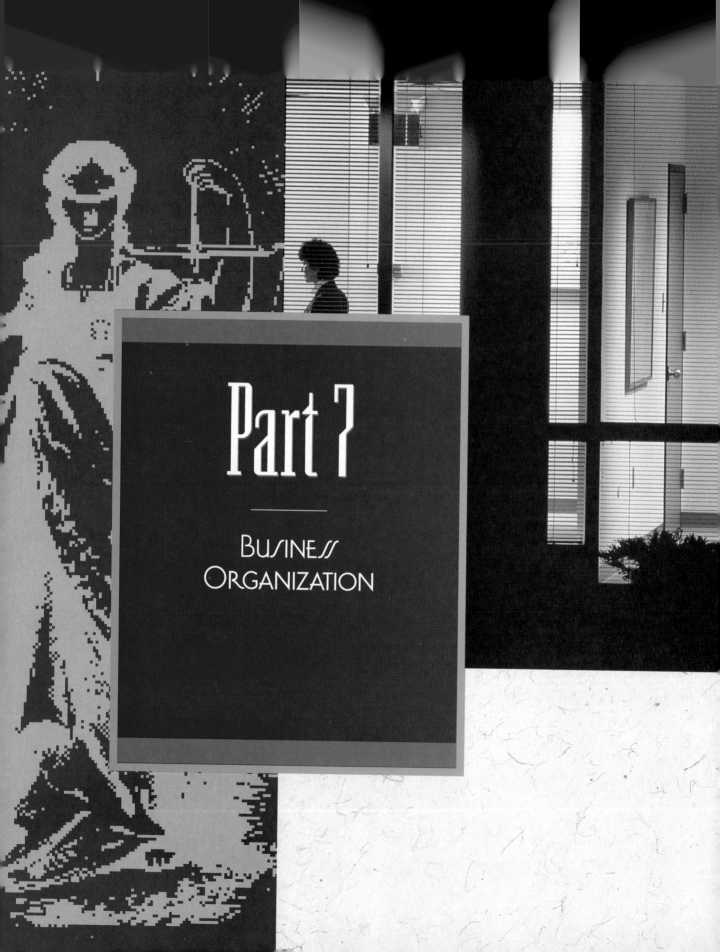

Part 7

Business Organization

Chapter 32

INTRODUCTION TO BUSINESS ORGANIZATION

LEARNING OBJECTIVES

After studying this chapter you should be able to:

1 Discuss the differences in setting up a sole proprietorship, a partnership, and a corporation.

2 Explain the most important disadvantages of sole proprietorships and partnerships.

3 Give two reasons why the corporate form of business organization is important.

Preview Case

J. David Cassilly was a partner in Glen Park Properties, a general partnership for real estate development. He entered into an agreement with Schnuck Markets, Inc., to share the cost of extending a sewer line to certain property. Glen Park did not pay its share of the construction costs. Schnuck sued Glen Park for damages. Glen Park defended by saying that Cassilly did not have the authority to contract for Glen Park. Did Cassilly have such authority?

An individual who is contemplating starting a business has a choice of several common types of business organizations. The number of owners, the formality in setting up the business, and the potential for personal liability are some of the factors that help distinguish the three most widely used types of business organization: sole proprietorship, partnership, and corporation.

SOLE PROPRIETORSHIP

Sole Proprietorship
Business owned and carried on by one person

Proprietor
Owner of sole proprietorship

L.O.1 ....

A **sole proprietorship** is a business owned and carried on by one person, called the **proprietor.** A sole proprietorship, the simplest and most common form of business, has a unique nature different from other businesses. It also has significant advantages and disadvantages as a result of the fact that one individual owns and runs it.

Nature

The proprietor directly owns the business. This means that the proprietor owns every asset of the business including the equipment, inventory, and real estate just as personal assets are owned. Although owned and run by one person, the business may have any number of employees and agents. However, the proprietor has ultimate responsibility for business decisions.

To start a sole proprietorship, an individual need only begin doing business. The law does not impose any formalities to begin and operate this form of business. A license may be needed for the particular type of business undertaken. However, the type of business imposes this requirement, not the form of business organization.

It is equally easy to end a sole proprietorship. The proprietor simply stops doing business. Because the proprietor directly owns all the business assets, the proprietor need not dispose of them in order to go out of business. A sole proprietorship normally ends at the death of the proprietor. Such a business may be willed to another, but the proprietor has no assurance the business will be continued.

Advantages

The sole proprietorship form of business has two major advantages.

1   Flexible management
2   Ease of organization

Flexible Management. As the sole owner, the proprietor has significant flexibility in managing the business. Other people do not have to be consulted before business decisions may be made. The proprietor has full control and has the freedom to operate the business in any way desired.

Fictitious Name Registration Statute
Law requiring operator of business under assumed name to register with state

Ease of Organization. Since an individual need do nothing but start doing business, the sole proprietorship is the simplest type of business to organize. The law imposes no notice, permission, agreement, or understanding for its existence. If the proprietor intends to operate the business under an assumed name, a state law will normally require registration of the name with the appropriate state official. These laws are called **fictitious name registration statutes.** A business operated under the proprietor's name and that does not imply additional owners does not have to be registered.

Unlimited Liability
Business debts payable from personal assets

Disadvantages

The most significant disadvantage of the sole proprietorship form of business is the **unlimited liability** of the owner for the debts of the business. Unlimited liability

L.O.2 .... means that business debts are payable from personal, as well as business, assets. If the business does not have enough assets to pay business debts, the proprietor's personal assets may also be taken by business creditors. The sole proprietor's financial risk cannot be limited to the investment in the business.

In addition to unlimited liability, a sole proprietorship has additional disadvantages of limited management ability and capital. Since only one person runs a sole proprietorship, the management ability of just the proprietor limits the business. The business also has only whatever capital the proprietor has or can raise. This may limit the size of the business.

A sole proprietor has liability for the activities of the business because the proprietor is the sole manager of the business. The proprietor is in a sense the business. The responsibility for all business decisions rest with the proprietor. A sole proprietor may not only be liable in damages for torts committed by the business, but also criminally liable for crimes.

PARTNERSHIP

Partnership

Association of two or more people to carry on business for profit

A **partnership** is a voluntary association of two or more people who have combined their money, property, or labor and skill, or a combination of these, for the purpose of carrying on as co-owners some lawful business for profit. The agreement of individuals to organize a partnership and run a business forms this type of organization. The individuals who have formed a partnership and constitute its members are called **partners.** They act as agents for the partnership.

Partner

Member of a partnership

The partnership must be formed for the purpose of operating a lawful business. The attempt to form a partnership to operate an unlawful business does not result in a partnership. Furthermore, a partnership may not be formed for the purpose of conducting a lawful business in an illegal manner.

A hunting club, a sewing circle, a trade union, a chamber of commerce, or other nonprofit association cannot be treated as a partnership because the purpose of a partnership must be to conduct a trade, business, or profession for profit.

Classification

Several different kinds of partnerships exist depending on the liabilities of the partners and the business carried out. Partnerships may be classified as follows:

1 Ordinary, or general, partnerships
2 Limited partnerships
3 Trading and nontrading partnerships

Ordinary or General Partnership

Partnership with no limitation on rights and duties of partners

Ordinary, or General, Partnerships. An **ordinary or general partnership** forms when two or more people voluntarily contract to pool their capital and skill to conduct some business undertaking for profit. An ordinary partnership results in no limitations upon a partner's rights, duties, or liabilities. The Uniform Partnership Act governs this type of business organization in most states.[1] This act aims to bring about uniformity in the partnership laws of the states.

[1]The Uniform Partnership Act has been adopted in all states except Louisiana.

J. David Cassilly was a partner in Glen Park Properties, a general partnership for real estate development. He entered into an agreement with Schnuck Markets, Inc., to share the cost of extending a sewer line to certain property. Glen Park did not pay its share of the construction costs. Schnuck sued Glen Park for damages. Glen Park defended by saying that Cassilly did not have the authority to contract for Glen Park. The court said that every partner of a general partnership is an agent of the partnership and binds the partnership when carrying on in the usual way the business of the partnership. Glen Park had to pay.

Limited Partnership

Partnership with partner whose liability is limited to capital contribution

Limited Partnerships. A **limited partnership** is one in which one or more partners have their liability for the firm's debts limited to the amount of their investment. This type of partnership cannot operate under either the common law or the Uniform Partnership Act. However, all states now permit limited partnerships. Most do so because of passage of the Uniform Limited Partnership Act or the Revised Uniform Limited Partnership Act. A limited partnership cannot be formed without a specific state statute prescribing the conditions under which it can operate. If the limited partnership does not comply strictly with the enabling statute, courts hold it to be an ordinary partnership.

Trading Partnership

One engaged in buying and selling

Nontrading Partnership

One devoted to professional services

Trading and Nontrading Partnerships. A **trading partnership** is one engaged in buying and selling merchandise. A **nontrading partnership** is one devoted to providing services, such as accounting, medicine, law, and similar professional services. The distinction matters because the members of a nontrading partnership usually have considerably less apparent authority than the partners in a trading partnership. For example, one partner in a nontrading partnership cannot borrow money in the name of the firm and bind the firm. One dealing with a nontrading partnership must exercise more responsibility in ascertaining the actual authority of the partners to bind the firm than a person dealing with a trading partnership.

Who May Be Partners?

As a contractually based entity, any person competent to make a contract has the competence to be a partner. A minor may become a partner to the same extent to which a contract may be made about any other matter. The law holds such contracts voidable, but a minor acting as the agent of the other partner or partners can bind the partnership on contracts within the scope of the partnership business. A minor partner also incurs the liabilities of the partnership. The states disagree as to whether a minor who withdraws from a partnership can withdraw the entire contribution originally made or whether a proportion of any losses must first be deducted.

Kinds of Partners

The members of a partnership may be classified as follows:

1   General partner
2   Silent partner
3   Secret partner
4   Dormant partner
5   Nominal partner

General Partner

One actively and openly engaged in business

General Partner.

A **general partner** is one actively and openly engaged in the business and held out to everyone as a partner. Such a partner has unlimited liability in respect to the partnership debts. A general partner appears to the public as a full-fledged partner, assumes all the risks of the partnership, and does not have any limitations of rights. This is the usual type of partner.

A limited partnership, the Quinn-L Baton Rouge Partnership, was formed to build an apartment complex. The Quinn-L Corporation was a general partner. Thomas R. Elkins was a limited partner. The corporation became the managing general partner. When the project proved to be more expensive than anticipated, the corporation loaned substantial money to the partnership. After construction was completed, the corporation was removed as managing general partner and replaced by Elkins. Three years later the corporation had received no payments on its loan. It sued the partnership and the partners. The court said that, having become the managing general partner, Elkins had the unlimited liability of a general partner.

Silent Partner

Partner who takes no part in firm

Silent Partner.

A **silent partner** is one who, though possibly known to the public as a partner, takes no active part in the management of the business. In return for investing in the partnership capital, such a partner has a right as a partner only to share in the profits in the ratio agreed upon. Why would a person invest money but take no active part in the management? Because such a partner gains limited liability and no share of the losses beyond the capital contribution. People frequently refer to this type of partner as a **limited partner** when known to the public as a partner.

Limited Partner

Partner who takes no active part in management and who is known to public as a partner

Secret Partner

Partner active but unknown to public

Secret Partner.

An active partner who attempts to conceal that fact from the public is a **secret partner.** Such a partner tries to escape the unlimited liability of a general partner but at the same time take an active part in the management of the business. Should such a partner's relationship to the firm become known to the public, however, unlimited liability cannot be escaped. Secret partners differ from silent partners in that secret partners: (1) are unknown to the public and (2) take an active part in the management of the business. Secret partners may feign the status of employees or may work elsewhere, but they meet frequently with the other partners to discuss management problems.

Dormant or Sleeping Partner

Partner unknown to public with no part in management

Dormant Partner.

A **dormant partner** (sometimes referred to as a **sleeping partner**) usually combines the characteristics of both the secret and the silent partner. A dormant partner is usually unknown to the public as a partner and takes no part in the management of the business of the firm. When known to the public as a partner, a dormant partner has liability for the debts of the firm to the same extent as a general partner. In return for limited liability so far as the other partners can effect it, a dormant partner foregoes the right to participate in the management of the firm. In addition, such a partner may agree to limit income to a reasonable return on investment, since no services are contributed.

Nominal Partner

Person who pretends to be a partner

Nominal Partner.

Nominal partners hold themselves out as partners or permit others to do so. In fact, however, they are not partners, since they do not share in the management of the business nor in the profits; but in some instances they may be held liable as a partner.

In order to open a McDonald's, Ralph Baker borrowed $107,000 from the Bank of River Oaks. He had a franchise and lease on a restaurant from McDonald's. To obtain additional capital, Baker and his wife, as general partners, formed a limited partnership, B/K Limited Partnership, with Arnold Kramer as a limited partner. At the same time, the Bakers signed a note to Kramer for $90,000, the amount of his investment. The business closed shortly after opening. When sold, the business equipment brought in just enough money to pay off the bank's note. Kramer sued, alleging that he had a right to have payment on his note. The court held that since the $90,000 was paid at the time of the formation of the limited partnership, it was intended as Kramer's contribution of capital to the partnership, not a loan. Since there were no profits, Kramer was not entitled to any return on his investment.

Advantages of the Partnership

By the operation of a partnership instead of a proprietorship, capital and skill may be increased, labor may be made more efficient, the ratio of expenses per dollar of business may be reduced, and management may be improved. Not all of these advantages will accrue to every partnership, but the prospect of greater profits by reason of them leads to the formation of a partnership.

Disadvantages of the Partnership

A partnership has the following disadvantages:

1   The unlimited liability of each partner for the debts of the partnership.
2   The relative instability of the business because of the danger of dissolution by reason of the death or withdrawal of one of the partners.
3   The divided authority among the partners, which may lead to disharmony.

Organizations Similar to Partnerships

Some business organizations resemble partnerships. However, they differ from them. These include joint-stock companies, joint ventures, and limited liability companies.

Joint-Stock Company
Entity that issues shares of stock, but investors have unlimited liability

Joint-Stock Companies. A **joint-stock company** resembles a partnership, but shares of stock, as in a corporation, indicate ownership. The ownership of these shares may be transferred without dissolving the association. Thus, one of the chief disadvantages of the general partnership is overcome. Shareholders in a joint-stock company do not have the authority to act for the firm. The joint stockholders have liability, jointly and severally, for the debts of the firm while members. For this reason, joint-stock companies do not offer the safeguards of a corporation. Some states permit joint-stock companies to operate by special statutes authorizing them, or in some states, without statute, as common-law associations.

Joint Venture
Business relationship similar to partnership, except existing for single transaction only

Joint Ventures. A **joint venture** is a business relationship in which two or more persons combine their labor or property for a single undertaking and share profits and losses equally or as otherwise agreed. For example, two friends enter into an agreement to get the rights to cut timber from a certain area and market the lumber.

A joint venture resembles a partnership in many respect, the primary difference being that a joint venture exists for a single transaction, though its completion may take several years. A partnership generally constitutes a continuing business.

Limited Liability Companies. The states have enacted statutes providing for the formation of a business organization similar to a partnership but without the disadvantage of unlimited liability. This is a **limited liability company** or LLC. The owners, who also run an LLC, are called members. The initial members sign an operating agreement or articles of organization, the contract that governs the operations of the LLC. This contract must be filed with the appropriate state office. Most states require two members for an LLC, which may be formed for any legal business purpose.

Limited Liability Company
Partnership-type organization but with limited liability

CORPORATIONS

Corporation
Association of people created by law into an entity

The Supreme Court described a **corporation** as "an association of individuals united for some common purpose, and permitted by law to use a common name and to change its members without dissolution of the association." The law creates a corporation—it does not exist merely by agreement of private individuals. It comes into existence by the state's issuing a charter. A corporation may be organized for any lawful purpose, whether pleasure or profit.

The law recognizes a corporation as an "entity," something that has a distinct existence separate and apart from the existence of its individual members. The law views a corporation as an artificial person substituted for the natural persons responsible for its formation who manage and control its affairs. When a corporation makes a contract, the contract is made by and in the name of this legal entity, the corporation, and not by and in the name of the individual members. It has almost all the rights and powers of an individual. It can sue and be sued, it can be fined for violating the law, and it has recourse to the Constitution to protect its liberties.

Importance of Corporations

L.O.3 ....

There are two major reasons why the corporation has such importance as a form of business organization. Corporations allow:

1   Pooling of capital from many investors
2   Limited liability

Pooling of Capital. The rapid expansion of industry from small shops to giant enterprises required large amounts of capital. Few people had enough money of their own to build a railroad or a great steel mill, and people hesitated to form partnerships with any but trusted acquaintances. In addition, even though four or five people did form a partnership, insufficient capital was still a major problem. Such a business needed hundreds or even thousands of people, each with a few hundred or a few thousand dollars, to pool their capital for concerted undertakings. The corporate form of business provided the necessary capital from any number of investors.

Limited Liability

Capital contribution is maximum loss

Limited Liability. Incorporation is attractive to business persons as a means of obtaining **limited liability.** Limited liability means that the maximum amount an investor can lose equals that person's actual investment in the business. Suppose three people with $20,000 each form a partnership with capital of $60,000. Each partner risks losing not only this $20,000 but also almost everything else owned, because of personal liability for all partnership debts. If a corporation is formed and each investor contributes $20,000, this amount is the maximum that can be lost, since an investor has no liability for corporate debts beyond the investment. Many businesses that formerly would have been organized as either a partnership or a sole proprietorship are today corporations in order to have the benefit of limited liability. The partners or the sole proprietor simply own all, or virtually all, the stock of the corporation.

Piercing the Corporate Veil

Ignoring the corporate entity

Piercing the Corporate Veil. Courts will, however, ignore the corporate entity under exceptional circumstances. When courts do, they say they are **piercing the corporate veil.** This can occur if one individual or a few individuals own all the stock of a corporation and ignore the corporate entity. Instead of avoiding the disadvantage of unlimited liability of a sole proprietorship and a partnership, a corporate investor can thus be held personally liable.

Richard J. Fenick owned all the stock in Advisory Associates, Inc. Advisory, by its president, Fenick, had signed a note payable to Jack M. Robertson. Fenick turned over the sole assets of Advisory, at no charge, to a corporation of which his son was president. No corporate resolution authorized Fenick to do this and Advisory never held any corporate meetings. When sued personally for payment of the note, Fenick said he should not be liable because Advisory was a legitimately organized corporation. The court found that since Fenick was the sole beneficiary of the corporation's activities, since he directed and managed its activities, and since he used the corporate name at his pleasure, he operated it as a sole proprietorship and therefore he had personal liability on the note.

Disadvantages of Corporations

In a sole proprietorship, the investor completely manages the business. In a partnership, each investor has an equal voice in the management of the business. In a corporation, the people who own or control a majority of the voting stock have not merely a dominant voice in management but the sole voice. If there are 15 stockholders, but one owns 51 percent of the voting stock, this stockholder is free to run the corporation as desired. The stockholder who owns the majority of the voting stock has the ability to dominate the board of directors and therefore the corporate officers. People who invest their savings in a business in the hope of becoming "their own boss" will not find the corporate type of business organization the most desirable unless they can control a majority of the voting stock.

QUESTIONS

1   What formalities must a person go through in order to set up a sole proprietorship.

2   What is a fictitious name registration statute?

3 What is the most serious disadvantage of a sole proprietorship?

4 What are the advantages of a partnership?

5 What is the difference between an ordinary partnership and a limited partnership?

6 a. Who may be a partner?

b. Can a minor be held to a partnership agreement?

7 What is the potential liability of a silent partner?

8 What is a limited liability company?

9 Explain the two reasons for the importance of the corporate form of business organization?

10 What are the main differences between a corporation and a partnership?

CASE PROBLEMS

L.O.1

1 The partnership agreement for Antiques Etc., a general partnership, stated, "Each partner hereto shall be a general partner . . . and may bind the other partner only as to the partnership business and assets." It stated that neither partner could bind the other as to the partners' personal assets. The partners were Raymond L. Gugelman and Marian E. McCoy. McCoy executed a number of promissory notes to obtain funds used in the operation of the partnership. The bank sued Gugelman for payment of the notes. Was he liable?

L.O.1

2 John Hackney owned a building that housed "Johnny's Barbeque." He leased the building and equipment to Luther Massengil, Sammie Hunt, and Doris Johnson for five years. Massengil, Hunt, and Johnson operated the restaurant and occupied the premises for a short time, but trouble occurred. Hackney, Massengil, and Hunt executed a release of each other from the lease. Johnson refused to sign and sued Hackney for eviction. Hackney argued that the business arrangement among Massengil, Hunt, and Johnson constituted a partnership and as agents of a trading partnership, Massengil and Hunt bound the partnership by the release. Johnson said giving the release did not constitute a transaction in the ordinary course of the business because without the lease there could be no business. Did the release bind Johnson?

L.O.1, 2

3 The Plastex Company sold goods to Central Pump and Supply Company between March and October. Plastex sued Homer Johnson and Monte Bunch as partners for the balance due. Plastex produced a bank signature card dated March 3 with Johnson's and Bunch's signatures. Johnson owned the property on which Central Pump and Supply did business and loaned Bunch $8,000 in June without requiring any collateral. Plastex received a letter signed by both Johnson and Bunch asking for credit with an attached financial statement showing Johnson's assets. A bank received a security agreement signed by Johnson showing the debtor as H. Johnson d/b/a/ (doing business as) Central Pump and Supply. Johnson claimed Plastex sold goods to Central without knowing about all these items; therefore, it did not sell on the basis of a partnership. Should the court hold Johnson liable?

L.O.1 ....

4 Dr. Joseph Martinez belonged to a medical partnership with two other physicians. He and his wife, Freida Martinez, had their marriage dissolved. Freida claimed that with the dissolution, she became the owner of a one-sixth interest in the partnership. She sued Joseph and the partnership for that interest. Did Freida become a partner in the partnership to the extent of half of Joseph's interest in it?

L.O.3 ....

5 A corporation, Unlimited Business Exchange of North Dakota, Inc. (UBE), was formed by Richard Collins and other investors. Collins later bought out the interests of the other investors. As the sole owner and the only person receiving benefit from UBE, Collins considered the corporation to be a sole proprietorship. He conducted the business as a sole proprietorship called UBE. UBE leased office space for 24 months from John A. Larson. Less than a year later, UBE informed Larson that it would be moving out at the end of only 12 months. Larson sued UBE and Collins for unpaid rent. Do the facts warrant the decision that the corporation was in fact a sole proprietorship?

Chapter 33

CREATION AND OPERATION OF A PARTNERSHIP

LEARNING OBJECTIVES

After studying this chapter you should be able to:

1 Describe how a partnership is created.

2 Specify the duties the law imposes upon partners.

3 Identify the rights and liabilities every partner has.

4 Understand how partnership profits and losses are shared.

Preview Case

For $260,500, Al Shacket and Leroy Helfman purchased options to buy land. They assigned the options to Hulett, Inc. Before Hulett closed the purchase of the land, Shacket and Helfman offered to buy the land for $525,000. After this offer was accepted, Shacket and Helfman assigned their purchase rights to a partnership they had with Harold Jaffa and Irving Taran, and the partnership bought the property from Hulett. The partnership agreement required Shacket and Helfman to transfer the property "at their cost." Jaffa and Taran sued, alleging Shacket and Helfman violated their duty to give to the other partners full and true information of all things affecting the partnership, because they failed to disclose that they had purchased the options for only $260,500. Shacket and Helfman alleged there is no violation of the duty to disclose information so long as there is no concealment of profit. Did Shacket and Helfman violate the duty to inform?

A partnership results from a contract, written or oral, express or implied, just as all other business commitments result from a contract. The parties to the contract must give the utmost fidelity in all relationships with the other partners. If any partner fails in this duty, the other partners have several legal remedies to redress the wrong.

PARTNERSHIP AGREEMENTS

The partnership agreement must meet the five tests of a valid contract as set out in Chapter 5. A partnership may also be created when two or more parties act in such a way as to lead third parties to believe that a partnership exists.

Written Agreement

L.O.1 ....

Articles of Partnership
Written partnership agreement

The partners ordinarily need not have a written agreement providing for the formation of a partnership. However, having an agreement in writing helps avoid disputes over rights and duties. If the parties choose to put their agreement in writing, in the absence of a statute to the contrary, the writing need not be in a particular form. The written partnership agreement is commonly known as the **articles of partnership.** Articles of partnership will vary according to the needs of the particular situation, but ordinarily they should contain the following:

1   Date
2   Names of the partners
3   Nature and the duration of the business
4   Name and the location of the business
5   Individual contributions of the partners
6   Sharing of profits, losses, and responsibilities
7   Keeping of accounts
8   Duties of the partners
9   Amounts of withdrawals of money
10 Unusual restraints upon the partners
11 Provisions for dissolution and division of assets
12 Signatures of partners

Implied Agreement

A partnership arises whenever the persons in question enter into an agreement that satisfies the definition of a partnership. Thus, three persons who agree to contribute property and money to the running of a business as co-owners for the purpose of making a profit, even though they do not in fact call themselves partners, have formed a partnership. Conversely, the mere fact that persons say "we are partners now" does not establish a partnership if the elements of the definition of a partnership are not satisfied.

Prima Facie
On the face of it

Prima Facie Evidence
Evidence sufficient on its face, if uncontradicted

In many instances, the death of witnesses or the destruction of records makes proof of exactly what happened impossible. Because of this, the Uniform Partnership Act provides that proof that a person received a share of profits is **prima facie** evidence of a partnership. This means that in the absence of other evidence, it should be held that a partnership existed. This **prima facie evidence** can be overcome, and the conclusion then reached that no partnership existed, by showing that the share of profits received represented wages or payment of a debt, interest on a loan, rent, or the purchase price of a business or goods.

Brothers George and Clarence Simandl owned 6.638 acres of land on which they operated a gas station, delicatessen, and magazine stand. Clarence conveyed his share of the land to George, and a year later George reconveyed the property to Clarence. The conveyances were to aid the brothers' ability to get credit. When Clarence sold 5.5 acres of the land to nonfamily members, George and Clarence divided the proceeds equally. They shared in the receipts of the businesses, and both signed contracts for the purchase of goods sold. The brothers made business decisions only after consulting each other, and each bound the other. After they both died, George's widow sued for half the real property and business. The court said a partnership can be found when there was a sharing of net profits from a continuing business and each person is able to bind the business. This was a partnership.

Partnership by Estoppel

The conduct of persons who in fact are not partners could be such as to mislead other persons into thinking they are partners. The situation resembles that in which a person misleads others into thinking that someone is an authorized agent. In a case of a false impression of a partnership, the law will frequently hold that the apparent partners are estopped from denying that a partnership exists; otherwise, third persons will be harmed by their conduct.

Under a written agreement, Carmen Allen and Sandy Newsome engaged in business using the name Newsome Carpets. Allen agreed to invest $5,000 and Newsome agreed to invest an equal value of carpet stock, fixtures, and equipment. Newsome also agreed to supply purchasing power and John Robertson agreed to supply credit backing. The parties agreed to divide profits 50 percent to Newsome, 40 percent to Allen, and 10 percent to Robertson. Eight months later Allen and Newsome signed a partnership agreement that referred to each as "partners" with a 50 percent interest. Allen did share in profits from the business, gave business advice, and signed documents as a general partner of Newsome Carpets. Orders Distributing Company sued Allen and Newsome as partners for carpet stock delivered to Newsome Carpets. Allen claimed she was not a partner. The court found Allen and Newsome acted like partners so even if they were not, Allen was estopped to deny it.

PARTNERSHIP FIRM NAME

The law does not require a firm name for a partnership, but it makes identification convenient. Any name that does not violate the rights of others or the law may be adopted by the firm. The partnership name may be changed at will by agreement. In some states the name of a person not a member of the firm or the words *and Company* unless the term indicates an additional partner(s) may not be used. Many of the states permit the use of fictitious or trade names but require the firm to register its name, address, purpose, and the names and addresses of the partners.

A partnership may sue or be sued either in the firm name or in the names of the partners. Under the Uniform Partnership Act any partnership property, whether real or personal, may be owned either in the names of the partners or in the name of the firm. To hold partnership property in the names of the partners, the owner should convey the property to the partners d/b/a (doing business as) the partnership.

PARTNER'S INTEREST IN PARTNERSHIP PROPERTY

Tenancy in Partnership

Ownership of partner in partnership property

In a a **tenancy in partnership** (also called *owner in partnership*), each partner owns and can sell only a pro rata interest in the partnership as an entity. The purchaser of one partner's share cannot demand acceptance as a partner by the other partners. The purchaser acquires only the right to receive the share of profits the partner would have received. A surviving partner does not get full ownership upon the death of the other partner, as is the case in joint tenancy. One partner may not freely sell an interest in partnership property. The personal creditors of one partner cannot force the sale of specific pieces of property of the partnership to satisfy personal debts, nor can they force the sale of a fractional part of specific assets. The personal creditors of one partner can ask a court to order that payments due the debtor partner from the partnership be made to the creditors. They also can force the sale of a debtor partner's interest in the partnership.

DUTIES OF PARTNERS

L.O.2

Five common duties that one partner owes to the others include:

1 Duty to exercise loyalty and good faith.
2 Duty to work for the partnership.
3 Duty to abide by majority vote.
4 Duty to keep records.
5 Duty to inform.

Exercise Loyalty and Good Faith

Partners owe each other and the firm the utmost loyalty and good faith. As an agent of the firm, each partner has a fiduciary duty to the firm, so strict fidelity to the interests of the firm must be observed at all times. No partner may take advantage of the co-partners. Any personal profits earned directly as a result of one's connection with the partnership must be considered profits of the firm. If the personal interest or advantage of the partner conflicts with the advantage of the partnership, the partner has a duty to put the firm's interest above personal advantage. This duty lasts as long as the enterprise exists.

Henry Slingerland and Raymond Hurley were partners under a written partnership agreement covering a real estate project. When the partnership first purchased the real estate, the contract of sale did not indicate that $35,000 of partnership funds was used to pay off a prior debt owed by Hurley to the seller. Hurley alleged that since the seller would not sell without the debt's being paid, the $35,000 was a "necessary cost of doing business." The court held that the fact that the $35,000 payment was necessary to make the purchase did not excuse it. In all matters in which faith and trust are placed in a fiduciary, the fiduciary's conduct must be above reproach. Hurley had to repay the partnership the $35,000.

The partnership contract must be observed scrupulously. Each partner has the power to do irreparable damage to the co-partners by betraying their trust. For this reason, the law holds each partner to the utmost fidelity to the partnership agreement. Any violation of this agreement gives the other partners at least two rights: First, they can sue the offending partner for any loss resulting from the failure to abide by the partnership agreement; second, they may elect also to ask a court to decree a dissolution of the partnership. A trivial breach of the partnership agreement will not justify a dissolution, however.

Work for the Partnership

Unless provided otherwise in the partnership agreement, each partner has a duty to work on behalf of the partnership. In working for the partnership, partners must use reasonable care and skill in conducting the firm's business. Each partner has liability for partnership debts, but any loss resulting to the firm because of a partner's failure to use adequate care and skill in transacting business must be reimbursed by that partner. If the partnership supplies expert services, such as accounting services or engineering services, then each partner must perform these services in a manner that will free the firm from liability for damages for improper services. However, honest mistakes and errors of judgment do not render a partner liable individually nor the partnership liable collectively.

Dr. Donald Schwartz prescribed Poly-vi-flor for a child, Daniel Keech. The doctor instructed the parents to use the tablet form of Poly-vi-flor. When Keech tried to swallow a tablet he suddenly choked on it and could not breathe. He suffered massive brain damage. The parents sued Schwartz, his medical partnership, and his partner, Joan Magee, for failure to use adequate care and skill as physicians. The court removed Magee as a party saying that she did not have personal liability. Any liability on Magee resulted from her participation in the partnership.

Abide by Majority Vote

A partnership operates on the basis of a majority vote. Unless the partnership agreement provides otherwise, the majority of the partners bind the firm on any ordinary matters in the scope of the partnership business. A decision involving a basic change in the character of the enterprise or the partnership agreement requires the unanimous consent of the partners. Therefore, the majority rule does not apply to such actions as an assignment for the benefit of creditors, disposition of the firm's good will, actions that would make carrying on the firm's business impossible, confession of a judgment, or submitting a firm claim to arbitration.

Keep Records

Each partner must keep such records of partnership transactions as required for an adequate accounting. If the partnership agreement provides for the type of records to be kept, a partner fulfills this duty when such records are kept, even though they may not be fully adequate. Since each partner must account to the partnership for all business transactions including purchases, sales, commission payments, and receipts, this accounting should be based upon written records.

Inform

Each partner has the duty to inform the other partners about matters relating to the partnership. On demand, true and full information of all things affecting the partnership must be rendered to any partner or the legal representative of any deceased partner or partner under legal disability.

For $260,500, Al Shacket and Leroy Helfman purchased options to buy land. They assigned the options to Hulett, Inc. Before Hulett closed the purchase of the land, Shacket and Helfman offered to buy the land for $525,000. After this offer was accepted, Shacket and Helfman assigned their purchase rights to a partnership they had with Harold Jaffa and Irving Taran, and the partnership bought the property from Hulett. The partnership agreement required Shacket and Helfman to transfer the property "at their cost." Jaffa and Taran sued, alleging Shacket and Helfman violated their duty to give to the other partners full and true information of all things affecting the partnership, because they failed to disclose that they had purchased the options for only $260,500. Shacket and Helfman alleged there is no violation of the duty to disclose information so long as there is no concealment of profit. The court held that information means all relevant information regardless of whether it relates to profit.

RIGHTS OF PARTNERS

L.O.3 .... Every partner, in the absence of an agreement to the contrary, has five well-defined rights:

1. Right to participate in management
2. Right to inspect the books at all times
3. Right of contribution
4. Right to withdraw advances
5. Right to withdraw profits

Participate in Management

In the absence of a contract limiting these rights, each partner has the right by law to participate equally with the others in the management of the partnership business. The exercise of this right often leads to disharmony. It is a prime advantage, however, because the investor maintains control over the investment. The right of each partner to a voice in management does not mean a dominant voice. With respect to most management decisions, regardless of importance, the majority vote of the individual partners is controlling.

Rex Hammons and Donald Ball began a business, Hammons Heating and Air Conditioning, in which Ball was not active. A few years later, Hammons and Ball moved their business from Raleigh to Laurel and adopted a new name, Shady Grove TV and Appliance. When they got into severe financial difficulties, they petitioned to have their debts discharged in bankruptcy. The Bankruptcy Court found that Hammond and Ball had established a new business under a new name at Laurel, with both serving as active partners. The appellate court, however, held that Ball's becoming active in the business did not mean that they formed a new business. Every partner has a right to participate in the management and conduct of the business.

Inspect the Books

Each partner must keep a clear record of all transactions performed for the firm. The firm's books must be available to all partners, and each partner must explain on request the significance of any record made that is not clear. All checks written must show the purpose for which they are written. There may be no business secrets among the partners.

Contribution

A partner who pays a firm debt or liability from personal funds has a right to contribution from each of the other partners.

The Uniform Partnership Act states that "the partnership must indemnify every partner in respect of payments made and personal liabilities reasonably incurred by him in the ordinary and proper conduct of its business or for the preservation of its business or property." The partner has no right, however, to indemnity or reimbursement when (1) acting in bad faith, (2) negligently causing the necessity for payment, or (3) previously agreeing to bear the expense alone.

Clyde Hensley, one of eight partners in Mary Gail Coal Company, owned a truck destroyed by the alleged negligence of the company's employees. Hensley sued the partners for the damage to his truck. He argued that a partner who has paid a debt of the firm has a right to contribution from the co-partners; therefore, he should receive reimbursement for the loss he incurred for the partnership. The court agreed that Hensley could obtain reimbursement from his partners.

Withdraw Advances

A partner has no right to withdraw any part of the original investment without the consent of the other partners. One partner, however, who makes additional advances in the form of a loan, has a right to withdraw this loan at any time after the due date. Also, a partner has a right to interest on a loan unless there is an agreement to the contrary. A partner has no right to interest on the capital account. Therefore, the firm should keep each partner's capital account separate from that partner's loan account.

Withdraw Profits

Each partner has the right to withdraw a share of the profits from the partnership at such time as specified by the partnership agreement. Withdrawal of profits could be by express authorization by vote of the majority of the partners in the absence of a controlling provision in the partnership agreement.

LIABILITIES OF PARTNERS

A partner's liabilities include the following:

1   Liability for contracts

2   Liability for torts
3   Liability for crimes

Contracts

Every member of a general partnership has individual liability for all the enforceable debts of the firm. A partner who incurs a liability in the name of the firm but acted beyond both actual and apparent authority, has personal liability. The firm has no liability for such unauthorized acts. The firm also has no liability for illegal contracts made by any member of the firm, since everyone is charged with knowledge of what is illegal. Thus, if a partner in a wholesale liquor firm contracted to sell an individual a case of whiskey, the contract would not be binding on the firm in a state where individual sales are illegal for wholesalers.

Torts

A partnership has liability for the torts committed by a partner in the course of partnership business and in furtherance of partnership interests. When such liability occurs, the responsible partner has liability for indemnifying the partnership for any loss it sustains. The partnership does not have liability for deeds committed by one partner outside the course of partnership business and for the acting partner's own purposes unless the deeds have been authorized or ratified by the partnership.

In addition to the partnership's liability, a partner has liability for the torts of another partner committed in the course of partnership business. This rule applies to negligent as well as intentional acts, such as embezzlement of funds, even if the innocent partner has no knowledge of the acts.

Crimes

Courts will not imply criminal liability. In order to be liable for a crime, an individual partner must somehow have agreed to or participated in the crime. The individual partners could not be punished if they are free of personal guilt. However, the partnership has liability for any penalty incurred by the act of a partner in the ordinary course of business. *In the ordinary course of business* means while the partner acts as a partner in the business and in the promotion of partnership interests. The partnership has liability to the same extent as the acting partner. Thus, the criminal acts of one partner can justify a fine levied on partnership assets.

Without having a mine drainage permit, the King Coal Company, a partnership, conducted mining operations. Robert Woods, the managing partner who directed the mining, and the company were both charged with operating a surface mine without a mine drainage permit. The partnership was guilty because the conduct was performed by its agent in the scope of employment and acting in its behalf. Woods was guilty because he was a partner who caused unlawful conduct to be performed on the partnership's behalf.

NATURE OF PARTNERSHIP LIABILITIES

The partners have joint liability on all partnership contractual liabilities unless the contract stipulates otherwise. They have joint and several liability on all tort liabilities. For joint liabilities, the partners must be sued jointly. If the firm does not have adequate assets to pay the debts or liabilities of the firm, the general partners, of course, have individual liability for the full amount of debts or liabilities. If all the partners but one are insolvent, the remaining solvent partner must pay all the debts even though the judgment is against all of them. The partner who pays the debt has a right of contribution from the other partners but, as a practical matter, may be unable to collect from the other partners.

Withdrawing partners have liability for all partnership debts incurred up to the time they withdraw unless these partners are expressly released from liability by the creditors. Under the Uniform Partnership Act, incoming partners have liability for all debts as fully as if they had been partners when the debt was incurred, except that this liability for old debts is limited to their investment in the partnership. Withdrawing partners may contract with incoming partners to pay all old debts, but this does not bind creditors.

AUTHORITY OF A PARTNER

A partner has an authority expressly given by the partnership agreement or by the action of the partnership. In addition, a partner has all powers that it is customary for partners to exercise in that kind of business in that particular community. As in the case of an agent, any limitation on the authority the partner would customarily possess does not bind a third person unless made known. The firm, however, has a right to indemnity from the partner who causes the firm loss through violation of the limitation placed on the authority.

Customary or Implied Authority

Each partner in an ordinary trading partnership has the following customary or implied authority:

1 To compromise and release a claim against a third party.
2 To receive payments and give receipts in the name of the firm.
3 To employ or to discharge agents and employees whose services are needed in the transaction of the partnership business.
4 To draw and indorse checks, to make notes, and to accept drafts.
5 To insure the property of the partnership, to cancel insurance policies, or to give proof of loss and to collect the proceeds.
6 To buy goods on credit or to sell goods in the regular course of business.

Authority Not Implied

A partner does not have the implied power to do and must obtain express authorization for the following acts:

1 To assign the assets of the firm for the benefit of creditors.
2 To indorse a negotiable instrument as an accommodation.
3 To submit a partnership controversy for arbitration.

4   To discharge a personal debt by agreeing that it will be set off against one due the firm.

5   To dispose of the goodwill of the business or to do any other act that would make impossible the continuance of the business.

SHARING OF PROFITS AND LOSSES

L.O.4 ....

The partnership agreement usually specifies the basis upon which the profits and the losses are to be shared. This proportion cannot be changed by a majority of the members of the firm. If the partnership agreement does not fix the ratio of sharing the profits and the losses, they will be shared equally and not in proportion to the contribution to the capital. In the absence of a provision in the partnership agreement to the contrary, the majority of the partners may order a division of the profits at any time.

QUESTIONS

1   Must a partnership agreement be in writing? Explain.

2   How might two or more parties be held to have formed a partnership when they had no intention to form one?

3   Are partnerships required to have a firm name?

4   Are the assets of a partnership subject to sale by a personal creditor of one of the partners?

5   If one partner is able to make a personal profit as a result of membership in the firm, must this profit be shared with the other partners?

6   What action might partners take if another partner violates the partnership agreement?

7   If *A* and *B* form a partnership for the purpose of operating a public accounting office, who is personally liable if *A*, through ignorance of accounting principles, loses $10,000 of the firm's money?

8   What is a partner's right to participate in the management of the firm?

9   What is a partner's potential liability for the torts of another partner?

10   How are profits and losses shared among partners?

CASE PROBLEMS

L.O.3 ....

1   The Second National Bank of Clearwater sued Donald and Betty Myrick on unpaid promissory notes. After obtaining a judgment, the bank instructed the sheriff to levy on and sell the Myricks' interest in a partnership known as Port Richey Shopping Village. The Myricks alleged that because a person's interest in a partnership is personal property, the business could not be levied upon and sold. Can the bank have the business sold?

L.O.3 ....

2   C. R. Royal, a partner in Paseo Apartment Development Co., sued the partnership, alleging the other partners refused to allow him access to the partnership books. In order to maintain the action, Royal had to show Griffis refused

access to the books. Royal testified that Griffis had access to the books for an interim period, but it was not clear whether Royal requested to see them during that period. Griffis denied having custody of the books but later testified that he packed them in cartons and sent them to another partner who was being audited by the IRS. When asked if he ever took custody of the books, he replied, "Never. They were sent to Dallas, and that is all I know about handling the books." Did Griffis refuse Royal access to the books?

L.O.1 ....

3 Wilton and Janet Jackson, husband and wife, and their adult son, Walter Jackson, filed a voluntary petition under the Bankruptcy Code. The petition purported to be a partnership filing. They operated a hog farm. Wilton and Janet, on the one hand, and Walter, on the other, were to share profits and losses equally. However, all the losses were absorbed by Wilton and Janet, and there never were any profits. Walter testified that his wife, Carol, was a member of the partnership, while his parents said she was not. The three could not agree on when the alleged partnership was formed. Was there a partnership?

L.O.1 ....

4 Johnny Wood and Oscar Simmons were partners in Wood and Simmons Investments. On May 21, Wood deeded real property to "Johnny L. Wood and Oscar Harold Simmons d/b/a Wood and Simmons Investments, a partnership." The property was then leased to Quick-Stop Food Mart, Inc. When later dissolving the partnership, Johnny L. Wood and wife, Zula Wood, deeded to Oscar Harold Simmons and wife, Jacqueline B. Simmons, "all of their one-half undivided interest" in the property. Oscar then conveyed the property to Jacqueline. A lawsuit to determine the rights of Jacqueline and Quick-Stop to the property resulted. At issue was the effect of the May 21 deed. If it conveyed title to the partnership in the partnership name, there was never any conveyance out of the partnership name and the property was still owned by it. If the deed resulted in the property being held as partnership property in the names of Wood and Simmons, title had been conveyed out, ultimately to Jacqueline. Who has title to the property?

L.O.1 ....

5 Richard Missan was hired as a lawyer by the law firm of Gerald Schoenfeld and Bernard B. Jacobs. The firm received a large fee for work on an estate, and Missan sued, claiming a right to share in the fee as a partner. He alleged he was represented as a partner on the firm's letterhead, opinion letters, tax returns, professional directories, pension plan, and professional liability insurance policy. He also alleged that the parties had entered into an agreement admitting him as a member of the firm to receive a percentage of the profits. Schoenfeld and Jacobs submitted a written agreement that provided they would practice law as partners for one year. It also stated: "unless this agreement is extended by an agreement in writing . . . it shall terminate in all respects" and "This agreement constitutes the entire understanding among the parties." The agreement was executed many years before the suit and was not extended in writing. Schoenfeld and Jacobs contended Missan was barred from alleging an oral partnership agreement. Was he?

L.O.2 ....

6 Charles Gross withdrew from the partnership of Newburger, Loeb & Co. The partnership agreement required that at least 85 percent of the "partnership interest" of a withdrawn general partner remain in the firm, at the risk of the business, for one year following withdrawal. Under financial pressure, the remaining partners decided to transfer the assets of the partnership to a corporation. Gross and other withdrawn partners refused to consent to the transfer. The assets were transferred to a corporation anyway. In the resulting lawsuit, Gross alleged that the transfer was a breach of the fiduciary obligation of good faith, since without the withdrawn partners' consent, it violated state law. Did the partnership have a duty of good faith to the withdrawn partners?

L.O.4 ....

7   Zyck and his wife had a partnership in the operation of a real estate agency. Zyck was primarily responsible for obtaining listings and making sales. His wife held the brokerage license, and Zyck was licensed only as a salesman. Mrs. Zyck was at the office daily to supervise and discharge the normal duties associated with it. How should the shares of the profits of Zyck and his wife in the partnership be apportioned?

L.O.3 ....

8   A partnership named Fort George Associates, by means of an Agreement of Sale signed by one of the partners, John Collins, agreed to sell a liquor license to International Restaurant Corporation, owned by Antonio Pinero. The agreement provided the sellers sold "the Class B Seven-Day Liquor License owned by them" for $12,500. When International did not make the payments for the license, the partnership sued it. Pinero counterclaimed, alleging the partnership and the partners were liable for fraud and deceit. The license had expired before the agreement was signed. If Collins is liable for punitive damages, are the partnership and the other partners also liable?

L.O.1, 4 ....

9   Ronald Dreier withdrew from the law partnership of which he had been a member. The oral partnership agreement made no provision for withdrawal of a partner. Dreier sued his former partners for his share of the firm's earnings during the term of his membership. What should happen to fees that were unpaid or unbilled when Dreier withdrew?

Chapter 34

DISSOLUTION OF A PARTNERSHIP

LEARNING OBJECTIVES

After studying this chapter you should be able to:

1 Explain the difference between dissolution and termination of a partnership.

2 List the methods of dissolution of a partnership.

3 Explain who should be notified of a partnership dissolution.

Preview Case

Gerald Olivet, Bennett Marcus, and Edgar Lucidi were members of Whittier Leasing Company, a partnership that engaged in sale–lease-back transactions with Whittier Hospital. The partnership would purchase equipment from the hospital and lease it back at favorable rates. The partnership was successful because seven of the partners (other than Olivet, Marcus, and Lucidi) were members of the board of directors of Whittier Hospital. These seven, together with the other two directors of the hospital, formed a competing partnership, named Friendly Hills Leasing Company, which then got all the lease-back business of the hospital. Olivet, Marcus, and Lucidi sued for dissolution of the Whittier partnership, alleging misconduct on the part of the other seven partners. Was this misconduct?

L.O.1

Dissolution
Change in relation of partners by elimination of one

Winding Up
Taking care of outstanding obligations and distributing remaining assets

The change in the relation of the partners caused by any partner's ceasing to be associated in the carrying on of the business is called **dissolution of a partnership**. The withdrawal of one member of a going partnership normally dissolves the partnership relation, and the partnership cannot thereafter do any new business. The partnership continues to exist for the limited purpose of **winding up** or cleaning up its outstanding obligations and business affairs and distributing its remaining assets to creditors and partners. After all this has been completed, the partnership is deemed terminated and goes out of existence.

If a partner wrongfully withdraws, the remaining partners may continue the business.

DISSOLUTION BY ACTS OF THE PARTIES

L.O.2 ....

Acts of the partners that dissolve a partnership include:

1 Agreement
2 Withdrawal or alienation
3 Expulsion

Agreement

At the time they form the partnership agreement, the partners may fix the time when the partnership relation will cease. Unless they renew or amend the agreement, the partnership is dissolved on the agreed date. If no date for the dissolution is fixed at the time the partnership is formed, the partners may by mutual agreement dissolve the partnership at any time. Even when a definite date is fixed in the original agreement, the partners may dissolve the partnership prior to that time. In this case the subsequent decision to dissolve the partnership does not bind the partnership unless all the partners consent to the dissolution.

Sometimes the parties do not fix a date for dissolving the partnership, but the agreement sets forth the purpose of the partnership, such as the construction of a building. In this event the partnership is dissolved as soon as the purpose has been achieved.

Withdrawal or Alienation

The withdrawal of one partner at any time and for any reason unless wrongful normally dissolves the partnership. In a partnership for a definite term, any partner has the power, but not the right, to withdraw at any time. A withdrawing partner has liability for any loss sustained by the other partners because of the withdrawal. If the partnership agreement does not set a dissolution date, a partner may withdraw at will without liability. After creditors are paid, the withdrawing partner is entitled to receive capital, undistributed profits, and repayment of any loans to the partnership.

If the partnership agreement or a subsequent agreement sets a dissolution date, the withdrawing partner breaches the contract by withdrawing prior to the agreed date. When a partner withdraws in violation of agreement, the damages suffered by the firm may be deducted from that partner's distributive share of the assets of the partnership.

Similar to withdrawal, the sale of a partner's interest either by a voluntary sale or an involuntary sale to satisfy personal creditors does not of itself dissolve the partnership. But the purchaser does not become a partner by purchase, since the remaining partners cannot be compelled to accept as a partner anyone who might be persona non grata to them. The buying partner has a right to the capital and profits of the withdrawing partner but not a right to participate in the management.

Expulsion

The partnership agreement may, and should, contain a clause providing for the expulsion of a member, especially if the partnership has more than two members.

This clause should spell out clearly the acts for which a member may be expelled and the method of settlement for such a partner's interest. The partnership agreement should also set forth that the remaining partners agree to continue the business upon expulsion of a partner; otherwise, it will be necessary to wind up the partnership business and distribute all the assets to the creditors and partners, thereby terminating the partnership's existence.

DISSOLUTION BY COURT DECREE

Under certain circumstances a court may issue a decree dissolving a partnership. The chief reasons justifying such a decree include:

1   Insanity of a partner
2   Incapacity
3   Misconduct
4   Futility

Insanity of a Partner

A partner may obtain a decree of dissolution when a court declares another partner insane or of unsound mind.

Incapacity of a Partner

If a partner develops an incapacity that makes it impossible for the partner to perform the services to the partnership that the original partnership agreement contemplated, a petition may be filed to terminate the partnership on that ground. A member of an accounting firm who goes blind would probably be incapacitated to the extent of justifying a dissolution. The court, not the partners, must be the judge in each case as to whether or not the partnership should be dissolved.

As a rule, the incapacity must be permanent, not temporary, to justify a court decree dissolving the partnership. A temporary inability of one partner to perform duties constitutes one of the risks that the other partners assumed when they formed the partnership.

A question may arise as to whether an illness or other condition causing a partner's inability to perform duties is temporary or not. The safest procedure is for the remaining partners to seek a court order determining the matter.

Misconduct

If one member of a partnership engages in misconduct prejudicial to the successful continuance of the business, the court may, upon proper application, decree a dissolution of the partnership. Such misconduct includes habitual drunkenness, dishonesty, persistent violation of the partnership agreement, irreconcilable discord among the partners as to major matters, and abandonment of the business by a partner.

Gerald Olivet, Bennett Marcus, and Edgar Lucidi were members of Whittier Leasing Company, a partnership which engaged in sale–lease-back transactions with Whittier Hospital. The partnership would purchase equipment from the hospital and lease it back at favorable rates. The partnership was successful because seven of the partners (other than Olivet, Marcus, and Lucidi) were members of the board of directors of Whittier Hospital. These seven, together with the other two directors of the Hospital, formed a competing partnership, named Friendly Hills Leasing Company, which then got all the lease-back business of the Hospital. Olivet, Marcus, and Lucidi sued for dissolution of the Whittier partnership, alleging misconduct on the part of the other seven members. The court held that if partners elect to compete with the partnership, the remaining partners are entitled to a court-ordered dissolution.

Futility

All business partnerships are conducted for the purpose of making a profit. If this objective clearly cannot be achieved, the court may decree a dissolution. One partner cannot compel the other members to assume continued losses after the success of the business becomes highly improbable and further operation appears futile. A temporarily unprofitable operation does not justify a dissolution. A court will issue a decree of dissolution only when the objective reasonably appears impossible to attain.

Sheldon Mandell, Howard Mandell, Jerome Mandell, and Norman Mandell were limited partners in Frontier Investment Associates with Centrum Frontier Corporation and William Thompson. Frontier's only asset was Park Place, an apartment building. To purchase Park Place, a $22 million loan had been obtained from Continental Illinois National Bank. Continental had required the limited partner to pledge $1.6 million in securities to guarantee the loan. Frontier managed Park Place for 17 months, during which time it suffered cash losses of $2,123,825. The losses were increasing because the floating interest rate on the loan had increased. There had been losses for all but two months of the 17-month operation. If the losses continued, they were to be paid by selling the $1.6 million of securities pledged by the limited partners. They sued for dissolution. The court held that the history of losses indicated that profits were not to be expected in the future and ordered dissolution.

DISSOLUTION BY OPERATION OF LAW

Under certain well-defined circumstances, a partnership will be dissolved by operation of law; that is to say, it will be dissolved immediately upon the happening of the specified event. No decree of the court is necessary to dissolve the partnership. The most common examples include:

1. Death
2. Bankruptcy
3. Illegality

Death

The death of one member of a partnership automatically dissolves the partnership unless the agreement provides it shall not be dissolved. A representative of the deceased may act to protect the interest of the heirs but cannot act as a partner. This is true even when the partnership agreement provides that the partnership is not to be dissolved by the death of a member.

The partnership agreement can provide for an orderly process of dissolution upon the death of a member. Thus, a provision that the surviving partners shall have twelve months in which to liquidate the firm and pay the deceased partner's share to the heirs binds.

Bankruptcy

Persons who have their debts discharged in bankruptcy no longer have responsibility for paying most of their debts, including those connected with the partnership. This destroys the unlimited liability of the partner that could otherwise exist, and the partner is not a good credit risk. Because of this, the law regards bankruptcy of a partner as automatically terminating the partnership. The trustee in bankruptcy has the right to assume control of the debtor partner's share of the partnership business, but the trustee does not become a partner. The trustee merely stands in the place of the partner to see that the creditors' interests are protected.

The bankruptcy of the partnership also terminates the partnership. The partnership cannot continue doing business when in the course of the bankruptcy proceeding all of its assets have been distributed to pay its creditors.

Illegality

Some types of business are legal when undertaken, but because of a change in the law, they later become illegal. If a partnership is formed to conduct a lawful business and later this type of business becomes illegal, the partnership is automatically dissolved. A partnership formed for the purpose of operating an insurance underwriting business is dissolved by a law restricting this type of business to corporations.

Paul Williams and Richard Burrus signed a written agreement to buy the Skagit Inn Restaurant. The Skagit Inn had a class H liquor license. According to the agreement, Williams would put up the collateral necessary for Burrus to secure a bank loan to buy the Inn. They agreed the business would be in Burrus' name, and he agreed to apply for transfer of the liquor license without disclosing Williams' interest in the Inn because they knew the State Liquor Control Board would not license him. The Board would not issue a license to a partnership unless it found all the partners qualified to hold a license. Later Williams sued Burrus to dissolve the partnership and for a share of its assets. The court refused saying a partnership is dissolved by an event making the business illegal.

EFFECTS OF DISSOLUTION

Dissolution terminates the right of the partnership to exist and must be followed by the liquidation of the business. Existing contracts may be performed. New contracts cannot be made, except for minor contracts that are reasonably necessary for completion of existing contracts in a commercially reasonable manner. If a part of the assets of the firm are goods in process, and additional raw materials must be purchased before the goods in process can be converted into finished goods, these raw materials may be purchased.

After dissolution, a third person making a contract with the partnership stands in much the same position as a person dealing with an agent whose authority has been revoked by the principal. If the transaction relates to winding up the business, the transaction is authorized and binds the partnership and all partners just as though there had not been a dissolution. If the contract constitutes new business, it is not authorized, and the liability of the partnership and of the individual partner so acting depends upon whether notice of dissolution has been properly given.

Dissolution does not relieve the partners of their duties to each other. These duties remain until they wind up the business.

NOTICE OF DISSOLUTION

L.O.3 .... When a partnership is dissolved, the change may not become known to creditors and other third parties who have done business with the old firm. For the protection of these third parties, the law requires that when dissolution is caused by an act of the parties, third persons who have done business with the firm must be given notice of the dissolution. If notice is not given, every member of the old firm may be held liable for the acts of the former partners that are committed within the scope of the business.

A partnership usually gives notice to customers and creditors by mail. It is sufficient to give the general public notice by publication, such as in a newspaper. When a new partnership or corporation has been organized to continue the business after dissolution and termination of the original partnership, the notice of dissolution will also set forth this information as a matter of advertising. If the name of the dissolved partnership included the name of a withdrawing partner, this name should be removed from the firm name on all stationery so that the firm will no longer be liable for the contracts or torts of that person.

Notice of dissolution is usually not deemed necessary:

1   To those who were partners.
2   When the partnership was dissolved by the operation of law.
3   When the partnership was dissolved by a judicial decree.
4   When a dormant or a secret partner retired.

DISTRIBUTION OF ASSETS

After the dissolution of a partnership, the partners share in the assets remaining after payment of the debts to creditors. The distribution of the remaining assets among the partners is usually made in the following order:

1   Partners who have advanced money to the firm or have incurred liabilities in its behalf are entitled to reimbursement.
2   Each partner is next entitled to the return of the capital that was contributed to the partnership.

3 Remaining assets are distributed equally, unless a provision in the partnership contract specifies an unequal distribution.

When a firm sustains a loss, the loss will be shared equally by the partners, unless the partnership agreement provides to the contrary.

QUESTIONS

1 What is the difference between termination and dissolution of a partnership?

2 If a partnership agreement fixes the date for dissolution of the partnership, is there any way that date can be changed?

3 What liability does a withdrawing partner incur in a partnership for a definite term and in a partnership that does not have a definite term?

4 Does expulsion of a partner require dissolution of the partnership?

5 If one member of a firm becomes ill and cannot perform a share of the work, what recourse do the other partners have?

6 Explain when a court will dissolve a partnership for futility.

7 When one member of a partnership dies, what effect does this have on the partnership?

8 Discuss the effects of dissolution of a partnership.

9 Patton and Ferguson dissolved their partnership but failed to give any notice. What is their potential liability?

10 After the dissolution of a partnership, how are the assets divided?

CASE PROBLEMS

L.O.2 ....

1 Metro U.S. Construction Corporation and James Riley were partners in Metro-Riley Associates, which owned an apartment complex. There were disputes between the partners, but a settlement agreement provided that Metro would make a $125,000 loan to the partnership (the Metro Debt) due and payable in ten years. The partnership agreement was amended to add that if Metro loaned additional cash, "the amount of additional cash paid to the partnership shall be added to . . . the 'Metro Debt,' and repayment . . . shall be on the same terms and provisions." Metro loaned an additional $73,000 to the partnership. Metro was also to use all "excess depreciation" available for income tax purposes. The partners continued to disagree on the running of the business, and Metro filed suit to dissolve Metro-Riley, alleging that the $73,000 loan was payable on demand, that Metro-Riley did not have the cash to repay the loan, and that the partners could not agree on how to get the money to repay it; therefore, the business should be operated only at a loss and should be dissolved. Should it?

L.O.2 ....

2 A partnership, the Lebanon Trotting Association, was to conduct the business of harness horse racing. The partnership agreement provided Lebanon should last for 20 years. The principal asset of Lebanon was a lease of a racetrack at the Warren County Fairgrounds, which lease extended beyond the term of the partnership. After the expiration of the 20 years, Lebanon brought suit regarding the dissolution of the partnership. It was alleged that the fact that

Lebanon entered into a lease that extended beyond the term of the partnership indicated an intention to continue it. Did it?

L.O.2 ....   **3** Chester S. and Margaret McDonald, husband and wife, operated a partnership with their four sons, Ronald, James, Chester R., and Robert. The parents were each to receive one-third of the profits, and each of the sons one-twelfth. The wills of the parents bequeathed their property equally among their four sons and two daughters. The father died, and Margaret, as executor, agreed with the sons that the father's estate would receive none of the partnership profits. Ronald later became the executor of the father's and Margaret's estates. The sons agreed the father's estate would continue to receive none of the profits, and Margaret's estate would receive one-fifth. The daughters received no profits of the business through the father's estate and one-sixth of one-fifth through Margaret's. In an action to dissolve the partnership, the daughters claim the executor is required to secure for the estate either interest on a deceased partner's share of ownership of the partnership or profits attributable to the continued use of that share. What, if anything, are the estates of the parents entitled to during winding up?

L.O.3 ....   **4** While George and Alice Long operated a partnership, Long's Auto Sound, Jensen Sound Laboratories extended credit to it. About six months later, the Longs incorporated their partnership as Long's Sound Systems, Inc. They continued to do business with Jensen for two years. The only notice Jensen had of the incorporation were corporate checks received to pay bills. These showed the name change. The corporation was dissolved owing Jensen money. It sued the Longs claiming they had personal liability because they did not adequately notify it of the incorporation. Should the court find the Longs personally liable?

L.O.1, 2 ....   **5** Charles Fowler, Marion Smith, Robert Wiggins Sr., and Robert Wiggins Jr., formed a partnership named J.D.M. Productions and Delta Sound Studio. The partnership borrowed $25,000 from Peoples Bank of Indianola, and all the partners signed a note as partners and individuals. In addition, Bobby Chrestman and Doris Smith, Marion's wife, signed the note. Fowler went bankrupt, and the partnership failed to pay the note, which the bank assigned to Smith & Hitt Construction Co. Smith & Hitt sued J.D.M. and those who signed the note. What is the significance of Fowler's bankruptcy?

L.O.3 ....   **6** Emil Heimos and Milton Lawrence had a partnership, H & G Equipment Co. Heimos and his wife signed a guaranty for any current or future debts of H & G to Lemay Bank. Heimos and Lawrence later dissolved the partnership. Two years later H & G executed a series of four notes renewing a $22,000 debt owed Lemay. All the notes contained the signatures of both Lawrence and Heimos, but only Lawrence signed them at Lemay. Lawrence would take each note to obtain Heimos' signature. When Lawrence returned, the notes bore what appeared to be Heimos' signature. However, those signatures were forged. Lawrence went bankrupt, so Lemay sued the Heimoses. They claimed they had no liability because of the dissolution of the partnership. Decide the case.

L.O.1 .... **7** Leland McElmurry was a partner in MHS Enterprises. MHS owed Commonwealth Capital Investment Corporation $1,000,000. It sued McElmurry as a partner in MHS. McElmurry contended that since MHS was dissolved before Commonwealth filed suit, a judgment could not be rendered against MHS. Thus, McElmurry could not be liable as a partner when no judgment could be rendered against the partnership. Does dissolution relieve McElmurry of all liability for MHS' debts?

Chapter 35

NATURE OF A CORPORATION

LEARNING OBJECTIVES

After studying this chapter you should be able to:

1 List the different classifications and kinds of corporations.

2 Discuss how a corporation is formed and potential promoter liability.

3 Name the types of powers a corporation has and the significance of ultra vires contracts.

Preview Case

Richard Bielinski and Richard Miller prepared a written agreement for a corporation they were organizing. At a meeting of incorporators it was voted that the capital stock of the corporation would be 500 shares and that 100 shares each to Bielinski and Miller were to be issued for $1,000 cash. The corporation was formed, but at a board meeting Bielinski resigned from the board and presidency because of illness. Pursuant to a law allowing a shareholder in a closely held corporation to seek judicial relief, Bielinski later filed suit to again have a say in running the corporation. Did Bielinski have a right to file the suit?

Corporations have become a widely used form of business organization. No matter what the size of a business, a corporation may be formed to run it. Because of the variety of uses to which corporations may be put, there are different types of corporations. They are also classified by the state of incorporation because, as an entity of the state, they are governed by the laws of the state of incorporation.

CLASSIFICATION BY PURPOSE

Corporations may be classified according to their purpose or function as public or private.

L.O.1 ....

Public Corporations

Public Corporation
One formed for governmental function

A **public corporation** is one formed to carry out some governmental function. Examples of public corporations include a city, a state university, and a public hospital. The powers and functions of public corporations may be much greater than those of private corporations conducted for profit. Public corporations may, for example, have the power to levy taxes, impose fines, and condemn property. Public corporations are created by the state primarily for the purpose of facilitating the administration of governmental functions.

Quasi Public Corporation
Public body with powers similar to corporations

Some public bodies, such as school boards, boards of county commissioners, and similar bodies, are not true public corporations but have many similar powers. Such powers include the right to sue and be sued; the power to own, buy, and sell property; and the power to sign other contracts as an entity. These bodies are called **quasi public corporations,** *quasi* meaning "as if" or "in the nature of."

Private Corporations

Private Corporation
One formed to do nongovernmental function

Private corporations are those formed by private individuals to perform some nongovernmental function. They in turn include:

1 Not-for-profit corporations
2 Profit corporations

Not-for-Profit Corporation
One formed by private individuals for charitable, educational, religious, social, or fraternal purpose

Not-for-Profit Corporations. A **not-for-profit corporation** is one formed by private individuals for some charitable, educational, religious, social, or fraternal purpose. This corporation is not organized for profit, and it does not issue stock. As a legal entity like any other corporation, it can sue and be sued as a corporation, can buy and sell property, and otherwise operate as any other corporation. A person acquires membership in a not-for-profit corporation by agreement between the charter members in the beginning and between the present members and new members thereafter.

Profit Corporation
One organized to run a business and earn money

Profit Corporations. A **profit corporation** is one organized to run a business and earn money. In terms of number and importance, stock corporations organized for profit constitute the chief type. Certificates called shares of stock represent ownership in a **stock corporation.** The number of shares of stock owned and the charter and the bylaws of the corporation determine the extent of one's rights and liabilities.

Stock Corporation
One in which ownership is represented by stock

A profit corporation that has a very small number of people who own stock in it is called a **close corporation** or a **closely held corporation.** Because of the small number of stockholders, they normally expect to be and are active in the management of the business.

Close or Closely Held Corporation
One with very small number of shareholders

Many close corporations choose to be designated Subchapter S corporations for federal income tax purposes. Unlike other corporations, a Subchapter S corporation files only an information tax return. It does not pay corporate income tax. The owners report the profit of the corporation as income on their personal income tax returns. This results in a tax savings. The corporation's profits are not taxed twice—once when shown on a corporate tax return and second when shown as income from the corporation to the owners on their personal tax returns.

CLASSIFICATION BY STATE OF INCORPORATION

Domestic Corporation
One chartered in the state

Corporations may be classified depending on where they were incorporated. A corporation is a **domestic corporation** in the state where it received its initial charter; it is a **foreign corporation** in all other states. If incorporated in another country, a corporation may be referred to as an **alien corporation.** The corporation can operate as a foreign corporation in any other state it chooses as long as it complies with the registration or other requirements of the other states.

FORMATION OF A CORPORATION

L.O.2

Foreign Corporation
One chartered in another state

Alien Corporation
One chartered in another country

Promoter
One who takes initial steps to form corporation

The initial steps of forming a corporation are usually taken by one who acts as the **promoter.** A corporation can be organized in any state the promoter chooses. A lot of preliminary work must be done before the corporation comes into existence. The incorporation papers must be prepared, a registration statement may need to be drawn up and filed with the Securities and Exchange Commission (SEC) and the appropriate state officials, the stock must be sold, and many contracts entered into for the benefit of the proposed corporation. Filing with the SEC is not required in the case of smaller corporations.

Minor defects in the formation of a corporation may generally be ignored. In some instances the defect is of a sufficiently serious character that the attorney general of the state that approved the articles of incorporation of the corporation may obtain the cancellation or revocation of such articles. In other cases, the formation of the corporation is so defective that the existence of a corporation is ignored, and the persons organizing the corporation are held liable as partners or joint venturers.

LIABILITY ON PROMOTER'S CONTRACTS AND EXPENSES

The corporation does not automatically become a party to contracts made by the promoter. After the corporation is organized, it will ordinarily approve or adopt the contracts made by the promoter. The approval may be either express or by the corporation's conduct. Once approved, such contracts bind the corporation, and it may sue thereon.

The promoter may avoid personal liability on contracts made for the benefit of the corporation by including a provision in the contract that the promoter incurs no personal liability if the corporation does or does not adopt the contract. In the absence of such a provision, the promoter may have liability. The wording of the contract determines whether it binds the promoter either pending the formation of the corporation or after it has come into existence.

Clinton Investors Company owned property it leased for three years to The Clifton Park Learning Center, Inc. Berne Watkins executed the lease on behalf of Clifton Park and represented himself as its treasurer. The state did not issue a certificate of incorporation for Clifton Park until eight months later. A year later Clifton Park had failed to pay all the rent due. Clinton sued Watkins. The court found that because no corporation existed when Watkins executed the lease on behalf of Clifton Park, he signed as a promoter. Since the parties did not agree that Watkins should not be bound by the contract, the court held him liable on it.

Along with the adoption of the promoter's contracts, the corporation may or may not pay the expenses of the promoter in organization of the corporation. After the corporation comes into existence, the corporation customarily reimburses the promoter for all necessary expenses in forming the corporation. This may be done by a resolution passed by the board of directors.

ISSUANCE OF STOCK

Subscriber

One who agrees to buy stock in proposed corporation

When a new corporation is about to be formed, agreements to buy its stock will generally be made in advance of actual incorporation. In such a case the purchase agreement or subscription to stock by a prospective stockholder or investor, called a **subscriber,** constitutes merely an offer to buy. In most jurisdictions this offer may be revoked anytime prior to acceptance. As the offeree, the corporation cannot accept the subscription until the state issues the charter. If an existing corporation sells stock, it can accept all subscriptions immediately and make them binding contracts. If the promoter is to be paid by means of a stock option, the corporation can make such a contract with the promoter before any services are performed. Most state laws provide that a minimum amount of stock must be sold and paid for before the corporation can begin operations.

Once a valid subscription agreement is signed, the subscriber has rights in the corporation even if the stock certificates have not been received or issued.

Richard Bielinski and Richard Miller prepared a written agreement for a corporation they were organizing. At a meeting of incorporators it was voted that the capital stock of the corporation would be 500 shares and that 100 shares each to Bielinski and Miller were to be issued for $1,000 cash. The corporation was formed, but at a board meeting Bielinski resigned from the board and presidency because of illness. Pursuant to a law allowing a shareholder in a closely held corpora-tion to seek judicial relief, Bielinski later filed suit to again have a say in running the corporation. The court found he was eligible to file suit because he was a subscriber to 50 percent of the stock. When he and Miller agreed to take and pay for 100 shares of stock, they clearly expressed an intention to become sub-scribers. This subscription offer was impliedly accepted by the corporation. A valid subscription gives a subscriber the rights of a stockholder.

ARTICLES OF INCORPORATION

Articles of Incorporation

Document stating facts about corporation required by law

Incorporators

People initially forming a corporation

The written document setting forth the facts prescribed by law for issuance of a certificate of incorporation or a charter and asserting that the corporation has complied with legal requirements is the **articles of incorporation.** Once approved by the state, the articles determine the authority of the corporation. This document constitutes a contract between the corporation and the state. So long as the corporation complies with the terms of the contract, the state cannot alter the articles in any material way without obtaining the consent of the stockholders. The articles include such information as the name of the corporation, the names of the people forming the corporation (the **incorporators**), and the amount and types of stock the corporation has authorization to issue. The incorporators elect a board of directors and begin business which constitutes acceptance of the charter and binds all parties.

POWERS OF A CORPORATION

L.O.3 .... A corporation has three types of powers: express, incidental, and implied.

Express Powers

The statute or code under which the corporation is formed and to a lesser degree the corporation's articles determine its express powers. In a few instances, the state constitution sets forth the powers of a corporation. The statutes limit a corporation's powers to what they grant, and a corporation may not do what statutes prohibit.

Incidental Powers

Certain powers always incidental to a corporation's express powers or essential to its existence as a corporation include:

1 To have a corporate name.
2 To have a continuous existence.
3 To have property rights.
4 To make bylaws and regulations.
5 To engage in legal actions.
6 To have a corporate seal.

Corporate Name. A corporation must have a corporate name. The members may select any name they wish, provided it does not violate the statutes or another firm or corporation within the state does not use it. Many of the states have statutes regulating corporate names. For example, statutes may require the name to end with "Corporation" or to be followed by the word "Incorporated," an abbreviation thereof, or other indication of corporate status.

Continuous Existence. The existence of the corporation continues for the period for which the state grants the charter. This feature of a corporation makes this form of organization valuable. The death of a stockholder does not dissolve the organization. Sometimes people refer to this characteristic as perpetual, or continuous, succession.

Property Rights. A corporation has the right to buy, sell, and hold property necessary in its functioning as a corporation and not foreign to its purpose.

Bylaws and Regulations. The organization needs rules and regulations to govern it and to determine its future conduct. They must conform to the statutes and must not be contrary to public policy. The corporation's board of directors adopt these rules, called the corporation **bylaws.**

Bylaws

Rules enacted by directors to govern corporation's conduct

Legal Actions. Long considered incidental to corporate existence is the corporation's power to sue in its own name. Since a corporation may be composed of hundreds or thousands of stockholders, it would be a cumbersome, if not impossible, task to secure the consent of all the stockholders each time a suit needed to be brought by a corporation. A corporation may likewise be sued in the corporate name.

Corporate Seal. A corporation has the incidental power to have and to own a seal. Normally a corporation need not use a seal except (1) in executing written instruments that require the use of a seal when executed by natural individuals, or (2) in carrying out transactions where special statutory requirements require the use of the seal.

Implied Powers

In addition to incidental or express powers conferred upon all corporations, a corporation has the implied power to do all acts reasonably necessary for carrying out the purpose for which the corporation was formed. A corporation may borrow money and contract debts if such acts are necessary for the transaction of the corporate business. It may make, indorse, and accept negotiable instruments. It has the power to acquire and convey property and to mortgage or lease its property in case such transactions are necessary for carrying on its business. Corporation codes as a rule expressly list the various implied powers described above so that they constitute express powers.

ULTRA VIRES CONTRACTS

Ultra Vires Contract

Contract exceeding corporation's powers

Any contract entered into by a corporation that goes beyond its powers is called an **ultra vires contract.** As between the parties to the contract, the corporation and the third person, the contract generally binds them. However, a stockholder may bring an action to prevent the corporation from entering into such a contract or to recover damages from the directors or officers who have caused loss to the corporation by such contracts. In extreme cases, the attorney general of a state may obtain a court order revoking the articles of incorporation of the corporation for frequent or serious improper acts that make it proper to impose such an extreme penalty.

Billy Mansell organized J.F.K. Carwash, Inc. He sold a one-third interest in it to Charles James and to David Grubbs. James later wanted to get out of the business, so the three agreed to have the corporation repurchase James' stock. The corporation executed a note for the repurchase, which note Mansell and Grubbs guaranteed. On the day of the execution, the corporation had a deficit and no unrestricted earned surplus, so the repurchase violated state law. When the corporation failed to make the note payments, James sued J.F.K., Mansell, and Grubbs. They contended the note was void since it was ultra vires. The court stated the note was not void and held it binding between the corporation and James.

QUESTIONS

1   What is the difference between a public and a private corporation?

2   How does a person acquire membership in a corporation that does not issue stock?

3   Why are stock corporations significant?

4   How is a corporation formed, and for what is the promoter potentially personally liable?

5   What is the importance of a corporation's articles of incorporation?

6   What are the limitations imposed on a corporation in selecting a corporate name?

7   What are a corporation's implied powers?

8   What action may the state take if a corporation engages in an ultra vires act?

CASE PROBLEMS

L.O.2

1   Douglas McLeod, Lauren McLeod, and Allan Jones met with Edward Hamilton, the president of Peter Glenn Shops, Inc., and agreed that a corporation named Fashion Sports, Inc., would be formed, with the McLeods and Jones each owning 50 percent of the stock. Fashion Sports was to operate a ski shop. Glenn was to order and supply the company's inventory. The shop began operation, but Fashion Sports was never incorporated. Jones and the McLeods signed a note and Jones signed a renewal note for $30,000, which was used to pay for inventory from Glenn. Jones and the McLeods were supposed to invest $10,000 each but never did. Hamilton became concerned, and a new agreement was reached that Hamilton would invest $5,000, Jones $5,000, and the McLeods $10,000. This was never done because credit from Glenn was cut off, and the shop was closed. In a suit on the $30,000 note, Jones alleged Hamilton or Glenn, as promoters of Fashion Sports, should be liable for debts of the business. Should they?

L.O.3

2   The Country Club of Tyler, a corporation, owned a large tract of land with a lake. It permitted its members, after obtaining permission from the board of directors, to build boat houses or cottages on the land. Because the members did not have title to the land, they could not easily sell their improvements. At a stockholders meeting, the stockholders authorized the club to convey the title to all sites then occupied by stockholders to the respective stockholders. Some sites had significantly grater value than others. The minority stockholders who had improvements on the less valuable sites sued to prevent the conveyances. They alleged the conveyances would benefit individual stockholders personally and not the corporation and therefore were ultra vires. Discuss whether they would be ultra vires and whether the plaintiffs have standing to sue.

L.O.2

3   Roy Lathan signed a contract on behalf of Royal Development and Management Corp. with Guardian 50/50 Fund V Ltd. By the contract, Guardian agreed to sell Royal 23 lots on a closing date set by North Carolina National Bank (NCNB). NCNB set the date, but Guardian had not removed construction debris as required, so Royal refused to close. Guardian sued Royal and Lathan for breach of contract. Lathan contended he should not be personally liable because he did not know when he signed the contract that Royal had not been incorporated. Lathan signed the articles of incorporation three days after executing the contract. Should Lathan have personal liability on the contract?

L.O.3 ....

4 L & S Boat Company, Inc., and Hydroswift requested a financing arrangement by which Hydroswift would sell boats to L & S, which would assign trust receipts to Westinghouse Credit, which would then advance money to Hydroswift. L & S was to keep boats in the showroom as security for payment, and when they were sold Westinghouse was to be paid. Westinghouse said it would not agree unless Hydroswift would, in writing, be a guaranty of the L & S account. A guaranty, signed by the president of Hydroswift, was delivered to Westinghouse, and on the basis of it business was carried on. L & S went bankrupt and Westinghouse sued Hydroswift. Hydroswift alleged the guaranty was invalid because it was not authorized by its board of directors, thus ultra vires. Was it binding?

L.O.2 ....

5 William Putnam approached Robert Williams about starting a franchise of a soccer league. Williams orally agreed to put up $75,000 "seed money" in return for 50 percent of the stock of a future corporation, Georgia Soccer, Inc. Neither the franchise nor Georgia Soccer, Inc., materialized, and Williams' only investment amounted to an advance of $2,500. Putnam sued Williams alleging breach of a stock subscription agreement. Does Williams have any liability on this agreement?

L.O.2 ....

6 Bill Weiss orally agreed to give Clifford Anderson temporary possession of a lot and building in exchange for monthly rental payments. For two years Anderson sent checks payable to and accepted by Weiss. These checks constituted rental payments while Anderson was in possession. The first two checks were drawn on Capital Rentals & Import Repair and subsequent ones on Import Repair Self Service, Inc. Anderson's business, Import Repair & Body Shop, Inc., was not incorporated until five months after the lease began. Weiss alleged Anderson had not paid enough rent and sued him. Anderson alleged Import Repair Self Services, Inc., not he personally, should be liable for any rent due. Is Anderson liable?

L.O.3 ....

7 The state Blue Cross and Blue Shield corporation requested approval from the commissioner of insurance to buy a life insurance company, United Trust Life Insurance Company. Several competing insurance companies opposed the purchase. The single purpose for which Blue Cross was organized was to establish, maintain, and operate "a health-care service plan" for subscribers. Is the selling of life insurance beyond the powers of Blue Cross?

L.O.3 ....

8 Perry Doyle had been in business under the name Doyle Plumbing Company for many years. Vincent J. Doyle organized a corporation named V. J. Doyle Plumbing Company, Inc. As the corporation's business grew, so did confusion caused by the similarity of names. It interfered with communications between the parties and the public. Perry Doyle asked a court to order V. J. Doyle Plumbing Company, Inc., not to use the name Doyle and the words *Plumbing* and *Company* in its corporate name and advertising. Should the corporation be prevented from using its corporate name?

L.O.2 ....

9 Under an agreement with Indian Head Tennis Club, Inc., Steward Becker, Ltd., purchased 25 percent of the corporate stock for $150,000, with $75,000 to be paid in monthly installments. The shares were to be held in escrow until full payment was made. The agreement gave Becker voting rights and the right to dividends from the shares. Becker sued for dissolution of the corporation, stating the shareholders were so divided that votes required for action by the board of directors could not be secured. The law under which it sued allowed the holders of stock to request dissolution. Should Becker be allowed to maintain the action?

Chapter 36

OWNERSHIP OF A CORPORATION

LEARNING OBJECTIVES

After studying this chapter you should be able to:

1 Define capital stock.

2 Explain what dividends are and how they may be paid.

3 List the various types of stock and stock rights.

4 Name the various laws regulating the sale of securities, exchanges, and brokers.

Preview Case

James Junker owned stock in Reco Investment Corporation. At a stockholders' meeting, Frederick Heisler, the attorney for Reco and the Road Equipment Company, Inc., suggested that since Reco could not pay a debt it owed to Road, the solution was to merge Reco into another company such as Road. The merger passed. The merger formula for exchanging Reco stock for Road stock used book values despite the fact Reco's property was located in an area where real estate values and the cost of building had greatly increased. Two months after the merger, Junker was notified that Road's annual report would show a loss. This had not been mentioned at the stockholders' meeting. Junker sued, alleging violation of the federal Securities Act. This Act establishes a cause of action for a purchaser of securities against a person who sold the securities by means of oral communication that includes an untrue statement of material fact or omits a material fact required to render the statements not misleading. Did Heisler violate the Act?

L.O.1

Capital Stock
Declared value of outstanding stock

Share
Unit of stock

The **capital stock** of the corporation is the declared money value of its outstanding stock. The owners subscribe and pay for this stock. Generally, not all the stock a corporation may issue need be subscribed and paid for before the corporation begins operation. The amount of capital stock authorized in the charter cannot be altered without the consent of the state and a majority of the stockholders. The capital stock is divided into units called **shares.**

General Export Iron and Metal Company of Louisiana authorized the issuance to Sam Goltzman of 12 shares of stock. Sam paid for the stock, and General issued and delivered certificate number 004 for 12 shares in Sam's name. Ronald Goltzman, the president, and Grace Kennedy, the secretary-treasurer, had not signed the certificate. Sam endorsed the certificate and transferred the 12 shares to Ronald, his son. Sam delivered the certificate to Ronald who signed it as president and had Kennedy sign it. Sam later filed suit to compel General to issue 12 shares of stock. He alleged that the defectiveness of the first certificate meant he had not owned the 12 shares and could not have transferred them to Ronald. The court held that the certificate was not the actual shares of stock. It was simply evidence of ownership of stock. Sam owned 12 shares when he endorsed and transferred the certificate to Ronald.

OWNERSHIP

Shareholder or Stockholder

Person who owns stock

A person achieves ownership in a stock corporation by acquiring title to one or more shares of stock. Owners are known as **shareholders** or **stockholders.** A person may obtain shares of stock by subscription either before or after organization of the corporation, or shares may be obtained in other ways, such as by gift or purchase from another shareholder.

DIVIDENDS

L.O.2 ....

Dividends

Profits distributed to owners

The profits of a corporation belong to the corporation until the directors set them aside for distribution by declaring a **dividend.** Dividends may be paid in cash, stock, or other property.

A cash dividend usually can be paid only out of retained earnings with two exceptions. A cash dividend may be paid out of donated or paid-in surplus. Also, for corporations with depleting assets, such as coal mines, oil companies, lumber companies, and similar industries, cash dividends may be paid out of capital.

Stock dividends may be in the corporation's own stock or in stock the corporation owns in another corporation. When in the corporation's own stock, they are usually declared out of retained earnings, but they can be paid out of other surplus accounts. A stock dividend of the corporation's own stock cannot be declared if the corporation has no surplus of any kind. Dividends also may be paid in the form of property that the corporation manufactures, but this seldom happens.

The declaration of a dividend on either common or preferred stock depends almost entirely upon the discretion of the directors. The directors, however, must act reasonably and in good faith. This means minority stockholders can ask the court to require a corporation to declare a dividend out of surplus profits only when they clearly have a right to a dividend.

Once the directors declare a cash dividend, it cannot later be rescinded. It becomes a liability of the corporation the minute the directors declare it. A stock dividend, on the other hand, may be rescinded at any time prior to the issuance and delivery of the stock.

STOCK CERTIFICATE

The amount of ownership (the number of shares owned) is evidenced by a stock certificate. It is not the actual stock, just written evidence of ownership of stock.

The certificate shows on its face the number of shares represented, the par value of each share if the stock has a par value, and the signatures of the officers.

CLASSES OF STOCK

Stock is divided into many classes. The laws under which the corporation is organized and the articles of incorporation determine the classes. The two principal classes of stock are:

1 Common stock
2 Preferred stock

Common Stock

L.O.3 ....

Common Stock

Stock that entitles owner to vote

Common stock is the simplest form of stock and the normal type of stock issued. The owners of common stock control the corporation because they may vote for members of the board of directors. The board in turn hires the individuals who manage and operate the corporation. Unless selected as a director or appointed as an officer, a stockholder has no voice in the running of the corporation beyond the annual vote for the board of directors.

Common stockholders have the right to a share of the assets of a corporation upon dissolution.

Preferred Stock

Preferred Stock

Stock giving special advantage

Preferred stock differs from common stock in that the holder of this stock has some sort of special advantage or preference. In return for a preference, the preferred stockholders usually give up two rights common stockholders retain—the right to vote in stockholders' meetings and the right to participate in profits beyond the percentage fixed in the stock certificate.

The preference granted may pertain to the division of dividends, to the division of assets upon dissolution, or to both of these. Most often, the preference relates both to dividends and assets. Calling particular stock preferred does not tell what preference the holder has. The stock certificate will indicate the type of preference, although the certificate of incorporation governs the exact rights of preferred shareholders. Preferred stock may be preferred as to assets, preferred as to dividends, participating, or nonparticipating.

Rothschild International Corp. owned 7 percent cumulative preferred stock in Liggett Group, Inc. Rothschild sued on behalf of all such stockholders challenging a tender offer and merger that eliminated the 7 percent cumulative preferred at a price of $70 per share instead of the $100 per share liquidation preference provided in Liggett's certificate of incorporation. Rothschild argued that the tender offer and merger essentially liquidated the company, entitling the 7 percent preferred stockholders to the $100 liquidation value. The court said the express provisions of the certificate of incorporation governed preferred rights since they were contractual. Since the certificate provided the $100 liquidation preference only upon "any liquidation of the assets of the Corporation," and the merger did not liquidate Liggett's assets, the $100 did not have to be paid.

Preferred as to Assets. Stock preferred as to assets gives the holder an advantage only in the event of liquidation. Preferred stockholders receive their proportionate share of the corporation's assets prior to any share going to common shareholders.

Preferred as to Dividends. Stock preferred as to dividends means the preferred stockholders receive a dividend before any common stockholders do. Preferred stock usually states the percentage it receives. Once this percentage has been paid to preferred stockholders, any money remaining may be paid as a dividend to holders of common stock. This right to preference as to dividends may be cumulative or noncumulative.

Cumulative Preferred Stock
Stock on which all dividends must be paid before common dividends

Noncumulative Preferred Stock
Stock on which current dividends must be paid before common dividends

Cumulative preferred stock is preferred stock on which all dividends must be paid before the common stock receives any dividend. These dividends on cumulative preferred stock must be paid even for years in which the corporation did not earn an adequate profit to pay the stated dividend.

Noncumulative preferred stock is preferred stock on which dividends have to be paid only for the current year before common stock dividends are paid. Thus, dividends do not have to be paid for years the corporation does not make a profit or even for years in which the directors simply do not declare a dividend.

The difference between cumulative and noncumulative preferred stock can be significant if the corporation operates at a loss in any given year or group of years. For example, a corporation that has $1 million outstanding common stock and $1 million outstanding 7-percent preferred stock operates at a loss for two years and then earns 21-percent net profit the third year. Noncumulative preferred stock would be entitled to only one dividend of 7 percent. The common stock is entitled to the remaining 14 percent. Cumulative preferred stock would be entitled to three preferences of 7 percent, or 21 percent in all, before the common stock is entitled to any dividend. If the company earned a net profit each year equal to only 7 percent on the preferred stock, the directors could, if the preferred stock was noncumulative, pass the dividend the first year and declare a 7-percent dividend on both the common and the preferred stocks for the second year. Since the common stockholders elect the directors, the common stockholders could easily elect directors who would act in ways to help them as much as possible. For that reason, the law provides that preferred stock be cumulative unless specifically stated to be noncumulative. All this can occur, however, only when the corporation earns a profit but fails to declare a dividend. Unless the stock certificate expressly states that it is cumulative, the preference does not cumulate in the years during which the corporation operated at a loss.

Participating Preferred Stock
Stock that shares with common stock in extra dividends

Nonparticipating Preferred Stock
Stock on which maximum dividend is stated percentage

Shareholders with participating preferred stock are entitled to share equally with the common shareholders in any further distribution of dividends made after the common shareholders have received dividends equal to those that the preferred shareholders have received by virtue of their stated preference. Thus, 7-percent participating preferred stock may pay considerably more than 7 percent annually. If the preferred stock is to participate, this right must be expressly stated on the stock certificate and in the articles of incorporation. It can participate only according to the terms of the articles of incorporation. The articles may provide that the preferred stock shall participate equally with the common stock. On the other hand the articles may provide, for example, that the preferred stock is entitled to an additional 1 percent for each additional 5 percent the common stock receives.

Nonparticipating preferred stock is stock on which the maximum dividend is the percentage stated on the stock. If it is 7-percent nonparticipating preferred, for example, 7 percent annually would be the maximum to which the preferred stockholders would be entitled no matter how much the corporation earned. The law presumes stock is nonparticipating in the absence of a provision to the contrary in the articles of incorporation.

KINDS OF STOCK

In addition to the fact of two *classes* of stock, stock comes in several different *kinds*. These include par-value stock, no-par-value stock, treasury stock, and watered stock.

Par-Value Stock

Par-Value Stock
Stock with assigned face value

Stock to which a face value, such as $25, $50, or $100, has been assigned and that has this value printed on the stock is **par-value stock.** Preferred stock usually has a par value. The law requires that when a corporation issues par-value stock in return for payment in money, property, or services, the par value of the stock must be equal in value to the money, property, or services. This relates only to the price at which the corporation may issue the stock to an original subscriber. It has no effect upon the price paid as between a shareholder and a buyer thereafter. The price a buyer pays a shareholder ordinarily equals the market price, which may be more or less than the par value. If a corporation sells par-value stock at a discount, the purchaser incurs liability to subsequent creditors of the corporation for the discount.

No-Par-Value Stock

No-Par-Value Stock
Stock without face value

Stock to which no face value has been assigned is **no-par-value stock.** A corporation may issue no-par-value stock at any price, although some states do set a minimum price, such as $5, for which it can be issued. Common stock may be either par-value or no-par-value stock.

Treasury Stock

Treasury Stock
Stock reacquired by a corporation

If a corporation purchases stock that it has sold, this reacquired stock is referred to as **treasury stock.** When a corporation first offers stock for sale, less sales resistance may be encountered if the prospective purchaser can be assured that the corporation will repurchase the stock upon request. Treasury stock may also be reacquired by gift. The reacquired stock may be sold at any price fixed by the directors. Until the corporation resells it, no dividends can be paid on it nor can it be voted.

Ampco-Pittsburgh Corp. attempted to buy all Buffalo Forge Company stock at $25 a share. Buffalo resisted the acquisition and contracted to merge with Ogden Corporation. By the contract, Ogden bought 425,000 shares of Buffalo treasury stock for $32.75. Ogden also obtained an option to buy 143,400 more treasury shares. A bidding war between Ampco and Ogden ended with Ampco offering $37.50 per share. Ogden tendered its 425,000 shares of Buffalo stock, but Ampco refused to buy them. Ampco also refused to allow Ogden to exercise its option to buy the additional 143,400 treasury shares. Ampco sued for recission of the treasury stock sale and option claiming Buffalo's directors had breached their duty by selling the trea- sury stock at too low a price. The court held that Buffalo could sell the treasury shares at any price it wanted.

Watered Stock

Watered Stock

Stock paid for with property of inflated value

Stock issued as fully paid up, but paid with property of inflated values, is said to be **watered stock.** If someone conveys real estate actually worth $40,000 for stock having a par value of $100,000, the stock is watered to the extent of $60,000. Watering stock may be prohibited outright, but in any case it cannot be used to defraud creditors. In the event of insolvency, the creditors may sue the original recipients of watered stock for the difference between the par value and the actual purchase price. This may not be true, of course, if the creditors knew the stock was watered. Although creditors are allowed these rights, most state statutes do not prohibit the watering of stock by corporations other than public utility companies.

If a person pays for stock with overvalued real estate, the extent of the watering can be determined with reasonable accuracy. If a person pays in the form of patents, trademarks, blueprints, or other similar assets, the extent of the watering may be difficult to determine.

TRANSFER OF STOCK

A stock certificate indicates the manner in which the stock may be transferred to another party. The owner may use a blank form on the back of the certificate in making a transfer. The signature of the previous owner gives the new holder full possession and the right to exchange the certificate for another made out by the corporation to the new owner. Whenever an owner transfers stock, the new owner should have the certificate exchanged for a new one showing the correct name so that the corporation's books will show the correct stockholders' names. Stockholders not registered do not have to the rights and privileges of a stockholder and will not receive any declared dividends.

Under the Uniform Stock Transfer Act, the unregistered holder of stock has a right to the distribution that represents a return of capital. As under common law, the unregistered holder has no right to any distribution that represents a share of the profits.

STOCK OPTIONS

Stock Option

Right to purchase shares at set price

A **stock option** is a contract entered into between a corporation and an individual. The contract gives the individual the option for a stated period of time to purchase a prescribed number of shares of stock in the corporation at a given price. If a new corporation sells stock to the public at $2 a share, the individual having the option must also pay $2 but may be given two, five, or even ten years in which to exercise the option. If the corporation succeeds, and the price of the stock goes up, the individual will of course want to exercise the option and buy at the low option price and then resell at the higher market price. If the corporation fails, the option does not have to be exercised. Existing corporations may give officials of the corporation an option to purchase a given number of shares of stock in lieu of a salary increase. If the market price of the stock rises, an official may make a capital gain by buying the stock, holding it the required time, and selling it. The income tax on a capital gain may be considerably less than that on other income. This type of compensation may be more attractive to top management officials than a straight increase in salary, enabling a corporation to retain their services at a lower cost than with a salary increase. If the corporation makes stock available to all the corporation's employees, the option price may be less than the fair market value.

LAWS REGULATING STOCK SALES

In order to protect investors in corporations, a number of laws have been enacted. These laws seek to prevent fraudulent activities and protect investors from loss as a result of stockbrokers becoming insolvent.

Blue-Sky Laws

L.O.4 ....

Blue-Sky Laws
State laws to prevent sale of worthless stock

The purpose of so-called **blue-sky laws** is to prevent fraud through the sale of worthless stocks and bonds. State blue-sky laws apply only to intrastate transactions.

These security laws vary from state to state. Some prescribe criminal penalties for engaging in prohibited transactions. Others require that dealers be licensed and that a state commission approve sales of securities before a corporation offers them to the public.

Securities Act, 1933

Prospectus
Document giving speci-
fied information about a
corporation

Because the state blue-sky laws apply only to intrastate sales of securities, in 1933 the Congress passed the federal Securities Act to regulate the sale of securities in interstate commerce. Any corporation offering a new issue of securities for sale to the public must register it with the SEC and issue a **prospectus** containing specified information. This Act does not apply to the issuance of securities under $5 million nor does the act regulate the sale or purchase of securities after they have been issued by the corporation.

In addition to filing the registration statement with the SEC, a corporation must furnish a prospectus to each purchaser of the securities. Full information must be given relative to the financial structure of the corporation. This information must include the types of stock to be issued; types of securities outstanding, if any; the terms of the sale; bonus and profit-sharing arrangements; options to be created in regard to the securities; and any other data the SEC may require.

James Junker owned stock in Reco Investment Corporation. At a stockholders' meeting, Frederick Heisler, the attorney for Reco and the Road Equipment Company, Inc., suggested that since Reco could not pay a debt it owed to Road, the solution was to merge Reco into another company such as Road. The merger passed. The merger formula for exchanging Reco stock for Road stock used book value despite the fact Reco's property was located in an area where real estate values and the cost of building had greatly increased. Two months after the merger Junker was notified that Road's annual report would show a loss. This had not been mentioned at the stockholders' meeting. Junker sued, alleging violation of the federal Securities Act. This Act establishes a cause of action for a purchaser of securities against a person who sold the securities by means of oral communication that includes an untrue statement of material fact or omits a material fact required to render the statements not misleading. The court held that the exchange of Reco stock for Road stock by the merger made Junker a purchaser; Heisler's participation in the sales transaction was a substantial factor in causing the transaction to take place, so he was a seller, and he did violate the Act.

The registration statement must be signed by the company, its principal officers, and a majority of the board of directors. If either the registration statement or the prospectus contains misstatements or omissions, the SEC will not permit the corporation to offer the securities for sale. If the corporation sells them before the SEC ascertains the falsity of the information, an investor may rescind the contract and sue for damages any individual who signed the registration statement. Any failure to comply with the law also subjects the responsible corporate officials to criminal prosecution.

Securities Exchange Act, 1934

The security exchanges and over-the-counter markets constitute the chief markets for the sale of securities after the initial offerings. In 1934 Congress passed the Securities Exchange Act to regulate such transactions. The Act requires the registration of stock exchanges, brokers, and dealers of securities traded in interstate commerce and SEC-regulated, publicly held corporations. The law also requires regulated corporations to make periodic disclosure statements regarding corporate organization and financial structure.

Under rule-making authority of the Securities Exchange Act, the SEC has declared it unlawful for any broker, dealer, or exchange to use the mails, interstate commerce, or any exchange facility to knowingly make an untrue statement of a material fact or engage in any other act that would defraud or deceive a person in the purchase or sale of any security. This provision applies to sellers as well as buyers.

Insider
Officer, director, or owner of more than 10 percent of stock

The Act requires certain disclosures of trading by **insiders**—officers, directors, and owners of more than 10 percent of any class of securities of the corporation. Any profits made by an insider in connection with the purchase and sale of the corporation's securities within a six-month period may be recovered by the corporation or its stockholders suing in behalf of the corporation.

A 1975 amendment to this Act attempts to foster competition among securities brokers by reducing regulation of the brokerage industry.

Securities Protection Act of 1970

In order to protect investors when the stockbroker or investment house with which they did business had severe financial difficulty that threatened financial loss to the customers, Congress passed the Securities Protection Act. This federal law requires generally that all registered brokers and dealers and the members of a national securities exchange contribute a portion of their gross revenue from the securities business to a fund regulated by the Securities Investor Protection Corporation (SIPC).

The SIPC is a not-for-profit corporation whose members are the contributors to the fund. If the SIPC determines that any of its members has failed or is in danger of failing to meet its obligations to its customers and finds any one of five other specified indications of its being in financial difficulty, the SIPC may apply to the appropriate court for a decree adjudicating the customers of such member in need of the protection provided by the Act. If the court finds the requisite financial problems, it will appoint a trustee for liquidation of the SIPC member. The SIPC fund may be used to pay certain customers' claims up to $50,000 for each customer.

QUESTIONS

1   What is capital stock?
2   How may a person obtain shares of stock?
3   What are dividends and how may they be paid?
4   Discuss the difference in the ability of a corporation to rescind a cash dividend and a stock dividend.
5   What evidences ownership of stock in a corporation?
6   What is the difference between common and preferred stock?
7   Who exercises voting rights and receives dividends on treasury stock?
8   What is a stock option?
9   What is a prospectus?
10   What laws regulate the sale of securities, brokers, and exchanges?

CASE PROBLEMS

L.O.3 ....

1   Charles Naekel, president of a corporation, Arkota Industries, did not invest in Arkota, but received 450 shares of its par-value stock, and his sons received 250 shares. Several years later the directors fired Naekel and canceled the stock because of questions about whether he had paid adequate consideration for it. The parties reached a settlement by which Naekel received cash and 50 shares of stock. Two years later, Naekel sued Arkota for wrongfully canceling most of the stock. In the suit, a question arose as to the value of the sons' stock. Since it was par-value stock, the trial court stated the market value equaled the par value. Does the market value of stock equal its par value?

L.O.2 ....

2   Lawrence Gay owned 24.5 percent of the stock in Gay's Super Markets, Inc. The board of directors failed to declare a dividend for the year, and Gay sued to compel the corporation to pay a dividend. The corporation contended it did not declare a dividend because it needed capital for a planned expansion in two towns and the threat of competition from a new grocery chain in its area. Should the court order declaration of a dividend?

L.O.1 ....

3   Kirk's Auto Electric, Inc., issued shares of stock to Billy Bone, Andre Bone, and Joe Bone. In return, the Bones executed unsecured, interest-bearing,

demand promissory notes which they delivered to the corporation. They had made no payment on the notes. Clarence Kirk, a shareholder, sued the corporation and the Bones alleging the shares were void for nonpayment. Are the shares void, outstanding shares of the corporation?

L.O.3 ....

4   Rose Udoff was a stockholder in a corporation that had granted stock options to officers and employees. The directors of the corporation lowered the exercise price of the stock to the market price under the authority of and in accordance with the option plan. Udoff filed suit. Was the reduction in the price actionable as detrimental to the corporation?

L.O.2 ....

5   John Greco was a shareholder in Tampa Wholesale Company, a corporation. He did not agree to an agreement by which Lucky Stores, Inc., would acquire the assets of Tampa. He sued under a state law to receive the fair market value of his stock on the day preceding the date of the vote approving the agreement. Subsequent to the vote a dividend had been paid by Tampa, and Greco received a dividend check. The court ruled in his lawsuit that he was entitled to the fair market value of his stock. Is he allowed to keep the dividend?

L.O.3 ....

6   Paul Joseph was employed by Wilson Leasing Company. He was told by Lawrence Wilson, the president of the corporation, that he would receive 10,000 shares of Class B stock at the same cost as the Wilson family. Later, Wilson told him he would receive 2,000 or 4,000 shares. Joseph quit because the amount was less than the 10,000 promised. Wilson asked if he would return to work if he got 10,000 shares. Joseph agreed, and Wilson sent a memo to his attorney that stated:

> *Please arrange an immediate transfer of 2,000 of my shares plus 1,000 each from my parents.*
> *Also draft an agreement to allow P. J. to buy 2,000 additional shares on each of the next three years. Then he'll have 10,000 shares of B convertible to 11,000 A—all bought at our base cost.*

Joseph paid for and received only 4,000 shares. He was asked to resign in May, 1972, before he had purchased any more stock. The value of the stock was $5 per share, and the base cost was 20 cents. Joseph sued for breach of the agreement, alleging it was a contract of sale. Wilson alleged it was a stock option granted as an incentive for continued employment, so future right to purchase stock was dependent on Joseph's continued employment. Was Joseph entitled to purchase any stock?

Chapter 37

MANAGEMENT AND DISSOLUTION OF A CORPORATION

LEARNING OBJECTIVES

After studying this chapter you should be able to:

1 Discuss how a corporation is managed and the control of management by stockholders.

2 Specify the requirements for taking action at stockholders' meetings and how votes are cast.

3 Identify the rights of stockholders.

4 Describe how a corporation is combined or dissolved.

Preview Case

Washington Preferred Life Insurance Company called a stockholders' meeting to vote on a proposed merger. Washington mailed notice of the meeting to stockholders of record and published it in two legal newspapers. The published notice indicated that the meeting was for the purpose of voting on the merger; that proxies, proxy statements, and notices were mailed to stockholders at their last known addresses; and that if anyone was a stockholder of record and had not received the material, inquiry should be made to the company at the address given. A week later Washington asked a court to appoint a representative for missing shareholders in accordance with state law. This law allowed for such appointment if addresses of the shareholders were lost or inadequate and if the purpose of the meeting required a two-thirds vote. The law stated that approval by the court of the representative's findings acted as an affirmative vote at the stockholders' meeting by the missing shareholders. The court appointed a representative, who approved the merger. James Watson, a Washington stockholder, asked the court to vacate the order of appointment because the notice to the allegedly missing stockholders was insufficient. The notice did not inform stockholders that if they did not attend the meeting, a person would be appointed to vote their shares. Was the notice inadequate?

As an artificial being, existing only in contemplation of law, a corporation can perform business transactions only through actual pesons, acting as agents. The directors as a group act as both fiduciaries and agents. To the corporation, they are trustees and have responsibility for breaches of trust. To third parties, directors as a group constitute agents of the corporation.

L.O.1 ....

The board of directors selects the chief agents of the corporation, such as the president, the vice president, the treasurer, and other officers, who perform the managerial functions. The board of directors is primarily a policy-making body. The chief executives in turn appoint subagents for all the administrative functions of the corporation. These subagents constitute agents of the corporation, however, not of the appointment executives.

The directors and officers manage the corporation. Since the stockholders elect the board of directors, they indirectly control it. However, neither the individual directors nor a stockholder, merely by reason of membership in the corporation, can act as an agent or exercise any managerial function.

Even a stockholder who owns 49 percent of the common stock of a corporation has no more right to work or take a direct part in running the corporation than another stockholder or even a stranger would have. In contrast, a person who owns even 1 percent of a partnership, has just as much right to work for the partnership and to participate in its management as any other partner.

STOCKHOLDERS' MEETINGS

L.O.2 ....

In order to make the will of the majority binding, the stockholders must act at a duly convened and properly conducted stockholders' meeting.

A corporation usually holds a regular meeting such as its annual meeting at the place and time specified in the articles of incorporation or in the bylaws; notice of the meeting is ordinarily not required (see Illustration 37.1). A special meeting may be called by the directors of the corporation or, in some instances, by a particular officer or a specified number of stockholders. The corporation must give notice specifying the subjects to be discussed for a special meeting.

Washington Preferred Life Insurance Company called a stockholders' meeting to vote on a proposed merger. It mailed notice of the meeting to stockholders of record and published it in two legal newspapers. The published notice indicated that the meeting was for the purpose of voting on the merger; that proxies, proxy statements, and notices were mailed to stockholders at their last known addresses; and that if anyone was a stockholder of record and had not received the material, inquiry should be made to the company at the address given. A week later Washington asked a court to appoint a representative for missing shareholders in accordance with state law. This law allowed for such appointment if addresses of shareholders were lost or inadequate and if the purpose of the meeting required a two-thirds vote. The law stated that approval by the court of the representative's findings acted as an affirmative vote at the stockholders' meeting by the missing shareholders. The court appointed a representative who approved the merger. James Watson, a Washington stockholder, asked the court to vacate the order of appointment because the notice to the allegedly missing stockholders was insufficient. The court found that the notice did not inform stockholders that if they did not attend the meeting, a person would be appointed to vote their shares. Normally, absence from a stockholders' meeting constitutes a negative vote, so the notice was inadequate.

Meetings of the stockholders theoretically act as a check upon the board of directors. Corporations must have one annually. If the directors do not carry out the will of the stockholders, they can elect a new board that will carry out the stockholders' wishes. In the absence of fraud or bad faith on the part of the directors, this

Illustration 37-1   Notice of a Stockholders' Meeting

WATERS, MELLEN AND COMPANY
900 West Lake Avenue
Cincinnati, Ohio 45227

NOTICE OF ANNUAL MEETING OF STOCKHOLDERS
August 22, 19--

The Annual Meeting of Stockholders of Waters, Mellen and Company, a Delaware corporation, will be hold in the Auditorium, Building C, at the headquarters of the Company, 900 West Lake Avenue, Cincinnati, Ohio, on Wednesday, August 22, 19-- at 10:00 A.M. for the following purposes:

1. To elect a Board of thirteen Directors of the Company;

2. To consider and vote upon the ratification of the appointment of Arthur Andrews & Co. as independent public accountants for the Company for the fiscal year May 1, 19-- through April 30, 19--; and

3. To transact such other business as may properly come before the meeting or any adjournment thereof.

The Accompanying Proxy Statement provides additional information relating to the above matters.

The Board of Directors has fixed the close of business on Friday, July 6, 19-- as the record date for the determination of stockholders entitled to notice of and to vote at this meeting or any adjournment thereof. The stock transfer books will not be closed.

Please sign and mail the accompanying proxy in the envelope provided. If you attend this meeting and vote in person, the proxy will not be used.

By order of the Board of Directors.

RICHARD P. ROBERTS
Secretary

July 18, 19--

IMPORTANT—You can help in the preparation for the meeting by mailing your proxy promptly.

procedure constitutes the only legal means by which the investors can exercise any control over their investment.

Quorum

Quorum
Minimum number of shares required to be represented to transact business

A stockholders' meeting, in order to be valid, requires the presence of a **quorum,** or a minimum number of shares that must be represented in order that business may be lawfully transacted. At common law a quorum consisted of the stockholders actually assembled at a properly convened meeting. A majority of the votes cast by those present expressed the will of the stockholders. Statutes, bylaws, or the articles of incorporation now ordinarily require that a majority of the outstanding stock be represented at the stockholders' meeting in order to constitute a quorum. This representation may be either in person or by proxy.

Voting

L.O.3 ....

The right of a stockholder to vote is the most important right, because only in this way can the stockholder exercise any control over investment in the corporation. Only stockholders shown by the stockholders' record book have a right to vote. A person who purchases stock from an individual does not have the right to vote until the corporation makes the transfer on its books. Subscribers who have not fully paid for their stock, as a rule, may not vote.

State corporation laws control the right to vote. Voting and nonvoting common stock may be issued if the law permits.

Two major classes of elections are held during stockholders' meetings in which the stockholders vote. They include the annual election of directors and the elections to approve or disapprove some corporate acts that only the stockholders can authorize. Examples of some of these acts are consolidating with another corporation, dissolving, increasing the capital stock, and changing the number of directors.

Giving Minority Stockholders a Voice. Each stockholder normally has one vote for each share of common stock owned. In the election of a board of directors, the candidates receiving a majority of the votes of stock actually voting win. In corporations with 500,000 stockholders, control of 10 percent of the stock often suffices to control the election. In all cases the owners of 51 percent of the stock can elect all the directors. This leaves the minority stockholders without any representation on the board of directors. To alleviate this situation, two legal devices exist that may give the minority stockholders a voice, but not a controlling voice, on the board of directors. These devices are:

1 Cumulative voting
2 Voting trusts

**Cumulative
Voting**
Stockholder has votes
equal to shares owned
times number of directors
to be elected

Some state statutes provide that in the election of directors, a stockholder may cast as many votes in the aggregate equal to the number of shares owned multiplied by the number of directors to be elected. This method of voting is called **cumulative voting.** Thus, if a stockholder owns ten shares and ten directors are to be elected, 100 votes may be cast. All 100 votes may be cast for one director. As a result, under this plan of voting the minority stockholders may have some representation on the board of directors, although still a minority.

Voting Trust
Device whereby stock is
transferred to trustee to
vote it

Under a **voting trust,** stockholders give up their voting privileges by transferring their stock to a trustee and receiving in return voting trust certificates. This is not primarily a device to give the minority stockholders a voice on the board of directors; but it does do that, and often in large corporations it gives them a controlling voice. Twenty percent of the stock always voted as a unit has more effect than individual voting. State laws frequently impose limitations on voting trusts, as by limiting the number of years that they may run.

Absentee Voting. Under the common law only stockholders who were present in person were permitted to vote. Under the statutory law, the articles of incorporation, or the bylaws, stockholders who do not wish to attend a meeting and vote in person may authorize another to vote their stock for them. The person authorized to

Proxy

Person authorized to vote for another; written authorization to vote for another

vote for another is known as a **proxy.** The written authorization to vote is also called a proxy (see Illustration 37-2). While corporations send proxy forms to shareholders, the law does not require any special form for a proxy.

As a rule, a stockholder may revoke a proxy at any time. If a stockholder should sign more than one proxy for the same stockholders' meeting, the proxy having the later date would be effective. A proxy may be good in some states for only a limited period of time. If the stockholder attends the stockholders' meeting in person, this acts as a revocation of the proxy.

A property settlement agreement signed by Jack Lewis and Cecilia, his former wife, granted Cecilia 175,000 shares of Health Concepts IV, Inc., titled in her name and 175,000 shares titled in Jack's name. However, the agreement granted Jack the voting rights to all those shares. The agreement required Cecilia to execute a proxy designating Jack as the person authorized to vote the stock. At a stockholders' meeting, Jack voted Cecilia's 175,000 shares under the authority of the settlement agreement since she had not executed a formal proxy. A stockholder sued for a determination of whether Jack could validly vote Cecilia's shares. The court said he could since a proxy need only appoint someone to vote the shares and have the signature of the stockholder.

The management of a corporation may legally solicit proxies for candidates selected by the board of directors. However, proxies secured by means of fraudulent representations to stockholders may not be voted.

Proxy Wars

Stockholders dissatisfied with the policies of the present board of directors can try to elect a new board. Electing a new board is often a difficult or impossible task. If one

Illustration 37-2   Proxy

WATERS, MELLEN AND COMPANY

PROXY
ANNUAL MEETING AUGUST 22, 19--

KNOW ALL MEN BY THESE PRESENTS, That the undersigned shareholder of WATERS, MELLEN AND COMPANY hereby constitutes and appoints O. W. PRESCOTT, A. B. BROWN, and GEORGE CONNARS, and each of them, the true and lawful proxies of the undersigned, with several power of substitution and revocation, for and in the name of the undersigned, to attend the annual meeting of shareholders of said Company, to be held at the Main Office of the Company, 900 West Lake Avenue, Cincinnati, Ohio, on Thursday, August 22, 19--, at 10:00 o'clock A.M., Standard Time, and any and all adjournments of said meeting, receipt of the notice of which meeting, stating the purposes thereof, together with Proxy Statement, being hereby acknowledged by the undersigned, and to vote for the election of a Board of thirteen directors for the Company, to vote upon the ratification of the appointment of Arthur Andrews & Co. as independent public accountants for the fiscal year May 1, 19-- through April 30--, and to vote as they or he may deem proper upon all other matters that may lawfully come before said meeting or any adjournment thereof.

Signed the _____ 1st _____ day of March

_____ Wanda Klimecki _____

or even several people own a majority of the voting stock, the objecting stockholders cannot obtain a majority of the voting stock to ensure success. If the voting stock is widely held, and no group owns a majority of the voting stock, then the objecting stockholders at least have a chance to elect a new board. To do this a majority of the stock represented at a stockholders' meeting must be controlled by this dissatisfied group. To ensure success, the leaders of the group will obtain proxies from stockholders who cannot attend the stockholders' meeting in person. The current board members will also attempt to secure proxies. This is known as a **proxy war.** The present board of directors may in most instances pay the cost of this solicitation from corporate funds. The "outsiders" generally must bear the cost of the proxy war out of their personal funds. If there are one million shareholders, the cost of soliciting their proxies is enormous. For this reason proxy wars seldom happen.

Proxy War

Attempt by competing sides to secure majority of stockholders' votes

RIGHTS OF STOCKHOLDERS

The stockholders of a corporation enjoy several important rights and privileges. Three of these rights that have already been discussed include the following:

1   A stockholder has the right to receive a properly executed certificate as evidence of ownership of shares of stock.
2   A stockholder has the right to attend corporate meetings and to vote unless this right is denied by express agreement, the articles of incorporation, or statutory provisions.
3   A stockholder has the right to receive a proportionate share of the profits when profits are distributed as dividends.

In addition, each stockholder has the following rights:

4   The right to sell and transfer shares of stock.
5   The right, when new stock is issued by the corporation, to subscribe for new shares in proportion to the shares the stockholder owns. For example, a stockholder who owns 10 percent of the original capital stock has a right to buy 10 percent of the shares added to the stock. If this were not true, stockholders could be deprived of their proportionate share in the accumulated surplus of the company. This is known as a **preemptive right.** Only stockholders have the right to vote to increase the capital stock.
6   The right to inspect the corporate books and to have the corporate books inspected by an attorney or an accountant. This right is not absolute, since most states have laws restricting the right. These laws tend to be drawn to protect the corporation from indiscriminate inspection, not to hamper a stockholder in this right.
7   The right, when the corporation is dissolved, to share pro rata in the assets that remain after all the obligations of the company have been paid. In the case of certain preferred stock, the shareholders may have a preference in the distribution of the corporate assets upon liquidation.

Preemptive Right

Right to purchase new shares in proportion to shares owned

DIRECTORS

A board of directors elected by the stockholders manages every corporation. Laws normally require every board to consist of at least three members; but if the number exceeds three, the articles of incorporation and the bylaws of the corporation fix the number, together with qualifications and manner of election.

The directors, unlike the stockholders, cannot vote by proxy. Nor can they make corporate decisions as individual directors. All decisions must be made collectively and in a called meeting of the board.

The functions of the directors can be classified as:

1   Powers
2   Duties
3   Liabilities

Powers

Law, the articles of incorporation, and the bylaws limit the powers of the board of directors. The directors have the power to manage and direct the corporation. They may do any legal act reasonably necessary to achieve the purpose of the corporation so long as this power is not expressly limited. They may elect and appoint officers and agents to act for the corporation, or they may delegate authority to any number of its members to so act. If a director obtains knowledge of something while acting in the course of employment and in the scope of authority with the corporation, the corporation is charged with this knowledge.

Duties

The directors have the duty of establishing policies that will achieve the purpose of the corporation, selecting executives to carry out these policies, and supervising these executives to see that they efficiently execute the policies. They must act in person in exercising all discretionary power. The directors may delegate ministerial and routine duties to subagents, but the duty of determining all major corporate policies, except those reserved to the stockholders, must be assumed by the board of directors.

Liabilities

As fiduciaries of the corporation, the directors incur liability for bad faith and for negligence. They do not incur liability for losses when they act with due diligence and reasonably sound judgment. Directors make countless errors of judgment annually in operating a complex business organization. Only when these errors result from negligence or a breach of good faith can a director be held personally liable.

The test whether the directors failed to exercise due care depends upon whether they exercised the care that a reasonably prudent person would have exercised under the circumstances. If they did that, they were not negligent and do not incur liability for the loss that follows. The test of whether they acted in bad faith is whether they acted in a way that conflicted with the interests of the corporation. The corporate directors have a duty of loyalty to the corporation similar to the duty of loyalty an agent has to a principal or a partner has to the partnership and the other partners.

Directors may be held liable for some acts without evidence of negligence or bad faith either because the act is illegal or bad faith is presumed. Paying dividends out of capital and ultra vires acts constitute illegal acts. Loaning corporate funds to officers and directors constitutes an act to which the court will impute bad faith.

The members of the board of directors incur civil and criminal liability for their corporate actions. This means a director does not get any immunity or protection from the legal consequences of actions taken. Because of this, individual directors who do not agree with action taken by the other directors must be careful to protect themselves by having the minutes of the meeting of the directors show that they dissented from the board's action. Otherwise stated, every director present at a board meeting is conclusively presumed to have assented to the action taken unless the director takes positive action to overcome this presumption. If the directors present who dissent have a record of their dissent entered in the minutes of the meeting, then they cannot be held liable for the acts of the majority.

James and Geneva Bobb, officers and directors of Queen City Grain Company, which operated grain elevators, engaged in commodity trading resulting in losses to the corporation of more than $1,500,000. The transactions violated the law. The trustee in bankruptcy of Queen City sued the Bobbs alleging they had breached their duty to the corporation by speculating in commodities in violation of the law. The court held that by violating the law, the Bobbs had acted in bad faith and breached their duty to the corporation.

OFFICERS

In addition to selecting and removing the officers of a corporation, the board of directors authorizes them to act on behalf of the corporation in carrying out the board's policies. As agents of the corporation, the principles of agency apply to the officers' relationship with the corporation and define many of their rights and obligations.

State statutes may specify a few of the officers that corporations must have. The corporation's bylaws will specify what additional officers the corporation must have and the duties of each officer. A corporation commonly has a president, vice president, secretary, and treasurer. In small corporations, some of these offices may be combined. Additional officers may be assistant secretaries or treasurers, additional vice presidents, and a chief executive officer. The chief executive officer is frequently the president or the chairman of the board of directors. The board of directors creates or deletes some positions.

A corporate officer or agent who commits a tort or crime incurs personal liability even when the act was done for the corporation in a corporate capacity. In this case, both the corporation and the individual could be jointly liable. Only personal liability is imposed when the acts are detrimental to the corporation and outside the scope of the officer's authority. Thus, an officer has liability when actions are improper or unjustified, such as when based on spite toward the injured party. Federal law even imposes liability on officers and agents for aiding and abetting lower-ranking employees in the commission of crimes. Specific statutes may impose liability on officers if they have a duty to ensure violations do not occur and to seek out and remedy violations that do occur. Corporate officers and agents are not personally liable for acts in which they do not participate, authorize, consent to, or direct.

CORPORATE COMBINATIONS

L.O.4 ....

Merger
One corporation absorbed
by another

Consolidation
Combining two corpora-
tions to form a new one

When two corporations wish to combine, they frequently do so by means of a merger or a consolidation. A **merger** of two corporations occurs when they combine so that one survives and the other ceases to exist. One absorbs the other. A **consolidation** occurs when two corporations combine to form a new corporation. Both of the two previous corporations disappear.

It has become a rather common practice recently for a corporation to try to take over another corporation. This may be done by the acquiring corporation's making a formal tender offer, an offer to buy stock in the target corporation at a set price. Since attempts at takeovers usually cause the price of the stock of the target company to rise, the acquiring corporation may try to obtain the amount of stock it wants in its target through the purchase of large blocks of the target's stock. The purchase of a large amount of stock cannot be kept quiet for long, however, because the Securities Exchange Act requires any person who acquires 5 percent of any class of stock to file a schedule reporting the acquisition within ten days.

DISSOLUTION

A corporation may terminate its existence by paying all its debts, distributing all remaining assets to the stockholders, and surrendering its articles of incorporation. The corporation then ceases to exist and completes its dissolution. This action may be voluntary on the part of the stockholders, or it may be involuntary by action of the court or state. The state may ask for a dissolution for any one of the following reasons:

1   Forfeiture or abuse of the corporate charter.
2   Violation of the state laws.
3   Fraud in the procedurement of the charter.
4   In some states, failure to pay specified taxes for a specified number of years.

When a corporation dissolves, its existence is terminated for all purposes except to wind up its business. It cannot sue, own property, or form contracts except for the purpose of converting its assets into cash and distributing the cash to creditors and stockholders.

In the event that assets cannot cover the corporation's debts, the stockholders do not incur personal liability. This is one of the chief advantages to business owners of a corporation over a sole proprietorship or partnership. It is an advantage from the stockholders' standpoint, but a disadvantage from the creditors' standpoint.

QUESTIONS

1   Discuss the management of a corporation and how stockholders control management.
2   What are the notice requirements for taking action at stockholders' meetings?
3   Who may vote at a stockholders' meeting?

4   What are the two major classes of elections held during stockholders' meetings in which the stockholders vote?

5   What is cumulative voting?

6   Explain how a shareholder who cannot attend a stockholders' meeting can vote at it.

7   What is the purpose of giving stockholders a preemptive right?

8   By what are the powers of the board of directors limited?

9   When does a corporate officer alone have liability for a tort or a crime?

10 a. How is a corporation dissolved?

    b. Under what conditions may the state order a dissolution of a corporation against the stockholders' objection?

CASE PROBLEMS

L.O.3 ....

1   At a directors meeting of Covington Grain Company, Morris Rabren, the president and a director, explained that the company engaged in commodities trading as legal hedges not as risky speculation. An independent CPA said he saw no reason to recommend an audit of the company's commodities transactions. The directors told Rabren not to engage in speculation and he agreed. At the time, Covington had a profit. It filed bankruptcy four months later. The trustee in bankruptcy sued the directors for negligence in allowing Rabren to control Covington and engage in speculation. The trustee's witnesses testified that after Rabren opened the hedging account, it would have been extremely difficult to detect that he had engaged in speculative transactions. Should the court find the directors negligent?

L.O.3 ....

2   Crawford and Thibaut, Inc., held its annual meeting at which John Thibaut held a proxy for two-thirds of a share owned by Jerry Boyce. However, Boyce had not signed the proxy, so the chairman of the meeting did not allow John Thibaut to vote the two-thirds share. The stockholders elected three directors by a vote of 60 to 59$\frac{1}{3}$. John Thibaut sued the elected directors challenging the election. How should the court rule regarding the validity of the proxy?

L.O.2 ....

3   Jan Chin died owning the 300 outstanding shares of stock in Jan Chin, Inc., and by will left his property to his widow, Toy See Chin. Legal title to the stock vested in his estate's executor, Donald Delahunt. At Toy Chin's request, Delahunt distributed 85 shares to her, and she gave them to her son, Chin Chak Ping and his children. Chin Chak Ping, the president of Jan Chin, Inc., called a meeting to elect directors. He and Toy Chin waived notice of the meeting. Delahunt was not notified of the meeting, and he did not attend. Toy Chin and Chin Chak Ping elected themselves directors and elected Chin Chak Ping to all the corporate offices. During the years, stock was issued to Toy Chin, who distributed 145 shares to her son and his family. Delahunt was never notified of any meetings and never attended any. Toy Chin died, and Delahunt assigned to her executor the stock he held. This executor brought a suit to cancel distribution of the 145 shares and have the election of directors and officers declared void, alleging that, as the beneficial owner, Toy Chin did not have the power to waive notice of the meeting and vote the stock. Did she?

L.O.3 .... **4** Jerry Ward, a shareholder of Cook Inlet Region, Inc., sent a proxy solicitation to all shareholders. The solicitation started with a cartoon showing a group of Cook shareholders saying to management, "Hey! We want our money NOW." It further stated: "If we each want a big chunk of land then let's give it to ourselves 'NOW'" and "If we were to go ahead and sell just the coal for its estimated value that would be over three hundred thousand dollars . . . for every man, woman, and child owner of Cook." Ward received a large number of proxies from this solicitation. The resulting lawsuit alleged that the proxy solicitation was materially false or misleading. Cook did not have large amounts of land it could distribute to shareholders, and there was no current prospect of selling coal reserves for anything like $300,000 per shareholder. Was the solicitation misleading?

L.O.3 .... **5** Robert Nanney was a stockholder and president of Robert Nanney Chevrolet Co. The corporation was in financial trouble and owed money on loans personally endorsed by James Austin, the majority stockholder. Concerned about his personal liability, Austin took steps to liquidate the corporation. Nanney hired Evans and Moses, a law firm, to defeat Austin's efforts to liquidate. Nanney and Austin settled their dispute. Nanney issued a check on the corporation, payable to Evans and Moses. The check had two signature lines, but the check was signed only by Nanney. The check was not paid because two signatures were required. Evans and Moses sued the corporation for payment of the check. Austin, who had succeeded as president, testified Nanney did not have authority from the corporation to hire the firm or issue the check. Was the check valid?

L.O.2 .... **6** The John A. Nugent Trust, John Nugent, trustee, owned half of the stock in Midwest Machinery Movers. The Riemore Nugent Trust with Riemore Collins as trustee owned the other half. Nugent died and Beverly Nugent, his surviving spouse and executor of his estate, sued Midwest and Riemore Collins to require annual meetings of the corporation. The defendants claimed a meeting of the corporation had taken place at a hospital. The corporate records did not contain minutes of any such meeting. Should the court order annual meetings?

L.O.3 .... **7** MBPXL Corporation and ConAgra signed a merger agreement that contained a "best efforts" clause requiring MBPXL's officers and directors to take all action necessary or appropriate to effectuate the merger. The agreement also stated that it did not relieve the directors of their duties to their stockholders. Meanwhile, Cargill Holdings, Inc., bought 22 percent of MBPXL's stock from several individuals and made a public offer to buy the rest of MBPXL's stock at $27 a share. ConAgra sued to prevent Cargill from interfering with its merger with MBPXL. Investment bankers hired by MBPXL indicated that Cargill's offer was superior to ConAgra's merger terms for MBPXL stockholders. The MBPXL board of directors approved a resolution canceling the stockholders meeting scheduled for voting on the merger and recommending the stockholders accept Cargill's offer. Did this action violate the "best efforts" provision of the merger agreement?

Summary Cases

BUSINESS ORGANIZATION

1. Darden, Doman & Stafford Associates (DDS), a partnership, executed a renovation contract with "Building Design and Development Inc. (in formation) John A. Goodman, President." DDS knew the corporation was not in existence, but Goodman had told them he would form a corporation to limit his personal liability. The work was to be completed by October 15, and disputes were to be settled by arbitration. The first check in payment for the work was made out to "Building Design and Development Inc.—John Goodman." Goodman crossed out his name and indorsed it "Bldg. Design & Dev. Inc., John A. Goodman, Pres." and told DDS to make payments only to the corporation. The work was not finished by October 15 and DDS claimed it was of poor quality. A corporate license for Building Design and Development Inc. was issued on November 2. DDS served a demand for arbitration and named the corporation and Goodman. DDS testified it never agreed to make the contract only with the corporation; therefore, Goodman should be a party to the arbitration. Should he? [*Goodman* v. *Darden, Doman & Stafford Associates*, 670 P. 2d 648 (Wash.)]

2. The Timely Investment Club (TIC), a partnership, was formed to educate the partners in investing and allow them to invest on a regular basis. The partnership agreement provided that when partners withdrew, TIC was required to redeem units of ownership of the withdrawing partners from the funds available. Eight partners withdrew. Was the partnership dissolved by their withdrawal? [*Cagnolatti* v. *Guinn*, 189 Cal. Rptr. 151 (Cal. Ct. App.)]

3. Jerold Murphy and three others were the incorporators and original stockholders of Country House, Inc. For nine years they all worked as full-time employees of Country House and were paid wages. Twice they were paid "bonuses" which were authorized when fiscal reports indicated sufficient corporate earnings. Murphy terminated his employment but kept his stock. Then Country House paid stockholder-employee bonuses in addition to their wages. No dividends were ever paid. Murphy brought suit, alleging the bonuses were really dividends and, as a stockholder, money was due him, too. Were the payments dividends? [*Murphy* v. *Country House, Inc.*, 349 N.W. 2d 289 (Minn. Ct. App.)]

4. Paul Wright and John Termeer were partners in an auto repair business. Interstate Motors, Inc., brought in a car for repairs. The car was accepted by Wright, who then drove it to Houston and into a lake, causing significant damage. Is Termeer liable for Wright's negligence? [*Termeer* v. *Interstate Motors, Inc.*, 634 S.W. 2d 12 (Tex. Ct. App.)]

5. United Electronics Co. (UE) borrowed money from Factors and Note Buyers and pledged stock it owned in Frost Controls Corp. UE defaulted on the loan,

so Factors foreclosed. Factors offered the stock for sale publicly and then bought it itself. Frost's president, Arthur Thomson, started a new company, which bought Frost's assets. UE sued Thomson and his new company. To win the lawsuit UE had to have owned the Frost stock when Frost's assets were sold. To establish that it owned the stock at that time, UE tried to show the foreclosure sale was invalid because Factors, trying to sell the Frost stock, was an "underwriter" as defined in the Securities Act. UE alleged that Factors, with a view to the distribution of the securities, sold the stock for UE, which controlled Frost. Since the Frost stock was unregistered, it alleged the public foreclosure sale violated the Securities Act. Did the sale violate the Securities Act? [*A.D.M. Corp.* v. *Thomson*, 707 F. 2d 25 (1st Cir.)]

6   Chet Ellingson, a licensed real estate broker, told Gregory Walsh that he owned real estate with "some partners" and that it was for sale. A buy-sell agreement was executed by Walsh and Ellingson, and Walsh gave Ellingson $1,000 in earnest money. The closing was set for April 5. Four Seasons Motor Inn owned the real estate with Ellingson as tenants in common. On April 5, Walsh told Ellingson he was ready to close, but Ellingson told Walsh he could not get his partners to sell. The real estate had a building on it that Ellingson managed. There had been a prior land holding between Ellingson and Four Seasons by which they had owned property as tenants in common and then sold it and divided the profits equally. Walsh sued for specific performance of the buy-sell agreement, alleging Ellingson had a partnership with Four Seasons and as an agent of the partnership bound it to sell. Was there a partnership? [*Walsh* v. *Ellingson Agency*, 613 P. 2d 1381 (Mont.)]

7   Glenn C. Shaw died on March 17 and by will bequeathed his property to the Abby Tarr–Glenn C. Shaw Foundation, a charitable, educational, and benevolent corporation. The Foundation was incorporated by his attorney on May 21. Shaw's heirs alleged that a bequest to a nonexistent charitable corporation is invalid and fails. Testamentary dispositions are assumed to take effect at the death of the testator, but a legal doctrine states a bequest made to a charitable corporation that is not in existence will not fail if there is an intention to devote the property to charitable purposes, not just to make a gift to a designated corporation. Shaw's will provided: "in the event any individual should prove themselves to be an heir at law and entitled to any portion of my estate then . . . I . . . bequeath to each such individual . . . the sum of one dollar only, it being my intention and desire that . . . my entire estate should go to the above-named foundation." It also designated Shaw's attorney to handle "all other legal proceedings . . . including all legal and management services in connection with the handling of the Abby Tarr–Glenn C. Shaw Foundation." Should the estate go to the corporation or the heirs? [*Matter of Estate of Shaw*, 620 P. 2d 483 (Okla. Ct. App.)]

8   Bernard Susman and members of the Asher family were partners in a real estate business. They had a dispute concerning whether the partnership was to develop a portion of the property or whether it was to be sold to a developer. Their dispute became so heated the Ashers told Susman he was no longer a partner, changed the partnership tax returns to show Susman's interest was zero, kept him out of partnership business, refused to give him information concerning the business, and refused to account for expenses of the partnership. Susman sued for breach of the partnership agreement. Were the breaches

serious enough to order dissolution? [*Susman* v. *Venture*, 449 N.E. 2d 143 (Ill. App. Ct.)]

9   W. E. Groves and Lloyd Lindsey signed an act of exchange. One of the provisions was that Groves transfer his "ownership in Rosemound Improvement Association, Inc., represented by the following stock certificates" to Lindsey. No certificates were described and none were signed over by Groves. Rosemound's charter provided: "Stock certificates herein shall not be transferable except back to the corporation." After the act of exchange was signed, the parties became dissatisfied, and the provisions were not all fulfilled. Groves sued to require Rosemound to recognize his right to vote at shareholders' meetings. Is Groves entitled to vote? [*Groves* v. *Rosemound Improvement Association, Inc.*, 413 S. 2d 925 (La. Ct. App.)]

10 Harold, Jane, and Prudence Miller; Joanne and Theodore Lilley; Achsah Graham; Darrell Schroeder; and Miller Redwood Co. applied for a reduction in assessments on land to which they held title in a variety of combinations. Harold and Jane were married, and Prudence, Achsah, and Joanne were their daughters. Theodore was Joanne's husband, and Darrell Schroeder was a key employee of the family lumber business. Miller Redwood was a wholly owned subsidiary of Stimson Lumber Company, at least 90 percent of which was owned by the individuals. A web of contractual rights bound the land together. The individuals regarded themselves as partners, operated their business jointly, and disbursed profits in accordance with their ownership interests. Was there a partnership? [*Cochran* v. *Board of Supervisors of Del Norte County*, 149 Cal. Rptr. 304 (Cal. Ct. App.)]

11 Jack Alpert and others owned 26 percent of the stock of 79 Realty Corp., which had an office building as its principal asset. Another corporation, 28 William St. Corp., purchased more than two-thirds of 79 Realty's stock. The board of directors of 79 Realty was replaced, and the new board approved a merger of 28 William St. into 79 Realty. The minority shares would be canceled, and title to the office building would end up in Madison 28 Associates, a partnership. The minority shareholders were to be paid the same price per share as had been paid to acquire the majority interest. The merger was to get more capital for necessary renovation and realize tax savings by owning as a partnership rather than as a corporation. The minority shareholders sued to rescind the merger. There was no showing of fraud, illegality, or self-dealing. Should the merger be rescinded? [*Alpert* v. *28 Williams St. Corp.*, 457 N.Y.S. 2d 4 (N.Y. App. Div.)]

Part 8

RISK-BEARING DEVICES

Chapter 38

PRINCIPLES OF INSURANCE

LEARNING OBJECTIVES

After studying this chapter you should be able to:

1 Identify important terms used in insurance.

2 Explain who may obtain insurance.

3 List the five aspects of the law of contracts that have special significance for insurance contracts.

Preview Case

Freddie Long obtained a life insurance policy from Mutual Benefit Life Insurance Company of New Jersey. Richard Chisholm was the beneficiary. Question 15 in the application for the insurance asked if the applicant "had any surgery, treatment, observation, or routine examination in doctor's office, hospital, clinic . . . ?" It instructed, "For routine physical examinations indicating only good health . . . state 'routine exams' beside your 'yes' answer." Long marked "yes" and stated "routine exams." Long died five months later in a car accident. Mutual denied Chisholm's claim for payment, stating that in answering Question 15 Long had failed to disclose that after an auto accident he had received hospital treatment for minor injuries for which the prognosis was good. Mutual's underwriting department indicated the injuries were of no underwriting concern. Was there concealment?

I nsurance provides a fund of money when a loss covered by the policy occurs. Life is full of unfavorable financial contingencies. Not every financial peril in life can be shifted by insurance, but many of the most common perils can. **Insurance** is a contract whereby a party transfers a risk of financial loss to the risk bearer, the insurance company, for a fee.

Every insurance contract specifies the particular risk being transferred. The name that identifies the policy does not control either the coverage or protection of the policy. For example, a particular contract may carry the name "Personal Accident Insurance Policy," but this name may not clearly indicate the risk being

Insurance

Contract that transfers risk of financial loss for a fee

assumed by the insurance company. A reading of the contract may reveal that the company will pay only if an accident occurs while the insured is actually attending a public school. In such a case, in spite of the broad title of the policy, the premium paid covers only the described protection against a financial loss due to an accident, not the loss due to any accident. The contract determines the risk covered, and it binds the parties.

TERMS USED IN INSURANCE

L.O.1

Insurer
Company writing insurance

Insured
Person protected against loss

Beneficiary
Person who receives proceeds of life insurance

Policy
Written contract of insurance

Face
Maximum insurer pays for loss

Premium
Consideration paid by insured

Risk or Peril
Danger of loss

Hazards
Factors that contribute to uncertainty

The company agreeing to compensate a person for a certain loss is known as the **insurer,** or sometimes as the *underwriter*. The person protected against the loss is known as the **insured,** or the *policyholder*. In life insurance the person who will receive the benefits or the proceeds of the policy is known as the **beneficiary**. In most states the insured may make anyone the beneficiary.

Whenever a person purchases any kind of insurance, a contract is formed with the insurance company. The written contract is commonly called a **policy.** The maximum amount that the insurer agrees to pay in case of a loss is known as the **face** of the policy, and the consideration the insured pays for the protection is called the **premium.**

The danger of a loss of, or injury to, property, life, or anything else, is called a **risk** or **peril**; when the danger may be covered by insurance, it is known as the insurable risk. Factors, such as fire, floods, and sleet, that contribute to the uncertainty are called **hazards.**

An insurance company assumes the risks caused by normal hazards. The insured must not do anything to increase the risk. Negligence by the insured constitutes a normal hazard. Gross negligence indicating a criminal intent does not. When a loss occurs, the insured must use all due diligence to minimize it. The insured has no responsibility for an increased risk over which the insured has no control or knowledge. For example, the insured must remove household effects from a burning building or keep a car involved in an accident from being vandalized if it can be done safely.

Kevin Cumiskey leased property for a restaurant and had to insure the property. The property was insured in the name of Kevin Cumiskey, d/b/a "Chiripa's." Later the insurance lapsed and the business was incorporated as K.S.J., Inc., with Kevin and his parents, Stephanie and John, as stockholders and officers. One summer Stephanie and John were to run the restaurant. They insured the property in the same name as previously. The restaurant consistently lost money, and a series of explosions and fire damaged the property.

Circumstantial evidence indicated John had set the fire. The insurance company filed for a declaratory judgment, an action asking the court to decide the rights of the parties. The court found a declaratory judgment action was proper because there were many issues, and the possible guilt of John in setting the fire raised the question of the company's liability. Where an officer, director, stockholder, or managing agent deliberately set a fire, the insurer has a good defense to a claim on the policy.

Rider
Addition to insurance policy to modify, extend, or limit base contract

A **rider** on an insurance policy is a clause or even a whole contract added to another contract to modify, extend, or limit the base contract. A rider must be clearly incorporated in, attached to, or referred to in the policy so that there is no doubt the parties wanted it to become a part of the policy.

Eza Rozas had hospital and medical insurance with Louisiana Hospital Service, Inc. She had a severe headache and dizziness, was hospitalized, and was found to have two aneurysms and a large blood clot in her brain. Louisiana refused to pay her hospital bill because riders to her policy excluded coverage. The riders were stapled to her application for insurance, which had been put inside the policy and given to her. Rozas alleged the riders were not effective because they were not physically attached to the policy. The court held that Rozas had the entire contract in her possession at all times, and to require the riders to have been attached by staples, paper clips, or glue would be an absurd and unintended result.

TYPES OF INSURANCE COMPANIES

There are two major types of insurance companies:

1 Stock companies
2 Mutual companies

Stock Companies

Stock Insurance Company

Corporation of stock-holder-investors

A **stock insurance company** is a corporation for which the original investment was made by stockholders and whose board of directors conducts its business. As in all other corporations, the stockholders elect the board of directors and receive the profits as dividends. Unlike other corporations, insurance companies must place a major portion of their original capital in a reserve account. As business volume increases, the reserve must be increased by setting aside part of the premiums.

Mutual Companies

Mutual Insurance Company

Company of policyholder-investors

Assessment Mutual Company

Mutual insurance company in which losses are shared by policyholders

In a **mutual insurance company** the policyholders are the members and owners and correspond to the stockholders in a stock company. In these companies the policyholders are both the insurer and the insured, but the corporation constitutes a separate legal entity. A person who purchases a $10,000 fire insurance policy in a mutual company that has $10 million of insurance in force, owns $1/_{1,000}$ of the company and is entitled to share the profits in this ratio. Losses may also have to be shared in the same ratio if it is an **assessment mutual company.** A policyholder is not subject to assessment where the policy makes no provision for it. In a stock company, policyholders never share the losses.

WHO MAY BE INSURED

L.O.2 ....

To contract for a policy of insurance, an individual must be competent to contract. Insurance does not constitute a necessary; thus, a minor who wishes to disaffirm is not bound on insurance contracts. A minor who disaffirms a contract may demand the return of any money. Since insurance contracts provide protection only, this cannot be returned. Some states hold that because of this a minor can demand only the unearned premium for the unexpired portion of the policy. A few states have passed laws preventing minors from disaffirming some insurance contracts by reason of minority.

Insurable Interest

Interest in nonoccurrence of risk insured against

To become a policyholder, one must have an insurable interest. An **insurable interest** means that the policyholder has an interest in the nonoccurrence of the risk insured against, usually because there would be financial loss. The insurance contract is in its entirety an agreement to assume a specified risk. If the insured has no interest to protect, there can be no assumption of risk, and hence no insurance. The law covering insurable interest is different for life insurance and for property insurance.

Life Insurance

The insured has an insurable interest in his or her own life. When people insure another's life, however, and make themselves or someone else the beneficiary, they must have an insurable interest in the life of the insured at the time the policy is taken out. That interest does not need to exist at the time of the death of the insured.

A person has an insurable interest in the life of another when such a relationship exists between them that a reasonable expectation of benefit will be derived from the continued existence of the other person. The relationships most frequently giving rise to an insurable interest are those between parents and children, husband and wife, partner and copartner, and a creditor in the life of the debtor to the extent of the debt. There are numerous other relationships that give rise to an insurable interest. With the exception of a creditor, if the insurable interest exists, the amount of insurance is irrelevant.

Property Insurance

One must have an insurable interest in the property at the time the policy is issued and at the time of the loss to be able to collect on a property insurance policy. Ownership is, of course, the clearest type of insurable interest; but there are many other types of insurable interest. Insurable interest occurs when the insured would suffer a monetary loss by the destruction of the property. Common types of insurable interest other than ownership include:

1   The mortgagee has an insurable interest in the property mortgaged to the extent of the mortgage.
2   The seller has an insurable interest in property sold on the installment plan when the seller retains a security interest in it as security for the unpaid purchase price.
3   A bailee has an insurable interest in the property bailed to the extent of possible loss. The bailee has a potential loss from two sources. Compensation as provided for in the contract of bailment might be lost. Secondly, the bailee may be held legally liable to the owner if the bailee's negligence or the negligence of the bailee's employees causes the loss.
4   A partner has an insurable interest in the property owned by the firm to the extent of the possible loss.
5   A tenant has an insurable interest in property to the extent of the loss that would be suffered by damage to or destruction of the property.

A change in title or possession of the insured property may destroy the insurable interest, which in turn may void the contract, because insurable interest must exist at the time of the loss.

H. N. Henderson and his wife executed a mortgage to American National Bank when they bought their house. They then contracted to sell the house to Edward and Robin Benefield. The Benefields wanted to assume the mortgage, and to do so American National required insurance on the house. Henderson arranged with Baldwin Mutual Insurance Co. for the insurance. The Hendersons deeded the property to the Benefields a few days before Baldwin issued the policy. The house burned. Baldwin refused to pay on the policy claiming the Hendersons did not have an insurable interest at the time the policy was issued because they no longer had title. The court said the Benefields had assumed the mortgage, but the Hendersons still remained liable on it. Thus, they had an insurable interest.

SOME LEGAL ASPECTS OF THE INSURANCE CONTRACT

L.O.3 ....

The laws applicable to contracts in general apply to insurance contracts. Five aspects of the law, however, have special significance for insurance contracts:

1   Concealment
2   Representation
3   Warranty
4   Subrogation
5   Estoppel

Concealment

Concealment

Willful failure to disclose pertinent information

An insurer must rely upon the information supplied by the insured. This places the responsibility of supplying all information pertinent to the risk upon the insured. A willful failure to disclose this pertinent information is known as **concealment.** To affect the contract the concealed facts must be material; this means they must relate to matters that would affect the insurer's decision to insure the insured and the determination of the premium rate. Also, the concealment must be willful. The willful concealment of a material fact renders the contract voidable.

Freddie Long obtained a life insurance policy from Mutual Benefit Life Insurance Company of New Jersey. Richard Chisholm was the beneficiary. Question 15 in the application for the insurance asked if the applicant "had any surgery, treatment, observation or routine examination in doctor's office, hospital, clinic . . . ?" It instructed, "For routine physical examinations indicating only good health . . . state 'routine exams' beside your 'yes' answer." Long marked "yes" and stated "routine exams." Long died five months later in a car accident. Mutual denied Chisholm's claim for payment, stating that in answering Question 15 Long had failed to disclose that after an auto accident he had received hospital treatment for minor injuries for which the prognosis was good. Mutual's underwriting department indicated the injuries were of no underwriting concern. The court held that there was no concealment.

The rule of concealment does not apply with equal stringency to all types of insurance contracts. In the case of property insurance, where the agent has an opportunity to inspect the property, the insurance company waives the right to void the contract. Concealment arises in ocean marine insurance whenever the insured withholds pertinent information, even if there is no intent to defraud.

Representation

False Representation

Misstatement of material fact

An oral or written misstatement of a material fact by the insured prior to the finalization of the contract is called a **false representation.** If the insured makes a false representation, the insurer may avoid the contract of insurance. This results whether or not the insured made the misstatement purposely.

Insurance policies now usually provide that if the age of the insured is misstated, the policy will not be voided; however, the face amount paid on the policy "shall be that sum which the premium paid would have provided for had the age been correctly stated."

Roy McAllister owned a plane he insured with Avemco Insurance Co. until 12:01 A.M. on May 25. At that time the policy expired. That day, McAllister filled out and returned a renewal proposal. One of the questions on the renewal form asked if the plane had passed an annual inspection during the past year. McAllister answered "yes" even though he had not had the plane inspected during the past year. The plane crashed causing damage to it, a building, and injuring three people. The failure to have the annual inspection did not contribute to the crash. Avemco refused to pay under the policy because of McAllister's misrepresentation. McAllister said he did not intend to mislead Avemco. The court held the misrepresentation allowed Avemco to avoid the policy because if McAllister had answered the question "no," Avemco would not have renewed the policy.

Warranty

Warranty

Statement of insured that relates to risk and appears in contract

A **warranty** is a statement or promise of the insured that relates to the risk and appears in the contract or another document incorporated in the contract. Untrue statements or unfulfilled promises permit the insurer to declare the policy void.

Warranties differ from representations in several ways. The insurance company includes warranties in the actual contract of insurance or incorporates them in it by reference. Representations are merely collateral or independent, such as oral statements or written statements appearing in the application for insurance or other writing separate from the actual contract of insurance.

Also, in order to void the contract of insurance, the false representations must concern a material fact, whereas the warranties may concern any fact or be any promise. A representation need only be substantially correct, whereas a warranty must be absolutely true or strictly performed.

Several states have enacted legislation that eliminates any distinction between warranties and representations and does not require a showing of materiality for a warranty or that the insured intended to defraud. In these states, a breached warranty does not void the policy. Even in states without such statutes, courts are reluctant to find policies invalid and will construe warranties as representations whenever possible and interpret warranties strictly against the insurer so as to favor the insured.

Subrogation

Subrogation

Right of insurer to assume rights of insured

In insurance, **subrogation** is the right of the insurer under certain circumstances to assume the legal rights of, or to "step into the shoes" of, the insured. Subrogation particularly applies to some types of automobile insurance. If the insurer pays a claim to the insured, under the law of subrogation the insurer has a right to any claims that the insured had because of the loss. For example, *A* has a collision insurance policy on a car. *B* negligently damages the car. The insurance company will pay *A* but then has the right to sue *B* to be repaid.

Estoppel

Estoppel

One party leads the other to a conclusion the other relies on and by which the other would be harmed if the first party were allowed to show the conclusion was false

Neither party to an insurance contract may claim the benefit of a violation of the contract by the other party. Each party is said to be **estopped** from claiming the benefit of such violation. An estoppel arises whenever a party, by statements or actions, leads another party to a conclusion that the latter relies upon and by which the latter would be harmed if the first party were allowed to show that the conclusion is not true. For example, if the insurer gives the insured a premium receipt, the insurer would be estopped from later asserting that the insured had not paid the premium in accordance with the terms of the policy.

Jack McGeehee called a Farmers Insurance Co. agent and told him he wanted to get insurance on a house he owned. McGeehee told the agent his son, Howard McGeehee, lived in the house and Jack also wanted to get insurance on Howard's furniture. The agent had a homeowner's insurance policy issued, which covered the house and its contents, showing Howard as the insured and Jack as the mortgagee. Jack paid the premiums. Four years later, fire destroyed the house. Farmers paid for the destroyed contents, but refused to pay for the destruction of the house since the policy showed Howard as the insured and he did not own the house. The court held that since the agent made the choice as to how to insure the property and thus as to "insurable interest," Farmers was estopped to deny liability on its policy.

QUESTIONS

1   What is the purpose of insurance?
2   Identify the parties to a contract of insurance.
3   What is the insured's responsibility with respect to property when a loss occurs?
4   a.   When must a person have an insurable interest for life insurance purposes?
     b.   Give three examples of relationships giving rise to an insurable interest for life insurance.
5   a.   When must a person have an insurable interest for property insurance purposes?
     b.   Give three examples of persons who have an insurable interest in property.
6   How does a mutual insurance company differ from a stock insurance company?
7   What is the effect of the insured's concealing material facts in applying for insurance?
8   What is the difference between a warranty and a representation?
9   What is subrogation as applied to insurance contracts?
10   What is estoppel as applied to insurance contracts?

CASE PROBLEMS

L.O.2 .... **1** Hildegard and Lenard Price contracted to buy a house and lot, Lot 3, from Roy and Deanna Clemence, and the Prices took possession. The Clemences later refused to sell, and a lawsuit resulted. The Prices bought a fire insurance policy from Trinity Universal Insurance Company, and the house was damaged by fire. The court held that the contract to buy the house was void for mutual mistake of fact. When Trinity would not pay for the fire loss, the Prices sued. Did the Prices have an insurable interest in the house?

L.O.3 .... **2** An application for insurance asked the following questions: "Do you have or have you ever had or been treated for: . . . disorder of the stomach . . . any . . . mental disorder, . . ." "Have you ever been . . . counseled . . . because of . . . drug use?" and "Have you consulted any doctor or been hospitalized in the past five years for any reason . . . ?" Roger Johnson answered them all in the negative, and a policy of insurance was issued by State Farm Life Insurance Co. A month later Johnson was killed in a car accident. He had been hospitalized for an intestinal disorder a year and a half before answering the questions. He had also taken Valium, and his doctor had counseled him regarding the fact that he was taking too many drugs. State Farm refused to pay the insurance benefits, claiming misrepresentation. Was this misrepresentation?

L.O.3 .... **3** Gary and Patricia Lighton insured their house with Madison-Onondaga Mutual Fire Insurance Co. A fire damaged the house and Madison-Onondaga refused to pay under the policy. It asserted the Lightons had concealed the fact that a few months before applying for the policy a fire had occurred in their basement. The fire investigator had called that fire suspicious and told the Lightons. Madison-Onondaga said it would not have issued the policy if it had known about the previous, suspicious fire. The company had not asked the Lightons about any prior fires. Should the court find concealment?

L.O.3 .... **4** Barbara Garnes had two Bose speakers stolen from her. Her insurance company paid her for the loss. The thief pawned the speakers at King's Pawn Shop, owned by Jerry King. The police seized them as evidence. In court proceedings to determine to whom the speakers should go, King argued he purchased them in good faith and had a right to them against everyone but the true owner—Garnes. Having paid Garnes, the insurance company claimed it was entitled to subrogation and could assert Garnes' superior rights to the speakers. Who should get the speakers?

L.O.2 .... **5** While married to James, Dorothy Morgan bought insurance on the home they shared from American Security Insurance Co. The policy listed the named insured as Dorothy and any relative living in the home. The Morgans divorced and Dorothy deeded James her interest in the house. He bought insurance on the house from another company. A month later, fire destroyed the house. James' insurance company paid the limits of its policy. The Morgans also sought recovery from American on Dorothy's policy. American refused claiming no insurable interest existed on the policy at the time of the fire. Did either Morgan have an insurable interest?

L.O.3 ....

6 Barbara Washington purchased two fire insurance policies on her home and contents from Interstate Fire Insurance Company. The application asked, "If this policy is issued, will the building be insured by any other policy?" It was answered "no." The application also stated, "NO APPLICATION WILL BE APPROVED . . . WHEN THE BUILDING OR CONTENTS TO BE INSURED ARE ALREADY INSURED" and "said answers . . . shall form the basis of a contract of fire insurance . . ."

After the agent prepared a premium payment book, he hung it on a nail at Washington's request. Hanging on the nail was a premium payment book for a fire insurance policy she had already purchased. A few days later she purchased another fire insurance policy, and ten days later her home was totally destroyed by fire. Interstate refused to pay, alleging misrepresentation. Was it?

L.O.3 ....

7 Kevin Mulvihill bought a credit life insurance policy on the life of his wife. He had bought a car for her, and the insurance was to pay for the car in the event of her death. The insurance company did not ask for information concerning her health. Less than three weeks after the policy was obtained, she died of cancer. The company refused to pay, claiming Mulvihill had a duty to disclose his wife's terminal cancer. Did he?

L.O.3 ....

8 A teenager, William Bertram, was in a fight with another boy, Clinton Griggs. Bertram promptly gave notice to his insurer, Franklin Mutual Insurance Company. Three months later Franklin sent an investigator to interview Bertram. Four months later, Griggs made a claim for injuries, and Bertram sent it to Franklin, which made no effort to find or interview other witnesses or to obtain a physical examination of Griggs. Twenty months after the fight, Griggs filed suit, and Bertram promptly sent the papers to Franklin. A month later, Franklin refused coverage because intentional torts were excluded by the insurance policy. Bertram defended the action himself. He also alleged Franklin was liable to him on the basis of estoppel. He charged Franklin had a duty to promptly tell him that he might not be covered by the policy so that he could make his own investigation and preparation. Is Franklin liable?

L.O.3 ....

9 Kimberly and Walter Goodwin applied for a life insurance policy on Walter from Investors Life Insurance Co. through its agent, Charles Toomey. Toomey asked the Goodwins questions from the application and filled out the form. One question asked, "Within the past two years have you had your driver's license suspended or had two or more moving violations or accidents?" Toomey checked the box indicating "no." Kimberly knew Walter's license had been suspended three months previously and that he had two moving violations as well as two accidents within two years. The Goodwins signed the application, which stated they had read it and given complete and true answers. Investors issued the policy. Eight months later Walter died from massive head trauma received in an accident while racing at 70 mph in a 35 mph zone. Investors found out about Walter's driving record and refused to pay claiming false representation. Should Investors have to pay?

L.O.2 ....   **10**   Sam Rich, Sylvera Rich Class, Charles Rich, and Mamie Rich were partners in an investment business. Class died, and included in her estate were five life insurance policies on the life of Sam. The partnership agreement provided that upon the death of any partner, the partnership should terminate as to that partner, and the net worth of the partnership interest of the deceased partner should be paid to the deceased's personal representative. When, if ever, did Class have an insurable interest in Sam's life?

Chapter 39

TYPES OF INSURANCE

LEARNING OBJECTIVES

After studying this chapter you should be able to:

1 Explain the nature of life insurance and its normal limitations.

2 Define property insurance.

3 Identify the types of coverage afforded by automobile insurance.

Preview Case

After the court entered a decree of divorce for Joseph and Marcia Hortega, it ordered Joseph to keep Lonna and Josiah Hortega as the primary beneficiaries of his life insurance with Northern Illinois Gas Co. until they reached 21. However, six months later, Joseph completed a new beneficiary card naming his wife, Mary Hortega, as primary beneficiary. Joseph died, and the insurance company, Aetna Life Insurance Co., asked the court to determine who should receive the insurance proceeds. What should the court order?

Insurance companies provide many types of policies to help people protect against financial loss. Three types that most people purchase include:

1 Life insurance
2 Property insurance
3 Automobile insurance

LIFE INSURANCE

L.O.1

Life insurance is a contract by which the insurer agrees to pay a specified sum or sums of money to a beneficiary upon the death of the insured. An insured generally obtains life insurance to protect the beneficiary from financial hardship resulting from the death of the insured.

Types of Life Insurance Contracts

The most important types of life insurance policies include:

1 Term insurance
2 Endowment insurance
3 Whole life insurance
4 Combinations

Term Insurance

Life Insurance
Contract of insurer to pay money on death of insured

Term insurance contracts are those whereby the company assumes for a specified period of time the risk of the death of the insured. The term may be for only 1 year; or it may be for 5, 10, or even 50 years. The term must be stated in the policy.

Many variations of term policies exist. In short-term policies, such as five years, the insured might have the option of renewing it for another equal term without a physical examination. This is called **renewable term insurance.** The cost is higher for each renewal period. In nonrenewable term insurance the insured does not have the right to renew unless the company consents.

Term Insurance
Contract whereby insurer assumes risk of death of insured for specified time

Renewable Term Insurance
Term insurance renewable without physical examination

Term policies also may be either level term or decreasing term. In level term, the face of the policy is written in units of $1,000. The face amount remains the same during the entire term of the policy. In decreasing term contracts, the policy may be written in multiples of an amount of monthly income. For example, a person aged twenty could purchase a decreasing term policy of 50 units, or $500 a month, covering a period of 600 months, or 50 years. If the insured dies the first month after purchasing the policy, the beneficiary would draw $500 a month for 600 months, or $300,000 ultimately. If the insured dies at the end of 25 years, the beneficiary would draw $500 a month for 300 months, or $150,000 ultimately. Some decreasing term insurance is paid in a lump sum rather than periodically.

All term policies have one thing in common—they are pure life insurance. They shift the specific risk of loss as a result of death and nothing more.

Endowment Insurance

Endowment Insurance
Decreasing term insurance plus savings account

An **endowment insurance** policy is decreasing term insurance plus a savings account. Part of the premium pays for the insurance, and the remainder earns interest so that at the end of the term the savings will equal the face amount of the policy. If the insured dies during the term of the policy, the beneficiary will collect the face. If the insured is still living at the end of the term, the insurance company pays the face to the insured or a designated beneficiary.

Whole Life Insurance

All life insurance contracts are either term insurance or endowment insurance. A whole life insurance policy is one that continues, assuming the premium is paid, until age 100 or death, whichever occurs first. If the insured is still living at age

100, the face of the policy is collected as an endowment. A whole life policy might correctly be defined as endowment insurance at age 100.

Combinations

The three basic life insurance contracts—term, endowment, and whole life—can be combined in an almost endless variety of combinations to create slightly different contracts. In the case of universal life insurance, any premiums paid that exceed the current cost of term insurance are put into a fund and earn interest. The fund can be withdrawn by the owner or paid to the beneficiary at the death of the insured. The Family Income Policy, for example, is merely a straight life policy with a 20-year decreasing term policy attached as a rider.

Insurors frequently add several other riders to life insurance policies for an added premium. The disability income rider may be attached to any policy and pays an income to an insured who becomes disabled. A rider requiring the insurer to make a greater payment, customarily twice the ordinary amount when death is caused by accidental means, is called **double indemnity.**

Double Indemnity

Policy requiring insurer to pay twice ordinary policy amount if death is accidental

Limitation on Risks in Life Insurance Contracts

Two common limitations upon the risk covered by life insurance include: (1) suicide and (2) death from war activity.

Suicide

Life insurance policies commonly refuse payment when death occurs from suicide. Other suicide clauses stipulate that the company will not pay if the suicide occurs within two years from the date of the policy.

Farmers New World Life Insurance Co. issued two policies on the life of Lawrence Malcom. They each contained the following clause: "Suicide, whether sane or insane, will not be a risk assumed during the first two policy years. In such a case we will refund the premiums paid." Within two years of the issuance, Lawrence committed suicide. Farmers refused to pay the face of the policies. The beneficiaries sued alleging the suicide provision was not plain and clear. The court found the words of the clause understandable, and Farmers did not have to pay the face of the policies.

Death from War Activity

A so-called war clause provides that if the insured dies as a consequence of war activity the company will not pay. If a member of the armed forces dies a natural death, the company must pay. In order to refuse payment, the insurance company has the burden of proving war activity caused the death.

Payment of Premiums

If the premiums are not paid when due, and the policy so provides, it either will lapse automatically or may be declared forfeited at the option of the insurer. The policy or a statute of the state may provide that after a certain number of premiums have been paid, an unpaid premium results in the issuance of a smaller, paid-up policy for the same term. By the payment of an additional premium the insured may generally obtain a policy containing a waiver of premiums that becomes effective if the insured becomes disabled. When disability occurs, the insured does not have to pay premiums for the period of time during which the disability exists.

Grace Period

Grace Period
30- or 31-day period in which late premium may be paid without policy lapsing

The law requires life insurance companies to provide a **grace period** of 30 or 31 days in every life insurance policy. This grace period gives the insured 30 or 31 days from the due date of the premium in which to pay it without the policy's lapsing. Without this provision, if the insured paid the premium one day late, the policy either might lapse or be forfeited by the insured. The insured might be able to obtain a reinstatement of the policy but might be required to pass a new physical examination. To buy a new policy, the insured might have to pass a physical examination and would have to pay a higher rate for the current age.

Incontestability

Life insurance policies are incontestable after a certain period of time, usually one or two years. After that time, the insurance company usually cannot contest the validity of a claim on any ground except nonpayment of premiums.

Change of Beneficiary

Life insurance policies ordinarily reserve to the insured the right to change the beneficiary at will. Policies also permit the insured to name successive beneficiaries so that if the first beneficiary should die before the insured, the proceeds would pass to the second named or contingent beneficiary.

Courts uphold divorce decrees or separation agreements fixing beneficiaries of insurance policies. Later attempts by the insured to change a beneficiary required by a court order do not succeed.

After the court entered a decree of divorce for Joseph and Marcia Hortega, it ordered Joseph to keep Lonna and Josiah Hortega as the primary beneficiaries of his life insurance with Northern Illinois Gas Co. until they reached 21. However, six months later, Joseph completed a new beneficiary card naming his wife, Mary Hortega, as primary beneficiary. Joseph died, and the insurance company, Aetna Life Insurance Co., asked a court to determine who should receive the insurance proceeds. The court held that the proceeds should go to Lonna and Josiah as the divorce decree required.

Assignment of the Policy

The policy of insurance may be assigned (or the rights in the policy may be transferred to another) by the insured. The assignment may be either absolute or as collateral security for a loan that the insured obtains from the assignee, such as a bank.

A beneficiary may also make an assignment; however, the assignee of the beneficiary is subject to the disadvantage that the insured may change beneficiaries. If the assignment is made after the insured has died, the assignment is an ordinary assignment of an existing money claim.

Annuity Insurance

Annuity Insurance

Contract that pays monthly income to insured while alive

An **annuity insurance** contract pays the insured a monthly income from a specified age, generally age 65, until death. It is a risk entirely unrelated to the risk assumed in a life insurance contract, even though both contracts are sold by life insurance companies. Someone has defined life insurance as shifting the risk of dying too soon and annuity insurance as shifting the risk of living too long, or outliving one's savings. An individual aged 65 who has $50,000 and a life expectancy of 72 years could use up the $50,000 over the expected 7 additional years of life by using approximately $600 a month for living expenses. However, if the individual lives for more than seven years, there would be no money left. An annuity insurance policy could be purchased for $50,000, and the monthly income would be guaranteed no matter how long the insured lives. If the annuity contract calls for the monthly payments to continue until the second of two insureds dies, it is called a **joint and survivor annuity.** Couples who wish to extend their savings as long as either one is still living frequently use this type of annuity.

Joint and Survivor Annuity

Annuity paid until second of two people die

PROPERTY INSURANCE

L.O.2 ....

Property Insurance

Contract by which insurer pays for damage to property

Property insurance is a contract whereby the insurer, in return for a premium, agrees to reimburse the insured for loss or damage to specified property caused by the hazard covered. A contract of property insurance is one of indemnity or compensation for loss that protects the policyholder from actual loss.

If a building actually worth $40,000 is insured for $45,000, the extra premiums that were paid for the last $5,000 worth of coverage do not provide any benefit for the insured. The actual value, $40,000, is the maximum that can be collected in case of total loss. On the other hand, if a building is insured for only $20,000 and is totally destroyed, the insurance company has to pay only $20,000. The maximum amount paid for total loss of property is the lesser of the face of the policy or the value of the property.

Losses Related to Fire

Hostile Fire

Fire out of its normal place

Friendly Fire

Fire contained where intended

Normally, fire insurance covers damage to property caused only by hostile fires. A **hostile fire** is defined as one out of its normal place, whereas a **friendly fire** is one contained in the place where it is intended to be. Scorching, searing, singeing, smoke, and similar damages from a friendly fire are not covered under a fire policy. For a fire policy to cover damage, an actual fire must occur. The policy does not cover loss caused by heat without fire. In one case several thousand bales of cotton were under water during a flood. After the flood receded, heat in the bales of cotton was so intense smoke poured forth for days, but no flame was ever detected. The court held there was no fire.

Washington State Hop Producers, Inc., carried fire insurance with Harbor Insurance Company. Hop Producers discovered that 253 bales of hops in its warehouse were damaged by "browning." Heat generated by chemical oxidation causes browning. It may happen without flame, glow, or light, and none of those things were observed. The policy insured "against all direct loss by fire ..." When Harbor refused coverage, Hop Producers sued, alleging fire damaged the hops. The court held that since the damage can occur without flame and no evidence of flame existed, no fire damage occurred.

Business Interruption Insurance

Insurance covering loss of profits while business building is repaired

Leasehold Interest Insurance

Covers cost of higher rent when leased building is damaged

Extended Coverage

Riders covering loss from additional risks

Open Policy

Policy that requires insured to prove loss sustained

Valued Policy

Policy that fixes values for insured items

Specific Policy

Insurance that applies to only one item

Blanket Policy

Policy on many items in different places or different items in one place

Floating Policy

Coverage no matter where property located

Homeowners' Policy

Coverage of many perils plus liability for owners living in their houses

Fire insurance also does not cover economic loss that results from a fire. A hostile fire may cause many losses other than to the property insured, yet the fire policy on the building and contents alone will not cover these losses. An example is the loss of profits while the building is being restored. This loss can be covered by a special policy called **business interruption** insurance. If one leases property on a long-term, favorable lease and the lease is canceled because of fire damage to the building, the tenant may have to pay a higher rent in new quarters. This increased rent loss can be covered by a **leasehold interest insurance policy** but not by a fire policy.

The typical fire policy may also cover the risks of loss by windstorm, explosion, smoke damage from a friendly fire, falling aircraft, water damage, riot and civil commotion, and many others. Each of these additional risks must be added to the fire policy by means of riders. This is commonly known as **extended coverage.**

The Property Insurance Policy

The property insurance policy will state a maximum amount that will be paid by the insurer. When only a maximum is stated, the policy is called an **open policy,** and in the event of partial or total loss, the insured must prove the actual loss that has been sustained. The policy may be a **valued policy,** in which case, instead of stating a maximum amount, it fixes values for the insured items of property. Once a policyholder shows a covered total destruction of the property, the insurer pays the total value. If only a partial loss occurs, the insured under a valued policy must still prove the amount of loss, which amount cannot exceed the stated value of the property.

Insurance policies also may be specific, blanket, or floating. A **specific policy** applies to one item only, such as one house. A **blanket policy** covers many items of the same kind in different places or different kinds of property in the same place, such as a building, fixtures, and merchandise in a single location. **Floating policies** are used for trucks, theatrical costumes, circus paraphernalia, and similar items that are not kept in a fixed location. A floating policy is also desirable for items that may be sent out for cleaning, such as rugs or clothes, and articles of jewelry and clothes that may be worn while traveling. An insurance policy on household effects covers for loss only at the named location. The purpose of the floating policy is to cover the loss no matter where the property is located at the time of the loss.

Most people who own their homes obtain homeowners' insurance. A **homeowners' policy** protects the house and also its contents from almost every peril. It covers damage from such perils as fire, wind, lightning, hail, and theft. It also covers liability of the homeowner in case someone suffers injury on the property. A tenant can obtain similar insurance that protects the tenant's personal property but not the building itself.

Reporting Form for Merchandise Inventory

Policy allowing periodic reporting of inventory on hand to vary coverage amount

Another type of insurance policy of particular interest to merchants is the **Reporting Form for Merchandise Inventory.** This policy permits the merchant to report periodically, usually once a month, the amount of inventory on hand. This enables the merchant to carry full coverage at all times and still not be grossly over-insured during periods when inventory is low.

DESCRIPTION OF THE PROPERTY

All property and its location must be described with reasonable accuracy in order to identify the property and to inform the insurer of the nature of the risk involved. It is not accurate to describe a house with asphalt brick siding as brick. Personal property should be so described that in the event of loss, its value can be determined. The general description "living room furniture" may make it difficult to establish the value and the number of items. A complete inventory should be kept. If this is done, such description as "household furniture" in the policy is adequate.

Since the location of the property affects the risk, it must be specified. If personal property used in a brick house on a broad paved street is moved to a frame house on an out-of-the-way dirt road, the risk from fire may be increased considerably. To retain coverage, express permission must always be obtained from the insurer when property is moved except under a floating policy. Most homeowners' policies sold today continue coverage at a new location for several days together with coverage during the moving trip. If a loss occurs during the specified period, the company must pay, even though it received no notice of the changed location.

COINSURANCE

Coinsurance

Insured recovers in ratio of insurance to amount of insurance required

Under the principle of **coinsurance,** the insured recovers on a loss in the same ratio as the insurance bears to the amount of insurance that the company requires. Many policies contain an 80-percent coinsurance clause. This clause means the insured may carry any amount of insurance up to the value of the property, but the company will not pay the full amount of a partial loss unless insurance is carried for at least 80 percent of the value of the property. If a building is worth $50,000 and the insured buys a policy for $20,000, the company under the 80-percent coinsurance clause will pay only half of the damage and never more than $20,000. The 80-percent clause requires the insured to carry $40,000, or 80 percent of $50,000, to be fully protected from a partial loss. Since only half of this amount is carried, only half of the damage can be collected.

The coinsurance clause may be some percentage other than 80 percent. In burglary insurance it may be as low as 5 or 10 percent. On rare occasions it is as high as 100 percent in fire insurance.

REPAIRS AND REPLACEMENTS

Most insurance contracts give the insurer the option of paying the amount of loss or repairing or replacing the property. The amount the insurance company will pay for a loss will vary depending on whether market value or replacement cost is used to measure the amount of loss. Which measure is used will depend on the policy. If the property is repaired or replaced, materials of like kind and quality must be used. The work must be completed within a reasonable time. The option to replace is seldom exercised by the insurer. The insurer also may have the option of taking the property at an agreed valuation and then paying the insured the full value of the damaged property.

AUTOMOBILE INSURANCE

L.O.3 .... Automobile insurance includes two major classes of insurance: physical damage insurance (including fire, theft, and collision) and public liability insurance (including bodily injury and property damage). To understand the law one must know what specific risk the insurance carrier assumes and the terms of the policy covering that specific risk. The term *automobile insurance* refers to insurance that the insured obtains to cover a car and the injuries that the insured and other members of the family may sustain. The term also refers to liability insurance, which protects the insured from claims that third persons may make for injuries caused them or damage to their property caused by the insured.

Physical Damage Insurance

Physical Damage Insurance
Insurance for damage to car itself

As the name implies, **physical damage insurance** covers the risks of injury or damage to the car itself. It includes:

1　Fire insurance
2　Theft insurance
3　Collision insurance
4　Comprehensive coverage

Fire Insurance

Much of the law of property insurance discussed in the preceding pages applies to automobile insurance. The fire policy covers loss to a car damaged or destroyed by the burning of any conveyance upon which the car is being transported, such as a barge, boat, or train. Fire insurance can be obtained separately but is normally included in comprehensive coverage.

Theft Insurance

Theft
Taking another's property without consent

Conversion
Obtaining possession of property and converting it to own use

Robbery
Taking property by force

Theft is taking another's property without the owner's consent with the intent to wrongfully deprive the owner of the property. Automobile theft insurance either by law or by contract normally covers a wide range of losses. Obtaining possession of a car and converting it to one's own use to the exclusion of or inconsistent with the rights of the owner is known as **conversion.** Taking another's car by force or threat of force is known as **robbery.** In some states the automobile theft policy must cover all these losses. The policy itself may define theft broadly enough to cover theft, conversion, and robbery. Unless the policy is broadened either by law or by the wording of the policy, a theft policy covers only the wrongful deprivation of the car without claim of right.

Automobile theft insurance usually covers pilferage of any parts of the car but not articles or clothes left in the car. It also covers any damage done to the car either by theft or attempted theft. It does not cover loss of use of the car unless the policy specifically provides for this loss.

Cyrus See had an auto insurance policy with St. Paul Insurance Company. The policy covered theft of equipment from his vehicle "only if the equipment at the time of the loss . . . was permanently installed in or upon" the vehicle. See had removed a citizens band radio and microphone from the mounting bracket on the dashboard of his truck and put them out of sight on the floor behind the driver's seat. To do this he had disconnected the electrical and aerial wires before leaving the truck. When he returned, the truck had been broken into, and the radio and microphone were missing. He sued St. Paul for the value of them. The court held that they were not permanently installed in the truck at the time of the theft, so St. Paul was not liable.

Collision Insurance

The standard collision policy covers all damage to the car caused by a collision or upset. A collision occurs whenever an object strikes the insured car or the car strikes an object. Both objects need not be automobiles nor be moving. Frequently collision policies require the collision to be "accidental." A court held that rolling rock that crashed into a parked car constituted a collision. Likewise, there was a collision when a horse kicked the door of the insured automobile. However, no collision occurs when the colliding object consists of a natural phenomenon, such as rain or hail.

Practically all collision policies void or suspend coverage if a car hauls a trailer unless insurance of the same kind carried on the car is placed on the trailer. The question of interpretation then arises as to what constitutes a "trailer." A small boat trailer and a small two-wheel trailer generally are not considered trailers but horse or cattle trailers are.

If a car has collision insurance but not fire insurance, the policy will, in most states, pay both the fire loss and the collision loss occurring in the same wreck so long as the fire ensues after collision and is a direct result of it.

Deductible Clause

Insurance provision whereby insured pays damage up to specified amount; company pays excess up to policy limits

Most collision insurance policies have a **deductible clause.** A deductible clause provides that the insurance company will pay for damages to the car in excess of a specified amount. The specified amount, called the "deductible," is usually $100 to $250. The insured must pay this amount. Suppose a collision results in $850 in damages to a car covered by $250 deductible collision insurance. The insured must pay the first $250 and the insurance company pays the remainder—$600. Policies without any deductible clause have extremely high rates. It is much cheaper for the insured to assume some of the risk.

An insurance company may pay the insured a claim for collision damage caused by someone else's negligence. If so, under the law of subrogation the company has the right to sue this other party to the collision for the damages.

Comprehensive Coverage

Insurance companies will write automobile insurance covering almost every conceivable risk to a car, such as windstorm, earthquake, flood, strike, spray from trees,

Comprehensive Policy

Insurance covering large number of miscellaneous risks

Public Liability Insurance

Insurance designed to protect third persons from bodily injury and property damage

malicious mischief, submersion in water, acid from the battery, riot, glass breakage, hail, and falling aircraft. A **comprehensive policy** may include all of these risks plus fire and theft. A comprehensive policy covers only the hazards enumerated in the policy, and collision is normally excluded.

Public Liability Insurance

The second major division of automobile insurance, **public liability insurance,** protects third persons from bodily injury and property damage.

Bodily Injury Insurance

Bodily injury insurance covers the risk of bodily injury to the insured's passengers, pedestrians, or the occupants of another car. The insurance company obligates itself to pay any sum not exceeding the limit fixed in the policy for which the insured may be personally liable. If the insured has no liability for damages, the insurance company has no liability except the duty of defending the insured in court actions brought by injured persons. This type of insurance does not cover any injury to the person or the property of the insured.

Coverage under an automobile liability policy is usually written as 10/20/5, 25/50/10, 100/300/15, or similar combinations. The first number indicates that the company will pay $10,000, $25,000, or $100,000, respectively, to any one person for bodily injury in any one accident. The middle number fixes the maximum amount the company will pay for bodily injury to more than one person in any one accident. The third figure sets the limit the company will pay for property damage. This usually is the damage to the other person's car but may include damage to any property belonging to someone other than the insured.

Defense Clause

Policy clause in which insurer agrees to defend insured against damage claims

Under a **defense clause** the insurer agrees to defend the insured against any claim for damages. The insured reserves the right to accept or reject any settlement offered out of court.

A bodily injury insurance policy does not cover accidents occurring while an under-age person drives the car. It may not cover accidents occurring while the car is rented or leased unless specifically covered, while the car is used to carry passengers for a consideration, while the car is used for any purpose other than that named in the policy, or while it is used outside the United States and Canada. Some policies exclude accidents while the car is being used for towing a trailer or any other vehicle used as a trailer. These are the ordinary exclusions. Policies may have additional exclusions of various kinds.

The insured may not settle claims or incur expenses other than those for immediate medical help. In the event that the insurance company pays a loss, it is subrogated to any rights that the insured has against others because of such losses.

Property Damage Insurance

In automobile property damage insurance the insurer agrees to pay, on behalf of the insured, all sums the insured may be legally obligated to pay for damages arising out of the ownership, maintenance, or use of the automobile. The liability of the insurer, however, is limited as stated in the policy.

The policy usually provides that the insurer will not be liable in the event that the car is being operated, maintained, or used by any person in violation of any state or federal law as to age or occupation. The insurer has no liability for damage to property owned by, leased to, transported by, or in charge of the insured.

Medical Payments and Uninsured Motorist Insurance

In addition to physical damage and public liability insurance, there is insurance that covers injury to the insured or passengers in the insured's car. Medical payments cover bodily injury and are paid regardless of other insurance. Uninsured motorist coverage protects the insured when injury results from the negligence of another driver who does not have liability insurance.

Notice to the Insurer

In the event of an accident, the policyholder has the duty to give the insurer written notice and proof of loss regarding the damages resulting from the accident. The notice must identify the insured and give such information as the names and address of injured persons, the owner of any damaged property, witnesses, and the time, place, and detailed circumstances of the accident. This notice must be given within a reasonable time.

> Injured in an automobile accident, Brazil failed to notify his insurer, Government Employees Insurance Company, until 38 months later. The policy required Brazil to give notice as soon as possible and he offered no excuse for the delay in notification. When Government denied coverage, Brazil sued. The court held that the unexcused delay of 38 months in notification constituted an unreasonable delay.

If a claim or a suit is brought against the insured, every demand, notice, or summons received must immediately be forwarded to the insurance company. The insured must give the fullest cooperation to the insurer, who normally has the right to settle any claims or lawsuits as it deems best.

Recovery Even When at Fault

Last Clear Chance
Negligent driver recovers if other driver had one last clear chance to avoid injury

Comparative Negligence
Contributory negligence reduces but does not bar recovery

Normally the injured party must prove the driver of the insured car was negligent or at fault before the insurer becomes liable. Frequently, both drivers are negligent. Formerly, if the driver bringing suit negligently contributed even slightly to the accident, no recovery could be had. This harsh rule has been replaced in most states by the **last clear chance** rule. This rule states that if one driver is negligent but the other driver had one last clear chance to avoid hitting the negligent driver and did not take it, then the driver who had the last clear chance is liable.

In a number of states the harshness of the common-law rule as to contributory negligence has also been modified by **comparative negligence** statutes. These statutes provide that the contributory negligence of the plaintiff reduces the recovery but does not completely bar recovery from a negligent defendant. That means, the court balances the negligence of each party against that of the other. Suppose

Roemer and Griffero have an automobile accident. Both were negligent. It is determined that the damage to Roemer's car was caused 60 percent by Griffero and 40 percent by Roemer's own negligence. If the total damage to Roemer's car is $2,500, Griffero will have to pay 60 percent or $1,500.

Some states have established **no-fault insurance.** Under this plan, insurance companies pay for injuries suffered by their insureds no matter who has responsibility for negligence. States use this no-fault plan for a limited amount of damages. Above this amount, the fault rules apply.

No-Fault Insurance

Insurance companies pay for this insured's injury regardless of fault

Required Insurance

People with poor driving records might find it difficult or impossible to obtain mandatory automobile insurance. When the law requires a person to carry insurance in order to be permitted to drive but no insurance company will sell a policy, a state agency will assign this driver to an insurance company. The company must issue the policy under the "assigned risk" rule. States require all insurance companies to accept the drivers assigned in this manner.

QUESTIONS

1   What do all term life insurance policies have in common?
2   What is the importance of a grace period in a life insurance policy?
3   When may the insured change the beneficiary of a life insurance policy?
4   What is the maximum amount an insured can recover for the total loss of property?
5   Why must the property and its location be described accurately when obtaining insurance on it?
6   What is coinsurance?
7   What is a collision for auto insurance purposes?
8   Why do most automobile collision insurance policies have a deductible clause?
9   If an insured has no liability for damages after an auto accident, does this mean the insurance company has no responsibility under the insured's bodily injury insurance coverage?
10   Under what theories or programs may the injured party recover even when at fault?

CASE PROBLEMS

L.O.1 ....

1   Franklin Summers applied for life insurance, paid one month's premium, and received a Conditional Receipt for Advance Payment with Application for Life Insurance. The medical requirements of the application were completed on November 10, and by the terms of the Conditional Receipt, the policy became effective that day. The formal policy was issued on December 15. On November 18, two years later, Summers committed suicide. The suicide clause in the policy stated: "If the insured shall commit suicide . . . within two years from the Date of Issue of this contract, the amount payable will be

limited to the premiums paid." "Date of Issue" was not defined in the policy. The company argued that date of issue meant the date of issue on the face of the policy. The beneficiary argued that date of issue meant the effective date of the policy; otherwise there would effectively be two policies, one during the conditional coverage period with no suicide clause and the formal policy. What was the date of issue?

L.O.3 ....

2 Leon D. McCormick & Sons, Inc., carried collision insurance on its dump truck with Auto-Owners Insurance Company. The truck was loaded with wet limestone, and the driver attempted to empty the load. The load emptied from the right-hand side of the truck first so that a large amount of wet limestone was on the left side of the dump bed. The uneven distribution caused the dump bed to twist. A rear hinge pin on the dump body broke, and the dump body tipped over onto the ground. The truck stayed upright. The policy covered damage to the vehicle "and its equipment caused by accidental collision with another object or by accidental upset." The dump body was within the definition of equipment. Auto-Owners refused to pay for the damage. Should it pay?

L.O.3 ....

3 While driving a car owned by Roy Matheney, Alan Conley fell asleep and drove off the highway causing damage to the car. Alan was covered by automobile liability and collision coverage with Farmers Insurance Company of Arkansas. The policy stated it did not apply under Liability Insurance Coverage "to damage to . . . property . . . in charge of the insured other than a residence or private garage." Farmers denied liability, so Matheney sued it. He had already obtained a judgment against Conley, so Conley's liability was clear. Matheney argued that if a nonowner-driver is liable for negligence in causing collision damage, then his insurance policy ought to be interpreted, if possible, to cover him for such liability. Was Farmers liable?

L.O.2 ....

4 Arlene Schnitzer purchased from South Carolina Insurance Company two blanket insurance policies insuring five buildings for $2,136,000. One of the buildings was destroyed by fire. The policies stated: "THIS COMPANY SHALL BE LIABLE FOR NO GREATER PROPORTION OF . . . LOSS THAN THE AMOUNT OF INSURANCE SPECIFIED . . . BEARS TO THE PERCENTAGE SPECIFIED ON THE FIRST PAGE OF THIS POLICY ON THE ACTUAL CASH VALUE OF THE PROPERTY DESCRIBED . . . AT THE TIME OF LOSS, NOR FOR MORE THAN THE PROPORTION WHICH THE AMOUNT OF INSURANCE SPECIFIED . . . BEARS TO THE TOTAL INSURANCE ON THE PROPERTY DESCRIBED . . . AT THE TIME OF LOSS." The percentage was 90 percent. The destroyed building was valued at $574,209, and the total value of the buildings was $3,887,499. Does the coinsurance clause apply?

L.O.3 ....

5 Sheila Blaylock bought a car for $8,500. Three months later she was informed by the police that the car had been stolen from its owner. They took the car and it was never returned. She filed suit against her insurance company, alleging it was liable on her comprehensive auto insurance. The policy stated it did "not apply to loss or damage . . . which may be caused by war, declared or undeclared, invasion, directly or indirectly, insurrection, civil war, military or usurped power, or to confiscation by duly constituted governmental or civil authority." Is the company liable?

L.O.1 ....

6 On March 21, John D'Allessandro applied for life insurance with Durham Life Insurance Co. He signed an application, a copy of which was given him, indicating that he had not consulted a doctor or been hospitalized within five years and had no heart trouble, chest pains, or other health problem. He actually had been treated and hospitalized within five years for heart and kidney problems. The policy was issued July 1, and D'Allessandro died of coronary artery disease on October 14. The incontestability clause in the policy stated: "no . . . statement shall be used in defense of a claim hereunder unless a copy of the instrument containing the statement has been furnished to the person making the claim." Durham furnished the beneficiary with a copy of the instrument after D'Allessandro died. She claimed the misrepresentations could not be raised by Durham because she had not been given a copy of the instrument before D'Allessandro died. Did the incontestability clause apply?

L.O.3 ....

7 B. R. Justice owned a pickup truck that was insured by Government Employees Insurance Company. He bought a camper for use on the pickup. It was bolted on with chains and tighteners. Justice had an accident, and the pickup and camper were extensively damaged. Government refused to pay for the damage to the camper. The auto insurance policy provided coverage to "the automobile, including its equipment." Justice sued Government. Is Government liable for the damage to the camper?

Chapter 40

SECURITY DEVICES

LEARNING OBJECTIVES

After studying this chapter you should be able to:

1   State the general nature of contracts of guaranty or suretyship.

2   Identify ways contracts of guaranty and safetyship are discharged.

3   Discuss the rights of the parties in a secured credit sale.

4   Discuss the rights of the seller and buyer in a secured credit sale.

Preview Case

Yvonne Sanchez defaulted on her auto payments to MBank El Paso. MBank hired two men to repossess the car. They found the car in Sanchez' driveway and hooked it to a tow truck. Sanchez ordered them to leave. When they did not, she jumped into the car, locked the doors, and refused to get out. The men towed the car at a high speed to a repossession yard; parked the car; and padlocked the gate to the yard. A Doberman pinscher guard dog roamed loose in the yard. Sanchez remained in the car until rescued by her husband and police. Did the bank properly repossess the car?

T his chapter discusses two types of security devices: (1) guaranty and suretyship contracts and (2) secured credit sales.

GUARANTY AND SURETYSHIP

L.O.1

A contract of guaranty or suretyship is an agreement whereby one party promises to be responsible for the debt, default, or obligation of another. Such contracts generally arise when one person assumes responsibility for the extension of credit to another, as in buying merchandise on credit or in borrowing money from a bank.

A person entrusted with money of another, such as a cashier, a bank teller, or a county treasurer, may be required to have someone guarantee the faithful performance of the duties. This contract of suretyship is commonly referred to as a **fidelity bond.**

In recent years **bonding companies** have taken over most of the business of guaranteeing the employer against losses due to the dishonesty of employees. These bonding companies are paid sureties, which means they receive money for entering into the suretyship. The bonding company's obligation arises from its written contract with the employer. This contract of indemnity sets out in detail the conditions under which the surety will be liable.

Parties

A contract of guaranty or of suretyship involves three parties. The party who undertakes to be responsible for another is the **guarantor,** or the **surety**; the party to whom the guaranty is given is the **creditor**; and the party who has primary liability is the *principal debtor,* or simply the **principal.**

Distinctions

The words *surety* and *guarantor* are often used interchangeably, and they have many similarities. Some states have abolished any distinction between them. However, in other states their legal usages differ. In a contract of suretyship, the surety has liability coextensive with that of the principal debtor. The surety has direct and primary responsibility for the debt or obligation just as the primary debtor. The surety's obligation, then, is identical with the debtor's.

A guarantor's obligation is secondary to that of the principal debtor. The promise to pay comes into effect only in the event the principal defaults. The guarantor's obligation does not arise simultaneously with the principal's. The obligation depends upon the happening of another event, namely, the failure of the principal to pay.

For the most part, the law of suretyship applies with equal force to both paid sureties and accommodation sureties. A bail bondsman is a paid surety. An accommodation surety agrees to be a surety as a favor to the principal. A parent who cosigns a note for a teenager constitutes an accommodation surety. In some instances the contract of a paid surety will be interpreted strictly. Thus, in the case of acts claimed to discharge the surety, courts sometimes require paid sureties to prove that they have actually been harmed by the conduct of the principal before allowing recovery.

Importance of Making a Distinction

In states that recognize a difference between guarantors and sureties, the distinctions involve three aspects:

1 Form
2 Notice of default
3 Remedy

Fidelity Bond

Suretyship for someone who handles another's money

Bonding Company

Paid surety

Guarantor or Surety

Party who agrees to be responsible for obligation of another

Creditor

Party who receives guaranty

Principal

Party primarily liable

Form. All the essential elements of a contract must be present in both contracts of guaranty and contracts of suretyship. However, a contract of guaranty must be in writing (see Illustration 40-1), whereas most contracts of suretyship may normally be oral.

The Uniform Commercial Code provides: "The promise to answer for the debt, default, or obligation of another must be in writing and be signed by the party to be charged or by his authorized agent." This provision should apply to a promise that

Illustration 40-1   A Letter of Guaranty

WATERS, MELLEN AND COMPANY
900 West Lake Avenue
Cincinnati, Ohio 45227

May 16, 19--

Ms. Norma Rae
201 E. Fifth Street
CAmpton, KY 41301

Dear Ms. Rae

In consideration of the letting of the premises located at 861 South Street, this city, to Mr. William H. Prost for a period of two years from date, I hereby guarantee the punctual payment of the rent and the faithful performance of the covenants of the lease.

Very truly yours

Orvinne L. Meyer

Orvinne L. Meyer
Vice-President, Personnel

creates a secondary obligation, which means an obligation of guaranty, not to a promise that creates a primary obligation or suretyship.

Notice of Default. As parties primarily liable for the debt, a creditor need not notify sureties if the principal defaults. Guarantors, on the other hand, must be notified by the creditor. In some states, failure to give notice does not of itself discharge the guarantyship. A guarantor damaged by the failure to receive notice may offset the amount of the damage against the claim of the creditor.

Thomas Gentry was a guarantor on a promissory note executed by Baytown Sports Center, Inc., to Highlands State Bank. Sports Center defaulted on the note and Highlands foreclosed on the security. After foreclosure and sale of the collateral, there was a deficiency of $172,000 still owing on the note. Highlands filed suit against Gentry as guarantor. The trial court entered summary judgment against him. The appellate court held that in order to recover, Highlands had to establish that notice had been given to Gentry. Since the court record did not show such notice, the trial court ruling was reversed.

Remedy. In the case of suretyship, the surety assumes an original obligation. The surety must pay. Sureties have liability as fully and under the same conditions as if the debt were theirs from the beginning. The rule is different in many contracts of guaranty. In a conditional guaranty, the guarantor has liability only if the other party cannot pay.

Arnold writes, "Let Brewer have a suit; if he cannot pay you, I will." This guaranty depends upon Brewer's ability to pay. Therefore, the seller must make all reasonable efforts to collect from Brewer before collecting from Arnold. If Arnold had written, "Let Brewer have this suit, and I will pay you," an original obligation would have been created for which Arnold would have been personally liable. Therefore, Arnold would be deemed a surety if the understanding was that Arnold was to pay for the suit.

Rights of the Surety and the Guarantor

A guarantor and a surety have the following rights:

1 Indemnity
2 Subrogation
3 Contribution
4 Exoneration

Indemnity
Right of guarantor to be
reimbursed by principal

Indemnity. A guarantor or surety who pays the debt or the obligation of the principal has the right to be reimbursed by the principal, known as the right of **indemnity.** The guarantor or the surety may be induced to pay the debt when it becomes due to avoid the accumulation of interest and other costs on the debt.

Subrogation. When the guarantor or the surety pays the debt of the principal, the law automatically assigns the claim of the creditor to the guarantor or surety. The payment also entitles the guarantor or surety to all property, liens, or securities that were held by the creditor to secure the payment of the debt. This right of subrogation does not arise until the creditor has been paid in full, but it does arise if the surety or the guarantor has paid a part of the debt and the principal has paid the remainder.

Raymond Fulton guaranteed a lease of J. D. Edge's to South Oak Cliff State Bank. When Edge defaulted on the lease, the bank sued Edge. Fulton gave the bank his note in payment of his guaranty. Without Fulton's knowledge, the bank dismissed its suit against Edge with prejudice (meaning the same suit could not be refiled). The bank sued Fulton on his note. Fulton said he should not have to pay because when the bank dismissed the suit against Edge with prejudice, it made it impossible for Fulton to sue Edge on the transaction. The court held that once Fulton paid his guaranty, he acquired subrogation rights. The subrogation rights arose from payment of the guaranty, not from the lease on which the bank had sued Edge. Fulton could still sue Edge.

Coguarantors or Cosureties

Two or more people jointly liable for another's obligation

Contribution

Right of coguarantor to recover excess of proportionate share of debt from other coguarantor(s)

Exoneration

Guarantor's right to have creditor compel payment of debt

L.O.2 ....

Contribution. Two or more persons jointly liable for the debt, default, or obligation of a certain person are **coguarantors** or **cosureties.** Guarantors or sureties who have paid more than their proportionate share of the debt are entitled to recover from the other guarantors or sureties the amount in excess of their pro rata share of the loss. This is the right of **contribution.** It does not arise until the surety or the guarantor has paid the debts in full or has otherwise settled the debt.

Exoneration. A surety or guarantor may call upon the creditor to proceed to compel the payment of the debt; otherwise the surety or guarantor will be released. This is the right of **exoneration.** The creditor may delay in pressing the debtor to pay because of the security of the suretyship. In cases where the debtor can pay, failure of the creditor to compel payment when due releases the surety. The surety then has no uncertainty concerning potential liability.

Discharge of a Surety or a Guarantor

The usual methods of discharging any obligation, including performance, voluntary agreement, and bankruptcy, discharge both a surety and a guarantor. However, some additional acts that will discharge the surety or the guarantor include:

1 Extension of time
2 Alteration of the terms of the contract
3 Loss or return of collateral by the creditor

Extension of Time. If the creditor extends the time of the debt without the consent of the surety or the guarantor and for a consideration, the surety or the guarantor is discharged from further liability.

Alteration of the Terms of the Contract. A material alteration of the contract by the creditor without the surety's or guarantor's consent discharges the surety or guarantor. The change must be prejudicial to the surety or the guarantor. A reduction in the interest rate has been held not to discharge the surety, whereas a change in the place of payment has been held to be an act justifying a discharge of the surety. A material change in a contract constitutes substituting a new contract for the old. The surety guaranteed the payment of the old contract, not the new one.

Stuart and Marlene Engar executed a guaranty on a debt owed by a corporation to Capital Bank. As permitted by the guaranty, the Engars subsequently revoked the guaranty as to any new debts under the terms of the guaranty. Capital later restructured the corporate debt without the Engars' consent. By the restructuring, payments had to be applied first to a new personal debt of one of the principals in the corporation before being applied to the corporate debt. The Engars alleged the restructuring constituted a material and detrimental alteration of the debtor's contract with Capital. The court agreed and released the Engars from the guaranty.

Loss or Return of Collateral by the Creditor. If the creditor through negligence loses or damages collateral security given to secure the debt, a surety or a guarantor is discharged. The return of any collateral security to the debtor also discharges a surety or guarantor. Collateral must be held for the benefit of the surety until the debtor pays the debt in full.

Custom Leasing, Inc., a wholly owned subsidiary of Otoe County National Bank, purchased equipment from Carlson Stapler and Shippers Supply, Inc., to lease to Creative Buildings, Inc. Carlson executed a guaranty agreement for the lease. It provided, "in the event the LESSEE fails to perform . . . the DEALER agrees to Repossess the said equipment at his own expense and therwith [sic] simultaneously pay the LESSOR forthwith an amount equal to the number of remaining months . . . thereof under Lease Agreement." Custom assigned the lease to Otoe, which improperly filed a financing statement. Creative filed a bankruptcy petition. Custom advised Carlson of the bankruptcy and made demand for the amount owing. The trustee in bankruptcy claimed the equipment on the basis of the improper filing of the financing statement. It took 13 months from Custom's demand until the bankruptcy court granted possession of the equipment to Otoe. During this time the value of the equipment decreased from more than the amount owing to $8,500 less. Otoe assigned the lease to Custom, which sued for the $8,500 and costs of obtaining possession from the trustee. The court found that the action of Otoe in improperly filing the financing statement was the cause of the trustee's refusing possession of the equipment and the delay and loss of value; therefore, Carlson was released from liability to the extent of the injury caused by Custom and Otoe.

SECURED CREDIT SALES

L.O.3 ....

Secured Credit Sale

Sale in which seller retains right to repossess goods upon default

When goods are financed by someone other than the buyers (purchased on credit), a convenient way to protect creditors from loss is to allow them to have an interest in the goods. When sellers retain the right to repossess the items sold if the buyers breach the sales contracts, the transactions are **secured credit sales.** In such cases, the buyers obtain possession of the items, and the risk of loss passes to them. Article 9 of the UCC governs secured credit sales. A security interest cannot attach or become enforceable until the buyer and seller agree it shall attach, the seller gives value, and the buyer has the right to possess or use the item.

Security Agreement

Written agreement that creditor has a security interest in collateral signed by buyer

Security Agreement

A creditor may not enforce a security interest unless the buyer has signed a security agreement. The **security agreement** is a written agreement, signed by the buyer, that describes the collateral, or the item sold, and usually contains the terms of payment and names of the parties.

David Ziluck filled out and signed a Radio Shack credit card application. The space for his signature appeared on the front below the statement: "I have read the Radio Shack Credit Account and Security Agreement. . . . I agree to the terms of the Agreement and acknowledge receipt of a copy . . ." The back of the application had the title, "Radio Shack Credit Account and Security Agreement." Radio Shack issued Ziluck a credit card, which he used to buy several items. Ziluck later filed for bankruptcy and Radio Shack asked for possession of these items claiming a security interest in them. The bankruptcy court found that Ziluck had not "signed" the security agreement. The appellate court said signing the front underneath language indicating agreement to the terms of the security agreement constituted a signature by Ziluck.

Rights of the Seller

L.O.4

The rights of the seller, referred to as the secured party under the security agreement, may be transferred to a third person by assignment. In any sale, the buyer may have claims or defenses against the seller. In the case of consumer sales, the Federal Trade Commission requires the seller to include in the agreement a notice that any holder of the agreement is subject to all claims and defenses that the buyer could assert against the seller. Thus, an assignee would be subject to any claims or defenses. This protection for the buyer applies only to consumer transactions.

Rights of the Buyer

The buyer, also called the debtor, has the right to transfer the collateral and require a determination of the amount owed.

Transfer of Collateral. Even though there is a security interest in the collateral, the debtor may transfer the collateral to others. Such a transfer will usually be subject to the security interest.

Determination of Amount Owed. A buyer who wishes may sign a statement indicating the amount of unpaid indebtedness believed to be owed as of a specified date and send it to the seller with the request that the statement be approved or corrected and returned.

Perfection of Security Interest

Perfected Security Interest
Seller's right to collateral that is superior to third party's right

Inventory
Articles purchased with intention of reselling or leasing

Equipment
Goods for use in business

When the rights of the seller to the collateral are superior to those of third persons, the seller has a **perfected security interest.** The use to which the buyer puts collateral at the time of perfection of the security interest determines how the creditor perfects a security interest.

Inventory and Equipment. Articles purchased with the intention of reselling or leasing them are called **inventory. Equipment** consists of goods used or purchased for use in a business, including farming or a profession. In order to have a perfected security interest in inventory or equipment, the seller must usually file a financing statement in the appropriate public office. However, filing need not be made when the law requires a security interest to be noted on the document of title to the goods, such as in the case of noting a lien on a title to a motor vehicle. Buyers of inventory sold in the regular course of business and for value acquire title free of the security interest. For example, any time a customer goes into a store, buys, and pays for a TV, the customer obtains the TV free of any security interest. Any time an item subject to a security interest is sold at the direction of the secured party, the buyer takes it free of the security interest.

A **financing statement** is a writing signed by the debtor and the secured party that contains the address of the secured party, the mailing address of the debtor, and a statement indicating the types of or describing the collateral. A copy of the security agreement may serve as a financing statement if it contains the required items.

Financing Statement

Writing with signatures and addresses of debtor and secured party and description of collateral

Fixtures. Personal property attached to buildings or real estate is called a **fixture.** A creditor perfects a security interest in fixtures by filing the financing statement in the office where a mortgage on the real estate involved would be filed or recorded.

Fixture

Personal property attached to real estate

Pauline Fink bought a mobile home from Palmer Mobile Homes, Inc. Palmer retained a security interest that was assigned to Endicott Trust Company. Endicott filed a financing statement as if the mobile home were a chattel. Fink bought real property from Wemco Corp. and gave Wemco a mortgage on the property. A crawl space was dug on the property, footings were installed, a cinder block pillar was cemented to the footings to support the home, a septic tank system was installed, and water and electricity were run to it. The mobile home was delivered in two sections that were then bolted together. A roof cap was put over the joint and was cemented and nailed down. Siding was installed on the ends of the house and nailed over the joint in the two sections. Fink went bankrupt. Endicott claimed a security interest in the home. The court held the home was so annexed to the realty as to become a part of it; therefore the mobile home was a fixture. The financing statement should have been filed in the office where real estate mortgages would be recorded. Endicott's filing was improper, which meant that the security interest was not perfected. Because of this, the rights of Endicott to the collateral were not superior to the rights of third persons.

Consumer Goods. Consumer goods are items used or bought primarily for personal, family, or household purposes. A security interest in consumer goods is perfected as soon as it attaches and without filing in most cases. It is not perfected, however, against a buyer who purchases the item without knowledge of the security interest for value and for the buyer's own personal, family, or household use. The secured party can be protected against such a buyer only by filing a financing statement.

Consumer Goods

Items purchased for personal, family, or household purposes

Duration of Filing. Filed financing statements last for five years from their date. However, a continuation statement may be filed, which continues the effectiveness of the filing for five more years. Succeeding continuation statements may be filed, each of which lasts five years.

Effect of Default

Under the UCC, the seller has certain rights if the buyer fails to pay according to the terms of the security agreement or otherwise breaches the contract. These rights include repossession and resale. The buyer has the rights to redemption and an accounting.

Repossession. When the buyer has the right to possession of the collateral before making full payment and the buyer breaches the purchase contract, the seller may repossess, or take back, the collateral. If it can be done without a breach of the peace, the repossession may be made without any judicial proceedings. In any case, judicial action may be sought. The seller may retain the collateral in satisfaction of the debt unless the debtor, after being notified, objects.

Yvonne Sanchez defaulted on her auto payments to MBank El Paso. MBank hired two men to repossess the car. They found the car in Sanchez' driveway and hooked it to a tow truck. Sanchez ordered them to leave. When they did not, she jumped into the car, locked the doors, and refused to get out. The men towed the car at a high speed to a repossession yard; parked the car; and padlocked the gate to the yard. A Doberman pinscher guard dog roamed loose in the yard. Sanchez remained in the car until rescued by her husband and police. Sanchez sued MBank for damages alleging it had not repossessed the car without a breach of the peace. The court agreed.

Resale. After default, the seller may sell the collateral. A public or private sale may be used, and any manner, time, place, and terms may be used as long as the disposition is commercially reasonable and done in good faith. Advance notice of the sale must be given to the debtor unless the goods are perishable. If the buyer has paid 60 percent or more of the cash price of the goods, the seller must resell the goods within 90 days after possession of them unless the buyer, after default, has signed a statement waiving the right to require resale. The purpose of this requirement is to cause a sale before the goods decline in value.

Redemption. At any time prior to the sale or the contracting to sell of the collateral, the buyer may redeem it by paying the amount owed and the expenses reasonably incurred by the seller in retaking and holding the collateral and preparing for the sale. This includes, if provided in the agreement, reasonable attorney's fees and legal expenses.

Accounting. After the sale of the collateral, the creditor must apply payments in the following order: the expenses of retaking and selling the collateral, the amount owed on the security interest, and all amounts owed on any subordinate security interests. The seller must pay any surplus remaining to the buyer. The buyer has liability for any deficiency.

QUESTIONS

1   Who are the parties to a contract of guaranty or suretyship?
2   What is the difference between a paid surety and an accommodation surety?
3   In those states that recognize a difference, what is the difference between a contract of guaranty and one of suretyship?
4   What rights does a sole guarantor have by virtue of having paid the debt of the principal?
5   What is the right of contribution?
6   Why would a surety want to exercise the right of exoneration?
7   What acts, other than the usual methods of discharging any obligation, discharge a surety or guarantor?
8   What is a secured credit sale?
9   What are the rights of the seller and buyer in a secured credit sale?
10   How is a security interest in equipment perfected?

CASE PROBLEMS

L.O.3 ....

1 Farmers & Merchants Bank of Long Beach loaned $35,400 to Frank Hoffer to finance his tractor and trailer. Hoffer gave Farmers a security interest in them, and Farmers gave him the titles, which had no binding notation of the liens. The vehicles were then registered with no notation of the liens on the titles. Hoffer filed a petition under Chapter 11 of the Bankruptcy Code, and Farmers sought to foreclose its security interest on the vehicles. Does Farmers have a perfected security interest in the tractor and trailer?

L.O.2 ....

2 Robert Gandy was a guarantor on notes by U.S. National Mortgage Company to Park National Bank. The guaranty stated: "'indebtedness' . . . includes any and all advances, debts, obligations and liabilities . . . heretofore, now, or hereafter made . . ." and "This is a continuing guaranty relating to any indebtedness . . . which shall either continue the indebtedness or from time to time renew it. . . . This guaranty shall not apply to any indebtedness created after actual receipt by Bank of written notice of its revocation as to future transactions." A month later Gandy gave Park written notice of revocation. After that, Park extended the date of payment on the notes four times, on one extension increasing the rate of interest. When the notes were not paid, Park sued Gandy. Is he liable?

L.O.1 ....

3 General Insurance Company of America was surety on a bond running to the state as obligee to indemnify it for losses from the failure of any deputy registrar to faithfully perform the duties required by law. The bond stated, "the obligee shall notify the surety of any default . . . within a reasonable time after discovery . . . by the obligee" and "Within six months after discovery . . . of any default . . . the obligee shall file with the surety affirmative proof of loss. . . ." On May 6, the state auditor sent a claim memorandum to the attorney general regarding former deputy registrar Carol Shirk. Twenty-three months later a special counsel for the attorney general advised General that he had received the claim for collection eight months after the auditor's memo and four months later had secured a judgment against Shirk. This was General's first documentation from the state regarding the claim. The state sued General for payment on the bond. Is it liable?

L.O.3 ....

4 Vinod and Surekha Vashi leased a telephone system. The lease created a security interest. When the Vashis defaulted, General Electric Capital Corporation (GECC), the secured party, took possession of the equipment. GECC notified the Vashis it would sell the collateral, but GECC could not sell it because it was worthless. GECC obtained a deficiency judgment that gave the Vashis no credit for the equipment kept by GECC. The Vashis argued a court could not enter a deficiency judgment if GECC kept the collateral. Should the appellate court affirm the deficiency judgment?

L.O.2 ....

5 Curtis Carleton guaranteed the sales and use tax liability of Curtis Surgical Supply Co. The company incurred an unpaid tax liability of almost $15,000. It also executed two waivers extending the time during which the state Board of Equalization could issue a deficiency determination for the taxes. The board sued Carleton on his guaranty. Carleton said the waivers constituted a material alteration from the original obligation, discharging his guaranty. The board cited Carleton's guaranty, which stated: ". . . no . . . waivers, or modifications in the liability . . . between the taxpayer and the State Board of Equalization shall in any way relieve [Carleton] of his obligation herein." Did the alteration in Curtis' obligation for taxes discharge Carleton's guaranty?

L.O.3 .... **6** Glenn McFadden bought a video cassette recorder on which Walloch TV & Appliances, Inc., held a security interest. At the time, McFadden occasionally used the recorder for business purposes but more often for personal use. Sometime later, McFadden filed under Chapter 13 of the Bankruptcy Code, and Walloch filed a reclamation for the recorder, alleging it held a perfected security interest in the recorder. Walloch had not filed on the recorder with the secretary of state and the county clerk as was required for the perfection of a security interest in business equipment. Therefore the reclamation would be allowed only if the recorder were consumer goods and not business equipment. Was the recorder consumer goods or business equipment?

Chapter 41

BANKRUPTCY

LEARNING OBJECTIVES

After studying this chapter you should be able to:

1 Identify the purposes for bankruptcy and who may file for it.

2 Describe the procedures in a bankruptcy (liquidation) case.

3 Explain the effect of a discharge of indebtedness.

4 Summarize the effect of nonliquidation bankruptcy plans.

Preview Case

Veronica Scales filed a petition under Chapter 13 of the Bankruptcy Code. Under Chapter 13, a debtor with a regular income may work out a plan to pay creditors. By Scales' plan, she was to make weekly payments of $47.50 to the trustee for payment of claims. The form on which the plan was filed had blank spaces in which the amount of dividends to be paid secured and unsecured creditors was to be inserted but was not. At the confirmation hearing, Scales' lawyer advised that all secured and unsecured claims were to be fully paid over three years. Each claim in each of the two classes of creditors (secured and unsecured) was to be treated alike. Peoples Financial Corporation, a secured creditor, alleged that the plan was so deficient that it was not a plan. Was the plan proposed sufficient to qualify as a Chapter 13 plan?

L.O.1

Bankruptcy is a judicial declaration as to a person's (the debtor's) financial condition. The federal bankruptcy law has two very definite purposes: to give the debtor a new start and to give creditors an equal chance in the collection of their claims.

An honest debtor, hopelessly insolvent, may be tempted to cease trying even to earn a living. By permitting an insolvent debtor to give up all assets with a few minor exceptions and thereby get forgiveness of the debts, at least a new start can be made. The court prescribes an equitable settlement under the circumstances; and when these conditions are fully met, the debtor may resume full control of any business.

It is unfair to permit some unsecured creditors to get paid in full by an insolvent person while others receive nothing. By appointing a trustee to take over the debtor's property and pay each creditor in proportion to a claim, the trustee seeks to achieve a more equitable settlement. This arrangement promotes equity and wastes fewer assets and costs less money than for each creditor to separately sue the debtor.

WHO CAN FILE A PETITION OF BANKRUPTCY

Today any person who lives in, has a residence, place of business, or property in the United States can be a debtor under the Bankruptcy Code except banks, insurance companies, savings and loan associations, and some municipalities. Rehabilitation proceedings may be instituted against all of these exempted institutions except municipalities, but the proceedings may not be had under the Bankruptcy Code. There are several Chapters under the Code and only specified persons may be debtors under the particular Chapters. Chapter 7, providing for liquidation, applies to any person; Chapter 9 applies to municipalities; Chapter 11, providing for reorganization, applies to any person; and Chapter 13 applies to individuals with regular income.

KINDS OF DEBTORS

There are two kinds of debtors:

1   Voluntary
2   Involuntary

Voluntary Debtors

Anyone, except the institutions listed previously, may file a voluntary petition with the bankruptcy court under one of the four chapters of the Code. A husband and wife may file a petition for a joint case.

Involuntary Debtors

Under certain conditions one may be forced into involuntary bankruptcy. Generally if a debtor has 12 or more creditors, 3 must join the petition for involuntary bankruptcy. If a debtor has fewer than 12 creditors, one may sign. The creditors who sign must have aggregate claims amounting to $5,000 in excess of any collateral held as security. Involuntary petitions may not be filed under Chapters 9 or 13 or against farmers and charitable corporations.

A court will enter an order for relief upon the filing of an involuntary bankruptcy petition if either of the following two situations exist:

1   The debtor does not pay debts as they become due.
2   A custodian of the debtor's assets was established within 120 days preceding the filing of the involuntary petition.

Bankruptcy law uses the same procedure in liquidating the estate whether under a voluntary bankruptcy proceeding or an involuntary one. The filing of a petition automatically stays the filing or continuation of proceedings against the debtor that could have been begun or were to recover a claim against the debtor that arose before the bankruptcy petition.

PROCEDURE IN A LIQUIDATION CASE

L.O.2 ....

After filing a petition in bankruptcy creditors must be notified and a meeting of them called. These creditors elect a trustee to take over all the assets of the debtor. The trustee steps into the shoes of the debtor and collects all debts due the debtor, preserves all physical assets, sues all delinquent creditors of the estate, and finally distributes all money realized according to a definite priority that will be discussed later in this chapter.

EXEMPT PROPERTY

The federal bankruptcy law lists property that will not be used to pay debts. In addition each state has laws exempting property from seizure for the payment of debts. The debtor has a choice between federal or state exemptions unless state law specifies state exemptions must be used. The most common types of property excluded include a limited interest in a residence and vehicle, household effects, tools of the trade, such as a carpenter's tools, a dentist's equipment, and similar items within reasonable limits. The debtor may also exclude unmatured life insurance contracts owned other than credit life insurance.

Most states specifically exempt all necessary wearing apparel for the debtor and members of the family, such items as the family Bible, and all pictures of the members of the family even though some of these may be portraits of some value. Many of the federal exemptions set a limit on the value of items that may be excluded.

INCLUDED PROPERTY

The law includes some property acquired by the debtor after the bankruptcy proceedings have been instituted in the debtor's estate and uses it for the payment of creditors. This includes property acquired by inheritance, divorce, or as a beneficiary of life insurance within 180 days after the date of filing.

An involuntary Chapter 7 case was filed against Leon Lonstein. Ten years before, his mother's will had bequeathed Lonstein 10 percent of her estate. The will directed the executor to pay the 10 percent on a date a year after the filing of the bankruptcy case. Lonstein insisted the bequest should not be included in the Chapter 7 estate because the distribution would occur more than 180 days after the filing. The court said filing the bankruptcy petition created the Chapter 7 estate. That estate included all of the debtor's interests in property. Since Lonstein's interest in the bequest vested long before the bankruptcy filing, his interest in the bequest had to be included in his Chapter 7 estate.

If the debtor transfers property, normally within 90 days preceding the filing of the bankruptcy petition, to one creditor with the intent to prefer one creditor over another, the transfer may be set aside and the property included in the debtor's estate.

DUTIES OF THE DEBTOR

The debtor must cooperate fully with the trustee. When requested, the debtor must attend creditors meetings and must furnish all relevant evidence about debts due. The debtor must file with the trustee a schedule of all assets and all liabilities. This schedule must be in sufficient detail so that the trustee can list the secured creditors, the partially secured creditors, and the unsecured creditors. Failure of the debtor to cooperate with the trustee and to obey all orders of the referee not only may prevent discharge from bankruptcy but may also subject the debtor to criminal prosecution for contempt of court.

PROOF OF CLAIMS

All unsecured creditors must present proof of their claims to the court. The court sets a deadline for filing proof of claims, but they must generally be filed within 90 days after the date for the first meeting of creditors.

Chrysler Motors Corporation had a disputed claim of $500,000 against Jerome Schneiderman who had filed a petition in bankruptcy. Chrysler prepared a proof of claim and mailed it to the clerk of the bankruptcy court at the correct address. The postal service never returned the proof of claim to Chrysler and the bankruptcy court had no record of having received it. After the date for filing proof of claims had passed, Schneiderman moved to disallow the claim for failure to file with the court. The court said mailing is not filing with the court and disallowed the claim.

RECLAMATIONS

Frequently at the time the court discharges debts, the debtor has possession of property owned by others. This property takes the form of consigned or bailed goods, or property held as security for a loan. The true owner of the property is not technically a creditor of the debtor in bankruptcy. The owner should file a reclamation claim for the specific property so that it may be returned.

A person in possession of a check drawn by the debtor may or may not be able to get it paid depending on the circumstances. If the check is an uncertified check, the holder is a mere creditor of the debtor and cannot have it cashed. This occurs because a check is not an assignment of the money on deposit, and the creditor merely holds the unpaid claim the debtor intended the check to discharge. If the check has been certified, the creditor has the obligation of the drawee bank on the check, which may be asserted in preference to proceeding upon the claim against the drawer of the check.

TYPES OF CLAIMS

Claims of a debtor in bankruptcy may be classified as fully secured claims, partially secured claims, and unsecured claims.

Fully secured creditors may have their claims satisfied in full from the proceeds of the assets that were used for security. If these assets sell for more than enough to satisfy the secured debts, the remainder of the proceeds must be surrendered to the trustee in bankruptcy of the debtor.

Partially secured creditors have a lien on some assets but not enough to satisfy the debts in full. The proceeds of the security held by a partially secured creditor are used to pay that claim; and, to the extent any portion of a debt remains unpaid, the creditor has a claim as an unsecured creditor for the balance.

Unsecured claims are those for which creditors have no lien on specific assets.

PRIORITY OF CLAIMS

The claim with the highest priority is that for the administrative expenses of the bankruptcy proceedings (such as filing fees paid by creditors in involuntary proceedings and expenses of creditors in recovering property transferred or concealed by the debtor). Additional priority claims include debts incurred after the filing of an involuntary petition and before an order of relief or appointment of a trustee; wage claims not exceeding $2,000 for any one wage earner, provided the wages were earned not more than three months prior to bankruptcy proceedings; fringe benefits for employees; claims by individuals who have deposited money with the debtor for undelivered personal, family, or household goods; and tax claims.

DISCHARGE OF INDEBTEDNESS

L.O.3 ....

If the debtor cooperates fully with the court and the trustee in bankruptcy and meets all other requirements for discharge of indebtedness, the discharge will be granted. To be discharged, the debtor must not hide any assets or attempt to wrongfully transfer them out of the reach of creditors. A discharge voids any liability of the debtor on discharged debts and prevents any actions for collection of such debts.

August Perez filed a voluntary petition for relief under Chapter 7. Hibernia National Bank, to which Perez owed a considerable sum, contended the court should deny Perez a discharge. It alleged Perez failed to explain a loss of assets from Perez's distribution of tax refunds between himself and his wife. Under an agreement signed prior to their marriage, 85 percent of the tax refunds should have gone to August. However, he had divided them equally between himself and his wife because, he said, "She's on this check here, . . . so she's entitled to half." The tax refunds amounted to $300,000. The court found evidence of intent to defraud creditors and denied the discharge.

DEBTS NOT DISCHARGED

Certain obligations cannot be avoided by bankruptcy. The most important of these claims include:

1   Claims for alimony and child support.
2   All taxes incurred within three years.
3   Debts owed by reasons of embezzlement.
4   Debts due on a judgment for intentional injury to others, such as a judgment obtained for assault and battery.
5   Wages earned within three months of the bankruptcy proceedings.
6   Debts incurred by means of fraud.
7   Educational loans.

Under some other circumstances, bankruptcy does not discharge certain debts, but the list above includes the most common ones.

NONLIQUIDATION PLANS

The bankruptcy laws provide special arrangements that do not result in liquidation and distribution of the debtor's assets. These are business reorganization and Chapter 13 plans.

Business Reorganization

L.O.4 ....

Bankruptcy proceedings under Chapter 7 result in the liquidation and distribution of the assets of an enterprise. Under Chapter 11 the Bankruptcy Code provides a special rehabilitation system designed for businesses so that they may be reorganized rather than liquidated. Although designed for businesses, the language of Chapter 11 allows individuals not engaged in business to request relief.

Reorganization proceedings may be voluntary or involuntary. Normally the debtor will be allowed to continue to run the business; however, a disinterested trustee may be appointed to run the business in cases of mismanagement or in the interest of creditors. The debtor running its business has the first right, for 120 days, to propose a rehabilitation plan indicating how much and how creditors will be paid. The court will confirm a plan it finds fair, equitable, feasible, has been proposed and accepted in good faith, and all the payments made or proposed are found to be reasonable. If no acceptable plan of reorganization can be worked out, the business may have to be liquidated under Chapter 7.

Chapter 13 Plans

If the debtor is an individual, a Chapter 13 plan may be worked out. This Chapter attempts to achieve for an individual the same advantages that Chapter 11 gives to businesses. An individual with a regular income, except a stock or commodity broker, who has unsecured debts of less than $100,000 and secured debts of less than $350,000 may file a petition under Chapter 13. This Chapter is completely voluntary for the debtor. However, a majority of creditors can impose a settlement plan upon a dissenting minority. The debtor is as fully released from debts as under Chapter 7 of the Code. These arrangements help prevent the hardship of an immediate liquidation of all of the debtor's assets and give the debtor the opportunity to develop a plan for the full or partial payment of debts over an extended period. This plan benefits the creditors because they are likely, in the long run, to receive a greater percentage of the money owed them. The plan may not pay unsecured creditors less than the amount they would receive under a Chapter 7 liquidation.

Veronica Scales filed a petition under Chapter 13 of the Bankruptcy Code. By the plan, she had an obligation to make weekly payments of $47.50 to the trustee for payment of claims. The form on which the plan was filed had blank spaces on which the amount of dividends to be paid secured and unsecured creditors was to be inserted but was not. At the confirmation hearing, Scales' lawyer advised that all secured and unsecured claims were to be fully paid over three years. Each claim in each of the two classes of creditors was to be treated alike. Peoples Financial Corporation, a secured creditor, alleged that the plan was so deficient that it was not a plan. The court stated that it would have been better if the plan had listed the secured and unsecured creditors, indicated how much of their claims were to be paid, and stated the duration of the plan, but since these items were revealed at the first meeting of creditors, these defects in the plan were cured. The plan proposed was sufficient to qualify as a Chapter 13 plan.

QUESTIONS

1   What is bankruptcy?
2   Who may file a petition under the Bankruptcy Code?
3   What are the two bases for entering an order for relief on an involuntary bankruptcy petition?
4   Is all the debtor's property subject to the claims of creditors?
5   What are the procedures in a bankruptcy case?
6   What are the duties of a debtor in bankruptcy proceedings?
7   List three debts that bankruptcy does not discharge.
8   What claim is given the highest priority in bankruptcy proceedings?
9   What is the effect of a discharge of indebtedness?
10   What procedure may be followed rather than liquidating a business that cannot pay its debts as they are due?

CASE PROBLEMS

L.O.1

1   Almist held a note by Sundown Associates, which owned an apartment complex. Almist filed an involuntary petition under Chapter 11 against Sundown. Sundown moved to dismiss the case claiming it had more than 12 creditors, so an involuntary filing required filing by three or more claimants. Sundown asserted that all its tenants constituted unsecured creditors because it held their security deposits and therefore owed them money. Should the court dismiss the petition?

L.O.2

2   Harold Younger's ex-wife filed an involuntary Chapter 7 bankruptcy petition with Younger as the debtor. The U.S. Marshal arrested Younger to compel his

attendance at an examination as to location of marital assets. At the examination, Younger refused to testify, citing the Fifth Amendment to the Constitution. The judge granted him immunity and ordered him to testify. Younger refused again. What do you think will happen now?

L.O.3 ....

3   E. M. Radcliffe filed a voluntary petition under Chapter 7. Radcliffe was the president and sole shareholder of Delta Title Company. He transferred checks payable to him or other companies he owned, furniture, and three vehicles, including two Cadillacs, to Delta. He made these transfers without consideration from Delta. He pledged all the issued and outstanding stock of Delta, his only asset of value, to his long-time friend and attorney. He claimed the pledge represented payment for past due attorney fees. Some unsecured creditors objected to discharging Radcliffe. Should he receive a discharge?

L.O.4 ....

4   Thomas and Joyce White filed a petition under Chapter 11 of the Bankruptcy Code. Midland Bank & Trust Company, which had two claims, objected to the plan as not being proposed in good faith. Under the plan, Midland's first claim was to be secured by the accounts receivable of Thomas's surveying business and was to be paid in monthly installments with 12-percent interest until paid in full. The second claim of $88,200, to be secured by a security interest in an 87-acre farm, was to be paid under a ten-year term, and any funds from subdividing the land were to reduce the debt. There was testimony that in order to subdivide, a dirt road would have to be improved and water mains installed at a small cost. On the basis of the value of new projects in the surveying business, work in progress, accounts receivable, and general economic conditions, the business was projected to make enough money to provide the payments required on Midland's first claim. Was the plan proposed in good faith?

L.O.1 ....

5   When Charles Pettis filed an involuntary petition under Chapter 7 regarding International Teldata Corporation, the debt owed Pettis represented 52 percent of ITC's total debts. Another 30 percent was owed to insiders, officers of ITC. One officer testified that he and the other insider had voluntarily agreed to delay payment because ITC was unable to make payments on these debts. Pettis had obtained a judgment against ITC, but attempts at execution were unsuccessful. ITC argued it was paying all its debts when due except those owed Pettis and the insiders. Was ITC paying its debts as they became due?

L.O.2 ....

6   Carl and Shirley Miller defaulted on a mortgage to First Federal Savings and Loan Association of Monessen. It got a judgment against them and arranged a sheriff's sale of their house for May 10. On May 9, the Millers filed a petition in bankruptcy, staying the sheriff's sale. The Millers ultimately dismissed that case. First Federal scheduled another sheriff's sale for January 2. On December 31, the Millers filed another petition. The court notified them that day that the petition did not include certain, required schedules and statements and gave them until January 15 to file them. The filing stayed the second sheriff's sale. On January 15, the Millers filed a motion for an extension of time to file the papers. The court gave them until January 30. The Millers did not file the papers, so the court dismissed the case February 3 for the

Millers' failure to obey the order of the court requiring filing of certain documents. First Federal scheduled a third sale for April 2. Carl Miller filed another petition on April 1. The third petition lacked the same documents as the second and the court told Miller to file them by April 16. Miller filed a motion for an extension on April 28. The court gave him until May 15 and he finally complied. Bankruptcy law does not allow a person to be a debtor who during the previous 180 days had a case dismissed for willful failure to obey orders of the court. Did Miller accidentally fail to obey the court's orders or did he knowingly disobey?

L.O.1 .... **7** Charles and Shirley Cunningham were the debtors in a proceeding under the Bankruptcy Code. They petitioned the bankruptcy court to grant them a divorce because, they alleged, the filing of a divorce petition against a debtor in a state court would violate the automatic stay of judicial proceedings against debtors provided in the Bankruptcy Code. Is a divorce proceeding stayed by filing under the Bankruptcy Code?

L.O.3 .... **8** The Family Court entered an order directing Samuel Homyak to pay his wife, Linda, support. Later Samuel filed a divorce action, and Norman Essner was Linda's attorney. The court that heard the divorce action awarded Essner $900 for his fee. A month later, Homyak filed a petition under Chapter 7 of the Bankruptcy Code. After he was discharged, Essner filed a complaint to have his $900 claim declared nondischargeable because it was in the nature of alimony. Should this be a nondischargeable debt?

Summary Cases

RISK-BEARING DEVICES

1   Robert McCloskey obtained a life insurance policy from New York Life Insurance Company. The medical questionnaire asked, "Have you ever consulted a physician or . . . had or been treated for . . . heart attack . . . or any other disorder of the heart or blood vessels . . . or diabetes?" McCloskey answered no. He in fact had diabetes and had had a heart attack. A paramedical examination had revealed he was overweight, so the policy New York issued required a higher premium than was standard. Within a month of the issuance of the policy, McCloskey died. New York refused to pay on the policy, alleging misrepresentation. Was there misrepresentation? [*McCloskey* v. *New York Life Insurance Company,* 436 A.2d 690 (Pa. Super. Ct.)]

2   Evelyn Vlastos carried a fire insurance policy on her building. The policy included a section labeled Endorsement No. 4 that was incorporated into the policy and stated: "Warranted that the third floor is occupied as Janitor's residence." The building was destroyed by fire, and the insurers refused to pay on the policy, charging breach of warranty. Vlastos sued the insurers alleging there was no proof the provision in Endorsement No. 4 was a warranty, implying it was a representation. Which was it, and what difference would it make? [*Vlastos* v. *Sumitomo Marine & Fire Insurance Company (Europe) Ltd.,* 707 F.2d 775 (3rd Cir.)]

3   Merrimack Mutual Fire Insurance Company issued a fire insurance policy to James and Loree Stewart as owners. There was a mortgage clause requiring payment upon loss to Portland Savings Bank as mortgagee. The clause provided: "the mortgagee . . . shall notify this Company of any change of ownership . . . or increase of hazard. . . ." Portland later foreclosed on the property, and after the Stewarts' redemption period expired, it became the owner. It did not notify Merrimack of the foreclose and its ownership before there was a fire loss. Merrimack denied coverage because Portland had not notified it of the change in ownership. Was Merrimack liable under the policy? [*Hartford Fire Insurance Company* v. *Merrimack Mutual Fire Insurance Company,* 457 A.2d 410 (Me.)]

4   Rohde purchased an automobile public liability policy with a 20/50/5 coverage for each accident. The insured while driving negligently struck three motorcycles simultaneously. The drivers of the motorcycles were injured and their vehicles damaged. The total damages assessed were in excess of the limits of the policy if this was one accident. If there were three separate accidents, then the policy limits were adequate to cover all damages. Was this one accident or three accidents? [*Truck Insurance Company* v. *Rohde,* 303 P.2d 659 (Wash.)]

5   On August 13, Dennis and Diane Rose borrowed $1,034.10 from Huntington National Bank. In order to obtain this unsecured loan the Roses omitted $2,900 in unsecured loans from the loan application. A month later, having made no payments on the loan, the Roses filed a petition under Chapter 13 of the Bankruptcy Code. Their plan called for them to pay the $220 difference between their monthly income and expenses to the trustee for three years and pay only 10 percent to unsecured creditors. Huntington objected to the plan on the ground of bad faith. Should Huntington recover only 10 percent? [*Matter of Rose,* 40 B.R. 178 (Bankr. S.D. Ohio)]

6   Sheila Kercher sued for dissolution of her marriage, and on November 3, the court issued an order restraining her husband "from transferring . . . or in any way disposing of any property except in the usual course of business or for the necessities of life." He had a term life insurance policy on which Kercher was the beneficiary and which gave him the right to change the beneficiary. On November 11, he changed the beneficiary to his mother, Helen Tallent, and on December 11, committed suicide. Should Kercher or Tallent receive the proceeds of the life insurance? [*Metropolitan Life Insurance Company* v. *Tallent,* 445 N.E.2d 990 (Ind.)]

7   C. E. Youse purchased a fire insurance policy on her household goods and personal property. She removed a valuable ring from her finger and laid it on the table with some cleaning tissue. By mistake the maid threw the tissue and the ring into the wastepaper basket and then threw the contents of the basket into the backyard incinerator. She lighted the contents of the incinerator intentionally, and the ensuring fire stayed within the incinerator. About one week later the ring was discovered in the ashes in the incinerator. It had sustained about $900 damage by the fire. The insurance company refused to pay on the ground this was a friendly fire. Was this a friendly fire or a hostile fire? [*Youse* v. *Employers Fire Insurance Company,* 238 P.2d 472 (Kan.)

8   A car driven by James Hilton struck a parked trash truck that extended onto the travel lane of the highway. Two people in the Hilton car received severe head lacerations, and the car was considerably damaged. The truck was owned by Joe Blakeney and insured by Safeco Insurance Company of America. At the scene, Blakeney saw the damage and injury, was issued a traffic summons, and was told by a police officer to file an accident report within ten days. Seven weeks later, an attorney for the Hiltons wrote the insurance agent who had written the Safeco policy and advised him of the accident. He prepared an accident report form and sent it to Safeco. Its policy stated: "written notice . . . with respect to the time, place and circumstances . . . and the names and address of the injured and of available witnesses, shall be given by or for the insured to the company . . . as soon as practicable." Blakeney never notified anyone. Safeco denied coverage. Was it liable? [*Liberty Mutual Insurance Company* v. *Safeco Insurance Company,* 288 S.E.2d 469 (Va.)]

9   Devers Auto Sales financed its inventory with Thrift, Incorporated, which perfected its security interest in the inventory by filing a financing statement with the secretary of state in accordance with Article 9 of the UCC. The statement included a security interest in after-acquired inventory. A.D.E., Inc., agreed to sell three cars to Devers and gave it possession of them but not the titles. Thrift gave Devers the money for the cars, and Devers gave checks to A.D.E., but the checks were dishonored. Thrift took possession of Devers's inventory and demanded the titles from A.D.E. A.D.E. demanded the three cars. Did Thrift have a perfected security interest in the cars? [*Thrift, Inc.* v. *A.D.E., Inc.,* 454 N.E.2d 878 (Ind. Ct. App.)]

10   Smith sold a cruiser to Seal, who executed a security agreement and a note for $31,000 to the First National Bank of Linn Creek. A financing statement was filed by the bank. Seal decided not to keep the cruiser and asked Smith to sell it for him. Pieper bought it for $13,000 and his older boat. Smith applied the $13,000 to the note and told the bank it was received from the sale of the cruiser. Seal also told the bank he was going to sell the second boat. Five months later the bank repossessed the cruiser. Pieper sued for recovery of the cruiser. If the secured party has authorized a sale, the buyer takes free of the security interest. Was Pieper entitled to the cruiser? [*Pieper* v. *First National Bank of Linn Creek, Camdenton,* 453 S.W.2d 926 (Mo.)]

Part 9

Real Property

Chapter 42

NATURE OF REAL PROPERTY

LEARNING OBJECTIVES

After studying this chapter you should be able to:

1 Define real property, and explain the rules about vegetation, running water, and fixtures.

2 Name the types of multiple ownership of property.

3 List the estates and other interests in real property.

4 Identify the ways only real property can be acquired.

Preview Case

On August 12, Elwyn Groth sold all the Christmas trees growing on his land. He granted the buyers the right to enter upon the land to spray, prune, and care for the trees until they reached their appropriate growth. The buyers of the trees had the right to then harvest and remove the trees. Groth retained the right to sell any land that had no such trees and even land that had trees, but after they were harvested. About a year later, by warranty deed, Groth conveyed all the land to Ronald and Diane Stillson without reservation. The Stillsons alleged they did not have notice of the tree sale, so Groth asked the court to reform his deed to include a reservation of the trees. Christmas trees require care annually for six to eight years. Were the trees personal property or part of the land?

REAL PROPERTY

L.O.1

Real Property

Land and permanent attachments to land

Real property consists of land, including the actual soil, and all permanent attachments to the land, such as fences, walls, other additions and improvements, timber, and other growing things. It also includes minerals under the soil and the waters upon it.

DISTINGUISHING REAL PROPERTY

Through court interpretations we have accumulated a definite set of rules to guide us in identifying real property and distinguishing it from personal property. The most important of these rules pertain to the following specific items of property:

1   Vegetation—trees and perennial crops
2   Waters—rivers and streams
3   Fixtures

Trees and Perennial Crops

Vegetation may be real or personal property. Trees growing on the land, orchards, vineyards, and perennial crops, such as clovers, grasses, and others not planted annually and cultivated, are classed as real property until severed from the land. Annual crops and severed vegetation are personal property. When a person sells land, questions sometimes arise as to whether or not a particular item belongs to the land or constitutes personal property. The parties should agree before completing the sale just how to classify the item.

On August 12, Elwyn Groth sold all the Christmas trees growing on his land. He granted the buyers the right to enter upon the land to spray, prune, and care for the trees until they reached their appropriate growth. The buyers of the trees had the right to then harvest and remove the trees. Groth retained the right to sell any land that had no such trees and even land that had trees, but after they were harvested. About a year later, by warranty deed, Groth conveyed all the land to Ronald and Diane Stillson without reservation. The Stillsons alleged they did not have notice of the tree sale, so Groth asked the court to reform his deed to include a reservation of the trees. Christmas trees require care annually for six to eight years. The court held that the sale of the trees was the sale of a growing crop, and they were constructively severed from the land by the August 12 agreement. As personal property, they did not pass with the land.

Rivers and Streams

If a nonnavigable river flows through property, the person who owns the property owns the riverbed but not the water that flows over the bed. The water cannot be impounded or diverted to the property owner's own use in such a way as to deprive any neighbors of its use. If the river or the stream forms the boundary line, then the owner on each side of the river owns the land to the middle of the riverbed.

In most states where navigable rivers form the boundary, the owner of the adjoining land owns the land only to the low-water mark.

Fixture

Personal property so securely attached to real estate that it becomes part of it

Fixtures

Personal property attached to land or a building that becomes a part of it is known as a **fixture.** To determine whether or not personal property has become real estate, one or more of the following rules may be applied:

1   How securely is it attached? If the personal property has become a part of the real estate and lost its identity, such as the boards or bricks making up a house wall, it constitutes a fixture. If it is so securely attached that it cannot be removed without damaging the real property to which it is attached such as windows or light switches, then it also ceases to be personal property.

2   What was the intention of the one installing the personal property? No matter what one's intention, the personal property becomes real property if it cannot be removed without damaging the property. But, if it is loosely attached and the person installing the fixture indicates the intention to make the fixture real property, then this intention controls. Refrigerators have been held to be real property when apartments were rented unfurnished but contained refrigerators. In determining intention, courts frequently consider the purpose of the attachment and who did the attaching.

    a. What is the purpose of attachment? The purpose for which the fixture is to be used may show the intention of the one annexing it.

    b. Who attached the item? If the owner of a building installs personal property to the building, this usually indicates the intention to make it a permanent addition to the real property. If a tenant makes the same improvements, the court presumes that the tenant intended to keep the fixture as personal property unless a contrary intention can be shown.

John Taylor bought a sewage treatment system that was manufactured by Multi-Flo, Inc. It was installed at Taylor's residence in August. In October he began to have problems with the system. Over the next three years, service and repairs were made by three different companies, and a few months later Taylor sued Multi-Flo, claiming the system was defective and had been since installation. In installing it, a hole was dug and the base leveled with sand. The unit was put into the hole and leveled. The inlet and outlet lines were then hooked up and the wiring system installed from the aerator to the alarm box. Backfill was then placed around the system. The trial court said the action was barred by a two-year statute of limitations on personal property. The appellate court held that where the product has become a fixture the two-year statute of limitations does not apply.

MULTIPLE OWNERSHIP

L.O.2   Property can be owned by one person, or it can be owned by more than one person. When more than one person owns land, each person has the right to use and possess it. The most common ways real property can be owned by more than one person include:

1   Tenancy in common
2   Joint tenancy
3   Tenancy by the entirety
4   Community property

Tenancy in Common

Multiple ownership in which, at death, one owner's share passes as will directs or to heirs

Tenancy in Common

A **tenancy in common** occurs when two or more persons own property and when one dies, that owner's interest in the property passes to a person named in the deceased's will or, if no will exists, to the deceased's heirs. In this type of ownership, the other owner or owners have no automatic right to the deceased's share of the property. Each owner determines who gets the share of the property at his or her death.

The owners of property held as a tenancy in common each own an undivided fractional share of the property. For example, if two people equally own a piece of land, each tenant owns an undivided one-half interest in the land. Three people who own land equally each own an undivided one-third interest in the land. This means they do not own a specific portion of the land, but own a one-third interest in the entire piece of land. The land does not have to be owned equally. Two people could own a piece of property as tenants in common, and one could own a one-third interest and the other could own a two-thirds interest.

A tenant in common has the right not only to determine who becomes the owner of the fractional share upon death but to convey the property while alive. The property may be given away or sold. The new owner then becomes a tenant in common with the remaining owner or owners.

When more than one person takes title to property, the law presumes they hold the property as tenants in common. Thus when the type of ownership is not clearly spelled out, it will be held a tenancy in common.

Joint Tenancy

Joint Tenancy

Multiple ownership in which, at death of one, that share passes to remaining owners

A **joint tenancy** exists when two or more persons own property and upon the death of one, the remaining owners own the entire property free of any interest of the deceased. This means that a joint owner does not have the power to determine who owns the property at death. The remaining joint owner or owners automatically own the entire property. This automatic ownership of the entire property by the surviving owners is called the **right of survivorship.**

Right of Survivorship

Automatic ownership of property by survivors

As in the case of a tenancy in common, each joint owner owns an undivided interest in the property. No joint owner owns a specific portion of the property.

The law does not favor the creation of a joint tenancy so there must be a clear intention to create one. The language normally used conveys the property "to X and Y as joint tenants with right of survivorship."

A joint tenancy can be destroyed by one joint tenant selling or giving that tenant's interest to another person. The new owner becomes a tenant in common of the interest conveyed. If there are three or more joint tenants and one sells his or her interest, the new owner is a tenant in common and the remaining, original joint tenants remain joint tenants as between themselves.

Partition

Suit to divide joint tenancy

A joint tenancy can also be destroyed by one joint tenant suing for a division of the property, called a suit for **partition.** Any joint tenant may sue for partition.

Because a joint tenant's interest in the property disappears at the joint tenant's death, a joint tenant cannot dispose of such an interest by will. If a joint tenant purports to dispose of an interest in jointly held property by will, the will has no effect with regard to such property.

Tenancy by the Entirety

Co-ownership by husband and wife with right of survivorship

Tenancy by the Entirety

Similar to a joint tenancy, a **tenancy by the entirety** can exist only between a husband and wife. At the death of one, the other becomes the sole owner of the property. This type of tenancy is popular with married couples because most want the survivor to have title to the property and to get it without any court proceedings. Many couples also like this type of ownership because the creditors of just the husband or just the wife cannot claim the property. To have a claim against the property, a creditor must be a creditor of both spouses. Almost half the states recognize this form of ownership.

A joint tenancy differs in other ways from a tenancy by the entirety. In the case of property held as a tenancy by the entirety, neither the husband nor the wife alone may sell or otherwise dispose of it. Both parties must join in any conveyance of the property. A divorce changes the husband and wife from tenants by the entirety to tenants in common with respect to the property.

Community Property

Community Property

Property acquired during marriage owned separately and equally by both spouses

Eight states, mostly out west, recognize a form of ownership called **community property.** Community property is a type of ownership reserved for married couples, such that both spouses own a separate and equal share of the property no matter how titled. In these states, unless the parties agree it shall be separate property, property acquired by a husband and wife during their marriage constitutes community property. This is normally important if a couple divorces. In that case, each owns one-half of the property acquired during the marriage. Property owned by one spouse prior to the marriage normally is that spouse's separate property and not community property.

> Robert and Joyce Hilke married and lived in a community property state. They bought a house conveyed to them as joint tenants. They later got a divorce, and before the divorce court determined a division of property, Joyce died. Robert argued that as joint tenants, upon Joyce's death, the house became his sole property. The court said once the divorce was entered, no matter how the house was titled, it constituted community property. Thus Robert owned only a one-half interest in the house.

ESTATES IN PROPERTY

L.O.3 ....

Estate

Interest in property

An **estate** is the nature and extent of interest that a person has in real or personal property. The estate that a person has in property may be:

1 A fee simple estate
2 A life estate

Fee Simple Estate

Fee Simple Estate

Largest, most complete right in property

A **fee simple estate** is the largest and most complete right that one may possess in property. A fee simple owner of property, whether real or personal, has the right to possess the property forever. The owner of a fee simple estate may also sell, lease, or otherwise dispose of the property permanently or temporarily. At the death of such owner, the property will pass to the persons provided for in the owner's will or, if no will exists, to the heirs at law.

A fee simple owner of land has the right to the surface of the land, the air above the land "all the way to heaven," and the subsoil beneath the surface all the way to the center of the earth. The courts have held, however, that the right to the air above the land is not absolute. An individual cannot prevent an airplane from flying over the land unless it flies too low. It is possible for a person to own the surface of the land only and not the minerals, oil, gas, and other valuable property under the topsoil. A person may also own the soil but not the timber.

Life Estate

Life Estate

Estate for duration of a life

Reversion

Interest of grantor in life estate that returns to grantor on death of grantee

Remainder

Interest in life estate that goes to someone other than grantor on death of grantee

One may have an estate in property by which the property is owned for a lifetime, known as a **life estate.** At the death of the owner, the title passes as directed by the original owner. The title may revert, or go back, to the grantor, the one who conveyed the life estate to the deceased. In this case, the interest of the grantor is called a **reversion.** Alternatively, the property may go to someone other than the grantor. Such an interest is called a **remainder.**

OTHER INTERESTS IN REAL PROPERTY

While not classified as estates, other interests a person may have in real property exist. Two common ones are easements and licenses.

Easement

An interest in land for nonexclusive or intermittent use

An **easement** is a right to use land, such as a right-of-way across another's land or the use of another's driveway. An easement does not give an exclusive right to possession, but a right of permanent intermittent use. It is classified as an interest in land and created by deed or by adverse use for a period of time set by statute.

When Mr. and Mrs. Bogoson divorced, Mrs. Bogoson received half their land. She deeded the other half, which included a lot with a house on it and an adjacent vacant lot, to Mr. Bogoson. Mrs. Bogoson's deed stated it included "a way for ingress and egress from said property to U.S. Highway 1, along the south side thereof." Frank Wolfe acquired Mrs. Bogoson's half. Robert and Bobbie Jean Dotson acquired the lot with the house by a deed also conveying a "fifty foot wide road right-of-way for ingress and egress along the south side of the property to U.S. Highway No. 1." The Dotsons then acquired the vacant lot by a deed that included the same language as Mrs. Bogoson's deed. The Dotsons filed suit to determine what right they had across Wolfe's land. The court held they had an easement created by the deed from Mrs. Bogoson to Mr. Bogoson.

License

Right to do certain acts on land

A **license** is a right to do certain acts on the land but not a right to stay in possession of the land. It constitutes a personal right to use property for a specific purpose. A licensor normally may terminate a license at will.

Monarch Associates owned an apartment complex. It contracted with James Todd giving Todd the exclusive, ten-year right to install and maintain laundry machines in the complex. The contract stated it bound the successors and assigns of the parties. Ronald Krolick and his partners obtained title to the complex. They asked Todd to remove the machines, so he sued for a court order preventing removal of them during the term of the contract with Monarch. The court stated that the contract granted a license, not an easement or lease. As a license, Krolick and his partners could revoke it, which they did.

ACQUIRING REAL PROPERTY

L.O.4 ....

Real property may be acquired in many of the same ways as personal property (Chapter 14). However, some ways exist in which real property, but not personal property, can be acquired. These include accretion and adverse possession.

Accretion

Accretion

Addition to land by gradual water deposits

Accretion is the addition to land as a result of the gradual deposit by water of solids. It takes place most commonly when a stream, river, lake, or ocean constitutes the boundary line of property. If one's land extends to the low water mark of a navigable stream, title to some land may be acquired by the river's shifting its flow. This occurs slowly by the deposit of silt. Also, the accretion may be the result of dredging or channeling of the river. If the silt and sand are thrown up on the riverbank thereby increasing the acreage of the upland contiguous to the river, the added acreage belongs to the owner of the upland.

Adverse Possession

Adverse Possession

Acquiring title to land by occupying it for fixed period

An individual may acquire title to real property by occupying the land owned by another for a period fixed by statute. This is known as **adverse possession** and basically means the original owner may no longer object to a trespass. The statutory period required varies from 7 years in some states to 21 in others. Occupancy must be continuous, open, hostile, visible, actual, and exclusive. It must be apparent enough to give the owner notice of trespass. In colonial times this was known as "squatter's rights." To get title by adverse possession, one had to go one step further than the "squatter"; this meant the adverse possession had to continue for the statutory period.

Color of Title

One's apparent title

Possession for the statutory period then gave clear title to all the land one's color of title described. **Color of title** is a person's apparent title. It usually arises, but does not have to, from some defective document purporting to be a deed or a will or even a gift.

Marvel L. Gaddis purchased a home. The property was described as a rectangular tract 295 feet north and south by 73 feet 8 inches east and west. On the north portion of the property was a horse barn, flower garden, and orchard all located partially on the property and partially on a 20-foot by 295-foot strip of land to the east. At the eastern edge of the strip was a dropoff to farmland beyond. The strip was never cultivated with the cropland. Gaddis assumed her property extended to the cropland and maintained and used the strip as an integral part of her property. A septic tank for the house was installed on it. Only Gaddis used or had possession of the strip since her purchase. Seventeen years later, a survey revealed that the strip was not part of her rectangular tract. The statutory period for adverse possession was 10 years. Nebraska State Bank, which held a deed to the strip, asked a court to declare it the owner. The court found Gaddis was in actual, continuous, exclusive, notorious, and hostile possession of the strip for 10 years. She owned it by adverse possession.

QUESTIONS

1 What is real property? Give some examples.

2 Is vegetation real or personal property?

3 What is the difference in ownership rights of a person whose property borders on a nonnavigable river and a person whose property borders on a navigable river?

4 What are the two questions that must be answered in order to determine whether personal property has become a fixture?

5 What presumption does a court make when a tenant installs personal property in a building?

6 When property is owned by more than one person, what type of ownership does the law presume they have?

7 a. Which types of multiple ownership of property give the owners the right of survivorship?

    b. What does the right of survivorship mean?

8 What are the real property estates?

9 What is accretion?

10 Is it possible for a trespasser to acquire title to the property on which the trespass is made?

CASE PROBLEMS

L.O.1 ....

1 Mr. and Mrs. Simmons lived in a mobile home that had been bought with community-property funds. The home was in a mobile home park where they rented a lot. Mrs. Simmons had title to the home. She went to Cooper's Mobile Homes, Inc., and signed a number of documents relating to the purchase of a new mobile home. She signed over the title certificate of the old home to Cooper's as a down payment on a new home, intending to move the old home off the lot. Mr. Simmons objected to the arrangement and said he would not agree to it. Mrs. Simmons tried to cancel the agreement. The sale was never made, and Cooper's sued for breach of the contract to buy the new home. Mrs. Simmons alleged that the law that gives each spouse management authority over community property did not apply because the home was real property and both had to join in the conveyance. Was it real property?

L.O.2 ....

2 Robert Funches died. Gisele Funches claimed that since they had married and never divorced, she became Robert's widow. Robert and Pranee Funches had contracted a bigamous marriage and real property had been conveyed to them as tenants by the entirety. Gisele alleged that since a tenancy by the entirety between Robert and Pranee could not exist, they owned the property as tenants in common. As Robert's widow, Gisele claimed his share of the property. Pranee claimed a joint tenancy existed and Robert's share became hers upon his death. Considering the nature of the various tenancies involved, which type of tenancy is closest to what Robert and Pranee intended to establish?

L.O.4 ....

3 Some islands were formed as an accretion to the bed of the Missouri River. Continued accretion permanently joined them to the shore. The state of Iowa, as the owner of the bed of the river, claimed the land. As owners of land adjoining a navigable river, Harry Sorensen and other adjoining landowners owned only to the high water mark. However, once the islands became attached to the shore, they were no longer part of the riverbed and were not necessary for navigation or commerce. The state brought a lawsuit to establish its title to the land. Discuss the rights of the parties to the land.

L.O.3 ....

4   In 1941, a tract of land owned by Elizabeth Selig and her husband was taken by the United States. The Declaration of Taking stated that a full fee simple title, subject only to easements for pipelines, roads, and utilities, was taken. Many years later Selig filed suit against the United States, alleging the compensation paid in 1941 did not include compensation for the minerals. Who owned the minerals?

L.O.2 ....

5   Rafael Villarreal acquired title to a house by a deed conveying to him as a single person. Two months later, Rafael married Ludivina. Several years later Rafael and Ludivina divorced. Since they lived in a community property state, what should the court order regarding title to the house when making a property division?

L.O.1 ....

6   Key Bank loaned William DiBiase $2,580,000 secured by a mortgage on real property and covering after-acquired fixtures. DiBiase had an inn built on the property and bought 90 heating and air-conditioning units for each of the rooms. The units were purchased from Lewiston Bottled Gas Co. (LBG), which retained a security interest in the units. Bolted to the walls, they became part of the walls of the building. Their removal would leave a large hole in the wall of each room. Key Bank foreclosed on the real property, and a court had to determine whether it or LBG had priority over the units. The key question was whether they were fixtures or remained personal property. What were they?

L.O.3 ....

7   The town of Hempstead attached street light fixtures to telephone poles owned by the New York Telephone Company. Under the provisions of state law the telephone company had an unconditional right to erect poles for its line on public streets and highways. When the telephone company sued Hempstead to require it to remove the light fixtures, the town alleged that the right to attach the fixtures to utility poles is an interest in real property and subject to the power of the city to take property for public purposes. Is the telephone company's right to erect telephone poles an interest in real property?

Chapter 43

TRANƧFER OF REAL PROPERTY

LEARNING OBJECTIVES

After studying this chapter you should be able to:

1 Describe the means by which title to real estate is transferred.

2 Explain the provisions normally contained in a deed.

3 Summarize the steps taken to safely and effectively transfer title to real property after a deed is signed.

Preview Case

I. A. Rosenbaum conveyed land to T. S. McCaskey by quitclaim deed. The deed stated: "The grantor herein is to retain one-half of all oil, gas, and mineral rights in the above described lands. . . ." When this conveyance was made, Rosenbaum owned the surface and one-half of the mineral rights. After Rosenbaum died, his heirs sued to confirm title to the mineral rights. What did this deed convey to McCaskey?

A sale constitutes the most common reason for transferring title to real estate. In the ordinary case, the parties sign a contract of sale, and the seller delivers a deed to the buyer. One may, by means of a lease, transfer a leasehold title giving the rights to the use and possession of land for a limited period. The provisions of the deed or the lease determine the extent of the interest transferred.

Even when the owner makes a gift of real property, the transfer must be evidenced by a deed. As soon as the owner executes and delivers a deed, title vests fully in the donee. Acceptance by the donee is presumed.

DEEDS

L.O.1 ....

Deed

Writing conveying title to
real property

Grantor

Person conveying prop-
erty

Grantee

Person receiving title to
property

Quitclaim Deed

Deed that transfers what-
ever interest grantor has
in property

A **deed** is a writing, signed by the owner, conveying title to real property. The law
sets forth the form that the deed must have, and this form must be observed. The
parties to the deed include the **grantor,** or original owner, and the **grantee,** or
recipient. The two principal types of deeds are:

1   Quitclaim deeds
2   Warranty deeds

Quitclaim Deeds

A **quitclaim deed** is just what the name implies. The grantor gives up whatever
interest the grantor may have in the real property. However, the grantor makes no
warranty that the grantor has any claim to the property.

In the absence of a statute or an agreement between the parties requiring a warranty deed, a quitclaim deed may be used in making all conveyances of real property. A quitclaim deed transfers the grantor's full and complete interest as effectively as a warranty deed. When buying real property, however, one does not
always want to buy merely the interest that the grantor has. A buyer wants to buy a
perfect and complete interest so that the title cannot be questioned by anyone. A
quitclaim deed conveys only the interest of the grantor and no more. It contains no
warranty that the grantor has good title. In most real estate transactions therefore, a
quitclaim deed cannot be used because the contract will specify that a warranty
deed must be delivered.

I. A. Rosenbaum conveyed land to T. S. McCaskey by
quitclaim deed. The deed stated: "The grantor herein is
to retain one-half of all oil, gas, and mineral rights in
the above described lands. . . ." When this conveyance
was made, Rosenbaum owned the surface and one-
half of the mineral rights. After Rosenbaum died, his
heirs sued to confirm title to the mineral rights. The
court stated a quitclaim deed was only a conduit that
passed the grantor's interest to the grantee. To find out
what interest passed, it is necessary to determine
what interest the grantor had to convey and take from
it anything reserved in the quitclaim deed. This deed
reserved a one-half interest in the mineral rights and
conveyed what was left—the surface.

Warranty Deeds

Warranty Deed

Deed with guarantees

**General
Warranty Deed**

Warrants good title free
from all claims

A **warranty deed** not only conveys the grantor's interest in the real property but, in
addition, makes certain warranties or guarantees. The exact nature of the warranty
or guarantee depends upon whether the deed is a general warranty or a special warranty deed.

A **general warranty deed,** (see Illustration 43-1) not only warrants that the
grantor has good title to the real property but further warrants that the grantee "shall
have quiet and peaceable possession, free from all encumbrances, and that the
grantor will defend the grantee against all claims and demands from whomsoever
made." This warranty, then, warrants that all prior grantors had good title and that

Illustration 43-1   General Warranty Deed

WARRANTY DEED
Know All Men by These Presents:

That   Donald C. Coson and Millicent M. Coson, his wife

of Butler   County, Ohio

in consideration of   the sum of Forth-five Thousand Dollars ($45,000)

to them   *in hand paid by*   Eugene F. Acknor, the grantee, the receipt of
which is hereby acknowledged,

do hereby **Grant, Bargain, Sell and Convey**

to the said Eugene F. Acknor

h is   heirs

and assigns forever, the following described **Real Estate** *situated in the* City

of Hamilton   *in the County of*   Butler   *and State of* Ohio

Lot No. 10, Section 14, Range 62, Randall Subdivision, being a portion of
the estate of Horace E. Cresswell and Alice B. Cresswell

and all the **Estate, Right, Title and Interest** *of the said grantors in and to said premises;* **To have
and to hold** *the same, with all the privileges and appurtenances thereunto belonging, to said grantee ,his
heirs and assigns forever. And the Said*   Donald C. Coson and Millicent M. Coson

do   hereby **Covenant and Warrant** *that the title so conveyed is* **Clear, Free and
Unencumbered,** *and that they will* **Defend** *the same against all lawful claims of all persons whomsoever.*

In Witness Whereof, *the said grantors have hereunto set* their hand s ,this first

day of December   *in the year A.D. nineteen and* --

Signed and acknowledged in presence of us:

Michael R. Wiser	*Donald C. Coson*
Antonia C. Patricelle	*Millicent M. Coson*

State of   Ohio,   Butler **County, ss.**

On this first   *day of* December   *A.D. 19*   *, before me, a* Notary Public
in and for said County, personally came   Donald C. Coson and Millicent M. Coson

the grantor in the foregoing deed, and
acknowledged the signing thereof to be   their *voluntary act and deed.*

Witness *my official signature and seal on the day last above mentioned.*

Sarah M Evans

Sarah M. Evans
Notary Public, State of Ohio
My commission expires June 1, 19—

no defects exist in any prior grantor's title. The grantee does not have to assume
any risks as the new owner of the property.

A **special warranty deed** warrants that the grantor has the right to sell the real
property. The grantor makes no warranties of the genuineness of any prior grantor's
title. Trustees and sheriffs who sell land at a foreclosure sale use this type of deed.

**Special
Warranty Deed**

Warrants grantor has
right to convey property

Executors and administrators also use such a deed. These officials should not warrant anything other than that they have the legal right to sell whatever interest the owner has.

When a builder sells a new house, most courts now impose an implied warranty of fitness not found in the deed. The warranty amounts to a promise that the builder designed and constructed the house in a workmanlike manner, suitable for habitation by the buyer.

PROVISIONS IN A DEED

L.O.2 ....   Unless statutes provide otherwise, a deed usually has the following provisions:

1 Parties
2 Consideration
3 Covenants
4 Description
5 Signature
6 Acknowledgment

Parties

The grantor and the grantee must be identified, usually by name, in the deed. If the grantor is married, the grantor's name and that of a spouse should be written in the deed. If the grantor is unmarried, this fact should be indicated by using the word *single* or the phrase a *single person*.

Consideration

The amount paid to the grantor for the property is the consideration. The payment may be in money or in money's worth. A deed usually includes a statement of the consideration, although the amount specified need not be the actual price paid. Some localities have a practice of indicating a nominal amount, such as one dollar, although a much larger sum was actually paid. The parties state a nominal amount as the consideration to keep the sale price from being a matter of public record.

Covenant
Promise in a deed

Affirmative Covenant
Promise by grantee to do an act

Negative Covenant
Agreement by grantee not to do an act

Covenants

A **covenant** is a promise contained in a deed. There may be as many covenants as the grantor and the grantee wish to include. **Affirmative covenants** obligate the grantee to do something, such as agreeing to maintain a driveway used in common with adjoining property. In **negative covenants** the grantee agrees to refrain from doing something. Such covenants frequently appear in deeds for urban residential developments. The more common ones prohibit the grantee from using the property for business purposes and set forth the types of homes that can or cannot be built on the property. Most covenants run with the land, which means they bind all future owners.

Capitol Housing Corporation (CHC) bought land containing a building from the Harrisburg Redevelopment Authority (Authority). The deed incorporated covenants restricting the building to residential private housing for 40 years. The Pennsylvania Higher Education Assistance Agency contracted to buy the property and obtained permission from the city of Harrisburg to rent the second, third, and fourth floors for government offices. A lawsuit ensued. The court held that using three floors of the building for government offices violated the covenants and prohibited the sale to PHEAA.

Description

The property to be conveyed must be correctly described. Any description that will clearly identify the property suffices. Ordinarily, however, the description used in the deed by which the present owner acquired the title should be used if correct. The description may be by lots and blocks if the property is in a city; or it may be by metes and bounds or section, range, and township if the property is in a rural area. If the description is indefinite, the grantor retains title.

Lake Minnewaska Mountain Houses, Inc., owned land it contracted to convey to the Nature Conservancy. LMMH employed Albin Rekis and allowed him to live in a house located on five acres of the land. LMMH called Rekis to the office to sign some documents, including an agreement providing:

1. LMMH would execute a deed to real property to Rekis. LMMH would record it prior to the conveyance to the Nature Conservancy.
2. Rekis would execute a deed of property to LMMH.

It would be recorded after the conveyance to the Nature Conservancy.

The parties executed these deeds. The one Rekis signed contained no description of the property to be conveyed by the deed. Rekis later discovered that LMMH's contract with the Nature Conservancy excluded the five-acre parcel and the contract stated LMMH agreed to convey that parcel to Rekis. He sued LMMH. The court held that since the deed Rekis signed had no description it was void.

Signature

The deed should be signed by the grantor in the place provided for the signature. A married grantor must have the spouse also sign for the purpose of giving up the statutory right of the spouse. In some states the signatures must be attested by a witness or witnesses. If the grantor cannot sign the deed, it may be executed by an agent, the grantor with assistance, or the grantor making a mark, thus:

Maria Smith
Witness of the mark of
Henry Finn

$$\text{Henry} \left\{ \begin{array}{c} \text{His} \\ \text{X} \\ \text{Mark} \end{array} \right\} \text{Finn}$$

Acknowledgment

The statutes normally require that the deed be formally acknowledged before a notary public or other officer authorized to take acknowledgments. The acknowledgment allows the deed to be recorded. After a deed has been recorded, it may be used as evidence in a court without further proof of its authenticity. Recording does not make a deed valid, but it helps give security of the title to the grantee.

The **acknowledgment** is a declaration made by the properly authorized officer, in the form provided for that purpose, that the grantor has acknowledged signing the instrument as a free act and deed. In some states the grantor must also understand the nature and effect of the deed or be personally known to the acknowledging officer. The officer attests to these facts and affixes an official seal. The certificate provides evidence of these actions.

Acknowledgment

Declaration grantor has stated execution of instrument is free act

DELIVERY

L.O.3 ....

Delivery

Giving up possession and control

A deed has no effect on the transfer of an interest in real property until it has been delivered. **Delivery** consists of the grantor intending to give possession and control over the deed. So long as the grantor maintains control over the deed and reserves the right to demand its return before delivery of the deed to the grantee, there has been no legal delivery. If the grantor executes a deed and leaves it with an attorney to deliver to the grantee, there has been no delivery until the attorney delivers the deed to the grantee. Since the attorney is the agent of the grantor, the grantor has the right to demand that the agent return the deed. If the grantor, however, delivers the deed to the grantee's attorney, then there has been an effective delivery because releasing control constitutes evidence of intent that title pass. Once the grantor makes delivery, title passes.

Paul Carlile executed three deeds including a deed that gave an interest in minerals from a parcel of land to three of his children, Violet Enlow, Claude Carlile, and William Carlile. The other deeds were recorded, but the mineral deed was not. After Paul Carlile died, only a third son, J. C. Carlile knew the mineral deed's location. J. C. told Violet he would not record the deed unless the other siblings conveyed five acres of minerals to him. They refused and William and Violet sued. Violet testified that Paul had told her he was making a deed to equally divide the minerals. The next week Paul told her J. C. had the deeds and would record them. At trial J. C. produced an envelope in which Paul had put all three deeds. The court held that the mineral deed had been delivered along with the other two deeds.

RECORDING

Statutes in every state require grantees to file their deeds with a public official in the county in which the land lies. Any other instrument affecting title to real property in the county can also be filed. These public records of land transactions give notice of title transfers to all, particularly potential subsequent purchasers.

A deed need not be recorded in order to complete one's title. Title passes upon delivery of the deed. Recording the deed protects the grantee against a second sale by the grantor and against any liens that may attach to the property while still recorded in the grantor's name.

When the recording official receives a deed for recording, the law ordinarily requires the deed be stamped with the exact date and time the grantee leaves the deed for recording.

ABSTRACT OF TITLE

Abstract of Title
History of real estate

Before one buys real estate, an abstract of title may be prepared. An abstract company normally does this, but it may be done by an attorney. The **abstract of title** gives a complete history of the real estate. It also shows whether or not there are any unpaid taxes and assessments, outstanding mortgages, unpaid judgments, or other unsatisfied liens of any type against the property. Once an abstracting company makes the abstract, an attorney normally reads the abstract to see if it reveals any flaws in the title.

TITLE INSURANCE

Some defects in the title to real estate cannot be detected by an abstract. Some of the most common of these defects are forgery of signatures in prior conveyances; claims by adverse possession; incompetency to contract by any prior party; fraud; duress; undue influence; defective wills; loss of real property by accretion; and errors by title examiner, tax officials, surveyors, and many other public officials. A title insurance policy can be obtained that will cover these defects. The policy may expressly exclude any possible defects that the insurance company does not wish to be covered by the policy. The insured pays one premium for coverage as long as the property is owned. The policy does not benefit a subsequent purchaser or a mortgagee.

QUESTIONS

1   Is it necessary for the donee of real property to accept the property before title vests?
2   How is title to real estate transferred?
3   Who are the two parties named in a deed?
4   What interest in property does a quitclaim deed convey and how does it differ from a warranty deed?
5   What description of property is sufficient in a deed?
6   What is an acknowledgment?
7   When does a deed become effective?
8   a. Is it necessary to record a deed in order to complete one's title to the land?
    b. What does recording a deed do?
9   What is an abstract of title, and what is its significance when transferring real estate?
10 How may an owner of real property be protected against defects in title?

CASE PROBLEMS

L.O.2 ....

1   V.T.C. Lines, Inc., owned two pieces of real estate. On April 8 they were the subject of a deed to John Christian. The deed stated: "This deed of

Conveyance . . . between Logan Middleton, President of the V.T.C. Lines Incorporated . . . party of the first part, and John Christian . . . party of the second part." It was signed by Logan Middleton, President V.T.C. Lines, Incorporated. The only other reference to the corporation was in the attestation clause, where Logan Middleton was again designated president of the corporation. The next day Jerry and Donald Johnson secured a judgment against V.T.C. On June 12, Christian and his wife conveyed a one-half interest in the property to Johnny Pace. The Johnsons tried to execute on the property. Who owns it?

L.O.3 ....   **2**   Martha Wisdom executed a deed conveying certain real property to her son, Charles Smith. Wisdom put the deed in an envelope and asked Smith to hide the envelope with other papers in a wall heater in Wisdom's house, which he did. Wisdom had told Smith she had made a deed of the house to him. At a later time when at Wisdom's home, Smith went through the papers and found the deed. After Wisdom died, Smith recorded the deed. Smith's sister, Mildred Cecil, filed a suit to have the deed set aside based on failure of Wisdom, the grantor, to deliver the deed. Should the court find a valid delivery?

L.O.2 ....   **3**   Robert Young brought an action to quiet title (decide who has title) to 80 acres of land in U.S. Survey 691 on Prince of Wales Island. William Shilts alleged that as the sole heir of Aaron Shellhouse, he was the record owner of part of the property. Alaska Industrial Company received a grant to U.S. Survey 691. It later conveyed six blocks of land in that survey to Shellhouse. The 200-foot-square blocks were located by reference to named streets and were "more particularly described on Survey No. 691, made by Chas. S. Hubbell. . . ." That survey was not found, and the only map showing the survey did not indicate any lots or streets. The trial court determined the configuration of the lots from the street references in the deed and that the Shellhouse property was between Corner No. 1 and Point No. 2 on one of the exhibits and contained 400 feet of beachfront. Was the description in the deed adequate to convey the property?

L.O.2 ....   **4**   R. S. Farrar executed a deed of real estate to Ann and Larry Shrewsbury on the same day an agreement was signed by which the Shrewsburys agreed to provide a home for Farrar for the rest of his life. After Farrar's death, his sons filed an action to set aside the deed for failure of consideration. Regarding consideration, the deed stated: "For and in consideration of the sum of One Dollar ($1.00), and other good and valuable consideration, cash in hand paid . . . the receipt of which is hereby acknowledged. . . ." Farrar lived with the Shrewsburys for four months and then lived elsewhere but visited them often on weekends and was always welcome at their home. Should the deed be canceled for failure of consideration?

L.O.1 ....   **5**   Edmund and Maude Clarke, husband and wife, owned a home. They had one child, Fleur Van Pelt. After Maude died, Edmund married Enid and they lived in the home. Van Pelt and her husband executed a quitclaim deed to Edmund and Enid for the recited purpose of giving up any claim to the property.

Edmund died and his will did not specifically mention the property, so Van Pelt asked the court to determine its status. The court had to determine the effect of the quitclaim deed. What had that deed done to the title to the property?

L.O.3 ....   **6**   After Felix Dopieralla died, a sealed envelope containing a deed to his house was discovered in his home. The grantee on the deed was Pauline Adams. Adams said Dopieralla had delivered the deed to her at the home of a mutual friend, Mrs. Nielson. Adams testified she did not record or keep the deed because Dopieralla might not understand. The deed was left with Nielson. Adams returned the deed to Dopieralla when Nielson was leaving on an extended trip and did not want to keep it. Dopieralla lived in the house, exercised all rights of ownership over it, and paid the taxes on it. Was there a valid delivery of the deed to Adams?

L.O.2 ....   **7**   William Middleton owned a large tract of land that he conveyed in smaller parcels using deeds containing covenants restricting the land to residential use. The covenants stated they ran with the land. Two deeds, including one to Waldo Leynse, also specifically prohibited commercial logging on the property. Leynse divided his property and conveyed it to a number of people including Lawrence Holmes. Holmes Lumber Co. got approval from the state board of forestry for commercial logging on the property of Lawrence Holmes and others who had obtained their property from Leynse. Other owners of land originally in the Middleton tract filed suit against these landowners to prevent the logging, asking the court to enforce the restrictive covenants in the deeds. Should the court enforce the covenants?

Chapter 44

REAL E/TATE MORTGAGE/

LEARNING OBJECTIVES

After studying this chapter you should be able to:

1 Define and discuss the effect of a mortgage.

2 List the duties and rights of a mortgagor.

3 Explain the rights of parties upon foreclosure, sale, and assignment of the mortgage.

Preview Case

Ralph and Florence Manning, husband and wife, executed a mortgage on land they owned as tenants in common to Farmers Trust and Savings Bank to secure a loan for $69,000. The mortgage contained an open-end, or dragnet, provision that stated: "This mortgage shall stand as security . . . for any and all future and additional advances made to the Mortgagors by the holder . . . in such . . . amounts so that the total . . . outstanding . . . shall not exceed $100,000 and Mortgagee is hereby given authority to make such future . . . advances to Mortgagors herein." Subsequently, Ralph alone borrowed a total of $31,000. None of the additional notes were signed by Florence. When one came due, Ralph offered Farmers checks in payment on the condition Farmers would loan the money to cover them. Farmers refused and sued, invoking an acceleration clause to declare the entire indebtedness due. It claimed that the mortgage secured the additional notes executed only by Ralph. Did it?

L.O.1

Mortgage
Lien on real estate

Mortgagor
Person who gives mortgage

Mortgagee
Person who holds mortgage

A **mortgage** is a lien given upon real estate to secure a debt. The mortgage does not constitute the debt itself but the security for the debt. Land or any interest in land may be mortgaged. Land may be mortgaged separately from the improvements, or the improvements may be mortgaged apart from the land. A person who gives a mortgage as a security for a debt is a **mortgagor.** A person who holds a mortgage as security for a debt is a **mortgagee.**

The mortgagor normally retains possession of the property. In order for the mortgagee to obtain the benefit of the security, the mortgagee must take possession of the premises upon default or sell the mortgaged property at a foreclosure sale. In some states, the mortgagee may not take possession of the property upon default but may obtain the appointment of a receiver to collect the rents and income. If the sale of the property brings more than the debt and the costs, the mortgagor must be paid the balance.

THE MORTGAGE CONTRACT

A mortgage must be in writing. The contract, as a rule, must have the same form as a deed, which means it must be acknowledged. The mortgage, like all other contracts, sets forth the rights and the duties of the contracting parties (see Illustration 44-1).

A mortgagor normally gives a mortgage to raise money for the purchase price of real estate, but it may be given for other reasons. One may borrow money for any reason and secure the loan by a mortgage. One may assume a contingent liability for another, such as becoming a surety, and receive a mortgage as security.

The lien of the mortgage attaches to the property described in the mortgage. A mortgage generally also provides that the lien attaches to additions thereafter made to the described property; for example, the lien of the mortgage attaches to personal property, which thereafter becomes a fixture. A clause purporting to make the security clause of a mortgage cover future debts will be valid if the parties intended it to cover future debts.

Ralph and Florence Manning, husband and wife, executed a mortgage on land they owned as tenants in common to Farmers Trust and Savings Bank to secure a loan for $69,000. The mortgage contained an open-end, or dragnet, provision that stated: "This mortgage shall stand as security . . . for any and all future and additional advances made to the Mortgagors by the holder . . . in such . . . amounts so that the total . . . outstanding . . . shall not exceed $100,000 and Mortgagee is hereby given authority to make such future . . . advances to Mortgagors herein." Subsequently, Ralph alone borrowed a total of $31,000. None of the additional notes were signed by Florence. When one came due, Ralph offered Farmers checks in payment on the condition Farmers would loan the money to cover them. Farmers refused and sued, invoking an acceleration clause to declare the entire indebtedness due. It claimed the mortgage secured the additional notes executed only by Ralph. The court held that the express terms of the mortgage established it as security only on loans to both of the Mannings.

RECORDING

Depending upon the law of the state in which the land lies, the mortgage gives the mortgagee either a lien on the land or title to the land. The mortgagor's payment of the debt divests or destroys this title or lien. Recording the mortgage protects the mortgagee against subsequent creditors, since the public record normally constitutes notice to the whole world as to the mortgagee's rights. There may be both a first mortgage and subsequent mortgages. The mortgage recorded first normally has preference. This is not true when actual notice of a prior mortgage exists. However, a purchase money mortgage has preference over other claims arising through the mortgagor. The mortgage is also recorded to notify subsequent purchasers that as much of the purchase price as is necessary to pay off the mortgage must be paid to the mortgagee. Recording must be proper, otherwise the purpose of the mortgagee providing notice to others cannot be accomplished.

Illustration 44-1   Mortgage Contract

MORGAGE
WITH POWER OF SALE (Realty)

KNOW ALL MEN BY THESE PRESENTS:

THAT .... Walter A. Righetti .... and

.... Susan L. Righetti .... husband and wife, GRANTORS, for and in consideration of the sum of One Dollar ($1.00), to GRANTORS in hand paid, the receipt of which is hereby acknowledged, and in consideration of the premises hereinafter set forth, do hereby grant, bargain, sell and convey unto ...... Third National Bank of Russellville .... , GRANTEE, (Whether one or more) and unto GRANTEE'S ~~heirs~~ (Successors) and assigns forever, the following property, situatedin .... Pope .... County, Arkansas:

Lot 37 in GREENE HEIGHTS SUBDIVISION

TO HAVE AND TO HOLD the same unto the said GRANTEE, and unto GRANTEE's ~~heirs~~ (successors) and assigns forever, with all appurtenances thereunto belonging; and all rents, income, and profits therefrom after any default herein.

We [I] hereby covenant with the said GRANTEE, GRANTEE's ~~heirs~~ (successors) and assigns, that said lands are free and clear of all encumbrances and liens, and will forever warrant and defend the title to said property against all lawful claims. And, we, GRANTORS, ... Walter A. Righetti and Susan L. Righetti .... , for the consideration aforesaid do hereby release unto the said GRANTEE and unto GRANTEE's ~~heirs~~ (successors) and assigns forever, all our rights and possibility of dower, curtesy and homestead in and to the said lands.

The sale is on the condition, that whereas, GRANTORS are justly indebted unto said GRANTEE in the sum of ..... Sixty .... Thousand and 00/100 .... Dollars ($ .... 60,000.00 ....), evidenced by .... their .... promissory note .... dated ...... October 17 .... , 19 .--., in the sum of $ .... 60,000.00 .... bearing interest from date until due at the rate of .... 10 .. % per annum and thereafter until paid at the rate of .... 10 ... % per annum, payable as follows:

$ 545 per month, due and payable on the first day of the month, beginning November 1, 19-- and continuing for 25 years.

This mortgage shall also be security for any other indebtedness of whatsoever kind that the GRANTEE or the holders or owners of this mortgage may hold against GRANTORS by reason of future advances made hereunder, by purchase or otherwise, to the time of the satisfaction of this mortgage.

In the event of default of payment of any part of said sum, with interest, or upon failure of GRANTORS to perform the agreements contained herein, the GRANTEE, GRANTEE's ~~heirs~~ (successors) and assigns, shall have the right to declare the entire debt to due and payable; and

GRANTORS hereby covenant that they will keep all improvements insured against fire, with all other full coverage insurance, loss payable clause to holder and owner of this mortgage; that said improvements will be kept in a good state of repair, and waste will neither be permitted nor committed,; that all taxes of whatever nature, as well as assessments for improvements will be paid when due, and if not paid GRANTEE may pay same and shall have a prior lien upon said property for repayment, with interest at the rate of 10% per annum; now,

THEREFORE, if GRANTORS shall pay all indebtedness secured hereby, with interest, at the times and in the manner aforesaid, and perform the agreements herein contained, then this conveyance shall be void. In case of nonpayment or failure to perform the agreements herein contained, the said GRANTEE, GRANTEE'S ~~heirs~~ (successors) and assigns, shall have the right and power to take possession of the property herein conveyed and expel any occupant therefrom without process of law; to collect rents and profits and apply same on unpaid indebtedness; and with or without possession to sell said property at public sale, to the highest bidder for cash, (or ....), at .... the county courthouse .... of .... Pope .... County, Arkansas, public notice of the time, terms and place of sale having first been given twenty days by advertising in some newspaper published in said County, by at least three insertions, or by notices posted in five public places in the County, at which sale any of the parties hereto, their heirs (successors), or assigns, may bid and purchase as any third person night do; and GRANTORS hereby authorize the said GRANTEE, GRANTEE'S ~~heirs~~ (successors), or assigns to convey said property to anyone purchasing at said sale, and to convey an absolute title thereto, and the recitals of such conveyance shall be taken as *prima facie* true. The proceeds of said sale shall be applied, first to the payment of all costs and expenses attending said sale; second to the payment of all indebtedness secured hereby, with interest; and the remainder, if any, shall be paid to said GRANTORS. GRANTORS hereby waive any and all rights of appraisement, sale, redemption, and homestead under the laws of the State of Arkansas, and especially under the Act approved May 8, 1899, and acts amendatory thereof.

WITNESS ..... our ..... hand s.. and seal s.. this .... 17th .... day of .... October ..... , 19 ....

            Walter A. Righetti .... (seal)
      .... *Susan L. Righetti* .... (seal)

(ACKNOWLEDGMENT BEFORE A NOTARY FOLLOWS)

Burl Brunson borrowed $50,000 from Howard Savings Bank securing the loan by a mortgage on real estate. This mortgage was properly recorded but not properly indexed. Two years later, Brunson conveyed the property by deed to Jesus and Celeste Ijalba, and the Ijalbas executed a mortgage on the property to Chrysler First Financial Services Corp. This mortgage was properly recorded and indexed. Chicago Title Insurance Co. conducted a thorough title search and, finding no mortgage under Brunson's name, issued a title insurance policy on the property to Chrysler. Six months later, Howard filed a foreclosure suit against Chrysler and Ijalba claiming its mortgage had priority. The court said the law requires recording to give notice to subsequent purchasers and encumbrancers of real estate. Because each county has thousands of record books, each with at least 1,000 pages, a mortgage cannot be duly recorded without being properly indexed. Howard's mortgage did not have priority over the one to Chrysler.

DUTIES OF THE MORTGAGOR

L.O.2 ....

The mortgagor assumes three definite duties and liabilities when placing a mortgage upon real estate. These pertain to:

1   Interest and principal
2   Taxes, assessments, and insurance premiums
3   Security of the mortgagee

Interest and Principal

The mortgagor must make all payments of interest and principal as they become due. Most mortgages call for periodic payments, such as monthly, semiannually, or annually. These payments are used to pay all accrued interest to the date of payment, and the mortgagee applies the balance on the principal. Other mortgages call for periodic payment of interest and for the payment of the entire principal at one time. In either case, a failure to pay either the periodic payments of interest and principal or of interest only constitutes a default. A default gives the mortgagee the right to foreclose. Most mortgages contain a provision that if the mortgagor does not make an interest or principal payment when due or within a specified time after due, the mortgagee may declare the entire principal immediately due. This is known as an **acceleration clause.**

Acceleration Clause

Clause allowing entire principal to be due

If the mortgagor wishes to pay off the mortgage debt before the due date so as to save interest, that right must be reserved at the time the mortgage is given.

Taxes, Assessments, and Insurance Premiums

The mortgagor, who is the owner of the land regardless of the form of the mortgage, must continue to make such payments as would be expected of an owner of land. The mortgagor must pay taxes and assessments. If the mortgagor does not, the mortgagee may pay them and compel a reimbursement from the mortgagor. If the mortgage contract requires the mortgagor to pay these charges, a failure to pay them becomes a default.

The law does not require the mortgagor to keep the property insured nor to insure it for the benefit of the mortgagee. This duty must be imposed on the mortgagor by contract. Both the mortgagor and the mortgagee have an insurable interest in the property to the extent of each one's interest or maximum loss.

Security of the Mortgagee

The mortgagor must do no act that will materially impair the security of the mortgagee. Cutting timber, tearing down buildings, and all acts that waste the assets impair the security and give the mortgagee the right to seek legal protection. Some state statutes provide that any one of these acts constitutes a default. This gives the mortgagee the right to foreclose. Other statutes provide only that the mortgagee may obtain an injunction in a court of equity enjoining any further impairment. Some states provide for the appointment of a receiver to prevent waste. Many state laws also make it a criminal offense to willfully impair the security of mortgaged property.

Alfred and Donna Allen and James and Patricia Simpson had executed a 20-year mortgage to Michael Bodwitch. It contained a provision "that no building on the premises shall be removed or demolished without the consent of the mortgagee." The city condemned the building on the mortgaged property as a safety hazard because part of it collapsed. It notified the Allens and Simpsons that they had to demolish the building. They, Bodwitch, and a demolition contractor signed a contract for the demolition. Bodwitch then sued the Allens and Simpsons alleging they had breached the mortgage agreement. The court said the purpose of the provision regarding demolition of a building was to protect the security of the mortgagee. However, in this case the mortgagee lost any security when the building collapsed, not from its demolition.

RIGHTS OF THE MORTGAGOR

The mortgagor has four rights:
1   Possession of the property
2   Rents and profits
3   Cancellation of lien
4   Redemption

Possession of the Property

The mortgagor usually has the right to retain possession of the mortgaged property. Upon default the mortgagee usually may take possession to collect rents and profits and apply them to the mortgage debt in compliance with a duty as a fiduciary to the mortgagor. In some states possession cannot be taken, but the appointment of a receiver to collect rents and profits may be obtained.

Rents and Profits

The mortgagor has the right to rents and profits from the property. In the absence of an express agreement to the contrary, the mortgagor has the right to all rents and profits obtained from the mortgaged property. The mortgagor may retain the profits. This rule or any other rule may, of course, be superseded by a contract providing otherwise.

Cancellation of Lien

The mortgagor has the right to have the lien canceled on final payment. As soon as the mortgagee receives the mortgage, it becomes a lien upon the mortgaged real estate. The clerk in the recorder's office cancels a mortgage lien by entering a notation, usually on the margin, certifying that the debt has been paid and that the lien is canceled. The mortgagee, not the mortgagor, must have this done. If the mortgagee does not, the mortgagor may institute court action to have this cloud removed from the title so that there may be a clear title.

Redemption

Redemption

Right to free property from lien of mortgage after default

The mortgagor has the right to free the mortgaged property from the lien of the mortgage after default, known as the right of **redemption.** Statutes in most states prescribe a specific time after the foreclosure and sale when this right may be exercised. In order to redeem the property, the mortgagor must pay the amount of the mortgage and the costs of the sale.

Usually the right of redemption may be exercised only by a person whose interests will be affected by foreclosure. This includes the executor or administrator and heirs of the mortgagor, and frequently a second mortgagee.

FORECLOSURE

L.O.3 ....

Foreclosure

Sale of mortgaged property to pay debt

If the mortgagor fails to pay the debt secured by the mortgage when it becomes due, or fails to perform any of the other terms set forth in the mortgage, the mortgagee has the right to foreclose for the purpose of collecting the debt. **Foreclosure** usually consists of a sale of the mortgaged property. The sale is made under an order of a court and generally by an officer of the court. The mortgagor must be properly notified of the foreclosure proceedings.

Earnestine and Henry Henderson mortgaged their home to the Farmers Home Administration (FmHA) as security for a loan. They defaulted on the loan, so FmHA accelerated the debt and foreclosed on the property. When sued for eviction, the Hendersons alleged the notice of foreclosure FmHA sent them misrepresented the law regarding what they had to pay to avoid foreclosure. The law stated: "The debtor . . . may at any time before a sale . . . stop a threatened sale . . . by paying the amount actually past due . . . rather than the amount accelerated." The amount past due was $1,200. The notice from FmHA stated: "The indebtedness . . . consists of $8,585.77 plus interest of $477.77. . . . You are hereby notified that unless said indebtedness is paid in full within 20 days . . . the United States . . . will take action to foreclose. Any negotiation by the United States . . . of any remittance tendered by you . . . will not constitute a waiver of this acceleration or institution of foreclosure action." This notice was faulty because it indicated that foreclosure could have been avoided only by payment of the entire amount owed. Notice is required to give debtors the opportunity to make the payments to avoid foreclosure. The incorrect notice negated the very reason for it.

Foreclose literally means a legal proceeding to shut out all other claims. A first mortgage may not necessarily constitute a first claim on the proceeds of the sale. The cost of foreclosure and taxes always takes precedence over the first mortgage.

Mechanics' Lien

Lien of people who have furnished materials or labor on property

People who furnish materials for the construction of a house and workers who work on it have a claim under what is known as a **mechanics' lien.** A mechanics' lien takes precedence over unrecorded mortgages. The law varies somewhat among the states, but normally a mortgage recorded before a mechanics' lien attaches has priority. The foreclosure proceedings establish the existence of all prior claims and the order of their priority. Foreclosure proceedings are fixed by statutory law and therefore vary in different states.

If the proceeds of the sale of mortgaged property exceed the amount of the debt and the expenses of foreclosure, the surplus must be used to pay off any other liens such as second mortgages. Any money remaining belongs to the mortgagor.

If a deficiency results, however, the mortgagee may secure a deficiency judgment for this amount. In that case the unpaid balance of the debt will stand as a claim against the mortgagor until payment of the debt.

When the mortgagor has given a mortgage for the purpose of purchasing the property, some states limit the amount of a deficiency judgment. The deficiency cannot be greater than the amount by which the debt exceeds either the fair market value or the selling price, whichever amount is smaller. This gives protection to the mortgagor from the mortgagee buying the property at foreclosure for a very low price. For example, suppose A mortgages property to B for $50,000, and the value of the property declines to $40,000. A defaults and B forecloses. B buys the property at foreclosure for $30,000.

	Fair Market Value	Selling Price
Amount of debt	$50,000	$50,000
Less amount "received"	40,000	30,000
Deficiency	$10,000	$20,000

B may obtain a deficiency judgment of $10,000 because it is the lesser of the two amounts.

SALE OF MORTGAGED PROPERTY

The owner frequently sells property on which a mortgage exists. The purchaser may agree to "assume the mortgage," which means to be primarily liable for its payment. "Assuming" the mortgage differs from buying the property "subject to the mortgage." In the first case the buyer agrees to be liable for the mortgage obligation as fully as the original mortgagor. If the buyer takes the property "subject to the mortgage" and default occurs, the property may be lost, but no more.

A sale of the mortgaged property does not automatically release the original mortgagor whether the purchaser assumed the mortgage or bought it subject to the mortgage. The mortgagor remains fully liable in both cases.

To excuse the mortgagor from liability under a mortgage, a novation must take place. This can occur if the parties involved sign a written agreement releasing the mortgagor. Courts have also found novations if the mortgagee extends the time of payment for the purchaser of the property without the mortgagor's consent. Accepting an interest payment after the principal of the mortgage has become due constitutes an extension of the mortgage. If the mortgagee does this without the mortgagor's consent, a novation results and releases the mortgagor from all liability under the mortgage. However, the action of the mortgagee must amount to an extension of time of payment.

Carteret Savings Bank extended a home equity credit line to Mayer and Linda Weiner secured by a mortgage on their home. They each had access to the credit line by writing a check. They had marital difficulties. Linda tried to negotiate a check on the credit line and found that Mayer had closed the account. Mayer withdrew $12,000 after reopening the account. Linda closed the account. While closed, Carteret refused to honor a check by Mayer for $8,800. Carteret told Linda it had opened the account again, so she withdrew the balance of $9,000. The Weiners defaulted and Carteret sued them both for foreclosure. The trial court said closing the account constituted a termination of it. Reopening the account, that court found, constituted a new agreement. The appellate court said reopening the account at one party's request did not result in a novation. It did not constitute a new, written agreement by the parties or extend the time of payment of the debt.

ASSIGNMENT OF THE MORTGAGE

The rights of the mortgagee under the mortgage agreement may be assigned. The assignee, the purchaser, obtains no greater rights than the assignor had. To be protected, the assignee should require the assignor to produce an estoppel certificate signed by the mortgagor. This certificate should acknowledge that the mortgagor has no claims of any kind in connection with the mortgage. This would bar the mortgagor from subsequently claiming the right of offset.

The assignee of a mortgage should have this assignment recorded. In the event that the mortgagee assigns the mortgage to more than one party, the one who records an assignment first has preference. This can be important when the proceeds are not adequate to pay both assignees.

DEED OF TRUST

Deed of Trust
Deed that transfers property to trustee for benefit of creditor

Trustee
One who holds title to property for another

In a number of states, parties commonly use a deed of trust instead of a mortgage for securing a debt with real estate. A mortgage involves two parties, a debtor and a creditor. A **deed of trust** involves three parties. It conveys title to the property to a disinterested party, called a **trustee.** The trustee holds the property in trust for the benefit of the creditor. Most courts treat a deed of trust like a mortgage. If a default in payment occurs, the trustee forecloses on the property and applies the proceeds to the payment of the debt. The right to redeem under a deed of trust, when it exists, is similar to the right of redemption under a mortgage.

The advantage to the creditor in using a deed of trust instead of a mortgage is in the power held by the trustee. In the event a mortgagor defaults in the payments, the mortgagee who holds an ordinary mortgage can foreclose. In most states, however, the mortgagee must go into court and have a judicial foreclosure in order to have the mortgaged property sold to satisfy the debt. A trustee of a deed of trust may sell the mortgaged property at public auction if the debtor defaults. No time-consuming court foreclosure proceedings are necessary. Hence, the property can be more quickly sold at a trustee's sale.

MORTGAGE INSURANCE

Private companies and several agencies of the federal government insure or guarantee mortgages against default by the mortgagor. The government agrees to pay in case of default by the mortgagor in order to make it easier for some people to obtain a mortgage. The most frequently used government programs are those administered by the Federal Housing Administration (FHA) and the Veterans Administration (VA).

FHA-insured mortgages require a smaller down payment than conventional mortgages. Anyone who meets the financial qualifications may obtain an FHA loan. Because FHA mortgages are insured, the interest rate is slightly less than for a conventional mortgage. The FHA sets a maximum amount that may be mortgaged. The FHA bases this amount on the average sale price in the area for a home. The mortgagor pays premiums for this mortgage insurance.

The VA guarantees mortgages for people who have served on active duty in the armed forces for a minimum period of time. The mortgage must be on owner-occupied property. The VA charges the mortgagor a percentage of the loan amount for its guarantee. It sets the interest rate charged. As a benefit to veterans, it sets this rate less than the market rate for conventional loans. A VA mortgage may be for up to 100 percent of the value of the real estate. This means no down payment is required. The maximum loan amount is $144,000.

QUESTIONS

1   What property can be the subject of a mortgage?
2   a. Define a mortgage.
     b. What is the effect of a mortgage?
3   For what reasons may a person secure a loan by a mortgage?
4   If two mortgages are executed on the same land, which mortgagee normally has priority?
5   If there is a street assessment for $1,000 against mortgaged property, who must pay this, the mortgagor or the mortgagee?
6   Who has possession of mortgaged property?
7   How may the mortgagor redeem property after it has been sold under a foreclosure sale?
8   If the proceeds of a foreclosure sale of property are not enough to pay off the mortgage, how is the balance of the debt canceled?
9   What is the difference in the liability of the purchaser when mortgaged property is purchased "subject to the mortgage" and "assuming the mortgage"?
10   What is a deed of trust and how is it used?

CASE PROBLEMS

L.O.3 ....

1   Acting on behalf of the senior lienholder, Pacific Loan Management Corp. (PLMC) conducted a foreclosure sale of Dennis and Nina Armstrong's real estate. The U.S. Small Business Administration (SBA) purchased the property at the sale. SBA had a second mortgage on the property. After paying the

senior mortgage, $31,000 remained. The Armstrongs and the SBA both claimed it. Who should get it and why?

L.O.2 ....

2 HNC Mortgage and Realty Investors lent M.L.W. Construction Corp. $5.85 million to build a series of condominiums on a tract of land mortgaged to secure the debt. M.L.W. defaulted after HNC had advanced $2.9 million, so HNC assumed control of the project and went into possession. Pursuant to a contract with M.L.W., Myers-Macomber Engineers had done site-preparation work in the amount of $11,000. Myers-Macomber sued HNC for this sum. What duty did HNC have as mortgagee in possession, and to whom did it owe this duty?

L.O.1 ....

3 Joseph Lettieri managed the John Lettieri Corp., which was incorporated as a closely held family corporation. It owned real property in Wethersfield, which it quitclaimed to the members of the Lettieri family. No one recorded this quitclaim deed. At the same time, Joseph negotiated a loan on behalf of the corporation from the American Savings Bank and offered to secure the loan with a mortgage on the Wethersfield property. The bank searched the title records and since the quitclaim deed did not appear, the bank made the loan and the corporation mortgaged the property. The corporation later defaulted. A lawsuit ensued involving the priorities of the quitclaim deed and the mortgage. Which should have priority?

L.O.3 ....

4 Dale Vandenberg bought Warren's Bait Shop from Richard Warren by a contract. Vandenberg executed a mortgage on the property to First National Bank of Aitkin and gave the bank a quitclaim deed. First National recorded the mortgage and contract. The bait shop later burned down and Alvin Cox contracted to rebuild it for Vandenberg. Cox began construction, but Vandenberg did not pay him, so Cox filed a mechanics' lien. Which lien has priority, the mortgage or the mechanics' lien?

L.O.1 ....

5 Turabo Shopping Center, Inc., owned and operated the Plaza del Carmen Shopping Center. In order to build it, Turabo had executed a mortgage to Chase Manhattan Bank. The mortgage provided that Chase was to be repaid by assignment of rent due Turabo from tenants of the Plaza. Chase instituted foreclosure proceedings and asked for the appointment of a receiver to manage the Plaza during the action. The value of the Plaza was probably not enough to cover the amount owed Chase, and three tenant companies run by the sister of Turabo's president paid no rent for a substantial time. Turabo allowed its lawyer to set up a restaurant without paying rent and withheld $100,000 in rent from Chase to defend the foreclosure action and get an appraisal to be used in that action. Should a receiver be appointed?

L.O.3 ....

6 Victor Paulos, Dan Lamountt, and Stanley Stephen formed Westridge Court Joint Venture to build an apartment complex. Westridge borrowed $1.9 million secured by a deed of trust on the complex's property to finance construction. After construction, Paulos, Lamountt, and Stephen did not like the occupancy rate and sold the project to DFAI. DFAI defaulted on the loan and the mortgagee foreclosed. The mortgagee made the only bid at the foreclosure sale and purchased the project for $957,000. The court entered a deficiency judgment against DFAI for $1.9 million—the difference between the debt and the price bid at the foreclosure sale. Discuss the rights of the parties depending on whether or not the state has a law regarding the sufficiency of the sale price at a foreclosure.

L.O.1 ....

7 The Henry S. Miller Company executed deeds of trust to Harold and Ruth Wood and Warren and Ruth Ann Wood to secure payment of notes. There was default, so the Woods foreclosed and bought the property at foreclosure. Later they paid taxes assessed during the term of the mortgage and sued Miller for reimbursement. The deeds of trust stated: "The undersigned shall have no personal liability for the payment of the note secured hereby, and in the event of default, the holder of said note shall have the mortgaged property alone as security for payment of said note." The deeds of trust also stated: "If the undersigned shall fail . . . to pay such taxes, . . . said taxes may be paid by the legal holder of said note, and sums so expended shall . . . become part of the debt hereby secured." Was Miller liable for reimbursement of the taxes?

L.O.3 ....

8 American Bankers Life Assurance Company of Florida held a first mortgage on real property. Development International Corporation of Florida held a second mortgage. American Bankers then secured a third mortgage in reliance on a subordination agreement from Development yielding priority of its second mortgage to a "new mortgage." Prior to the subordination agreement, Development had made, and there was recorded, a collateral assignment of its mortgage to Security Mortgage Investors. Security later executed a general release to Development and assigned the second mortgage to Williams, Salomon, Kanner & Damian. There was default, and foreclosure proceedings resulted. American Bankers alleged its "new mortgage" had priority over Williams's second mortgage. Did it?

Chapter 45

LANDLORD AND TENANT

LEARNING OBJECTIVES

After studying this chapter you should be able to:

1 Explain the nature and formation of the landlord/tenant relationship.

2 Name the various types of tenancies.

3 List the rights and duties of tenants and landlords.

4 Explain how a lease may be terminated.

Preview Case

William H. Waldrop leased property from Erwin Siebert under a written lease for two years. The lease stated: "Lessor grants to Lessee the option to renew at the end of term for an additional term of Three (3) years, and year to year thereafter." Waldrop exercised the option for the additional three years. Prior to the expiration of that period, Waldrop notified Siebert he intended to renew the lease for a year and enclosed a check for the annual rent. Siebert returned the check and gave notice to quit. When sued for possession, Waldrop alleged the lease contained an option to renew from year to year forever. What was the effect of the option?

L.O.1

Landlord or Lessor
Owner of leased property

Tenant or Lessee
Possessor of leased property

A contract whereby one person agrees to lease land or a building to another creates the relationship of landlord and tenant. Such an agreement does not require special words or acts for creation unless the lease lasts for more than a year, in which case it must be in writing. The tenant's temporary possession of the premises and payment of rent for its use constitute the chief characteristics that determine the relationship of landlord and tenant. The landlord may retake possession of the property at the end of the lease period.

The owner of the property is known as the **landlord**, or **lessor.** The person given possession of the property is the **tenant**, or **lessee.** The contract between the

Lease
Contract between land-
lord and tenant

Rent
Amount paid landlord for
use of property

two parties is called a **lease** (see Illustration 45-1). The amount the tenant agrees to pay the landlord for the use of the property is the **rent.**

A tenant differs from a lodger or roomer in that the former has the exclusive legal possession of the property, whereas the latter has merely the right to use the premises subject to the control and supervision of the owner.

THE LEASE

The lease may be oral or written, express or implied, formal or simple, subject, however, to the general statutory requirements that a lease of land for a term longer than one year must be in writing. If a dispute arises between the tenant and the landlord over their rights and duties, the court will look to the terms of the lease and the general body of landlord and tenant law to determine the decision.

Russell Ratliff rented a house to Johnny and Mary Gorman. The Gormans became delinquent in their rent to Ratliff and he asked them to vacate the house. The written lease provided that if the Gormans did not pay any rent when due, Ratliff "may, if desired, take immediate possession . . . removing and storing at the expense of said lessees all property contained therein." Relying on such provisions in the lease, Ratliff entered the house in the Gormans' absence, removed all their personal property, and put it in storage. State law provided that "carrying away the goods of the party in possession . . ." constituted the offense of forcible entry and detainer. The Gormans sued Ratliff. The court said that although the lease gave Ratliff the authority to take possession of the Gormans' property, state law invalidated that portion of the lease.

In order to avoid disputes, a lease should be in writing and should cover all terms of the contract. The parties should include such items as a clear identification of the property, the time and place of payment of rent, the notice required to vacate, the duration or the nature of the tenancy, and any specific provision desired by either party, such as the right of the landlord to show the property to prospective purchasers or agreement requiring the landlord to redecorate.

TYPES OF TENANCIES

L.O.2 ....

Four separate and distinct classes of tenancies exist, each of which has some rule of law governing it that does not apply to any other type of tenancy. The four classes of tenancies are:

1 Tenancy for years
2 Tenancy from year to year
3 Tenancy at will
4 Tenancy by sufferance

Tenancy for Years

**Tenancy for
Years**
Tenancy for any definite
period

A **tenancy for years** is a tenancy for a definite period of time, whether it be one month, 1 year, or 99 years. The lease fixes the termination date. However, most states limit the length of time a lease may last. A lease for a time greater than the statutory limit is void. The payment of the rent may be by the month even when a

Illustration 45-1   Lease

House Lease

THIS INDENTURE *made the*   19th   *day of*   April   *,19 --*

BETWEEN   Richard T. Mowbray   *, Lessor (whether one or more);*
             Cincinnati, Ohio

AND   Edward J. and Doris R. Caldwell   *, Lessee (whether one or more);*
             Cincinnati, Ohio

WITNESSETH*: that for and in consideration of the payments of the rents, and the performance of the covenants contained herein, on the part of the said Lessee, and in the manner hereinafter specified, said Lessor does hereby lease, demise and let, unto the said Lessee, that certain dwelling house and its appurtenances*

situated at   single-family
                   2668 Russel Road, Cincinnati, Ohio 45250

for the term of   one (1) year   *, commencing on the*

             1st   *day of,*   May   *19, --   and ending on the*

             30th   *day of,*   April   *19, --   at the total rent or*

sum of   Six thousand ($6,000)   *Dollars,*

payable   monthly *in advance on the*   1st   *day of each and every*

calendar month of said term in equal   monthly   *payments of*

      Five hundred ($500)   *Dollars,*

AND *the said Lessee does hereby promise and agree to pay to the said Lessor the said rent, herein reserved in the manner herein specified.*

AND *not to let or sublet the whole or any part of said premises, nor to assign this lease, and not to make or suffer any alteration to be made therein without the written consent of the said Lessor. And it is further agreed, that the said Lessor shall not be called upon to make any improvements or repairs whatsoever upon the said premises, or any part thereof, but the said Lessee agrees to keep the same in good order and condition at*   their   *own expense.*

AND *it is agreed, that if any rent shall be due and unpaid or if default shall be made in any of the covenants herein contained, then it shall be lawful for the said Lessor to re-enter the said premises and to move all persons therefrom.*

AND THAT *at the expiration of the said term or any sooner determination of this lease the said Lessee will quit and surrender the premises hereby demised, in as good order and condition as reasonable use and wear thereof will permit, damage by the elements excepted. And if the Lessee shall hold over the said term with the consent, expressed or implied, of the Lessor, such holding shall be construed to be a tenancy only from month to month, and Lessee will pay the rent as above stated for such term as*   they   *hold the same.*
             Lessee   *agrees to pay the water rate during the continuance of this lease.*

IN WITNESS WHEREOF*: the said parties have hereunto set their hands and seals the day and year first above written.*

                         Richard L. Mowbray   (Seal)
                         Edward J. Caldwell   (Seal)
                         Doris R. Caldwell   (Seal)

tenancy for a specified number of years exists. No notice to terminate the tenancy need be given by either party when the lease fixes the termination date. Most leases provide that they will continue to run on a year-to-year basis after the termination date, unless the tenant gives notice to the landlord not less than a specified number of days before the termination date that the tenant intends to leave on that date.

Tenancy from Year to Year

Tenancy from Year to Year
Tenancy for indefinite period with yearly rent

A tenancy for an indefinite period of time with rent set at a yearly amount, is known as a **tenancy from year to year.** Under such a tenancy, a tenant merely pays the rent periodically, and the lease lasts until proper notice of termination has been given. A tenancy of this kind may also be by the month or any other period agreed upon. If by the month, it is called a *tenancy from month to month.* The length of the tenancy is usually determined by the nature of the rent stated or paid although there could be a tenancy from year to year with the rent paid quarterly or monthly.

Notice to terminate this type of tenancy must exactly follow the state law governing it. Notice must normally be in writing. In a tenancy from month to month, the law usually requires notice 30 days before a rent due date.

> William H. Waldrop leased property from Erwin Siebert under a written lease for two years. The lease stated: "Lessor grants to Lessee the option to renew at the end of term for an additional term of Three (3) years, and year to year thereafter." Waldrop exercised the option for the additional three years. Prior to the expiration of that period, Waldrop notified Siebert he intended to renew the lease for a year and enclosed a check for the annual rent. Siebert returned the check and gave notice to quit. When sued for possession, Waldrop alleged the lease contained an option to renew from year to year forever. The court held that the option transformed the tenancy from a tenancy for years to a tenancy from year to year terminable by either party after proper notice.

Tenancy at Will

Tenancy at Will
Tenancy for uncertain period

A **tenancy at will** exists when the tenant has possession of the property for an uncertain period. Either the tenant or the landlord can terminate the tenancy at will, since both must agree to the tenancy. This tenancy, unlike any of the others, automatically terminates upon the death of the tenant or the landlord, if the tenant attempts to assign the tenancy, or if the landlord sells the property.

Tenancy at Sufferance

Tenancy at Sufferance
Holdover tenant without landlord's permission

When a tenant holds over the tenancy after the expiration of the lease without permission of the landlord, a **tenancy at sufferance** exists until the landlord elects to treat the tenant as a trespasser or as a tenant. The landlord may treat the tenant as a trespasser, sue for damages, and have the tenant removed by legal proceedings. If the landlord prefers, payment of the rent due for another period may be accepted, and thus the tenant's possession may be recognized as rightful.

RIGHTS OF THE TENANT

L.O.3

A lease gives the tenant certain rights, as follows:

1   Right to possession
2   Right to use the premises
3   Right to assign or sublease

Right to Possession

By signing the lease, the landlord warrants the right to lease the premises and that the tenant shall have possession during the period of the lease. During the term of the lease, tenants have the same right to exclusive possession of the premises as if they owned the property. If someone questions the owner's right to lease the property, the landlord must defend the tenant's right to exclusive possession. Failure of the landlord to give possession on time or to protect the tenant's rights subjects the landlords to liability for damages.

A nuisance that disturbs the tenant's quiet enjoyment of the property often causes disputes between landlords and tenants. Courts have held failure to remove dead rats from the wall, failure to stop disorderly conduct on the part of other tenants, and frequent and unnecessary entrances upon the property by the landlord or agents constitute acts that destroy the tenant's right to quiet enjoyment and constitute a breach of warranty on the part of the landlord.

If the nuisance existed at the time the tenant leased the property and the tenant knew of its existence, the right to complain will be deemed to have been waived. Also, if the landlord has no control over the nuisance, the tenant cannot avoid the contract even though the nuisance arose subsequent to the signing of the lease. If the landlord fails or refuses to abate a nuisance over which the landlord has control, the tenant not only may terminate the lease but may sue for damages. In other cases the tenant may seek an injunction compelling the landlord to abate a nuisance.

Right to Use the Premises

Unless the lease expressly restricts this right, the tenant has the right to use the premises in any way consistent with the nature of the property. A dwelling cannot be converted into a machine shop, nor can a clothing store be converted into a restaurant. Damage to leased property other than that which results from ordinary wear and tear is not permissible. In the case of farming land, the tenant may cut wood for personal use but not to sell.

Right to Assign or Sublease

Assignment
Transfer to another of tenant's rights

Sublease
Transfer of less than a tenant's full rights under a lease

If the tenant transfers all interest in the lease to another party who agrees to comply with its terms, including the payment of the rent to the landlord, there is an **assignment.** In an assignment, the assignee pays the rent directly to the landlord. Assignment must include the entire premises. In a **sublease,** the tenant transfers the premises for a period less than the term of the lease or transfers only a part of the premises. The tenant usually collects the rent from the subtenant and pays the landlord. Ordinarily a written lease prohibits assigning or subleasing the premises unless the lessor gives written consent thereto first. Residential leases commonly restrict the use of the premises to the tenant and the immediate family or to a certain number of persons. Unless the lease expressly prohibits both assignment and subleasing, either may be done. If the lease prohibits only subleasing, then the lease may be assigned.

Joint occupancy closely relates to subleasing. A provision in the lease prohibiting subleasing does not forbid a contract for a joint occupancy. In joint occupancy the tenant does not give up exclusive control of any part of the premises. The tenant merely permits another party to jointly occupy all or a part of the premises.

DUTIES OF THE TENANT

The lease imposes certain duties upon the tenant:

1   To pay rent
2   To protect and preserve the premises

To Pay Rent

The tenant's primary duty is to pay the rent. This payment must be made in money unless the contract provides otherwise, such as a share of the crops. The rent is not due until the end of the term, but leases almost universally provide for rent in advance.

Landlords commonly appoint an agent for the purpose of collecting the rent. The death of the principal automatically terminates such a principal-agent relationship. Any rent paid to the agent after this termination and not remitted to the proper party must be paid again.

If the tenant fails to pay rent on time, the landlord may terminate the lease and order the tenant to vacate, or the landlord may permit the tenant to continue occupancy and sue for the rent. Under the common law the landlord could seize and hold any personal property found on the premises. This right has been either curtailed or abolished by statute.

To Protect and Preserve the Premises

Traditionally, a tenant had to make repairs on the premises. This was because a tenant had a duty to keep the leased property in as good condition as the landlord had it when the lease began. Some states have enacted statutes requiring the landlord to make repairs. Other states find a warranty of habitability, which makes the landlord responsible for keeping the premises livable. Some statutes even give tenants a form of self-help. The tenant must notify the landlord of needed repairs. If the landlord does not make the repairs, the tenant may fix things and deduct the cost from the rent. Tenants, however, must repair damage caused by their negligence. In states in which statutes have not altered the traditional responsibility, tenants must repair damage except reasonable wear and tear and damage by the elements.

Bobenal Investment, Inc., leased 15,000 square feet of a 45,000 square-foot building to Giant Super Markets, Inc. The agreement between the parties allowed Giant to remove all its fixtures and equipment. When Giant moved out, it inadvertently removed a downspout, which resulted in flooding of the building. Within two days Giant mopped up and swept away the water and then had the floor scrubbed and cleaned by a professional janitorial contractor. When Bobenal later filed a suit, the court found Giant had substantially repaired the damage caused by its error.

RIGHTS OF THE LANDLORD

The landlord has three definite rights under the lease:

1 To regain possession
2 To enter upon the property to preserve it
3 To assign rights

To Regain Possession

Upon termination of the lease, the landlord has the right to regain peaceable possession of the premises. If the tenant refuses this possession, the most common remedy is to bring an **action of ejectment** in a court of law. Upon the successful completion of this suit the sheriff will forcibly remove the tenant and any property.

Action of Ejectment

Action to have sheriff remove tenant

When the landlord repossesses the property, all permanent improvements and fixtures may be retained. Courts determine whether or not the improvements have become a part of the real estate. If they have, they cannot be removed.

To Enter upon the Property to Preserve It

The landlord has a right to enter upon the property to preserve it. Extensive renovations that interfere with the tenant's peaceable occupancy cannot be made. If the roof blows off or becomes leaky, the landlord may repair it or put on a new roof. This occasion cannot be used to add another story. A landlord who enters the property without permission may be treated as a stranger. A landlord has no right to enter the premises to show the property to prospective purchasers or tenants unless the lease reserves this right.

To Assign Rights

The landlord has the right to assign the rights under the lease to a third party. The tenant cannot avoid any duties and obligations by reason of the assignment of the lease. Like all other assignments, the assignment does not release the assignor from the contract without the consent of the tenant. If, for example, the tenant suffers injury because of a concealed but defective water main cover, and the landlord knew of this condition, the landlord has liability even though rights under the lease were assigned before the injury.

DUTIES OF THE LANDLORD

The lease imposes certain duties upon the landlord:

1 To pay taxes and assessments
2 To protect the tenant from concealed defects
3 To mitigate damages upon abandonment by the tenant

To Pay Taxes and Assessments

Although the tenant occupies and uses the premises, the landlord must pay all taxes and special assessments. Sometimes the lease provides that the tenant shall pay the taxes. In such event, the tenant has no liability for special assessments for sidewalks, street paving, and other improvements.

To Protect the Tenant from Concealed Defects

The landlord has liability to the tenant if the tenant suffers injury by concealed defects that were known or should have been reasonably known to the landlord at the time of giving the tenant possession of the premises. Such defects might be contamination from contagious germs; concealed, unfilled wells; and rotten timbers in the dwelling. The tenant bears the risk of injury caused by apparent defects or defects reasonably discoverable upon inspection at the time that the tenant enters into possession. Most cities and many states have tenement laws that require the landlord to keep all rental property habitable and provided with adequate fire escapes. Any damage due to a failure to observe these laws may subject the landlord to liability for damages.

To Mitigate Damages upon Abandonment by Tenant

Unless the landlord accepts the abandonment, a tenant who abandons leased property before the end of the lease term still has an obligation to pay the rent due through the end of the term. However, the landlord has a duty to mitigate the tenant's damages by attempting to secure a new tenant. If a new tenant occupies the premises, the landlord's damage from the first tenant abandoning the property equals the difference between the rent the original tenant had to pay and the rent the new tenant pays. In this way, the original tenant's obligation amounts to less than the original rent called for by the lease and the new tenant's payments mitigate the landlord's damage due from the original tenant.

The National Bank and Trust Company of South Bend leased some commercial real estate to Radio Distributing Company. Before the end of the lease term, Radio Distributing moved out. The bank allowed the Council for the Retarded to move into the building and remain in possession without paying any rent for several years. The bank had exercised reasonable efforts to relet the property and let the Council occupy it in order to maintain property and casualty insurance on it. When sued by National, Radio alleged the bank had not acted to mitigate its damages. The court said that as long as National had made reasonable efforts to relet the property and only let the Council use it in order to keep the property insured, National had carried out its obligation to mitigate damages.

TERMINATION OF THE LEASE

L.O.4 ....

A lease for a fixed time automatically terminates upon the expiration of that period. The death of either party does not ordinarily affect the lease. If the leased property consists of rooms or apartments in a building and fire or any other accidental cause destroys them, the lease terminates without liability on the part of the tenant. In the case of leases of entire buildings, serious problems arise if fire, tornado, or any other cause destroys the property. Under the common law the tenant had to continue to pay rent even though the property was destroyed. Some states retain this rule while other states have modified it. A landlord who has a ten-year lease on a $100,000 building destroyed by fire one year after signing the lease would not be inclined to rebuild if fully covered by fire insurance. The landlord would find it more profitable to invest the $100,000 and continue to collect the rent. To prevent this, statutes may provide that if the landlord refuses to restore the property, the lease terminates. The lease itself may contain a cancellation clause. If it does not, the tenant can carry fire insurance for the amount of possible loss. Even when the lease will thus terminate, the tenant will probably wish to carry fire insurance for personal property and, if the premises are used for a business purpose, may carry insurance to indemnify for business interruption or loss of business income.

The landlord may agree to the voluntary surrender of the possession of the premises before the lease expires. An abandonment of the premises without the consent of the landlord does not constitute a surrender, however, but a breach of contract.

If the lease runs from year to year or from month to month, the party wishing to terminate it must generally give the other party a written notice of this intention (see Illustrations 45-2 and 45-3). Statutes prescribe the time and the manner of giving notice; they may also specify other particulars, such as the grounds for a termination of the tenancy.

Illustration 45-2   Landlord's Notice to Leave the Premises

NOTICE TO LEAVE THE PREMISES

To __Mr. C. Harold Whitmore__

You will please take notice that __I__ *want you to leave the premises you now occupy, and which you have rented of* __me__ *, situated and described as follows:*

__Suite 4__

__Lakeview Apartment__

__Lake Shore Drive at Overview Street__

in __Cleveland__ *County of* __Cuyahoga__ *and State of* __Ohio__

Your compliance with this Notice __July 31__

will prevent legal measures being taken by __me__ *to obtain possession of the same, agreeably to law.*

Yours respectfully,

H. L. Simpson

__May 1__ *19* __--__

Illustration 45-3   Tenant's Notice that the Tenant Is Leaving the Premises

January 2, 19—

Mr. George A. Hardwick
1719 Glenview Road
St. Louis, Missouri 65337

Dear Mr. Hardwick

This is to notify you that on March 31, 19—, I
intend to vacate the premises now leased from
you and located at 1292 Clarendon Road, St.
Louis, Missouri. In accordance with the terms of
our written lease, this letter constitutes
notice of the termination of said lease as of
March 31, 19—.

Sincerely

John N. Richter

JOHN N. RICHTER

If either party fails to give proper notice, the other party may continue the tenancy for another period.

Eviction

Eviction

Expulsion of tenant from leased property

Tenants sometimes refuse to give up possession of the property after the expiration of the lease or fail to perform required duties. In such a case, a landlord may seek an **eviction** of the tenant. Eviction is the expulsion of the tenant from the leased

Forcible Entry and Detainer Action
Summary action by landlord to regain possession

property. The laws of the states vary, but all have some form of summary eviction law. The summary action brought by the landlord is called a **forcible entry and detainer action.** The tenant has a right to written notice and a court hearing. However, the court will set an early date, usually 7 to 15 days after notification of the tenant, for the trial. If the landlord wins, law enforcement officers may enforce the eviction in a few days. The proceedings permit quick recovery of real property by the one legally entitled to it.

IMPROVEMENTS

Tenants frequently make improvements during the life of the lease. Many disputes arise as to the tenant's right to take these improvements after the lease is terminated. Courts must determine whether an improvement has become a fixture, which must be left on the land, or whether it remains personal property. If the improvements are **trade fixtures,** or fixtures used in business, and can be removed without substantial injury to the leased property, the tenant may remove them. If a farm tenant builds a fence in the normal way, the fence is a fixture, and the tenant has no right to remove it upon leaving. A poultry house built in the usual way is a fixture and cannot be removed. In a similar case the tenant built the poultry house on sled-like runners. When ready to leave, the tenant had the poultry house hauled away and took it when vacating. The court held the shed had not become a fixture but remained personal property.

Trade Fixtures
Fixtures used in business

Unless prohibited by law, one may freely contract away rights or may waive them, so the parties may agree as to how to treat fixtures. In one case a tenant built a permanent frame house on leased property with the landlord's agreement that the house could be moved at the end of the lease. The landlord was bound by this contract.

Discrimination

Federal law prohibits landlords from discriminating against tenants or proposed tenants because of race, color, religion, sex, familial status, or national origin. The term familial status refers to whether the tenant has children. Additionally, some states have laws that prohibit discrimination based on physical or mental handicaps, age, or marital status.

QUESTIONS

1   How is the relationship of landlord and tenant created?
2   Under what circumstances must a least be in writing?
3   Explain what a tenancy for years is and how long it may last.
4   How long does a tenancy from year to year last?
5   What rights does the tenant have when property is leased?
6   Explain the difference between subleasing and assigning.
7   Explain the primary duty of a tenant.
8   a. If a hurricane breaks all the windows in a dwelling, must the tenant replace these windows?

b. If leased property is destroyed by fire, must the tenant continue to pay rent?

9   If a tenant builds a garage on the property, may the garage be taken when the tenant moves? Explain.

10   How may a lease be terminated?

CASE PROBLEMS

L.O.3 ....

1   David and Jeanie Fossati executed a written lease on a house and dealt with Nancy Calhoun, one of the owners. The Fossatis made two lease payments in cash and then Calhoun died. The Fossatis told Calhoun's administrator they had an oral agreement with Calhoun to apply toward the rent the cost of materials used to improve the house. The administrator accepted receipts for materials for the third month's rent. The Fossatis paid the fourth month's rent in cash, but made no payments for the following two months. Dean Quitta and the other remaining owners, skeptical of any oral agreement, made repeated demands for the unpaid rent. Quitta told the Fossatis that if they did not pay cash rent, he would have the sheriff get them out. The Fossatis moved out and when sued for the rent claimed the equivalent of eviction relieving their obligation to pay it. Were they evicted, and did they owe rent?

L.O.1 ....

2   The lessee of a long-term lease for a radio broadcasting tower site assigned the lease to Towers of Texas, Inc. The lease's description of the site gave latitude and longitude coordinates and an elevation but also gave the lessee "exclusive use of the space on top of said Double Mountain." The original lessee built the tower on a flat place on top of the mountain because the coordinates described a single point on the side of the mountain not suitable in location or size for the tower and which did not coincide with the elevation given. The lessors built a second radio tower on the top of the mountain, and Towers sued them. Was Towers' lease limited to the coordinate-described point, or was that description ambiguous?

L.O.3 ....

3   JBA, Inc., leased a commercial warehouse from Properties Investment Group of Mid-America (PIGOMA). Before the end of the term, JBA moved out and PIGOMA refused to accept termination of the lease. PIGOMA interviewed realtors to list the property for sale or lease and listed it with a realtor a month after JBA moved out. The realtor advertised and showed the property for a year. PIGOMA then retained a certified property manager for three months to assist it in selling or leasing the property and negotiated a sale itself that fell through. Other Realtors also showed the property during those three months until PIGOMA signed another listing agreement with one. When PIGOMA sued JBA for unpaid rent, JBA alleged PIGOMA had not taken reasonable steps to mitigate its damages. Had it?

L.O.4 ....

4   The East Harlem Pilot Block Building 1 Housing Development Fund Corp. leased an apartment for a specified period to Jose Serrano who died during the term of the lease. The Fund then brought an eviction proceeding for non-payment of rent against the deceased. To decide who the proper party defendant was in the proceeding the court had to decide whether the lease terminated with Serrano's death. Does a lease automatically terminate when the tenant of a tenancy for years dies?

L.O.3 ....

5   Lawrence Frazier leased 26,000 acres of grazing land from Phillip Kern. The lease stated: "The Lessee shall not assign this lease or enter into any sublease without first obtaining the written consent of the Lessor." Frazier made an arrangement with Ronnie Bloxham to graze Bloxham's cattle at a fee of $7 per head. Frazier would control the range and movement of the cattle, supply salt and hay, repair fences and gates, and generally supervise the cattle. Bloxham was to supply hay if the winter was really bad, haul the cattle in and out, and take care of problem cattle. When Kern learned of this agreement, he sent a notice to declare a forfeiture, alleging Frazier had subleased or assigned the lease without written consent. Was the agreement a breach of the lease?

L.O.1 ....

6   By the terms of two agreements called leases, United Coin was to install, maintain, and service coin-operated laundry equipment in two apartment complexes. The agreements described the premises as "laundry space provided by OWNER . . . located in an area measuring approximately 10 feet by 10 feet in the 'Laundry area(s)' in the . . . building(s)." The owner of the complexes was to keep the laundry rooms clean and safely maintained. The complexes were sold to Craig Gibson, who removed United's equipment and installed some other. United sued Gibson, alleging breach of the "lease." Were the agreements leases?

Chapter 46

WILLS AND INHERITANCES

After studying this chapter you should be able to:

1 Describe a will, its characteristics, and the limitations on disposition of property.

2 Explain the normal formalities required for executing the various types of wills.

3 Name the ways in which a will may be changed or revoked.

4 Discuss the requirements for probate and administration.

Preview Case

By the terms of her will, Eloise Williams devised her 103-acre "home place" to her nephews and nieces. The residue of the estate was bequeathed to the Masonic Home or Homes for Crippled Children. Three months before her death, Williams sold the "home place" and received an $80,000 note secured by a deed of trust. What effect does the sale of the property have on the devises?

L.O.1

Will

Document providing disposition of property after death

Estate

Property left by a person who has died

Title to all property, both real and personal, may be transferred by a will. A **will** is an instrument prepared in the form prescribed by law that provides for the disposition of a person's property and takes effect after death. The property left by a person who has died is called the **estate.**

The person making the will is called a **testator** (**testatrix** if a woman). Testators do not have to meet as high a standard of capacity to make a will as a person does in order to make a contract. They must have the mental capability at the time of making the will to know the natural objects of their bounty, understand

Testator or
Testatrix

Person making a will

the nature and extent of their property, understand that they are making a will, and have the ability to dispose of their property by means of a plan they have formulated. Even if they do not have the mental capacity to carry on a business or if they make unusual provisions in the will, this does not necessarily mean that they do not have capacity to make a will. An insane person lacks sufficient capacity; however, an insane person who has intervals of sanity has capacity during sane intervals to make a will. Any person, other than a minor, of sound mind ordinarily has the competence to make a will. In a few states minors can, under limited circumstances, make a will.

LIMITATIONS ON DISPOSITION OF PROPERTY

The law places few restrictions on the right to dispose of property by will. However some restrictions include:

Right to Take
Against the Will

Spouse's right to share of estate provided by statute if will leaves smaller share

1   A spouse may elect to take that share of property that would have been received had the deceased died without leaving a will, or the share provided by statute, if the spouse's will does not leave as large a share, called the **right to take against the will.**

Most state laws now provide that when an individual dies without leaving a will, a spouse has the right to a set portion of all the property the deceased spouse owned at the time of death. The spouse's portion varies depending on the number of children or other heirs who survive. The surviving spouse in some states may also claim an interest in property conveyed by the deceased spouse during the marriage without the consent of the surviving spouse.

The right to take against the will can be barred by actions of the surviving spouse. If the surviving spouse commits acts that would have justified the deceased in securing a divorce, the surviving spouse generally cannot elect to take against the will.

Except for the cases of a surviving spouse electing to take against the will and in some cases of a subsequent marriage, birth, or adoption, the testator may exclude or disinherit any person from receiving any portion of the estate. If the testator gives the entire estate to someone else, all persons who would inherit in the absence of a will are excluded. The testator does not even have to mention in a will those persons disinherited with the exception of children, nor does a nominal sum have to be left to those disinherited.

2   One cannot control by will the distribution of property in perpetuity (for all time). The common-law rule against perpetuities requires that an interest in property must vest, if at all, within 21 years after the death of persons living on the date the owner of the property creates the interest. When the interest is created by will, the date of death of the owner constitutes the date of creation.

TERMS COMMON TO WILLS

Devisee

One receiving real estate by will

A number of terms may refer to individuals named or gifts given in a will. The one receiving a gift of real estate (the beneficiary) is called the **devisee;** the beneficiary of personal property is a **legatee.** A **devise** is real property given by will. A

Legatee
One receiving personal property by will

Devise
Real property left by will

bequest, or a **legacy,** is a gift by will of personal property. The person named in a will as the one to administer the estate is an **executor.** One who dies without having made a will is said to die **intestate.** A person appointed by a court to settle the affairs of an intestate is an **administrator** (man) or an **administratrix** (woman).

DISTINGUISHING CHARACTERISTICS OF A WILL

Bequest or Legacy
Personal property left by will

Executor
Person named in will to administer estate

Intestate
One who dies without a will

A will has the following outstanding characteristics that distinguish it from many other legal instruments:

1 The courts construe a will with less technical strictness than a deed or any other kind of written document.
2 A will devising real property must be executed in conformity with the law of the state in which the property is situated. The law of the state in which the testator was domiciled (had permanent residence) at the time of death governs a will bequeathing personal property.
3 A will may be revoked at any time during the life of the testator.

FORMALITIES

L.O.2 ....

Administrator or Administratrix
Person appointed by court to administer estate of intestate

All states prescribe formalities for wills. These formalities must be strictly followed. A will almost always must be in writing and signed by the testator.

A will written in the testator's own handwriting and dated need not be witnessed in a number of states. In almost all states the will must be witnessed by at least two, and in some states three, disinterested witnesses regardless of how it is written. Usually, the witnesses and the testator must sign in the presence of each other. Many states also require the testator to inform the witnesses that the instrument being signed is the testator's will. This is called **publication.**

Florence Griffin lived with Ethel Lockwood. One room of the Lockwood home acted as the town clerk's office. Griffin had told Lockwood that she was writing her will. Griffin entered the clerk's office with a sheet of paper containing some writing. She asked Lockwood and Rita Wood to witness her signature on the paper and had Mrs. Wood type an attestation clause on the paper. Wood and Lockwood signed the paper and Griffin returned to the living room. Wood left. Griffin returned and asked Lockwood to staple four pieces of paper together. Griffin put them in an envelope, sealed it, and then gave the envelope to Robert Davis. After Griffin's death the document was offered for probate, but refused. The court said that a testator must tell the witnesses that the instrument the witnesses are signing is the testator's will. Since Griffin did not make publication of this instrument, it would not be probated.

Publication
Testator's informing witnesses that document signed is will

When the law requires subscribing witnesses, they must be available at the time of probate of the will to identify their signatures and the signature of the testator and to state that they were present when the testator signed the will. If the witnesses cannot be found, two persons must normally identify the signature of the testator on the will. They base their opinion regarding the testator's signature upon their experience through prior correspondence or business records involving the testator's signature. A will executed in another jurisdiction is valid if correctly executed in the other jurisdiction. If a person's will is not drawn according to the legal requirements, the court may disregard it and the property may be disposed of in a manner entirely foreign to the testator's wishes.

SPECIAL TYPES OF WILLS

Under special circumstances, testators can make valid wills that are less formal than usual. Three special types of wills include:

1 Holographic wills
2 Nuncupative wills
3 Soldiers' and sailors' wills

Holographic Wills

Holographic Will

Will written out by testator

Holographic wills are written entirely in longhand by the testator. Some states make no distinction between holographic and other wills. In other states variations of the general law of wills exist for holographic wills. In still other states holographic wills may not be recognized.

David Horwitz had a son, also named David, from a previous marriage. David Sr., died leaving two-thirds of his estate to Margaret, his wife, and one-third to David Jr. Margaret died 25 years later. A nephew found pages of writing paper, folded together, on Margaret's bedside table. The pages contained only Margaret's handwriting in several colors of ink, with interlineations, corrections, and marginal notations. The first page began, "Being of sound mind I, Margaret Macleod Horwitz, declare the following to be my last will and testament." The pages contained many numbered bequests to people including David Jr., his wife, and daughter. The last bequest gave the remainder of the estate to five nephews and listed their names. Margaret did not sign at the end. The court received the document for determination of its status. The court said that the document described itself as a will; it contained specific bequests and a residuary clause that disposed of all of Margaret's property; and it seemed reasonable and complete. Therefore the court found it a valid, holographic will.

Nuncupative Wills

Nuncupative Will

Oral will made during last illness

Nuncupative wills are oral wills declared by the testator in the presence of witnesses. Usually such a will can only be made during the testator's last illness. A nuncupative will only applies to personal property, and sometimes only a limited value of personal property may be so disposed. The witnesses frequently must reduce the will to writing within a specified number of days and they must agree as to how the deceased disposed of the property.

During the last of several hospital stays, Mr. Kay told Shirley Macow that he wanted to change his will. She called Mr. Engelhardt, his attorney, who went to see Kay at the hospital. While alone with Engelhardt, Kay told him what terms he wanted in his will. During this conversation, Kay did not tell Engelhardt that he was making an oral will. Engelhardt drafted a new will for Kay, but when he took it to Kay's office, Kay had had a heart attack and died. Mike Kay alleged the new will constituted a nuncupative will that revoked a prior will. The court found the alleged nuncupative will invalid because the law required three witnesses to agree to the words spoken by the deceased. Only Engelhardt heard Kay, and Kay did not indicate the words he spoke constituted his will.

Soldiers and Sailors

Most states make special provision for members of the armed forces. They are allowed to make oral or written wills of personal property without complying with the formalities required of other wills. These wills are in force even after the testator returns to civilian life. They must be revoked in the same manner as other wills.

THE WORDING OF A WILL

Any words that convey the intention of the testator suffice (see Illustration 46-1). No matter how rough and ungrammatical the language may be, if the intention of the testator can be ascertained, the court will order that the provisions of the will be carried out. Since the court will order the terms of a will to be carried out exactly, the wording of the will should express the exact wishes of the testator.

REVOCATION

L.O.3 ....

A will may be revoked at any time prior to the death of the testator. The revocation may take any one of several forms.

CODICILS

Codicil
Writing that modifies a will

A **codicil** is a separate writing that modifies a will. Except for the part modified, the original will remains the same. A codicil must be executed with all the formalities of the original will.

Destruction or Alteration

If the testator deliberately destroys a will, this constitutes a revocation. If the testator merely alters the will, this may or may not revoke it, depending upon the nature and the extent of the alteration. If the testator merely obliterates a part of the will, this in most states does not revoke the will.

Marriage and Divorce

If a single person makes a will and later marries, the marriage may revoke the will in whole or in part, or the will may be presumed to be revoked unless made in contemplation of the marriage or unless it made provision for a future spouse. In some states a marriage will not revoke a will completely, but only so that the spouse will get the estate that would have been received in the absence of a will. A divorce automatically revokes a will to the extent of the property left to the divorced spouse if the court orders a division of property; otherwise, a divorce usually in no way affects the will.

Illustration 46-1   Will

```
                    WILL OF FRANK JOSEPH ROSE

        I, Frank Joseph Rose, of the City of Chicago and State of
   Illinois, revoke all prior wills and codicils and declare that
   this is my will.
        FIRST: If she survives me, I give to my beloved daughter,
   Anna Rose, now residing in Crestwood, Illinois, that certain
   piece of real estate, with all improvements thereon, situated at
   341 Hudson Avenue, Crestwood, Illinois. If my daughter prede-
   ceases me, I give this real estate to my brother, James Earl
   Rose, now residing in Crestwood Illinois.
        SECOND: All the remainder and residue of my property I give
   to my beloved wife, Mary Ellen Rose, if, she survives me. If my
   wife predeceases me, I give the remainder and residue of my
   property to my daughter, Anna. If both my wife and my daughter
   predecease me, I give the remainder and residue of my property
   to my brother, James.
        THIRD: I hereby nominate and appoint my wife, Mary Ellen
   Rose, executrix of this will. If my wife is unable or unwilling
   to act as executrix, I nominate and appoint my daughter, Anna,
   executrix. I direct that neither Mary Ellen nor Anna be required
   to give bond or security for the performance of duties as
   executrix.
        IN WITNESS WHEREOF, I have subscribed my name this tenth day
   of October, in the year nineteen hundred --.


                              Frank Joseph Rose
                              Frank Joseph Rose

   We, the undersigned, certify that the foregoing instrument was,
   on the tenth day of October, signed and declared by Frank Joseph
   Rose to be his will, in the presence of us who, in his presence
   and in the presence of each other, have, at his request, here-
   unto signed our names as witnesses of the execution thereof,
   this tenth day of October, 19--.



                                         4316 Cottage Grove Avenue
   Constance O. Moore        residing at Chicago, Illinois 60600

                                         1313 East 63 Street
   Sarah J. King             residing at Chicago, Illinois 60600

                                         2611 Elm Street
   Stewart S. Samuels        residing at Joliet, Illinois 60400
```

Grady Miles made a will leaving his "friend," Georgia Hall, his car and a life interest in his home. Georgia had rejected numerous marriage proposals from Grady. More than a year later, Grady and Georgia got married. Grady died seven months later without having changed his will. Georgia filed suit claiming the marriage revoked the will. The court said that while Grady did make some provision for Georgia in the will, he made no indication that the bequest was made in contemplation of marriage. In fact Georgia had refused to marry him many times and it took more than a year for Grady to persuade her to marry him. The will, not having been made in contemplation of marriage, was revoked by the marriage.

Execution of a Later Will

The execution of a later will automatically revokes a prior will if the terms of the second conflict with the first will. If the second will merely changes a few provisions in the first will and leaves the bulk of it intact, then a second revokes the first will only to the extent of such inconsistency.

After-Born Child

A child may be born or adopted after a person makes a will. If the original will does not provide for subsequent children or the testator makes no codicil to provide for the child, then this will revoke or partially revoke the will.

ABATEMENT AND ADEMPTION

Abatement

Proportionate reduction in monetary bequest because of insufficient funds

Ademption

Failure of bequest because property not in estate

An **abatement** occurs when a testator makes bequests of money in the will and the estate does not have enough money to pay the bequests. The legatees will receive a proportionate share of the bequests.

An **ademption** occurs when a testator makes a bequest of specific property and the estate does not have the property at death. In this case, the legatee gets nothing.

If a testator leaves $20,000 to his son John, $10,000 to his sister Mary, and a painting to his brother Adam, there could be both an abatement and an ademption. If the estate has only $15,000 in cash left after paying all debts, the cash gifts to John and Mary will abate. Each will receive a proportionate share, in this case fifty percent, or $10,000 and $5,000 respectively. If the testator had sold the painting, given it away, or someone had stolen, destroyed, or lost the painting before the death of the testator, Adam would get nothing. The bequest to him is adeemed since the property was not in the estate at the testator's death. He has no right to its cash value or any other substitute item of property.

> By the terms of her will, Eloise Williams devised her 103-acre "home place" to her nephews and nieces. The residue of the estate was bequeathed to the Masonic Home or Homes for Crippled Children. Three months before her death, Williams sold the "home place" and received an $80,000 note secured by a deed of trust. The court held that the devise of the "home place" was adeemed by the sale, and the $80,000 note passed under the residuary clause of the will.

PROBATE OF A WILL

L.O.4

Probate

Court procedure to determine validity of will

When a testator dies leaving a will, the will must be probated. **Probate** is the court procedure that determines the validity of a will. The will normally names an executor to preserve and handle the estate during probate and distribute it to the rightful individuals. An executor has liability to legatees, creditors, and heirs for loss to the estate as a result of negligence, bad faith, or breach of trust and must comply with any instructions in the will. A will may expressly provide that the executor continue a business owned by the deceased. If the will does not so provide, an executor frequently can obtain permission of the appropriate court to continue the business. With but few exceptions, anyone may be appointed executor. The executor may be excused by the testator from furnishing a bond which would be an expense to the estate. If the will does not name an executor, then upon petition of one of the beneficiaries the court will appoint an administrator.

If a person contests the will, the court must hear the contest to determine the validity of the will. A contest of the will differs from litigation over the meaning or interpretation to be given the will. If the contest alleges and proves fraud, undue influence, improper witnessing, mental incapacity of the testator, revocation of the will, or any other infirmity in the will affecting its legality, the court will find the will nullified. It will then distribute the property of the testator according to the law of descent described later in this chapter.

WHEN ADMINISTRATION IS UNNECESSARY

Of course, if an individual does not own any property at the time of death, no need for administration exists. Also, all property jointly owned with someone else who acquires the interest by right of survivorship does not require administration.

Some states have special statutes allowing the administration procedures to be shortened for very small estates. In many states all the persons interested in the estate, relatives and creditors, can agree on the share each one is to receive and can divide the estate without formal court proceedings.

TITLE BY DESCENT

When a person dies intestate, the property is distributed in accordance with the state law of descent. Every state has such a law. Although these laws vary slightly, on the whole they provide as follows: The property of the intestate goes to any children subject to the rights of the surviving spouse. If no spouse, children, or grandchildren survive, the father and mother, as the next of kin, receive the property. If no parents survive, the brothers and sisters become the next of kin, followed by grandparents, aunts and uncles, and so on. Some statutes permit any person related by blood to inherit when no nearer related relative exists. Other statutes do not permit those beyond first cousins to inherit. In any case, if no proper person to inherit survives, the property passes to the state.

Title to real estate is passed by the administrator conveying by means of an administrator's deed. When approved by the court, the grantee obtains good title to the property.

PER CAPITA AND PER STIRPES DISTRIBUTION

Per Capita
Per head

The lineal descendants of a decedent include the children and grandchildren. If all the children were living at the time of an intestate's death, and the spouse was dead, the property would be distributed **per capita,** meaning per head, or equally (see Illustration 46-2). If one child predeceased the intestate and left three surviving children, then the property would be divided into equal parts on the basis of the

Illustration 46-2   Per Capita Distribution

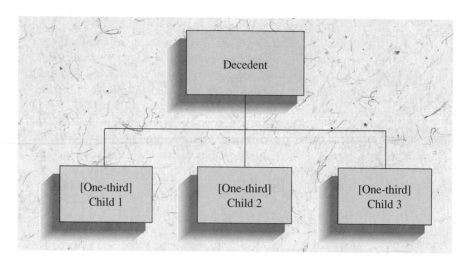

number of children the intestate had. The dead child's part would then be divided into three equal parts with one of these parts going to each of the grandchildren. When this happens, the property is said to be divided **per stirpes** (see Illustration 46-3). If the deceased child left no children or other lineal descendants, then the surviving children of the intestate would take the deceased child's share.

Per Stirpes

Distribution among heirs according to relationship to deceased

Illustration 46-3   Per Stirpes Distribution

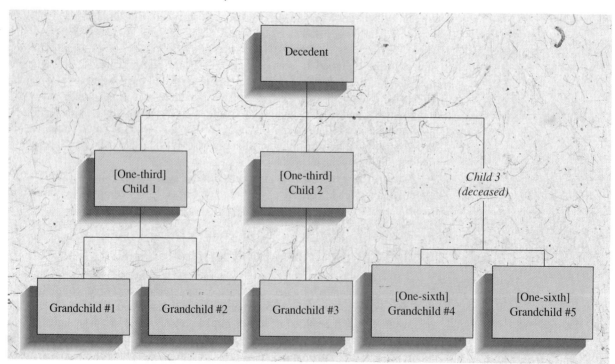

ADMINISTRATORS

For the most part the duties and responsibilities of administrators resemble those of executors with two significant differences. First, in the appointment of an administrator, some states have a clear order of priority. The surviving spouse has first priority, followed by children, grandchildren, parents, and brothers or sisters. Second, an administrator must in all cases execute a bond guaranteeing the faithful performance of the duties.

The prime duty of administrators is the same as that of executors—to preserve the estate and distribute it to the rightful parties. Administrators must act in good faith, with prudence, and within the powers conferred on them by law. If any part of the estate is a going business, with only a few exceptions the business must be liquidated. However, the administrator may obtain leave of court to continue the business for either a limited time or an indefinite time, depending largely upon the wishes of those entitled to receive the estate. Third parties dealing with administrators, as well as executors, must know of limitations upon their authority.

QUESTIONS

1   What standard of capacity must testators meet?
2   What restrictions are there upon one's right to leave property by will to anyone desired?
3   What characteristics distinguish a will from other legal instruments?
4   What are the formalities required for executing a will?
5   What is a holographic will?
6   How do holographic wills differ from nuncupative wills?
7   What are the ways in which a will may be revoked?
8   What is the difference between ademption and abatement?
9   What is the difference between distributing property per capita and per stirpes?
10   What are the two ways in which the duties and responsibilities of an administrator differ from those of an executor?
11   What is the major duty of executors and administrators?

CASE PROBLEMS

L.O.2

1   Lillian Burke did not sign her will on the line provided for her signature. She signed on one of the lines designed to be used by a witness at the end of the attestation clause following the line for her signature. After she signed, her name was typed into the attestation clause and the word "Testatrix" was typed above her signature. The will was contested. Was the will signed at the end by the testatrix?

L.O.2

2   The attorney who prepared a will for Edwin Lubin inserted a clause that stated it relieved the executor from liability "for any loss or injury to the property . . . except . . . as may result from fraud, misconduct, or gross negligence." In a court proceeding relating to the will the validity of this provision

arose. Is this provision in accordance with the liabilities and duties of an executor?

L.O.2 ....

3 William Lamb executed a will witnessed by Grier Shotwell and Hilda Johnson. After Lamb's death a will contest followed. Johnson, the only living witness, testified either Lamb or Shotwell, his attorney, in Lamb's presence, referred to the document as Lamb's will. Lamb then signed the document. Was this sufficient publication?

L.O.3 ....

4 William Cole executed a will naming Catherine Jackson the sole beneficiary and executrix. He specifically did not leave any property to any of his brothers. Six months later, he married Catherine Jackson. He died about 25 years later. As his executrix, Catherine executed a deed of William's real estate to herself. Catherine's will left the real estate to St. Pius Church. A question arose about the validity of the church's title, so Laureen D'Ambra, Catherine's executrix, filed a suit to clear it up. The issue before the court involved whether William's marriage after execution of his will revoked it. Did it?

L.O.1 ....

5 Tennie Joyner faced hospitalization and visited a neighbor, Jeff Permenter. She told him she wanted a paper prepared for her to sign so Calvin Britton could live in her home for his lifetime. Pat Shroud said she would type up a document. She asked Joyner if she wanted a will and Joyner said no. Joyner said she just wanted Britton to have a home if she died in the hospital. Five days later Joyner signed a paper that stated: "I, the undersigned, do hereby request, at the time of my death, that Calvin Britton . . . have my home and all the furnishings as long as he wants, or as long as he shall live." Two people witnessed Joyner's signature. Joyner died shortly thereafter. Was the paper a will?

L.O.2 ....

6 Alice C. Little executed a will in conformity with the laws of the state in which she lived by having three witnesses. She then moved to another state and died. Her only heir was an infant daughter. The state in which she lived at the time of her death required only two witnesses. A petition for the probate of her will was made and proofs of will executed by two witnesses were filed with the court. The state in which she executed her will permitted probate upon the testimony of only one witness where there was no objection and where there was written consent of the heirs. Should the will be admitted to probate?

L.O.4 ....

7 Myrtice Hogue became pregnant by Archie Hearn, so they got married and had a daughter, Mallery Clotille Hearn. Archie had no contact with the child after she was a month old, and Myrtice obtained a divorce. Fourteen years later Archie married Mamie Slack and 40 years later Archie died. Archie's will named Mamie executrix and bequeathed her his entire estate. Mamie petitioned to probate the will alleging that Archie died leaving no lawful descendants. The estate was probated and Mamie got Archie's property. Six years after Archie died, Mallery filed suit alleging Archie's estate was probated based on false statements by Mamie because she knew about Mallery. Did Mamie owe any duty to Mallery?

L.O.2   8   To write out her will Frances Black used three copies of a stationer's form designed to be used for a one-page will. In the clause at the top of each page she filled in her signature and residence. She also filled in the name and gender of her executor and used the appropriate blanks on the last page to give her city and state of residence and the date. She dated the top of the first page. The rest of the printed language was either stricken or ignored by her. She used almost all the remaining area on all three pages for a specific disposition of her estate. No other person's handwriting appeared on the three pages. The court denied probate of the will because Black "incorporated" portions of the form in her will so it was not entirely in her own handwriting. Should the will be admitted to probate?

Summary Cases

PROPERTY

1 Jacobson by oral contract sold some standing timber to Sorensen. Sorensen started immediately to cut and haul the timber. Since there was no time limit set on when the timber was to be removed, two years later much timber remained to be cut. Jacobson then served written notice on Sorensen that he had only ten days more to complete the contract. When the ten days expired, there were about 70,000 board feet of logs on the ground that had not been removed. Jacobson refused to let him haul these away even though Sorensen was willing to pay for them. The question was raised to what extent an oral contract for the sale of an interest in land can be enforced. Was this oral contract enforceable? [*Sorensen et al.* v. *Jacobson,* 232 P.2d 332 (Mont.)]

2 The Wade family owned the west half of Section 5, Township 7 North, Range 11 East in Newton County. Robert Grisson owned the east half of said section. Grisson claimed the west half by adverse possession and hired Jake Smith, Harvey Cleveland, and Bobby Gregory to cut timber from part of the west half. The timber was cut and delivered to Bay Springs Forest Products, Inc. The Wades sued Bay Springs to recover the value of the timber. Having determined that Grisson did not own the west half by adverse possession, the court had to consider the type of property the timber was. What was it? [*Bay Springs Forest Products, Inc.* v. *Wade,* 435 So. 2d 690 (Miss.)]

3 Cecil Carruth sent a letter to Paul McDaniel in which he agreed to deed McDaniel some land for $260,000. He stated that the deed would be delivered to McDaniel upon payment of the $30,000 down payment. Carruth later told McDaniel he was not going to sell him the land, and McDaniel filed suit for specific performance or conversion of his real estate. Carruth admitted he had told his lawyer to hold the deed until McDaniel paid the $30,000. McDaniel alleged a deed was executed and delivered for his benefit to the attorney and was either wrongfully taken or still in the possession of the attorney. Did the facts establish that McDaniel had title to the land? [*McDaniel* v. *Carruth,* 637 S.W. 2d 498 (Tex.)]

4 Arthur H. Kelley executed a deed to his home to his son. The deed was complete in every detail. When Kelley handed it to his son, he said, "Here is the deed to the home property. . . . The only request I want to make is that you do not record the deed until after my death." The father made many statements after this to the effect he had not given his son the property except on the condition that he die from a serious operation he was to undergo. The son's acts corroborated these statements by his failure to assume possession of the property, pay tax on it, or in any way assert ownership during his father's lifetime. Since a deed cannot serve as a will, this deed was not effective unless there was a delivery for the purpose of passing title. Was the son the owner? [*Kelley*

v. *Bank of America, National Trust and Savings Association*, 246 P.2d 92 (Colo.)]

5 B-L-S Construction Company, Inc., orally agreed to lease property to St. Stephen Knitwear, Inc., for four months at $4,500 a month. The parties had planned to sign a written lease but did not. St. Stephen paid one month's rent and then abandoned the property. B-L-S sued for the rent remaining under the oral lease. Was there a valid lease? [*B-L-S Construction Company, Inc.* v. *St. Stephen Knitwear, Inc.*, 281 S.E.2d 129 (S.C.)]

6 Robert Daly died, and his will was offered for probate. The first witness, Ronald Witkowski, stated he was employed by Daly and was called into Daly's office and asked to sign a document. Witkowski did not know what he was singing and was not told it was Daly's will. Daly did not sign it in his presence. The second witness, Leo Hodge, was also employed by Daly and asked to witness a document. Hodge insisted on knowing what he was signing, so Daly showed him the front, which indicated it was Daly's will. Hodge was not sure whether Daly's signature was on the will or not. Daly's widow and three children, who were left very little by the will, filed objections to its probate alleging it was not properly executed. Was it? [*Matter of Will of Daly*, 402 N.Y.S.2d 747 (N.Y.)]

7 Edd Campbell entered into an oral contract by which he gave Brad Miller the right to remove dirt and rock from an old hole on Campbell's property for a stated price per cubic yard. The contract required Miller to repair any damages as a result of the removal and refill the old hole and any new ones created. Campbell died and his wife, Mary Alice, was appointed administratrix of his estate. She sued alleging that while Edd had received payment under the contract, Miller had not repaired the damages nor filled the hole. Miller alleged that as administratrix, Mary Alice did not have authority to bring the suit. Does an administratrix have such authority? [*Campbell* v. *Miller*, 562 S.W.2d 827 (Tenn. Ct. App.)]

Glossary

(Other legal terms are defined elsewhere in the text. Refer to the Index for them.)

A

Abandon: relinquish possession of personal property with intent to disclaim title.

Abatement: a proportionate reduction in monetary bequests because the estate does not have sufficient funds to pay all bequests in full.

Abrogate: recall or repeal; abolish.

Absolute liability: liability for an act that causes harm even though the doer was not at fault.

Abstract of title: history of the transfers of title to a given piece of land, briefly stating the parties to and the effect of all deeds, wills, and judicial proceedings relating to the land.

Acceleration clause: provision in a contract or any legal instrument that upon the occurrence of a certain event the time of the performance of specified obligations shall be advanced.

Acceptance: an accepted draft; the assent by the person on whom a draft is drawn to pay it when due. The agreement to an offer resulting in a contract. The assent of the buyer of goods to become the owner.

Acceptor: one who assents to an order, draft, or receipt of goods.

Accession: acquisition of title to property by virtue of the fact that it has been attached to property already owned.

Accessory after the fact: one who after the commission of a felony knowingly assists the felon.

Accessory before the fact: one who is absent at the commission of the crime but who aided and abetted its commission.

Accommodation party: a person who signs a negotiable instrument as a favor to another.

Accord and satisfaction: an agreement made and executed in satisfaction of the rights one has acquired under a former contract.

Accretion: acquisition of title to additional land when the owner's land is built up by gradual deposits made by the natural action of water.

Acknowledgment: the admission of the execution of a writing made before a competent officer; the formal certificate made by an officer.

Acquittal: the action of a jury in a finding of not guilty.

Act of God: an act of nature that is not reasonably foreseeable.

Action: proceeding at law.

Action of ejectment: an action brought by the landlord to have the sheriff remove a tenant.

Active fraud: fraud caused when a party engages in action that causes the fraud.

Ademption: the inability to make a bequest of specific property because the property is not in the testator's estate.

Adjudication: a judicial determination.

Administrative agency: a governmental commission or board given authority to regulate particular matters.

Administrator (Administratrix): a man (woman) appointed by the court to take charge of the estate of a deceased person.

Admission: an acknowledgment by the party to a lawsuit that a certain fact is true, or a matter of law is decided so it does not have to be proved in court.

Adult: one who has reached full legal age.

Adverse possession: the hostile possession of real estate, which when actual, visible, notorious, exclusive, and continued for the required number of years, will place title to the land in the person in possession.

Affidavit: a voluntary, sworn statement in writing.

Affirm: to declare to tell the truth under a penalty of perjury; to confirm.

Affirmative covenant: an express undertaking or promise in a contract or deed to do an act.

Agency: the relationship that exists between a person identified as a principal and another by virtue of which the latter may make contracts with third parties on behalf of the principal.

Agency by estoppel: agency which arises when a person leads another person to believe that a third party is the first person's agent.

Agency coupled with an interest in the authority: an agency in which the agent has given a consideration or has paid for the right to exercise the authority.

Agency coupled with an interest in the subject matter: an agency in which, for a consideration, the agent is given an interest in the property with which the agent is dealing.

Agency shop: a union contract provision requiring that nonunion employees pay the union the equivalent of union dues in order to retain their employment.

Agent: one who is authorized by the principal to make contracts with third parties on behalf of the principal.

Alien corporation: a corporation chartered in a foreign country.

Alienate: to transfer voluntarily the title to property.

Alimony: an allowance made to the dependent spouse living apart from the supporting spouse.

Allegation: a statement to be proved in a legal proceeding.

Allonge: a paper so firmly attached to an instrument as to become a part of it.

Alteration: Any material change of the terms of a writing fraudulently made by a party thereto.

Ambiguity: doubtfulness: the state of having two or more possible meanings.

Annexation: attachment of personal property to realty in such a way as to make it become real property.

Annuity: a contract by which the insured pays a lump sum to the insurer and later receives fixed, regular payments.

Annulment: the act of making void.

Answer: a written statement of the defendant's position regarding the facts alleged in a lawsuit; a response.

Antedate: to place date prior to the true one on an instrument.

Anti-injunction acts: statutes prohibiting the use of injunctions in labor disputes except under exceptional circumstances; notably the Norris-LaGuardia Act.

Anticipatory breach: when, prior to the time the other party is entitled to performance, one party announces an intention not to perform.

Antitrust laws: laws designed to prevent one individual or group from controlling too large a share of the market for a product.

Apparent authority: the authority an agent is believed by third parties to have because of the behavior of the principal.

Appeal: taking a case to a reviewing court to determine whether the judgment of the lower court was correct.

Appellate jurisdiction: the authority of a court to hear and decide a given class of cases on appeal from another court or administrative agency.

Arbitration: the settlement of disputed questions, whether of law or fact, by one or more disinterested persons by whose decision the parties agree to be bound.

Arraign: to accuse; to impeach; to read the charge of an indictment.

Articles of incorporation: the written document setting forth the facts about a corporation prescribed by law for issuance of a charter and asserting the corporation has complied with legal requirements.

Articles of partnership: a written partnership agreement.

Assault: to attempt or threaten to harm another while having the apparent present ability to do so.

Assent: to consent; to concur.

Assessment mutual company: a mutual insurance company in which losses are shared by policyholders in the ratio of their insurance to the company's total insurance in force.

Assets: property available for the payment of debts.

Assign: to transfer property or a right to another.

Assignee: one to whom property has been assigned.

Assignment: transfer of a right. Used in connection with personal property rights, as rights under a contract, a negotiable instrument, an insurance policy, or a mortgage.

Assignor: the party who makes an assignment.

Assumption of risk: the common law rule that an employee could not sue the employer for injuries caused by the ordinary risks of employment on the theory that the employee had assumed such risks by undertaking the work.

Attachment: the legal process by which property is seized in process of a debt settlement.

Attest: to bear witness.

Attorney: one legally appointed to act for another.

Attorney in fact: a general agent appointed by a written authorization.

Attractive nuisance doctrine: a rule imposing liability on a landowner for injuries sustained by small children playing on the land when the landowner permits a condition to exist or maintains equipment that the landowner should realize would attract small children who would not realize the danger.

Auction: a means of selling goods in which the seller or an agent of the seller orally asks for bids on the goods and orally accepts the highest bid.

Automated teller machine: an electronic fund transfer terminal which can perform a number of routine banking services.

Avoid: to make void; to annul.

Award: the decisions of arbitrators.

B

Bacteria: a rogue program that replicates itself to the capacity of the system and prevents a computer from processing.

Bad check: a check the drawee bank refuses to pay for such reasons as insufficient funds or no account.

Bad check laws: statutes making it a crime to issue, with intent to defraud, a check that will not be paid by the bank.

Baggage: articles of necessity or personal convenience usually carried for personal use by passengers of common carriers.

Bail: security given for the appearance of a person in court.

Bailee: the person in possession of bailed property.

Bailee's lien: a specific, possessory lien of the bailee on the bailed goods for work done to them. Commonly extended by statute to any bailee's claim for compensation and eliminating the necessity of retention of possession.

Bailiff: a court executive officer.

Bailment: the relation that exists when personal property is delivered into the possession of another under an agreement, express or implied, that the identical property will be returned or will be disposed of in accordance with the agreement.

Bailor: the person who gives up possession of property when there is a bailment.

Bank draft: a check drawn by one bank on another bank.

Bankruptcy: a procedure by which one unable to pay debts (the debtor) may have all assets in excess of an exemption claim surrendered to the court for administration and distribution to creditors. The debtor is then given a discharge that releases the debtor from the unpaid balance due on most debts.

Battery: the unlawful touching of another.

Bearer: the person in physical possession of a negotiable instrument payable to bearer.

Bearer paper: commercial paper made payable to the bearer.

Beneficiary: the person to whom the proceeds of a life insurance policy are payable; a person for whose benefit property is held in trust; a person who is given property by a will.

Bequest: a gift of personal property by will.

Bidder: the person who makes an offer at an auction.

Bilateral contract: a contract which consists of mutual promises to perform some future acts.

Bill of exchange (draft): an unconditional order in writing by one person upon another, signed by the person giving it, and ordering the person to whom it is directed to pay or deliver on demand or at a definite time a sum certain in money to order or to bearer.

Bill of lading: a document issued by a carrier showing the receipt of goods and the terms of the contract of transportation.

Bill of Rights: the first ten amendments to the Constitution, enacted by the first Congress to protect the civil rights and liberties of citizens and the states.

Bill of sale: a writing signed by the seller showing that the seller has sold to the buyer the personal property described.

Binder: a memorandum delivered to the insured stating the essential terms of a policy to be executed in the future, when it is agreed that the contract of insurance is to be effective before the written policy is executed.

Blank indorsement: an indorsement that does not state to whom the instrument is to be paid.

Blanket policy: an insurance policy which covers many items of the same kind in different places or different kinds of property in the same place.

Blue-sky laws: statutes designed to protect the public from the sale of worthless stocks and bonds.

Boardinghouse keeper: one regularly engaged in the business of offering living accommodations to permanent lodgers or boarders as distinguished from transient guests.

Bona fide: in good faith; without deceit or fraud; genuine.

Bond: an obligation or promise in writing and sealed, generally of corporations, personal representatives, or trustees.

Bonding company: a paid surety.

Boycott: a combination of two or more persons to cause harm to another by refraining from patronizing or dealing with such other person in any way or inducing others to so refrain.

Breach: in contracts, the violation of an agreement or obligation.

Bribery: offering or paying something of value to influence the action of an official's discharge of a legal or public duty.

Brief: written arguments or authorities furnished by a lawyer to a court.

Broker: a special agent whose job is to bring two contracting parties together.

Bulk sales acts: statutes to protect creditors of a bulk seller by preventing that seller from obtaining cash for the goods and then leaving the state. Expanded to "bulk transfers" under the UCC.

Burglary: the unlawful entering of a building with the intent to commit a felony.

Business crime: a crime against a business or committed by using a business.

Business interruption insurance: insurance which covers the loss of business profits while a damaged building is being repaired.

Business law: the rules of conduct prescribed by government for the performance of business transactions.

Business trust: a form of business organization in which the owners of the property to be devoted to the business transfer the title of the property to trustees with full power to operate the business.

Bylaws: the rules enacted by the directors to govern a corporation's conduct.

C

Cancellation: a crossing out of a part of an instrument or a destruction of all legal effect of the instrument, whether by act of a party, upon breach by the other party, or pursuant to agreement or decree of court.

Capital: net assets of a corporation.

Capital stock: the declared money value of the outstanding stock of the corporation.

Carrier: an entity engaged in the business of transporting goods and/or people.

Case: an occurrence upon which an action in court is based.

Cash surrender value: the sum that will be paid the insured upon surrender of a policy to the insurer.

Cashier's check: a check drawn by a bank on its own funds and signed by the cashier or another official of the bank.

Cause of action: the right to damages or other judicial relief when a legally protected right of the plaintiff is violated by an unlawful act of the defendant.

Caveat emptor: let the buyer beware.

Cease and desist: an order to stop a practice, usually issued by a court or administrative agency.

Certificate of deposit: an acknowledgment by a bank of a receipt of money with an engagement to repay it with interest.

Certified check: an ordinary check accepted by a bank official who writes "certified," or some similar word, on it and signs it.

Chancery courts: courts of equity.

Charter: the grant of authority from a government to exist as a corporation.

Chattel: any article of personal property.

Chattel mortgage: a security device by which the owner of personal property transfers the title to a creditor as security for the debt owed by the owner to the creditor.

Check: an order by a depositor on the bank to pay a sum of money to a payee; a bill of exchange drawn on a bank and payable on demand.

Check truncation: a system of in some way shortening the trip a check makes from the payee to the drawee bank and then the drawer.

Circuit court: a state court of record.

Circumstantial evidence: circumstances surrounding the facts in dispute from which the trier of fact may deduce what had happened.

Civil action: action brought to enforce or protect private rights.

Civil court: a court with jurisdiction to hear and determine controversies relating to private rights and duties.

Civil law: the body of law concerned with private or purely personal rights.

Claims Court: the federal trial court which hears cases involving claims against the US. government.

Clerk of the court: the person who keeps the records for a court.

Close corporation: a corporation which has a very small number of shareholders.

Closed shop: a place of employment in which only union members may be employed. Now generally prohibited by statutes.

Closely held corporation: *see* Close corporation.

Code: a compilation of laws by public authority.

Codicil: a writing which modifies a will.

Coguarantor: one of two or more people jointly liable for another's debt, default, or obligation.

Coinsurance: a principle that the insured recovers on a loss in the same ratio as the insurance bears to the amount of insurance which the company requires.

Collateral note: a note secured by personal property.

Collateral security: a thing of value which may be used to satisfy an obligation which is past due and unpaid.

Collective bargaining: the process by which the terms of employment are agreed upon through negotiations between the employer and the union or other bargaining representative of the employees.

Collective bargaining unit: a group of employees who are by statute authorized to select a bargaining representative to represent all the employees within that unit in bargaining collectively with the employer.

Collusion: a secret agreement between two or more people that is designed to obtain an object forbidden by law or to defraud another.

Color of title: a person's apparent title.

Commercial paper: negotiable instrument.

Commission merchant: a bailee to whom goods are consigned for sale.

Common carrier: a carrier that holds out its facilities to serve the general public for compensation without discrimination.

Common law: the body of unwritten principles originally based on the usages and customs of the community which were recognized and enforced by the courts.

Common stock: stock that has no right or priority over any other stock of the corporation as to dividends or distribution of assets upon dissolution.

Communication: telling something to a third person.

Community property: the co-tenancy held by husband and wife in property acquired during their marriage under the law of some of the states.

Comparative negligence: the rule that contributory negligence reduces but does not completely bar recovery from a negligent person.

Competency: legal power, adequacy, or ability.

Complaint: initial pleading filed by the plaintiff in many actions; a petition.

Composition of creditors: an agreement among creditors that each shall accept a part payment as full payment in consideration of the other creditors' doing the same.

Comprehensive policy: an automobile insurance policy which covers a large number of risks to a car such as wind, earthquake, flood, riot.

Compromise: a settlement reached by mutual concessions.

Computer crimes: crimes that are committed with the aid of a computer or that exist because of computers.

Computer trespass: the unauthorized use of or access to a computer.

Concealment: a withholding of information which one has a duty to reveal.

Conditional sale: a credit transaction by which the buyer purchases on credit and promises to pay the purchase price in installments, while the seller retains the title to the goods, together with the right of repossession upon default, until the condition of payment in full has been satisfied.

Conflict of laws: the body of law that determines which state's law is to apply when two or more states are involved in the facts of a given case.

Confusion of goods: the mixing of goods of different owners that under certain circumstances results in one of the owner's becoming the owner of all the goods.

Confusion of source: representing goods or services as being those of another.

Consanguinity: relationship by blood.

Consideration: the promise or performance by the other party that the promisor demands as the price of the promise.

Consignee: one to whom goods are shipped.

Consignment: the transfer of possession of personal property for the purpose of selling it.

Consignor: one who ships goods by a common carrier.

Consolidation: a combination of two corporations into a new one.

Constable: executive officer of an inferior court.

Constitution: the document which contains the fundamental principles of government of a country or state including the relationships of the parts of the government to each other and of the government to its citizens.

Constructive bailment: a bailment imposed by the law when someone finds and takes possession of lost property.

Constructive notice: information or knowledge the law presumes everyone knows.

Consumer: one who purchases goods primarily for household, personal, or family use.

Consumer goods or services: goods or services for use primarily for personal, family, or household purposes.

Contempt of court: an act against the dignity or authority of a court for which a fine or imprisonment may be summarily imposed.

Contingent beneficiary: the person to whom the proceeds of a life insurance policy are payable in the event that the primary beneficiary dies before the insured.

Contingent liability: a responsibility to pay which usually does not arise until someone with primary liability defaults.

Contract: a binding agreement based upon the genuine assent of the parties, and for a lawful object, between competent parties, in the form required by law, and generally supported by consideration.

Contract carrier: a carrier which transports on the basis of individual contracts that it makes with each shipper.

Contract of record: the name sometimes given to a judgment of a court.

Contract rate: the maximum rate of interest allowed by law to be demanded of a debtor.

Contract to sell: a contract to make a transfer to title in the future as contrasted with a present sale.

Contribution: the right of coguarantors or cosureties who have paid more than their proportionate share of the debt to recover the excess from the other guarantors or sureties.

Contributory negligence: negligence of the plaintiff that contributes to the injury and at common law bars the plaintiff from recovery from the defendant although the defendant may have been more negligent than the plaintiff.

Conversion: the unauthorized exercise of ownership rights over another's property.

Conveyance: a transfer of an interest in land, ordinarily by the execution and delivery of a deed.

Convict: a person who has been found guilty of a major criminal offense by a court.

Cooperative: a group of two or more persons or enterprises that act through a common agent with respect to a common objective, as buying or selling.

Corporation: an artificial legal person or being created by law, which for many purposes is treated as a natural person.

Corporeal: material; tangible; substantial.

Cosurety: *see* Coguarantor.

Counterclaim: a claim that the defendant in an action may make against the plaintiff.

County court: a state court of record.

Coupon bond: a bond with detachable, individual coupons representing the interest payments, which coupons are to be presented for payment when due.

Court of appeals: one of thirteen federal courts which hear appeals of cases from federal district courts, administrative agencies, special federal courts, and US. territories. Also, a state intermediate appellate court.

Court of International Trade: the federal trial court which hears cases involving the rates of duty on imported goods, the collection of the revenues, and similar controversies.

Court of original jurisdiction: a court of record in which a case, either criminal or civil, is first tried.

Court of record: a trial court at which an official, permanent record is kept of the trial showing such things as testimony, evidence, and statements of the parties.

Covenant: a promise contained in a conveyance or other instrument relating to real estate; a solemn compact.

Credit sale: the exchange of goods for a promise to pay later.

Creditor: the person to whom money is owed; the party in a contract of guaranty to whom the guaranty is given.

Creditor beneficiary: a person to whom the promisee of a contract owes an obligation or duty which will be discharged to the extent that the promisor performs the promise.

Crime: a violation of the law that is punished as an offense against the state or government.

Criminal law: That branch of the law which classifies offenses against society as crimes and provides for the punishment of the people who commit the offenses.

Cumulative preferred stock: preferred stock on which dividends must be paid for all years before any common stock dividends may be paid.

Cumulative voting: a system of voting for directors of a corporation in which each stockholders has as many votes as the number of voting shares owned multiplied by the number of directors to be elected, which votes can be distributed for the various candidates as desired.

Custody: care and control of property or of a person.

Customary authority: agent's authority which arises because by custom such agents ordinarily possess such power.

D

Damages: a sum of money recovered to redress or make amends for a legal wrong or injury.

Debenture: an unsecured bond or note issued by a business firm.

Debt: an obligation to pay in money or goods.

Deceit: a device of false representation by which one person misleads another to the latter's injury.

Decree: the decision of a court of equity or admiralty.

Dedication: acquisition by the public or a government of title to land

when it is given over by its owner to use by the public and such gift is accepted.

Deductible clause: an insurance provision whereby the insured pays for damage up to a specified amount and the company pays for any excess.

Deed: an instrument by which the grantor (owner of land) conveys or transfers the title to a grantee.

Deed of trust: a deed that transfers land to a trustee for the benefit of the creditor when real estate is used to secure payment of a debt; commonly used as a form of mortgage.

Defamation: publication of a false statement about another by means of a writing.

Default: the nonperformance of a duty or an obligation.

Defendant: a person against whom a suit is brought.

Defense: that which is relied upon by a defendant to defeat an action.

Defense clause: an insurance policy clause by which the insurer agrees to defend the insured against claims for damages.

Delegation: the transfer to another of the power to do an act.

Delivery: giving up possession and control of something.

Demurrage: a charge made by the carrier for the unreasonable detention of cars by the consignor or consignee.

Deposition: the testimony of a witness taken out of court before a person authorized to administer oaths.

Descent: hereditary succession to an estate.

Devise: a gift of real estate made by will.

Devisee: a person who receives real estate by a will.

Directors: the individuals vested with control of the corporation, subject to the elective power of the shareholders.

Disability: incapacity to perform a legal act.

Disaffirmance: the repudiation of or election to avoid a voidable contract.

Discharge in bankruptcy: an order of a bankruptcy court discharging the debtor from the unpaid balance of most of the claims against him or her.

Discharge of contract: termination of a contract by performance, agreement, impossibility, acceptance of breach, or operation of law.

Discovery: the procedure for obtaining unprivileged information from another party to a legal case.

Dishonor: when a presentment is made and a due acceptance or payment is refused or cannot be obtained in time.

Dissolution: the change in the relation of the partners caused by any partner's ceasing to be associated in the carrying on of the business; the termination of a corporation's operation except for activities needed for liquidation.

District court: the trial court in the federal judicial system. Also, a state court of record in some states.

Dividends: corporate profits declared by the board of directors for distribution to the shareholders.

Divorce: the dissolution of marriage ties.

Document of title: a document that shows ownership.

Domestic bill of exchange: a draft drawn in one state and payable in the same or another state.

Domestic corporation: a corporation in the state in which it was incorporated.

Domestic relations court: a court which has jurisdiction over divorce and child custody cases.

Domicile: the home of a person or the state of incorporation of a corporation, to be distinguished from a place where a person lives but which that person does not regard as home, or a state in which a corporation does business but in which it was not incorporated.

Donee beneficiary: a third party beneficiary to whom no legal duty is owed and for whom performance is a gift.

Dormant partner: a partner who is unknown to the public as a partner and takes no part in the management of the business.

Double jeopardy: the principle that a person who has once been placed in jeopardy by being brought to trial and the proceedings progressed at least as far as having the jury sworn cannot thereafter be tried a second time for the same offense.

Draft: *see* Bill of exchange.

Drawee: the person who is ordered to pay a draft.

Drawer: the person who executes a draft.

Due care: the degree of care that a reasonable person would exercise to prevent the realization of harm, which under all the circumstances was reasonably foreseeable in the event that such care were not taken.

Due date: the time at which payment is required and after which payment is delinquent.

Duress: constraint or compulsion.

E

Easement: the right that one person has to use the land of another for a special purpose.

Electronic fund transfer: a transfer of funds initiated by means of an electronic terminal, telephonic instrument, or computer or magnetic tape which instructs or authorizes a financial institution to debit or credit an account.

Eleemosynary corporation: a corporation organized for a charitable or benevolent purpose.

Embezzlement: the fraudulent appropriation of property by a person to whom it has been entrusted.

Emblements: growing crops that have been sown or planted.

Eminent domain: the power of a government to take private property against the objection of the owner, provided the taking is for a public purpose and just compensation is made therefor.

Enact: to make into a law.

Encumbrance: a right held by a third person in, or a lien or charge against, property, as a mortgage or judgment lien on land.

Endowment insurance: term insurance policy which combines decreasing term insurance and a savings account.

Equipment: goods used or purchased for use in a business.

Equitable: just; fair; right; reasonable.

Equity: the body of principles based on fairness that originally developed because of the inadequacy of the rules then applied by the common law courts of England.

Erosion: the loss of land through a gradual washing away by tides or currents, with the owner losing title to the lost land.

Escrow: a conditional delivery of property or of a deed to a custodian or escrow holder, who in turn makes final delivery to the grantee or transferee when a specified condition has been satisfied.

Estate: an interest in property; the property left by the deceased.

Estate in fee simple: the largest estate possible in which the owner has the absolute and entire interest in the land.

Estoppel: the principle by which a person is barred from pursuing a certain course of action or of disputing the truth of certain matters because that person's conduct was such that it would be unjust to permit him or her to do so.

Ethics: the study of the morality of conduct, its motives, and duties.

Eviction: the expulsion of an occupant of real property.

Evidence: that which is presented to the trier of fact as the basis on which the trier is to determine what happened.

Ex parte: upon or from one side only.

Executed contract: a contract that has been fully performed by all parties to it.

Execution: the carrying out of a judgment of a court, generally directing that property owned by the defendant be sold and the proceeds first be used to pay the execution or judgment creditor.

Executive officer of a court: the person who serves process and maintains order and acts as a guard in a court.

Executor (executrix): the man (woman) named by the maker of a will to carry out its provisions.

Executory contract: a contract whose terms have not been fully carried out by all parties.

Existing goods: goods that are in being and owned by the seller.

Exoneration: the guarantor's or surety's right to have the creditor compel payment of the debt.

Express authority: the authority of an agent which is stated in the document or agreement creating the agency.

Express contract: a contract in which the parties state their intentions by words, either written or oral, when agreement is made.

Express warranty: the statement by the seller in which the article sold is guaranteed.

Extended coverage: riders to a fire insurance policy covering loss from additional risks.

Extradition: the surrender by one government to another of a person charged with a crime.

Extraordinary bailment: a bailment in which the bailee is subject to unusual duties and liabilities, as a hotelkeeper or common carrier.

F

F.O.B.: free on board; the designated point to which a seller bears the risk of loss and expense of delivery.

Factor: a bailee to whom goods are consigned for sale.

Factor del credere: a commission merchant who sells the goods on credit and guarantees the purchase price will be paid.

Fair employment practice acts: statutes designed to eliminate discrimination in employment on the basis of race, religion, national origin, or sex.

Fair labor standards acts: laws, particularly the federal statute, designed to prevent excessive hours of employment, low pay, and the employment of young children.

Featherbedding: the exaction of money for services not performed or not to be performed, which is made an unfair labor practice generally and a criminal offense in connection with radio broadcasting.

Fee simple estate: the largest and most complete right which one may possess in property.

Fellow-servant rule: a common law defense of the employer that barred an employee from suing an employer for injuries caused by a fellow employee.

Felony: a criminal offense that is punishable by confinement in prison or by death, or that is expressly stated by statute to be a felony.

Fictitious name registration statute: a law requiring the person who operates a business under an assumed name to register the name.

Fidelity bond: a contract of suretyship for someone who handles another's money.

Fiduciary: person in a relation of trust or confidence.

File: to make a matter of public record or notice by registering with the proper authorities.

Financial responsibility laws: statutes that require a driver involved in an automobile accident to provide financial responsibility in order to retain a driver's license.

Financing statement: a writing with the signatures and addresses of the debtor and the secured party and a description of the collateral.

Firm offer: a merchant's signed, written offer to sell or purchase goods saying it will be held open.

Fixture: personal property that has become so attached to or adapted to real estate that it has lost its character as personal property and is part of the real estate.

Floating policy: an insurance policy which covers property no matter where it is at the time of the loss.

Forbearance: refraining from doing a legal act.

Forcible entry and detainer action: a summary action brought by the landlord to regain possession of leased property.

Foreclosure: procedures for enforcing a mortgage resulting in the public sale of the mortgaged property and less commonly in merely barring the right of the mortgagor to redeem the property from the mortgage.

Foreign (international) bill of exchange: a bill of exchange made in one nation and payable in another.

Foreign corporation: a corporation incorporated under the laws of another state.

Foreign draft: *see* Foreign bill of exchange.

Forfeiture: the loss of some right or privilege.

Forgery: the fraudulent making or altering of an instrument that apparently creates or alters a legal liability of another.

Formal contract: a contract that must be in a special form or created in a certain way.

Franchise: a right or privilege conferred by law.

Fraud: the making of a false statement of a past or existing fact with knowledge of its falsity or with reckless indifference as to its truth with the intent to cause another to rely thereon, and the other is injured by relying thereon.

Fraud in the execution: false statement that causes a party to sign a contract when unaware contract is being signed.

Fraud in the inducement: false statement made about the terms or obligations of a transaction between parties and not about the nature of the document signed.

Friendly fire: a fire burning in its normal or intended place.

Fungible goods: goods of a homogeneous nature of which any unit is the equivalent of any other unit or is treated as such by mercantile usage.

Future goods: goods which are not both existing and identified.

G

Gambling contract: an agreement by which the parties stand to win or lose based on pure chance.

Garnishment: a process whereby a person's money or property which is held by another is applied to payment of the former's debt to a third person.

General agent: one authorized to carry out the principal's business of a particular kind, or all the principal's business at a particular place even though it is not all of one kind.

General partner: a partner who is actively and openly engaged in the business and is held out as a partner.

General partnership: a partnership in which the partners conduct as co-owners a business for profit, and each partner has a right to take part in the management of the business and has unlimited liability.

General warranty deed: a deed which warrants good title in the grantee, free from claims of all persons.

Gift: a transfer of ownership of property without any consideration.

Goods: movable personal property.

Grace period: a period of 30 or 31 days in which a late life insurance premium may be paid without the policy lapsing.

Grant: convey real property; an instrument by which such property has been conveyed, particularly in the case of a government.

Grantee: the person who receives title to property.

Grantor: the person who conveys property.

Gratuitous bailment: a bailment in which the bailee does not receive any compensation or advantage.

Group boycott: a concerted refusal to deal; an agreement among competitors not to deal with a third party.

Guarantor: one who undertakes the obligation of guaranty.

Guaranty: an undertaking to pay the debt of another if the creditor first sues the debtor and is unable to recover the debt from the debtor or principal.

Guardian: one who is responsible for the care of a person or another's property.

Guest: a transient receiving accommodations in a hotel.

H

Hazards: factors which contribute to the uncertainty of the danger of a loss insured against.

Heirs: those persons specified by statute to receive the estate of a decedent not disposed of by will.

Holder: a person in possession of a commercial paper payable to the person as payee or indorsee, or a person in possession of a commercial paper payable to bearer.

Holder in due course: a holder of a commercial paper under such circumstances that the holder is treated as favored and is given an immunity from certain defenses.

Holder through a holder in due course: a person who does not meet the requirements of a holder in due course but is a holder of the paper after it was held by some prior party who was a holder in due course, and who is given the same rights as a holder in due course.

Holographic will: a will written by the testator in the testator's own hand.

Horizontal territorial restraint: an agreement by competitors to divide a geographic area among them so they will not compete.

Hostile fire: a fire which is out of its normal place.

Hot cargo agreement: agreement between an employer and a union that the employer will not use nonunion materials.

Hotelkeeper: one regularly engaged in the business of offering living accommodations to all transients.

I

Identified goods: goods which the seller and the buyer have agreed are to be received by the buyer or have been picked out by the buyer.

Implied authority: an agent's authority to do things not specifically authorized in order to carry out express authority.

Implied contract: a contract expressed by conduct or implied or deduced from the facts.

Implied warranty: a warranty imposed by law.

Incidental authority: authority of an agent that is reasonably necessary to execute the agent's express authority.

Incidental beneficiary: a person not a party to a contract who is not specifically intended to, but does, benefit from its performance.

Incontestability clause: a provision that after the lapse of a specified time the insurer cannot dispute the policy on the grounds of misrepresentation or fraud of the insured or similar wrongful conduct.

Incorporators: the people who initially form a corporation.

Indemnity: a compensation for loss sustained; the right of the guarantor to be reimbursed by the principal.

Independent contractor: a person who undertakes to perform a specified task according to the terms of a contract but over whom the other contracting party has no control except as provided for by the contract.

Indictment: a formal accusation of crime made by a grand jury which accusation is then tried by a petty or trial jury.

Indorsee: the person who becomes the holder of a negotiable instrument by an indorsement naming him or her as the person to whom the instrument is negotiated.

Indorsement: the signature of the holder on the back of an instrument including any directions or limitations regarding payment of the instrument.

Indorser: payee who signs the back of the instrument.

Inducing breach of contract: a third party's causing a party to a contract to breach the contract.

Infant: any person not of full legal age.

Inferior courts: trial courts of state court systems which hear only cases involving minor criminal offenses and disputes between citizens.

Inheritance: the estate which passes from a decedent to the heirs.

Injunction: a judicial order or decree forbidding the doing of a certain act.

Injunctive powers: the power to issue cease and desist orders.

Injurious falsehood: a false statement of fact that degrades the quality of another person's goods or services.

Inland draft: *see* Domestic bill of exchange.

Innocent misrepresentation: a false statement made in the belief that it is true.

Insolvency: the state of being unable to pay one's debts as they become due.

Instrument: a written document.

Insurable interest: an interest in the nonoccurrence of the risk insured against, generally because such occurrence would cause financial loss, although sometimes merely because of the close relationship between the insured and the beneficiary.

Insurance: a plan of security against risks by charging the loss against a fund created by the payments made by policyholders.

Insured: the person protected against the loss stated in an insurance policy.

Insurer: the company that agrees to compensate a person for a loss under an insurance contract.

Intangible personal property: evidences of ownership of personal property such as stock of a corporation, checks, and copyrights.

Interference with prospective advantage: the unjustified interference with a person's reasonable expectation of future economic benefit.

International bill of exchange: an instrument made in one nation and payable in another.

Interrogatories: in a lawsuit, written questions from one party to another party which must be answered in writing.

Intestate: one who dies without having made a valid will.

Invalid: void, of no legal effect.

Inventory: articles purchased with the intention of reselling or leasing them.

Issue: to release control over a negotiable instrument to the payee.

J

Joint and several contract: a contract in which two or more people are obligated or are entitled to recover individually and as a unit.

Joint contract: a contract in which two or more people are, as a unit, liable or entitled to performance under the contract.

Joint stock company: an association in which the shares of the members are transferable and control is delegated to a group or board.

Joint tenancy: estate held by two or more jointly with the right of survivorship between them.

Joint venture: a relationship in which two or more people combine their labor or property for a single undertaking and share profits and losses equally unless otherwise agreed.

Judge: the chief officer of a court.

Judgment: a decision of a court.

Judicial admission: a fact acknowledged by a party in the course of legal proceedings.

Jurisdiction: the power of a court to hear and determine a given class of cases; the power to act over a particular defendant.

Justice of the peace: chief officer of an inferior court.

Justice-of-the-peace court: an inferior court.

Juvenile court: a court which has jurisdiction over cases involving delinquent, dependent, and neglected children.

L

Landlord: the owner of leased premises.

Larceny: taking and carrying away the property of another without the consent of the person in possession and with the intent of depriving the possessor of the property.

Last clear chance rule: the rule that allows a negligent driver to recover if the other driver had one last clear chance to avoid the accident.

Law: a governmental rule of conduct prescribing what is right and what is wrong, with penalties provided for its violation.

Law merchant: the rules applied by courts set up by merchants in England prior to 1400.

Lawyer: a person legally appointed to act for another; an attorney.

Lease: an agreement between the owner of property and a tenant by which the former agrees to give possession of the property to the latter in consideration of the payment of rent. (Parties—landlord or lessor, tenant or lessee)

Leasehold: the estate or interest the tenant has in the land rented.

Legacy: a gift of personal property by will.

Legal: authorized or prescribed by law.

Legal rate of interest: the rate which is set by statute to apply when interest is to be paid but no rate is specified.

Legal tender: such form of money as the law recognizes as lawful and declares that a tender thereof in the proper amount is a proper tender which the creditor cannot refuse.

Legatee: one to whom personal property is left by a will.

Lessee: person given possession of leased property.

Lessor: owner of leased premises.

Levy: to take possession of property to satisfy a judgment.

Libel: written defamation of another without legal justification.

License: a personal privilege to do some act or series of acts upon the land of another, not amounting to an easement or a right of possession, as the placing of a sign thereon.

Lien: a right to control, hold, and retain, or enforce a charge against another's property as security for a debt or claim.

Life estate: an estate for the duration of a life.

Life insurance: a contract by which the insurer agrees to pay a sum of money to a beneficiary on the death of the insured.

Limited defense: a defense which cannot be raised against a holder in due course.

Limited liability: loss of contributed capital as maximum liability.

Limited liability company: a type of business organization similar to a partnership but without the disadvantage of unlimited liability.

Limited partnership: a partnership in which at least one partner has a liability limited to the loss of the capital contribution made to the partnership, and such a partner neither takes part in the management of the partnership or appears to the public to be a partner.

Liquidated damages: the amount agreed upon in advance by the parties to a contract, to be paid in case of a breach.

Liquidation: the process of converting property into money.

Litigation: a suit at law, a judicial contest.

Lost property: property unintentionally left with no desire to discard it.

Lottery: any plan by which a consideration is given for a chance to win a prize.

M

Magistrate court: an inferior court.

Magistrate: chief officer of an inferior court.

Majority: of age, as contrasted with being a minor; more than half of any group, as a majority of stockholders.

Maker: the person who executes a promissory note.

Malfeasance: the doing of some wrongful act.

Malice: ill will towards some person.

Malpractice: the failure to perform a contract with the ability and care normally exercised by people in the specific profession.

Marshal: the executive officer of a federal court.

Mechanics' lien: protection afforded by statute to various types of laborers and people supplying materials, by giving them a claim against the building and land that has been improved or added to by them.

Merchant: a person who deals in goods of the kind or otherwise by occupation purports to have knowledge or skill peculiar to the practices or goods involved in the transaction.

Merger: an absorption, union, or extinguishment of one contract or interest in another; combination of two corporations so that one survives.

Minor: any person not of full legal age.

Misdemeanor: a criminal offense which is neither treason nor a felony.

Misrepresentation: a false statement of fact made innocently without any intent to deceive.

Model: a replica of the article in question.

Money order: an instrument issued by a bank, post office, or express company indicating that the payee may request and receive the amount indicated on the instrument.

Monopoly: the condition of an industry when one or a few entities control the supply of a product.

Mortgage: an interest in land given by the owner to a creditor as security for the payment of a debt, the nature of the interest depending upon the law of the state where the land is located. (Parties—mortgagor, mortgagee)

Mortgagee: the person who holds a mortgage as security for a debt.

Mortgagor: the person who gives a mortgage as security for a debt.

Moveable personal property: all physical property with the exception of real estate.

Municipal court: an inferior court.

Mutual insurance company: an insurance company in which the policyholders are the members and owners.

Mutual mistake: mistake made by both parties to a contract.

N

Necessaries: items required, or proper and useful, for sustaining a human being at an appropriate living standard.

Negative covenant: an agreement in a deed to refrain from doing an act.

Negligence: the omission to do what a reasonable, prudent person would do, or doing what such a person would not have done.

Negotiability: transferability.

Negotiable instrument: draft, promissory note, or check in such form that greater rights may be acquired thereunder than by taking an assignment of a contract might.

Negotiation: the transfer of ownership of a negotiable instrument by indorsement and delivery by the person to whom then payable in the case of order paper, and by physical transfer in the case of bearer paper.

No-fault insurance: insurance arrangement by which insurance companies pay for injuries suffered by their insureds no matter who is at fault.

No-par-value stock: stock to which no face value has been assigned.

Nominal damages: a small sum given for the violation of a right where no actual loss has resulted.

Nominal partner: a person who in fact is not a partner but who purports to be a partner or permits others to represent him/her as a partner.

Noncumulative preferred stock: preferred stock on which only current dividends must be paid before common stock dividends may be paid.

Nonparticipating preferred stock: stock on which the maximum dividend is the percentage stated on the stock.

Nonresellable goods: unusual goods that are specifically made for the buyer and are not suitable for sale in the ordinary course of the seller's business.

Nontrading partnership: a partnership which provides professional services.

Not-for-profit corporation: a corporation formed by private individuals for charitable, educational, religious, social, or fraternal purposes.

Notice and comment rule making: enacting administrative rules by publishing the proposed rule and then the final rule without holding formal hearings.

Notice of dishonor: notice given to parties secondarily liable that the primary party to the instrument has refused to accept the instrument or to make payment when it was properly presented for that purpose.

Novation: the discharge of a contract between two parties by their agreeing with a third person that such third person shall be substituted for one of the original parties to the contract, who shall thereupon be released.

Nuisance: something which wrongfully disturbs, annoys, or injures another.

Nuncupative will: an oral will, generally made during the testator's last illness, made and declared by the testator in the presence of witnesses to be his or her will.

O

Obligation: a duty.

Occupation: taking and holding possession of property; a method of acquiring title to personal property that has been abandoned.

Offer: a proposal, the agreement to which makes a contract.

Offeree: the person to whom an offer to contract is made.

Offeror: the person who makes an offer to contract.

Open-end mortgage: a mortgage given to secure additional loans to be made in the future as well as the original loan.

Option contract: a contract to hold an offer to make a contract open for a fixed period of time.

Order bill of lading: contract between the shipper and the carrier that allows delivery of shipped goods to the bearer.

Order paper: commercial paper made payable to the order of a named person.

Ordinance: a rule of law passed by the legislative body of a city.

Ordinary partnership: a partnership in which there are no limits on the rights and duties of the partners; a general partnership.

P

Par-value stock: stock to which a face value has been assigned.

Parol evidence: oral testimony.

Parol evidence rule: the rule that prohibits the introduction into evidence of oral statements made prior to or contemporaneously with the execution of a complete written contract, deed, or instrument, in the absence of clear proof of fraud, accident, or mistake.

Parole: conditional, supervised freedom of a prisoner.

Participating preferred stock: stock which shares with common stock in additional dividends made after common stockholders have received dividends equal to those preferred shareholders have received by virtue of their preference.

Partner: an owner-member of a partnership.

Partnership: an association of two or more people to carry on a business.

Passive fraud: fraud caused by failure to disclose information when there is a duty to do so.

Past consideration or past performance: something that has been performed in the past and which

therefore cannot be consideration for a promise made in the present.

Patent: the grant to an inventor of an exclusive right to make and sell an invention for a term of years; a grant of privilege, property, or authority made by a government to a private person.

Pawn: a pledge of tangible personal property.

Payee: the party to whom an instrument is made payable.

Per capita: per head; distribution among heirs equally.

per se: in, through, or by itself.

Per se violations: activities that are illegal regardless of their effect.

Per stirpes: according to the root or by way of representation. Distribution among heirs related to the decedent in different degrees, the property being divided into lines of descent from the decedent and the share of each line then divided within the line by way of representation.

Perfected security interest: what the seller has when the rights of the seller to the collateral are superior to those of third persons.

Peril: risk.

Perjury: willful false testimony under oath in a judicial proceeding.

Perpetual succession: a phrase describing the continuing life of the corporation unaffected by the death of any stockholder or the transfer by stockholders of their stock.

Person: natural (living) people or artificial persons, as corporations, which are created by act of government.

Personal property: all property which is not real property.

Petition: initial pleading filed by the plaintiff in many actions; a complaint.

Physical damage insurance: automobile insurance which covers the risks of damage to the car itself.

Picketing: placing people outside places of employment or distribution so that by words or banners they may inform the public of the existence of a labor dispute.

Piercing the corporate veil: when a court ignores the existence of a corporate entity.

Plaintiff: one who brings an action in a court.

Pledge: a bailment given as security for the payment of a debt or the performance of an obligation owed to the pledgee. (Parties—pledgor, pledgee)

Point-of-sale system: electronic fund transfers that are begun at retailers where consumers pay for goods or services.

Police power: the power to govern; the power to adopt laws for the protection of the public health, welfare, safety, and morals.

Policy: a paper evidencing the contract of insurance.

Policyholder: the insured.

Polygraph testing: testing with lie detector devices.

Possession: exclusive domain and control of property.

Possessory lien: a right to retain possession of property of another as security for some debt or obligation owed the lienor, which right continues only as long as possession is retained.

Postdate: to insert or place a later date on an instrument than the actual date on which it was executed.

Power of attorney: a written authorization to an agent by the principal.

Preauthorized debit: the authorized, automatic deduction of a bill payment from a checking account customer's account.

Preemptive right: the right of a shareholder to purchase newly issued stock in proportion to the shares owned.

Preferred stock: stock that has a priority or preference as to payment of dividends or upon liquidation, or both.

Prejudicial: something which substantially adversely affects one's rights.

Premium: the consideration paid by the insured for an insurance policy.

Prescription: the acquisition of a right to use the land of another, as an easement, through the making of hostile, visible, and notorious use of the land, continuing for the period specified by local law.

Presentment: the demand for acceptance or payment of commercial paper.

Price: the consideration for a sale of goods.

Price fixing: an agreement or any other arrangement among competitors that interferes with free market forces setting the price for a product.

Prima facie: at first view, apparently true; on the first appearance.

Prima facie evidence: evidence that is sufficient on its face if it is uncontradicted.

Primary beneficiary: the person designed as the first one to receive the proceeds of a life insurance policy, as distinguished from a contingent beneficiary who will receive the proceeds only if the primary beneficiary dies before the insured.

Primary liability: the liability to pay commercial paper without any condition being met other than that the paper is due.

Principal: one who employs an agent to act on his or her behalf; the person who in a suretyship is primarily liable to the third person or creditor.

Private carrier: a carrier which transports goods or people only in particular instances and only for those it chooses to contract with, such as a company's own fleet of trucks.

Private corporation: a corporation formed to perform some non-governmental function.

Privileged communication: information which the witness may refuse to testify to because of the relationship with the person furnishing the information, as husband-wife, attorney-client.

Privity: a succession or chain of relationship to the same thing or right, as a privity of contract, privity of estate, privity of possession.

Probate: a court having jurisdiction over individuals' estates; the process of proving a will as the testator's.

Procedural law: law that specifies how actions are filed and what trial procedure to follow.

Process: a writ or order of court generally used as a means of acquiring jurisdiction over the person of the defendant by serving the defendant with process.

Profit corporation: a corporation organized to run a business and earn money.

Promissory estoppel: the doctrine that a promise will be enforced although not supported by consideration when the promisor should have reasonably expected that the promise would induce action or forbearance of a definite and substantial character on the part of the promisee, and injustice can only be avoided by enforcement of the promise.

Promissory note: an unconditional promise in writing made by one person to another, signed by the maker, engaging to pay on demand, or at a definite time, a sum certain in money to order or bearer. (Parties—maker, payee)

Promoters: the people who plan the formation of a corporation and sell or promote the idea to others.

Property: the rights and interests one has in anything subject to ownership.

Property insurance: a contract whereby the insurer pays the insured for damage to specified property caused by the hazard covered.

Proprietor: the owner of a sole proprietorship.

Prosecute: to proceed against by legal means.

Protest: formal certification that proper presentment of a commercial paper was made to the primary party and that the primary party defaulted.

Proximate cause: the act which is the natural and reasonably foreseeable cause of the harm or event which occurs and injures the plaintiff.

Proximate damages: damages which in the ordinary course of events are the natural and reasonably foreseeable result of the defendant's violation of the plaintiff's rights.

Proxy: a written authorization by a shareholder to another person to vote the stock owned by the shareholder; the person who is the holder of such a written authorization.

Proxy war: an attempt by two competing sides to secure the majority of the stockholders' votes by obtaining proxies to be voted at a stockholders' meeting.

Public corporation: a corporation formed to perform governmental function.

Public domain: public or government-owned lands.

Public liability insurance: automobile insurance designed to protect third persons from bodily injury and property damage.

Publication: the testator's informing witnesses that the instrument being signed is the testator's will.

Punitive damages: damages in excess of those required to compensate the plaintiff for the wrong done, which are imposed in order to punish the defendant because of the particularly wanton or willful character of the wrongdoing.

Purchase-money mortgage: a mortgage given by the purchaser of land to the seller to provide security for the payment of the unpaid balance of the purchase price.

Purchase: to acquire ownership of property by making payment for it.

Purchaser in good faith: a person who purchases without any notice or knowledge of any defect of title, misconduct, or defense.

Q

Qualified acceptance: an acceptance of a draft that varies the order of the draft in some way.

Qualified indorsement: an indorsement that includes words such as "without recourse" evidencing the intent of the indorser not to be held liable for the failure of the primary party to pay the instrument.

Quantum meruit: an action brought for the value of the services rendered the defendant when there was no express contract as to the payment to be made.

Quasi: as if, as though it were, having the characteristics of; a modifier employed to indicate that the subject is to be treated as though it were in fact the noun which follows the word "quasi"; as in quasi contract and quasi-corporation.

Quasi public corporation: a public body which has powers similar to those of a corporation.

Quitclaim deed: a deed by which the grantor purports only to give up whatever right or title the grantor may have in the property without specifying or warranting that any particular interest is being transferred.

Quorum: the minimum number of persons, shares represented, or directors who must be present at a meeting in order that business may be lawfully transacted.

R

Ratification: confirming an act which was executed without authority or an act which was voidable.

Real estate mortgage note: a note given to evidence a debt which is secured by a mortgage on real estate.

Real property: land and all rights in land.

Realty: real property.

Reasonable care: that degree of care that a reasonable person would take under all the circumstances then known.

Recall: the process by which regulatory agencies demand that a manufacturer inform consumers of a product's defects and remedy them or replace the product.

Receipt: the taking possession of goods.

Receiver: a person appointed by a court to take charge of property pending litigation.

Recognizance: a formal contract entered into before a court by which a person agrees to do a specified act required by law.

Redemption: buying back one's property which has been sold because of a default.

Referee: an impartial person selected by the parties or appointed by a court to determine facts or decide matters in dispute.

Reformation: judicial correction of a contract.

Registered bond: a bond payable to a named person and recorded under that name by the organization issuing the bond.

Reimbursement: the right of one paying money on behalf of another, which the other person should have paid, to recover the amount of the payment from the person paying.

Release: the surrender or relinquishment to another of a right, claim, interest, or estate.

Remainder: the interest a person other than the grantor of a life estate has when title goes to that person upon death of the holder of the life estate.

Remedy: the action or procedure that is followed in order to enforce a right or to obtain damages for injury to a right.

Renewable term insurance: term life insurance which may be renewed for another equal term without a physical examination.

Rent: the amount paid to the landlord for the use of property.

Renunciation: a unilateral act of the holder giving up rights in an instrument or against a party to the instrument.

Reorganization of corporation: procedure devised to restore insolvent corporations to financial stability through readjustment of debt and capital structure under the supervision of a bankruptcy court.

Replevin: an action to recover possession of property unlawfully detained.

Reporting form for merchandise inventory: a property insurance policy that permits periodic reporting of the inventory on hand to vary the amount of coverage.

Repossession: the power of the credit seller to take back goods because of the buyer's failure to meet the obligation specified in the credit agreement.

Representations: statements, whether oral or written, made to give the insurer the information which it needs in writing the insurance, and which if false and relating to a material fact will entitle the insurer to avoid the contract.

Representative capacity: action taken by one on behalf of another, as an executor acting on behalf of a decedent's estate, or action taken both on one's behalf and on behalf of others, as a stockholder bringing a representative action.

Rescind: to set a contract or offer aside.

Rescission: cancelling, annulling, avoiding.

Res ipsa loquitur: the rebuttable presumption that the thing speaks for itself when the circumstances are such that ordinarily the plaintiff could not have been injured had the defendant not been at fault.

Reservation: the creation by the grantor of a right that did not exist before, which the grantor reserves or keeps upon making a conveyance of property.

Respondeat superior: the doctrine that the principal or employer is vicariously liable for the unauthorized torts committed by the agent or employee while acting within the scope of the agency or the course of the employment, respectively.

Restraining order: a judicial order or decree temporarily forbidding the doing of a certain act.

Restrictive covenants: covenants in a deed by which the grantee agrees to refrain from doing specified acts.

Restrictive indorsement: an indorsement that prohibits the further transfer, constitutes the indorsee the agent of the indorser, vests the title in the indorsee in trust for or to the use of some other person, is conditional, or states it is for collection or deposit.

Reversion: the interest of the grantor of a life estate when title reverts to the grantor upon the death of the owner of the estate.

Revocation: the annulment or cancellation of an instrument, act, or promise by one doing or making it.

Rider: a paper executed by the insurer and intended to be attached to the insurance policy for the purpose of changing it in some respect.

Right to take against the will: the right of a spouse to the share of the estate provided by statute if the will leaves a smaller share.

Riparian rights: the right of a person through whose land runs a natural watercourse to use the water free from unreasonable pollution or diversion by the upper riparian owners and from blockage by lower riparian owners.

Risk: the peril or contingency against which an insured is protected by the contract of insurance.

Robbery: taking another's property by force or threat of force.

Rogue program: a set of software instructions which produces abnormal or unexpected computer behavior.

Rule of reason: a court's examination and ruling on the anticompetitive effect of a particular activity on a case-by-case basis.

S

Sale: the transfer of title to goods from the seller to the buyer for a consideration called the price.

Sale or return: a sale in which the title to the property passes to the buyer at the time of the transaction but the buyer is given the option of returning the property and restoring the title to the seller.

Sample: a portion of a whole mass that is the subject of the transaction.

Scope of employment: the area within which an employee is authorized to act with the consequence that a tort committed while so acting imposes liability upon the employer.

Seal: at common law, an impression on wax or other material attached to the instrument. Under modern law, any mark not ordinarily part of the signature is a seal when so intended, including the letters "L.S." and the word "seal," or a pictorial representation of a seal.

Secondary boycott: an attempt by employees to cause a third party to a labor dispute to stop dealing with the employer.

Secondary liability: the liability to pay commercial paper which has been presented, dishonored, and for which notice of dishonor has been given.

Secondary meaning: the special meaning of a mark for goods which distinguishes the goods in such a way as to warrant trademark protection.

Secret partner: a partner who takes an active part in the management of the partnership but is not known to the public as a partner.

Secured transaction: a credit sale of goods or a secured loan that provides special protection for the creditor.

Security agreement: a written agreement, signed by the buyer of goods, which describes the collateral and usually contains the terms of payments.

Sentence: the penalty pronounced upon a person convicted of a crime.

Set off: the process in a case by which a defendant seeks to deduct from the plaintiff's claim amounts owed to the defendant by the plaintiff.

Severable contract: a contract the terms of which are such that one part may be separated from the other, so that a default as to one part is not necessarily a default as to the entire contract.

Several contracts: separate or independent contracts made by different persons undertaking to perform the same obligation.

Severalty: sole ownership of property by one person.

Share: a unit of a corporation's stock.

Shareholder: a person who owns stock in a corporation.

Shareholder's derivative action: an action brought by one or more shareholders on behalf of the shareholders generally and of the corporation to enforce a cause of action of the corporation against third parties.

Sheriff: the executive officer of a state court of record.

Shoplifting: taking possession of goods in a store with the intent to use them as the taker's own without paying the purchase price.

Shop right: the right of an employer to use an employee's invention without payment of a royalty.

Sight draft: a draft or bill of exchange payable on sight or when presented for payment.

Silent partner: a partner who takes no active part in the business, regardless of whether known to the public as a partner.

Simple contract: a contract which is not formal.

Sitdown strike: a strike in which the employees remain in the plant and refuse to allow the employer to operate it.

Slander: defamation of character by spoken words or gestures.

Sleeping partner: *see* Dormant partner.

Slowdown: a reduction in production by employees without actual stoppage of work.

Small claims court: an inferior court.

Sole proprietorship: a business owned and carried on by one person.

Special agent: an agent authorized to perform a specific transaction or to do a specific act.

Special damages: damages that do not necessarily result from the injury to the plaintiff but at the same time are not so remote that the defendant should to be held liable therefor, provided that the claim for special damages is properly made in the action.

Special federal courts: federal trial courts whose jurisdiction is limited by the laws creating them, such as the US. Tax Court and the US. Claims Court.

Special indorsement: an indorsement that specifies the person to whom the instrument is indorsed.

Special warranty deed: a deed which warrants good title in the grantee free of claims by all persons claiming by, through, or under the grantor.

Specific (identified) goods: goods which are so identified to the contract that no other goods may be delivered in performance of the contract.

Specific lien: the right of a creditor to hold particular property or assert a lien on any particular property of the debtor because of the credi-

tor's having done work on or having some other association with the property, as distinguished from having a lien generally against the assets of the debtor merely because the debtor is indebted.

Specific performance: an action brought to compel the adverse party to perform a contract on the theory that merely suing for damages for its breach will not be an adequate remedy.

SS. or ss.: abbreviation for the Latin word *scilicet*, meaning to wit; namely; that is to say.

Stale check: a check presented more than six months after its date.

Stare decisis: the principle that the decision of a court should serve as a guide or precedent and control the decision of a similar case in the future.

Statute of Frauds: a law which, in order to prevent fraud through the use of perjured testimony, requires that certain types of transactions be evidenced by a writing in order to be binding or enforceable.

Statute of Limitations: a law that restricts the period of time within which an action may be brought.

Statutes: laws enacted by the legislative branch of government.

Stock: an ownership interest in a corporation.

Stock corporation: a corporation, ownership in which is represented by shares of stock.

Stock insurance company: an insurance corporation in which stockholders were the original investors.

Stock option: a contract between a corporation and an individual giving the individual the right for a stated period to buy a set number of shares of stock at a given price.

Stockholder: person who owns stock in a corporation.

Stop payment order: a depositor's directive to the bank to refuse to make payment of the depositor's check when presented for payment.

Straight bill of lading: the contract between the shipper and the carrier requiring delivery of the goods only to the consignee.

Strike: a temporary, concerted action by workers to withhold their services from their employer.

Sublease: a tenant's transfer of less than full interest in leased premises to a third person.

Subpoena: a writ commanding a person to appear as a witness.

Subrogation: the right of a party secondarily liable to stand in the place of the creditor after making payment to the creditor and to enforce the creditor's right against the party primarily liable in order to obtain indemnity.

Subscriber: a person who has contracted to purchase stock in a proposed corporation.

Subsidiary corporation: a corporation that is controlled by another corporation through the ownership by the latter of a controlling amount of the voting stock of the former.

Substantial performance: the equitable doctrine that a contractor substantially completing a contract in good faith is entitled to recover the contract price less damages for noncompletion or defective work.

Substantive law: the law that defines rights and liabilities.

Substitution: discharge of a contract by substituting another in its place.

Subtenant: one who rents all or part of the leased premises from the original tenant for a period of time less than the balance of the lease to the original tenant.

Suit: the prosecution of some claim in a court of justice.

Summons: a notice to a person to appear in court.

Superior court: a state court of record.

Supreme court: the highest tribunal in the US. court system with final decision in a case. Also, in most states, the highest tribunal in the state court system.

Surety: a guarantor.

Suretyship: an undertaking to pay the debt or be liable for the default of another.

Surrender: the yielding up of the tenant's leasehold estate to the lessor in consequence of which the lease terminates.

Survivorship: the right by which a surviving joint tenant or tenant by the entireties acquires the interest of the predeceasing tenant automatically upon the death of the predeceasing tenant.

Syndicate: an association of individuals formed to conduct a particular business transaction, generally of a financial nature.

T

Tangible personal property: personal property which can be seen, touched, and possessed.

Tax Court: the federal trial court which hears cases involving tax controversies with the US. government.

Tenancy at sufferance: the holding over by a tenant after the lease has expired without the permission of the landlord and prior to the time that the landlord has elected to treat the person as a trespasser or a tenant.

Tenancy at will: the holding of land for an indefinite period that may be terminated at any time by the landlord or by the landlord and tenant acting together.

Tenancy for years: a tenancy for a fixed period of time, even though the time is less than a year.

Tenancy from year to year: a tenancy which continues indefinitely from year to year until terminated.

Tenancy in common: the relation that exists when two or more people own undivided interests in property.

Tenancy in partnership: the ownership of a partner in the partnership property.

Tenant: the person given possession of leased property.

Tender of payment: an unconditional offer to pay the exact amount of money due at the time and place specified by the contract.

Tender of performance: an unconditional offer to perform at the time and in the manner specified by the contract.

Term insurance: life insurance contract whereby the insurer assumes the risk of death of the insured for a specific period of time.

Testamentary: designed to take effect at death, as by disposing of property or appointing an executor.

Testate: the condition of leaving a will upon death.

Testator (testatrix): a man (woman) who makes a will.

Testimony: the answers of witnesses under oath to questions given at the time of the trial.

Theft: taking another's property without the owner's consent with the intent to wrongfully deprive the owner of the property.

Third party beneficiary: a third person whom the parties to a contract intend to benefit by the making of the contract.

Time bomb: a rogue program set to go off at a specified time.

Time draft: a bill of exchange payable at a stated time after sight or a stated period after a certain date.

Title: evidence of ownership in property.

Title insurance: a form of insurance by which the insurer insures the buyer of real property against the risk of loss should the title acquired from the seller be defective in any way.

Tort: a private injury or wrong arising from a breach of a duty created by law.

Trade acceptance: a draft or bill of exchange drawn by the seller of goods on the purchaser at the time of sale and accepted by the purchaser.

Trade fixtures: articles of personal property which have been attached to the realty by a tenant and which are used for or are necessary to the carrying on of the tenant's trade.

Trade name: a name under which a business is carried on.

Trademark: a name, device, or symbol used by a manufacturer or seller to distinguish his or her goods from those of others.

Trademark or trade name infringement: the unauthorized use of or confusingly similar imitation of another's mark or name.

Trading partnership: a partnership engaged in buying and selling merchandise.

Trailing edge: the left side of a check when looking at it from the front.

Traveler's check: an instrument much like a cashier's check of the issuer except that it requires signature and counter-signature by its purchaser.

Treasury stock: stock of a corporation which the corporation has reacquired.

Trespass: an unwarranted invasion of another's right.

Trial court: the court in which a case is originally tried and decided.

Trojan horse: a desirable computer program containing a hidden code that performs an undesirable function.

Trust: a transfer of property by one person to another with the understanding or declaration that such property be held for the benefit of another, or the holding of property by the owner for the benefit of another, upon a declaration of trust, without a transfer to another person.

Trustee: one who holds property for the benefit of another.

Trustee in bankruptcy: an impartial person elected to administer the debtor's estate.

U

Ultra vires: an act or contract which the corporation does not have authority to do or make.

Unconscionable contract: a contract, the terms of which are so harsh as to shock the conscience of the community.

Underwriter: insurer.

Undisclosed principal: a principal on whose behalf an agent acts without disclosing to the third person the agency or the identity of the principal.

Undue influence: the influence that is asserted upon another person by one who dominates that person.

Unenforceable contract: an agreement which is not in the form required by law, but can be made so by the parties.

Unfair competition: the wrong of employing competitive methods that have been declared unfair by statute or an administrative agency: when the total impression of a product results in confusion as to its origin.

Unfair labor practice acts: statutes that prohibit certain labor practices and declare them to be unfair.

Unilateral: one-sided, applied to contracts where an act is done in consideration for a promise.

Unilateral mistake: mistake made by only one of the parties to a contract.

Unincorporated association: a combination of two or more people for the furtherance of a joint nonprofit activity.

Union contract: a contract between a labor union and an employer or group of employers prescribing terms of employment.

Union shop: a place of employment where nonunion workers may be employed for a period of not more than 30 days after which the nonunion worker must join the union or be discharged.

Unit pricing: stating the price for goods as the price per unit of measurement.

Universal agent: an agent authorized by the principal to do all acts that can lawfully be delegated to a representative.

Universal defense: a defense which can be raised against any holder.

Unjust enrichment: one person unfairly keeps money or otherwise benefits at the expense of another.

Unlimited liability: business debts are payable from personal assets.

Usury: lending money at greater than the maximum rate allowed by law.

V

Valid: legal.

Valued policy: a fire insurance policy which fixes values for the insured items of property.

Venue: the place where a trial is held.

Verdict: a decision rendered by a jury.

Virus: a rogue program that duplicates itself and attaches copies of itself to other programs, thus spreading from computer to computer.

Void: of no legal effect and not binding on anyone.

Voidable: a transaction that may be set aside by one party because of fraud or similar reason but which is binding on the other party until the injured party elects to set the transaction aside.

Voluntary subscription: a pledge, usually to a charitable enterprise, to donate funds in the future.

Voting trust: the transfer by two or more stockholders of their shares of stock on a corporation to a trustee who is to vote the shares and act for those shareholders.

W

Waiver: the voluntary surrender or relinquishment of a right or privilege.

Warehouse receipt: a receipt issued by the warehouser for goods stored. Regulated by the UCC, which clothes the receipt with some degree of negotiability.

Warehouser: a person regularly engaged in the business of storing the goods of others for compensation. If the warehouser purports to serve the public without discrimination, he or she is a public warehouser.

Warranty: an assurance by the seller that an article will conform to a certain standard or will operate in a certain manner; in insurance, a statement of the insured which relates to the risk and appears in the insurance contract.

Warranty deed: a deed by which the grantor conveys a specific estate or interest to the grantee and covenants that the transfer has been made with covenants of title.

Waste: damage or destruction to property done or permitted by a tenant.

Watered stock: stock issued by a corporation as fully paid when in fact it is not.

Will: an instrument executed with the formality required by law, by which a disposition of the signer's property is to take effect upon his or her death.

Winding up: taking care of the outstanding obligations of a partnership and distributing the remaining assets.

With reserve: a way of offering goods for sale at an auction by which the goods may be withdrawn for sale after the bidding starts.

Without reserve: a way of offering goods for sale at an auction by which the goods may not be withdrawn for sale after the bidding starts.

Witness: a person who gives testimony in court; one who sees a document executed and signs his or her name thereto.

Workers' compensation: a system providing for payments to workers because they have been injured or have contracted an occupational disease from a risk arising out of the course of their employment, payment being made without consideration of the negligence of any party.

Works of charity: in connection with Sunday laws, acts involved in religious worship or aiding people in distress.

Works of necessity: in connection with Sunday laws, acts that must be done at the particular time in order to save life, health, or property.

Worm: a rogue program which resides in the memory of a computer and erases the contents.

Writ: a formal written command issued by a court of law.

Writ of certiorari: an order from a higher court requiring a lower court to produce the record of a case for the higher court's review.

Z

Zoning restrictions: restrictions imposed by government on the use of the property for the advancement of the general welfare.

Index

Temple   drawer

drawel